Free Black Heads of Households in the New York State Federal Census, 1790-1830

Free Black Heads of Households in the New York State Federal Census, 1790-1830

Alice Eichholz

Assistant Professor
Department of Special Programs
Queens College
Flushing, New York

James M. Rose

Ethnic Studies Internship Coordinator
Queens College
Flushing, New York

CLEARFIELD

Reprinted, with permission, for
Clearfield Company, Inc. by
Genealogical Publishing Co., Inc.
Baltimore, Maryland
2003

International Standard Book Number: 0-8063-5199-3

Made in the United States of America

To
CADY AND KATRINA

VITAE

Alice Eichholz is an assistant professor at Queens College, City University of New York, in the department of special programs. She is codirector, with Rose, of the Ethnic Genealogy Center at Queens College, and research associate for the Institute for Psychohistory. Dr. Eichholz received her M.Ed. from Wayne State University, and Ph.D. from New York University. She coedited, with Rose, BLACK GENESIS (Gale, 1978), published two books on her family, the Linvilles, and has written several articles on pregnancy.

James M. Rose is an ethnic studies internship coordinator at Queens College, City University of New York. He received his master's degree at Queens College, and his Ph.D. at Union Graduate School. He has published numerous articles and books on genealogical studies of the Afro-American family.

CONTENTS

ACKNOWLEDGMENTS

Genealogy projects such as this one are laborious, time-consuming and, at times, monotonous. It has been five years since we started this index with no funds except for the purchase of microfilm and some indirect support from Queens College, of the City University of New York. We are consequently deeply appreciative of the Alumni Association and Computer Center for their support in these areas.

What started out as a class learning project with nearly one hundred students quickly became an enormous task for two people also employed in full-time jobs. That left little time for checking and rechecking names, spellings and page numbers. With everything nearly completed, we were exhausted at the thought of keypunching all the data. Consequently, the project could not have been completed without the help of two individuals. Mrs. Ruth Vermont of the Financial Aid Office at Queens College was persistent and conscientious in locating a graduate student, Wesley Campbell, eligible for College Work Study. Wesley's diligence and commitment to the project inspired both of us to carry on and complete it. When his grant time was used up, the Division of Social Sciences was able to compensate him for a few additional hours. Beyond that Wes donated his own time--having a strong desire to finally see all those keypunch cards produce a comprehensive index.

Finally, we are continually indebted to J. Carlyle Parker for his vision in understanding the usefulness of such an index in black genealogical research.

Alice Eichholz
James M. Rose

INTRODUCTION

The New York State Federal Census records for 1790-1830 reflect the interesting history of slavery in New York State. During that period of time, the legislature passed a number of bills for the gradual emancipation of slaves. Consequently, by the 1830 census all blacks in New York State were counted as free.

Unfortunately, a high percentage of blacks, especially in urban areas, still resided with white families. This index, therefore, does not include those blacks since their names do not appear. Originally, the index was to cover the 1840 and 1850 censuses as well. But the enormity of the task and lack of funds necessitated the elimination of that material.

What follows is an alphabetical index of free black heads of households. Where last names were not available in the original records, the first names are alphabetized with the surnames. The year of the census, an abbreviation for the New York county, the county's township, and the page number of the census follows each name.

For the 1790 census, the page number refers to the popularly available HEADS OF FAMILIES AT THE FIRST CENSUS OF THE UNITED STATES TAKEN IN THE YEAR 1790: NEW YORK compiled by Bureau of Census of the Department of Commerce and Labor and published by the Government Printing Office in 1908. Most research libraries have this volume which contains all the information found in the original records.

Page numbers for the 1800, 1810, 1820, and 1830 census records are from the microfilm editions of the original records available on interlibrary loan from the Fort Worth Regional Center of the National Archives. In most cases, the page numbers are written on the originals in heavy black ink. If no written number was available, the number designated during the microfilming process was used. However, this is definitely the exception.

The process of checking and rechecking names, spelling, and pages used to compile this index should have eliminated most errors. However, in reading nineteenth-century handwriting, some errors are still possible. Changes in name spelling, depending on the skills of census takers, obviously adds to this problem. Vowels are persistently difficult to decifer, and consonants can also be misread. Consequently, variations in spelling should be checked according to sound and similarity in strokes of the pen.

This index should be used in conjunction with the wealth of information on blacks in New York State (see BLACK GENESIS edited by Rose and Eichholz, Detroit: Gale Research Co., Gale Genealogy and Local History Series, vol. 1, 1978). Then a more thorough historical picture of blacks, as they moved from slavery to freedom, can be developed.

COUNTY AND TOWNSHIP ABBREVIATIONS

ALBANY—ABNY

Albany City -no ward	-Abny
Albany City Ward 1	-WD01
Albany City Ward 2	-WD02
Albany City Ward 3	-WD03
Ballstown	Ball
Bem	Bern
Bethlehem	Beth
Catskill	Cats
Coeymans	Coey
Coxsackie	Coxs
Duanesburgh	Dubg
Easton	East
Freehold	Free
Guiderland	Guid
Halfmoon	Half
Hoosick	Hoos
Pittstown	Pitt
Rensselaerville	Renv
Rensselaerwick	Renw
Saratoga	Sara
Schaghticoke	Schg
Schenectady	Scne
Schoharie	Schr
Stephentown	Step
Stillwater	Stil
Watervilet	Watv
Westerlo	West

ALLEGANY—ALLE

Almond	Almd
Angelica	Ange
Birdsall	Bird

Caneadea	Cane
Friendship	Fdsp
Grove	Grov
Haight	Haig
Nunda	Nund
Orcean	Orce
Rushford	Rush
Scio	Scio

BROOME—BROM

Chinago	Chin
Conklin	Conk
Owego	Oweg
Union	Unon
Vestal	Vest
Windsor	Wind

CATTARAUGUS—CATT

Perrysburgh	Pery
Randolph	Rand

CAYUGA—CAYU

Auburn	Aubn
Aurelius	Aure
Brutus	Brut
Cato	Cato
Ellicot	Elct
Genoa	Geno
Ledyard	Ledy
Milton	Milt
Owasco	Owas
Scipio	Scip
Semprontus	Semp
Springport	Sprg
Venice	Veni

CHAUTAUGUA—CHAT

Busti	Bust
Chautangua	Chat
Ellicot	Elct
Hanover	Hano
Pomfret	Pomf

Ripley	Ripy
Sheridan	Sher

CHENANGO—CHEN

Bainbridge	Bain
Brookfield	Brok
Carnovia	Carn
Greene	Gren
McDonough	Mcdn
North Berlin	Nber
Norwich	Norw
Oxford	Oxfo
Plymouth	Plym
Roxbury	Roxb
Sherburne	Sher
Smyrna	Smya

CLINTON—CLNT

Beekmantown	Beek
Champlain	Cham
Chasy	Chas
Crown Point	Crpt
Peru	Peru
Plattsburgh	Plat
Wellsburgh	Well

COLUMBIA—COLU

Ancram	Ancm
Austerlitz	Aust
Canaan	Cann
Chatham	Chat
Claverback	Clav
Clermont	Cler
Copake	Copa
Gallatin	Gala
Germantown	Germ
Ghent	Ghen
Granger	Gran
Hillsdale	Hill
Hudson	Huds
Kinderhook	Kind
Lebonon	Lebn
Laughkanick	Laug
Livingston	Livg

Stuyvesant   Stuy

CORTLAND—CORT

Cortlandville   Cort
Preble   Preb
Scott   Scot
Virgil   Virg

DELAWARE—DELA

Colchester   Colc
Davenport   Dave
Delhi   Deli
Franklin   Fran
Hamden   Hamd
Harpersfield   Harp
Kortright   Kort
Meredith   Meri
Middletown   Midd
Sidney   Sidn
Stamford   Stam
Tompkins   Tomp
Walton   Walt

DUTCHESS—DUTC

Amenia   Amen
Beekman   Beek
Carmel   Carm
Clinton   Clnt
Dover   Dove
Fishkill   Fish
Franklin   Fran
Frederickson   Frdk
Hyde Park   Hypk
Lagrange   Lagr
Milan   Miln
Northeast   Nort
Patterson   Patt
Pawling   Pawl
Philipstown   Phil
Pine Plains   Pine
Pleasant Valley   Plea
Poughkeepsie   Pgkp
Rhinebeck   Rhin
Red Hook   Redh

Southeast	Sout
Stanford	Stan
Union Vale	Unva
Washington	Wash

ERIE—ERIE

Buffalo	Buff
Erie	Erie
Evans	Evan
Hamburg	Hamb

ESSEX—ESEX

Chesterfield	Ches
Elizabeth	Eliz
Essex	Esex
Jay	Jay
Keene	Kene
Point	Pint
Schroon	Shon
Ticonderoga	Tico
Willisborough	Will

FRANKLIN—FRAN

Constable	Cons
Fort Covington	Forc
Malone	Malo
Westville	West

GENESEE—GENE

Alabama	Alab
Batavia	Bata
Bergen	Berg
Caladonia	Cala
Castle	Cast
Gates	Gate
Leicister	Leic
Leroy	Lroy
Perry	Pery
Riga	Riga
Stafford	Staf
Sweden	Swed

GREENE—GREN

Athens	Athn
Cairo	Cair
Catskill	Cats
Coxsackie	Coxe
Durham	Durh
Greenville	Gren
Hunter	Hunt
New Baltimore	Newb
Windham	Wind

HERKIMER—HERK

Columbia	Colu
Danube	Danu
Fairfield	Fair
Frankfort	Fran
Germanflats	Germ
Herkimer	Herk
Little Falls	Ltfa
Manheim	Mani
Newport	Newp
Norway	Norw
Russia	Russ
Salisbury	Salb
Schuyler	Schu
Stark	Star
Warren	Warr
Winfield	Winf

JEFFERSON—JEFF

Brownsville	Bron
Champion	Cham
Ellisburgh	Elis
Hounsfield	Houn
Leray	Lray
Lorraine	Lorr
Orleans	Orln
Pamelia	Pame
Philadelphia	Phil
Watertown	Wate
Wilna	Wiln

KINGS—KING

Bradford	Brad
Brooklyn	Bryn
Bushwick	Bush
Flatbush	Flat
Flatlands	Flan
Gravesend	Grav
New Lotts	Nlot
New Utrecht	Neut
Watabaut	Wata
Williamsburg	Will

LEWIS—LEWI

Brantingham	Bran
Denmark	Denm
Leyden	Leyd
Lowville	Lowv
Watson	Wats

LIVINGSTON—LIVI

Avon	Avon
Conesus	Cone
Genesco	Genc
Groveland	Grov
Leicester	Leic
Sparta	Spar
Springwater	Spwt
York	York

MADISON—MADI

Hamilton	Haml
Lebonan	Lebn
Lenox	Lenx
Nelson	Nels
Smithfield	Smit
Sullivan	Sull

MONROE—MONR

Brighton	Brig
Brockport	Brkp
Gates	Gate

County and Township Abbreviations

Greece	Grec
Mendon	Mend
Penfield	Penf
Perrinton	Pert
Pittsford	Pits
Rochester Ward 1	Rwd1
Rochester Ward 2	Rwd2
Rochester Ward 3	Rwd3
Rush	Rush
Sweden	Swed

MONTGOMERY—MONT

Amsterdam	Amst
Broadablin	Broa
Canajoharie	Canj
Caughnawaga	Cghw
Charlestown	Char
Chemung	Chem
Chenango	Chen
Ephrata	Ephr
Florida	Flor
Germanflats	Germ
Glen	Glen
Harpersfield	Harp
Herkimer	Herk
Johnstown	John
Manheim	Manh
Mayfield	Mayf
Minden	Mind
Mohawk	Moha
Oppenheim	Open
Otsego	Otse
Palantine	Plan
Root	Root
Whites	Whit

NEW YORK COUNTY—NYCO

Dock Ward	Dock
East Ward	East
Harlem	Harl
Montgomery Ward	Mont
New York City – no ward	NYCI
New York City Ward 1	WD01
" " " Ward 2	WD02
" " " Ward 3	WD03
" " " Ward 4	WD04
" " " Ward 5	WD05

New York City Ward 6	WD06
" " " Ward 7	WD07
" " " Ward 8	WD08
" " " Ward 9	WD09
" " " Ward 10	WD10
" " " Ward 11	WD11
" " " Ward 12	WD12
" " " Ward 13	WD13
" " " Ward 14	WD14
North Ward	Nort
Out Ward	Outw
South Ward	Sout
West Ward	West

NIAGARA—NIAG

Buffalo	Buff
Cambria	Camb
Hartland	Hart
Lewiston	Lews
Lockport	Lock
New Fane	Newf
Niagara	Niag
Olean	Olen
Pendelton	Pend
Royalton	Royl

ONEIDA—ONID

Amisville	Amis
Augusta	Augu
Boonville	Boon
Bridgewater	Brid
Canton	Cant
Deerfield	Deer
Florence	Flor
Kirkland	Kirk
Lisburn	Lisb
Madrid	Mard
Marcellus	Marc
Marshall	Mars
New Hartford	Nwht
Paris	Pari
Remsen	Rems
Rome	Rome
Trenton	Tren
Utica	Utic
Vernon	Vern

Western	West
Westmoreland	Wesm
Whitetown	Whtt

ONONDAGO—ONON

Camillus	Cami
Clay	Clay
Cicero	Cice
Lafayette	Lafy
Lysondin	Lyso
Manilus	Manl
Marcellus	Marc
Onondago	Onon
Otisco	Otis
Pompey	Pomp
Salina	Sali
Skaneatelas	Skan
Van Buren	Vanb

ONTARIO—ONTA

Avon	Avon
Benton	Bent
Bloomfield	Blom
Boyle	Boyl
Brighton	Bton
Bristol	Bris
Canandaigua	Cana
Charlston	Char
Erwin	Erwn
Farmington	Farm
Freeport	Free
Genesee	Gene
Gorham	Gorh
Hartford	Hart
Hopewell	Hope
Italy	Ital
Jerusalem	Jeru
Lyons	Lyon
Manchester	Manc
Middlesex	Midd
Northhampton	Noth
Palmyra	Palm
Penfield	Penf
Phelps	Phel
Richmond	Rich
Rush	Rush
Seneca	Sene

Sodus	Sodu
Victor	Vict

ORANGE—ORNG

Bloominggrove	Blom
Calhoun	Calh
Cheesecocke	Chee
Cornwall	Corn
Cranford	Cran
Deer Park	Deer
Goshen	Gosh
Hamptonburgh	Hbgh
Haverstraw	Have
Minisink	Mini
Montgomery	Mont
Monroe	Monr
Newburgh	Newb
New Cornwall	Newc
New Windson	Neww
Orange	Orng
Wallkill	Wall
Warwick	Warw

ORLEANS—ORLE

Albion	Albn
Murray	Mura

OSWEGO—OSWE

Amboy	Ambo
Granby	Gran
Hannibal	Hann
Hasting	Hast
Scriba	Scri
Volney	Voln

OTSEWGO—OTSG

Burlington	Burl
Butternut	Butt
Cherry Valley	Chrv
Decatur	Deca
Hartwick	Hart
Laurens	Laur
Maryland	Mary

Middlefield	Midd
Plainfield	Plan

PUTNAM—PUTM

Carmel	Carm
Kent	Kent
Paterson	Pate
Phillips	Phil
Southeast	Sout

QUEENS—QUEN

Flushing	Flus
Jamaica	Jama
Newtown	Newt
North Hempstead	Nhem
Oyster Bay	Oyst
South Hempstead	Shem

RENSSELAER—RENS

Berlin	Berl
Brunswick	Brun
Grafton	Graf
Greenbush	Gren
Hoosick	Hoos
Lansingbush	Lans
Nassau	Nass
Petersburgh	Pete
Pittstown	Pitt
Sandlake	Sand
Scashtikoke	Scas
Schodach	Scho
Stephentown	Step
Troy	Troy

RICHMOND—RICH

Castletown	Cast
Northfield	Nort
Southfield	Sout
Westfield	West

County and Township Abbreviations

ROCKLAND—ROCK

Clarkstown	Clar
Haverstraw	Hver
Hempstead	Hemp
Malta	Malt
Ramapoo	Rpoo
Orangetown	Orgt

ST. LAWRENCE—STLR

Massena	Mass
Oswegatchie	Oswe
Potsdam	Pots

SARATOGA—SARA

Ballston	Ball
Charlton	Char
Clifton Park	Cfpk
Concord	Conc
Edinburgh	Edin
Galway	Galw
Greenfield	Gren
Hadley	Hadl
Halfmoon	Half
Malta	Malt
Milton	Milt
Moreau	More
Northumberland	Nort
Providence	Prov
Saratoga Springs	Sasp
Stillwater	Stil
Waterfield	Wate
Wilton	Wilt

SCHENECTADY—SCNE

Duanesburgh		Duan
Glenville		Glen
Princetown		Prin
Rotterdam		Rott
Schenectady		Scne
"	Ward 1	WD01
"	Ward 2	WD02

County and Township Abbreviations

SCHOHARIE—SCHR

Blenheim	Blen
Broome	Brom
Brown	Brow
Cobbleskill	Cobl
Fulton	Fult
Jefferson	Jeff
Middleburgh	Midd
Schoharie	Schr
Sharon	Shar
Summit	Summ

SENECA—SENE

Covert	Cove
Falls	Fall
Fayette	Faye
Galen	Gale
Hector	Hect
Junius	Junu
Lodi	Lodi
Ovid	Ovid
Romulus	Romu
Tyre	Tyre
Varick	Vari
Waterloo	Wloo

STEUBEN—STEU

Bath	Bath
Howard	Howa
Pottney	Pott
Prattsburgh	Prat
Reading	Read
Urbana	Urba
Wayne	Wayn
Wheeler	Whel

SUFFOLK—SUFF

Brookhaven	Brok
Easthampton	East
Huntington	Hunt
Islip	Islp
Riverhead	Rivh
Shelter Island	Shel
Smithtown	Smit

Southhampton	Sham
Southhold	Sout

SULLIVAN—SULL

Bethel	Beth
Lumberland	Lumb
Mamakating	Mama
Neversing	Neve
Thompson	Thom

TIOGA—TIOG

Barton	Bart
Berkshire	Berk
Caroline	Caro
Catharine	Cath
Chemungo	Chem
Damby	Damb
Elmira	Elmi
Lisle	Lisl
Newtown	Newn
Nicholas	Nich
Owego	Owgo
Southport	Sopo
Spencer	Spen
Veteran	Vetr

TOMPKIN—TOMP

Caroline	Caro
Danby	Danb
Enfield	Enfd
Hector	Hect
Ithaca	Itca
Lansing	Lans
Newfield	Newf
Ulysses	Ulys

ULSTER—ULST

Esopus	Esop
Hurley	Hurl
Kingston	King
Mamakating	Maka
Marbletown	Marb
Marlborough	Marl

County and Township Abbreviations

Middletown	Midd
Montgomery	Mont
Navisink	Navi
New Marlborough	Nmar
New Paltz	Npal
New Windsor	Nwin
Newburgh	Newb
Olive	Oliv
Plattekill	Plat
Rochester	Roch
Saugerties	Saug
Shandaken	Shan
Shawangunk	Shaw
Wallkill	Walk
Wawarsing	Wawa
Woodstock	Wood

WARREN—WARR

Queensbury	Quen

WASHINGTON—WASH

Argyle	Argy
Bottom	Bott
Cambridge	Camb
Caston	Cast
Chester	Ches
Easton	Eatn
Fort Edward	Fted
Granville	Gran
Greenwich	Gren
Hampton	Hamp
Hartford	Hart
Hebron	Hebr
Jackson	Jack
Kingsbury	King
Queensbury	Quen
Salem	Salm
Thurman	Thur
Westfield	West
White Creek	Wtck
Whitehall	Whit
Youcumb	Youc

WAYNE—WANE

Arcadia	Arca
Galen	Gale
Lyons	Lyon
Macedon	Mace
Ontario	Onta
Palmyra	Palm
Sodus	Sodo

WESTCHESTER—WEST

Bedford	Bedf
Castle	Cast
Cortland	Cort
Eastchester	East
Fort Ann	Fann
Greenburgh	Gren
Harrison	Harr
Mamaroneck	Mama
Morrisania	Morr
Mt. Pleasant	Mtpl
New Castle	Newc
New Rochelle	Newr
North Castle	Norc
North Salem	Nors
Parkchester	Pche
Pelham	Pelh
Pound Ridge	Poun
Rye	Rye
Salem	Sale
Scarsdale	Scar
Somers-Sumers	Summ
Stephen	Step
Thurman	Thur
Westchester	West
Westfield	Wesf
White Plains	Wtpl
Yonkers	Yonk
Yorktown	York

YATES—YATE

Benton	Bent
Italy	Ital
Jerusalem	Jeru
Middlesex	Msex
Milo	Milo

FREE BLACK HEADS OF HOUSEHOLDS

NAME	YR	CO	TWP	PG
AAKLY, PROMPLY	1820	SUFF	HUNT	278
AARON	1790	QUEN	JAMA	150
AARON	1800	WEST	SCAR	639
AARON, JACOB	1820	NYCO	WD04	312
AARON, POMPE	1790	ORAN	WARW	148
ABBETY, ELIZABETH	1820	ABNY	ABNY	149
ABBEY, LABAN	1830	MADI	----	188
ABBY	1810	NYCO	WD07	576
ABBY, PRINCE	1800	CAYU	AURE	688
ABE	1790	QUEN	OYST	155
ABEEL, JOSEPH	1810	DELA	DELH	531
ABEEL, PETER	1820	GREN	CATS	160
ABERCROMBIE, ISAAC	1830	NYCO	WD06	399
ABIGAIL	1790	NYCO	SOUT	132
ABIGAIL	1790	QUEN	NHEM	152
ABIJAH	1790	QUEN	OYST	153
A BLACK FAMILY	1810	NYCO	WD06	416
A BLACK FAMILY	1810	NYCO	WD06	437
ABO, SAMUEL	1820	COLU	KIND	73
ABO, SARAH	1820	COLU	KIND	73
ABRAHAM	1790	NYCO	NORT	127
ABRAHAM	1800	QUEN	OYST	578
ABRAHAM	1800	SUFF	BROK	9
ABRAHAM	1810	NYCO	WD07	546
ABRAHAM	1820	SUFF	BROK	355
ABRAHAM	1820	ULST	MARB	54
ABRAHAM, SAMUEL	1830	SARA	CTPK	135
ABRAHAMS, CYRUS	1810	NYCO	WD06	460
ABRAHAMS, DAVID	1830	MONR	RWD1	196
ABRAHAMS, SILAS	1800	RICH	SOUT	952
ABRAHAMS, WILLIAM	1820	NYCO	WD07	705
ABRAMS, MRS.	1830	KING	WD04	310
ABRAMS, TAMOUR	1830	NYCO	WD06	366
ABURTS, LANDERT	1830	ULST	NPAL	209
ABWELL, MARY	1820	NYCO	WD10	954
ACHILLES, JANE	1830	SUFF	SHAM	204
ACKER, JONATHAN	1830	ULST	PLAT	269
ACKLEY	1810	NIAG	BUFF	235
ACKLEY	1820	PUTM	PATE	101
ACKLEY, P.	1830	ERIE	BUFF	5
A COLURED FAMILY	1810	NYCO	WD06	410
ADAM	1790	QUEN	NHEM	152
ADAM	1800	SUFF	BROK	10
ADAMA, JACK	1820	ORNG	NEWW	493
ADAMS, ADAM	1820	ROCK	ORNG	85
ADAMS, ANNA	1830	COLU	HUDS	106
ADAMS, ANTHONY	1830	ORNG	MINI	269
ADAMS, ARCH	1820	ROCK	HAVE	107
ADAMS, FRANK	1810	COLU	HUDS	142

NAME	YR	CO	TWP	PG
ADAMS, FRANK	1810	COLU	HUDS	149
ADAMS, FRANK	1820	COLU	HUDS	4
ADAMS, FRANK	1830	ONID	UTIC	43
ADAMS, GEORGE	1810	NYCO	WD06	425
ADAMS, J.	1820	NYCO	WD10	1028
ADAMS, JACOB	1820	OTSG	PLAN	174
ADAMS, JAMES	1810	NYCO	WD06	423
ADAMS, JAMES	1820	NYCO	WD07	621
ADAMS, JOHN	1830	NYCO	WD10	114
ADAMS, JOHN	1830	NYCO	WD13	365
ADAMS, JOHN	1830	ORNG	NEWW	96
ADAMS, JOHN	1830	RENS	TROY	15
ADAMS, JOHN	1830	WANE	PALM	43
ADAMS, JOSEPH	1820	ONTA	CANA	210
ADAMS, JOSEPH	1830	ONTA	CANA	118
ADAMS, KING	1800	NYCO	WD02	674
ADAMS, LYDIA	1820	NYCO	WD07	686
ADAMS, MARGARET	1790	ULST	WALK	184
ADAMS, MC	1820	NYCO	WD10	983
ADAMS, MRS.	1830	KING	WD03	286
ADAMS, RICHARD	1830	ROCK	HVER	141
ADAMS, SAMUEL	1830	NYCO	WD06	388
ADAMS, SAMUEL	1830	QUEN	NEWT	5
ADAMS, THOMAS	1810	NYCO	WD06	419
ADAMS, THOMAS	1820	ABNY	ABNY	150
ADAMS, THOMAS	1820	NYCO	WD06	496
ADAMS, THOMAS	1830	MONT	ROOT	42
ADAMS, THOMAS	1830	NYCO	WD06	431
ADAMS, WILLIAM	1830	NYCO	WD12	278
ADAMS, WILLIAM	1830	ROCK	CLAR	126
ADDISON, TOBIAS	1820	ABNY	ABNY	149
ADKINS, ADAM	1820	DUTC	FISH	61
ADKINS, ISAAC	1830	DUTC	FISH	479
ADKRINS, RICHARD	1810	SARA	MILT	795
ADLER, HANNAH	1830	NYCO	WD05	257
AFFRICANE, EDWARD	1830	NYCO	WD14	484
AFRICANIS, EDWARD	1820	NYCO	WD06	501
AGEE, NICHOLAS	1820	PUTM	CARM	101
AGNEW, NANCY	1820	NYCO	WD07	635
AGNEW, PHOEBE	1810	NYCO	WD06	401
AGNEW, SAMUEL	1810	NYCO	WD06	424
AGUSTUS	1830	NYCO	WD13	341
AKAY, JANUS	1810	SEÑE	OVID	258
AKERLEY, JAMES	1810	QUEN	OYST	239
AKERLEY, RICHARD	1830	SUFF	BROK	192
ALARR, SIBBY	1830	WEST	CORT	55
ALART, JESSE	1830	WEST	CORT	63
ALBANY, STEPHEN	1810	SUFF	HUNT	505
ALBANY, STEPHEN	1820	SUFF	HUNT	274

NAME	YR	CO	TWP	PG
ALBANY, STEPHEN	1830	SUFF	HUNT	304
ALBERT	1790	QUEN	NHEM	153
ALBERT, WILLIAM	1830	KING	WD03	279
ALBERTRON, JOSEPH	1830	QUEN	NHEM	112
ALBERTSON, HEDER	1810	SUFF	RIVH	551
ALDERMAN, MR.	1830	NYCO	WD10	19
ALDREDGE, DANIEL	1810	NYCO	WD05	317
ALDRIDGE, DANIEL	1800	NYCO	WD02	674
ALDRIDGE, DANIEL	1830	NYCO	WD08	229
ALDRIDGE, JOSHUA	1830	NYCO	WD08	217
ALDRIDGE, SOPHIA	1830	SUFF	SOUT	347
ALESWORTH, ARTHUR	1830	SUFF	BROK	164
ALEXANDER	1810	NYCO	WD10	697
ALEXANDER, BLACK	1830	ULST	NPAL	223
ALEXANDER, CALEB	1830	NYCO	WD05	328
ALEXANDER, CATO	1830	NYCO	WD12	280
ALEXANDER, CESAR	1830	NYCO	WD05	257
ALEXANDER, GEORGE	1820	ORNG	NEWB	509
ALEXANDER, GEORGE	1830	STEU	BATH	268
ALEXANDER, JOHN	1800	NYCO	WD03	697
ALEXANDER, JOHN	1830	NYCO	WD05	260
ALEXANDER, JOHN	1830	NYCO	WD09	349
ALEXANDER, JOHN	1830	NYCO	WD10	118
ALEXANDER, JOSEPH	1810	NYCO	WD02	99
ALEXANDER, MOSES	1830	STEU	BATH	273
ALEXANDER, MRS.	1820	KING	BRYN	126
ALEXANDER, PATO	1820	NYCO	WD09	938
ALEXANDER, THOMAS	1800	NYCO	WD07	887
ALEXANDRIA, JOHN	1810	DUTC	CLNT	378
ALEY, JOHN BATTIS	1800	NYCO	WD07	889
ALFERD, PERRE	1830	JEFF	ORLN	305
ALFERTS, FANNY	1830	NYCO	WD08	246
ALFORD, BENJAMIN	1830	NYCO	WD10	20
ALFRED, JOHN	1820	NYCO	WD06	455
ALICE	1790	WEST	HARR	199
ALIRANDER, MOSES	1820	STEU	BATH	227
ALKINS, FRANCIS F.	1830	DUTC	FISH	458
ALKINS, FRANCIS P.	1830	DUTC	FISH	459
ALLAIR, FRASER	1800	WEST	GREN	686
ALLEN, BACE VANE	1830	RENS	SHOD	252
ALLEN, FRANCIS	1830	NYCO	WD12	262
ALLEN, FRANCIS	1830	ONON	SALI	11
ALLEN, GEORGE	1830	SCNE	WD02	217
ALLEN, JOHN	1810	ORNG	NEWB	920
ALLEN, JOHN	1820	NYCO	WD07	631
ALLEN, JOHN	1820	ORNG	NEWC	695
ALLEN, JOSEPH	1810	NYCO	WD04	174
ALLEN, JOSEPH	1820	NYCO	WD02	115
ALLEN, MARY	1810	NYCO	WD02	102

NAME	YR	CO	TWP	PG
ALLEN, MR.	1830	NYCO	WD11	196
ALLEN, NATHANIEL	1830	NYCO	WD05	300
ALLEN, NELSON	1830	QUEN	FLUS	138
ALLEN, PETER	1830	DUTC	FISH	504
ALLEN, PRINCE	1800	DUTC	NORT	147
ALLEN, RICHARD	1820	NYCO	WD04	278
ALLEN, RICHARD	1830	RENS	TROY	17
ALLEN, SETH	1810	QUEN	FLUS	198
ALLEN, SHARP	1830	LEWI	DENM	407
ALLEN, TOBR	1820	HERK	NEWP	37
ALLEN, TOBY	1830	ONID	BOON	310
ALLEN, WILLIAM	1830	NYCO	WD08	169
ALLISON, RICHARD	1820	ORNG	GOSH	749
ALLMAN, HENRY	1830	NYCO	WD13	378
ALLURD, WILLIAM	1810	QUEN	NHEM	218
ALSDORF, GEORGE	1830	ULST	SHAW	254
ALSOP	1790	WEST	NORS	203
ALSOP, JACOB	1830	QUEN	OYST	41
ALSOP, MICAH	1810	QUEN	OYST	247
ALSTON, TIMOTHY	1810	QUEN	NHEM	212
ALSTYNE, JOHN	1830	RENS	PITT	143
ALTHOUSE, SAMUEL	1830	SUFF	HUNT	304
ALVANDOL, FRANCIS	1830	NYCO	WD05	321
AMBERMAN, ANTHONY	1830	NYCO	WD12	286
AMBERMAN, JAMES	1830	QUEN	FLUS	151
AMBERMAN, THOMAS	1820	QUEN	----	38
AMBERS	1790	SUFF	HUNT	163
AMBROSE	1800	QUEN	FLUS	543
AMBY, THOMAS	1800	NYCO	WD06	993
AMERGY, JAMES	1830	NYCO	WD05	354
AMES, BENHADAD	1790	DUTC	PAWL	86
AMEY	1790	QUEN	NHEM	153
AMHERST, MORRIS	1830	ORNG	GOSH	286
AMOS	1790	WEST	NORC	203
AMOS	1810	NSAL	SCHO	548
AMOS, ELIJIAH	1810	WEST	HARR	1105
AMOS, JAMES	1830	NYCO	WD08	215
AMOS, JOHN	1810	WEST	EAST	1155
AMOS, JOHN	1820	WEST	CORT	308
AMOS, STEPHEN	1830	NYCO	WD12	298
AMOS, THOMAS	1790	ABNY	WD02	13
AMUS	1820	SUFF	BROK	363
AMY	1800	NYCO	WD06	816
AMY, BENJAMIN	1810	NYCO	WD02	124
AMY, JERIMIAH	1810	NYCO	WD04	203
AMY, PRINCE	1810	NYCO	WD04	220
ANANIAS	1790	QUEN	OYST	153
ANBESMAN, THOMAS	1830	QUEN	JAMA	133

NAME	YR	CO	TWP	PG
ANDERS, THOMAS	1810	NYCO	WD03	83
ANDERSON	1810	NYCO	WD07	584
ANDERSON, CHARLES	1810	NYCO	WD05	318
ANDERSON, CHARLES	1820	NYCO	WD06	494
ANDERSON, CORNEALIA	1820	KING	BRYN	142
ANDERSON, CORNELIUS	1830	KING	BRYN	358
ANDERSON, CORNELIUS	1830	KING	FLAT	400
ANDERSON, CUFFEE	1830	KING	GRAV	405
ANDERSON, DARRICH	1820	NYCO	WD10	953
ANDERSON, DURHAM	1800	NYCO	WD05	775
ANDERSON, ESTHER	1830	NYCO	WD08	217
ANDERSON, GEORGE	1830	NYCO	WD06	437
ANDERSON, HARRY	1810	NYCO	WD05	370
ANDERSON, HENRY	1820	NYCO	WD06	528
ANDERSON, HENRY	1820	NYCO	WD08	841
ANDERSON, HENRY	1830	NYCO	WD08	174
ANDERSON, HENRY	1830	NYCO	WD09	413
ANDERSON, HENRY	1830	NYCO	WD10	46
ANDERSON, ISSAC	1810	ORNG	MONR	957
ANDERSON, ISSAC	1810	ORNG	MONT	957
ANDERSON, ISAAC	1820	ORNG	MONT	809
ANDERSON, ISAAC	1830	KING	WD05	327
ANDERSON, JAMES	1820	NYCO	WD04	237
ANDERSON, JAMES	1830	NYCO	WD09	431
ANDERSON, JANE	1830	NYCO	WD08	248
ANDERSON, JOEL	1830	ORNG	WALL	149
ANDERSON, JOHN	1810	NYCO	WD05	262
ANDERSON, JOHNATHAN	1830	NYCO	WD14	461
ANDERSON, JOHNATHAN	1830	NYCO	WD14	472
ANDERSON, JOSIAH	1800	NYCO	WD03	706
ANDERSON, JULIAN	1830	MONR	RWD2	204
ANDERSON, MARY	1810	NYCO	WD05	320
ANDERSON, MARY	1820	NYCO	WD03	169
ANDERSON, MARY	1830	NYCO	WD05	271
ANDERSON, MICHAEL	1830	KING	WD04	299
ANDERSON, NATHAN	1830	NYCO	WD14	455
ANDERSON, PETER	1820	JEFF	HOUN	417
ANDERSON, RICHARD	1820	WEST	HARR	467
ANDERSON, RICHARD	1830	KING	BUSH	384
ANDERSON, ROBERT	1830	HERK	SCHU	103
ANDERSON, S.	1830	NYCO	WD13	395
ANDERSON, SAMUEL	1820	COLU	HILL	1
ANDERSON, SAMUEL	1820	KING	BRYN	137
ANDERSON, SAMUEL	1830	KING	WD04	319
ANDERSON, SAMUEL	1830	NYCO	WD05	301
ANDERSON, SAMUEL	1830	NYCO	WD07	58
ANDERSON, SAMUEL	1830	NYCO	WD07	65
ANDERSON, SIMON	1820	ONID	UTIC	208
ANDERSON, STEPHEN	1830	NYCO	WD05	343

Anderson

NAME	YR	CO	TWP	PG
ANDERSON, THOMAS	1830	KING	WD04	321
ANDERSON, WILLIAM	1800	NYCO	WD07	888
ANDERSON, WILLIAM	1820	KING	BRYN	133
ANDERSON, WILLIAM	1830	NYCO	WD08	201
ANDERSON, WILSON	1800	NYCO	WD01	659
ANDREA, PETER	1800	NYCO	WD06	831
ANDREW	1790	QUEN	FLUS	150
ANDREW	1810	RICH	CAST	613
ANDREW	1820	KING	BRYN	175
ANDREW	1820	NYCO	WD05	341
ANDREW, JAMES	1810	NYCO	WD05	325
ANDREWS, MOSIER	1830	NYCO	WD06	435
ANDREWS, MRS.	1810	NYCO	WD03	45
ANDREWS, THOMAS	1800	NYCO	WD05	763
ANER	1790	QUEN	OYST	155
ANGAR, ALEXANDER	1800	NYCO	WD05	781
ANGELINE, GEORGE	1810	NYCO	WD04	177
ANGEVINE, ANN	1830	NYCO	WD05	344
ANHERST, DAVID	1830	ORNG	NEWB	59
ANLIGHT, PETER	1800	SUFF	SHAM	72
ANN	1790	QUEN	NHEM	152
ANN	1790	QUEN	FLUS	149
ANN	1790	QUEN	OYST	254
ANN	1800	ABNY	WD02	8
ANNOW, JOHNATHAN A.	1830	NYCO	WD10	46
ANSO, CUNEY	1830	SUFF	ISLP	285
ANTHEM, ELIJAH	1830	MONR	RWD3	231
ANTHON, THOMAS	1830	COLU	CHAT	43
ANTHONEY, ALEXANDER	1820	NYCO	WD08	733
ANTHONEY, ANTHONEY	1820	NYCO	WD09	940
ANTHONY	1790	NYCO	MONT	122
ANTHONY	1790	NYCO	MONT	124
ANTHONY	1790	NYCO	NORT	127
ANTHONY	1790	NYCO	OUTW	131
ANTHONY	1790	NYCO	HARL	137
ANTHONY	1790	QUEN	FLUS	149
ANTHONY	1790	QUEN	OYST	154
ANTHONY	1790	QUEN	OYST	155
ANTHONY	1790	SUFF	HUTT	163
ANTHONY	1800	SUFF	SMIT	60
ANTHONY	1800	SUFF	SHAM	74
ANTHONY	1810	GREN	COXE	290
ANTHONY	1820	WEST	PELH	207
ANTHONY, ABRAHAND	1830	RENS	SHOD	253
ANTHONY, ANDREW	1830	SARA	WATE	36
ANTHONY, ANTHONY	1830	NYCO	WD12	258
ANTHONY, CASPER	1810	COLU	HUDS	138
ANTHONY, CHARLES	1810	NYCO	WD10	657
ANTHONY, CHARLES	1820	DUTC	CLNT	39

NAME	YR	CO	TWP	PG
ANTHONY, CHRISTOPHER	1820	COLU	HUDS	4
ANTHONY, CORNELIA	1830	NYCO	WD06	449
ANTHONY, DIANA	1820	NYCO	WD08	789
ANTHONY, DINAH	1820	ABNY	ABNY	150
ANTHONY, FONDA	1830	DUTC	PGKP	355
ANTHONY, FRANCES	1820	DUTC	STAN	136
ANTHONY, FRANCIS	1830	DUTC	WASH	436
ANTHONY, GEORGE	1830	SCNE	GLEN	261
ANTHONY, JACOB	1830	COLU	KIND	142
ANTHONY, JACOB	1830	RENS	BRUN	221
ANTHONY, JOHN	1800	NYCO	WD04	737
ANTHONY, JOHN	1830	COLU	STUY	69
ANTHONY, JOSEPH	1820	SCHR	SCHR	436
ANTHONY, MILTON	1830	NYCO	WD14	460
ANTHONY, PETER	1810	NYCO	WD05	323
ANTHONY, RUBEN	1820	NYCO	WD07	636
ANTHONY, SAMUEL	1830	ABNY	BETH	536
ANTHONY, SAMUEL	1830	NYCO	WD05	335
ANTHONY, THOMAS	1820	COLU	CHAT	1
ANTHONY, THOMAS	1830	NYCO	WD09	291
ANTHONY, TONEY	1790	SUFF	BROK	162
ANTHONY, WILLIAM	1810	NYCO	WD04	213
ANTHONY, WILLIAM	1820	NYCO	WD07	686
ANTHONY, WILLIAM	1830	NYCO	WD04	182
ANTONIA, POLLY	1820	NYCO	WD07	677
ANTONIO, PETER	1810	NYCO	WD06	407
ANTONY, ANTHONY	1810	NYCO	WD05	369
ANTRIM, --	1790	NYCI	MONT	124
APINBE, DANIEL	1810	QUEN	NHEM	210
APPELBY, ELIJAH	1820	QUEN	----	67
APPLEBY, ANDREW	1830	QUEN	NHEM	104
APPLEBY, CHARLES	1810	QUEN	OYST	238
APPLEBY, ELIJAH	1830	QUEN	NHEM	117
APPLER, JONAS	1830	RENS	LANS	93
ARABELLA	1790	NYCO	MONT	123
ARAY, ABRAHAM	1830	WEST	CORT	59
ARAY, JACOB	1820	SENE	ROMU	352
ARCH	1790	QUEN	OYST	154
ARCH, ISAAC	1830	SUFF	SHAM	230
ARCH, JAMES	1830	SUFF	ISLP	278
ARCH, JAMES	1830	SUFF	SHAM	224
ARCH, JOHN	1820	SUFF	SOUT	349
ARCH, JOHN	1830	SUFF	BROK	181
ARCH, JOSHUA	1810	SUFF	BROK	483
ARCHBOUL, KESIAH	1830	SUFF	SMIT	273
ARCHI, SAMUEL	1820	SUFF	SMIT	318
ARCHIBALD	1800	QUEN	OYST	573
ARCHIBALD	1800	SUFF	ISLP	62

NAME	YR	CO	TWP	PG
ARCHIBALD	1810	SUFF	SMIT	540
ARCHIBALL	1820	SUFF	SMIT	323
ARCOS, CHARLES	1830	NYCO	WD08	244
ARDEN, JAMES	1830	NYCO	WD10	66
ARDEN, PHEOBY	1830	WEST	WEST	120
ARDEN, RICHARD	1820	PUTM	PHIL	101
ARDIS, JANE	1810	NYCO	WD06	424
ARLEN, POLLY	1820	NYCO	WD07	635
ARMER, JACOB	1820	NYCO	WD10	1054
ARMONG, CHARLES	1810	NYCO	WD05	290
ARMSTRONG, ABRAHAM	1830	DUTC	STAN	405
ARMSTRONG, ELIAS	1790	DUTC	NORT	86
ARMSTRONG, ELIAS	1800	COLU	HUDS	450
ARMSTRONG, HENRY	1820	QUEN	----	20
ARMSTRONG, JULIA	1800	ORNG	NEWC	394
ARMSTRONG, MARY	1830	QUEN	SHEM	85
ARMSTRONG, PETER	1830	DUTC	STAN	405
ARMSTRONG, PETING	1820	DUTC	STAN	137
ARMSTRONG, RICHARD	1820	DUTC	CLNT	28
ARNOLD, EBENEZER	1790	DUTC	FRDK	81
ARNOLD, EBENEZER	1800	DUTC	PAWL	128
ARNOLD, NOEL	1810	NYCO	WD05	290
ARNWOOD, WHITTINGTON	1830	CAYU	LEDY	275
ARRANT, PRINCE	1830	MONT	MIND	7
ARROUX, NOEL	1830	NYCO	WD06	369
ARROW, ABEL	1790	ULST	SHAW	183
ARTHUR, NOEL	1810	SUFF	SMIT	539
ARVILL, CHARLES P.	1830	ORNG	BLOM	122
ASBORN	1820	PUTM	PATE	101
ASBORNS, DENCE	1820	SUFF	BROK	328
ASH, CHARLES	1820	KING	BRYN	115
ASH, JAMES	1820	KING	BRYN	118
ASH, MRS.	1830	KING	WD03	280
ASHE, ROBERT	1810	NYCO	WD06	444
ASHLEY, HENRY	1820	COLU	KIND	1
ASHLEY, HENRY	1830	COLU	STUY	63
ASHLEY, ROBERT	1810	COLU	HUDS	133
ASHMAN, H.	1830	ERIE	BUFF	33
ASHTON, AMANDA	1800	NYCO	WD06	849
ASON	1810	NYCO	WD10	688
ASTOR, PHILLIP	1820	NYCO	WD10	964
ASURE, RICHARD	1820	SCNE	WD02	129
ASURE, SAMUEL	1820	SCNE	WD02	127
ATEAN, BENNET	1820	NYCO	WD05	382
ATHON, SHARBE	1810	NYCO	WD05	259
ATKIN, JOSEPH	1830	NYCO	WD05	267
ATKINS, ADAM	1830	DUTC	FISH	476
ATKINS, CHARLES	1820	NYCO	WD07	628
ATKINS, FRANCIS P.	1820	DUTC	FISH	68

NAME	YR	CO	TWP	PG
ATKINS, JAMES	1830	SCNE	WD02	223
ATKINS, JOHN	1830	ROCK	HVER	155
ATKINS, JONATHAN	1810	ROCK	HVER	649
ATKINS, RICHARD	1820	SARA	MILT	236
ATKINS, RICHARD	1820	SARA	MILT	231
ATKINS, THOMAS	1830	DUTC	FISH	463
ATKINSON, CHRISTOPHER	1830	NYCO	WD08	224
ATKINSON, SARAH	1830	NYCO	WD05	264
ATTIS, CHARLES	1810	NYCO	WD07	568
AUCKERTON, JOHN	1830	NYCO	WD01	34
AUDROVETT, WILLIAM	1820	BROM	UNON	28
AUGUSTA, ELEXABETH	1820	NYCO	WD08	781
AUGUSTINE	1790	WEST	RYE	205
AUGUSTINE, CHRISTOPHER	1810	NYCO	WD06	399
AUGUSTUS, CESAR	1830	GREN	ATHN	205
AUGUSTUS, GALLY	1820	NYCO	WD10	1055
AUGUSTUS, GEORGE	1800	NYCO	WD06	817
AUGUSTUS, GEORGE	1810	NYCO	WD05	312
AUGUSTUS, ISAAC	1830	NYCO	WD08	184
AUGUSTUS, PETER	1820	NYCO	WD05	339
AUGUSTUS, RICHARD	1830	NYCO	WD01	48
AUGUTUS, BENJAMIN	1800	NYCO	WD07	889
AUSTIN, JOHN	1810	NYCO	WD05	371
AUSTIN, JOHN	1830	NYCO	WD06	463
AUSTIN, THOMAS	1830	SUFF	SHAM	217
AVERY, AMOS	1800	DUTC	STAN	125
AVERY, CESAR	1820	WASH	SALM	186
AVERY, JACK	1810	NYCO	WD06	417
AVERY, JOHN	1830	NYCO	WD12	298
AVERY, LOUISA	1820	NYCO	WD04	242
AVERY, SOLOMON	1820	PUTM	PHIL	101
AVERY, THOMAS	1830	MONR	RWD1	197
AXWELL, JONE	1830	QUEN	JAMA	134
AYLESWORTH, ARTER	1810	SUFF	BROK	471
AZURE, SAMUEL	1830	SCNE	WD01	203
B...., MICHAEL B.	1810	NYCO	WD04	224
BABCOCK, JOSEPH	1820	ONTA	SENE	269
BABTEST, JOHN	1800	NYCO	WD05	781
BABTIS, JOHN	1800	NYCO	WD06	820
BABTIST, JOHN	1800	NYCO	WD06	849
BABTIST, JOHN	1810	NYCO	WD02	108
BABYLON, PRENTICE	1830	NYCO	WD10	72
BACCUS, THOMAS	1820	SCNE	ROTT	578
BACKUS, RICHARD	1830	WANE	PALM	40
BADGER, CHARLES	1830	NYCO	WD10	38
BADGER, CHARLES	1830	NYCO	WD10	125
BAGGOT, THOMAS	1830	NYCO	WD12	262

NAME	YR	CO	TWP	PG
BAGIT, LEWIS	1810	NYCO	WD10	628
BAGO, CESAEREZER	1790	ORNG	MINI	143
BAGO, RACHEL	1810	ORNG	GOSH	1121
BAILEY, EDWARD	1820	NYCO	WD07	633
BAILEY, GEORGE	1830	NYCO	WD08	248
BAILEY, ISAAC	1830	SUFF	SMIT	276
BAILEY, MARY ANN	1830	NYCO	WD14	443
BAILEY, MRS.	1830	NYCO	WD11	158
BAILEY, PETER	1830	SCHR	MIDD	49
BAILEY, THOMAS	1830	DUTC	FISH	480
BAILEY, WILLIAM	1820	ONTA	SENE	272
BAILEY, WILLIAM	1830	KING	WD05	329
BAIN, PETER	1810	NYCO	WD05	371
BAIR, JOHN O.	1810	NYCO	WD06	468
BAIRD, SIMON	1830	ONID	WEST	318
BAKEMAN, BENJAMIN	1830	ONON	ONON	189
BAKEMAN, HENRY	1810	ONON	CICE	586
BAKEMAN, HENRY	1820	OSWE	GRAN	12
BAKEMAN, JACOB	1830	OSWE	GRAN	173
BAKEMAN, JAMES	1830	ONON	CAMI	201
BAKEMAN, JOSEPH	1830	WEST	MTPL	44
BAKER, ABRAHAM	1830	RENS	BRUN	224
BAKER, BARSLEY	1830	MONR	RWD1	199
BAKER, FRANCES	1800	NYCO	WD07	872
BAKER, FRANCES	1810	WEST	HARR	1131
BAKER, FRANCIS	1830	NYCO	WD10	99
BAKER, IZABEL	1820	DUTC	FISH	62
BAKER, JACOB	1830	SARA	CTPK	139
BAKER, JAMES	1820	NYCO	WD03	189
BAKER, JAMES	1830	RENS	LANS	100
BAKER, JAUK	1830	SCHR	MIDD	36
BAKER, JOHN	1830	MONT	CANJ	29
BAKER, LEWIS	1810	DUTC	BEEK	278
BAKER, LEWIS	1830	DUTC	BEEK	188
BAKER, MRS.	1830	NYCO	WD11	213
BAKER, RACHAEL	1830	NYCO	WD14	526
BAKER, WILLIAM	1830	NYCO	WD10	19
BALD, ARCHIBALD	1830	MONR	BRIG	14
BALDWIN, ANTHONY	1820	ONTA	BENT	264
BALDWIN, J.	1810	MADI	SMIT	877
BALDWIN, JAMES	1830	SUFF	ISLP	284
BALDWIN, JOHN	1830	MADI	----	419
BALDWIN, PHILIP	1810	QUEN	OYST	241
BALDWIN, SUSAN	1830	NYCO	WD08	241
BALDWIN, THOMAS	1820	PUTM	SOUT	100
BALDWIN, WILLIAM	1810	NYCO	WD05	377
BALDWIN, WILLIAM	1820	NYCO	WD06	495
BALDWIN, WILLIAM	1830	NYCO	WD06	381
BALEY	1820	PUTM	PATE	101

NAME	YR	CO	TWP	PG
BALEY, LEVY	1820	PUTM	SOUT	100
BALEY, ROWLAND	1820	PUTM	KENT	100
BALL, GEORGE	1830	NYCO	WD08	256
BALL, SARAH	1810	NYCO	WD05	345
BALL, SOLOMAN	1800	NYCO	WD06	814
BALLARD, ALEXANDER	1810	NYCO	WD04	235
BALTIMORE, HARRY	1830	CAYU	SEMP	306
BALTIMORE, JAMES	1830	ABNY	WD04	320
BALTIMORE, SAMUEL	1830	RENS	TROY	15
BAMAN, THOMAS	1830	DUTC	FISH	462
BANBRIDGE, WILLIAM	1830	ONTA	SENE	85
BAND, ANTHONY	1820	NYCO	WD07	705
BANE, JOHNATHAN	1830	NYCO	WD14	432
BANE, PETER	1820	NYCO	WD02	122
BANE, PETER	1830	NYCO	WD05	341
BANE, ROBERT	1830	GREN	CATS	221
BANEKER, JOHN	1800	NYCO	WD05	753
BANK, MR.	1830	NYCO	WD11	196
BANK, ROBERT	1820	NYCO	WD10	977
BANKER, JANE	1810	SCNE	WD01	935
BANKER, TOBY	1820	NYCO	WD09	939
BANKLEY, JAMES	1810	NYCO	WD05	286
BANKS, GEORGE	1830	WEST	RYE	99
BANKS, HILLIS	1830	NYCO	WD06	444
BANKS, POMP	1830	WEST	NORC	195
BANKS, R.	1830	ERIE	BUFF	5
BANKS, SAMUEL	1830	ULST	SHAW	255
BANKS, WILLIAM	1830	NYCO	WD10	87
BANTA, NICHOLAS	1830	ORNG	WARW	78
BANYAN, GEORGE	1820	NYCO	WD07	701
BAPTEST, JOSEPH	1820	NYCO	WD03	152
BAPTIS, JOHN	1800	NYCO	WD06	847
BAPTIS, JOHN	1800	NYCO	WD06	830
BAPTIST, ANDREW	1810	NYCO	WD06	435
BAPTIST, JOHN	1810	NYCO	WD05	322
BAPTIST, JOHN	1810	NYCO	WD06	439
BAPTIST, JOHN	1810	NYCO	WD06	416
BAPTIST, JOHN	1810	NYCO	WD06	458
BAPTIST, JOHN	1810	NYCO	WD06	398
BAPTIST, JOHN	1810	NYCO	WD07	576
BAPTIST, JOHN	1810	NYCO	WD07	591
BAPTISTE, JOHN	1810	NYCO	WD04	159
BAPTISTE, JOHN	1820	NYCO	WD06	528
BARAGA, ANDREW	1820	NYCO	WD06	536
BARBAREE, PEGGY	1810	NYCO	WD02	120
BARBARIE, ADAM	1800	NYCO	WD03	705
BARBARU, CHARLOTTE	1820	NYCO	WD05	391
BARBER, CHARLOTTE	1810	NYCO	WD05	307
BARBER, JOHN	1800	NYCO	WD06	846

Barber

NAME	YR	CO	TWP	PG
BARBER, PRINCE	1820	COLU	HUDS	5
BARBER, SAMUEL	1800	NYCO	WD06	449
BARBER, SAMUEL	1820	NYCO	WD04	290
BARBER, WILLIAM	1830	NYCO	WD14	495
BARBERRY, CHARLOTTE	1830	NYCO	WD05	331
BARCLAY, SIMEON	1810	NYCO	WD05	321
BARDONE, DINAH	1820	ONID	WHTT	303
BARDUE, SALEM	1820	WASH	JACK	190
BAREMAKER, GEORGE	1820	NYCO	WD03	155
BARENT, SIMEON	1830	CHEN	GREN	48
BARKER, RICHARD	1830	WEST	HARR	214
BARKER, THOMAS	1820	WEST	WEST	186
BARLEY, FRANCIS	1820	ORNG	NEWB	513
BARLOW, THOMAS	1800	NYCO	WD06	473
BARNARD, J.	1830	NYCO	WD11	155
BARNARD, JAMES	1830	NYCO	WD06	427
BARNARD, MARY	1800	NYCO	WD01	23
BARNARD, SIMON	1820	ONID	WEST	155
BARNES, DINA	1830	SUFF	EAST	259
BARNES, JOHN	1820	NYCO	WD01	51
BARNES, JOHN	1830	NYCO	WD01	8
BARNES, MARY	1830	NYCO	WD08	131
BARNES, SAMUEL	1830	NYCO	WD04	178
BARNET, GEORGE	1830	NYCO	WD10	26
BARNET, ROSANNA	1800	NYCO	WD04	181
BARNET, SAMUEL	1800	NYCO	WD06	835
BARNETT, JOHN A.	1830	NYCO	WD01	35
BARNEY, ISAAC	1830	NYCO	WD08	186
BARNEY, MARIA	1820	NYCO	WD08	797
BARNS, CATO	1820	SUFF	EAST	295
BARNS, EASOP	1800	WEST	RYE	1164
BARNS, EASOP	1830	WEST	HARR	214
BARNS, JOHN	1800	NYCO	WD06	830
BARNS, JOHN	1820	ABNY	ABNY	156
BARNS, SAMUEL	1800	NYCO	WD04	231
BARNS, WILLIAM	1820	ABNY	BETH	217
BARNUM, STEPHEN	1820	PUTM	SOUT	100
BARON, DIANA	1800	NYCO	WD06	494
BARRIAN, CORNELIUS	1820	ORNG	BLOM	718
BARRIS, EASOP	1820	WEST	NORC	466
BARRON, STEPHEN	1830	ABNY	WD01	224
BARRY, JAS	1820	NYCO	WD08	773
BARTHOLOMEW, M.	1800	NYCO	WD05	291
BARTO, JERRY	1800	WEST	EAST	1156
BARTON, ANN	1830	NYCO	WD08	217
BARTON, JARED	1830	BROM	UNON	34
BARTON, JOHN	1820	COLU	HUDS	3
BARTON, NICHOLAS	1830	NYCO	WD10	19

NAME	YR	CO	TWP	PG
BARTON, THOMAS	1830	COLU	KIND	147
BARTOR, THOMAS	1830	ORNG	GOSH	274
BARTOW, LUKE	1800	WEST	NEWR	625
BARTOW, NICKOLAS	1800	NYCO	WD06	493
BARTUM, JOHN	1800	NYCO	WD07	885
BARYER, MANN	1830	RICH	NORT	22
BASET, DAVID	1800	NYCO	WD07	535
BASS, ASA.	1820	ONTA	PENF	148
BASS, ASA	1830	MONR	PENF	347
BASS, JENNY	1800	QUEN	JAMA	545
BASS, JOHN	1810	NYCO	WD06	425
BASSETTERRY, LETTY	1820	NYCO	WD07	619
BASSTON, QUACK	1830	WASH	SALM	210
BASTON, WILLIAM	1830	QUEN	JAMA	124
BAT	1800	ROCK	ORNG	636
BATAMON, JAMES	1820	LEWI	DENM	277
BATES, BENJAMIN	1830	QUEN	OYST	34
BATES, BENJAMIN	1830	QUEN	FLUS	154
BATES, CATO	1820	QUEN	----	57
BATES, ISAAC	1830	WEST	EAST	133
BATES, SILVANUS	1830	KING	BRYN	367
BATES, JEREMIAH	1830	ABNY	WD01	221
BATEY, ANDREW	1820	WEST	SUMM	356
BATIS, M.	1810	NYCO	WD05	280
BATTE, PETER	1810	NYCO	WD07	553
BATTES, SYLVESTER	1820	ABNY	WATV	259
BATTEY, LOUIS	1830	NYCO	WD06	450
BATTICE, JOHN	1830	NYCO	WD06	435
BATTIN, JOSEPH	1830	NYCO	WD06	432
BATTIS, CHARLES	1820	NYCO	WD06	465
BATTIS, ELIZA	1830	NYCO	WD10	18
BATTIS, JOHN	1820	NYCO	WD05	352
BATTIS, JOHN	1820	NYCO	WD05	393
BATTIS, JOHN	1830	NYCO	WD05	266
BATTIS, JUDAH	1810	NYCO	WD01	23
BATTIS, JUDITH	1800	NYCO	WD06	844
BATTIS, MADAM	1830	NYCO	WD06	431
BATTIS, P.	1830	NYCO	WD10	37
BATTIS, PETER	1800	NYCO	WD07	889
BATTIS, PETER	1820	NYCO	WD07	635
BATTIST, JOHN	1820	NYCO	WD03	146
BATTIST, JOHN	1820	NYCO	WD03	185
BAUKY, MINTO	1800	NYCO	WD03	696
BAUMAN, JAMES	1810	NYCO	WD03	87
BAUN, ANTHONY	1830	NYCO	WD05	328
BAUR, ANTHONY	1830	SCHR	COBL	149
BAUSER, GEORGE	1830	NYCO	WD06	383
BAYA, ROBERT	1810	NYCO	WD10	658
BAYARD, HENRY	1810	NYCO	WD03	59

NAME	YR	CO	TWP	PG
BAYARD, LAPICE	1800	NYCO	WD06	798
BAYARD, SIMON	1820	ONID	WEST	155
BAYLEY, AGNES	1830	NYCO	WD07	40
BAYMAN, JIM	1790	QUEN	FLUS	149
BAYON, MARY	1810	NYCO	WD05	250
BAYS, DAVID	1820	ORNG	WARW	626
BAYS, DAVID	1830	ORNG	WARW	78
BAYS, WILLIAM	1830	ORNG	WARW	76
BEACH, SAMUEL	1820	NYCO	WD07	621
BEADLE, JACOB	1820	GREN	NEWB	20
BEADLY, GILES	1810	SUFF	BROK	478
BEAGLE, WILLIAM	1820	ORNG	BLOM	731
BEAGLE, WILLIAM	1830	ORNG	MONR	220
BEAM, WILLIAM	1830	NYCO	WD05	264
BEAN	1810	NYCO	WD06	450
BEAN, LEWIS	1800	NYCO	WD06	844
BEAN, RICHARD	1800	NYCO	WD06	797
BEAR, MARY O.	1830	NYCO	WD06	367
BEARD, SIMON	1810	MONT	CANJ	84
BEARMAKER, GEORGE	1800	NYCO	WD01	667
BEARSHAKER, GEORGE	1810	NYCO	WD05	249
BEASE, JOHN	1810	NYCO	WD05	269
BECKER, DIANAH	1820	ABNY	BETH	218
BECKER, JACOB	1830	ABNY	BETH	548
BECKER, JANE	1820	ABNY	BETH	218
BECKER, JOHN	1830	CAYU	LEDY	283
BECKER, SAMUEL A.	1830	ABNY	BETH	536
BECKET, GEORGE A.	1830	NYCO	WD08	219
BECKLIS, GEORGE	1800	NYCO	WD01	667
BECKMAN, HENDRICK	1790	ABNY	BALL	15
BECOMBUS, JACOB	1830	ORNG	WALL	148
BEDDENCE, BENJAMIN	1800	NYCO	WD06	808
BEDELL, JACK	1830	RICH	WEST	9
BEDELL, JACOB	1830	GREN	NEWB	174
BEDELL, LAWRENCE	1830	RICH	NORT	30
BEEKMAN, CESAR	1830	NYCO	WD09	295
BEEKMAN, HENRY	1790	MONT	MOHA	110
BEEMAN, THOMAS	1830	SUFF	SOUT	348
BEEN, IRA	1820	NYCO	WD10	981
BEERS, CHARLES	1830	NYCO	WD07	61
BEES, JOHN	1830	NYCO	WD08	212
BEGELL, SAMUEL	1790	RICH	SOUT	159
BEGLE, BENJAMIN	1800	NYCO	WD07	912
BEGRAFF, JOHN	1820	GREN	COXE	43
BEIDOUT, MARIA	1820	NYCO	WD07	621
BELCHER, ISSAC	1820	DELA	DAVE	55
BELDING, JERIMAH	1810	NYCO	WD03	78
BELDING, JOHN	1800	DUTC	AMEN	134
BELFAST, WILLIAM	1800	NYCO	WD06	810

NAME	YR	CO	TWP	PG
BELIMORE, JOHN	1830	NYCO	WD06	379
BELL, H.	1830	NYCO	WD11	162
BELL, JACK	1830	ROCK	ORGT	115
BELL, JEREMIAH	1830	MONR	RWD3	231
BELL, LUCRETIA	1810	NYCO	WD03	368
BELL, LUCRETIA	1830	NYCO	WD06	435
BELL, S.	1830	NYCO	WD13	343
BELL, SOLOMON	1810	NYCO	WD05	319
BELLA, SOPHIA	1830	NYCO	WD14	426
BELLINGER, AARON	1830	HERK	DANU	181
BELSHER, ISAAC	1830	DELA	HAMD	96
BEMET	1810	DUTC	PGKP	324
BEN	1790	QUEN	OYST	154
BEN	1800	QUEN	OYST	579
BEN	1800	QUEN	OYST	576
BEN	1800	QUEN	OYST	575
BEN	1800	SUFF	BROK	3
BEN	1820	QUEN	----	75
BENADICT, ELIJAH	1820	NYCO	WD06	537
BENDETT, MARIA	1830	NYCO	WD14	438
BENEDECT, JOSEPH	1820	NYCO	WD10	976
BENEDICT, ISAAC	1830	NYCO	WD10	91
BENEDICT, ISAAC	1830	NYCO	WD12	255
BENEDICT, JOHN	1830	NYCO	WD06	431
BENEDICT, JOSEPH	1810	NYCO	WD07	605
BENEDICT, PHILLIS	1830	NYCO	WD05	342
BENET, ABRAHAM	1810	WEST	NEWR	1079
BENET, TIM	1810	WEST	NEWR	1079
BENIT, ATLON	1830	NYCO	WD05	260
BENJAMIN	1790	QUEN	NHEM	153
BENJAMIN	1790	QUEN	OYST	153
BENJAMIN	1790	QUEN	OYST	154
BENJAMIN	1790	QUEN	OYST	155
BENJAMIN	1800	QUEN	NHEM	559
BENJAMIN	1800	QUEN	NHEM	551
BENJAMIN	1800	QUEN	OYST	573
BENJAMIN	1800	SUFF	HUNT	39
BENJAMIN	1810	KING	BRYN	638
BENJAMIN	1810	NYCO	WD07	617
BENJAMIN	1810	ONTA	PALM	800
BENJAMIN	1820	QUEN	----	66
BENJAMIN, ADAM	1830	NYCO	WD10	85
BENJAMIN, BEN	1810	NYCO	WD05	280
BENJAMIN, CHARLES	1830	NYCO	WD06	404
BENJAMIN, JEREMIAH	1830	SUFF	ISLP	284
BENJAMIN, JOHN	1820	NYCO	WD07	628
BENJAMIN, LEWIS	1830	OTSG	SPFD	79
BENJAMIN, PECK	1820	ULST	KING	78
BENJAMIN, PETER	1810	SUFF	SOUT	571

17

Benjamin

NAME	YR	CO	TWP	PG
BENJAMIN, PETER	1820	SUFF	SOUT	345
BENJAMIN, PETER	1830	QUEN	NHEM	112
BENJAMIN, ROBERT	1830	NYCO	WD14	438
BENJAMIN, SUSAN	1830	NYCO	WD08	172
BENJAMIN, THOMAS	1820	NYCO	WD06	447
BENJAMIN, THOMAS	1830	NYCO	WD04	188
BENKIS, SIRUS	1790	RICH	SOUT	159
BENNET, ABNER	1830	DELA	DELH	42
BENNET, AMOS	1830	DELA	DELH	42
BENNET, BENJAMIN	1830	MADI	----	232
BENNET, JAMES JR.	1830	ORNG	HBGH	124
BENNET, LEWIS	1810	NYCO	WD05	25
BENNET, LOUISA	1800	NYCO	WD06	802
BENNET, SOLMON	1830	DELA	MERI	134
BENNET, TIMOTHY	1810	DELA	DELH	529
BENNET, WILLIAM W.	1830	DELA	DELH	42
BENNETT	1810	NYCO	WD05	283
BENNETT, CHARLES	1820	NYCO	WD08	733
BENNETT, TIMOTHY	1800	DELA	DELH	1324
BENNETT, TIMOTHY	1820	DELA	DELH	55
BENOIT, LOUIS	1830	NYCO	WD05	267
BENSEN, LEN	1820	QUEN	----	478
BENSON, BENJAMIN	1830	NYCO	WD10	122
BENSON, BENJAMIN	1830	ROCK	RPOO	101
BENSON, CHARITY	1830	NYCO	WD06	383
BENSON, CRANDUS	1820	QUEN	----	74
BENSON, CROSS	1820	NYCO	WD05	365
BENSON, ISAAC	1810	WEST	NEWR	1083
BENSON, ISAAC	1830	NYCO	WD06	408
BENSON, JAMES	1830	QUEN	OYST	49
BENSON, JOHN	1800	ORNG	GOSH	356
BENSON, JOHN	1820	NYCO	WD05	395
BENSON, JOHN	1820	NYCO	WD05	418
BENSON, JOHN	1830	KING	FLAN	412
BENSON, JOHN	1830	NYCO	WD06	386
BENSON, JORDAN	1830	NYCO	WD07	40
BENSON, LIMON	1820	QUEN	----	20
BENSON, PHILLIS	1830	NYCO	WD05	262
BENSON, SHARP	1810	NYCO	WD06	452
BENTHISEN, ALEXANDER	1820	NYCO	WD05	398
BENTON, DANIEL	1820	JEFF	PAME	460
BENTON, DANIEL	1830	JEFF	LRAY	327
BENTON, JOHN	1830	NYCO	WD08	148
BENTON, MATTHEW	1820	JEFF	PAME	462
BENTON, THOMAS	1830	COLU	CLER	272
BENUETT, LEWIS	1820	NYCO	WD06	490
BEOISS	1790	NYCO	MONT	123
BERDUE, THOMAS	1830	SUFF	BROK	158
BERGELOW, RICHARD	1830	NYCO	WD14	451

NAME	YR	CO	TWP	PG
BERGEN, JOHN	1830	GREN	NEWB	174
BERGER, HENRY	1810	NYCO	WD03	80
BERGS, HARRY	1830	SCHR	SCHR	14
BERIAN, J.O.	1830	NYCO	WD11	133
BERKLET, BENJAMIN	1820	ABNY	ABNY	151
BERNARD, JOHNATHAN	1830	NYCO	WD14	492
BERRIAN, CORNELIUS	1830	ORNG	BLOM	118
BERRY, CEASAR	1810	NYCO	WD03	85
BERRY, CHARLES	1830	NYCO	WD05	305
BERRY, DANIEL	1810	NYCO	WD06	445
BERRY, DINAH	1810	NYCO	WD05	360
BERRY, DOROTHEA	1830	NYCO	WD05	329
BERRY, ELIZABETH	1830	NYCO	WD08	175
BERRY, JAMES	1810	NYCO	WD07	553
BERRY, JOHN	1820	ROCK	ORGT	86
BERRY, JOHN	1830	ROCK	ORGT	111
BERRY, JOSEPH	1830	NYCO	WD08	195
BERRY, JOSEPH	1830	NYCO	WD08	257
BERRY, MARY	1830	NYCO	WD14	468
BERRY, PATRICK	1820	NYCO	WD04	313
BERRY, WIDOW	1820	NYCO	WD04	299
BERRY, WILLIAM	1810	NYCO	WD05	277
BERRY, WILLIAM	1830	NYCO	WD08	249
BERTEN, MAGDALEN	1810	NYCO	WD06	404
BERTHOLF, POMP	1820	ORNG	WARW	644
BERTHOLF, POMPEY	1830	ORNG	WARW	64
BERTHOLF, SUSAN	1830	ORNG	WARW	87
BERTHOLIMERE, H.	1800	ONID	MADR	255
BERTINE, HARRY	1810	WEST	RYE	1168
BERTOLF, POMP	1810	ORNG	WARW	973
BESHEL, BENJAMIN	1810	NYCO	WD06	457
BESS	1810	DUTC	FISH	238
BEST, CAESAR	1830	COLU	KIND	138
BEST, CORNELIUS	1830	COLU	GHEN	165
BEST, GEORGE	1830	HERK	LTFA	86
BET	1800	ABNY	WD01	263
BET	1800	ABNY	WD02	286
BET	1800	ABNY	WATV	95
BET	1820	SARA	STIL	191
BETEY	1810	RENS	TROY	388
BETSEY	1800	SUFF	SMIT	57
BETSEY	1810	NYCO	WD06	406
BETT	1790	QUEN	JAMA	150
BETTE	1800	SUFF	BROK	7
BETTE	1800	SUFF	BROK	8
BETTEY	1810	NYCO	WD05	364
BETTIS, E.	1820	NYCO	WD05	391
BETTRINGO	1790	QUEN	FLUS	149
BETTS, LUCRETIA	1830	NYCO	WD06	380

NAME	YR	CO	TWP	PG
BETTS, TICE	1810	QUEN	NEWT	168
BETTY	1790	NYCO	MONT	121
BETTY	1790	QUEN	NEWT	151
BETTY	1790	QUEN	OYST	154
BETTY	1800	NYCO	WD05	748
BETTY	1800	QUEN	FLUS	540
BETTY	1800	RENS	GREN	721
BETTY	1810	COLU	HUDS	143
BETTY	1810	NYCO	WD05	304
BETTY	1810	RENS	TROY	389
BETTY	1830	KING	FLAT	397
BETU	1790	NYCO	MONT	122
BEVIER, ABRAHAM	1830	ULST	SHAW	241
BEZ, JOSEPH	1810	NYCO	WD06	441
BIARA, EDWARD	1820	QUEN	----	56
BIARD, SEAZER	1830	WEST	NEWR	112
BIAS, MRS.	1830	TOMP	ITCA	332
BICKEL, ISHMAEL	1810	ONTA	CANA	888
BIJAH	1800	QUEN	OYST	580
BILL	1790	NYCO	WEST	133
BILL	1790	QUEN	FLUS	149
BILL	1790	QUEN	NHEM	152
BILL	1790	WEST	NEWR	201
BILL	1800	QUEN	OYST	570
BILL	1800	QUEN	OYST	575
BILL	1800	RENS	SCAS	777
BILL, INDIAD	1830	WEST	HARR	215
BILL, LUCRETIA	1800	NYCO	WD02	672
BILLINGS, THOMAS	1800	NYCO	WD06	797
BILLSON, JOHN	1790	ORNG	GOSH	139
BILSON, LUCY	1810	ORNG	GOSH	1129
BIN, SUSANNA	1820	WEST	MAMA	367
BINAH	1800	SUFF	EHAM	95
BINGS, JOHN	1830	WEST	NEWR	114
BINKS, ANN	1820	NYCO	WD06	450
BINKS, ANN	1830	NYCO	WD06	389
BINKS, BENJAMIN	1820	NYCO	WD05	422
BINKS, JOHN	1820	NYCO	WD09	944
BINNIS, JOHN	1810	NYCO	WD07	556
BIRCH, HANNAH	1830	NYCO	WD04	159
BIRCHUM, EDWARD	1800	NYCO	WD04	733
BIRD, GEORGE	1820	NYCO	WD07	721
BIRD, GEORGE	1820	NYCO	WD07	631
BIRD, JOHN	1820	SUFF	SHEL	331
BIRD, MARIA	1830	NYCO	WD06	408
BIRD, POLLY	1800	NYCO	WD07	858
BIRDS, RICHARD	1800	DELA	KORT	8
BIRTCH, ISIAH	1820	DUTC	BEEK	18
BISHOP, BRISTER	1800	NYCO	WD07	916

NAME	YR	CO	TWP	PG
BISHOP, EDWARD	1830	RENS	TROY	17
BISHOP, GEORGE	1820	GENE	PERY	230
BISHOP, JACOB	1820	WEST	NEWR	211
BISHOP, JOHN	1830	ONON	SKAN	136
BISHOP, LEWIS	1800	WEST	CORT	811
BISHOP, SAMUEL	1830	GENE	PERY	261
BISHOP, WILLIAM H.	1830	ONON	SKAN	136
BITUS	1810	NYCO	WD06	416
BIX, HENRY	1830	ORNG	NEWB	46
BLACK	1810	NYCO	WD06	444
BLACK	1810	QUEN	OYST	231
BLACK, AARON	1820	SUFF	SHAM	320
BLACK, ABRAHAM	1810	SUFF	ISLP	499
BLACK, BETSY	1820	NYCO	WD06	447
BLACK, BILL	1810	WEST	NORC	1176
BLACK, CAESAR	1800	ORNG	GOSH	361
BLACK, CAR...	1810	QUEN	OYST	237
BLACK, CEASER	1810	SUFF	SMIT	540
BLACK, CHRISTENE	1820	SCNE	SCNE	130
BLACK, CLORAH	1790	SUFF	BROK	162
BLACK, CUFF	1790	DUTC	PGKP	91
BLACK, EPHAIM	1820	SUFF	BROK	356
BLACK, GEORGE	1820	NYCO	WD03	188
BLACK, GEORGE	1820	NYCO	WD04	227
BLACK, GEORGE	1820	NYCO	WD10	982
BLACK, HAGER	1810	SUFF	RIVH	543
BLACK, HARRY	1810	WEST	HARR	1135
BLACK, HARRY A.	1830	SARA	MILT	21
BLACK, HENRY	1830	ULST	MARL	283
BLACK, ISAAC	1800	NYCO	WD04	722
BLACK, ISAAC	1810	SUFF	SMIT	536
BLACK, ISABELLA	1830	NYCO	WD06	385
BLACK, JACK	1810	QUEN	OYST	231
BLACK, JACOB	1820	NYCO	WD06	467
BLACK, JACOB	1830	NYCO	WD06	384
BLACK, JAMES	1820	QUEN	----	38
BLACK, JEREMIAH	1830	TOMP	CARO	500
BLACK, JOB	1830	NYCO	WD11	230
BLACK, JOCKA	1820	SCNE	ROTT	134
BLACK, JOE	1830	SARA	CTPK	135
BLACK, JOHN	1810	NYCO	WD07	558
BLACK, JOHN	1820	NYCO	WD06	471
BLACK, JOHN	1820	NYCO	WD06	502
BLACK, JOHN	1820	SUFF	SHAM	323
BLACK, JOHN	1830	KING	GRAV	407
BLACK, JOSEPH	1820	NYCO	WD07	634
BLACK, LYDIA A.	1820	NYCO	WD05	425
BLACK, MOSES	1810	ORNG	MINI	1137
BLACK, NATHANIEL	1810	SUFF	ISLP	499

Black

NAME	YR	CO	TWP	PG
BLACK, NELLY	1810	QUEN	JAMA	188
BLACK, NEPTON	1810	QUEN	OYST	252
BLACK, PETER	1810	SUFF	BROK	492
BLACK, PRINCE	1820	SUFF	SMIT	327
BLACK, R.	1830	ERIE	BUFF	8
BLACK, RACHEL	1810	SUFF	HUNT	310
BLACK, SUSAN	1810	SUFF	SHAM	462
BLACK, SUSAN	1830	NYCO	WD06	381
BLACK, THOMAS	1820	NYCO	WD05	430
BLACK, TITE	1820	SUFF	ISLP	307
BLACK, TONY	1820	SUFF	SOUT	352
BLACK, WILLIAM	1800	NYCO	WD04	779
BLACK, WILLIAM	1820	NYCO	WD05	384
BLACKAMORE, JOHN	1800	WEST	CORT	816
BLACKMAN	1810	CLNT	PLAT	897
BLACKMAN, ANNIBAL	1800	WEST	BEDF	723
BLACKMAN, CAMELIA	1800	SARA	BALL	1056
BLACKMAN, CATO	1800	WEST	YORK	742
BLACKMAN, HENRY	1790	DUTC	PGKP	91
BLACKMAN, KEAGA	1800	SARA	BALL	1053
BLACKMAN, ROBERT	1800	WEST	NORC	730
BLACKMAN, TONICA	1800	SARA	BALL	1054
BLACKSON, C.	1830	ERIE	BUFF	5
BLAINES, SAMUEL	1820	NYCO	WD05	433
BLAIR, ALEXANDER	1820	NYCO	WD06	460
BLAIR, ELISA	1820	NYCO	WD07	677
BLAIR, JAMES	1810	NYCO	WD05	299
BLAIR, THOMAS	1810	NYCO	WD03	57
BLAKE, A.	1830	NYCO	WD11	150
BLAKE, ABRAHAM	1830	ULST	MARL	279
BLAKE, ADAM	1820	ABNY	ABNY	152
BLAKE, ADAM	1830	ABNY	WD05	347
BLAKE, ANDREW	1810	NYCO	WD05	368
BLAKE, DAVID	1820	NYCO	WD10	1055
BLAKE, DAVID	1830	NYCO	WD10	88
BLAKE, FRANCIS	1800	DUTC	RHIN	153
BLAKE, FRANCIS	1820	ORNG	NEWB	520
BLAKE, GEORGE	1800	NYCO	WD07	929
BLAKE, GEORGE	1830	ORNG	MONR	160
BLAKE, HARRY	1820	DUTC	CLNT	25
BLAKE, HARRY	1820	NYCO	WD09	929
BLAKE, JOHN J.	1830	ONID	UTIC	8
BLAKE, MR.	1830	NYCO	WD13	369
BLAKE, SARAH	1820	NYCO	WD05	328
BLAKE, THOMAS	1810	NYCO	WD05	330
BLAKE, THOMAS	1820	NYCO	WD05	377
BLAKE, THOMAS	1830	NYCO	WD05	341
BLAKE, TUNIS	1830	COLU	HUDS	104
BLAKE, WILLIAM	1830	NYCO	WD08	279

NAME	YR	CO	TWP	PG
BLAMES, SAMUEL	1830	NYCO	WD05	325
BLAND, JOHN	1820	ONTA	SENE	269
BLAND, JOHN	1830	ONTA	SENE	85
BLAND, ROBERT	1830	ONTA	SENE	85
BLANDER	1800	NYCO	WD06	831
BLANSHAN, ROBIN	1810	ULST	WARW	791
BLATE, J.	1830	ERIE	BUFF	21
BLEAK, JAMES	1820	ORNG	BLOM	727
BLINPER, MRS.	1820	NYCO	WD07	618
BLOAH, SILVEY	1810	NYCO	WD05	278
BLONDY	1790	NYCO	WEST	133
BLOOD, ORAN	1810	MONT	JOHN	26
BLOOD, TOBIAS	1830	MONT	GLEN	75
BLOODGOOD, THOMAS	1810	SCNE	WD01	940
BLOODOW, HARRY	1830	MONT	FLOR	100
BLOOM, EPINETUS	1800	DUTC	BEEK	6
BLOOM, JEMIMA	1820	DUTC	CLNT	44
BLOOM, JOSEPH	1820	KING	BRYN	157
BLOOM, NANCY	1820	DUTC	PGKP	97
BLOOM, NANCY	1830	NYCO	WD05	325
BLOOM, PEGGY	1830	KING	WD04	311
BLOOMER, DANIEL	1830	ORNG	HBGH	130
BLOOMER, WILLIAM	1820	NYCO	WD07	670
BLOOMFIELD, CATO	1830	NYCO	WD08	247
BLOOMFIELD, CUFF	1810	NYCO	WD06	413
BLOOMFIELD, DAVID	1830	MONR	RWD2	204
BLOW, CEASAR	1810	QUEN	FLUS	191
BLUCKE, MARGART	1800	NYCO	WD03	694
BLUE, HENRY	1830	MONT	EPHR	183
BLUE, ROBERT	1830	NYCO	WD04	203
BLUE, WILLIAM	1810	NYCO	WD10	690
BLUE, WILLIAM	1810	QUEN	NHEM	218
BLUMS, HENRY	1820	WEST	SUMM	344
BLURCH, CATO	1790	SUFF	BROK	162
BLY, SARAH	1790	NYCO	MONT	120
BLYDENBURG, OLIVER	1830	SUFF	HUNT	325
BOARDMAN, ADAM	1810	NYCO	WD05	269
BOAZ, DINA	1820	NYCO	WD05	434
BOB	1790	WEST	MAMA	200
BODKINS, SUSAN	1830	NYCO	WD05	300
BOERUM, JAMES	1830	KING	BRYN	347
BOES, BLATHER	1810	NYCO	WD07	545
BOFFON, QUAUCK	1820	WASH	SALE	186
BOGARDUS, HARRIS	1820	COLU	HUDS	1
BOGARDUS, HARRY	1830	COLU	HUDS	98
BOGARDUS, THOMAS	1820	ONTA	SENE	269
BOGART, CHARLES	1820	QUEN	----	73
BOGART, CHARLES	1830	QUEN	OYST	24
BOGART, HENRY	1820	NYCO	WD10	1048

NAME	YR	CO	TWP	PG
BOGART, PETER	1830	ORNG	WARW	75
BOGART, RICHARD	1810	DUTC	FISH	228
BOGERT, DICK	1820	DUTC	FISH	65
BOGERT, PRINCE	1830	NYCO	WD12	310
BOGERT, RICHARD	1830	ULST	MARB	158
BOGERT, ROBERT	1820	DUTC	FISH	75
BOGERT, ROBERT	1830	DUTC	FISH	490
BOGUYN, WILLIAM	1820	ORNG	WARW	643
BOKER, WILLIAM	1830	NYCO	WD14	503
BOLD, PETER	1820	DUTC	DOVE	47
BOLDEN, R.	1830	KING	WD04	310
BOLES, JAMES	1830	DUTC	DOVE	214
BOLES, THOMAS	1820	DUTC	PAUL	95
BOLICE, JOHN	1830	WEST	CORT	74
BOLSON, PHOEBE	1830	NYCO	WD06	447
BOLT, JOHN	1810	NYCO	WD03	80
BOMAN, HARRY	1830	DUTC	FISH	489
BOMAN, SAMUEL	1830	DUTC	FISH	499
BOMON, ANTHONY	1830	DUTC	FISH	474
BON, PETER	1820	SUFF	SMIT	316
BOND, ELLEA	1830	NYCO	WD14	427
BOND, HARRY	1820	BROM	UNON	25
BOND, HENRY	1830	BROM	VEST	73
BOND, JAMES	1810	WEST	HARR	1135
BONN, JAMES	1820	NYCO	WD06	485
BONNER, PETER	1820	NYCO	WD08	731
BONNET, ABIN	1830	NYCO	WD10	78
BONNETT, ABRAHAM	1820	WEST	NEWR	217
BONNETT, ABRAHAM	1830	WEST	NEWR	107
BONNETT, ABRAHAM	1830	WEST	NEWR	108
BONNETT, JAMES	1810	NYCO	WD06	424
BONNETT, STEPHEN	1820	NYCO	WD06	490
BONNETT, THOMAS	1830	WEST	NEWR	107
BONNETT, TIMOTHY	1820	WEST	NEWR	216
BONNETT, TIMOTHY	1820	WEST	NEWR	217
BONNETT, TIMOTHY	1830	WEST	NEWR	108
BONO, ANN	1830	NYCO	WD08	234A
BONT, MINK	1830	SCHR	MIDD	36
BONTI, PHILIP	1830	NYCO	WD05	254
BOODHEAD, H.	1820	ULST	MARB	62
BOOKER, JAMES	1800	NYCO	WD05	753
BOON, ISAAC	1820	ONTA	PALM	342
BOON, JAMES	1830	NYCO	WD08	214
BOORMAN, JOHN	1830	NYCO	WD06	435
BOORMAN, THOMAS	1830	NYCO	WD08	229
BOOTES, JOHN	1810	DUTC	FISH	210
BOOTH, DORCAS	1820	SUFF	SOUT	332
BOOTON	1820	QUEN	----	27
BOOWAN, BENJAMIN	1810	ULST	MARB	805

NAME	YR	CO	TWP	PG
BORDEN, ADAM	1800	NYCO	WD06	840
BORDLEY, SARAH	1830	NYCO	WD01	31
BORLAN, ABRAHAM	1830	QUEN	NEWT	4
BOROUGHS, JOHN	1830	DUTC	FISH	481
BORTLE, ABRAHAM	1830	MONT	JOHN	222
BOSKER, MR.	1820	NYCO	WD05	337
BOSS, FREDERICK	1820	NYCO	WD06	465
BOSS, JACK	1790	QUEN	JAMA	150
BOSTON	1800	QUEN	OYST	572
BOSTON	1810	NYCO	WD06	399
BOSTON	1810	SARA	MILT	797
BOSTON, JACOB	1800	NYCO	WD06	848
BOSTON, JACOB	1810	KING	GRAV	663
BOSTON, JACOB	1810	NYCO	WD06	489
BOSTON, JAMES	1830	QUEN	NEWT	15
BOSTON, JAMES	1830	SCHR	SCHR	20
BOSTON, MARK	1830	ONID	UTIC	8
BOSTON, MRS.	1830	KING	GRAV	405
BOSTON, RICHARD	1830	STLR	MASS	65
BOSTON, ROBERTSON	1820	NYCO	WD06	490
BOSTON, SAMUEL	1830	WASH	SALM	216
BOSTOW, JACOB	1820	KING	BRYN	167
BOSTWICK, CHARLES	1820	ABNY	ABNY	154
BOSTWICK, HANNAH	1830	NYCO	WD05	334
BOSTWICK, RICHARD	1800	NYCO	WD02	677
BOSTWICK, RICHARD	1810	NYCO	WD05	288
BOSTWICK, RICHARD	1820	NYCO	WD05	426
BOSTWICK, ROBERT	1810	NYCO	WD05	306
BOSTWICK, SAMUEL	1810	NYCO	WD03	83
BOSTWICK, THOMAS	1810	NYCO	WD05	305
BOSTWICK, THOMAS	1820	NYCO	WD06	475
BOTHEL, MARY	1830	NYCO	WD04	190
BOTTS, JESSE	1830	NYCO	WD05	328
BOUDETT, JACOB A.	1830	NYCO	WD06	436
BOULD, JOSEPH	1830	NYCO	WD06	372
BOUND, RYLEY	1830	QUEN	OYST	42
BOUNE, SAMUEL	1830	NYCO	WD10	76
BOUNTY, CHARLES	1830	ORNG	GOSH	284
BOUNTY, DINAH	1810	NYCO	WD02	124
BOURK, CHARLES	1800	NYCO	WD05	759
BOURY, SAM	1810	ORNG	MONT	965
BOUSHEL, AMOSE	1820	CHEN	NORW	378
BOWEN, LEWIS	1830	NYCO	WD06	431
BOWER, SAMUEL	1800	ORGN	MONR	295
BOWER, THOMAS	1820	NYCO	WD06	506
BOWERS, LUKE	1830	KING	WD02	275
BOWERS, SAMUEL	1810	NYCO	WD03	89
BOWERS, SAMUEL	1830	ORNG	MONR	163
BOWLES, PETER	1820	NYCO	WD09	891

Bowline

NAME	YR	CO	TWP	PG
BOWLINE, THOMAS	1830	DUTC	PAWL	290
BOWLIS, PETER	1830	NYCO	WD10	78
BOWMAKER, WILLIAM	1810	NYCO	WD04	205
BOWMAN, BEN	1810	QUEN	FLUS	201
BOWMAN, HARRY	1820	DUTC	FISH	57
BOWMAN, SAMUEL	1820	ORNG	MONR	669
BOWN, JOHN	1830	WEST	RYE	105
BOWNE, JIM	1790	QUEN	OYST	157
BOWNE, JOSIAH	1800	NYCO	WD07	858
BOWNES, JOSEPH	1830	SUFF	ISLP	282
BOWSER, D.J.	1820	NYCO	WD06	476
BOWSER, JAMES D.	1830	NYCO	WD06	429
BOWSER, THOMAS	1830	NYCO	WD05	331
BOWSER, THOMAS	1830	NYCO	WD08	246
BOWYN, THOMAS	1830	ULST	MARB	166
BOYD	1820	NYCO	WD05	428
BOYD, EBENIZAR	1820	PUTM	KENT	100
BOYD, HENRY	1830	NYCO	WD10	37
BOYD, JOHN	1800	NYCO	WD05	789
BOYD, JOHN	1800	SARA	HALF	1031
BOYD, JOHN	1810	NYCO	WD06	440
BOYD, R.	1830	NYCO	WD11	162
BOYD, ROBERT	1830	DUTC	REDH	375
BOYER, ANDREW	1820	NYCO	WD05	383
BOYER, CONSTANTINE	1830	NYCO	WD05	331
BOYERT, CAESAR	1820	NYCO	WD09	935
BOYERT, WILLIAM	1820	NYCO	WD09	935
BRABOY, SARAH	1800	NYCO	WD06	794
BRACEBY, JOHN H.	1830	NYCO	WD07	116
BRACUY, TILES	1820	SUFF	BROK	343
BRADBERRY, THOMAS	1810	NYCO	WD05	286
BRADDINGTON, ABRAHAM	1830	WANE	SODU	130
BRADENTON, ABRAHAM	1820	ONTA	SODU	121
BRADFORD, ABRAHAM	1820	NYCO	WD04	267
BRADFORD, ABRAHAM	1830	DUTC	PGKP	355
BRADFORD, CATO	1820	DUTC	PGKP	111
BRADFORD, JAMES	1820	DUTC	FISH	77
BRADFORD, JAMES	1830	DUTC	PGKP	361
BRADFORD, NANCY	1830	DUTC	PGKP	326
BRADFORD, SAMUEL	1820	DUTC	PAUL	90
BRADFORD, THOMAS	1830	DUTC	PGKP	330
BRADLEY, GILES	1790	SUFF	SOUT	168
BRADLEY, GILES	1830	SUFF	BROK	179
BRADLEY, JANE	1830	NYCO	WD08	234A
BRADLEY, JOSEPH	1790	DUTC	PAWL	88
BRADLEY, JOSEPH	1810	DELA	MIDD	493
BRADLEY, LEWIS	1810	DUTC	BEEK	278
BRADLEY, NATHANIEL	1830	NYCO	WD08	231
BRADLY, ENOCH	1830	QUEN	FLUS	146

NAME	YR	CO	TWP	PG
BRADY	1830	NYCO	WD02	95
BRADY, LEWIS	1820	DUTC	BEEK	18
BRADY, LEWIS	1830	WEST	MTPL	35
BRAG, SAMUEL	1830	SCNE	GLEN	272
BRAGG, ISABEL	1830	HERK	NEWP	34
BRAND, HENRY	1830	KING	WD03	287
BRANDON, DAVID	1820	GREN	ATHN	7
BRANDOW, DAVID	1830	GREN	ATHN	210
BRANSON, MARY	1830	NYCO	WD09	416
BRASHER, YORK	1800	NYCO	WD05	753
BRASS, DAVID	1800	NYCO	WD06	837
BRATMAN, JACOB	1820	NYCO	WD06	472
BRATON, JOHN	1830	OTSG	HART	92
BRATT, JACOB	1790	ABNY	WATV	52
BRATT, JACOB	1800	ABNY	WATV	123
BRAVEBOY	1820	WEST	HARR	463
BRAWBERRIE, JACK	1830	ROCK	ORGT	118
BRAY, BETSEY	1810	NYCO	WD06	424
BRAY, CEARAR	1800	NYCO	WD01	661
BRAY, JOHN	1820	HERK	MANH	39
BRAY, SAMSON	1810	SCNE	----	974
BRAY, SAMUEL	1810	KING	BRYN	633
BRAY, SAMUEL	1820	SCNE	GLEN	147
BRAY, SARAH	1810	NYCO	WD05	255
BRAY, WILLIAM	1830	WEST	YONK	3
BRAYTON, JOHN	1820	OTSG	LAUR	139
BREACHERD, THOMAS	1810	NYCO	WD05	5
BREED, EPHRAIM	1820	CHEN	NORW	378
BREED, EPHRAIM	1830	CHEN	NORW	165
BRENSON, MARGARET	1830	NYCO	WD08	236
BRESHARD, M. MARY	1810	NYCO	WD06	437
BREUVER, HENRY J.	1830	NYCO	WD14	432
BREWER, DANIEL	1830	SUFF	SHAM	228
BREWSTER, AUGUSTUS	1830	COLU	CHAT	51
BREWSTER, CHARLES	1830	GREN	COXE	186
BREWSTER, DAVID	1810	QUEN	OYST	244
BREWSTER, DAVID	1830	SUFF	HUNT	304
BREWSTER, HARRY	1830	SARA	SARA	148
BREWSTER, JEFFRY	1830	NYCO	WD07	44
BREWSTER, RICHARD	1830	QUEN	OYST	27
BREWSTER, STEPHEN	1830	ONID	NWHT	64
BRIAN, JAMES O.	1830	NYCO	WD14	525
BRIAN, JOHN	1820	NYCO	WD06	482
BRIAN, JOSEPH	1830	NYCO	WD08	230
BRIANT, GEORGE	1830	SENE	OVID	107
BRIDELL, MARY	1830	NYCO	WD08	227
BRIDGE, CAESAR	1800	NYCO	WD05	755
BRIEN, THOMAS O.	1830	NYCO	WD11	148
BRIER, FRANCIS	1830	KING	FLAN	413

NAME	YR	CO	TWP	PG
BRIETER, AARON	1820	ONTA	PALM	331
BRIGGS, HENRY	1820	COLU	KIND	1
BRIGGS, HENRY	1830	COLU	STUY	65
BRIGGS, JACK	1820	COLU	KIND	1
BRIGGS, JACK	1830	COLU	STUY	68
BRIGGS, JACK	1830	WEST	WTPL	223
BRIGGS, JOHN	1800	ORNG	WALL	344
BRIGGS, MARCUS	1830	ORNG	MONR	168
BRIGGS, MARGARET	1790	ULST	NMAR	177
BRIGGS, MARGARET	1800	ULST	MARB	268
BRIGGS, MARTHA	1820	SCNE	SCNE	122
BRIGGS, MRS.	1800	ABNY	WD01	3
BRIGGS, NANCY	1830	ABNY	WD02	261
BRIGGS, PRINCE	1830	MONT	JOHN	232
BRIGGS, THOMAS	1810	ORNG	MONR	997
BRIGGS, THOMAS	1810	SCNE	WD01	938
BRIGHT, JANE	1810	NYCO	WD06	423
BRIGHT, LEWIS	1800	NYCO	WD07	868
BRIGS, NICHOLAS	1830	SCNE	WD02	223
BRINEHERKOFF, HENRY	1830	DUTC	PLEA	308
BRINK, PETER	1830	ULST	SAUG	107
BRINKERHOFF, H.	1830	KING	WD05	333
BRINKERHOOF, PETER	1830	ULST	MARL	276
BRINKERHOOF, SAMUEL	1830	DUTC	FISH	479
BRISBAN, EDWARD	1830	NYCO	WD07	16
BRISLOW, STEPHEN	1820	ONID	WHIT	303
BRISTER	1800	SUFF	RIVH	21
BRISTER	1810	LEWI	----	685
BRISTER, BENJAMIN	1820	ONTA	PALM	339
BRISTER, ISAAC	1830	NYCO	WD05	328
BRISTER, JOHN	1830	SUFF	SHAM	222
BRISTER, THOMAS	1830	KING	WD04	295
BRISTIL, THOMAS	1820	KING	BRYN	127
BRISTOL, ANTHONY	1820	NYCO	WD06	515
BRISTOL, BENJAMIN	1810	ONTA	PALM	792
BRISTOL, BETSEY	1830	WANE	PALM	39
BRISTOL, CHARLES	1820	DUTC	FISH	58
BRISTOL, CHARLES	1830	DUTC	LAGR	242
BRISTOL, LONDON	1800	WASH	WHIT	543
BRISTON, STEPHEN	1820	ONID	WATE	303
BRISTOR, AMOS	1820	SARA	SARA	198
BRITTON, ROBERT	1800	NYCO	WD04	733
BRIVELTAR, JOHN	1800	NYCO	WD06	843
BROAD, PETER	1820	NYCO	WD06	445
BROADHEAD, ANDSES	1830	ULST	MARB	168
BROADHEAD, GEORGE	1830	ULST	OLIV	134
BROADHEAD, HARRY	1830	ULST	WAWA	196
BROADHEAD, PETER	1820	ORNG	WALL	779
BROADHEAD, PETER	1830	ORNG	WALL	147

NAME	YR	CO	TWP	PG
BROADHEAD, SAMUEL	1820	ORNG	WALL	787
BROCKES, M.	1810	NYCO	WD05	293
BROMLEY, J.	1810	ONID	LISB	312
BROMLEY, JOHN	1820	ONID	REMS	171
BROMLEY, WILLIAM	1830	HERK	RUSS	20
BRONK, BENJAMIN	1830	GREN	COXE	187
BRONK, JUDAH	1820	GREN	ATHE	4
BRONK, THOMAS	1820	OTSG	OTSG	100
BRONK, THOMAS	1830	OTSG	OTSG	37
BRONSON, JAMES	1830	ORNG	WALL	149
BRONSON, TITUS	1830	ORNG	WALL	145
BROOK, ALBERT	1830	QUEN	NHEM	106
BROOKS, BENJAMIN	1820	NYCO	WD03	149
BROOKS, BENJAMIN	1830	NYCO	WD06	431
BROOKS, CHATHAM	1830	ORNG	WALL	151
BROOKS, HENRY	1830	NYCO	WD14	450
BROOKS, JACOB	1830	WANE	PALM	37
BROOKS, LEWIS	1830	ONTA	CANA	112
BROOKS, LUKE	1820	ONTA	CANA	210
BROOKS, LYDIA	1830	NYCO	WD10	84
BROOKS, MRS.	1830	NYCO	WD13	396
BROOKS, NOAH	1830	NYCO	WD05	334
BROOKS, WALTER	1830	ABNY	WD04	319
BROOKS, WILLIAM	1830	NYCO	WD07	66
BROOKS, WILLIAM L.	1820	NYCO	WD07	641
BROOM	1800	QUEN	OYST	579
BROOMFIELD, CUFF	1800	NYCO	WD06	831
BROTHERTON, DANIEL	1790	ABNY	SARA	40
BROTHERTON, GIDEON	1820	SUFF	SHAM	300
BROTHERTON, GIDEON	1830	SUFF	SHAM	219
BROUCH, JACOB	1830	GREN	COXE	186
BROUCH, THOMAS	1830	GREN	COXE	186
BROUEN, L.	1830	NYCO	WD13	349
BROVER, WILLIAM	1830	ROCK	ORGT	105
BROWBERRIE, TOBE	1830	ROCK	ORGT	116
BROWER, HARRY	1830	COLU	CLAV	80
BROWER, TONE	1830	ROCK	CLAR	132
BROWN	1800	QUEN	HEMP	566
BROWN	1810	NYCO	WD06	460
BROWN	1820	NYCO	WD07	636
BROWN	1820	PUTM	PATE	101
BROWN	1830	NYCO	WD05	276
BROWN	1830	NYCO	WD05	344
BROWN, A.	1830	KING	WD04	310
BROWN, ABRAHAM	1800	NYCO	WD06	797
BROWN, ABRAHAM	1820	NYCO	WD05	391
BROWN, ABRAHAM	1830	KING	BRYN	369
BROWN, ALBERT	1830	ORNG	MONR	166
BROWN, ALLEN	1830	WEST	BEDF	153

NAME	YR	CO	TWP	PG
BROWN, ALMON	1830	ABNY	BETH	536
BROWN, ANN	1800	QUEN	SHEM	557
BROWN, ANN	1820	WEST	BEDF	415
BROWN, ANTHONY	1830	NYCO	WD14	518
BROWN, ARTHUR	1810	NYCO	WD06	450
BROWN, AUTHOR	1820	NYCO	WD08	735
BROWN, BAABOY	1820	ORNG	GOSH	734
BROWN, BENJAMIN	1820	GREN	CATS	157
BROWN, BENJAMIN	1820	ORNG	MONT	807
BROWN, BENJAMIN	1830	GREN	CATS	237
BROWN, BENJAMIN	1830	NYCO	WD08	274
BROWN, BENJAMIN	1830	ORNG	MONR	166
BROWN, BENJAMIN	1830	ULST	KING	64
BROWN, BETSEY	1830	NYCO	WD08	236
BROWN, BETSY	1820	NYCO	WD05	386
BROWN, BRAVE	1830	ORNG	GOSH	276
BROWN, BRISTO	1810	ORNG	NEWB	927
BROWN, BURRELL	1800	NYCO	WD06	808
BROWN, BYALL	1810	NYCO	WD05	302
BROWN, CATHERINE	1830	QUEN	FLUS	143
BROWN, CATY	1820	ORNG	GOSH	750
BROWN, CHARATY	1820	NYCO	WD05	419
BROWN, CHARITY	1830	NYCO	WD07	46
BROWN, CHARITY	1830	ONTA	CANA	120
BROWN, CHARLES	1820	NYCO	WD03	165
BROWN, CUFF	1810	SARA	BALL	742
BROWN, CUFF	1830	WEST	RYE	99
BROWN, DANIEL	1800	NYCO	WD06	812
BROWN, DANIEL	1810	NYCO	WD05	313
BROWN, DANIEL	1830	ONON	SALI	32
BROWN, DAVID	1830	NYCO	WD06	438
BROWN, DIANA	1830	NYCO	WD08	184
BROWN, DIANA	1830	NYCO	WD08	235
BROWN, DINAH	1810	NYCO	WD02	116
BROWN, DUNBAR	1830	DUTC	HYPK	232
BROWN, EDWARD	1830	NYCO	WD12	254
BROWN, ELLEN	1830	NYCO	WD08	239
BROWN, ESSEE	1830	NYCO	WD09	365
BROWN, FRANCES	1830	KING	BUSH	382
BROWN, FRANCIS	1820	SARA	MILT	236
BROWN, GARRET	1800	NYCO	WD06	822
BROWN, GEORGE	1820	NYCO	WD05	394
BROWN, GEORGE	1830	NYCO	WD08	236
BROWN, GEORGE	1830	ONON	CICE	103
BROWN, H.	1830	NYCO	WD13	394
BROWN, HANNAH	1830	NYCO	WD05	334
BROWN, HARRY	1830	PUTM	PHIL	63
BROWN, HARRY	1830	WEST	HARR	215
BROWN, HENRY	1810	KING	BRYN	630
BROWN, HENRY	1810	NYCO	WD03	44

NAME	YR	CO	TWP	PG
BROWN, HENRY	1820	DUTC	WASH	140
BROWN, HENRY	1820	KING	BRYN	139
BROWN, HENRY	1820	NYCO	WD07	636
BROWN, HENRY	1820	NYCO	WD07	624
BROWN, HENRY	1820	WEST	RYE	372
BROWN, HENRY	1830	DUTC	WASH	447
BROWN, HENRY	1830	NYCO	WD08	204
BROWN, HENRY	1830	ORNG	NEWB	25
BROWN, HENRY	1830	QUEN	FLUS	
BROWN, HUGH	1830	NYCO	WD14	438
BROWN, IAS	1820	NYCO	WD10	988
BROWN, ISAAC	1820	NYCO	WD04	313
BROWN, ISAAC	1820	ORNG	GOSH	749
BROWN, ISAAC	1820	ORNG	MONT	812
BROWN, ISSAC	1820	ULST	SHAW	67
BROWN, ISAAC	1830	ORNG	MONR	166
BROWN, ISAAC	1830	ORNG	NEWB	60
BROWN, J.	1800	QUEN	FLUS	540
BROWN, J.	1830	KING	WD04	310
BROWN, JACK	1820	KING	BRYN	124
BROWN, JACK	1830	ULST	KING	69
BROWN, JACOB	1800	RENS	GREN	721
BROWN, JACOB	1810	NYCO	WD05	298
BROWN, JACOB	1810	RENS	GREN	483
BROWN, JACOB	1830	NYCO	WD05	336
BROWN, JACOB	1830	NYCO	WD09	424
BROWN, JACOB	1830	QUEN	FLUS	138
BROWN, JACOB	1830	RENS	WD05	79
BROWN, JAMES	1810	WEST	SUMM	1031
BROWN, JAMES	1820	ABNY	ABNY	156
BROWN, JAMES	1820	NYCO	WD10	967
BROWN, JAMES	1820	WEST	YORK	338
BROWN, JAMES	1830	ABNY	WD01	223
BROWN, JAMES	1830	NYCO	WD06	367
BROWN, JAMES	1830	NYCO	WD08	220
BROWN, JAMES	1830	ORNG	WALL	134
BROWN, JAMES	1830	ORNG	GOSH	282
BROWN, JAMES	1830	WEST	YORK	176
BROWN, JAMES	1830	YATE	BENT	302
BROWN, JENNE	1820	ABNY	ABNY	155
BROWN, JOHN	1800	NYCO	WD06	853
BROWN, JOHN	1820	ALLE	RUSH	5
BROWN, JOHN	1820	NYCO	WD06	450
BROWN, JOHN	1830	ALLE	BIRD	54
BROWN, JOHN	1830	KING	WD04	307
BROWN, JOHN	1830	NYCO	WD03	109
BROWN, JOHN	1830	NYCO	WD05	344
BROWN, JOHN	1830	NYCO	WD05	345
BROWN, JOHN	1830	NYCO	WD07	29

Brown

NAME	YR	CO	TWP	PG
BROWN, JOHN	1830	QUEN	NEWT	12
BROWN, JOHN	1830	QUEN	JAMA	128
BROWN, JOHN	1830	WEST	YONK	6
BROWN, JOHN	1830	WEST	YONK	11
BROWN, JOHN	1830	WEST	RYE	99
BROWN, JOHNATHAN	1830	OSWE	HANN	237
BROWN, JONATHAN	1830	ALLE	HAIG	122
BROWN, JOSEPH	1800	NYCO	WD06	842
BROWN, JOSEPH	1810	NYCO	WD04	163
BROWN, JOSEPH	1810	WEST	PELH	1159
BROWN, JOSEPH	1820	NYCO	WD04	221
BROWN, JOSEPH	1830	NYCO	WD08	175
BROWN, LAURENCE	1830	KING	WD05	333
BROWN, LEVY	1820	NYCO	WD05	392
BROWN, LEW	1810	WEST	SUMM	1037
BROWN, LEWIS	1810	NYCO	WD06	467
BROWN, LEWIS	1820	TOMP	HECT	10
BROWN, LEWIS	1830	TOMP	ENFD	375
BROWN, LIDDY	1810	KING	BRYN	639
BROWN, LUAM	1820	WEST	SUMM	354
BROWN, LUCINDA	1830	NYCO	WD14	457
BROWN, LYDIA	1830	NYCO	WD06	400
BROWN, MARGARET	1820	NYCO	WD06	482
BROWN, MARGARET	1830	NYCO	WD05	278
BROWN, MARGARET	1830	NYCO	WD06	383
BROWN, MARGARET	1830	WEST	BEDF	147
BROWN, MARGARETT	1820	NYCO	WD10	1016
BROWN, MARLAND	1830	ORNG	MONR	172
BROWN, MARLIN	1820	ORNG	MONT	841
BROWN, MARTIN	1820	NYCO	WD06	455
BROWN, MARY	1810	NYCO	WD06	403
BROWN, MARY	1830	NYCO	WD10	128
BROWN, MATTHIAS	1830	WEST	SALM	156
BROWN, MICHAEL	1820	WEST	HARR	467
BROWN, MICHAEL	1830	WEST	HARR	215
BROWN, MICHEAL	1810	WEST	HARR	1131
BROWN, MOSES	1830	NYCO	WD13	380
BROWN, MOSES	1830	OSWE	OSWE	134
BROWN, MRS.	1830	KING	WD04	310
BROWN, MRS.	1830	KING	WD04	319
BROWN, MRS. E.	1830	ERIE	BUFF	30
BROWN, NOAH	1820	ULST	MARB	63
BROWN, NANCY	1830	NYCO	WD06	444
BROWN, NEAL	1820	NYCO	WD08	814
BROWN, OBEDIAH	1820	PUTM	SOUT	100
BROWN, OLIVER	1810	QUEN	FLUS	200
BROWN, PATRICK	1830	NYCO	WD14	467
BROWN, PETER	1800	NYCO	WD07	919
BROWN, PETER	1820	ORNG	MONT	845

NAME		YR	CO	TWP	PG
BROWN,	PETER	1830	NYCO	WD12	255
BROWN,	PETER	1830	ORNG	MONR	173
BROWN,	PETER	1830	ORNG	MONR	174
BROWN,	PETER	1830	ORNG	MONR	175
BROWN,	PHILIP	1820	GREN	CATS	170
BROWN,	PHILIP	1830	GREN	CATS	228
BROWN,	POMP	1830	ROCK	ORGT	109
BROWN,	POMPE	1810	NYCO	WD05	378
BROWN,	PRENTICE	1830	CAYU	AUBN	157
BROWN,	PRINCE	1810	WEST	NORT	1039
BROWN,	PRINCE	1810	WEST	SUMM	1033
BROWN,	PRINCE	1820	NYCO	WD10	970
BROWN,	PRINCE	1830	WEST	SUMM	186
BROWN,	QUAM	1810	WEST	SUMM	1036
BROWN,	RICHARD	1800	NYCO	WD03	708
BROWN,	RICHARD	1810	NYCO	WD05	259
BROWN,	RICHARD	1820	WEST	SUMM	352
BROWN,	RICHARD	1830	ORNG	MONR	174
BROWN,	RICHARD	1830	RENS	BRUN	230
BROWN,	RICHARD	1830	WEST	SUMM	191
BROWN,	RICHARD	1830	WEST	WEST	119
BROWN	ROBER	1830	PUTM	SOUT	49
BROWN,	ROBERT	1800	NYCO	WD07	910
BROWN,	ROBERT	1810	WEST	NORT	1042
BROWN,	ROBERT	1810	WEST	SUMM	1029
BROWN,	ROBERT	1820	PUTM	SOUT	100
BROWN,	ROBERT	1820	ULST	MARB	53
BROWN,	ROBERT	1830	ORNG	CORN	203
BROWN,	ROBERT	1830	WEST	BEDF	151
BROWN,	ROBERT T.	1830	NYCO	WD07	66
BROWN,	RUBEN	1830	WEST	GREN	14
BROWN,	SALLY	1800	NYCO	WD03	695
BROWN,	SAMUEL	1810	WASH	BOTT	399
BROWN,	SAMUEL	1830	ORNG	NEWB	60
BROWN,	SAMUEL	1830	QUEN	NEWT	12
BROWN,	SAMUEL	1830	ROCK	ORGT	109
BROWN,	SAMUEL	1830	ULST	KING	64
BROWN,	SIMON P.	1830	CAYU	GENO	289
BROWN,	STEPHEN	1830	QUEN	FLUS	142
BROWN,	SUSAN	1820	NYCO	WD10	982
BROWN,	THOMAS	1810	SARA	MILT	796
BROWN,	THOMAS	1820	SCNE	ROTT	133
BROWN,	THOMAS	1830	KING	WD04	313
BROWN,	THOMAS	1830	NYCO	WD08	248
BROWN,	THOMAS	1830	NYCO	WD08	255
BROWN,	TIM	1790	QUEN	FLUS	149
BROWN,	TOM	1810	DUTC	CLNT	416
BROWN,	W.	1830	KING	FLAT	400
BROWN,	WALTER	1820	WEST	RYE	370

NAME	YR	CO	TWP	PG
BROWN, WILLIAM	1800	NYCO	WD03	695
BROWN, WILLIAM	1800	NYCO	WD05	751
BROWN, WILLIAM	1810	NYCO	WD02	102
BROWN, WILLIAM	1810	NYCO	WD04	160
BROWN, WILLIAM	1820	GREN	COXE	39
BROWN, WILLIAM	1820	NYCO	WD04	211
BROWN, WILLIAM	1820	NYCO	WD05	343
BROWN, WILLIAM	1820	NYCO	WD05	391
BROWN, WILLIAM	1820	NYCO	WD05	400
BROWN, WILLIAM	1830	NYCO	WD05	329
BROWN, WILLIAM	1830	NYCO	WD05	329
BROWN, WILLIAM	1830	NYCO	WD05	341
BROWN, WILLIAM	1830	NYCO	WD10	13
BROWN, WILLIAM	1830	NYCO	WD10	25
BROWNE	1810	NYCO	WD07	592
BROWNHILL, MARY	1820	NYCO	WD05	385
BRUCE, LOUDER	1830	NYCO	WD06	414
BRUCE, MICHAEL	1830	NYCO	WD04	201
BRUCE, WILLIAM	1830	NYCO	WD09	296
BRUCKERHOOF, PETER	1820	ULST	MARB	54
BRUISTER, SAMUEL	1820	PUTM	SOUT	100
BRUSE, ARTHUR	1800	NYCO	WD05	755
BRUSH, ANTHONY	1830	QUEN	FLUS	146
BRUSH, JOHN	1820	PUTM	SOUT	100
BRUSH, PETER	1810	SUFF	HUNT	528
BRUSH, PETER	1830	ABNY	WD05	338
BRUSH, SEASON	1830	QUEN	OYST	29
BRUSH, TAST V.	1820	PUTM	SOUT	100
BRUSH, VENUS	1810	SUFF	ISLP	500
BRUSHELL, THOMAS	1820	CHEN	NORW	378
BRUSSEL, AMOS	1830	CHEN	NORW	165
BRUSSEL, THOMAS	1830	CHEN	NORW	165
BRUSTER, DAVID	1820	SUFF	HUNT	274
BRUSTER, JOHN	1820	NYCO	WD07	721
BRUYN, TERRIS	1830	ULST	SHAW	248
BRYAN, GEORGE	1820	SENE	FAYE	382
BRYAN, PERRY	1830	NYCO	WD05	262
BRYANT	1820	PUTM	PATE	101
BRYANT, CHARLES	1810	SUFF	HUNT	517
BRYANT, HENRY	1830	QUEN	NHEM	115
BRYCE, WILLIAM	1830	NYCO	WD10	13
BUCH, THOMAS	1800	NYCO	WD05	816
BUCHANAN, JAMES	1830	NYCO	WD09	404
BUCHANAN, JANMS	1830	NYCO	WD05	300
BUCK, BENJAMIN	1820	JEFF	CHAM	386
BUCK, DANIEL	1830	JEFF	WATE	83
BUCK, SARRY	1820	JEFF	CHAM	386
BUCKBOUT, CHARLES	1830	WEST	SUMM	182

NAME	YR	CO	TWP	PG
BUCKLEE, EDWARD	1820	TOMP	ULYS	18
BUCKLEY, EDWARD	1830	TOMP	ENFD	375
BUCKLEY, JESSE	1830	ONID	WEST	319
BUCKLEY, MARY	1830	NYCO	WD05	336
BUCKLEY, MARY	1830	NYCO	WD13	336
BUCKNER, C.	1830	ERIE	BUFF	8
BUCKS, MARGARET	1830	SARA	SASP	164
BUCKWAY, JAMES	1820	DUTC	AMEN	7
BUDD, JOHN	1810	WEST	NEWR	1086
BUDD, PRIMUS	1830	SARA	SASP	163
BUDD, PRUMUS	1820	SARA	SARA	189
BUDD, SAMUEL	1800	SUFF	SHAM	67
BUEL, ELLENEER	1800	NYCO	WD06	792
BUEL, ENOS	1800	SUFF	SHAM	71
BUEL, LANY	1810	NYCO	WD05	258
BUELL, ENOS	1830	SUFF	SHAM	230
BUFFAWS, MRS.	1830	KING	WD03	289
BUFFET, CAESAR	1820	QUEN	----	26
BUFFET, CEASAR	1810	QUEN	OYST	258
BUFFETT, SAMUEL	1820	SUFF	SMIT	322
BUFFETT, SAMUEL	1830	QUEN	SHEM	78
BUFFETT, SCEZAR	1830	QUEN	OYST	46
BUFFIT, JAMES	1830	NYCO	WD10	26
BUG, AARON	1810	QUEN	NHEM	213
BUGGS, P.	1820	NYCO	WD10	991
BULEY, J.	1830	NYCO	WD13	337
BULL, DINAH	1810	NYCO	WD02	124
BULL, G.	1830	NYCO	WD13	387
BULL, PETER	1830	ORNG	WALL	147
BULLIS, SAMUEL	1810	NYCO	WD10	688
BULLOCK, JACK	1830	DUTC	PLEA	314
BUM, CHARITY	1810	SUFF	BROK	469
BUN, OLIVER	1820	SUFF	ISLP	309
BUNCE, CHARLES	1820	SUFF	HUNT	301
BUNCE, CHARLES	1820	SUFF	SMIT	323
BUNCE, CHARLES	1830	KING	WD03	286
BUNCE, JACOB	1830	KING	WD05	327
BUNCE, NELSON	1830	SUFF	HUNT	317
BUND, FRANK	1830	SUFF	ISLP	280
BUNDAY, FRANCIS	1830	NYCO	WD14	456
BUNDY, HENRY	1830	NYCO	WD07	107
BUNN, CHARLES	1810	SUFF	HUNT	523
BUNN, DAVID	1800	SUFF	ISLP	62
BUNN, FRANCES	1810	SUFF	ISLP	496
BUNN, JAMES	1800	SUFF	SHAM	67
BUNN, JAMES	1810	SUFF	SHAM	440
BUNN, JAMES	1830	SUFF	SHAM	215
BUNN, LUTHER	1830	SUFF	SHAM	215
BUNN, OLIVER	1810	SUFF	ISLP	497

Bunos

NAME	YR	CO	TWP	PG
BUNOS, DAVID	1820	QUEN	----	7
BUON, FRANCES	1800	SUFF	ISLP	61
BUOY, SUSAN	1810	NYCO	WD05	371
BURCHALL, NEPTUNE	1830	NYCO	WD06	389
BURCHEL, STEPHEN	1820	NYCO	WD05	384
BURCHELL, HESTER	1800	NYCO	WD07	885
BURCHILL, BETSY	1810	NYCO	WD02	101
BURCHILL, NEPTUNE	1820	NYCO	WD04	281
BURDEN	1820	PUTM	PATE	101
BURDEN, THOMAS	1820	NYCO	WD10	954
BURGER, HANNAH	1800	NYCO	WD03	701
BURGER, PATIENCE	1810	NYCO	WD06	450
BURGHER, JANE	1790	NYCO	MONT	123
BURGOINE, WILLIAM	1830	ORNG	BLOM	115
BURH, JACK	1820	DELA	SIDN	87
BURHAM, PRINCE	1820	ULST	KING	78
BURHANS, DINAH	1810	ULST	KING	756
BURHANS, FRANK	1810	ULST	SHAW	678
BURHANS, HARRY	1830	ABNY	RENV	440
BURHAUS, PRINCE	1830	ULST	KING	67
BURHITE, ROBERT	1830	GREN	WIND	104
BURK, CHARLES	1810	NYCO	WD06	469
BURK, LARCY	1830	JEFF	CHAM	141
BURK, LEWIS	1830	JEFF	CHAM	141
BURK, MARY	1810	NYCO	WD02	127
BURKE, GEORGE	1820	KING	BRYN	115
BURKELOE, SAMUEL	1810	NYCO	WD06	425
BURKER, WILLIAMS	1820	NYCO	WD10	1016
BURLING, AMOS	1820	QUEN	----	27
BURLING, AMOS	1830	QUEN	OYST	47
BURLING, CATO	1810	NYCO	WD02	127
BURLING, POMP	1810	DUTC	PATT	119
BURLING, POMPEY	1800	DUTC	FISH	171
BURLIP, JOHN	1830	NYCO	WD06	368
BURN, DAVID	1790	SUFF	ISLP	165
BURN, ISSAC	1810	NYCO	WD03	57
BURN, JAMES	1830	NYCO	WD03	109
BURN, M.	1820	NYCO	WD10	981
BURNES, HENRY	1830	NYCO	WD01	50
BURNES, PHILLIS	1830	ABNY	WD02	262
BURNET, HENRY	1820	ORNG	NEWW	481
BURNET, THOMAS	1830	DUTC	PLEA	312
BURNET, THOMAS JR.	1830	DUTC	PLEA	312
BURNETT, HENRY	1830	NYCO	WD09	416
BURNETT, ROBERT	1820	NYCO	WD10	984
BURNETT, THOMAS	1820	DUTC	CLNT	42
BURNHAM, JACK	1810	WASH	EAST	499
BURNIGHT, JOHN	1830	KING	WD02	267
BURNS, DAVID	1830	ABNY	BETH	536

NAME	YR	CO	TWP	PG
BURNS, DINAH	1800	NYCO	WD07	859
BURNS, FRANCIS	1820	SUFF	ISLP	306
BURNS, HAVERY	1810	MONT	CANJ	76
BURNS, HENRY	1820	ABNY	ABNY	153
BURNS, HENRY	1820	NYCO	WD02	131
BURNS, JOHN	1820	NYCO	WD03	142
BURNS, JOHN	1830	NYCO	WD05	345
BURNS, JUBITER	1800	NYCO	WD01	656
BURNS, MOSES	1830	NYCO	WD05	261
BURNS, SAMSON	1800	WASH	GREN	527
BURRAGER, CHARLES	1830	NYCO	WD09	383
BURRIS, DAVID	1810	QUEN	SHEM	307
BURRIS, JACOB	1820	ORNG	WARW	627
BURRIS, TREDWELL	1820	NYCO	WD08	795
BURROUGHS, PETER	1830	JEFF	BRON	279
BURROWS, GEORGE	1800	NYCO	WD07	926
BURROWS, ISAAC	1830	MONR	RWD3	226
BURROWS, SAMUEL	1800	NYCO	WD07	857
BURROWS, THOMAS	1830	TOMP	HECT	426
BURROWSE, JOHN	1820	DUTC	FISH	60
BURT, CHARLES	1820	CHEN	SHER	337
BURT, CHARLES	1830	NYCO	WD14	445
BURT, CHARLES W.	1830	MADI	----	346
BURTCH, ISAIAH	1810	DUTC	BEEK	278
BURTEEN, CALVIN	1820	SARA	HADL	178
BURTIS, JOHN	1810	NYCO	WD05	312
BURTIS, JOHN	1820	NYCO	WD10	1039
BURTIS, MRS.	1830	KING	WD04	307
BURTIS, SAMUEL	1820	NYCO	WD01	33
BURTISS, JOHN	1800	DUTC	PGKP	69
BURTON, BENJERMIN	1820	COLU	LIVG	1
BURTON, CALVIN	1830	WASH	WHIT	353
BURTON, GEORGE	1820	NYCO	WD05	393
BURTON, HENRY	1820	ABNY	ABNY	152
BURTON, JAMES	1830	NYCO	WD14	469
BURTON, M.	1830	ERIE	BUFF	26
BURTON, THOMAS	1820	COLU	CLER	1
BUSH, A.	1830	ERIE	ERIE	84
BUSH, ALSOP	1820	ABNY	ABNY	154
BUSH, CESAR	1830	ROCK	ORGT	114
BUSH, CHRISTOPHER	1810	NYCO	WD05	380
BUSH, DIANA	1830	NYCO	WD11	190
BUSH, HANNAH	1830	NYCO	WD08	125
BUSH, JACOB	1800	NYCO	WD07	857
BUSH, JOHN	1800	DUTC	CLNT	116
BUSH, JOHN	1810	DELA	SIDN	558
BUSH, JOHN	1830	DELA	SIDN	194
BUSH, MARY	1810	NYCO	WD05	311
BUSH, PETER	1820	ULST	MARB	62

Bush

NAME	YR	CO	TWP	PG
BUSH, PETER	1830	ULST	MARB	160
BUSH, ROBERT	1830	NYCO	WD10	9
BUSH, THOMAS	1830	ORNG	NEWB	46
BUSH, YORK	1830	ROCK	CLAR	131
BUSHMAN, SAMUEL	1810	QUEN	OYST	241
BUSK, SARAH	1830	DUTC	HYPK	234
BUSKER, THOMAS	1820	NYCO	WD10	1016
BUSKER, THOMAS JR.	1820	NYCO	WD10	1016
BUST, JOHN	1830	WASH	CAST	134
BUSTER	1820	SUFF	RIVH	359
BUSTER, CHARLES	1830	SUFF	BROK	193
BUSTER, DAVID	1830	SUFF	BROK	193
BUTCHER, AARON	1820	STEU	BATH	227
BUTCHER, AARON	1830	STEU	BATH	264
BUTLER, ABRAHAM	1810	QUEN	OYST	239
BUTLER, ANTHONY	1810	NYCO	WD04	231
BUTLER, BENJAMIN	1830	SUFF	SHAM	209
BUTLER, CHARLES	1830	DUTC	PLEA	303
BUTLER, DIANA	1830	NYCO	WD06	410
BUTLER, EDWARD	1810	QUEN	OYST	252
BUTLER, GEORGE	1820	NYCO	WD07	710
BUTLER, HANNAH	1820	NYCO	WD07	715
BUTLER, HENRY	1830	NYCO	WD01	48
BUTLER, HENRY	1830	NYCO	WD05	344
BUTLER, HENRY	1830	NYCO	WD10	26
BUTLER, J.J.	1830	NYCO	WD13	370
BUTLER, JACK	1830	RICH	WEST	8
BUTLER, JACOB	1820	QUEN	----	73
BUTLER, JACOB	1830	PUTM	CARM	13
BUTLER, JACOB	1830	QUEN	OYST	31
BUTLER, JAMES	1810	NYCO	WD05	324
BUTLER, JAMES	1820	NYCO	WD06	568
BUTLER, JAMES	1830	NYCO	WD10	11
BUTLER, JENET	1830	NYCO	WD09	399
BUTLER, JEREMIAH	1830	SUFF	SHAM	209
BUTLER, JOHN	1810	NYCO	WD05	279
BUTLER, JOHN	1830	ABNY	WD02	260
BUTLER, JOHN	1830	OTSG	MARY	25
BUTLER, JOHN	1830	QUEN	NEWT	17
BUTLER, JOSEPH	1830	NYCO	WD07	46
BUTLER, JUBA	1830	STEU	BATH	272
BUTLER, LEWIS	1800	ONTA	CANA	430
BUTLER, LEWIS	1830	ONTA	CANA	120
BUTLER, LIBRA	1810	NYCO	WD10	545
BUTLER, MARY	1830	NYCO	WD08	148
BUTLER, NICHOLAS	1800	NYCO	WD07	903
BUTLER, PATRICK	1830	NYCO	WD13	337
BUTLER, PETER	1830	ABNY	BETH	538
BUTLER, PHILLIP	1830	NYCO	WD06	385

NAME	YR	CO	TWP	PG
BUTLER, ROBERT	1830	NYCO	WD08	261
BUTLER, SAMUEL	1830	RICH	WEST	12
BUTLER, SARAH	1830	SENE	FALL	29
BUTLER, SAUL	1820	WEST	NORS	391
BUTLER, SIMEON	1810	COLU	CANN	111
BUTLER, SIMON	1800	DUTC	STAN	128
BUTLER, SIMON	1830	COLU	CANN	23
BUTLER, SOLOMON	1830	WEST	SUMM	185
BUTLER, SOLOMON	1830	WEST	SUMM	192
BUTLER, THOMAS	1830	RENS	BRUN	222
BUTLER, WILLIAM	1810	NYCO	WD05	318
BUTLER, BENJAMIN	1820	SUFF	SHAM	305
BUTTER, JOHN	1810	NYCO	WD10	690
BUTTER, PUBA	1820	STEU	BATH	227
BUTTER, WILLIAM	1820	NYCO	WD05	348
BUTTERFIELD, SAMUEL	1800	NYCO	WD06	845
BUTTON, E.	1830	ERIE	BUFF	39
BUTTON, GEORGE	1830	ERIE	BUFF	5
BUTY, BELLA	1830	NYCO	WD06	368
BYARDS, JANE	1810	WEST	WEST	1145
BYAS, SARAH	1810	NYCO	WD05	255
BYASS, THOMAS	1800	NYCO	WD03	696
BYERD, THOMAS	1820	COLU	HUDS	4
BYERS, DARIA	1820	QUEN	----	41
BYERSON, DINAA	1800	NYCO	WD06	799
BYRE, SAMUEL	1810	NYCO	WD04	177
BYRNES, JAMES	1810	NYCO	WD03	90
BYRNES, JOHN	1820	ABNY	ABNY	152
CABLE, PATIENCE	1820	ABNY	ABNY	161
CABLE, SAMUEL	1830	ORNG	WARW	64
CABLE, TIMOTHY	1820	ORNG	WARW	626
CABLE, TIMOTHY	1830	ORNG	WARW	92
CABS, JABES	1810	NYCO	WD10	664
CADET, SANON	1830	NYCO	WD05	302
CADOUSE, JOSEPH	1800	NYCO	WD07	867
CAESAR	1790	NYCO	NORT	126
CAESAR	1790	NYCO	MONT	120
CAESAR	1790	NYCO	OUTW	130
CAESAR	1790	QUEN	NEWT	151
CAESAR	1790	QUEN	NEWT	152
CAESAR	1790	QUEN	NHEM	152
CAESAR	1790	QUEN	OYST	154
CAESAR	1800	QUEN	OYST	571
CAESAR	1800	QUEN	OYST	575
CAESAR, JAMES	1830	COLU	STUY	70
CAESAR, JOSEPH	1790	ABNY	SCNE	44
CAESAR, TIMOTHY	1800	DUTC	NORT	143

NAME	YR	CO	TWP	PG
CAESER	1800	SUFF	HUNT	36
CAESER, ABRIEN	1820	MONT	AMST	279
CAFF, STEPHEN	1790	SUFF	BROK	161
CAGE	1810	NYCO	WD06	470
CAGGY, JOHN	1820	WEST	EAST	200
CAIN	1790	QUEN	OYST	154
CAIN	1800	SUFF	BROK	11
CAIN, LOT	1830	SCHR	SCHR	13
CAKMAN, JOHN	1800	RENS	TROY	880
CALDER, ADAM	1830	DUTC	PGKP	363
CALEB	1790	NYCO	OUTW	129
CALEB	1790	QUEN	OYST	153
CALEB	1800	QUEN	OYST	580
CALER, THOMAS	1810	NYCO	WD07	529
CALKINS, TIMOTHY	1790	DUTC	CLNT	76
CALORIS, TUCKING	1800	SUFF	SHAM	64
CALUE, LEWIS	1810	NYCO	WD05	280
CALWELL, DAVID	1820	NYCO	WD08	780
CAMBEE, MARGARET	1810	NYCO	WD04	179
CAMBELL, JACK	1830	SARA	SARA	147
CAMELIA	1800	SARA	BALL	1056
CAMER, CHLOE	1830	MADI	----	312
CAMITAU, THOMAS	1810	NYCO	WD07	521
CAMP, AMOS	1810	WASH	BOTT	399
CAMP, JOAN	1810	NYCO	WD05	262
CAMPBELL	1820	NYCO	WD07	635
CAMPBELL, JACK	1820	SARA	SARA	200
CAMPBELL, JOHN	1810	SARA	SARA	873
CAMPBELL, JOHN	1820	NYCO	WD05	423
CAMPBELL, JOHN	1830	ONID	UTIC	12
CAMPBELL, RICHARD	1810	NYCO	WD02	122
CAMPBELL, THOMAS	1820	ONID	AUGU	320
CANADA, BRACE	1830	WEST	HARR	216
CANADA, ROBERT	1820	FRAN	FORC	673
CANE, BENJAMIN	1820	COLU	HUDS	9
CANE, TESTUS	1820	SUFF	SOUT	344
CANES, ELIZABETH	1820	DUTC	FISH	90
CANIN, MOSES	1830	KING	FLAT	402
CANINE, JACK	1830	GREN	NEWB	174
CANINE, JACOB	1830	GREN	COXE	190
CANLER, HENRY	1820	MADI	SULL	2
CANNAN, JACOB	1830	NYCO	WD13	392
CANNASAY, SAMUEL	1810	ULST	MARB	805
CANNON, JACOB	1810	NYCO	WD07	552
CANNON, JACOB	1820	NYCO	WD07	635
CANNON, JOHN	1830	NYCO	WD05	312
CANO	1790	QUEN	NHEM	153
CANTINE, ADAM	1830	ULST	OLIV	132
CANTINE, CROSS	1830	ULST	WAWA	191

NAME	YR	CO	TWP	PG
CANTINE, HENRY	1810	NYCO	WD05	326
CANTINE, HENRY	1820	NYCO	WD04	212
CANTINE, HENRY	1830	DUTC	PLEA	313
CANTINE, PETER	1810	ULST	MARB	800
CANTINE, ROBERT	1830	ULST	SAUG	110
CANTINE, THOMAS	1830	ULST	MARB	159
CANTINE, WANE	1810	ULST	MARB	801
CANUN, ELLEN	1830	NYCO	WD08	179
CAP	1790	QUEN	NHEM	152
CAPMAN, CHRISTOPHER	1790	NYCO	NORT	127
CAPTAIN	1820	SUFF	SMIT	314
CARELISS, SIMON	1800	NYCO	WD03	705
CAREY, JAMES	1830	PUTM	SOUT	51
CAREY, SIMEON	1830	PUTM	SOUT	51
CAREY, THOMAS	1810	DUTC	DOVE	110
CAREY, ZACHARIAH	1830	NYCO	WD10	117
CARITY	1800	ABNY	WD01	263
CARL, PELEG	1830	SUFF	HUNT	315
CARL, PELEZ	1820	SUFF	HUNT	298
CARLE, LEWIS	1830	QUEN	OYST	50
CARLE, OSBOURNE	1830	NYCO	WD08	227
CARLE, STEPHEN	1820	QUEN	----	76
CARLE, STEPHEN	1830	QUEN	OYST	33
CARLEY, ABRAHAM	1820	MONT	CHAR	325
CARLEY, CHARLES	1830	SCHR	BROM	89
CARLINE	1810	COLU	CLAV	161
CARLON, J.	1810	MADI	SULL	797
CARLOS, FRANCES	1800	NYCO	WD06	832
CARMAN, ADAM	1830	NYCO	WD14	455
CARMAN, FRANCIS	1830	DUTC	LAGR	246
CARMAN, J.	1830	NYCO	WD11	163
CARMAN, JAMES	1830	SUFF	BROK	196
CARMAN, LEWIS	1810	QUEN	OYST	256
CARMAN, M.	1810	DUTC	WASH	162
CARMAN, MICHEL	1830	QUEN	SHEM	94
CARMAN, MONDESIE	1820	DUTC	BEEK	12
CARMAN, NANCY	1830	KING	WD03	284
CARMAN, RICHARD	1810	QUEN	SHEM	306
CARMAN, RICHARD	1830	QUEN	SHEM	94
CARMAN, THOMAS	1830	DUTC	UNVA	427
CARMAN, WILLIAM	1810	QUEN	SHEM	306
CARMAN, WILLIAM	1830	SUFF	ISLP	284
CARMEL, PETER	1820	QUEN	----	38
CARMEN, BEN	1820	QUEN	----	50
CARMEN, NICHORA	1820	QUEN	----	10
CARMEN, WILLIAM	1820	QUEN	----	18
CARMICHAEL, WARWICK	1820	SENE	GALE	428
CARNELL, JACOB	1820	QUEN	----	54
CARPENDER, FRANCIS	1820	ORNG	MONT	846

Carpent

NAME	YR	CO	TWP	PG
CARPENT, SILAS	1810	QUEN	OYST	232
CARPENTER, A.	1820	NYCO	WD10	977
CARPENTER, BETSEY	1830	ABNY	WD01	212
CARPENTER, CULL	1810	WEST	RYE	1162
CARPENTER, FRANCIS	1810	ORNG	GOSH	1121
CARPENTER, FREDERICK N.	1830	DUTC	STAN	409
CARPENTER, HARRY	1820	SUFF	ISLP	310
CARPENTER, HARRY	1830	SUFF	ISLP	286
CARPENTER, HENRY	1810	SUFF	ISLP	499
CARPENTER, ISAAC	1820	WEST	HARR	467
CARPENTER, ISMAEL	1830	QUEN	OYST	29
CARPENTER, JACK	1820	QUEN	----	78
CARPENTER, JOSEPH	1820	DUTC	CLNT	44
CARPENTER, NICHOLAS	1820	WEST	EAST	206
CARPENTER, NICHOLAS	1830	WEST	EAST	133
CARPENTER, NICK	1810	WEST	HARR	1133
CARPENTER, OLIVER	1820	GREN	ATHN	1
CARPENTER, ROBERT	1810	NYCO	WD04	153
CARPENTER, SAMUEL	1810	QUEN	OYST	236
CARPENTER, SAMUEL	1820	MADI	SULL	10
CARPENTER, SIMEON	1820	ORNG	NEWB	546
CARPENTER, STEPHEN	1830	QUEN	OYST	30
CARR, BENJAMIN	1800	QUEN	NHEM	553
CARR, BENJAMIN	1820	QUEN	----	38
CARR, ICHOBAL	1830	SCHR	SCHR	20
CARR, LEASER	1810	NYCO	WD10	696
CARR, SUSAN	1830	NYCO	WD08	245
CARR, THOMAS	1810	DUTC	DOVE	113
CARR, THOMAS	1820	DUTC	DOVE	46
CARR, THOMAS	1830	DUTC	DOVE	214
CARRICK, ROBERT	1830	DUTC	FISH	478
CARRINGTON, RICHARD	1830	ORNG	NEWB	39
CARRINGTON, SOFIHIA	1820	NYCO	WD08	784
CARROL, CHARLES	1830	NYCO	WD10	115
CARROL, JOHN	1830	NYCO	WD05	339
CARROLL, JAMES	1810	NYCO	WD05	309
CARROLL, JAMES	1820	NYCO	WD04	226
CARROW, HANNAH	1790	NYCO	NORT	125
CARSIER, JACOB	1830	WASH	KING	356
CARSON, CUFFY	1820	NYCO	WD10	983
CARTER, ABEL H.	1830	ORNG	NEWB	29
CARTER, CHARLES	1830	NYCO	WD08	140
CARTER, CHARLES	1830	NYCO	WD08	230
CARTER, DAVID	1830	NYCO	WD07	58
CARTER, ELISON	1830	NYCO	WD04	158
CARTER, HENRY	1830	NYCO	WD05	343
CARTER, J.	1830	NYCO	WD06	451
CARTER, JOHN	1800	NYCO	WD05	757
CARTER, JOHN	1820	NYCO	WD06	498

NAME	YR	CO	TWP	PG
CARTER, JOHN	1830	NYCO	WD06	379
CARTER, JOHN	1830	NYCO	WD10	26
CARTER, JONATHAN	1820	SCNE	WD01	65
CARTER, LEWIS	1830	NYCO	WD03	116
CARTER, OWEN	1830	NYCO	WD10	11
CARTER, SAMUEL	1800	NYCO	WD03	696
CARTER, SUSAN	1800	NYCO	WD06	821
CARTINE, JUDITH	1830	NYCO	WD05	272
CARTLANDT, ISAAC	1830	ORNG	GOSH	289
CARTRIGHT, JACOB	1790	ORNG	ORNG	146
CARTRIGHT, JACOB	1800	NYCO	WD06	808
CARTY, JOSEPH	1830	ONTA	GORH	6
CARY, PRINCE	1830	SARA	SASP	163
CARY, THOMAS	1800	DUTC	WASH	102
CARY, TOM	1810	DUTC	NORT	455
CASBERY, EDWARD	1830	NYCO	WD12	278
CASE, FESTUS	1830	SUFF	SOUT	353
CASE, JASON	1830	SUFF	SHEL	291
CASER	1800	QUEN	NHEM	550
CASEY, CORNELIUS	1810	NYCO	WD06	394
CASEY, LEWIS	1830	DUTC	WASH	436
CASEY, LEWIS C.	1810	NYCO	WD05	279
CASEY, WILLIAM	1820	DUTC	PAUL	90
CASH, JOHN	1830	NYCO	WD04	203
CASHORE, TOM	1830	SARA	SASP	174
CASMIRE	1810	NYCO	WD06	441
CASS, MOTT	1830	QUEN	NHEM	108
CASSAM, HENRY	1830	SARA	EDIN	201
CASSIDY, SAMUEL	1820	ABNY	ABNY	159
CASSON, PHILLIP	1830	QUEN	NHEM	116
CASTER, BEN	1810	WEST	NORC	1175
CASTER, CHARLES	1820	NYCO	WD10	992
CASTIN, BENJAMIN	1820	WEST	NORC	440
CASTO, MITCHEL	1820	NYCO	WD03	149
CASTON, BENJAMIN	1830	WEST	NORC	194
CASTON, HENRY	1830	WEST	NORC	194
CASTORS, PETER P.D.	1810	NYCO	WD04	212
CATAWAY, LOTT	1810	NYCO	WD02	138
CATER, ABRAHAM	1810	SCHR	SCHR	7
CATER, J.	1830	NYCO	WD11	154
CATHARINE	1790	NYCO	MONT	124
CATHARINE	1790	QUEN	NHEM	152
CATHARINE	1790	QUEN	OYST	155
CATHERINE	1800	ABNY	SCNE	3
CATHERINE	1800	NYCO	WD06	811
CATHERINE	1800	NYCO	WD05	748
CATHERINE	1800	SARA	CHAR	1074
CATHERINE	1810	NYCO	WD06	419
CATHERINE, MADAM	1810	NYCO	WD06	186

NAME	YR	CO	TWP	PG
CATO	1790	NYCO	MONT	120
CATO	1790	NYCO	MONT	121
CATO	1790	NYCO	WEST	135
CATO	1790	NYCO	WEST	136
CATO	1790	QUEN	FLUS	149
CATO	1790	QUEN	NHEM	153
CATO	1790	QUEN	SHEM	156
CATO	1800	ABNY	SCNE	7
CATO	1800	QUEN	OYST	577
CATO	1800	QUEN	OYST	579
CATO	1800	SUFF	SHAM	77
CATO	1810	DUTC	PGKP	169
CATO	1810	RENS	SCHO	549
CATO	1810	NYCO	WD07	559
CATO	1820	NYCO	WD07	621
CATO, ANTHONY	1830	QUEN	NHEM	105
CATO, JOHN	1820	NYCO	WD05	384
CATO, JUDAS	1830	SUFF	BROK	159
CATO, PHILIP	1830	MONT	FLOR	98
CATO, SILVANUS	1830	QUEN	NHEM	108
CATON, TOBINS	1820	DUTC	CLNT	27
CATOSON, CATO	1820	SCNE	WD02	129
CATS, HENRY	1810	NYCO	WD05	307
CATSKILL, PRIMUS	1820	DUTC	FISH	72
CATSKILL, PRIMUS	1830	DUTC	FISH	463
CATY	1790	NYCO	MONT	121
CAUS, WILLIAM	1800	NYCO	WD03	709
CAUSE, DAIRA	1820	QUEN	----	9
CAUSE, STEPHEN	1820	QUEN	----	77
CAUSNO, JOSEPH	1820	WEST	BEDF	415
CAUSS, JAMES	1830	QUEN	NHEM	105
CAUSS, MOSES	1830	QUEN	NHEM	112
CAUSS, STEPHEN	1830	QUEN	NHEM	106
CAVALIER, DANIEL J.	1830	NYCO	WD08	178
CAVELL, JAMES	1830	ONON	ONON	192
CAVERLY, RACHEL	1830	NYCO	WD01	40
CAVIER, HENRY	1820	MADI	SULL	2
CAWS, DAVID	1800	NYCO	WD07	887
CAZEMLINE, CATO	1800	QUEN	NHEM	553
CEAREN, JAMES	1820	SUFF	ISLP	309
CEARER, PAUL	1820	SUFF	BROK	330
CEARZER, GITTY	1830	ANBY	WD02	255
CEASAN	1820	QUEN	----	67
CEASAR	1790	SUFF	SMIT	166
CEASAR	1800	NYCO	WD07	881
CEASAR	1800	NYCO	WD07	900
CEASAR	1810	COLU	GRAN	204
CEASAR	1810	COLU	KIND	172
CEASAR	1810	RENS	TROY	381

NAME	YR	CO	TWP	PG
CEASAR	1810	SUFF	SMIT	538
CEASAR, FRANCIS	1820	NYCO	WD04	241
CEASAR, JOHN	1830	COLU	KIND	146
CEASAR, STEPHEN	1810	SUFF	BROK	469
CEASER	1820	QUEN	----	65
CEASER, BENJAMIN	1830	SUFF	SHAM	228
CEAVEN, STEPHEN	1820	SUFF	SOUT	333
CEAZER, RICHARD	1830	ABNY	WD01	219
CEBRA, JAMES	1790	QUEN	OYST	155
CELLIS	1790	NYCO	OUTW	129
CEAT, MARGARET	1810	NYCO	WD05	305
CEPHAS, CATO	1820	NYCO	WD06	531
CESAR	1790	NYCO	NORT	124
CESAR	1810	NYCO	WD05	360
CESAR, BARTH SHEEHY	1830	SUFF	EAST	259
CESAR, CALEB	1830	SUFF	BROK	161
CESAR, DANIEL	1830	SUFF	RIVH	233
CESAR, JAMES	1810	NYCO	WD04	160
CESAR, WILHELM	1830	COLU	GHEN	166
CETING, HARRY	1830	ULST	KING	63
CEVEST, THOMAS	1820	COLU	KIND	3
CEZAR	1810	MADI	SMIT	880
CHABA, STEPHEN	1820	NYCO	WD03	157
CHACY, CORNELUS	1820	SUFF	ISLP	311
CHAMBERS, JACOB	1830	ULST	MARB	154
CHAMBERS, SAMUEL	1820	ONTA	CANA	211
CHAMBERS, WILLIAM	1830	ABNY	WD01	200
CHAMPIN, PRIMUS	1810	ONON	POMP	513
CHANCELER, JAMES	1830	MONT	MAYF	279
CHANCELL, EPHRAIM	1830	MONT	JOHN	209
CHANCELOR, CUFFS	1820	MONT	JOHN	357
CHANCY, JOSEPH	1820	DUTC	BEEK	17
CHANDELON, COFFEE	1810	MONT	JOHN	31
CHANDLER, SOPHIA	1830	ORNG	MONR	163
CHAPEL, AARON	1800	DUTC	PAWL	44
CHAPEL, AARON	1830	CHEN	GREN	48
CHAPLIN, PRIMUS	1830	ONON	LAFY	300
CHAPPEL, JOSEPH	1820	QUEN	----	62
CHAPPEL, MORRIS	1810	NYCO	WD05	249
CHAPPEL, THOMAS	1820	QUEN	----	60
CHAPPEL, THOMAS	1830	QUEN	FLUS	155
CHAPPELL, AARON	1820	DUTC	DOVE	49
CHAPPELL, HENRY	1830	QUEN	NHEM	112
CHAPPLE, AARON	1810	DUTC	DOVE	115
CHAPPLE, AARON	1830	DUTC	DOVE	210
CHARITY	1790	QUEN	OYST	155
CHARITY	1800	ABNY	WD02	286
CHARLES	1790	NYCO	MONT	124
CHARLES	1790	QUEN	FLUS	150

NAME	YR	CO	TWP	PG
CHARLES	1790	QUEN	NEWT	151
CHARLES	1790	QUEN	NHEM	152
CHARLES	1790	QUEN	OYST	155
CHARLES	1790	QUEN	SHEM	156
CHARLES	1800	ABNY	WD02	284
CHARLES	1800	QUEN	NEWT	656
CHARLES	1800	QUEN	OYST	568
CHARLES	1800	QUEN	OYST	574
CHARLES	1800	QUEN	OYST	570
CHARLES	1800	QUEN	OYST	579
CHARLES	1800	QUEN	OYST	569
CHARLES	1800	RENS	GREN	721
CHARLES	1800	SUFF	HUNT	36
CHARLES	1800	SUFF	BROK	12
CHARLES	1800	SUFF	BROK	9
CHARLES	1800	WEST	HARR	652
CHARLES	1820	ABNY	COEY	125
CHARLES	1820	QUEN	----	28
CHARLES	1820	QUEN	----	57
CHARLES	1820	SUFF	BROK	353
CHARLES	1830	NYCO	WD11	179
CHARLES, DANIEL	1810	NYCO	WD01	28
CHARLES, H.	1810	ONID	----	377
CHARLES, HENRY	1800	WASH	EATN	463
CHARLES, HENRY	1820	ONID	AUGU	320
CHARLES, HENRY	1830	MADI	----	419
CHARLES, KING	1820	ABNY	ABNY	159
CHARLOTTE	1790	QUEN	SHEM	156
CHARLTON, CHARLES	1830	NYCO	WD10	11
CHARLTON, EDWARD	1810	NYCO	WD05	299
CHARLTON, JAMES	1810	NYCO	WD05	313
CHARLTON, LEONARD	1820	WEST	SUMM	344
CHARLTON, SAMUEL	1810	NYCO	WD02	99
CHARLTON, SIMON	1820	NYCO	WD06	504
CHARPENTER, JOHN	1820	QUEN	----	52
CHARTER, & DIXON	1830	NYCO	WD13	343
CHASE, ISAAC	1810	NYCO	WD04	230
CHASE, PETER	1810	NYCO	WD01	20
CHASE, RICHARD	1820	NYCO	WD01	36
CHASE, SAMUEL	1830	WASH	JACK	180
CHASE, TASON	1820	SUFF	SHEL	329
CHASMAN, DANIEL	1810	QUEN	FLUS	191
CHATHAN, SARAH	1810	NYCO	WD02	101
CHATKETE, LYRCONTIC	1800	NYCO	WD07	870
CHATTERTON, EDWARD	1830	NYCO	WD06	458
CHAVIN, SOOKE	1810	QUEN	NHEM	300
CHAWN, PETER	1830	QUEN	FLUS	150
CHECKER	1790	QUEN	OYST	155
CHEESEBROUGH, DOMINGO	1790	DUTC	BEEK	76

NAME	YR	CO	TWP	PG
CHEESEMAN, DANIEL	1830	QUEN	OYST	43
CHEESMAN, BENJAMIN	1830	NYCO	WD10	19
CHEESMAN, RICHARD	1810	NYCO	WD05	291
CHELOCK, GEORGE	1830	NYCO	WD10	30
CHERRIN, DUNCAN	1830	ABNY	WD01	224
CHEW, WILLIAM	1810	NYCO	WD05	256
CHICKENS, BENJAMIN	1800	DUTC	PAWL	48
CHIPHOME, HANNAH	1810	SUFF	ISLP	498
CHOLWELL, HARRY	1830	DUTC	REDH	368
CHOWAN, JOHN	1800	QUEN	SHEM	556
CHRISTIAN, JONATHAN	1800	NYCO	WD05	763
CHRISTIE, MARY	1820	NYCO	WD04	317
CHRISTOPHER	1820	QUEN	----	10
CHRISTOPHER, EUGENIA	1820	NYCO	WD06	462
CHRISTOPHER, FORTUNE	1830	RICH	NORT	23
CHRISTOPHER, JACOB	1830	NYCO	WD04	188
CHRISTOPHER, MARY	1830	NYCO	WD06	389
CHUGGEL, JOSEPH	1820	DUTC	FISH	77
CHURCH, MEDAD	1830	MONR	RWD3	219
CHURCH, PETER	1820	WEST	GREN	238
CHURCH, PETER	1830	NYCO	WD07	009
CHURCH, PRIMUS	1800	NYCO	WD07	903
CHURCH, ROBERT	1820	NYCO	WD09	924
CHURCHHILL, ARABELLA	1820	DUTC	PGKP	102
CHURCHHILL, JEREMIAH	1830	DELA	TOMP	209
CHURCHHILL, REUBEN	1830	DELA	TOMP	209
CHURCHHILL, ROBERT	1820	DUTC	REDH	114
CHURCHHILL, SARAH	1820	DUTC	PGKP	99
CHURCHILL, LEONARD	1830	DUTC	REDH	372
CHURCHILL, NELSON	1830	DUTC	PGKP	327
CHURCHILL, ROBERT	1830	DUTC	REDH	372
CIGGS, PERRY	1820	STEU	BATH	227
CINTHIA	1790	QUEN	FLUS	149
CIPSON, JOHN	1800	NYCO	WD07	896
CISCO, ANTHONY	1830	NYCO	WD05	324
CISCO, DANIEL	1810	NYCO	WD05	338
CISCO, ISABELLA	1830	NYCO	WD08	229
CISCO, ISIAH	1830	NYCO	WD14	491
CISCO, JAMES	1830	QUEN	NEWT	4
CISCO, JOHN	1830	ROCK	ORGT	107
CISCO, MARIA	1830	NYCO	WD08	262
CISCO, MRS.	1820	NYCO	WD05	419
CISCO, NICHOLAS	1820	NYCO	WD05	433
CISCO, NICHOLAS	1820	NYCO	WD08	844
CISCO, SUSANNAH	1810	NYCO	WD05	279
CISCO, THOMAS	1830	NYCO	WD08	202
CISCO, TUNIS	1820	NYCO	WD05	433
CISCO, WILLIAM	1830	NYCO	WD08	202
CISCO, WILLIAM	1830	ROCK	ORGT	109

Ciscoe

NAME	YR	CO	TWP	PG
CISCOE, THOMAS	1830	ORNG	GOSH	275
CISER, JACK	1820	COLU	KIND	3
CISRO, JAMES	1820	NYCO	WD08	827
CLADY, ROBERT	1830	MONT	ROOT	56
CLAP, JANE	1810	SUFF	BROK	491
CLAPP, DICK	1810	WEST	NORT	1171
CLAPP, RICHARD	1820	WEST	NORC	441
CLAPP, SAMUEL	1830	WEST	WEST	124
CLARCKSON, JOHN	1830	NYCO	WD01	36
CLARK, BETSEY	1820	ROCK	ORNG	86
CLARK, BETSEY	1830	NYCO	WD10	65
CLARK, BETTY	1820	DUTC	CLNT	29
CLARK, CEASAR	1820	DUTC	CLNT	27
CLARK, CESAR	1830	DUTC	HYPK	234
CLARK, CHARLES	1820	NYCO	WD04	227
CLARK, CIRUS	1830	NYCO	WD14	459
CLARK, CONGO	1810	NYCO	WD06	450
CLARK, DAVID	1820	CHAT	CHAT	54
CLARK, ELIZABETH	1830	DUTC	HYPK	227
CLARK, FREDERICK	1820	NYCO	WD03	185
CLARK, GILES S.	1810	GENE	CALA	115
CLARK, HANNAH	1810	DUTC	RHIN	431
CLARK, HARRIET	1830	NYCO	WD05	336
CLARK, HARRY	1820	DUTC	CLNT	29
CLARK, HENRY	1830	DUTC	HYPK	227
CLARK, HENRY	1830	NYCO	WD05	271
CLARK, ISABELLA	1820	NYCO	WD06	486
CLARK, JAMES	1820	NYCO	WD01	19
CLARK, JANE	1830	NYCO	WD10	96
CLARK, JOB	1830	CHAT	SHER	448
CLARK, JOSEPH	1820	NYCO	WD03	149
CLARK, JOSEPH	1830	NYCO	WD07	90
CLARK, LUIS	1830	NYCO	WD10	87
CLARK, MOSE	1810	NYCO	WD06	468
CLARK, ROBERT	1790	NYCO	WEST	133
CLARK, ROBERT	1810	NYCO	WD05	372
CLARK, ROBERT	1830	NYCO	WD07	61
CLARK, SAMUEL	1800	NYCO	WD01	667
CLARK, SAMUEL	1830	DUTC	HYPK	227
CLARK, STEPHEN	1810	QUEN	OYST	238
CLARK, STEPHEN	1830	ONTA	CANA	137
CLARK, WILLIS	1830	NYCO	WD05	336
CLARKSON, MR.	1830	NYCO	WD06	450
CLARKSON, PETER	1830	ORNG	NEWW	99
CLARKSON, PRIOR	1810	NYCO	WD03	84
CLARY, DICK	1810	RENS	GREN	455
CLARY, JACK	1820	MONT	CANJ	304
CLARY, RICHARD	1830	RENS	BRUN	221
CLASEN, JOHN	1830	SCNE	WD01	202

NAME	YR	CO	TWP	PG
CLASON, CATHARINE	1830	NYCO	WD05	252
CLASON, TOBIAS	1830	NYCO	WD09	356
CLASS	1800	ABNY	WD01	264
CLASS, SAMUEL	1830	NYCO	WD14	517
CLASSON, NICHOLAS	1820	SCNE	SCNE	123
CLAUS	1800	ABNY	SCNE	18
CLAUS	1800	ROCK	CLAR	1015
CLAUS, SAMUEL	1810	NYCO	WD02	108
CLAUSEN, JOHN	1830	SCNE	WD01	203
CLAUSEN, PETER	1830	SCNE	WD01	203
CLAUSON, ANTHONY	1830	DUTC	FISH	478
CLAUSON, THOMAS	1830	DUTC	FISH	480
CLAVER, JACOB	1830	NYCO	WD06	427
CLAXTER, JOHN	1810	NYCO	WD02	17
CLAXTON, NATHANIEL	1830	NYCO	WD05	328
CLAY, JACK	1800	NYCO	WD06	842
CLEFS, SAMUEL	1820	PUTM	SOUT	100
CLEGGETT, DAVID	1830	OSWE	AMBO	267
CLEMENT, FRANCIS	1830	NYCO	WD08	243
CLEMENT, MOSES	1820	SENE	PAYE	372
CLEMENTS, CHARLES	1830	QUEN	JAMA	130
CLEMENTS, MASON	1830	YATE	MILO	277
CLEMENTS, SAMUEL	1830	YATE	MILO	277
CLEMMENT, CHARLES	1800	NYCO	WD07	903
CLEVELAND, JACKLYN	1820	MONT	CANJ	305
CLEVELAND, JOHN	1830	MONT	ROOT	58
CLIFF, ANTHONY	1830	PUTM	SOUT	50
CLIFS, WILLIAM	1820	PUTM	SOUT	100
CLINE, JIM	1820	WASH	FANN	148
CLINLAR, NED	1810	MONT	UPEN	137
CLOCERY, JOHN M.	1820	ORNG	WALL	793
CLOCKERY, JOHN	1830	ORNG	WALL	136
CLOSSON, NICHOLAS	1820	NYCO	WD08	858
CLOSS	1810	COLU	CANN	110
CLOSS, NICHOLAS	1830	QUEN	NEWT	16
CLOSS, SAMUEL	1820	NYCO	WD03	184
CLOUSE, GILBERT	1810	QUEN	SHEM	296
CLOUSE, LEWIS	1810	QUEN	SHEM	305
CLOW, ABRAHAM	1820	SCHR	MIDD	520
CLOW, RICHARD	1830	DUTC	STAN	413
CLOW, RICHARD C.	1830	GREN	ATHN	201
CLOWER, BENJAMIN	1830	NYCO	WD06	431
CLOWS, GILBENS	1820	QUEN	----	23
CLOWS, GILBERT	1800	NYCO	WD01	658
CO, MARA	1800	NYCO	WD06	807
COATES, S.W.	1820	NYCO	WD06	490
COBBS, JOHN	1830	NYCO	WD08	227
COBERD, THOMAS	1820	NYCO	WD10	992
COC, HARRY	1830	ULST	NPAL	220

NAME	YR	CO	TWP	PG
COCHSURE, JONAS	1800	DUTC	PAWL	6
COCHY, LEWIS	1820	NYCO	WD05	397
COCK, CHARLES	1810	QUEN	OYST	250
COCK, DAVID	1810	QUEN	OYST	255
COCK, MOSES	1810	QUEN	OYST	250
COCK, OBADIAH	1810	QUEN	OYST	255
COCK, SAMUEL	1810	QUEN	OYST	251
COCK, THOMAS	1810	QUEN	OYST	250
COCK, WILLIAM	1830	QUEN	OYST	31
COCK, WILLIAM	1830	QUEN	NHEM	102
COCKBURN, ELIZABETH	1830	MONT	CANJ	22
COCKBURN, HARRY	1820	MONT	CANJ	304
COCKBURN, HARRY	1830	MONT	CANJ	38
COCKS, JENNY	1820	DUTC	CLNT	25
COCKS, LANA	1830	WEST	RYE	103
CODJA, JOHN	1830	WEST	EAST	136
CODURSE, HENRY	1820	QUEN	----	54
COE, ABRAHAM	1830	NYCO	WD14	445
COE, CHARLES	1820	NYCO	WD08	853
COE, EPHRAM	1810	QUEN	NEWT	167
COE, ISSAC	1800	ORNG	WARW	375
COE, JONES	1790	ORAN	WARW	148
COE, NEHEMIAH	1800	QUEN	FLUS	542
COE, YAST	1810	QUEN	NEWT	167
COEBRUN, PHOBE	1820	ULST	SAUG	83
COENHOVEN, HENRY	1820	NYCO	WD06	515
COFF	1810	DUTC	PGKP	24-167
COFFE, JAMES	1830	ABNY	WD04	298
COFFEE, AARON	1830	SUFF	ISLP	284
COFFES, JACK	1820	QUEN	----	63
COFFIN, JOSEPH	1830	ABNY	WD01	219
COFFIN, PRINCE	1820	COLU	GHIN	3
COGGIN, TIMOTHY	1800	DUTC	CLNT	108
COHESE, P.	1810	MADI	SULL	796
COKLE, HENRY	1830	GREN	DURH	270
COLBERT, JONATHAN	1830	ONTA	CANA	115
COLBERT, LLOYD	1830	ONTA	CANA	112
COLBURT, LOYD	1820	ONTA	CANA	210
COLDEN	1800	QUEN	FLUS	543
COLDEN, CATO	1830	DUTC	LAGR	247
COLDEN, HENRY	1820	ORNG	MONT	844
COLDEN, HENRY	1830	ORNG	MONR	176
COLDEN, JAMES	1800	NYCO	WD06	883
COLDEN, MARTIN	1830	DUTC	FISH	481
COLDEN, PRINCE	1830	DUTC	FISH	477
COLDER, MARGARET	1820	DUTC	PGKP	107
COLE, ALEXANDER	1830	ORNG	CORN	214
COLE, ANNA	1820	NYCO	WD05	393
COLE, CATEY	1820	NYCO	WD06	481

NAME	YR	CO	TWP	PG
COLE, DAVID	1800	NYCO	WD06	808
COLE, DINAH	1810	NYCO	WD03	57
COLE, EDWARD	1810	NYCO	WD03	83
COLE, HARRY	1830	RICH	WEST	4
COLE, JOHN	1790	QUEN	NEWT	151
COLE, JOHN	1810	NYCO	WD05	285
COLE, JOHN	1820	QUEN	----	46
COLE, MR.	1830	NYCO	WD13	341
COLE, PETER	1830	FRAN	FORC	41
COLE, PHILLIP	1820	NYCO	WD04	248
COLE, SIMON	1830	ULST	MARB	164
COLE, STEPHEN	1830	ORNG	MINI	246
COLE, TOM	1800	WEST	PCHE	604
COLE, WILLIAM	1830	ORNG	WARW	71
COLEMAN, BARNABAS	1810	ORNG	BLOM	1014
COLER, JOHN	1810	NYCO	WD06	442
COLES, ELIZABETH	1830	NYCO	WD10	13
COLES, JOHN	1830	NYCO	WD08	229
COLES, JOHN	1830	QUEN	NEWT	18
COLES, JOSEPH	1830	NYCO	WD10	43
COLES, MOSES	1830	QUEN	FLUS	154
COLES, RICHARD	1820	WEST	WEST	193
COLES, RICHARD	1830	WEST	WEST	121
COLES, STEPHEN	1820	SUFF	EAST	294
COLES, THOMAS	1810	WEST	WEST	1147
COLES, THOMAS	1820	WEST	WEST	196
COLIS, ABRAM	1810	QUEN	OYST	237
COLIS, JACOB	1810	QUEN	OYST	236
COLLINGS, JAMES	1820	ORNG	NEWW	491
COLLINS, ANN	1810	ORNG	NEWW	916
COLLINS, DANIEL	1800	NYCO	WD07	916
COLLINS, FRANCIS	1820	TOMP	LANS	37
COLLINS, FRANCIS	1830	TOMP	ITCA	332
COLLINS, GEORGE	1830	NYCO	WD05	333
COLLINS, GES	1820	NYCO	WD08	784
COLLINS, HENRY	1830	NYCO	WD05	268
COLLINS, JACOB	1820	NYCO	WD05	394
COLLINS, JACOB	1830	NYCO	WD05	337
COLLINS, JAMES	1800	NYCO	WD07	916
COLLINS, JAMES	1820	TOMP	LANS	37
COLLINS, JAMES	1830	NYCO	WD13	359
COLLINS, JAMES	1830	NYCO	WD14	440
COLLINS, JAMES	1830	TOMP	ITCA	332
COLLINS, MARTHA	1830	NYCO	WD04	190
COLLINS, MRS.	1830	NYCO	WD06	445
COLLINS, NICHOLAS	1820	NYCO	WD09	914
COLLINS, PHILIP	1830	COLU	KIND	146
COLLINS, PHILLIP	1820	COLU	KIND	17
COLLINS, REBECCA	1830	NYCO	WD07	49

NAME	YR	CO	TWP	PG
COLLINS, SAMUEL	1830	ABNY	WD01	210
COLLINS, SAMUEL	1830	NYCO	WD04	218
COLLINS, THOMAS	1830	KING	WD05	328
COLLINS, TRIM	1830	DELA	DELH	42
COLLINS, WILLIAM	1810	NYCO	WD05	313
COLLINS, WILLIAM	1820	NYCO	WD03	190
COLLY, SOPHIA	1800	ORNG	MONT	21
COLT, ISABELLA	1830	SUFF	ISLP	285
COLTER, WILLIAM	1810	GENE	CALA	116
COLUMBUS, HENRY	1810	ULST	KING	748
COLVINE, JOSEPH	1830	NYCO	WD14	499
COLWELL, DAVID	1830	NYCO	WD08	212
COLWELL, ISAAC	1830	NYCO	WD06	386
COLWELL, JOSEPH	1810	NYCO	WD06	422
COLWELL, VALENTINE	1810	NYCO	WD05	345
COMATHEA, BENJAMIN	1820	NYCO	WD05	427
COMBE, LEONARD	1810	NYCO	ULST	733
COMBS, JOHN	1800	NYCO	WD07	929
COMING, JACOB	1810	QUEN	FLUS	198
COMMERACO, THOMAS	1800	NYCO	WD07	905
COMMSON, JOHN	1820	NYCO	WD08	781
COMPLE, ROBERT	1830	DUTC	REDH	366
COMPTON, HENRY	1830	NYCO	WD06	385
COMSTOCK, SAMUEL	1820	CHAT	CHAT	50
COMWELL, WILLIAM	1820	ONON	DALI	244
CONARVAY, JOHN	1820	ULST	MARB	61
CONCKLIN, HELEN	1830	NYCO	WD10	99
CONEAR, H.	1810	MADI	SULL	791
CONGING, LEWIS	1830	QUEN	SHEM	77
CONINE, THOMAS	1830	ULST	WOOD	118
CONKLIN, EPHRAIM	1830	NYCO	WD07	59
CONKLIN, FEDAS	1830	SUFF	BROK	173
CONKLIN, FRANCIS	1820	SUFF	HUNT	276
CONKLIN, FRANCIS	1830	QUEN	NEWT	9
CONKLIN, FRANK	1810	SUFF	HUNT	509
CONKLIN, HECTOR	1820	SUFF	ISLP	308
CONKLIN, JAMES	1830	QUEN	OYST	47
CONKLIN, JOSIAH	1810	SUFF	HUNT	507
CONKLIN, JOSIAH	1820	QUEN	----	55
CONKLIN, JOSIAH	1830	QUEN	FLUS	146
CONKLIN, ZEBULOU	1820	QUEN	----	29
CONKLING, JACK	1810	ORNG	GOSH	1067
CONNER, AARON	1810	NYCO	WD04	159
CONNER, JOHN	1830	NYCO	WD08	201
CONNER, THOMAS	1820	ABNY	ABNY	157
CONNHOVEN, ABRAHAM	1830	QUEN	NHEM	117
CONNOR, AURON	1800	NYCO	WD03	694
CONNOR, BETSY	1810	NYCO	WD01	27
CONNOR, PETER	1810	NYCO	WD02	127

NAME	YR	CO	TWP	PG
CONOR, AARON	1830	NYCO	WD06	385
CONOVER, ISAAC	1830	NYCO	WD10	78
CONOVER, ISAAC C.	1830	NYCO	WD09	328
CONOVER, SAMUEL	1830	NYCO	WD12	278
CONQUE, JOHN BABTISTE	1810	NYCO	WD05	353
CONSIR, WILLIAM	1830	SUFF	SHAM	215
CONSOR, JOHN	1830	SUFF	SHAM	232
CONSTANDT, ROBERT	1830	ORNG	GOSH	287
CONUN, HARMAN	1830	NYCO	WD12	251
CONWAY, J.	1810	ONID	----	446
CONWAY, JOHN	1810	SCHO	MIDD	29
CONWELL, MOSES	1830	PUTM	PATE	26
CONYEA, JOHN	1830	NYCO	WD06	398
COOK, DICK	1800	ROCK	CLAR	1015
COOK, ELLINA	1810	NYCO	WD06	422
COOK, ELSEA	1820	NYCO	WD10	969
COOK, ENOCH	1800	QUEN	JAMA	547
COOK, FRANCIS	1830	NYCO	WD10	125
COOK, GEORGE	1830	MADI	----	418
COOK, HENRY	1830	ONID	MARS	133
COOK, ISSAC	1820	KING	BRYN	123
COOK, JACOB	1830	KING	WD03	291
COOK, JAMES	1830	NYCO	WD14	522
COOK, JOHN	1820	NYCO	WD10	1055
COOK, JOHN	1830	ONON	CAMI	202
COOK, MRS.	1820	NYCO	WD07	659
COOK, PEGGY	1800	ABNY	WATV	91
COOK, PEGGY	1820	SCNE	SCNE	125
COOK, ROBERT	1830	SCHR	SHAR	108
COOK, SYLVIA	1820	DUTC	PGKP	101
COOK, THOMAS	1800	NYCO	WD05	752
COOK, WILL	1820	SUFF	SHAM	315
COOKE, THOMAS	1800	NYCO	WD06	825
COOLEY, CHARLES	1830	DUTC	CLNT	203
COOLEY, DIANA	1830	DUTC	REDH	375
COOLEY, DIANA	1830	NYCO	WD06	435
COOLIDGE, CHARLY	1820	DUTC	MILN	79
COOLY, HERMAN	1810	COLU	GRAN	200
COOLY, TOM	1810	COLU	GRAN	201
COON, JACK	1820	DUTC	REDH	114
COON, JOHN	1790	DUTC	RHIN	92
COON, JOHN	1830	ULST	ROCH	174
COONS, JOHN	1830	ULST	HURL	147
COOPER	1810	NYCO	WD06	461
COOPER, ADAM	1810	DUTC	WASH	159
COOPER, BENJAMIN	1800	NYCO	WD05	760
COOPER, BENJAMIN	1810	NYCO	WD04	213
COOPER, CUNUL	1820	STEU	BATH	227
COOPER, DANIEL	1830	STEU	BATH	273

Cooper

NAME	YR	CO	TWP	PG
COOPER, DAVID	1820	ONTA	LODU	121
COOPER, DAVID	1830	WANE	SODU	130
COOPER, DINA	1820	NYCO	WD10	969
COOPER, ELIZA	1830	NYCO	WD07	67
COOPER, FANNY	1820	NYCO	WD06	482
COOPER, GAD	1830	SUFF	SHAM	224
COOPER, GADD	1820	SUFF	SHAM	313
COOPER, JAMES	1830	STEU	BATH	270
COOPER, JOHN	1810	NYCO	WD04	159
COOPER, JOSHUA	1830	NYCO	WD08	148
COOPER, MRS.	1820	NYCO	WD05	336
COOPER, REBECCA	1810	NYCO	WD05	313
COOPER, REBECCA	1830	NYCO	WD05	268
COOPER, SOLOMAN	1830	NYCO	WD14	522
COOPER, WILLIAM	1830	NYCO	WD14	428
COP, JOSEPH	1820	QUEN	----	30
COPELAND, MRS.	1820	KING	BRYN	118
COPELAND, THOMAS	1810	NYCO	WD05	262
COPENEN, WILLIS	1810	WEST	WEST	1148
COPPAW, WILLIAM	1830	KING	WD03	286
COPSIE, CATHARINE	1790	ULST	MARB	175
COPSIE, CATHERINE	1800	ULST	MARB	201
COREK, JOHN	1820	NYCO	WD10	981
COREY, ELVIA	1820	NYCO	WD03	189
CORLE, JOHN	1810	NYCO	WD06	442
CORNELL, CHARLES	1820	NYCO	WD08	789
CORNALL, LETTY	1830	QUEN	NHEM	112
CORNALL, MORRIS	1830	QUEN	NHEM	104
CORNALL, RICHARD	1830	QUEN	NHEM	111
CORNEALISAN, CEZER	1820	KING	BRYN	141
CORNEALISON, COZER	1830	KING	BRYN	370
CORNELISEN, HENRY	1830	NYCO	WD14	458
CORNELIUS	1790	NYCO	MONT	121
CORNELIUS	1790	NYCO	WEST	136
CORNELIUS	1790	QUEN	OYST	155
CORNELIUS	1790	QUEN	SHEM	155
CORNELIUS	1800	QUEN	OYST	568
CORNELIUS, CORNELIUS	1790	ABNY	SCHR	45
CORNELIUS, JOHN	1830	NYCO	WD10	27
CORNELIUS, MARY	1830	NYCO	WD14	428
CORNELIUS, ROSANNA	1830	NYCO	WD08	215
CORNELL, ABRAHAM	1820	WEST	NEWR	217
CORNELL, CANDIS	1830	NYCO	WD06	371
CORNELL, CEASER	1800	NYCO	WD03	702
CORNELL, CHARLES	1810	NYCO	WD03	83
CORNELL, ELIZA	1820	NYCO	WD02	129
CORNELL, ISAAC	1820	WEST	WTPL	459
CORNELL, JACK	1810	QUEN	NHEM	214
CORNELL, JAMES	1820	QUEN	----	77

NAME	YR	CO	TWP	PG
CORNELL, JANE	1830	NYCO	WD08	213
CORNELL, JUDE	1820	WEST	NEWR	212
CORNELL, JUPITER	1800	NYCO	WD04	735
CORNELL, LAVINIA	1800	NYCO	WD05	778
CORNELL, LOT	1810	DUTC	PHIL	99
CORNELL, MOSES	1820	WEST	MAMA	360
CORNELL, NANCY	1810	NYCO	WD02	116
CORNELL, POMPEY	1810	QUEN	NHEM	216
CORNELL, PRIMUS	1820	WEST	NORC	429
CORNELL, RICHARD	1820	WEST	NORC	429
CORNELL, RICHARD	1830	KING	WD02	269
CORNELL, SAUL	1810	QUEN	NEWT	176
CORNELL, SOLOMON	1820	QUEN	----	60
CORNELL, STEPHEN	1810	WEST	NEWR	1091
CORNER, FRANCIS	1820	ABNY	ABNY	157
CORNIL, MOSES	1810	WEST	PELH	1159
CORNISH, CHARLES	1820	NYCO	WD10	1028
CORNISH, JAMES	1830	NYCO	WD13	406
CORNISH, JOSEPH	1820	NYCO	WD09	874
CORNWELL	1820	PUTM	PATE	101
CORNWELL, ELISHA	1830	WEST	NORC	199
CORNWELL, HARRY S.	1830	WEST	RYE	101
CORNWELL, ISAAC	1830	WEST	WTPL	222
CORNWELL, JONATHAN	1810	WEST	NEWR	1089
CORNWELL, LOT	1820	PUTM	PHIL	101
CORNWELL, MOSES	1830	PUTM	SOUT	49
CORNWELL, P.	1830	NYCO	WD10	87
CORNWELL, PRINCE	1820	PUTM	SOUT	100
CORNWELL, PRINCE	1830	WEST	NORS	79
CORNWELL, PRINCE	1830	WEST	NORC	203
CORNWELL, WILLIAM	1830	ORNG	WARW	89
COROLING, JOHN	1830	NYCO	WD06	427
CORRE, ABRAHAM	1830	KING	BUSH	378
CORREL, JAMES	1820	NYCO	WD05	392
CORSAN, JOHN	1820	NYCO	WD07	621
CORSEY, WILLIAM	1830	NYCO	WD08	173
CORSON, CUFF	1820	NYCO	WD06	572
CORSON, CUFFE	1830	NYCO	WD08	217
CORSON, CUFFEE	1830	NYCO	WD08	237
CORSSICAN, JOHN	1830	NYCO	WD06	404
CORT, STEPHEN	1820	SUFF	ISLP	309
CORTELYOU, BETSEY	1830	NYCO	WD06	448
CORTER, ANTHONY	1830	KING	WD04	297
CORTLAUDT, HESTER	1810	NYCO	WD06	424
CORTLAUDT, SAMUEL	1810	QUEN	FLUS	202
CORTWRIGHT, HENRY	1810	ULST	MARB	802
CORTWRIGHT, JACOB	1820	NYCO	WD06	472
CORVAN, THOMAS	1810	NYCO	WD06	397
CORVIN, JENNING	1790	SUFF	SOUT	168

NAME	YR	CO	TWP	PG
COSENTON, IZABEL	1820	DUTC	FISH	62
COSNON, JOSEPH	1830	WEST	BEDF	139
COSS, DAVID	1830	QUEN	SHEM	94
COSS, ISAAC	1830	QUEN	SHEM	84
COSS, JAMES	1830	NYCO	WD07	89
COSTAIN, JOHN	1830	KING	WD02	270
COSTER, FLORA D.	1800	NYCO	WD03	705
COSTER, MICHAEL	1830	KING	GRAV	405
COSWELL, JONATHAN	1800	CAYU	MILT	600
COTER, JONATHAN	1830	SCNE	WD01	206
COTHOUD, RACHEL	1800	RENS	TROY	896
COTTENS, MARY	1810	NYCO	WD06	420
COTTON, PRINCE	1820	NYCO	WD04	236
COTTON, SAMUEL	1830	ORNG	NEWW	100
COTTRELL, PRINCE	1830	NYCO	WD13	345
COUGNACY, CHARLES	1830	NYCO	WD04	157
COUN, HENRY	1830	ORNG	NEWB	50
COUN, LEONARD	1830	ORNG	NEWB	55
COUNER, RICHARD	1800	NYCO	WD06	791
COUNTER, MARY ANN	1830	CAYU	AUBN	165
COURSEN, JAMES	1830	NYCO	WD05	288
COURT, JOHN	1800	DUTC	CLNT	107
COURTLAND, ROBERT	1820	ORNG	GOSH	748
COVEL	1820	PUTM	PATE	101
COVEY, JOHN	1810	NYCO	WD04	238
COW	1820	PUTM	PATE	101
COWANS, NABBY	1830	CAYU	AURE	180
COWDRY, JOHN	1830	LIVI	GENC	5
COWES, PHILLIS	1830	NYCO	WD05	310
COWES, SOLOMON	1810	NYCO	WD05	318
COX, ABRAHAM	1820	NYCO	WD01	19
COX, CHARLES	1830	NYCO	WD08	257
COX, DAVIA	1820	QUEN	----	29
COX, ELIJAH	1830	SUFF	SHAM	215
COX, FANNY	1800	NYCO	WD07	889
COX, JAMES	1830	NYCO	WD09	355
COX, JOHN	1810	NYCO	WD02	100
COX, JOHN	1810	NYCO	WD06	450
COX, JOHN	1810	NYCO	WD06	415
COX, JOHNATHAN	1830	NYCO	WD14	455
COX, JOSHUA	1830	NYCO	WD13	378
COX, MOSES	1800	NYCO	WD07	891
COX, MRS.	1820	NYCO	WD05	398
COX, R.	1830	NYCO	WD02	80
COXEN, SAMUEL	1810	NYCO	WD06	410
COXEN, WIDOW	1810	NYCO	WD07	536
COXEN, FLORA	1830	ONID	UTIC	45
COXSURE, JONAS	1810	DUTC	BEEK	304
COY, JOHN	1790	NYCO	MONT	120

NAME	YR	CO	TWP	PG
COZEN	1830	KING	NEUT	392
CRACHOW, SILAS A.	1830	RICH	SOUT	16
CRAFT, JACK	1790	QUEN	OYST	154
CRAIG, ERWIN	1810	NYCO	WD05	334
CRAIGER, SARY	1810	SUFF	SHAM	445
CRAMER, ANTHONY	1830	COLU	GALA	263
CRANE, JOHN	1820	PUTM	CARM	101
CRANE, JOSEPH	1820	PUTM	SOUT	100
CRANE, NIMROD	1830	PUTM	SOUT	51
CRANFORDM JOHN	1830	ORNG	WALL	136
CRANK	1790	SUFF	SHEL	165
CRANK	1800	SUFF	SHEL	85
CRAW, BETSEY	1830	DUTC	PLEA	307
CRAW, C.	1830	NYCO	WD13	327
CRAW, FEDERAL	1830	DUTC	WASH	437
CRAW, TOPHER·	1820	SUFF	SMIT	318
CRAWFORD, DONIS	1800	NYCO	WD06	803
CRAWFORD, GLASSGOW	1830	FRAN	FORC	42
CRAWFORD, JOHN	1830	ALLE	RUSH	172
CRAWFORD, JOHN	1830	ORNG	NEWW	105
CRAWFORD, MARGARET	1820	NYCO	WD05	341
CRAWFORD, WILLIAM	1830	ORNG	CRAW	194
CRAWYER, NANNY	1800	QUEN	NHEM	553
CRAYSON, CONGO	1820	ONTA	PHEL	303
CREADY, JAMES	1830	NYCO	WD14	435
CREED, YAPT	1830	QUEN	JAMA	133
CREEF, JOHN	1830	QUEN	OYST	22
CREEO, GARRETT	1830	NYCO	WD08	217
CREGE, BRISTEL	1820	COLU	CHAT	5
CREIGHTON, GEORGE	1830	NYCO	WD06	437
CREIGHTON, JANE	1830	NYCO	WD08	172
CRIMP, ABOM	1820	NYCO	WD06	485
CRIO, ANTHONY	1830	ULST	MARB	157
CRISPELL, JACK	1830	ULST	OLIV	136
CRISPELL, SAMUEL	1830	ULST	OLIV	134
CRIST, NICHOLAS	1830	ULST	NPAL	224
CRISTO, WILLIAM	1820	NYCO	WD06	445
CRITIS, CHRISTOPHER	1810	NYCO	WD03	50
CROESBECK, DEBORAH	1830	NYCO	WD06	435
CROFTS, DINA	1830	COLU	HUDS	120
CROGER, BENJAMIN	1820	KING	BRYN	139
CROM, JOHN	1790	ABNY	WD02	13
CROMEL, OLIVER	1820	SUFF	SHAM	319
CROMEL, PETER	1820	SUFF	HUNT	284
CROMWELD, BOSTON	1810	NYCO	WD04	161
CROMWELL, BOSTON	1820	NYCO	WD06	495
CROMWELL, BOSTON	1830	NYCO	WD06	385
CROMWELL, ISAAC	1830	CAYU	LEDY	281

NAME	YR	CO	TWP	PG
CROMWELL, JACOB	1800	NYCO	WD05	785
CROMWELL, JAMES	1800	NYCO	WD05	865
CROMWELL, JOHNATHAN	1830	NYCO	WD09	353
CROMWELL, NANCY	1830	SUFF	SMIT	273
CROMWELL, WILLIAM	1830	ONON	SKAN	155
CRONK, BRIDGET	1820	ORNG	WARW	615
CROOK, AARON	1830	SUFF	SHAM	227
CROOK, CATO	1810	SUFF	SHAM	462
CROOK, CATO	1820	SUFF	SHAM	309
CROOK, CATO	1830	SUFF	SHAM	221
CROOK, ENOS	1830	SUFF	ISLP	287
CROOK, JOHN	1810	NYCO	WD06	420
CROOK, JOSEPH	1810	ULST	KING	751
CROOK, LUCY	1830	SUFF	EAST	253
CROOK, PHILLIS	1820	NYCO	WD06	460
CROOK, REUBEN	1820	SUFF	ISLP	309
CROOK, REUBEN	1830	SUFF	ISLP	284
CROOK, RUFUS	1810	SUFF	ISLP	498
CROOK, RUFUS	1830	SUFF	BROK	178
CROOK, RULIN	1810	SUFF	ISLP	498
CROOK, SILAS	1830	QUEN	FLUS	
CROOKE, FELICITY	1830	NYCO	WD06	427
CROSBY, AGUSTUS	1820	PUTM	PATE	101
CROSBY, ENOCH	1820	PUTM	SOUT	100
CROSBY, ISAAC	1820	PUTM	SOUT	100
CROSBY, JAMES	1820	HERK	FRAN	61
CROSBY, JOSEPH	1800	NYCO	WD07	885
CROSIER, CUFF	1800	ABNY	WD01	266
CROSS, DAVID	1820	DUTC	REDH	117
CROSS, MARTIN	1830	GREN	CATS	237
CROSS, MATHEW	1810	DUTC	RHIN	376
CROSS, MATHIAS	1820	DUTC	REDH	117
CROSS, OLIVER	1810	NYCO	WD06	408
CROSS, OLIVER	1820	NYCO	WD03	192
CROSS, PHOEBE	1830	NYCO	WD07	115
CROSS, TITUS	1820	OTSG	CHRV	19
CROSSLEY, EDWARD	1830	NYCO	WD14	518
CROST, BASTIAN	1800	DUTC	RHIN	153
CROWKER, PETER	1810	KING	BRYN	640
CROWN	1810	RENS	PITT	403
CRUGAR, JOHN	1820	NYCO	WD04	314
CRUGER, B.	1830	KING	WD04	319
CRUGER, P.	1830	NYCO	WD11	163
CRUGER, PETER	1820	KING	BRYN	139
CRUGER, PETER	1830	KING	WD04	319
CRUM, HARRY	1810	NYCO	WD05	249
CRUM, RICHARD	1830	COLU	CLAV	90
CRUMO, ABRAHAM	1830	SARA	MILT	30
CRUMWELL, BAZEL	1810	NYCO	WD06	434
CRUSER, SAMUEL	1830	BROM	VEST	74

NAME	YR	CO	TWP	PG
CUDINGTON, POMP	1820	ORNG	MONT	837
CUDJO, CHARLES	1790	ABNY	CATS	22
CUDJO, JOSEPH	1830	DUTC	FISH	455
CUDJOE, CHARLES	1820	SCHR	BROM	159
CUDJOE, CHARLES	1820	SCHR	BROM	158
CUDJOY, FRANCIS	1820	NYCO	WD09	909
CUFF	1790	NYCO	MONT	122
CUFF	1790	NYCO	HARL	137
CUFF	1790	QUEN	NHEM	152
CUFF	1790	WEST	NORC	203
CUFF	1800	QUEN	OYST	579
CUFF	1810	RENS	TROY	441
CUFF	1810	SCHR	SCHR	6
CUFF, AARON	1810	SUFF	SHAM	440
CUFF, ABRAHAM	1810	SUFF	EHAM	433
CUFF, ABRAHAM	1810	SUFF	RIVH	548
CUFF, AMOS	1810	SUFF	SHAM	445
CUFF, AMOS	1810	SUFF	EHAM	437
CUFF, CALEB	1810	SUFF	SHAM	433
CUFF, CEASUR	1810	SUFF	HUNT	503
CUFF, CUFFE	1810	SUFF	EHAM	430
CUFF, EMUEL	1810	COLU	HUDS	141
CUFF, FREEMAN	1810	MONT	JOHN	32
CUFF, IRA	1810	SUFF	SHAM	439
CUFF, JARRET	1810	SUFF	RIVH	542
CUFF, JOHN	1810	QUEN	NHEM	214
CUFF, JOHN	1810	SUFF	SHAM	460
CUFF, MISHEEH	1810	SUFF	SHAM	440
CUFF, NOAH	1810	SUFF	SHAM	439
CUFF, OBADIAH	1810	SUFF	BROK	469
CUFF, SILAS	1810	SUFF	EHAM	431
CUFF, STEPHEN	1810	NYCO	WD07	543
CUFF, STEPHEN	1810	SUFF	SHAM	460
CUFF, WRIGHT	1830	QUEN	OYST	32
CUFFE	1820	RICH	SOUT	106
CUFFE, ABRAHAM	1820	SUFF	SMIT	321
CUFFE, ABRAM	1820	SUFF	RIVH	356
CUFFE, ABSOLAM	1800	SUFF	SMIT	57
CUFFE, ABSOLUM	1800	SUFF	SHAM	67
CUFFE, AMON	1820	SUFF	SHAM	318
CUFFE, AMOS	1820	SUFF	SHAM	314
CUFFE, CUFFE	1820	SUFF	EAST	288
CUFFE, IRA	1820	SUFF	SHAM	318
CUFFE, ISAAC	1820	SUFF	HUNT	290
CUFFE, JAMES	1820	SUFF	RIVH	353
CUFFE, JEREMIAH	1820	SUFF	SHAM	321
CUFFE, MACKE	1820	SUFF	SHAM	318
CUFFE, NOAH	1820	SUFF	SHAM	318
CUFFE, OBEDIAH	1830	SUFF	BROK	161

NAME	YR	CO	TWP	PG
CUFFE, OBY	1820	SUFF	BROK	330
CUFFE, PAUL	1790	SUFF	BROK	160
CUFFE, SALLY	1820	SUFF	EAST	295
CUFFE, STEPHEN	1820	SUFF	RIVH	354
CUFFE, TEMP	1820	SUFF	SHAM	309
CUFFE, VINCENT	1820	SUFF	SHAM	318
CUFFEE	1820	SARA	MILT	232
CUFFEE	1830	KING	GRAV	407
CUFFEE, AARON	1800	SUFF	SHAM	67
CUFFEE, ABRAHAM	1800	SUFF	EHAM	92
CUFFEE, ABRAHAM	1830	SUFF	SHAM	215
CUFFEE, AMOS	1800	SUFF	EHAM	95
CUFFEE, AMOS	1800	SUFF	SHAM	67
CUFFEE, AMOS	1830	SUFF	SHAM	215
CUFFEE, ANANIAS	1830	SUFF	SHAM	228
CUFFEE, ANAZIAH	1830	SUFF	SHAM	221
CUFFEE, CALEB	1800	SUFF	EHAM	92
CUFFEE, CUFFEE	1800	SUFF	EHAM	90
CUFFEE, ELISHA	1830	SUFF	HUNT	332
CUFFEE, JASON	1800	SUFF	SHAM	67
CUFFEE, JOHN	1830	SUFF	SHAM	220
CUFFEE, LEWIS	1830	SUFF	EAST	254
CUFFEE, MARGARET	1830	SUFF	RIVH	244
CUFFEE, MESHAC	1830	SUFF	SHAM	228
CUFFEE, NOAH	1830	SUFF	SHAM	228
CUFFEE, OLIVER	1830	SUFF	SHAM	221
CUFFEE, PAUL	1800	SUFF	SHAM	67
CUFFEE, REBECCA	1830	SUFF	BROK	185
CUFFEE, SALLY	1830	SUFF	SHAM	228
CUFFEE, SAMPSON	1800	SUFF	EHAM	95
CUFFEE, STEPHEN	1800	SUFF	SHAM	74
CUFFEE, STEPHEN	1830	SUFF	RIVH	235
CUFFEE, VINCENT	1830	SUFF	SHAM	215
CUFFEE, WICKS	1830	SUFF	SHAM	216
CUFFS, AMOS	1820	SUFF	EAST	289
CUFFY	1790	QUEN	FLUS	149
CUFS, MOSES	1820	QUEN	----	59
CUGOR, WILLIAM	1820	DUTC	CLNT	40
CUGOW, TEAT	1810	NYCO	WD05	308
CUL	1790	WEST	HARR	199
CULBART, JONATHAN	1820	ONTA	CANA	211
CULLIVER, MARY	1830	TOMP	ITCA	332
CULL	1790	QUEN	NEWT	152
CULY, PHILIP	1830	RICH	WEST	5
CUMBER, TINNANT D.	1800	NYCO	WD05	779
CUMING, ALEXANDER	1830	TOMP	ITCA	349
CUMMING, ABRAHAM	1810	NYCO	WD06	422
CUMMINGS, ABRAHAM	1820	NYCO	WD05	424
CUMMINGS, AMY	1810	NYCO	WD06	482

NAME	YR	CO	TWP	PG
CUMMINGS, GEORGE	1810	NYCO	WD07	535
CUMMINGS, HANNAH	1830	NYCO	WD07	46
CUMMINGS, PRINCE	1820	DUTC	WASH	147
CUMMINGS, SALLY	1820	COLU	HUDS	7
CUMMINGS, WILLIAM	1820	COLU	HUDS	7
CUMMINGS, WILLIAM	1830	COLU	HUDS	111
CUMMINGS, WILLIAM	1820	NYCO	WD06	496
CUMMINGS, WILLIAM	1830	NYCO	WD10	110
CUMMINS, CORNELIUS	1800	SARA	CHAR	1075
CUMPER, FRANCES	1800	NYCO	WD07	862
CURDY, HENRY	1830	NYCO	WD09	324
CURENTINE, POMPEY	1830	ORNG	CRAW	186
CURFUR, STARLING	1820	ROCK	CLAK	98
CURL, CECILLA	1830	NYCO	WD05	335
CURRIAN, ENUS	1820	SUFF	SHAM	317
CURRINGTON, DICK	1810	ORNG	NEWB	930
CURRY, AFTER	1830	QUEN	NEWT	17
CURSEN, CUFF	1810	NYCO	WD06	494
CURSY, JAMES	1820	NYCO	WD10	988
CURTIS, G.	1830	ERIE	BUFF	28
CURTIS, JAMES	1830	QUEN	JAMA	132
CURTIS, SAMUEL	1830	NYCO	WD05	337
CURTISS, JOHN	1830	NYCO	WD07	31
CURTISS, NELSON	1830	NYCO	WD07	38
CUSAR, MUNRO	1830	QUEN	JAMA	127
CUSS, HENRY	1810	NYCO	WD06	425
CUTLER, SAMUEL	1790	ABNY	HOOS	30
CUTLER, SHARICK P.	1830	ABNY	WD01	201
CUVE	1810	RENS	LANS	424
CUYGESS, HARRY	1830	GREN	CATS	237
CYPHER, MANASSA	1800	NYCO	WD03	706
CYRUS	1810	SUFF	SMIT	540
CYRUS	1820	QUEN	----	79
CYRUS	1820	SUFF	HUNT	294
DAAPHILLIPS, ASAS	1810	NYCO	WD07	515
DAEE, CHARLES	1830	TOMP	ITCA	332
DAILEY, JOHN	1820	WASH	SALM	186
DAILY, JOHN	1830	WASH	SALM	211
DAKEN, HARRY	1830	NYCO	WD01	16
DAL, DICK	1810	SCNE	WD01	933
DALBE, WILLIAM	1830	NYCO	WD06	434
DALE, LYDIA	1800	NYCO	WD03	701
DALLY, JAMES	1830	NYCO	WD14	522
DALTON, HIRAM	1830	NYCO	WD05	332
DALY, ISAAC	1830	QUEN	NEWT	15
DAMIYE, GEORGE	1830	NYCO	WD04	215
DAN	1790	QUEN	NHEM	152

NAME	YR	CO	TWP	PG
DANA, ABRAHAM	1820	MADI	LENX	13
DAN, JOHN	1820	MADI	LENX	12
DANDO, HETTY	1810	SCHR	SCHR	49
DANFORD, JACOB	1830	CLNT	PERU	350
DANFORD, JAMES	1820	SCNE	GLEN	148
DANFORD, PRINCE	1810	ORNG	NEWW	907
DANFORD, PRINCE	1820	ORNG	NEWW	490
DANFORTH, PRINCE	1790	ULST	NWIN	180
DANFORTH, PRINCE	1800	ORNG	NEWW	289
DANFORTH, PRINCE	1830	ORNG	NEWW	96
DANGORDUS	1800	SARA	BALL	1055
DANIEL	1790	NYCO	MONT	122
DANIEL	1790	QUEN	NEWT	151
DANIEL	1790	QUEN	FLUS	149
DANIEL	1800	QUEN	NEWT	659
DANIEL	1800	QUEN	OYST	571
DANIEL	1800	SUFF	SMIT	54
DANIEL	1810	NYCO	WD05	327
DANN, MAHILABLE	1810	SUFF	SHAM	458
DANNALS, WILLIAM	1830	MONR	BRIG	6
DANNY, JOHN	1800	CHEN	CARN	944
DANSEY, JOHN	1830	TOMP	ITCA	332
DANY, A.	1810	MADI	SULL	797
DARBY, ABEL	1830	ORNG	WALL	151
DARBY, ANNE	1810	NYCO	WD03	83
DARBY, EDWARD	1830	ORNG	MINI	252
DARBY, JAMES	1800	TIOG	LISL	246
DARIS, WILLIAM	1830	KING	BUSH	382
DARLING, CHARLES	1810	SUFF	HUNT	505
DARLING, CHARLES	1810	SUFF	HUNT	507
DARLING, JOHN	1830	ABNY	WD02	257
DARLING, SAMUEL	1820	DUTC	BEEK	18
DARROW, JACOB	1830	NYCO	WD06	389
DASSETT, GAMBO	1830	OTSG	UNAD	206
DAUGHTY, BENJAMIN W.	1820	QUEN	----	39
DAVENISH, JOHN	1800	NYCO	WD06	820
DAVENPORT, ABIDIAH	1820	WEST	RYE	370
DAVENPORT, OBEDIA	1830	WEST	HARR	216
DAVENPORT, OBID	1820	WEST	HARR	463
DAVERLY, CHARLES	1820	NYCO	WD08	780
DAVID	1790	NYCO	NORT	125
DAVID	1790	QUEN	JAMA	150
DAVID	1790	SUFF	BROK	161
DAVID	1800	QUEN	NHEM	558
DAVID	1800	SUFF	BROK	11
DAVID	1810	NYCO	WD07	602
DAVID	1820	QUEN	----	57
DAVID	1820	QUEN	----	79
DAVID, JOHN M.	1830	NYCO	WD08	219

NAME	YR	CO	TWP	PG
DAVIS, AMOS	1830	MONR	PENF	332
DAVIS, B.	1830	ERIE	BUFF	5
DAVIS, BENJAMIN	1810	NYCO	WD10	658
DAVIS, BENJAMIN	1820	SUFF	BROK	363
DAVIS, BENJAMIN	1830	SUFF	BROK	177
DAVIS, CATO	1820	NYCO	WD09	918
DAVIS, CHARLES	1820	NYCO	WD02	122
DAVIS, CHARLES	1820	SUFF	SHAM	313
DAVIS, CHARLOTTE	1830	NYCO	WD06	435
DAVIS, DAN	1820	NYCO	WD10	1072
DAVIS, EPIPNEY	1830	NYCO	WD10	26
DAVIS, F.	1830	NYCO	WD13	375
DAVIS, GEORGE	1800	NYCO	WD01	665
DAVIS, GEORGE	1810	NYCO	WD06	401
DAVIS, GEORGE	1830	NYCO	WD14	435
DAVIS, HENRY	1810	QUEN	JAMA	188
DAVIS, HENRY	1820	QUEN	----	55
DAVIS, HENRY	1830	NYCO	WD12	280
DAVIS, ISAAC	1830	ULST	MARB	164
DAVIS, ISHMAEL	1790	DUTC	PGKP	91
DAVIS, ISHMAEL	1800	DUTC	PGKP	62
DAVIS, ISRAEL	1830	ERIE	BUFF	12
DAVIS, J.	1830	ERIE	BUFF	33
DAVIS, J.	1830	NYCO	WD02	91
DAVIS, J.	1830	NYCO	WD11	158
DAVIS, J.	1830	NYCO	WD13	356
DAVIS, JACK	1830	KING	WD05	335
DAVIS, JACOB	1800	NYCO	WD03	708
DAVIS, JACOB	1820	NYCO	WD10	988
DAVIS, JACOB	1830	NIAG	LOCK	403
DAVIS, JAMES	1820	NYCO	WD08	780
DAVIS, JEREMIAH	1830	NYCO	WD09	362
DAVIS, JESSE	1810	NYCO	WD03	93
DAVIS, JESSE	1820	NYCO	WD01	18
DAVIS, JESSE	1830	NYCO	WD01	32
DAVIS, JESSE	1830	WEST	CORT	54
DAVIS, JOEL	1830	SUFF	ISLP	280
DAVIS, JOHN	1830	NYCO	WD06	409
DAVIS, JOHN	1830	ORLE	MURA	43
DAVIS, JOHN	1830	ORNG	MINI	246
DAVIS, JOHNATHAN	1830	NYCO	WD10	19
DAVIS, JOSEPHINE	1830	NYCO	WD05	331
DAVIS, JUDY	1830	NYCO	WD10	46
DAVIS, JULIA	1830	NYCO	WD10	78
DAVIS, LEWIS	1820	ABNY	ABNY	162
DAVIS, LEWIS	1830	ABNY	WD02	237
DAVIS, MISS	1820	NYCO	WD07	721
DAVIS, NATHANIEL	1800	ABNY	WD01	263
DAVIS, PEGGY	1800	NYCO	WD01	667

Davis

NAME	YR	CO	TWP	PG
DAVIS, PEPHERY	1820	NYCO	WD07	686
DAVIS, RACHEL	1830	OSWE	GRAN	173
DAVIS, ROBERT	1820	ABNY	ABNY	163
DAVIS, ROSANNA	1800	NYCO	WD03	694
DAVIS, SAMUEL C.	1830	NYCO	WD05	303
DAVIS, SOUTHEY	1830	NYCO	WD05	337
DAVIS, THOMAS	1820	SUFF	BROK	359
DAVIS, THOMAS	1830	QUEN	JAMA	128
DAVIS, THOMAS	1830	SUFF	BROK	173
DAVIS, THOMAS	1830	SUFF	SMIT	276
DAVIS, TIMOTHY	1830	QUEN	OYST	41
DAVIS, WILLIAM	1820	KING	WILL	181
DAVIS, WILLIAM	1830	KING	BUSH	378
DAVIS, WILLIAM	1830	NYCO	WD05	274
DAVIS, WILLIAM	1830	NYCO	WD07	51
DAVIS, WILLIAM	1830	NYCO	WD10	124
DAVIS, WILLIAM	1830	NYCO	WD11	221
DAVIS, ZACHARIAH	1820	ONTA	PENF	149
DAVIS, ZACHARIAH JR.	1820	ONTA	PENF	149
DAVIS, ZACHERIAH	1830	MONR	PENF	326
DAVIS, ZACHERIAH	1830	MONR	PENF	329
DAWLES, JOHN	1830	NYCO	WD14	433
DAWSON, SAMUEL	1820	NYCO	WD04	233
DAY, AARON	1830	NYCO	WD08	148
DAY, ABAM	1830	OSWE	VOLN	191
DAY, ABRAHAM	1820	ONON	ONON	206
DAY, DINAH	1830	GREN	CATS	240
DAY, ISAAC	1820	NYCO	WD09	921
DAY, ISAAC	1820	ONON	ONON	208
DAY, ISAAC	1830	NYCO	WD12	278
DAY, JACOB	1820	COLU	CHAT	7
DAY, JACOB	1820	ONON	ONON	206
DAY, JACOB	1830	COLU	CHAT	38
DAY, JACOB	1830	OSWE	VOLN	191
DAY, JAMES J.	1820	ONON	ONON	206
DAY, JOHN	1820	OSWE	VOLN	62
DAY, P.	1830	NYCO	WD12	283
DAY, PETER	1820	NYCO	WD09	921
DAY, SAMUEL	1800	NYCO	WD06	820
DAY, SANDERS	1820	ONTA	BRIS	53
DAY, SANDERS	1830	WANE	GALE	152
DAY, SOLOMON	1810	ONON	ONON	495
DAY, SOLOMON	1820	ONON	ONON	206
DAY, SOLOMON	1830	ONON	ONON	188
DAY, WILLIAM	1810	ONON	ONON	495
DAY, WILLIAM	1820	NYCO	WD09	924
DAY, WILLIAM	1820	ONON	ONON	206
DAY, WILLIAM	1830	MONT	ROOT	58
DAY, WILLIAM	1830	ONON	ONON	188

NAME	YR	CO	TWP	PG
DAY, WILLIAM	1830	ONON	ONON	189
DEACON, JEREMIAH	1810	NYCO	WD05	275
DEAL, JOSEPH	1820	NYCO	WD07	627
DEALY, WILLIAM	1820	NYCO	WD09	934
DEAMOND, THOMAS	1830	SARA	WATE	43
DEAN	1800	ABNY	WD01	263
DEAN	1800	ABNY	SCNE	13
DEAN, CATHERINE	1810	ORNG	NEWW	912
DEAN, CHARLES	1830	NYCO	WD10	110
DEAN, DAVID	1820	ORNG	GOSH	750
DEAN, DAVID	1830	ORNG	GOSH	289
DEAN, EDWARD	1830	NYCO	WD07	90
DEAN, FREDERICK	1820	NYCO	WD06	495
DEAN, RICHARD	1810	NYCO	WD03	88
DEAN, RICHARD	1820	NYCO	WD02	114
DEAN, SAUN	1800	NYCO	WD03	706
DEANE, CATO	1800	ORNG	NEWC	394
DEANE, PRINCE	1810	NYCO	WD10	696
DEARBORN, WILLIAM	1820	ORNG	NEWB	514
DEARIN, PRINCE	1820	DUTC	FISH	77
DEAS, JOSEPH	1810	NYCO	WD05	289
DEBBLE, DINAH	1830	GREN	CATS	229
DEBBY	1830	ALLE	ANGE	6
DE BEVOISE, ALFRED	1830	NYCO	WD09	390
DEBOIS, JOHN	1830	ONID	TREN	288
DEBROAT, JOHN	1830	ONON	ONON	192
DECKER	1830	NYCO	WD05	299
DECKER, BETSEY	1830	NYCO	WD01	35
DECKER, JACOB	1830	NYCO	WD09	347
DECKER, JOHN	1820	ORNG	GOSH	742
DECKER, JOHN	1830	CAYU	LEDY	281
DECKER, SAMUEL	1820	GREN	DURH	130
DECKER, SUSAN	1830	ORNG	CALH	18
DECKER, WILLIAM	1830	WEST	YONK	8
DE DAY, ANNE	1820	ONON	MANL	168
DEDRECH, WILLIAM	1830	GREN	CATS	222
DEDRECTO, THOMAS	1820	ULST	SAUG	81
DEELION, JOHN	1820	NYCO	WD05	404
DEFOREST, D.	1830	NYCO	WD13	346
DEGG	1790	SUFF	HUNT	164
DEGRANT, PRIMUS	1810	NYCO	WD08	718
DEGRASS, G.	1830	NYCO	WD11	183
DEGRASS, GEORGE	1820	NYCO	WD01	61
DEGRAVE, JAMES	1800	NYCO	WD07	856
DE GRAZE, JOHN	1800	ORNG	WARW	381
DEGROAT, CATHERINE	1810	NYCO	WD06	443
DEGROAT, JAMES	1820	ONON	ONON	207
DEGROAT, JAMES	1830	ONON	ONON	193
DE GROAT, JOSEPH	1830	ONID	AUGU	112

NAME	YR	CO	TWP	PG
DEGROAT, RICHARD	1830	ONON	ONON	160
DEGROODT, PRIMOS	1810	NYCO	WD06	396
DEGROTE, NICHOLAS	1830	RICH	CAST	45
DEHART, CATHERINE	1820	NYCO	WD06	554
DEHART, JAMES	1810	NYCO	WD05	283
DEHART, JOHN	1830	RICH	CAST	42
DEHART, RICHARD	1820	RICH	NORT	109
DEHART, RICHARD	1830	RICH	NORT	28
DEHART, THOMAS	1830	RICH	NORT	27
DEHART, WILLIAM	1830	RICH	CAST	42
DEIDRICK, ABRAHAM	1830	ONON	POMP	282
DEKAY, HENRY	1830	ORNG	MINI	261
DELAMAKER, JAMES	1810	NYCO	WD01	13
DELAMASTER, MINK	1830	ULST	OLIV	140
DELAMATER, HENRY	1810	COLU	HUDS	134
DELANCEY, J.	1820	NYCO	WD10	1058
DELANO, THOMAS	1820	DUTC	FISH	75
DELANY, JOE P.	1810	NYCO	WD08	772
DELARAN, SEZAR	1830	WEST	CORT	62
DELAVAN	1820	PUTM	PATE	101
DELAWARE, JACOB	1830	COLU	CANN	21
DELERET, JOSEPH	1830	NYCO	WD10	66
DELEWATER, RICHARD	1820	ULST	WOOD	47
DELILLA, THOMAS	1820	DUTC	CLNT	43
DELILLA, THOMAS	1830	DUTC	FISH	478
DELILLA, TONE	1820	DUTC	CLNT	43
DELLEVE, WILLIAM	1800	NYCO	WD07	867
DELONY, BENJAMIN	1800	SARA	HALF	1046
DEMARES, JOSEPH	1830	NYCO	WD04	163
DEMARIST, JACOB	1830	GREN	ATHN	214
DEMASS, RICHARD	1830	ABNY	WD03	284
DEMBA, JOHN	1830	ABNY	WD04	311
DEMBY, JOHN	1800	NYCO	WD05	770
DEME, CHARLES	1800	OTSG	PITT	627
DEMENIS, PETER	1830	NYCO	WD07	121
DEMEROY, SUSAN	1830	NYCO	WD10	66
DEMERRY, DAVID	1820	NYCO	WD07	677
DEMESNE, SAMUEL	1830	KING	BUSH	383
DEMING, AUGUST	1820	OTSG	DECA	77
DEMION, SAMUEL	1820	KING	WILL	181
DEMMING, JACK	1830	RENS	WD04	75
DEMONS	1820	PUTM	PATE	101
DEMORE, LEWIS	1810	NYCO	WD06	397
D EMOTT, LEWIS	1810	QUEN	SHEM	286
DEMOTTE, LEDIAN	1810	NYCO	WD06	439
DEMUN, AARON	1830	CAYU	AUBN	157
DEMUN, SOLOMAN	1830	CAYU	AUBN	158
DENISON, BENJAMIN	1830	ORNG	MINI	259
DENISON, NACHT	1830	MADI	----	360

NAME	YR	CO	TWP	PG
DENISON, PHILLIP	1830	ONON	MANI	378
DENISON, THOMAS	1820	ONON	CICE	185
DENISON, THOMAS	1830	ONON	MANI	365
DENNING, WILLIAM	1800	NYCO	WD06	839
DENNIS, ANTHONY	1830	MONT	AMST	128
DENNIS, C.	1830	NYCO	WD11	133
DENNIS, HENRY	1830	NYCO	WD09	415
DENNIS, JOHN	1800	NYCO	WD04	709
DENNIS, JOHN	1810	NYCO	WD05	311
DENNIS, MRS.	1810	NYCO	WD06	449
DENNIS, STEPHEN	1800	NYCO	WD05	775
DENNIS, STEPHEN	1820	NYCO	WD05	383
DENNIS, WIDOW	1810	NYCO	WD07	535
DENNISAH, JAMES	1830	KING	BUSH	381
DENNISON, EDWARD	1830	ONID	KIRK	87
DENNY, JOHN	1820	NYCO	WD06	488
DENNY, THOMAS	1810	DUTC	BEEK	294
DENNY, THOMAS	1820	DUTC	BEEK	21
DENNY, THOMAS	1830	DUTC	UNVA	423
DENSEY, ANN	1830	NYCO	WD14	488
DENTON, ANTHONY	1800	DUTC	BEEK	17
DENTON, ANTHONY	1800	ULST	PLAT	258
DENTON, DANIEL	1820	SUFF	RIVH	355
DENTON, MORRIS	1820	QUEN	----	25
DENTON, MORRIS	1830	QUEN	OYST	50
DENUES, FRANCIS	1810	NYCO	WD05	289
DENYEN, JOSEPH	1820	QUEN	----	74
DENYER, DAVID	1820	TOMP	ULYS	13
DEON	1810	COLU	CLAV	161
DEON, FRANCIS	1810	NYCO	WD05	257
DEP	1820	SUFF	EAST	294
DEP, CYRUS	1820	SUFF	EAST	295
DEP, PETER	1820	SUFF	EAST	289
DEP, PETER	1820	SUFF	EAST	295
DEPEYSTER, DINAH	1800	NYCO	WD03	703
DEPEYSTER, DINAH	1800	NYCO	WD04	718
DEPEYSTER, DINAH	1810	NYCO	WD01	13
DEPEYSTER, HARRY	1800	NYCO	WD03	710
DEPEYSTER, HENRY	1830	NYCO	WD08	135
DEPEYSTER, THOMAS	1830	NYCO	WD09	417
DEPU, JOHN	1830	DELA	TOMP	202
DEPUY, HENRY	1820	ONON	POMP	145
DEPUY, HENRY	1830	ONON	POMP	282
DEPUY, JAMES	1830	ONON	POMP	282
DEPUY, JOSEPH	1830	ULST	PLAT	269
DE PUY, PETER	1830	NYCO	WD12	278
DEPUY, PHILLIP	1830	ULST	ROCH	176
DEPUY, ROBERT	1830	ULST	ROCH	184
DERBY, ELIMUS	1830	SUFF	SHAM	207

Derby

NAME	YR	CO	TWP	PG
DERBY, RUFUS	1830	ONID	WHTE	200
DERE, CHARLES	1830	TIOG	SOPO	212
DERICKSON, CHARLES	1830	NYCO	WD08	244
DE RIDDER, PRINCE	1830	WASH	GREN	157
DERLIN, EMANUEL	1830	RENS	SCHO	246
DEROBY, LALORD	1810	NYCO	WD05	257
DEROMA, FRANCIS	1810	NYCO	WD06	478
DEROSE, SARAH	1810	NYCO	WD01	22
DEROYER, JACOB	1810	QUEN	OYST	240
DERRICK, MARVIN	1830	OTSG	UNAD	206
DERRICK, PRINCE	1820	OTSG	UNAD	91
DERRICK, PRINCE	1830	OTSG	UNAD	205
DERRICK, RICHARD	1820	OTSG	UNAD	91
DERRICK, WILLIAM	1830	OTSG	UNAD	205
DERRIVILLE, VINCENT	1800	NYCO	WD06	831
DERRY	1800	NYCO	WD06	667
DERRY, GEORGE	1830	NYCO	WD05	300
DERRY, LONDON	1820	KING	BRYN	116
DERRY, WILLIAM	1810	NYCO	WD02	113
DERRY, WILLIAM	1820	NYCO	WD06	457
DERVELLIA, TICTUM	1800	NYCO	WD05	748
DES BOWAS, ALEXANDER	1830	NYCO	WD03	114
DESIER, CHARLES	1810	NYCO	WD04	159
DESILBY, ANTHONY	1830	DUTC	PLEA	309
DESPARD, JOHN	1810	NYCO	WD05	301
DESSES, JOHN P.	1830	NYCO	WD07	95
DEVANEY, MR.	1810	NYCO	WD10	697
DEVINDORF, HENRY	1830	HERK	DANU	179
DEVION	1810	NYCO	WD10	657
DEVOE, NANCY	1830	DUTC	PGKP	355
DEVOE, PETER	1810	NYCO	WD05	260
DEVOE, PRINCE	1830	WEST	YORK	169
DEVONSHIER	1810	NYCO	WD07	527
DEVONSHIER, JANE	1810	NYCO	WD03	88
DEWALL, ANTHONY	1790	ULST	NPAL	179
DEWAUTTS, MICHAEL	1830	MONT	JOHN	210
DEWIT, CEASAR	1810	STEU	BATH	375
DEWIT, ELIZABETH	1820	NYCO	WD05	341
DEWIT, FRANCIS	1810	ONON	MACE	539
DEWIT, HARRY	1830	DELA	COLC	26
DEWIT, SAMUEL	1830	NYCO	WD05	266
DEWITH, CATO	1830	TOMP	LANS	539
DEWITT, ABRAHAM	1820	NYCO	WD07	721
DEWITT, ALEXANDER	1830	ONID	UTIC	46
DEWITT, ALEXANDER	1830	ONON	SALI	23
DEWITT, ANTHONY	1790	ULST	ROCH	183
DEWITT, ANTHONY	1800	ULST	ROCH	212
DEWITT, B.	1820	ULST	MARB	62
DEWITT, BETSEY	1830	ONTA	CANA	120

NAME	YR	CO	TWP	PG
DEWITT, BETTY	1820	ULST	HURL	50
DEWITT, CATO	1820	CORT	VIRG	638
DEWITT, CEAZEAR	1830	ULST	MARB	157
DEWITT, FRANCIS	1820	ONON	MARC	231
DEWITT, FRANCIS	1830	ONON	SKAN	156
DEWITT, FRANCIS	1830	ULST	MARB	156
DEWITT, GEORGE	1830	ULST	WAWA	187
DEWITT, HARRY	1820	ONTA	CANA	225
DEWITT, HARRY	1830	ULST	MARB	158
DEWITT, HENRY	1810	STEU	WAYN	390
DEWITT, HENRY	1830	NYCO	WD05	317
DEWITT, HENRY	1830	ORNG	HBGH	124
DEWITT, JACK	1810	ULST	KING	750
DEWITT, JACK	1820	DUTC	CLNT	27
DEWITT, JACK	1820	ULST	KING	78
DE WITT, JAMES	1830	DUTC	PGKP	351
DE WITT, JAMES	1830	ULST	ROCH	174
DE WITT, PHILIP	1810	STEU	BATH	373
DEWITT, PHILIP	1820	ONTA	CANA	214
DEWITT, PHILIP	1830	ONTA	CANA	120
DEWITT, PHILIP	1830	ULST	ESOP	81
DEWITT, PRIMUS	1820	GENE	LEIC	158
DEWITT, RICHARD	1820	TIOG	CATH	249
DEWITT, ROBERT	1820	NYCO	WD07	714
DEWITT, ROBERT	1830	NYCO	WD07	18
DEWITT, S.	1820	ULST	MARB	62
DEWITT, SAMUEL	1830	ONTA	SENE	73
DEWITT, TOM	1830	ULST	MARB	156
DEWITT, TONEY	1810	STEU	BATH	373
DEWITT, RICHARD	1830	ULST	MARB	158
DEWITT, OLIVER	1820	NYCO	WD09	930
DEXTER, EMAR	1830	ABNY	WD02	262
DEY, SAMSON	1800	NYCO	WD05	781
DEY, SOLOMAN	1810	ROCK	ORNG	637
DEY, SUSAN	1810	ROCK	ORNG	636
DEY, WILLIAM	1810	ROCK	ORNG	635
DEYCO, JACOB	1830	KING	WD03	:90
DEYO, JANE	1830	ULST	NPAL	227
DEYO, LEONARD	1830	ULST	PLAT	265
DEYO, NANCY	1830	ULST	NPAL	203
DEYO, WILLIAM	1830	ULST	SHAW	251
DEYOE, ANN	1830	ULST	MARL	274
DEYOE, JOHN	1830	ULST	PLAT	259
DIAH, DAVID	1800	SUFF	SHAM	67
DIALE, WILLIAM	1810	NYCO	WD07	550
DIAMOND, JACOB	1830	SCHR	MIDD	36
DIAMOND, MOSES	1830	SCHR	MIDD	36
DIAN	1800	ABNY	WATV	95
DIAN	1810	RENS	TROY	388

NAME	YR	CO	TWP	PG
DIANA	1790	NYCO	SOUT	132
DIANA	1820	COLU	HUDS	3
DIARH, SESAR	1810	NYCO	WD07	544
DIARTOIS, BENJAMIN	1830	NYCO	WD05	268
DIAS, JOHN	1810	NYCO	WD05	371
DIBBLE, JOSEPH	1820	ABNY	ABNY	163
DIBBLE, JOSEPH	1830	ABNY	WD01	201
DICK	1790	NYCO	MONT	120
DICK	1790	QUEN	FLUS	149
DICK	1790	QUEN	OYST	154
DICK	1790	QUEN	SHEM	156
DICK	1790	SUFF	ISLP	165
DICK	1790	WEST	HARR	199
DICK	1790	WEST	POUN	204
DICK	1800	ABNY	RENV	162
DICK	1800	COLU	LIVG	1119
DICK	1800	NYCO	WD07	927
DICK	1800	QUEN	NEWT	656
DICK	1800	QUEN	SHEM	560
DICK	1800	QUEN	OYST	580
DICK	1800	RENS	SCAS	814
DICK	1810	DUTC	PGKP	319
DICK	1810	RENS	LANS	422
DICK	1810	RICH	NORT	600
DICK	1810	WEST	CORT	1016
DICK	1820	SUFF	BROK	333
DICK, ANTHONY	1820	MONT	FLOR	345
DICK, MR.	1830	NYCO	WD13	358
DICK, PAUL	1810	SUFF	SHAM	445
DICK, POLLY	1820	SUFF	SHAM	314
DICKASON, RICHARD	1830	ONON	MANI	380
DICKASON, SANDERS	1830	TOMP	ITCA	332
DICKEN, JOSEPH	1820	COLU	HUDS	9
DICKENSON	1810	NYCO	WD07	607
DICKENSON, HARRY	1820	DUTC	FISH	74
DICKENSON, JAMES	1820	GREN	ATHE	13
DICKENSON, JOHN	1810	NYCO	WD02	100
DICKENSON, JOHN	1810	NYCO	WD06	492
DICKERSON, CHARLES	1830	ABNY	WATV	466
DICKERSON, CHARLES	1830	MONR	RWD3	230
DICKERSON, EDWARD	1830	NYCO	WD05	328
DICKERSON, HARVEY	1830	DUTC	FISH	478
DICKERSON, JOHN	1810	SUFF	BROK	491
DICKERSON, JOHN H.	1830	NYCO	WD08	257
DICKERSON, RAIF	1830	KING	WD02	265
DICKERSON, STEPHEN	1830	QUEN	OYST	39
DICKINSON	1810	NYCO	WD07	556
DICKINSON, JAMES	1810	NYCO	WD07	648
DICKINSON, JOHN	1830	RENS	BRUN	230

NAME	YR	CO	TWP	PG
DICKINSON, RICHARD	1820	ABNY	ABNY	163
DICKINSON, RICHARD	1830	RENS	TROY	7
DICKINSON, T.	1830	NYCO	WD11	153
DICKS, DAVID	1820	BROM	OWEG	33
DICKS, SAMUEL	1810	DUTC	CLNT	380
DICKSON	1810	NYCO	WD06	460
DICKSON, AUG'	1820	COLU	KIND	5
DICKSON, BERRY	1800	NYCO	WD07	862
DICKSON, ELENOR	1820	NYCO	WD07	621
DICKSON, FANNY	1830	NYCO	WD08	231
DICKSON, JAMES	1830	COLU	STUY	64
DICKSON, MICHAEL	1820	ONON	ONON	218
DICKSON, RICHARD	1820	COLU	KIND	5
DICKSON, SAMUEL	1800	NYCO	WD03	698
DICKSON, SUSAN	1830	NYCO	WD08	213
DIE, ALLISS	1830	NYCO	WD01	27
DIELS, JACK	1830	ABNY	BERN	379
DIERS, JOHNATHAN	1830	NYCO	WD09	430
DI ESPINVILLE, MARY ANN	1830	NYCO	WD05	267
DIETZ, HARRY	1830	SCHR	SCHR	18
DIEVENDORFF, DANIEL	1830	MONT	MIND	7
DIFOREST, BENJAMIN	1820	PUTM	SOUT	100
DIGROAT, RICHARD	1810	NYCO	WD07	611
DIHUN, JAMES	1820	NYCO	WD08	807
DILL, CASEAR	1830	ORNG	HBGH	125
DILL, HARRY	1800	NYCO	WD07	903
DILL, RICHARD	1830	ULST	SHAW	238
DILL, TONE	1810	ORNG	NEWW	917
DILWORTH, JOHN	1830	COLU	HUDS	103
DILWORTH, THOMAS	1830	COLU	GALA	262
DILWORTH, TOBIAS	1830	ULST	NPAL	228
DIMES, ELESABETH	1810	SUFF	SHAM	445
DIMES, TOM	1810	COLU	CLAV	157
DIMKERSON, JONAH	1810	SENE	FAYE	210
DIMON, SIAS	1830	ORNG	NEWW	96
DIMON, THOMAS	1820	SARA	WATE	241
DIMOND, PEGGY	1830	RENS	TROY	7
DIMOND, SARAH	1830	RENS	TROY	3
DIMRESS, ABRAHAM	1830	ONID	WHTE	201
DIMS, PETER	1820	COLU	HUDS	3
DINAH	1790	NYCO	OUTW	131
DINAH	1790	QUEN	OYST	155
DINAH	1800	ABNY	WATV	87
DINAH	1800	NYCO	WD01	658
DINAH	1800	NYCO	WD07	895
DINAH	1800	SUFF	SMIT	57
DINAH	1820	SUFF	BROK	360
DINAH, JAMES	1820	GREN	HUNT	112
DINER, JAMES	1810	GREN	WIND	331

Dinge

NAME	YR	CO	TWP	PG
DINGE, CHARLES	1810	SUFF	SMIT	535
DINGE, PETER	1810	QUEN	SHEM	306
DINGEE, ROSE	1820	NYCO	WD06	470
DINGLE, JACOB	1830	GREN	ATHN	202
DINGO, FRANCIS	1820	GREN	ATHN	1
DINGO, HARRY	1820	GREN	ATHN	1
DINGO, JACOB	1820	GREN	CATS	171
DINGO, RICHARD	1830	GREN	CATS	244
DINGY, CHARLES	1820	SUFF	SMIT	322
DINGY, CHARLES	1830	SUFF	SMIT	267
DINKS, JOSEPH	1820	SARA	SARA	189
DINN	1820	WEST	MTPL	279
DINN	1820	WEST	WEST	195
DIRCK	1810	DUTC	PGKP	171
DIRKUM, M.	1810	RENS	PITT	392
DISCO, NANCY	1810	NYCO	WD05	331
DISOSWAY, SAMUEL	1800	RICH	SOUT	962
DISREY, MARY	1820	NYCO	WD03	144
DISSOSSWAY, THOMAS	1830	NYCO	WD05	270
DISSOSWAY, DINAH	1810	NYCO	WD05	80
DISSOSWAY, GINREA	1800	NYCO	WD01	663
DITMUS, CISH	1820	QUEN	----	59
DITTON, JOHN	1830	ONTA	SENE	85
DIXEN, W.	1810	RENS	TROY	376
DIXON, BENJAMIN	1800	NYCO	WD06	814
DIXON, BENJAMIN	1810	NYCO	WD05	370
DIXON, CHARLES	1830	NYCO	WD08	243
DIXON, GEORGE	1830	NYCO	WD10	117
DIXON, HENRY	1820	NYCO	WD02	118
DIXON, ISABELLA	1820	NYCO	WD06	449
DIXON, JOSEPH	1810	NYCO	WD05	273
DIXON, JOSEPH	1820	NYCO	WD06	518
DIXON, M.	1820	QUEN	----	40
DIXON, PLATO	1800	NYCO	WD06	796
DIXON, RICHARD	1790	DUTC	FDRK	82
DIXON, RICHARD	1820	ABNY	ABNY	162
DIXON, RICHARD	1830	RENS	BRUN	228
DIXON, SALLY	1820	ABNY	ABNY	164
DIXON, SAMUEL	1800	NYCO	WD05	768
DIXON, SAMUEL	1830	ORNG	NEWB	33
DIXON, STEPHEN	1830	NYCO	WD12	298
DIXON, THOMAS	1820	NYCO	WD06	475
DIXON, THOMAS	1830	NYCO	WD05	328
DIXON, THOMAS	1830	NYCO	WD05	336
DIXON, WILLIAM	1820	WASH	KING	164
DIXON, WILLIAM	1830	STLR	POTS	132
DIXON, WILLIAM	1830	WASH	KING	356
DIXSON, JOHN	1830	ABNY	BETH	536
DOANE, SILVIA	1830	KING	WD01	254

NAME	YR	CO	TWP	PG
DOBBINS, HUGHY	1830	NYCO	WD08	229
DOBBINS, ISAAC	1800	NYCO	WD03	701
DOCKSTADER, HENRY	1830	MONT	JOHN	205
DODGE, CHARITY	1830	QUEN	OYST	22
DODGE, CHARLES	1810	NYCO	WD10	672
DODGE, CHARLES F.	1820	NYCO	WD07	655
DODGE, ELIZABETH	1830	NYCO	WD06	371
DODGE, JAMES	1820	QUEN	----	76
DODGE, JOHN	1800	NYCO	WD07	894
DOLBERRY, WILLIAM	1830	NYCO	WD14	458
DOLE, BETSEY	1830	RENS	TROY	7
DOLFSON, ROSANNA	1830	MONR	BRIG	35
DOLLRAS, HUGH	1830	NYCO	WD10	122
DOLPHIN, ELI	1800	ABNY	RENV	175
DOLPHIN, ELI	1810	SENE	OVID	272
DOLSEY, EDWARD	1830	STEU	BATH	269
DOMINE, JANE	1800	SUFF	SHAM	95
DOMING, CAROLINE	1820	SUFF	EAST	294
DON, PETER	1790	SUFF	SOUT	166
DOOLITTLE, ICHABAL M.	1820	PUTM	SOUT	100
DOOR, HENRY	1820	SENE	ROMU	345
DOPHINCE, JOHN B.	1800	NYCO	WD06	831
DOR, THOMAS	1830	MONT	FLOR	98
DORERS, JOHN	1810	NYCO	WD02	116
DORIS, PETER	1820	NYCO	WD03	152
DORLAND, HARRY	1830	DUTC	BEEK	188
DORLAND, HENRY	1820	DUTC	BEEK	15
DORLAND, PETER	1830	QUEN	NEWT	17
DORLAND, SAM	1810	DUTC	BEEK	274
DORLAND, SAMUEL	1830	DUTC	BEEK	192
DORNING, FINE	1820	SUFF	EAST	297
DOROTHY, EUGENE	1830	DUTC	HYPK	230
DORSAN, SAMUEL	1810	NYCO	WD04	161
DORSEY, FRANK	1830	WANE	PALM	40
DORTLAND, SAMUEL	1830	DUTC	BEEK	188
DORUS, W.	1830	NYCO	WD11	159
DOSSET, SAMBO	1820	CHEN	SHER	337
DOTY, BOBIN	1810	QUEN	OYST	247
DOTY, FRANK	1820	QUEN	----	26
DOTY, JAMES	1810	NYCO	WD03	63
DOTY, ROBERT	1820	QUEN	----	75
DOTY, ROBERT	1830	QUEN	OYST	38
DOUGE, DANIEL	1810	NYCO	WD05	290
DOUGHERTY, WILLIAM	1830	NYCO	WD06	434
DOUGHTY, DIANA	1820	NYCO	WD04	212
DOUGHTY, DICK	1810	NYCO	WD03	81
DOUGHTY, N.	1810	NYCO	WD01	18
DOUGLAS, GEORGE	1830	NYCO	WD10	124
DOUGLASS, HENRY	1830	SENE	FAYE	64

Dougless

NAME	YR	CO	TWP	PG
DOUGLESS, STEPHEN	1830	ABNY	WD02	262
DOUKINS, THOMAS	1830	NYCO	WD08	214
DOUSE, MARY	1830	NYCO	WD06	381
DOVER	1790	WEST	SALM	206
DOW, JACOB	1830	SCNE	WD02	223
DOW, JAN	1830	SCNE	WD01	206
DOWLEY, ABRAHAM	1820	ONTA	SODU	121
DOWLEY, ABRAHAM	1830	WANE	SODU	128
DOWNING, NAT	1810	DUTC	FISH	212
DOWNING, RICHARD	1830	NYCO	WD01	48
DOWNS, BENJAMIN	1810	NYCO	WD04	218
DOWNS, LETTICE	1830	ORNG	NEWB	41
DOWNS, LYMUS	1820	ORNG	CORN	702
DOX, JACK	1820	ABNY	WATV	260
DOX, JASPER	1820	ABNY	WATV	261
DOYE, ANDREW O.	1810	NYCO	WD04	399
DRAKE, ANTHONY	1810	ONTA	CANA	895
DRAKE, ANTHONY	1820	ONTA	CANA	210
DRAKE, DIANA	1830	NYCO	WD05	261
DRAKE, FRANCIS	1810	NYCO	WD03	83
DRAKE, FRANCIS	1820	NYCO	WD05	345
DRAKE, FRANCIS	1820	NYCO	WD06	470
DRAKE, FRANCIS	1830	NYCO	WD05	342
DRAKE, JEREMIAH	1830	RICH	SOUT	19
DRAKE, LEWIS	1820	WEST	YORK	339
DRAKE, LEWIS	1830	WEST	YORK	170
DRAKE, PHOEBE	1830	ONTA	CANA	112
DRAKE, RICHARD	1820	NYCO	WD05	394
DRAKE, WILLIAM	1830	NYCO	WD06	393
DRAKES, LEWIS	1830	COLU	CANN	21
DRAPER, GEORGE	1830	SUFF	SHAM	221
DRAWYA, MATTHIAS	1820	ORNG	GOSH	761
DRAWYER, MATTHIAS	1830	ORNG	GOSH	290
DRAWYER, WILLIAM	1800	QUEN	NHEM	552
DRAYTON, HENRY	1830	NYCO	WD08	206
DRAYTON, MOSES	1830	NYCO	WD08	226
DREW, CHARLES	1820	PUTM	SOUT	100
DRILL, WILLIAM	1820	NYCO	WD03	190
DRUMMONS	1810	NYCO	WD07	547
DUANSON, HARRY	1810	QUEN	OYST	250
DUBLIN, FLORA	1800	NYCO	WD02	676
DUBLIN, JOHN	1830	HERK	HERK	50
DUBLIN, RICHARD	1810	ORNG	NEWB	938
DUBOIS, CEAZAR	1830	ULST	NPAL	221
DUBOIS, CESAR	1830	CAYU	SEMP	327
DUBOIS, CESAR	1830	NYCO	WD05	264
DUBOIS, CHARLES	1830	NYCO	WD05	310
DUBOIS, CHARLES	1830	ULST	MARL	280
DUBOIS, CHARLES	1830	ULST	PLAT	267

NAME	YR	CO	TWP	PG
DUBOIS, DAVID	1830	NYCO	WD08	244
DUBOIS, DICK	1830	ULST	SHAW	238
DUBOIS, DINAH	1830	ULST	MARL	283
DUBOIS, FRANCIS	1830	ULST	NPAL	211
DUBOIS, GARRET	1830	ULST	NPAL	234
DUBOIS, GARRET	1830	ULST	MARL	279
DUBOIS, GLEASON	1820	ULST	NPAL	69
DUBOIS, HARRY	1830	ULST	NPAL	225
DUBOIS, HARRY	1830	ULST	PLAT	268
DUBOIS, ISSAC	1830	ULST	NPAL	209
DUBOIS, JACK	1830	ULST	NPAL	227
DUBOIS, JACOB	1820	ULST	SHAW	64
DUBOIS, JACOB	1830	ORNG	NEWB	32
DUBOIS, JANE	1830	ULST	NPAL	230
DUBOIS, JANE	1830	ULST	NPAL	230
DUBOIS, JOHN	1830	JEFF	ORLN	305
DUBOIS, JOHN	1830	NYCO	WD08	173
DUBOIS, LEWIS	1830	ULST	KING	65
DUBOIS, PETER	1830	ULST	MARL	281
DUBOIS, PHILIP	1830	ULST	NPAL	212
DUBOIS, SAMUEL	1820	NYCO	WD04	212
DUBOIS, SAMUEL	1830	DUTC	PLEA	307
DUBOIS, SAMUEL	1830	NYCO	WD05	317
DUBOIS, SAMUEL	1830	NYCO	WD05	327
DUBOIS, SARAH	1830	ULST	NPAL	230
DUBOISE, CEASAR	1830	NYCO	WD09	333
DUBOISE, COLES	1830	NYCO	WD01	34
DUBOISE, DINAH	1830	ORNG	NEWB	57
DUBOISE, JAMES	1810	NYCO	WD05	324
DUBOISE, JOHN	1830	ORNG	CALH	17
DUBOLS, BOAS	1820	SCNE	WD01	123
DUBOLS, JACOB	1820	DUTC	CLNT	39
DUBOLS, SAMUEL	1820	DUTC	FISH	59
DUDRASS, GEORGE	1810	NYCO	WD05	371
DUEBOYCE, HENRY	1830	NYCO	WD08	276
DUER, CAESAR	1800	NYCO	WD05	752
DUER, HENRY	1830	SENE	OVID	101
DUFFE, JOHN	1820	SENE	GALE	388
DUFFON, JOHN	1830	ONTA	SENE	85
DUFFY, AARON	1830	NYCO	WD06	436
DU FREYER, AMBROSE	1830	NYCO	WD08	246
DUKEN, JOHN	1830	RENS	STEP	286
DUKER, JOHN	1810	ORNG	GOSH	1121
DUKER, THOMAS	1830	NYCO	WD12	254
DUMOND, QUAM	1830	SENE	OVID	111
DUMONEY, HARK	1830	CAYU	SPRG	339
DUN, THOMAS	1830	KING	WD02	275
DUNBAR, ABRON	1830	ONON	SALI	5
DUNBAR, ASA	1810	ONTA	BOYL	647
DUNBAR, BENJAMIN	1810	NYCO	WD06	449

NAME	YR	CO	TWP	PG
DUNBAR, CALEB	1830	CHEN	SHER	137
DUNBAR, JACOB	1830	NIAG	ROYL	372
DUNBAR, JOHN	1830	JEFF	HOUN	175
DUNBAR, JOSHUA	1810	ONTA	SENE	832
DUNBAR, LUCY	1800	NYCO	WD01	663
DUNBAR, ROBERT	1820	DUTC	DOVE	49
DUNBAR, RUTH	1820	DUTC	DOVE	49
DUNBARACK, PRINCE	1810	DUTC	DOVE	115
DUNCAN, ELIZAH	1810	NYCO	WD06	423
DUNCAN, JACOB	1810	NYCO	WD08	714
DUNCAN, WALTER	1820	NYCO	WD04	231
DUNCAN, WILLIAM	1810	COLU	HUDS	143
DUNCANSON, JOHN	1830	SENE	FAYE	66
DUNGEE, JOHN	1830	RENS	TROY	9
DUNHAM, SARAH	1830	NYCO	WD06	385
DUNING, BAZILLA	1820	NYCO	WD02	114
DUNKERSON, JOHN	1820	SENE	FAYE	369
DUNKERSON, JONAH	1820	ONTA	SENE	266
DUNKERSON, ROBERT	1820	ONTA	SENE	269
DUNKIN, JAMES	1830	NYCO	WD14	433
DUNKLE, ANDREW	1830	MONT	CANJ	32
DUNLAP, HENRY	1830	NYCO	WD08	224
DUNMORE, CIRUS	1800	NYCO	WD07	903
DUNN, AMOS	1830	NYCO	WD05	329
DUNN, H.L.	1820	NYCO	WD07	686
DUNN, JAMES	1830	SULL	LUMP	19
DUNN, MOLLY	1810	TIOG	ELMI	620
DUNN, SIMON	1830	NYCO	WD10	26
DUNN, THOMAS	1800	NYCO	WD07	859
DUNN, THOMAS	1830	HERK	GERM	141
DUNN, THOMAS	1830	KING	WD02	275
DUNN, THOMAS	1830	NYCO	WD04	181
DUNNING, WILLIAM	1830	ORNG	GOSH	275
DUNNSCORIB, INS.	1820	NYCO	WD10	989
DUNSON, HENRY	1820	QUEN	----	74
DUNSON, HENRY	1830	NYCO	WD07	46
DUPLACY, BENJAMIN	1820	NYCO	WD05	332
DUPLESSE, BENJAMIN	1830	NYCO	WD05	261
DUPLEX, GEORGE	1830	TOMP	DANB	440
DUPLEX, PRINCE	1820	TIOG	DAMB	267
DUPOOLS, PETER	1820	WASH	EAST	174
DUPOY	1810	NYCO	WD06	480
DUPREE, JOHN	1810	NYCO	WD03	83
DUPREY, JEROME	1810	NYCO	WD07	522
DURBY, WILLIAM	1820	NYCO	WD06	485
DUREE, JOHN	1830	NYCO	WD10	84
DUREERDER, CHEENUN	1810	NYCO	WD05	307
DURELL, SARAH	1830	NYCO	WD08	173
DURHAM, ISAAC	1830	NYCO	WD04	218

NAME	YR	CO	TWP	PG
DURHAM, JOHN	1820	NYCO	WD06	536
DURLAND, BETSEY	1830	SUFF	HUNT	303
DURLEY, JAMES	1830	NYCO	WD09	415
DURLIN, ANTHONY	1810	NYCO	WD03	90
DURLIN, ISAAC	1830	NYCO	WD08	232
DURLING, CAESAR	1830	NYCO	WD08	239
DURLING, HENRY	1830	QUEN	'NEWT	14
DURLON, JACK	1820	QUEN	----	45
DURLON, JOHN	1810	NYCO	WD06	469
DURPHY, ISAAC	1830	CHEN	NORW	175
DURRELL, CHARLES	1830	QUEN	JAMA	128
DURYEA, JAMES	1830	QUEN	JAMA	128
DURYEA, JOSEPH	1830	QUEN	OYST	28
DURYEA, SAMUEL	1830	QUEN	JAMA	128
DURYEU, JOSEPH	1810	QUEN	OYST	246
DUSENBERRY, JOSEPH	1830	NYCO	WD14	516
DUSENBURY, HANNAH	1830	NYCO	WD07	46
DUSENBURY, LEWIS	1830	NYCO	WD09	301
DUSENBURY, MASA	1820	NYCO	WD08	788
DUSHING, GEORGE	1830	QUEN	NEWT	17
DUVOT, PHLOMEN	1810	NYCO	WD05	359
DYOMIT, OBE	1810	KING	BRYN	632
EADON, WINT	1830	RICH	WEST	4
EARBS, WILLIAM	1820	TOMP	HECT	8
EARL, CATO	1820	ORNG	MONR	665
EARLE, WILLIAM	1830	MONR	GATE	234
EARSON, CHARLES	1820	NYCO	WD09	935
EASTER	1790	SUFF	ISLP	165
EASTER	1800	SUFF	ISLP	62
EASTER, CEASER	1820	NYCO	WD02	103
EASTER, PHILIP	1810	NYCO	WD10	636
EASTER, S.	1830	NYCO	WD11	201
EASTERLEY, JOHN	1820	ORNG	GOSH	757
EASTERLY, JOHN	1830	ORNG	WARW	71
EASTON, CHARLES	1830	NYCO	WD14	435
EATO, JACOB	1830	QUEN	FLUS	144
EBBETS, JOHN	1830	QUEN	NEWT	7
EBENEZER	1810	RENS	STEP	570
EBO	1790	QUEN	OYST	155
EBO	1800	QUEN	OYST	571
EBOE, SAMUEL	1830	COLU	STUY	70
EBOE, SAMUEL JR.	1830	COLU	STUY	70
ECHERSON, THOMAS	1820	SCHR	MIDD	526
ECKERSON, THOMAS	1830	SCHR	MIDD	36
EDDIRSON, SARAH	1820	NYCO	WD10	982
EDESIL, THOMAS	1800	QUEN	NEWT	659
EDGE, SAMUEL	1830	ABNY	WD02	261

Edinburgh

NAME	YR	CO	TWP	PG
EDINBURGH, PETER	1790	RICH	CAST	158
EDMENDSON, CHRISTOPHER	1800	NYCO	WD06	837
EDMOND	1800	QUEN	OYST	574
EDMOND, FRANCIS	1830	KING	FLAN	411
EDMOND, J.	1800	NIAG	BUFF	234
EDMONDSON, JOHN	1830	NYCO	WD05	336
EDMONDSON, RICHARD	1820	TIOG	SPEN	275
EDMONSON, JOHN	1810	NYCO	WD05	309
EDMONSON, JOHN	1820	ORNG	NEWW	492
EDMONSON, RICHARD	1830	TIOG	SPEN	151
EDMUND	1790	QUEN	OYST	155
EDMUND, WILLIAM	1810	NYCO	WD06	448
EDSAL, THOMAS	1810	NYCO	WD05	330
EDSALL, ISAAC	1820	NYCO	WD07	700
EDWARD	1790	QUEN	SHEM	156
EDWARD	1790	SUFF	ISLP	165
EDWARD	1800	QUEN	OYST	571
EDWARD	1800	SUFF	BROK	15
EDWARD	1800	SUFF	ISLP	62
EDWARD	1800	SUFF	EHAM	92
EDWARD	1810	QUEN	OYST	231
EDWARD, D.	1830	NYCO	WD13	393
EDWARD, JOHN	1820	NYCO	WD05	389
EDWARDS, DIANA	1810	NYCO	WD05	345
EDWARDS, GEORGE	1810	NYCO	WD03	80
EDWARDS, GEORGE	1830	NYCO	WD09	301
EDWARDS, HENRY	1830	JEFF	PHIL	225
EDWARDS, JAMES	1830	ABNY	WD01	205
EDWARDS, JANE	1810	NYCO	WD05	271
EDWARDS, JANE	1830	NYCO	WD05	339
EDWARDS, JOHN	1820	NYCO	WD02	98
EDWARDS, JOHN	1830	ABNY	WD01	211
EDWARDS, MALTBY	1830	SUFF	SOUT	334
EDWARDS, MORRIS	1830	QUEN	OYST	21
EDWARDS, PETER	1830	NYCO	WD05	332
EDWARDS, RACHAEL	1820	NYCO	WD06	488
EDWARDS, SAMUEL	1830	NYCO	WD03	138
EDWARDS, SAMUEL	1830	YATE	MILO	227
EDWARDS, WILLIAM	1810	NYCO	WD03	84
EGBERTS, CESAR	1830	GREN	COXE	191
EGBERTSON, CEASAR	1820	GREN	COXE	37
EGBERTSON, SAMUEL	1830	GREN	NEWB	174
EGLESTON, JOHN	1830	NYCO	WD08	220
ELAR, CEZAR	1810	WEST	CORT	1001
ELBERT	1820	QUEN	----	77
ELDERD, ANTHONY	1830	QUEN	SHEM	68
ELDERT, GILBERT	1830	QUEN	SHEM	73
ELDRIGE, ANTHONY	1820	QUEN	----	22
ELENDORF, THOMAS	1830	ORNG	NEWB	53

NAME	YR	CO	TWP	PG
ELEXANDER, THOMAS	1810	NYCO	WD07	530
ELHIANDORF, PINNEY	1820	ULST	SAUG	83
ELI, JOHN	1830	DUTC	PGKP	351
ELIAS	1790	QUEN	JAMA	150
ELIAS	1820	QUEN	----	59
ELIFSON, CHARLES	1820	NYCO	WD06	460
ELIJAH	1790	QUEN	SHEM	156
ELIJAH	1800	QUEN	SHEM	559
ELIJAH	1810	DUTC	STAN	180
ELIJAH	1820	QUEN	----	71
ELISHA	1800	SUFF	ISLP	59
ELIZABETH	1790	NYCO	SOUT	132
ELIZABETH	1790	QUEN	JAMA	150
ELIZABETH	1790	QUEN	OYST	155
ELIZABETH	1810	NYCO	WD06	442
ELIZABETH	1810	NYCO	WD06	454
ELIZABETH	1810	RENS	PITT	408
ELLETT, ROBERT	1810	NYCO	WD05	371
ELLICH, GEORGE	1820	SARA	HALF	241
ELLICK, JOHN	1830	RENS	TROY	13
ELLIOT, THOMAS	1820	NYCO	WD06	477
ELLIOTT, HANNAH	1810	NYCO	WD06	403
ELLIOTT, SAMUEL	1830	RENS	LANS	88
ELLIS, BENJAMIN	1800	NYCO	WD07	893
ELLIS, BENJAMIN	1820	ORNG	GOSH	761
ELLIS, BENJAMIN	1830	ORNG	MINI	252
ELLIS, CHARTER	1800	ORNG	GOSH	357
ELLIS, EFFY	1800	NYCO	WD06	818
ELLIS, GEORGE	1830	NYCO	WD05	328
ELLIS, HANNAH	1820	NYCO	WD09	935
ELLIS, JOHN	1820	NYCO	WD07	665
ELLIS, MOSES	1830	WANE	MACE	90
ELLIS, MRS.	1830	NYCO	WD06	386
ELLISON, EDWARD	1810	ORNG	NEWB	919
ELLISON, OLIVER	1830	ORNG	MONR	176
ELLISTON, BENJAMIN	1830	NYCO	WD06	423
ELLSWORTH, PRINCE	1830	DUTC	REDH	367
ELLSWORTH, PRINCE JR.	1830	DUTC	REDH	381
ELMENDOR, FRANCIS	1830	NYCO	WD08	214
ELMENDORF, FLORA	1830	ULST	SAUG	105
ELMENDORF, HARRY	1830	DELA	WALT	221
ELMENDORF, HARRY	1830	DELA	WALT	215
ELMENDORF, PETER	1830	ABNY	WD01	225
ELMER, PHILEAS	1820	ORNG	GOSH	741
ELMONDORF, HARRY	1830	ULST	MARB	167
ELMONDORF, PHILIP	1830	ULST	HURL	145A
ELMONDORF, PRINCE	1830	ULST	SAUG	113
ELMONDORF, SAMUEL	1830	ULST	HURL	145
ELSEA, LITTLETON	1810	NYCO	WD06	450

NAME	YR	CO	TWP	PG
ELSEY, LITHLOW	1820	NYCO	WD10	1029
ELSLON, BENJAMIN	1820	NYCO	WD03	185
ELSTON, ALEXANDER	1830	NYCO	WD06	426
ELSTON, CESAR	1810	NYCO	WD05	312
ELSWORTH, ARTOR	1820	SUFF	SHEL	332
ELTING, BENJAMIN	1810	NYCO	WD05	250
ELTING, CEZAER	1830	ULST	NPAL	227
ELTING, PETER E.	1830	ORNG	CRAW	190
EMERTSON, PETER	1820	NYCO	WD10	998
EMERY, DIMOND	1830	RENS	PITT	129
EMERY, POLLY	1830	SARA	SASP	163
EMILY, CHLOE	1830	NYCO	WD10	11
EMLER, GARRITT	1830	NYCO	WD08	265
EMMINS, JOHN	1810	WEST	EAST	1153
EMMIS, SARAH	1820	NYCO	WD08	780
EMMIT, JOHN	1830	RICH	SOUT	17
EMMONS, JAMES	1830	NYCO	WD05	329
EMORE, JOHN	1820	NYCO	WD07	619
ENGLISH, BENJAMIN	1830	NYCO	WD14	521
ENNELS, ABRAHAM	1810	NYCO	WD04	194
ENNINGS, SAMUEL	1820	NYCO	WD06	517
ENNOLDS, SAMUEL	1830	NYCO	WD06	414
ENNONS, SAMUEL	1810	NYCO	WD07	553
ENOCH	1790	QUEN	NHEM	153
ENOCH	1790	QUEN	SHEM	155
ENOCH	1820	QUEN	----	67
ENOS, BETTE	1810	SUFF	SHAM	460
ENOS, PEGGY	1830	SUFF	SHAM	230
ENSLEY, MARGARET	1810	NYCO	WD05	368
ENUR, GEORGE	1790	NYCO	WEST	133
EPHRAIGM	1810	RENS	TROY	382
EPHRAIM, JAMES	1830	SCHR	BROM	93
EPHRAIMS, JAMES	1820	SCHR	BROM	161
EPIHAIM	1800	SUFF	BROK	13
EPOLET, DUBO	1810	NYCO	WD05	278
EPOLETT, MR.	1820	NYCO	WD05	337
EPPES, JOHN	1820	WASH	SALM	186
EPPS, JOHN	1830	WASH	SALM	214
EPRHRAIM	1790	NYCO	MONT	123
ERMIA, ISAIAH	1830	NYCO	WD06	398
ERVIL, EMOS	1830	DELA	WALT	217
ESSEX, ABION	1830	NYCO	WD05	332
ESSEX, WILLIAM	1810	NYCO	WD01	28
ESTEVE, HAUNTH	1810	NYCO	WD10	687
ETO, ANTHONY	1810	NYCO	WD07	535
ETO, ANTHONY	1820	QUEN	----	77
ETO, JACOB	1820	QUEN	----	56
ETO, SELVENUS	1820	QUEN	----	65
ETO, VENIS	1810	QUEN	NHEM	210

NAME	YR	CO	TWP	PG
ETUSON, RICHARD	1820	NYCO	WD10	988
EVAN, JOHN	1800	NYCO	WD06	837
EVANS, ANDREW	1820	NYCO	WD05	400
EVANS, ELLEN	1830	NYCO	WD06	451
EVANS, JEFFERY	1820	NYCO	WD08	790
EVANS, JEFFRIE	1830	NYCO	WD14	435
EVANS, JOHN	1800	NYCO	WD06	837
EVANS, JOHN	1810	NYCO	WD06	494
EVANS, JOHN	1810	NYCO	WD06	484
EVANS, JOHN	1830	NYCO	WD12	303
EVANS, MR.	1830	NYCO	WD06	451
EVANS, NEW YEAR	1800	NYCO	WD05	754
EVANS, PETER	1830	RENS	TROY	17
EVERETT, JOSEPH	1820	NYCO	WD09	900
EVERSON, E.	1830	NYCO	WD12	309
EVERSON, HARRY	1830	WEST	YONK	5
EVERSON, RUBEN	1830	WEST	YONK	4
EVERSON, WALL	1830	WEST	YONK	6
EVERSON, WILLIAM	1830	NYCO	WD06	388
EVERSON, WILLIAM H.	1830	MONT	JOHN	190
EVERSON, YAFF	1810	WEST	WEST	1153
EVERSON, YAFF	1830	WEST	YONK	10
EVERTON, JAMES H.	1820	DUTC	AMEN	3
EVESON, MOSES	1820	NYCO	WD09	929
EVINSON, WALTER	1820	WEST	YONK	225
EVINSON, YAFF	1820	WEST	YONK	220
EVIRY, ELIJAH	1830	NYCO	WD12	277
EWING, GEORGE	1830	NYCO	WD10	128
EZARD, RACHAEL	1830	NYCO	WD14	498
FAIR, MR.	1810	NYCO	WD06	460
FALIMMU	1820	WASH	WEST	190
FALISE, TOSTON	1820	NYCO	WD05	358
FALK, MORRIS	1830	ABNY	RENV	423
FALMSBEE, ROBERT	1830	RENS	SCHO	249
FAN	1790	QUEN	JAMA	150
FANAS, J.	1830	KING	WD04	310
FANNEY	1790	QUEN	JAMA	151
FANNING, COMAS	1830	SUFF	SHEL	291
FANNING, COMUS	1820	SUFF	SHEL	330
FANNING, MINGO	1790	SUFF	SHAM	168
FARBER, ISAAC	1830	ROCK	RPOO	91
FARMIN, JEFFERSON	1830	MONT	MIND	9
FARREN, DIANA	1830	NYCO	WD10	46
FARRET, T.	1810	NIAG	OLEN	249
FARWELL, W.	1810	ONID	LISB	328
FASSETT, ABBY	1830	RENS	WD02	23
FAULKNER, JAMES	1820	ORNG	GOSH	752

NAME	YR	CO	TWP	PG
FAULKNER, JANE	1830	MONR	RWD1	201
FAY, NICHOLAS	1800	NYCO	WD06	820
FEDINE, PRINCE	1830	ABNY	WD01	218
FEE, JOSEPH	1810	NYCO	WD06	415
FEELE, ADAM	1810	COLU	HUDS	143
FEELE, PETER	1810	COLU	HUDS	149
FEELE, PETER	1830	COLU	STUY	59
FEFUS, CATO	1810	NYCO	WD02	129
FEGAN, MRS.	1830	NYCO	WD06	368
FELEE, PETER P.	1830	COLU	STUY	64
FELIX, EDWARD	1830	NYCO	WD05	257
FELIX, JOHN	1830	NYCO	WD07	22
FELIX, JOHN A.	1830	NYCO	WD07	97
FELIX, JOSEPH	1820	NYCO	WD03	145
FELIX, MOAB	1830	SUFF	SMIT	270
FELIX, WILLIAM	1810	SUFF	BROK	487
FELLER, ABRAHAM	1820	DUTC	MILA	82
FEN EYCK, CESAER	1830	ONON	CLAY	42
FENNINGS, DORAS	1800	NYCO	WD04	717
FERDON, JOHN	1830	SARA	SASP	163
FERGUSON, ANDREW	1820	NYCO	WD04	246
FERGUSON, FRANCIS	1810	NYCO	WD03	79
FERGUSON, FRANCIS	1820	NYCO	WD03	152
FERMAN, HENNY	1820	CHEN	OXFO	233
FERMAN, JOSIAH	1820	CHEN	OXFO	233
FERNE, JOHNATHAN	1830	NYCO	WD14	455
FERNWIST, CASPER	1820	COLU	HUDS	11
FERRIS, CUFF	1810	NYCO	WD06	426
FERRIS, CYRUS	1820	SUFF	HUNT	286
FERRIS, EASTER	1810	NYCO	WD05	303
FERRIS, HARRY	1810	QUEN	FLUS	203
FERRIS, HENRY	1820	NYCO	WD09	944
FERRIS, WILLIAM	1820	MADI	SULL	4
FERRIS, WILLIAM	1830	CAYU	AURE	180
FERRIS, WILLIAM	1830	NYCO	WD06	377
FERRITH, JACK	1820	NYCO	WD07	620
FETCH, THOMAS	1800	NYCO	WD05	779
FETUS, STEPHEN	1820	ULST	SHAW	64
FIDEY, JOHN	1830	NYCO	WD05	335
FIDLER, G.	1810	MADI	SMIT	877
FIDLER, POMP	1810	SUFF	HUNT	514
FIELD, ALEXANDER	1810	NYCO	WD03	46
FIELD, CEASER	1820	QUEN	----	54
FIELD, DORRAS	1810	NYCO	WD08	722
FIELD, HANNAH	1820	NYCO	WD06	462
FIELD, JACOB	1810	NYCO	WD07	599
FIELD, QUAM	1830	DUTC	DOVE	221
FIELD, SAMUEL	1820	NYCO	WD08	827
FIELD, TIMOTHY	1820	WEST	MTPL	254

NAME	YR	CO	TWP	PG
FIELDS, DAVID	1820	ROCK	CLAK	92
FIELDS, DAVID	1830	WEST	GREN	13
FIELDS, EDWARD	1830	NYCO	WD05	337
FIELDS, HANNAH	1830	NYCO	WD03	112
FIELDS, JACOB	1830	DUTC	FISH	471
FIELDS, JOHN	1830	KING	WD04	297
FIELDS, QUAM	1820	DUTC	DOVE	51
FIELDS, ROBERT	1800	NYCO	WD03	702
FIELDS, SAMUEL	1830	NYCO	WD08	128
FIELDS, WILLIAM	1830	ERIE	BUFF	5
FIETLD, PETER	1800	NYCO	WD07	889
FIGAMO, JOHN F.	1830	ULST	MARL	279
FIGAR	1820	ULST	MARB	54
FILIAT, MAMELA	1810	NYCO	WD05	273
FILLYUELL, ANTHONY	1820	ORNG	MONT	843
FINE, JENNY	1800	NYCO	WD02	675
FINGER, SAMUEL	1830	DUTC	REDH	366
FINLEY, AARON	1820	WEST	HARR	467
FINMOCK, WILLIAM	1830	NYCO	WD03	129
FINN, NICHOLAS	1830	ORNG	CALH	18
FINNEY, ELIZABETH	1800	NYCO	WD02	683
FINNEY, JAMES	1830	NYCO	WD04	218
FINSELL, JOSEPH	1820	NYCO	WD07	634
FIRCHER, JANNIS	1820	WEST	NEWR	212
FIRD, ADAM	1830	NYCO	WD10	60
FIRGERSON, RICHARD	1820	NYCO	WD10	982
FISH, ALEXANDER	1790	DUTC	RHIN	92
FISH, ALEXANDER	1800	DUTC	RHIN	159
FISH, ALEXANDER	1820	DUTC	REDH	119
FISH, ISAAC	1810	QUEN	OYST	256
FISH, JACOB	1830	DUTC	REDH	366
FISH, MARGET	1810	KING	BRYN	632
FISH, MRS.	1830	KING	WD04	316
FISH, ROBBIN	1820	QUEN	----	79
FISHER	1810	NYCO	WD06	409
FISHER, ANTHONY	1830	NYCO	WD14	475
FISHER, CASTHAREIN	1820	NYCO	WD10	988
FISHER, CUFF	1820	WEST	SCAR	282
FISHER, ELEANOR	1830	NYCO	WD08	234A
FISHER, HENRY	1800	NYCO	WD07	869
FISHER, J.	1830	NYCO	WD13	403
FISHER, JACK	1810	ORNG	NEWB	927
FISHER, JACK	1830	COLU	CHAT	40
FISHER, JAM	1830	DUTC	AMEN	179
FISHER, JOHN	1820	DUTC	FISH	76
FISHER, JOHN	1820	ORNG	NEWB	514
FISHER, MENTOR	1830	NYCO	WD08	206
FISHER, MOSES	1800	NYCO	WD07	891
FISHER, MOSES	1810	NYCO	WD07	589

NAME	YR	CO	TWP	PG
FISHER, SUSAN	1830	NYCO	WD05	311
FISK, ALEXANDER	1810	DUTC	RHIN	436
FIT, MRS.	1820	NYCO	WD03	184
FITCH, HENRY	1830	SARA	MILT	25
FITCHET, RICHARD	1830	GREN	GREN	156
FITLAND, CHARLES	1810	SCNE	WD01	938
FITZGERALD, JAMES	1810	NYCO	WD05	318
FITZGERALDS, THOMAS	1820	JEFF	WILN	492
FITZSIMMONS, HENRY	1830	NYCO	WD09	340
FLEET, CHARLES	1820	NYCO	WD03	139
FLEET, PETER	1830	SUFF	HUNT	301
FLEMING, JANE	1830	NYCO	WD05	352
FLEMING, JOSEPH	1810	NYCO	WD05	286
FLEMING, PERINAS	1810	NYCO	WD05	370
FLEMING, SABINA	1820	NYCO	WD05	369
FLEMING, THOMAS	1810	NYCO	WD05	340
FLETCHER, A.	1810	DUTC	PGKP	324
FLETCHER, ARCHELAUS	1820	ONTA	CANA	210
FLETCHER, ARCHELAUS	1830	ONTA	CANA	119
FLETCHER, ARCHELES	1810	ONTA	CANA	888
FLETCHER, JAMES	1820	ONTA	CANA	210
FLETCHER, PHOEBE	1830	ONTA	CANA	119
FLETCHER, RUFUS	1830	SUFF	SHAM	212
FLETCHER, WILLIAM	1830	NYCO	WD01	16
FLINT, WILLIAM	1820	NYCO	WD09	875
FLORA	1820	SARA	STIL	190
FLORENCE, JANE	1830	NYCO	WD06	389
FLORIS	1790	NYCO	NORT	126
FLORNBECK, DIANAH	1820	ORNG	NEWB	518
FLORO, HANNAH	1830	NYCO	WD05	260
FLOWE, J.	1810	ONID	DEER	471
FLOYD, ABRAHAM	1830	NYCO	WD07	30
FLOYD, ISAAC	1820	SUFF	BROK	355
FLOYD, ISAAC	1830	SUFF	BROK	193
FLOYD, LEWIS	1810	QUEN	OYST	244
FLOYD, MICHAEL	1830	SUFF	SMIT	268
FLOYD, RUTH	1830	SUFF	BROK	167
FLOYD, TEMP	1810	SUFF	BROK	469
FLUT, STEPHEN	1810	QUEN	OYST	260
FO, THOMAS	1830	DUTC	FISH	504
FOD, SAMUEL	1800	NYCO	WD07	910
FOGDEN, CHARLES	1830	MONR	BRIG	15
FOGGUSON, MARY	1810	KING	BRYM	632
FOLLOWER, PETER	1830	NYCO	WD11	201
FOLLYS	1810	NYCO	WD05	250
FONDA, LONDON	1830	MONT	BROA	138
FOOT, ASHER	1820	ABNY	ABNY	167
FOOT, HARRY	1830	DUTC	PGKP	325
FOOT, PHILIP	1820	GREN	CATS	161

NAME	YR	CO	TWP	PG
FOOTE, HARARD	1810	NYCO	WD05	250
FOOTHER, JOHN	1820	NYCO	WD06	481
FORBUS, SARAH	1800	NYCO	WD05	773
FORD, DAVID	1830	WEST	CORT	74
FORD, NATHANIEL	1820	WEST	EAST	204
FORD, NATHANIEL	1830	WEST	EAST	131
FORD, NATHENIAL	1810	WEST	EAST	1155
FORD, PHILLIS	1800	WEST	EAST	619
FORD, THOMAS	1820	WEST	EAST	204
FORD, THOMAS	1830	WEST	EAST	134
FORDAM, SAMUEL	1820	KING	BRYN	117
FORDHAM, SIMAS	1820	SUFF	SHAM	303
FORDUM, CUFF	1820	ALLE	ORCE	94
FOREST, BETSY	1800	NYCO	WD05	757
FORGUS, JAMES	1800	NYCO	WD02	677
FORMAN, D.	1830	NYCO	WD11	155
FORREST, GLASGOW	1820	NYCO	WD06	455
FORREST, GLASPER	1810	NYCO	WD06	424
FORT, HAZARD	1800	NYCO	WD06	849
FORT, THOMAS	1830	DUTC	PLEA	313
FORTEN, PETER	1820	ROCK	ORGT	85
FORTUNE	1790	NYCO	NORT	126
FORTUNE	1790	QUEN	FLUS	149
FORTUNE	1820	RICH	NORT	109
FORTUNE, ENOCH	1790	MONT	WAIT	115
FORTUNE, CHARLES	1810	COLU	LIVG	224
FORTUNE, DAVID	1810	NYCO	WD05	316
FORTUNE, ENOCH	1800	ONID	DEER	109
FORTUNE, HARRY	1820	ONID	BRID	232
FORTUNE, HARRY	1830	OTSG	PITT	313
FORTUNE, ISAAC	1810	NYCO	WD04	188
FORTUNE, JOHN	1800	NYCO	WD05	784
FORTUNE, NANCY	1790	NYCO	DOCK	117
FORTUNE, PETER	1800	ROCK	ORGT	1032
FORTUNE, PETER	1810	ROCK	ORGT	636
FORTUNE, PETER	1830	ROCK	ORGT	112
FORTUNET, FRANCIS	1830	NYCO	WD10	75
FOSBURGH, POMP	1830	COLU	CLER	272
FOSTER, ANN	1820	NYCO	WD07	707
FOSTER, ANTHONY	1820	WEST	HARR	467
FOSTER, CEASAR	1820	ABNY	ABNY	167
FOSTER, FERDINANDO	1800	DUTC	NORT	146
FOSTER, JOHN	1810	NYCO	WD04	205
FOSTER, JOHN	1830	WEST	MTPL	51
FOSTER, MARY ANN	1830	NYCO	WD14	504
FOSTER, RICHARD	1800	SUFF	SHAM	67
FOSTER, RICHARD	1810	SUFF	SHAM	439
FOSTER, RICHARD	1820	SUFF	ISLP	309
FOSTER, SAMUEL	1830	KING	WD04	307

NAME	YR	CO	TWP	PG
FOSTER, WILLIAM	1830	NYCO	WD10	107
FOSTER, WILLIAM	1830	QUEN	JAMA	134
FOSTER, SARAH	1810	NYCO	WD10	672
FOUMENIAR, BENJERMIN	1820	COLU	HUDS	11
FOUNTAIN, JAMES	1830	ONID	UTIC	18
FOUNTAIN, PETER	1830	NYCO	WD14	457
FOWLER, ABEL	1790	DUTC	WASH	95
FOWLER, ABEL	1800	DUTC	NORT	146
FOWLER, ABEL	1810	DUTC	NORT	340
FOWLER, AMOS	1820	ONTA	ITAL	198
FOWLER, BENJAMIN	1830	ONID	MARS	134
FOWLER, BENJAMIN	1830	QUEN	OYST	34
FOWLER, BENJAMIN H.	1820	DUTC	NORT	87
FOWLER, CHAPMAN F.	1830	ORNG	MONR	161
FOWLER, DAVID	1800	DUTC	PGKP	67
FOWLER, GARAH	1820	NYCO	WD10	981
FOWLER, HARVEY	1830	DUTC	PINE	293
FOWLER, JOHN	1820	DUTC	NORT	84
FOWLER, JOHN	1830	CHEN	NORW	161
FOWLER, JOHN	1830	ORNG	NEWB	22
FOWLER, MRS.	1810	NYCO	WD06	429
FOWLER, NANCY	1830	NYCO	WD01	31
FOWLER, RICHARD	1830	NYCO	WD06	379
FOWLER, TOBIAS	1790	DUTC	FISH	81
FOWLER, WILLIAM	1820	NYCO	WD07	715
FOWLER, WILLIAM	1830	QUEN	FLUS	149
FOWLER, ZEP	1810	DUTC	STAN	180
FOWLER, ZEPHAMIAH	1820	DUTC	STAN	139
FOWLER, ZEPHANIAH	1830	DUTC	PINE	294
FOWLER, ZEPHENIAH	1800	DUTC	STAN	127
FOX, ANTHONY	1800	DUTC	PGKP	60
FOX, ANTHONY	1820	DUTC	PGKP	108
FOX, GEORGE	1830	NYCO	WD06	414
FOX, HARRY	1820	DUTC	PGKP	106
FOX, JAMES	1810	QUEN	NHEM	218
FOXHOLE, WILLIAM	1800	NYCO	WD03	708
FRALER, LEANDER	1830	COLU	HUDS	106
FRAM, A.	1830	NYCO	WD13	396
FRANCES	1810	COLU	HUDS	150
FRANCES, ADAM	1800	NYCO	WD03	708
FRANCES, BRISTERS	1830	WEST	EAST	131
FRANCES, CUFFY	1800	NYCO	WD07	927
FRANCES, DINAH	1800	NYCO	WD06	831
FRANCES, JACOB	1800	NYCO	WD06	797
FRANCES, JOHN	1800	NYCO	WD06	831
FRANCES, JOHN	1830	SCNE	WD02	219
FRANCES, LEWIS	1800	NYCO	WD06	843

NAME	YR	CO	TWP	PG
FRANCES, MR.	1830	KING	WD05	335
FRANCES, MR.	1830	NYCO	WD10	66
FRANCES, PAUL	1810	DUTC	CLNT	378
FRANCES, PERO	1800	NYCO	WD07	883
FRANCES, TIMOTHY	1830	WEST	EAST	135
FRANCIS	1790	QUEN	NEWT	151
FRANCIS	1790	WEST	NORC	203
FRANCIS	1800	RENS	TROY	899
FRANCIS	1810	NYCO	WD07	559
FRANCIS	1810	NYCO	WD07	574
FRANCIS	1820	NYCO	WD05	430
FRANCIS	1820	NYCO	WD07	627
FRANCIS, ADAM	1810	NYCO	WD04	223
FRANCIS, ANTHONY	1810	NYCO	WD03	80
FRANCIS, ASA	1830	NYCO	WD11	203
FRANCIS, BRISTER	1820	WEST	EAST	203
FRANCIS, CAPRICE	1820	ROCK	HAVE	104
FRANCIS, CAPRICE	1830	NYCO	WD08	246
FRANCIS, CEASAR	1810	NYCO	WD03	113
FRANCIS, CIPIO	1800	NYCO	WD05	775
FRANCIS, CUFFEE	1820	NYCO	WD10	1056
FRANCIS, DIANAH	1830	NYCO	WD05	338
FRANCIS, DICK	1820	DUTC	PGKP	106
FRANCIS, FRANCIS	1810	NYCO	WD04	208
FRANCIS, FRANCIS	1830	NYCO	WD04	159
FRANCIS, J.	1820	NYCO	WD10	1100
FRANCIS, JACOB	1810	NYCO	WD02	100
FRANCIS, JACOB	1830	NIAG	PEND	426
FRANCIS, JACOB	1830	NYCO	WD05	346
FRANCIS, JACOB	1830	NYCO	WD09	399
FRANCIS, JANE	1830	ABNY	WD04	299
FRANCIS, JANET	1810	NYCO	WD06	413
FRANCIS, JOHN	1810	NYCO	WD05	271
FRANCIS, JOHN	1810	NYCO	WD06	397
FRANCIS, JOHN	1810	NYCO	WD06	415
FRANCIS, JOHN	1820	QUEN	----	38
FRANCIS, JOHN	1830	MONT	FLOR	103
FRANCIS, JOHN	1830	NYCO	WD06	437
FRANCIS, JOHN	1830	NYCO	WD10	26
FRANCIS, JOHN	1830	RICH	SOUT	17
FRANCIS, JOHNATHAN	1830	NYCO	WD14	435
FRANCIS, JOHN S.	1830	NYCO	WD05	308
FRANCIS, JOSEPH	1810	NYCO	WD05	344
FRANCIS, JOSEPH	1820	NYCO	WD09	930
FRANCIS, LEWIS	1810	NYCO	WD06	436
FRANCIS, MARGARET	1810	NYCO	WD04	193
FRANCIS, MARGARET	1820	NYCO	WD10	980
FRANCIS, MARGARET	1830	DUTC	PGKP	322

NAME	YR	CO	TWP	PG
FRANCIS, MARGARET A.	1830	NYCO	WD08	216A
FRANCIS, MARY	1820	ABNY	ABNY	165
FRANCIS, MRS.	1830	KING	WD05	325
FRANCIS, PAUL	1820	DUTC	CLNT	43
FRANCIS, PAUL	1830	DUTC	PLEA	309
FRANCIS, PEGGY	1800	NYCO	WD05	765
FRANCIS, PETER	1810	SARS	MILT	795
FRANCIS, PETER	1820	SARA	MILT	236
FRANCIS, PETER	1830	SARA	MALT	56
FRANCIS, RICHARD	1830	ONID	WESM	456
FRANCIS, SAMUEL	1820	ALLE	RUSH	4
FRANCIS, SAMUEL	1820	NYCO	WD04	226
FRANCIS, SAMUEL	1830	ALLE	HAIG	121
FRANCIS, SAMUEL	1830	NYCO	WD14	488
FRANCIS, SARAH	1810	NYCO	WD10	698
FRANCIS, SARAH	1830	NYCO	WD10	66
FRANCIS, THOMAS	1800	DUTC	CLNT	121
FRANCIS, THOMAS	1800	NYCO	WD06	847
FRANCIS, THOMAS	1810	NYCO	WD06	419
FRANCIS, THOMAS	1820	NYCO	WD06	450
FRANCIS, THOMAS	1830	NYCO	WD08	271
FRANCIS, THOMAS A.	1810	NYCO	WD06	291
FRANCIS, TOM	1830	SARA	CTPK	139
FRANCIS, WD.	1830	SARA	MILT	30
FRANCIS, WIDOW	1830	NYCO	WD13	364
FRANCIS, WILLIAM	1810	NYCO	WD02	102
FRANCIS, WILLIAM	1830	NYCO	WD05	335
FRANCIS, WILLIAM	1830	RENS	TROY	15
FRANCIS, WILLIAM	1830	ROCK	ORGT	107
FRANEWAY, JOHN	1810	NYCO	WD05	314
FRANK	1790	NYCO	MONT	120
FRANK	1790	QUEN	JAMA	150
FRANK	1800	ABNY	WD02	281
FRANK	1800	COLU	LIVG	1108
FRANK	1810	NYCO	WD07	584
FRANK	1820	SUFF	SMIT	320
FRANK	1820	WASH	YOUC	205
FRANK, AARON	1830	NYCO	WD14	525
FRANK, JEREMY	1820	CHEN	NORW	176
FRANK, JEREMY	1820	CHEN	NORW	194
FRANK, PETER	1830	HERK	SALB	72
FRANKINSON, SYLVIA	1800	DUTC	----	138
FRANKLIN, FRANCIS	1790	DUTC	SOUT	93
FRANKLIN, HARRY	1830	KING	WD04	319
FRANKLIN, HENRY	1830	RENS	PETE	170
FRANKLIN, JAMES	1810	NYCO	WD03	83
FRANKLIN, JAMES	1810	NYCO	WD04	159
FRANKLIN, JAMES	1820	NYCO	WD07	686
FRANKLIN, JAMES	1830	NYCO	WD11	182
FRANKLIN, JOHN	1820	NYCO	WD10	1075
FRANKLIN, MARY	1810	NYCO	WD05	355

NAME	YR	CO	TWP	PG
FRANKLIN, NATHAN	1820	ONTA	CANA	224
FRANKLIN, NATHAN	1830	ONTA	CANA	122
FRANKLIN, NATHANIEL	1830	WEST	EAST	134
FRANKLIN, P.	1830	NYCO	WD13	392
FRANKLIN, R.	1810	NIAG	BUFF	234
FRANKLIN, SAMUEL	1830	ABNY	WD04	319
FRANKLIN, SAMUEL	1830	ULST	NPAL	213
FRANKLIN, STEPHEN	1830	NYCO	WD08	226
FRANKLIN, THOMAS	1830	KING	FLAN	412
FRANKLIN, WILLIAM	1820	NYCO	WD06	536
FRANKLIN, WILLIAM	1830	NYCO	WD09	390
FRASEE, ISABELLA	1810	NYCO	WD05	286
FRASER, ADAM	1800	DUTC	NORT	145
FRASER, ADAM	1820	DUTC	NORT	84
FRASER, ADAM	1830	DUTC	PINE	295
FRASER, AMANDA	1830	NYCO	WD06	466
FRASER, ANDREW	1820	DUTC	MILN	82
FRASER, DIANA	1830	NYCO	WD06	367
FRASER, FERDINANDO	1790	DUTC	NORT	85
FRASER, JAMES	1830	NYCO	WD06	441
FRASER, JAMES	1830	NYCO	WD08	220
FRASER, JOHN	1830	DUTC	AMEN	168
FRASER, NANCY	1810	NYCO	WD05	344
FRASER, ROBERT	1820	DUTC	MILN	82
FRASER, ROBERT	1830	DUTC	MILN	265
FRASER, ROBERT	1830	NYCO	WD05	336
FRASIER, ADAM	1810	DUTC	NORT	455
FRASKER, ANDREW	1820	DUTC	STAN	137
FRASUR, JOHN	1820	DUTC	STAN	135
FRAY, BOSS	1790	COLU	HUDS	66
FRAY, JANE	1790	COLU	HUDS	66
FRAYER, DINAH	1830	NYCO	WD05	260
FRAZER, ANDREW	1830	DUTC	STAN	405
FRAZER, GEORGE	1830	NYCO	WD05	281
FRAZIEL, ROBERT	1810	NYCO	WD06	410
FRAZIER, JANE	1820	NYCO	WD10	992
FRAZIER, JOHN	1830	QUEN	JAMA	124
FRAZIER, ROBERT	1820	NYCO	WD10	1006
FREDERICK, CHARLES	1810	COLU	HUDS	121
FREDERICK, PRINCE	1800	ORNG	MINI	321
FREDERICK, PRINCE	1810	ULST	PLAT	717
FREE, ISAAC	1800	WEST	NEWR	622
FREE, JACOB	1800	ORNG	DEER	313
FREE, JACOB	1820	ORNG	DEER	661
FREE, RHODA	1800	ORNG	GOSH	359
FREE, ROBERT	1830	ORNG	CALH	17
FREE, THOMAS	1820	RICH	WEST	101
FREEBORN, RICHARD	1830	NYCO	WD05	341
FREEDOM, RICHARD	1800	DUTC	PGKP	71
FREELAND, ANN	1810	NYCO	WD05	283

NAME	YR	CO	TWP	PG
FREELAND, JACK	1830	HERK	GERM	138
FREELAND, PRIMUS	1830	NYCO	WD06	446
FREELOVE	1790	QUEN	NHEM	152
FREEMAN, ABRAHAM	1820	NYCO	WD02	95
FREEMAN, ALEXANDER	1820	DUTC	FISH	74
FREEMAN, ALEXANDER	1830	NYCO	WD10	46
FREEMAN, ANDREW	1790	DUTC	RHIN	92
FREEMAN, ARTILLO	1810	WEST	WEST	1153
FREEMAN, BEN	1810	COLU	HUDS	141
FREEMAN, BENJAMIN	1830	ULST	MARB	154
FREEMAN, CASPER	1830	COLU	CLAV	75
FREEMAN, CEASAR	1820	DUTC	BEEK	18
FREEMAN, CESAR	1800	COLU	LIVG	1127
FREEMAN, CESAR	1830	DUTC	BEEK	187
FREEMAN, CHARLES	1800	DUTC	BEEK	16
FREEMAN, CHARLES	1810	DUTC	BEEK	274
FREEMAN, CHARLES	1820	DUTC	BEEK	18
FREEMAN, CHARLES	1820	ESEX	WILL	35
FREEMAN, CHARLES	1820	ESEX	WILL	460
FREEMAN, CHARLES	1820	NYCO	WD02	97
FREEMAN, CHARLES	1830	DUTC	BEEK	192
FREEMAN, CHARLES	1830	ESEX	WILL	336
FREEMAN, CHARLES	1830	NYCO	WD13	336
FREEMAN, CUFF	1810	NYCO	WD02	124
FREEMAN, CUFFEY	1800	NYCO	WD03	706
FREEMAN, DANEA	1820	NYCO	WD06	517
FREEMAN, DICK	1800	WEST	POUN	834
FREEMAN, DINAH	1830	NYCO	WD08	213
FREEMAN, ELIAS	1830	NYCO	WD10	95
FREEMAN, FRANCIS	1830	ORNG	WARW	76
FREEMAN, HANNIBAL	1790	DUTC	RHIN	92
FREEMAN, HARRY	1830	CAYU	AUBN	157
FREEMAN, HARRY	1830	ESEX	CHES	245
FREEMAN, HENRY	1800	NYCO	WD01	667
FREEMAN, HENRY	1830	MONT	OPEN	256
FREEMAN, JAMES	1830	NYCO	WD11	195
FREEMAN, JANE	1830	ROCK	RPOO	89
FREEMAN, JEREMIAH	1830	MADI	----	395
FREEMAN, JEREMIAH	1830	MONR	BRIG	8
FREEMAN, JETHERS	1830	MONT	PALA	165
FREEMAN, JOHN	1810	DUTC	FISH	258
FREEMAN, JOHN	1830	COLU	CLAV	75
FREEMAN, JOHN	1830	MONR	RWD1	195
FREEMAN, JOHN	1830	NYCO	WD06	447
FREEMAN, JOHNATHAN	1830	NYCO	WD09	385
FREEMAN, JOSEPH	1790	DUTC	PAWL	91
FREEMAN, JOSEPH	1810	NYCO	WD06	493
FREEMAN, JOSEPH	1830	MONT	FLOR	97
FREEMAN, JUDITH	1800	NYCO	WD01	66

NAME	YR	CO	TWP	PG
FREEMAN, JUDITH	1830	ALLE	BIRD	53
FREEMAN, LEWIS	1830	NYCO	WD12	310
FREEMAN, MARTIN	1810	DELA	DARP	598
FREEMAN, MARTIN	1820	SCNE	SCNE	129
FREEMAN, MARTIN	1830	SARA	MILT	30
FREEMAN, MATTHIAS	1790	DUTC	RINE	92
FREEMAN, MOSES	1830	LEWI	DENM	418
FREEMAN, NICHOLAS	1830	MONT	OPEN	255
FREEMAN, OBED	1820	ONID	AUGU	320
FREEMAN, OMPEDOR	1820	DUTC	PGKP	107
FREEMAN, PETER	1810	MONT	PALA	128
FREEMAN, PETER	1830	GREN	DURH	269
FREEMAN, PHELIP	1820	ONID	AUGU	320
FREEMAN, PHILIP	1820	ONID	AUGU	320
FREEMAN, PHILIP	1830	DUTC	FISH	487
FREEMAN, PHILIP	1830	MADI	----	416
FREEMAN, PHILLIP	1810	DUTC	FISH	218
FREEMAN, PHILLIP	1820	DUTC	FISH	59
FREEMAN, PHILLIS	1830	ORNG	DEER	9
FREEMAN, PLYMOUTH	1820	MADI	NELS	63
FREEMAN, PRIMUS	1800	DUTC	FISH	18
FREEMAN, R.M.	1830	NYCO	WD06	438
FREEMAN, RICHARD	1790	COLU	CLAV	62
FREEMAN, RICHARD	1800	NYCO	WD05	778
FREEMAN, RICHARD	1820	HERK	GERM	103
FREEMAN, RICHARD	1830	HERK	MANH	118
FREEMAN, RICHARD	1830	NYCO	WD06	458
FREEMAN, RICHARD	1830	ROCK	CLAR	132
FREEMAN, RICHARD	1830	ROCK	HVER	151
FREEMAN, ROBERT	1790	DUTC	FRED	84
FREEMAN, ROBERT	1810	ROCK	HVER	657
FREEMAN, ROBIN	1800	ULST	MARB	203
FREEMAN, SAMUEL	1790	ORNG	ORNG	146
FREEMAN, SAMUEL	1800	ROCK	ORGT	1035
FREEMAN, SAMUEL	1830	ROCK	RPOO	100
FREEMAN, SPENCER	1820	ONIC	WHIT	303
FREEMAN, SPENCER	1820	ONID	WATE	303
FREEMAN, SPENCER	1830	ONID	ROME	406
FREEMAN, STEPHEN	1830	NYCO	WD08	230
FREEMAN, SYLVANUS	1830	DUTC	BEEK	192
FREEMAN, SYLVENUS	1820	DUTC	BEEK	18
FREEMAN, THOMAS	1830	MONT	PALA	165
FREEMAN, THOMAS	1830	ROCK	HVER	150
FREEMAN, TRUMAN	1820	GREN	ATHE	7
FREEMAN, TRUMAN	1830	GREN	ATHN	210
FREEMAN, WILLIAM	1830	NYCO	WD09	342
FREEMAN, WILLIAM	1830	ROCK	ORGT	112
FREEMAN, WILLIAM	1830	ROCK	CLAR	132

NAME	YR	CO	TWP	PG
FREEMAN, WILLIAM M.	1830	NYCO	WD09	302
FREEMAN, YILLOW	1820	NYCO	WD05	427
FREEMAN, YORK	1820	CLNT	BEEK	429
FREEMAN, YORK	1830	NYCO	WD14	466
FREEMAN, ZACHARIAH	1810	ONON	CICE	589
FREEMAN, ZACHARIAH	1830	ONON	VANB	120
FREEMON, PHILLESA	1820	ORNG	MINI	575
FREER, JOHN A.	1810	ULST	NPAL	697
FREER, WILLIAM	1830	ULST	NPAL	228
FREER, WILLIAM A.	1830	ULST	NPAL	229
FREGAN, AUGUSTUS	1830	ABNY	WD02	274
FREMAN, ROBERT	1820	ROCK	HAVE	108
FREMAN, WILLIAMS	1830	MONR	RWD1	19
FREMEN, LEWIS	1830	COLU	STUY	60
FREMOR, THOMAS	1830	RICH	SOUT	17
FRENCH, BILLY	1810	QUEN	NEWT	173
FRENCH, JACK	1810	QUEN	NEWT	171
FRENCH, JOHN	1810	NYCO	WD06	470
FRENCH, JOHN	1830	ABNY	WD01	212
FRENCHY, RACHEL	1790	ULST	WOOD	185
FRENTY, PERRY	1830	NYCO	WD14	456
FRIMAN, DAVID S.	1820	COLU	CANN	5
FRINBY, INS	1820	NYCO	WD10	987
FRISBEE, JOHN	1830	KING	WD04	316
FRISBY, ALEXANDER	1830	NYCO	WD08	249
FROST, BENJAMIN	1810	NYCO	WD06	430
FROST, ISAAC	1820	SARA	SARA	198
FROST, ISSAC	1820	ULST	SAUG	83
FROST, ISAAC	1830	NYCO	WD07	18
FROST, ISAAC	1830	SCHR	BROM	92
FROST, MORRIS	1830	QUEN	OYST	43
FROST, WIDOW	1810	NYCO	WD07	549
FRUMAN, ARTELLO	1800	NYCO	WD06	827
FRUMAN, CACELIA	1810	NYCO	WD05	250
FRY, DANBY	1830	JEFF	PHIL	225
FRY, HARRY	1830	ONON	SALI	31
FRY, JAMES	1830	SENE	TYRE	37
FRY, WILLIAM	1830	SARA	WATE	38
FULER, BENJAMIN	1820	COLU	HUDS	11
FULLER	1820	ESEX	ELIZ	414
FULLER, ABEL	1800	GREN	COSE	1108
FULLER, ISAAC	1830	NYCO	WD14	503
FULLER, LEMUEL	1820	DUTC	PGKP	107
FULLER, P.	1820	COLU	KIND	7
FULLER, PRINCE	1810	NYCO	WD05	323
FULLER, PRINCE	1820	NYCO	WD08	810
FULTON, CHARLES	1830	ORNG	WALL	138
FULTON, GEORGE	1830	KING	BRYN	344
FULTON, ISAAC	1830	ORLE	ALBN	6

NAME	YR	CO	TWP	PG
FURGERSON, DIANNA	1830	KING	WD04	297
FURGESAN, ABRAHAM	1820	KING	BRYN	136
FURGESAN, MARY	1820	KING	BRYN	126
FURGESAN, MRS.	1820	KING	BRYN	130
FURGESON, HENRY	1830	KING	FLAN	412
FURGESON, JOHN	1800	NYCO	WD07	864
FURGESON, TENE	1830	KING	WD01	246
FURGISON, WILLIAM	1810	NYCO	WD07	591
FURGUSON, BENJAMIN	1800	NYCO	WD07	917
FURGUSON, C.	1830	NYCO	WD03	143
FURMAN, ABRAHAM	1830	NYCO	WD08	198
FURMAN, BENJAMIN	1810	DUTC	PHIL	100
FURMAN, BENJAMIN	1820	DUTC	PGKP	107
FURMAN, BENJAMIN	1830	KING	WD05	327
FURMAN, ELIAS	1820	KING	BRYN	133
FURMAN, GEORGE	1820	NYCO	WD07	620
FURMAN, JAMES	1810	QUEN	FLUS	191
FURMAN, JAMES	1830	NYCO	WD08	255
FURMAN, JOSEPH	1820	KING	BRYN	136
FURMAN, RICHARD	1820	NYCO	WD09	874
FURMAN, RICHARD	1830	NYCO	WD09	303
FURMAN, SALLY	1820	NYCO	WD06	477
FURMAN, SAMUEL	1810	ONTA	CANA	892
FURMAN, TOM	1790	QUEN	FLUS	149
FUROS, JOHN	1820	NYCO	WD09	927
FURY, WILLIAM	1820	QUEN	----	38
FUTHILL, ISAAC	1820	ORNG	GOSH	737
FUTHILL, JEREMIAH	1820	ORNG	BLOM	714
GABRICE, PETER	1820	SUFF	EAST	295
GABRIEL	1790	NYCO	NORT	127
GABRIEL, F.	1830	NYCO	WD13	384
GABRIEL, JOHN	1810	NYCO	WD05	367
GABRIEL, JOSEPH	1810	NYCO	WD04	159
GAINER, JOHN	1820	NYCO	WD10	989
GAINES, DAVID	1830	NYCO	WD08	255
GAINES, ROSANAH	1830	NYCO	WD10	14
GAIT, WILLIAM	1820	NYCO	WD02	86
GALATIAN, GEORGE	1830	ORNG	CRAW	184
GALB, JOSEPH	1810	QUEN	FLUS	197
GALBRIANE, WILLIAM	1820	NYCO	WD05	393
GALE	1810	DUTC	PGKP	171
GALE, ABRAHAM	1810	WEST	NORS	1043
GALE, ABRAHAM	1820	WEST	NORS	387
GALE, ANDREW	1830	ORNG	MINI	260
GALE, EASOB	1820	WEST	HARR	467
GALE, EASOP	1830	WEST	HARR	215
GALE, ELIAS	1810	ORNG	CORN	1028

Gale

NAME	YR	CO	TWP	PG
GALE, ELIAS JR.	1800	ORNG	NEWC	394
GALE, ELLIE	1820	ORNG	CORN	705
GALE, WIDOW	1830	NYCO	WD09	353
GALL, B.	1830	NYCO	WD13	391
GALL, DAVID	1830	QUEN	OYST	47
GALL, DICK	1810	WEST	HARR	1131
GALL, EDWARD	1810	QUEN	FLUS	256
GALL, ISAAC	1830	ORNG	GOSH	286
GALL, JACOB	1800	ORNG	WARW	379
GALL, JACOB	1820	ORNG	WARW	633
GALL, JACOB	1830	QUEN	JAMA	135
GALL, JAMES	1810	QUEN	FLUS	258
GALL, JAMES	1830	NYCO	WD11	159
GALL, LENROW	1820	ULST	SHAW	65
GALL, MARGARET	1810	ULST	MARB	730
GALL, MARGARET	1820	ULST	MARB	54
GALL, MOSS	1830	WEST	NORS	84
GALL, SAMUEL	1810	QUEN	OYST	256
GALL, SAMUEL	1830	WEST	WEST	120
GALL, SAMUEL	1790	SUFF	HUNT	164
GALL, SIMON	1810	NYCO	WD03	68
GALL, TOWNSEND	1800	NYCO	WD07	878
GALLANTEE, HARRY	1820	DUTC	CLNT	40
GALLARY, JOHN	1810	NYCO	WD07	558
GALLAWAY, JOHN	1810	WEST	NORC	1172
GALLET, HARRY	1830	WEST	WEST	117
GAMBA, GASSET	1810	CHEN	SHER	1079
GAMBLE, JANE	1830	ORNG	WARW	78
GAMPSON, IRMA	1820	NYCO	WD10	991
GANCY, WILLIAM	1830	NYCO	WD06	401
GANNOW, SUSANNAH	1810	NYCO	WD05	249
GANON	1810	MADI	SMIT	880
GANTRANG, JAMES	1830	NYCO	WD09	334
GARDEN, CLARRISA	1830	MONR	RWD1	197
GARDEN, FLORA	1830	NYCO	WD08	257
GARDEN, SIMEON	1830	ORNG	MINI	246
GARDENER, HIRAM	1830	NYCO	WD06	430
GARDENER, JAMES	1810	DUTC	BEEK	294
GARDENER, JOHN	1830	NYCO	WD06	457
GARDENER, LUCE	1810	SUFF	EHAM	437
GARDENER, PAUL	1810	SUFF	SMIT	541
GARDENER, PETER	1810	QUEN	FLUS	201
GARDENER, THOMAS	1810	NYCO	WD07	531
GARDENIER, JOHN	1830	MADI	----	402
GARDINER, ABEL	1800	NYCO	WD05	775
GARDINER, BILLS	1820	SUFF	EAST	294
GARDINER, CATO	1820	SUFF	EAST	295
GARDINER, DAVID	1800	ORNG	GOSH	354
GARDINER, JAMES	1790	DUTC	PAWL	88

NAME	YR	CO	TWP	PG
GARDINER, JAMES	1800	DUTC	BEEK	11
GARDINER, NANCY	1830	WASH	KING	358
GARDINER, RICHARD	1830	ONON	SALI	3
GARDINER, SUCE	1820	SUFF	EAST	294
GARDINER, WILLIAM	1800	ONID	WHIT	185
GARDINER, WILLIAM	1830	SUFF	EAST	259
GARDINIER, THOMAS	1830	ABNY	WD02	256
GARDINIER, THOMAS	1830	MONT	JOHN	233
GARDINN, JOHN	1800	NYCO	WD04	736
GARDNER, AMY	1810	ORNG	GOSH	1131
GARDNER, DAVID	1810	ORNG	GOSH	1133
GARDNER, DUBLIN	1830	ORNG	GOSH	289
GARDNER, HENRY	1820	ORNG	CORN	711
GARDNER, HENRY	1830	ORNG	BLOM	114
GARDNER, HENRY	1830	ORNG	BLOM	118
GARDNER, ISAAC	1830	ONID	AUGU	112
GARDNER, JAMES	1830	NYCO	WD14	475
GARDNER, JOSEPH	1820	GREN	CATS	158
GARDNER, JULIA	1830	NYCO	WD10	97
GARDNER, MITCHELL	1830	NYCO	WD05	241
GARDNER, PETER	1800	NYCO	WD07	883
GARDNER, PHILLIS	1830	RENS	STEP	278
GARDNER, SAMUEL	1810	HERK	WARR	463
GARDNER, SAMUEL G.	1830	NYCO	WD04	158
GARDNER, SARAH	1830	QUEN	FLUS	147
GARDNER, ZEBEDEE	1810	WASH	GRAN	432
GARDORER, PRUDANA	1810	NYCO	WD05	353
GARISON, DAVID	1810	DUTC	NORT	341
GARNEFS, J.	1820	NYCO	WD10	999
GARNER	1830	NYCO	WD05	313
GARNER, GEORGE	1830	ONTA	MANC	172
GARNER, HARRY	1830	WEST	CORT	66
GARNER, JAMES	1820	DUTC	BEEK	21
GARNER, JAMES	1830	DUTC	UNVA	424
GARNER, SAMUEL	1820	DUTC	FISH	76
GARNET, GEORGE	1830	NYCO	WD08	246
GARNET, SOLOMON	1830	DUTC	MILN	257
GARNETT, WILLIAM	1820	NYCO	WD05	400
GARRETSON, HENRY	1830	RICH	WEST	8
GARRISON, CHARLES	1810	NYCO	WD06	410
GARRISON, DAVID	1820	DUTC	MILA	80
GARRISON, FORTUNE	1820	NYCO	WD07	625
GARRISON, GEORGE	1830	KING	BRYN	358
GARRISON, HANNAH	1810	NYCO	WD05	281
GARRISON, HARRY	1800	COLU	HILL	1190
GARRISON, HARRY	1830	DUTC	HYPK	232
GARRISON, HARRY	1830	NYCO	WD08	192
GARRISON, PETER	1810	NYCO	WD01	27
GARRISON, RICHARD	1810	NYCO	WD07	570

Garrison

NAME	YR	CO	TWP	PG
GARRISON, RICHARD	1820	NYCO	WD07	686
GARRISON, ROSE	1810	COLU	HILL	121
GARRISON, WILLIAM	1830	QUEN	FLUS	143
GARRISSON, CHRISTOPHER	1830	NYCO	WD06	398
GARRISSON, KING	1830	WEST	YORK	173
GARRITT, JOHN	1830	NYCO	WD08	226
GARTER, SAMUEL	1820	ORNG	MINI	579
GASAWAY, CHARLES	1830	QUEN	OYST	28
GASTON, JOHN	1810	NYCO	WD05	250
GASTON, JOSEPH	1830	NYCO	WD03	126
GATON, GODFRY	1830	STEU	POTT	382
GATON, JOHN JR.	1820	SENE	FAYE	372
GATTUS, J.	1820	NYCO	WD10	1055
GAUL, EDWARD	1820	QUEN	----	28
GAUL, HANNAH	1820	QUEN	----	28
GAUL, JACOB	1830	ORNG	WARW	92
GAUL, JAMES	1820	QUEN	----	27
GAUL, TOM	1790	QUEN	OYST	154
GAULD, ARCHIBALD	1820	STEU	READ	271
GAULDEN, GEORGE	1830	ABNY	WD02	245
GAUNTON, ANN	1800	ORNG	WARW	375
GAWN, LEMUEL	1820	DUTC	CLNT	43
GAYTON, HENRY	1830	ONTA	SENE	72
GAYTON, JOHN	1830	SENE	FAYE	62
GEAMAN, T.	1830	NYCO	WD11	234
GEDION, JOHN	1810	NYCO	WD05	294
GEIZER, JOHNATHAN	1830	NYCO	WD09	353
GELBY, CHARLES	1810	QUEN	OYST	256
GELEHNIST, JOSEPH	1810	NYCO	WD08	714
GELSTON, SALLY	1830	DUTC	REDH	375
GENIN, CYRUS	1820	SUFF	ISLP	306
GEORGE	1790	NYCO	MONT	120
GEORGE	1790	NYCO	OUTW	130
GEORGE	1790	NYCO	OUTW	131
GEORGE	1790	NYCO	WEST	134
GEORGE	1790	QUEN	FLUS	149
GEORGE	1790	QUEN	NHEM	152
GEORGE	1790	QUEN	OYST	155
GEORGE	1800	NYCO	WD05	757
GEORGE	1800	QUEN	FLUS	541
GEORGE	1800	QUEN	OYST	568
GEORGE	1800	WEST	PCHE	606
GEORGE	1810	COLU	CLAV	151
GEORGE	1810	COLU	GRAN	195
GEORGE	1810	NYCO	WD05	322
GEORGE	1830	KING	GRAV	406
GEORGE	1830	NYCO	WD11	166
GEORGE, CHARLES	1820	NYCO	WD05	350
GEORGE, DEBORAH	1830	NYCO	WD10	26

NAME	YR	CO	TWP	PG
GEORGE, HANNAH	1830	SUFF	SHAM	227
GEORGE, ISAAC	1820	NYCO	WD04	228
GEORGE, LOUISA	1800	NYCO	WD05	759
GEORGE, NANCY	1830	NYCO	WD06	388
GEORGE, PETER	1810	DUTC	PAWL	155
GEORGE, PRINCE	1790	DUTC	FRDK	82
GEORGE, PRINCE	1800	DUTC	FRAN	169
GEORGE, PRINCE	1820	DUTC	BEEK	18
GEORGE, SAMUEL	1800	NYCO	WD03	702
GERARD, CATO	1820	NYCO	WD05	383
GERARD, JOHN	1820	NYCO	WD06	489
GERARDUS	1790	QUEN	OYST	153
GERHARDY, JACOB	1820	KING	BRYN	143
GERLS, MARY	1800	SARA	GALW	1087
GERMAN, SUSAN	1830	NYCO	WD05	339
GERRY	1800	NYCO	WD06	810
GERRY, MARGARET	1830	NYCO	WD09	399
GERSEA, DAVID	1820	NYCO	WD10	1079
GIBBONS, JAMES	1830	NYCO	WD06	448
GIBBS, ISAAC	1830	MONR	RWD3	231
GIBBS, THOMAS	1810	NYCO	WD07	550
GIBBS, WILLIAM	1830	NYCO	WD08	219
GIBON, ABIGAIE	1820	QUEN	----	38
GIBSON, DARCUS	1830	NYCO	WD04	185
GIBSON, HENRY	1820	NYCO	WD05	348
GIBSON, JOHN	1830	NYCO	WD08	257
GIBSON, JOHN	1830	NYCO	WD10	18
GIBSON, THOMAS	1800	NYCO	WD06	848
GIDDY, DENNIS	1820	WEST	WEST	195
GIDEON	1790	SUFF	ISLP	165
GIDEON	1800	SUFF	ISLP	62
GIDNER, PRINCE	1810	WEST	GREN	1128
GIDNEY, PRINCE	1820	WEST	WTPL	461
GIDNEY, PRINCE	1830	WEST	WTPL	224
GIDNEY, RICHARD	1820	ORNG	NEWB	512
GIDNEY, RICHARD	1830	ORNG	NEWB	60
GIDNEY, ROBERT	1800	WEST	NEWR	623
GIDNEY, ROBERT	1810	WEST	NEWR	1081
GIDNEY, SIMON	1810	ULST	SHAW	689
GIDNEY, STEPHEN	1820	WEST	NEWR	215
GIDNEY, STEPHEN	1830	WEST	NEWR	112
GIGSBY, BARTLE	1810	NYCO	WD05	298
GILBERT	1800	SUFF	RIVH	19
GILBERT	1810	DUTC	WASH	162
GILBERT	1810	NYCO	WD06	491
GILBERT	1830	NYCO	WD11	178
GILBERT, CHARITY	1830	NYCO	WD09	430
GILBERT, CUFFEE	1830	NYCO	WD04	228
GILBERT, DINAH	1800	NYCO	WD03	705

NAME	YR	CO	TWP	PG
GILBERT, EDWARD	1830	ULST	WAWA	195
GILBERT, GILBERT	1810	KING	BRYN	636
GILBERT, JAMES	1830	NYCO	WD14	426
GILBERT, JOSIAH	1830	COLU	HUDS	102
GILBERT, MRS.	1830	NYCO	WD11	163
GILBERT, NATHAN	1800	CHEN	CARN	932
GILBERT, NATHAN	1810	MONT	MAYF	202
GILBERT, PETER	1830	HERK	FAIR	2
GILBERT, PETER S.	1830	STEU	PRAT	453
GILBERT, SAMUEL	1830	HERK	GERM	140
GILBORN, DANNA	1830	RENS	TROY	14
GILCHRIST, SOLOMON	1830	NYCO	WD07	46
GILCHRIST, SOLOMON	1830	NYCO	WD10	60
GILEAD, JABESH	1800	DUTC	WASH	101
GILECHRIST, MARY	1820	NYCO	WD06	502
GILES, ANGELICA	1830	ORNG	GOSH	290
GILES, ANN	1820	NYCO	WD05	390
GILES, DANIEL	1830	NYCO	WD06	377
GILES, JAMES	1820	NYCO	WD07	621
GILES, JEREMIAH	1830	NYCO	WD10	9
GILES, JOHN	1810	NYCO	WD03	83
GILES, PETER	1830	ROCK	HVER	147
GILES, PHILLIP	1800	NYCO	WD05	756
GILES, SAMUEL	1820	NYCO	WD08	731
GILES, SAMUEL	1830	NYCO	WD14	468
GILES, WILLIAM	1810	NYCO	WD04	154
GILIAND, PHILIP	1830	ONTA	SENE	85
GILISND, PHILLIP	1830	ONTA	SENE	85
GILL, DOCT	1820	KING	BRYN	132
GILLESPIE, DIANAH	1830	ULST	SHAW	248
GILLESPIE, JOHN	1810	NYCO	WD06	424
GILLESPIE, PETER	1820	ORNG	WARW	621
GILLESPIE, SIMON	1830	ULST	SHAW	251
GILLET, B.	1810	RENS	TROY	378
GILLET, BATTUS	1830	RENS	TROY	14
GILLET, PETER	1830	RENS	TROY	8
GILLISPIE, DIANNA	1810	ULST	SHAW	688
GILLOM, JOHN	1820	ONTA	SENE	277
GILLOM, PHILIP	1820	ONTA	SENE	269
GILMORE, RICHARD	1830	NYCO	WD08	175
GIMPSON, EPHRAIM	1830	RENS	BRUN	223
GINN	1820	SUFF	SMIT	321
GIRAUD, ELIZABETH	1830	NYCO	WD06	384
GIVENS, ANTHONY	1830	WEST	EAST	136
GIVENS, JOHN	1830	WEST	EAST	136
GIVENS, THOMAS	1810	ULST	KING	743
GIVENS, THOMAS	1830	SULL	NEVS	86
GLADDIN, PETER	1820	NYCO	WD07	671
GLANTIN, PRIMUS	1830	DUTC	PGKP	344

NAME	YR	CO	TWP	PG
GLARY, CHARLES	1820	DUTC	FISH	67
GLASLEY, JAMES	1810	NYCO	WD07	550
GLAWSON, THOMAS	1830	MONT	AMST	122
GLEN, THOMAS	1820	SCNE	WD02	130
GLONTON, JOHN	1810	DUTC	CLNT	392
GLORIANNA	1800	SUFF	HUNT	44
GOALD, MRS.	1810	NYCO	WD06	450
GOBB, PAUL	1820	LEWI	LOWV	51
GODFREE, JOHN	1800	RENS	STEP	929
GODFREE, SPENSER	1800	NYCO	WD07	878
GODFREY, EDWARD	1810	NYCO	WD04	236
GODFREY, GEORGE	1830	NYCO	WD07	38
GODFREY, SPENCER	1810	NYCO	WD10	668
GODNEY, MARGARET	1820	ULST	SHAW	67
GOELET, GEORGE	1830	NYCO	WD04	159
GOES, ABRAHAM	1810	COLU	KIND	174
GOES, OPE	1800	COLU	KIND	770
GOETEHES, HARRY	1820	GREN	CATS	162
GOETEHUS, TONI	1820	GREN	CATS	161
GOFF, HENRY	1820	ABNY	ABNY	170
GOFF, JOHN	1820	NYCO	WD06	527
GOGGILL, JACOB	1830	KING	WD04	321
GOIN, ELIZABETH	1830	NYCO	WD05	260
GOLB, JOSEPH	1810	QUEN	JAMA	7
GOLD, ISHAMEL	1810	DUTC	FISH	258
GOLD, LEWIS	1810	DUTC	FISH	244
GOLD, SHEM	1800	DUTC	FISH	29
GOLDEN, GEORGE	1820	ABNY	ABNY	170
GOLDEN, JAMES	1830	NYCO	WD06	410
GOLDEN, ROBERT	1800	ORNG	GOSH	280
GOLDERE, SAMUEL	1820	DUTC	FISH	71
GOLDING, SIMEON	1800	SUFF	ISLP	62
GOLDMAN, BENJAMIN	1810	NYCO	WD04	161
GOLDS, THEODORE	1830	DUTC	PGKP	326
GOLDSBURY, HENRY	1830	NYCO	WD04	197
GOLDSMITH, AMOS W.	1830	MONT	CANJ	36
GOLDSMITH, MATTY	1820	SUFF	SOUT	351
GOLDSMITH, MULLBY	1810	SUFF	SOUT	561
GOLDSMITH, RICHARD	1830	ORNG	MINI	260
GOLFY, AARON	1830	NYCO	WD11	203
GOLFY, JUDA	1830	NYCO	WD11	203
GOLLETT, BRISTER	1830	WEST	WEST	117
GOMAN, NERO	1810	SARA	BALL	748
GOMAN, THOMAS	1820	SARA	BALL	209
GOMAR, JOSEPH	1830	NYCO	WD05	336
GOMAR, MARIA	1830	SARA	BALL	10
GOMAS, SOPHIA	1830	NYCO	WD05	261
GOMER, RICHARD	1810	ULST	KING	757
GOMER, SAMUEL	1820	DUTC	FISH	71

NAME	YR	CO	TWP	PG
GOMER, SAMUEL	1830	DUTC	FISH	498
GOMER, SOL	1820	DUTC	FISH	76
GOMER, WARNER	1830	DUTC	PGKP	326
GOMES, LUCY	1830	NYCO	WD05	261
GOMEZ, B.	1830	NYCO	WD02	91
GOMEZ, JOHN	1820	NYCO	WD05	343
GOMMER, JOHN	1830	NYCO	WD05	303
GONUE, JAYNE	1830	SUFF	SHAM	215
GOODMAN, BRADLEY	1830	NYCO	WD10	6
GOODWIN, MRS.	1830	NYCO	WD06	455
GOODWIN, RACHAEL	1820	NYCO	WD10	975
GOOLD, FRANCES	1800	NYCO	WD03	702
GOOLEY, ADAM	1810	SUFF	BROK	492
GOOLO, CECLIA	1820	NYCO	WD02	131
GOORLACH, EDWARD	1800	NYCO	WD05	770
GOOSBERRY, THOMAS	1810	SCNE	WD02	953
GOOSNER, JOHNSON	1820	COLU	GHEN	7
GORAM, JACOB	1800	WEST	YORK	742
GORDEN, STEPHEN	1820	CLNT	CHAS	441
GORDENERE, RICHARD	1830	RENS	SCHO	248
GORDON, ABRAHAM	1830	NYCO	WD01	49
GORDON, ALBINA	1830	NYCO	WD06	399
GORDON, ANN	1830	NYCO	WD04	203
GORDON, PRINCE	1820	WASH	GRAN	136
GORDON, THOMAS	1800	WEST	YONK	610
GORGEN, ABRAHAM	1810	NYCO	WD02	108
GORGEN, JOHN	1810	NYCO	WD07	565
GOSEN, JAMES	1800	WASH	WHIT	548
GOSLIN, DAVID	1810	KING	BRYN	630
GOTH, P.	1810	MADI	HAML	845
GOTRON, JAS	1820	NYCO	WD08	853
GOUGH, HARVEY	1830	ABNY	WD05	339
GOULD, LEWIS	1820	DUTC	FISH	74
GOULD, LEWIS	1830	DUTC	FISH	469
GOULD, SIMEON	1830	DUTC	FISH	480
GOULDEN, SAMUEL	1830	DUTC	AMEN	170
GOURHIM, LEWIS	1820	NYCO	WD05	386
GOUSSAINT, VELMINERE	1800	NYCO	WD07	830
GRAHAM, ADAM	1810	WEST	YORK	1025
GRAHAM, ALEXANDER	1810	ONTA	SENE	846
GRAHAM, CHARLES	1830	MONR	RWD1	202
GRAHAM, ELIZABETH	1830	ONTA	SENE	85
GRAHAM, ELSE	1810	NYCO	WD03	44
GRAHAM, FEDRICK P.	1830	NYCO	WD06	402
GRAHAM, HECTOR	1800	ABNY	WD01	265
GRAHAM, HENRY	1820	ORNG	WALL	794
GRAHAM, HENRY	1830	QUEN	NEWT	15
GRAHAM, JAMES	1830	NYCO	WD13	336
GRAHAM, JOHN	1820	NYCO	WD08	784

NAME	YR	CO	TWP	PG
GRAHAM, JOHN	1830	ONTA	SENE	85
GRAHAM, JOHN	1830	WEST	SUMM	185
GRAHAM, JOHNNY	1820	WEST	SUMM	353
GRAHAM, MARY	1810	ORNG	NEWW	914
GRAHAM, MISS	1820	ONID	DEER	238
GRAHAM, MOSES	1830	ULST	SHAW	246
GRAHAM, PETER	1810	QUEN	FLUS	200
GRAHAM, PETER	1820	QUEN	----	54
GRAHAM, POMPEY	1810	QUEN	FLUS	201
GRAHAM, POMPEY	1820	QUEN	----	54
GRAHAM, S.	1830	NYCO	WD11	165
GRAHAM, WILLIAM	1820	NYCO	WD10	987
GRAMER, J.	1830	NYCO	WD13	346
GRAMMIR, GEORGE	1810	NYCO	WD10	551
GRANDISON, JOHN	1830	ONID	UTIC	18
GRANLEY, DAMERIS	1830	WANE	ARCA	72
GRANNIS, JOHN	1830	HERK	HERK	51
GRANT, ALEXANDER	1820	NYCO	WD05	350
GRANT, BENONA	1830	MONR	BRIG	26
GRANT, CATO	1830	DUTC	PAWL	287
GRANT, CUFF	1820	JEFF	HOUN	417
GRANT, JEHU	1810	SARA	GREN	842
GRANT, RENONI	1820	CORT	HARR'	516
GRANT, SARAH	1820	DUTC	REDH	114
GRANT, TOM	1830	SARA	MILT	19
GRANT, WILLIAM	1830	SARA	MILT	21
GRANTUM, PRIMUS	1820	DUTC	FISH	54
GRASON, POPA	1830	ONTA	MANC	179
GRASSON, CONGO	1830	SENE	JUNU	42
GRAVES, ADAM	1800	NYCO	WD07	912
GRAVES, ARCHY	1830	NYCO	WD06	432
GRAVES, HENRY	1830	NYCO	WD09	383
GRAVES, THOMAS	1810	SCNE	WD02	946
GRAVES, THOMAS	1820	SCNE	WD01	124
GRAVES, WILLIAMS	1820	ONTA	SENE	267
GRAY	1820	PUTM	PATE	101
GRAY, ADAM	1830	CAYU	AUBN	165
GRAY, BEN	1790	QUEN	FLUS	150
GRAY, CHARLES	1830	ABNY	WD04	312
GRAY, DANIEL	1830	ERIE	BUFF	5
GRAY, GEORGE	1790	NYCO	SOUT	131
GRAY, JANE	1810	NYCO	WD03	81
GRAY, JOE	1800	NYCO	WD01	663
GRAY, JOHN	1810	NYCO	WD07	529
GRAY, JOHN	1820	DUTC	DOVE	51
GRAY, JOHN	1830	DUTC	DOVE	223
GRAY, JOSEPH	1800	NYCO	WD06	796
GRAY, PETER	1800	NYCO	WD06	723
GRAY, THOMAS	1820	SARA	HALF	227

Gray

NAME	YR	CO	TWP	PG
GRAY, THOMAS	1830	NYCO	WD04	178
GRAY, WILLIAM	1830	NYCO	WD10	117
GRAY, WILLIAM	1830	SARA	CTPK	136
GRAYFIELD, DAVID	1830	QUEN	OYST	31
GRAYHAM, ALEXANDER	1820	ONTA	SENE	269
GRAYHAM, JOHN	1820	ONTA	SENE	264
GRAYHAM, POMPEY	1830	QUEN	FLUS	142
GRAYHAM, TONE	1810	WEST	HARR	1131
GREAVES, MOSES	1830	NYCO	WD07	15
GREEN, ALBERT	1830	NYCO	WD10	66
GREEN, ALLEN	1830	WEST	RYE	101
GREEN, BALAAM	1830	ORNG	WALL	155
GREEN, CANN	1830	WEST	YORK	177
GREEN, CATHARINE	1830	NYCO	WD05	336
GREEN, CATO	1820	SARA	STIL	191
GREEN, CHARLES	1820	NYCO	WD05	334
GREEN, CLOE	1830	NYCO	WD14	430
GREEN, CUNI	1820	WEST	YORK	329
GREEN, DANIEL	1820	SCNE	WD02	129
GREEN, DAVID	1800	NYCO	WD07	929
GREEN, EDMOND	1830	ORNG	MINI	252
GREEN, FRANCIS	1820	NYCO	WD05	337
GREEN, GEORGE	1830	NYCO	WD10	78
GREEN, HARRY	1810	KING	BRYN	639
GREEN, HENRY	1830	NYCO	WD10	26
GREEN, HOLET	1830	NYCO	WD08	213
GREEN, JACK	1800	WEST	PCHE	603
GREEN, JACK	1810	WEST	WEST	1147
GREEN, JACOB	1810	WEST	WEST	1147
GREEN, JAMES	1830	SCHR	SHAR	108
GREEN, JAMES	1830	WEST	RYE	100
GREEN, JANE	1830	NYCO	WD07	18
GREEN, JEREMIAH	1830	NYCO	WD06	447
GREEN, JOHN	1830	ABNY	WD02	261
GREEN, JOHN	1830	NYCO	WD10	26
GREEN, JOSEPH	1830	MONR	BRIG	4
GREEN, LEWIS	1830	CATT	PERY	219
GREEN, LEWIS	1830	NYCO	WD05	335
GREEN, NANCY	1830	KING	WD02	260
GREEN, PETER	1830	KING	WD05	340
GREEN, PETER	1830	RENS	LANS	100
GREEN, ROBERT	1830	WEST	SUMM	191
GREEN, SAMPSON	1820	NYCO	WD04	237
GREEN, SAMPSON	1820	SUFF	ISLP	307
GREEN, SAMPSON	1830	NYCO	WD09	431
GREEN, TERSHA	1830	SUFF	ISLP	284
GREEN, TOBIAS	1820	NYCO	WD01	43
GREEN, TOBIAS	1830	NYCO	WD05	339
GREEN, WILLIAM	1810	NYCO	WD03	83

NAME	YR	CO	TWP	PG
GREENE, BETSEY	1820	NYCO	WD10	992
GREENE, F.	1830	NYCO	WD12	308
GREENE, GROVE	1830	NYCO	WD12	281
GREENE, HENRY F.	1830	NYCO	WD12	288
GREENE, J.	1830	NYCO	WD13	394
GREENE, JAMES	1820	NYCO	WD10	998
GREENE, JOHN	1820	NYCO	WD04	290
GREENE, MRS.	1830	NYCO	WD13	391
GREENE, RACHEL	1810	ORNG	BLOM	1015
GREENE, ROBERT	1830	NYCO	WD12	278
GREENFIELD, PETER	1830	ULST	HURL	145A
GREENHOLD, ISAAC	1820	DUTC	PAUL	95
GREENLEAF, GARRIT	1830	ORNG	HBGH	124
GREGERY, JOSEPH	1830	WEST	GREN	16
GREGORY, ABRAHAM	1820	ORNG	WARW	643
GREGORY, JOSEPH	1820	WEST	WTPL	461
GREY, CAESAR	1820	PUTM	PATE	101
GREY, JOHN	1820	NYCO	WD06	564
GREY, JOHN	1820	NYCO	WD06	565
GREY, STEPHEN	1820	WEST	WEST	194
GREY, TOM	1830	SARA	CTPK	141
GREYFIELD, JAMES	1810	QUEN	OYST	247
GRIER, H.	1820	NYCO	WD10	1048
GRIFF, ANTHONY	1820	NYCO	WD09	918
GRIFFEN, HANNAH	1830	NYCO	WD06	449
GRIFFEN, HANNAK	1820	NYCO	WD08	790
GRIFFEN, JUDA	1830	DUTC	PGKP	343
GRIFFEN, MARY	1810	NYCO	WD05	299
GRIFFEN, PETER	1830	NYCO	WD07	116
GRIFFEN, PETER	1830	NYCO	WD14	475
GRIFFEN, ROBERT	1830	DUTC	RHIN	391
GRIFFEN, THOMAS	1820	NYCO	WD08	790
GRIFFENS, GRIFFEN	1830	DUTC	HYPK	233
GRIFFIN, ABRAHAM	1810	WEST	SCAR	1160
GRIFFIN, ABRAHAM	1830	WEST	HARR	215
GRIFFIN, HANNAH	1810	NYCO	WD05	258
GRIFFIN, JOHN	1800	HERK	NORW	565
GRIFFIN, JOHN	1800	NYCO	WD06	817
GRIFFIN, JOHN	1820	HERK	NEWP	37
GRIFFIN, KING	1820	WEST	YONK	224
GRIFFIN, KING	1830	WEST	YONK	6
GRIFFIN, PARNAL	1820	JEFF	LORR	450
GRIFFIN, PETER	1820	DUTC	CLNT	27
GRIFFIN, PETER	1830	DUTC	HYPK	230
GRIFFIN, SAMUEL	1800	NYCO	WD07	890
GRIFFIN, SIRIS	1820	WEST	YONK	222
GRIFFIN, WILLIAM	1830	CHAT	POMF	407
GRIFFINS, GRIFFINS	1820	DUTC	CLNT	27
GRIFFINS, PRIMUS	1820	WEST	BEDF	418

Griffis

NAME	YR	CO	TWP	PG
GRIFFIS, PETER	1810	NYCO	WD05	282
GRIFFLING, JOHN	1830	HERK	NEWP	36
GRIGGS, JOHN	1830	ORNG	CORN	210
GRIGNA (?), LEVI	1820	NYCO	WD02	131
GRIGSBY, BATTLE	1820	NYCO	WD03	144
GRIGUES, CYNTHIA	1830	NYCO	WD05	300
GRIM, HECTOR	1800	NYCO	WD06	807
GRINDER, JACK	1820	SCHR	SCHR	182
GRINGS, JSS.	1820	NYCO	WD08	750
GRINNELL, LEWIS	1820	NYCO	WD06	485
GRITH, L.	1820	NYCO	WD10	966
GROCE, JOHN	1830	KING	WD04	320
GRODUS	1800	QUEN	OYST	579
GROESBECK, PARIS	1830	NYCO	WD05	276
GROESBECK, RICHARD	1830	NYCO	WD08	179
GROMAN, THOMAS	1820	QUEN	----	47
GROOM, DINAH	1830	GREN	ATHN	212
GROOM, JACK	1820	GREN	ATHN	11
GROOM, JOHN	1830	NYCO	WD05	270
GROOMER, AMELIA	1820	NYCO	WD07	706
GROOMER, CANE	1820	COLU	AUST	7
GROOMS, MR.	1830	NYCO	WD13	393
GROSHON, LEWIS	1820	NYCO	WD06	488
GRUMER, CANO	1830	COLU	LABN	15
GRUN, WILLIAM	1800	NYCO	WD04	722
GUEST, ADAM	1830	NYCO	WD14	499
GUEST, SARAH	1820	ABNY	ABNY	168
GUI, JEREMIAH	1820	ORNG	MONR	666
GUILLET, ISADOICE	1830	NYCO	WD09	425
GUINEA	1790	QUEN	OYST	155
GUION, NED	1830	WEST	EAST	131
GULIVER, JAMES	1830	ROCK	CLAR	133
GUMAR, SAUL	1800	DUTC	FISH	40
GUMBEY, THOMAS	1820	GENE	GATE	130
GUMS, TITUS	1820	COLU	CANN	5
GUNBOAT, GRACE	1800	NYCO	WD06	820
GUNDIWAY, EZAKIEL	1830	NYCO	WD05	257
GUNDY, JEREMIAH	1820	SARA	SARA	169
GUNDY, JEREMIAH	1830	RENS	TROY	7
GUNN, JAMES	1830	NYCO	WD08	226
GUNN, LEMUEL	1830	NYCO	WD08	151
GUR, PRINCETON	1800	NYCO	WD06	801
GURY, ANN	1810	NYCO	WD05	330
GUTCHES, LUCY	1830	ORNG	MONR	173
GUTCHES, SAMUEL	1810	ULST	SHAW	687
GUY, A.	1820	NYCO	WD10	1068
GUY, AARON	1830	SUFF	HUNT	304
GUY, JEREMIAH	1830	ORGT	GOSH	274
GUY, JOHN	1810	ROCK	ORGT	637

NAME	YR	CO	TWP	PG
HABEN, JAMES	1830	TOMP	CARO	498
HABURY, JAMES	1820	SUFF	SHAM	320
HACHET, SIMON	1810	NYCO	WD10	693
HACKETT, DIANA	1830	NYCO	WD06	399
HACKETT, MRS.	1830	NYCO	WD01	9
HACKNEY, GEORGE	1830	NYCO	WD08	247
HACKNEY, SAMUEL	1830	NYCO	WD08	255
HACKS, THOMAS	1830	KING	BRYN	373
HADDEN, CEZER	1800	WEST	BEDF	720
HADDEN, DENNIS	1790	WEST	WEST	207
HADDEN, FRANK	1800	WEST	NEWC	730
HADDEN, LAZARUS	1800	WEST	NEWC	736
HADLEY, JAMER	1810	NYCO	WD06	495
HAFFERMAH, MRS.	1810	NYCO	WD06	417
HAFSKILL, BENJAMIN	1820	NYCO	WD06	501
HAGAMAN, JAMES	1810	QUEN	NHEM	213
HAGAN, PETER	1820	NYCO	WD05	352
HAGAR	1790	QUEN	FLUS	149
HAGARD, TIMOTHY	1820	MADI	SULL	1
HAGARMAN, ALBERT	1810	ONON	CICE	590
HAGER	1810	SUFF	BROK	492
HAGERMAN, ALBERT	1830	MONR	RWD3	225
HAGERMAN, JACK	1800	WEST	PCHE	620
HAGERMAN, WILLIAM	1830	ONTA	MANC	172
HAIGHT, HARVEY	1830	WEST	NEWR	107
HAILLS, DANIEL	1830	NYCO	WD01	31
HAINES, ARON	1820	PUTM	SOUT	100
HAINES, EDWARD	1810	NYCO	WD05	313
HAINES, EDWARD	1820	NYCO	WD05	352
HAINES, EDWARD	1830	KING	WD02	265
HAINES, ELIZABETH	1800	ORNG	NEWB	282
HAINES, O.	1830	NYCO	WD13	394
HAINES, THOMAS	1820	CLNT	PLAT	459
HAINS, UNICE	1810	ULST	MARL	729
HAISTEAD, JOHN	1830	DUTC	HYPK	234
HAIT, WILLIAM	1810	NYCO	WD10	650
HAK, H.	1820	NYCO	WD10	987
HALB, NERO	1830	COLU	LABN	7
HALE, LANE	1820	NYCO	WD05	348
HALEY, PETER	1800	NYCO	WD05	781
HALICUS, JOSEPH	1830	DELA	ROXB	177
HALL, A.P.	1830	KING	WD04	295
HALL, AVIS	1830	NYCO	WD14	525
HALL, BENJAMIN	1820	QUEN	----	29
HALL, DOLLY	1820	NYCO	WD10	1068
HALL, EPHRAIM	1830	NYCO	WD12	268
HALL, JACK	1810	DUTC	WASH	161
HALL, JAMES	1830	NYCO	WD10	107
HALL, JAMES	1830	TIOG	CATH	196

NAME	YR	CO	TWP	PG
HALL, JOHN	1800	NYCO	WD07	859
HALL, JOHN	1810	NYCO	WD07	535
HALL, JOHN	1810	NYCO	WD10	645
HALL, JOHN	1820	NYCO	WD04	237
HALL, MARY ANN	1830	NYCO	WD08	246
HALL, RUFUS	1820	ONID	WEST	155
HALL, SAMUEL	1830	MONR	RWD1	197
HALL, WILLIAM	1830	ERIE	BUFF	11
HALL, WILLIAM	1830	NYCO	WD10	78
HALLACH, ABRAHAM	1810	SUFF	BROK	492
HALLARD, JEPTHA	1810	COLU	HUDS	147
HALLENBECK, GEORGE	1830	SARA	EDIN	201
HALLENBECK, PETER	1830	ABNY	WD04	299
HALLENBECK, RICHARD	1830	SARA	EDIN	202
HALLENBEECK, ANTHONY	1820	GREN	ATHE	1
HALLENBEECK, JOSEPH	1820	GREN	ATHE	3
HALLENBEECK, RICHARD	1820	GREN	COXE	32
HALLET, HENRY	1830	QUEN	FLUS	148
HALLETT, ANDREW	1820	NYCO	WD05	395
HALLETT, DAVID	1820	NYCO	WD05	395
HALLICK, CATO	1800	NYCO	WD05	770
HALLICK, ISAAC	1820	ORNG	GOSH	738
HALLIDAY, FREEBORD	1830	NYCO	WD14	456
HALLOCK, ISAAC	1830	ORNG	GOSH	275
HALSEY, CUFF	1800	OTSG	BURL	646
HALSEY, CUFF	1830	CHAT	SHER	448
HALSEY, JABEZ	1830	CHAT	SHER	448
HALSEY, JACK	1820	ORNG	GOSH	750
HALSEY, JACOB	1830	NYCO	WD10	40
HALSEY, JOHN	1830	ORNG	GOSH	281
HALSEY, JOHN	1830	ORNG	NEWB	39
HALSEY, PETER	1810	SUFF	SHAM	458
HALSEY, PETER	1820	SUFF	ISLP	310
HALSEY, PRIME	1800	NYCO	WD05	768
HALSEY, PTERS	1830	COLU	CHAT	38
HALSEY, RUBEN	1810	SUFF	SHAM	458
HALSEY, THOMAS	1830	ORNG	NEWW	107
HALSEY, THOMAS	1830	SUFF	SHAM	215
HALSON, HENRY	1810	NYCO	WD10	553
HALSTEAD, LEWIS	1830	WEST	EAST	134
HALSTEAD, PRINCE	1830	WEST	SALM	158
HAM, MRS.	1830	NYCO	WD11	163
HAMAR, JAMES	1820	SUFF	SMIT	315
HAMBLETON, ABRAM	1830	SENE	WL00	8
HAMBLIN, JEFFY	1830	NYCO	WD06	466
HAMER, DANIEL	1830	ALLE	BIRD	54
HAMER, J.	1830	NYCO	WD13	413
HAMER, JACK	1830	TIOG	CHEM	261
HAMEY	1800	SUFF	EHAM	95

NAME	YR	CO	TWP	PG
HAMILTON	1820	PUTM	PATE	101
HAMILTON, ABRAHAM G.	1820	ONTA	PHEL	283
HAMILTON, ALEXANDER	1830	NYCO	WD10	11
HAMILTON, CHARLOT	1800	NYCO	WD05	778
HAMILTON, DIANA	1810	NYCO	WD06	439
HAMILTON, ELI	1830	NYCO	WD04	218
HAMILTON, FRANCIS	1830	NYCO	WD09	409
HAMILTON, HENRY	1830	RICH	CAST	39
HAMILTON, JOHN	1830	NYCO	WD06	454
HAMILTON, PRINCE	1820	ABNY	GUID	247
HAMILTON, RACHEAL	1830	NYCO	WD01	31
HAMILTON, ROBERT	1830	NYCO	WD09	430
HAMILTON, SARAH	1830	NYCO	WD10	107
HAMILTON, W.	1820	NYCO	WD10	989
HAMILTON, WILLIAM	1800	NYCO	WD04	724
HAMILTON, WILLIAM	1800	NYCO	WD07	859
HAMILTON, WILLIAM	1810	NYCO	WD10	535
HAMILTON, WILLIAM	1820	NYCO	WD03	197
HAMILTON, WILLIAM	1830	NYCO	WD01	50
HAMILTON, WILLIAM	1830	NYCO	WD09	383
HAMILTON, WILLIAM	1830	NYCO	WD12	293
HAMILTON, WILLIAM	1830	ORNG	MONR	176
HAMILTON, WILLIAM JR.	1830	NYCO	WD12	293
HAMLEN, THOMAS	1830	GREN	DURH	277
HAMMICK, ISAIAH	1830	DELA	MERI	129
HAMMOND, BENJAMIN	1820	SUFF	HUNT	284
HAMMOND, CHARITY	1830	SUFF	HUNT	324
HAMMOND, ELISHA	1830	ABNY	WD01	225
HAMMOND, JAMES	1810	NYCO	WD03	113
HAMMOND, JAMES	1810	NYCO	WD03	108
HAMMOND, JAMES	1820	NYCO	WD01	17
HAMMOND, MAGERETE	1830	MADI	----	335
HAMMOND, MINA	1830	NYCO	WD08	247
HAMMOND, SAM	1810	WEST	HARR	1133
HAMMOND, SAMUEL	1820	SUFF	HUNT	286
HAMMOND, SAMUEL	1820	WEST	HARR	467
HAMMOND, WILLIAM	1820	NYCO	WD06	476
HAMON, BEN	1820	SUFF	BROK	334
HAMPSHIRE, H.	1830	NYCO	WD11	214
HAMPTON, BILL	1800	WASH	ARGY	498
HAMPTON, HANNAH	1830	WASH	FTED	305
HAMPTON, HENRY	1820	NYCO	WD03	187
HAMPTON, JOHN	1830	MONT	JOHN	203
HAMPTON, WILLIAM	1810	WASH	KING	352
HAMPTON, WILLIAM	1820	WASH	KING	165
HAMWOOD, WITTY	1820	ONON	SALI	253
HANBY, HENRY	1810	DUTC	RHIN	375
HAND, PETER	1830	SUFF	EAST	259
HANDEN, WILLIAM	1820	DUTC	PGKP	97

NAME	YR	CO	TWP	PG
HANDEY, GEORGE	1830	NYCO	WD08	243
HANDY, ISAAC	1830	NYCO	WD06	410
HANEBAL, STEPHEN	1800	NYCO	WD07	901
HANER, JOHN	1800	WEST	NORS	754
HANER, MICHAEL	1830	MADI	----	416
HANES, WILLIAM	1830	ORNG	GOSH	292
HANFORD, ELIJAH	1820	ONON	MANL	167
HANIBAL, STEPHEN	1830	NYCO	WD05	343
HANN, MARCY	1830	ALLE	CANE	79
HANNAH	1790	NYCO	MONT	122
HANNAH	1790	NYCO	NORT	126
HANNAH	1790	QUEN	NHEM	152
HANNAH	1790	QUEN	OYST	155
HANNAH	1800	SUFF	ISLP	62
HANNAH	1800	SUFF	SHAM	72
HANNAH	1810	NYCO	WD02	128
HANNAH	1810	NYCO	WD06	444
HANNAH	1830	ROCK	CLAR	122
HANNIBAL, HANNAH	1820	SUFF	BROK	330
HANNIBAL, JOHN	1790	KING	BUSH	97
HANOR, MAT	1830	COLU	CLAV	80
HANS, THOMAS	1810	NYCO	WD07	552
HANSEN, BETSY	1810	NYCO	WD03	44
HANSEN, JOHN	1810	ULST	MARB	731
HANSON, JOHN	1830	LIVI	AVON	21
HANSUNAN, H.	1830	NYCO	WD11	133
HARBROOK, JAMES	1830	ORNG	BLOM	120
HARBROOK, TITUS	1830	ORNG	WALL	148
HARCOURT, FRANK	1830	ULST	MARL	276
HARDECK, JACK	1830	COLU	HUDS	128
HARDEN, CAESAR	1820	ONID	PARS	285
HARDEN, ELLIAS	1800	NYCO	WD07	879
HARDEN, MRS.	1830	KING	WD04	305
HARDEN, SAMUEL	1810	NYCO	WD02	116
HARDEN, WILLIAM	1830	DUTC	PGKP	322
HARDENBAUGH, ROBERT	1830	NYCO	WD08	241
HARDENBERG, BENJAMIN	1830	ULST	MARB	154
HARDENBERG, GEORGE	1830	ULST	SCHO	239
HARDENBERG, HENRY	1830	ULST	MARB	161
HARDENBERG, JAMES	1830	ULST	NPAL	224
HARDENBERG, JAMES B.	1830	DUTC	RHIN	399
HARDENBERG, JULIA	1830	ABNY	WD01	211
HARDENBERG, LUCAS	1830	ULST	MARB	154
HARDENBERG, PHILIP	1830	ULST	MARB	164
HARDENBERG, THOMAS	1830	ULST	ROCH	170
HARDENBURGH, DANIEL	1830	DUTC	MILN	263
HARDER, ANTHONY	1830	COLU	STUY	68
HARDER, CAESAR	1830	NIAG	LEWS	385
HARDER, THOMAS	1820	COLU	LABO	7

NAME	YR	CO	TWP	PG
HARDICK, PUNCH	1830	COLU	HUDS	106
HARDIN, BENJAMIN	1810	KING	BRYN	632
HARDIN, CHARLES	1830	ABNY	GUID	401
HARDIN, ELEAZER	1830	NYCO	WD05	314
HARDIN, JOHN	1830	NYCO	WD05	345
HARDIN, THOMAS	1810	NYCO	WD01	25
HARDING, ALEXANDER	1830	ORNG	CORN	215
HARDING, BENJAMIN	1800	QUEN	NHEM	552
HARDING, HARRY	1830	TIOG	OWGO	289
HARDING, ISABELLA	1830	NYCO	WD06	367
HARDING, JOHN	1830	ABNY	WD02	262
HARDING, MR.	1820	NYCO	WD05	389
HARDING, SAMUEL	1820	NYCO	WD06	572
HARDING, WILLIAM	1810	NYCO	WD05	307
HARDING, WILLIAM	1830	NYCO	WD06	368
HARDY, BEAL	1830	ONTA	SENE	76
HARDY, EMERY	1830	NYCO	WD10	88
HARDY, HARRY	1820	BROM	OWEG	31
HARDY, ISAAC	1830	NYCO	WD14	451
HARDY, JOSEPH	1820	ONTA	LYON	110
HARDY, JOSEPH	1830	ONTA	SENE	52
HARDY, NICHOLAS	1820	SCNE	WD02	129
HARDY, NICOLAS	1830	SCNE	WD02	219
HARDY, PEAT	1820	ONTA	SENE	270
HARDY, SAMUEL	1830	NYCO	WD12	278
HARISON, ABIGAIL	1820	QUEN	----	25
HARISON, S.	1830	NYCO	WD11	171
HARLEY, FRANCIS	1830	NYCO	WD08	225
HARLEY, THOMAS	1830	ULST	KING	58
HARMAN, C.	1830	NYCO	WD11	163
HARMAN, GEORGE	1830	NYCO	WD12	262
HARMAN, JACOB	1820	DUTC	RHIN	129
HARMAN, MR.	1830	NYCO	WD10	40
HARMANS, JANE	1830	NYCO	WD01	35
HARNEY, WILLIAM	1820	KING	BRYN	124
HARPEN, JOSEPH	1830	QUEN	FLUS	143
HARPER, JOSEPH	1810	QUEN	FLUS	197
HARPER, JOSEPH	1820	QUEN	----	54
HARR, CHARLES	1830	NYCO	WD10	87
HARRESON, CHARLES	1830	MONR	RWD1	197
HARRETT, MAJOR	1830	NYCO	WD07	46
HARREY, MRS.	1830	KING	BUSH	383
HARRIET, MISS	1820	KING	BRYN	134
HARRIETT	1800	NYCO	WD06	836
HARRINGTON, ELIJAH	1830	WEST	RYE	102
HARRINGTON, JACOB	1830	NYCO	WD06	380
HARRINGTON, JOHN	1830	RENS	SHOD	253
HARRINS, JOSEPH	1820	NYCO	WD07	686
HARRIS	1800	ABNY	SCNE	13

Harris

NAME	YR	CO	TWP	PG
HARRIS, ANN	1820	NYCO	WD09	944
HARRIS, BETSY	1820	NYCO	WD10	963
HARRIS, CEAZAR	1800	NYCO	WD01	663
HARRIS, CESAR	1810	NYCO	WD01	27
HARRIS, CESEAR	1820	NYCO	WD04	227
HARRIS, CHARLES	1830	KING	BUSH	377
HARRIS, CHARLES	1830	SARA	CHAR	127
HARRIS, CUFFEE	1820	SCNE	WD02	129
HARRIS, DANIEL	1820	NYCO	WD08	780
HARRIS, DANIEL	1830	NYCO	WD13	336
HARRIS, EDWARD	1810	NYCO	WD01	30
HARRIS, ELISABETH	1820	NYCO	WD05	428
HARRIS, HATH	1820	NYCO	WD08	738
HARRIS, HENRY	1800	NYCO	WD05	764
HARRIS, HENRY	1810	NYCO	WD05	367
HARRIS, HENRY	1820	NYCO	WD10	982
HARRIS, HENRY	1830	KING	WD04	313
HARRIS, HENRY	1830	NYCO	WD09	324
HARRIS, HENRY	1830	NYCO	WD10	19
HARRIS, HENRY	1830	NYCO	WD14	522
HARRIS, HENRY	1830	ORNG	WARW	72
HARRIS, HUFF	1830	SCNE	WD02	223
HARRIS, JACOB	1810	NYCO	WD10	543
HARRIS, JACOB	1810	NYCO	WD10	553
HARRIS, JAMES	1830	NYCO	WD05	329
HARRIS, JAMES	1830	NYCO	WD12	303
HARRIS, JANE	1820	SCNE	WD03	135
HARRIS, JOHN	1800	NYCO	WD06	803
HARRIS, JOHN	1820	ABNY	ABNY	174
HARRIS, JOHN	1820	NYCO	WD10	1016
HARRIS, JOHN	1830	NYCO	WD14	504
HARRIS, JOHNATHAN	1830	NYCO	WD14	468
HARRIS, MARRY	1800	NYCO	WD06	844
HARRIS, MARY	1800	NYCO	WD06	839
HARRIS, MARY	1820	NYCO	WD09	931
HARRIS, MERELD	1820	ORNG	GOSH	735
HARRIS, MRS.	1810	NYCO	WD06	408
HARRIS, NATHAN	1810	NYCO	WD06	472
HARRIS, NATHANEAL	1830	NYCO	WD14	475
HARRIS, PETER	1800	DUTC	RHIN	153
HARRIS, THOMAS	1820	NYCO	WD07	705
HARRIS, THOMAS	1830	ABNY	WATV	463
HARRIS, THOMAS	1830	NYCO	WD07	46
HARRIS, WILLIAM	1820	NYCO	WD09	892
HARRIS, WILLIAM	1830	CHAT	BUST	266
HARRIS, WILLIAM	1830	NYCO	WD08	232
HARRISM, JANE	1830	SCNE	ROTT	247
HARRISON, CALEMNIUS	1830	NYCO	WD05	343
HARRISON, DINAH	1830	ABNY	WD01	201

NAME	YR	CO	TWP	PG
HARRISON, GEORGE	1830	NYCO	WD08	173
HARRISON, HENRY	1820	DUTC	FISH	63
HARRISON, HENRY	1830	HERK	LTFA	90
HARRISON, JACK	1820	ABNY	ABNY	173
HARRISON, JEMIMA	1820	NYCO	WD08	795
HARRISON, JOHN	1830	NYCO	WD05	313
HARRISON, L.	1820	NYCO	WD10	1075
HARRISON, LEWIS	1830	NYCO	WD06	426
HARRISON, PETER	1830	NYCO	WD14	525
HARRISON, ROBERT	1820	ABNY	ABNY	174
HARRISON, ROSANNA	1820	NYCO	WD06	445
HARRISON, SAMUEL	1830	NYCO	WD14	460
HARRISON, THOMAS	1830	ORNG	WARW	76
HARRISON, TOBIAS	1820	SCHR	SCHR	447
HARRISON, TOBIAS	1830	SCHR	SCHR	27
HARRISON, TOM	1820	ABNY	WATV	263
HARRY	1790	NYCO	OUTW	131
HARRY	1800	ABNY	WD02	282
HARRY	1810	DUTC	PGKP	325
HARRY	1820	ABNY	COEY	129
HARRY	1820	ABNY	RENV	64
HARRY	1820	ABNY	WEST	96
HARRY	1820	RICH	SOUT	106
HARRY	1820	SARA	MILT	234
HARRY	1830	ALLE	ALMD	11
HARRY	1830	ALLE	ANGE	4
HARRY	1830	KING	WD04	306
HARRY (MOLATTA)	1790	COLU	HUDS	67
HARRY, BLACK	1830	KING	FLAN	411
HARRY, HEWLITT	1800	QUEN	NHEM	553
HARRY, JOHN	1810	NYCO	WD06	452
HARRY, JOHN	1820	NYCO	WD06	528
HARRY, JON	1810	RICH	NORT	601
HARSAN, TIMOTHY	1830	MADI	----	389
HARSON, ABRAHAM	1820	WEST	WEST	196
HART, ANA	1820	SUFF	SMIT	324
HART, ANTHONY	1810	NYCO	WD10	699
HART, CHARLES	1830	WEST	SCAR	77
HART, HENRY	1830	NYCO	WD10	26
HART, JACK	1830	ULST	SHAW	254
HART, JACK	1830	WEST	RYE	106
HART, JENNEY	1830	NYCO	WD01	15
HART, JOHN	1810	NYCO	WD03	61
HART, LEWIS	1800	NYCO	WD03	71
HART, OLIVER	1830	NYCO	WD10	26
HART, RICHARD	1820	NYCO	WD05	389
HART, THOMAS	1830	WEST	RYE	106
HART, WILLIAM	1810	NYCO	WD06	423
HARTLEY, JAMES	1820	SCNE	WD02	130

NAME	YR	CO	TWP	PG
HARTLEY, SARAH	1820	SCNE	SCNE	554
HARTON, JACK	1820	SUFF	SOUT	339
HARVEY, CEPHAS	1830	ONTA	SENE	73
HARVEY, HARRY	1820	COLU	CLER	3
HARVEY, JAMES	1830	NYCO	WD08	160
HARVEY, JOSEPH	1810	NYCO	WD05	309
HARVEY, WILLIAM	1810	NYCO	WD06	467
HARVEY, WILLIAM	1830	KING	WD05	324
HARVEY, WILLIAM	1830	NYCO	WD06	383
HARVY	1820	QUEN	----	57
HARVY	1820	QUEN	----	63
HARVY, DANIA	1830	WEST	NEWR	107
HARVY, DAVID	1830	WEST	MAMA	228
HASBROCK, THOMAS	1830	ULST	NPAL	203
HASBROOK, CASAR	1830	ORNG	NEWW	105
HASBROOK, JOSIAH	1830	ORNG	NEWB	34
HASBROOK, TOBIAS	1830	ORNG	MONR	181
HASBROUCK, ALEXANDER	1830	ULST	NPAL	211
HASBROUCK, JACK	1830	ULST	NPAL	212
HASBROUCK, RICHARD	1830	ULST	MARB	158
HASBROUCK, SIMON	1830	DUTC	PGKP	343
HASBROUCK, SUH	1820	ULST	MARB	53
HASBROUK, HARRY	1830	ULST	ROCH	180
HASCO, JACOB	1830	NYCO	WD09	406
HASER, BALTES H.	1830	MONT	FLOR	94
HASER, CHRISTIAN	1830	MONT	FLOR	102
HASHBROUK, RICHARD	1830	ORNG	MONR	181
HASTINGS, RUFUS	1810	GENE	CALA	116
HASTINGS, RUFUS	1820	GENE	CALA	116
HASWELL, THOMAS	1830	ABNY	WD01	199
HATFIELD, JESSE	1830	WEST	WTPL	224
HATFIELD, MOSES	1830	WEST	NORC	203
HATFIELD, PLATO	1830	WEST	WTPL	224
HATFIELD, ROBERT	1800	NYCO	WD06	799
HATFIELD, WILLIAM	1830	NYCO	WD10	26
HATTENTOTT, CATO	1810	QUEN	FLUS	203
HAVENS, CHARLES	1820	SUFF	BROK	359
HAVENS, CHARLES	1830	CHAT	SHER	451
HAVENS, CHARLES	1830	SUFF	HUNT	297
HAVENS, H.	1830	SUFF	HUNT	326
HAVENS, IRA	1830	SUFF	ISLP	286
HAVENS, JACK	1830	MONT	CHAR	60
HAVENS, JEREMIAH	1820	SUFF	HUNT	284
HAVENS, JOHN	1830	MONT	GLEN	83
HAVENS, JUDE	1820	SUFF	HUNT	301
HAVENS, JUDE	1830	SUFF	HUNT	297
HAVENS, TONE	1820	SUFF	SMIT	323
HAVENS, VIOLET	1820	SUFF	SHEL	331
HAVENS, VIOLET	1830	SUFF	SHEL	290

NAME	YR	CO	TWP	PG
HAVEY, ANN	1830	SUFF	SHAM	215
HAVILAND, JACOB	1830	NYCO	WD10	95
HAWES, JOHNATHAN	1830	NYCO	WD09	431
HAWKINS, ABRAHAM	1820	SUFF	BROK	353
HAWKINS, ABRAM	1830	SUFF	BROK	192
HAWKINS, BENJAMIN	1830	SUFF	BROK	162
HAWKINS, DINAH	1830	NYCO	WD08	231
HAWKINS, H.	1830	ERIE	BUFF	30
HAWKINS, ISAAC	1820	SARA	SARA	189
HAWKINS, ISAAC	1830	SARA	SASP	165
HAWKINS, PAUL	1830	SUFF	BROK	162
HAWKINS, STEPHEN	1830	NYCO	WD08	217
HAWKINS, SUSANNAH	1800	HERK	GERM	473
HAWKINS, TOBIAS	1820	NYCO	WD02	118
HAWKINS, TOBIAS	1830	NYCO	WD08	180
HAWN, WILLIAM	1830	MONT	CANJ	22
HAYDOCK, REDER	1830	NYCO	WD09	304
HAYES, GEORGE	1810	ONTA	BLOM	612
HAYNES, SAMUEL	1830	WASH	GRAN	246
HAYNES, THOMAS	1830	CLNT	PLAT	257
HAYS, GEORGE	1810	NYCO	WD05	306
HAYSE, GEORGE	1830	MONR	RWD3	228
HAYT, RICHARD	1820	PUTM	PATE	101
HAYWOOD, MAJOR	1830	NYCO	WD07	34
HAZARD, AVERY	1830	WASH	SALM	222
HAZARD, EBENEZER	1830	CAYU	AURE	185
HAZARD, ELIJAH	1820	HERK	MALI	167
HAZARD, ELIJAH	1830	TIOG	VETR	175
HAZARD, ELIZABETH	1790	QUEN	NEWT	151
HAZARD, JOSEPH	1790	DUTC	PAWL	88
HAZARD, NELLY	1830	NYCO	WD08	244
HAZARD, SARAH	1800	NYCO	WD05	762
HAZARD, STEPHEN	1800	NYCO	WD02	681
HAZEL, ANN	1830	ONID	FLOR	360
HAZEL, CUFFE	1820	MONT	FLOR	347
HAZEL, SAMUEL	1820	ONID	FLOR	194
HAZER, BALTIS	1830	MONT	FLOR	103
HAZZARD	1790	COLU	HUDS	66
HEACOCK, CORNELIUS	1820	DUTC	FISH	70
HEACOCK, PETER	1830	DUTC	FISH	477
HEADEY, JACOB	1820	PUTM	PHIL	101
HEADING, JACOB	1810	DUTC	PHIL	99
HEADY, D.	1830	NYCO	WD11	159
HEARD, WILLIAM	1830	ABNY	WD02	261
HEARD, ROBERT	1830	ORNG	GOSH	274
HEBBARD, ROBERT	1830	DUTC	UNVA	422
HEBE	1790	NYCO	MONT	120
HEBER, WILLIAM	1820	GREN	CATS	160
HECOCK, HENRY	1830	DUTC	LAGR	251

NAME	YR	CO	TWP	PG
HECTOR, WILLIAM	1790	DUTC	PAWL	86
HECTOR, WILLIAM	1800	DUTC	PAWL	54
HECTOR, WILLIAM	1810	DUTC	PAWL	153
HEDDEN, DENNIS	1820	NYCO	WD05	429
HEDDEN, DENNIS	1830	NYCO	WD08	148
HEDDEN, ELIJAH	1830	NYCO	WD14	456
HEDDEN, JACOB	1800	DUTC	PHIL	81
HEDDY, DENNIS	1800	WEST	PCHE	602
HEDDY, DENNIS	1810	NYCO	WD05	255
HEDDY, DENNIS	1810	NYCO	WD06	450
HEDDY, DENNIS	1810	WEST	WEST	1146
HEDDY, DENNIS	1830	NYCO	WD10	87
HEDDY, HARRY	1830	WEST	WEST	117
HEDDY, HENRY	1800	NYCO	WD03	699
HEDDY, HENRY	1810	NYCO	WD04	172
HEDDY, ISSAC	1810	NYCO	WD06	445
HEDDY, JACOB	1830	WEST	YORK	180
HEDDY, JOHN	1820	NYCO	WD06	503
HEDDY, JONATHAN	1810	DUTC	FISH	240
HEDDY, JONATHAN	1830	DUTC	FISH	484
HEDDY, LEWIS	1830	WEST	NEWC	96
HEDDY, SOLOMON	1830	WEST	YORK	178
HEDGES, CYRUS	1810	SUFF	EHAM	437
HEDGES, PEG	1820	SUFF	EAST	288
HEEDY, HENRY	1820	NYCO	WD06	498
HEGEMAN, TITUS	1830	QUEN	OYST	41
HEGEMON, JANES	1820	QUEN	----	68
HEICKS, L.	1820	KING	BRYN	112
HEICKS, MRS.	1820	KING	BRYN	114
HEICKS, PHILLIP	1820	KING	BRAD	157
HEICKS, SIMON	1820	KING	BRYN	129
HEICKS, THOMAS	1820	KING	BRYN	126
HEIRS, WILLIAMS	1830	QUEN	NEWT	11
HELEN, POMP	1830	COLU	HUDS	99
HELLEBRONT, JOHN	1820	ABNY	BETH	223
HELLICUS, ALEXANDER	1830	GREN	WIND	111
HELLIS, ROBBIN	1810	SUFF	BROK	488
HELM, DAVID	1820	SUFF	HUNT	292
HELME, POMPEY	1800	SUFF	SHEL	85
HELMER, NICHOLAS	1820	SARA	CLAR	213
HELMES, JOHN	1790	ABNY	HALF	28
HELMES, JUDE	1830	SUFF	BROK	180
HELMES, POMP	1810	SUFF	RIVH	549
HELMS, ALFRED	1830	NYCO	WD04	178
HELMS, JAMES	1820	SUFF	ISLP	309
HELMUS, JACK	1810	SCNE	WD02	947
HELMUS, JOHN	1800	ABNY	SCNE	8
HELSY, JOE	1820	SUFF	SHAM	309
HELVES, BEN	1790	SUFF	BROK	162

NAME	YR	CO	TWP	PG
HEMAN, PLINE	1820	ORNG	MONT	819
HEMPSTEAD, DAVID	1830	SUFF	SHEL	291
HEMSTEAD, DAVID	1810	SUFF	SHEL	465
HEMTHAN, DAVID	1820	SUFF	SHEL	330
HENDERSON, C.	1830	NYCO	WD04	160
HENDERSON, HENRY	1830	QUEN	NEWT	18
HENDERSON, JOHN	1830	NYCO	WD06	370
HENDERSON, MR.	1830	KING	WD05	335
HENDERSON, WILLIAM	1820	SENE	JUNU	400
HENDERSON, WILLIAM	1830	SENE	FALL	20
HENDINAN, A.	1830	NYCO	WD11	186
HENDRICKS, ABAGAIL	1820	NYCO	WD05	436
HENDRICKS, ISAAC	1830	NYCO	WD06	406
HENDRICKS, ROBERT	1830	COLU	KIND	147
HENDRICKSON, BENJAMIN	1830	QUEN	JAMA	125
HENDRICKSON, CHARLES	1810	NYCO	WD06	404
HENDRICKSON, DINAH	1830	NYCO	WD08	175
HENDRICKSON, HARRY	1810	NYCO	WD05	360
HENDRICKSON, HENRY	1800	NYCO	WD07	903
HENDRICKSON, JACOB	1830	QUEN	JAMA	128
HENDRICKSON, SCOTT	1830	KING	WD04	320
HENDRICKSON, THOMAS	1830	KING	WD05	327
HENERY, MARY	1830	NYCO	WD06	434
HENLES, THOMAS	1800	TIOG	NEWN	332
HENRY	1800	SUFF	HUNT	39
HENRY	1810	NYCO	WD05	368
HENRY	1810	ORNG	CORN	1036
HENRY	1830	NYCO	WD12	298
HENRY, A.	1830	ERIE	BUFF	7
HENRY, ANTHONY	1820	NYCO	WD06	457
HENRY, CHARLOTTE	1810	NYCO	WD06	449
HENRY, CHARLOTTE	1820	NYCO	WD05	392
HENRY, CHARLOTTE	1830	NYCO	WD06	380
HENRY, CORNELIUS	1830	NYCO	WD12	288
HENRY, CUFFEE	1790	ABNY	WD01	12
HENRY, DATHNY	1810	NYCO	WD06	430
HENRY, DAVID	1830	DUTC	REDH	370
HENRY, FRANCIS	1810	NYCO	WD10	722
HENRY, FRANCIS S.	1830	NYCO	WD09	320
HENRY, GEORGE	1800	NYCO	WD03	696
HENRY, GEORGE	1810	NYCO	WD04	182
HENRY, GEORGE	1820	NYCO	WD06	481
HENRY, GEORGE	1830	HERK	FAIR	3
HENRY, H. MILLER, H.	1830	NYCO	WD11	221
HENRY, HAIMAN	1810	NYCO	WD07	560
HENRY, HANNAH	1810	NYCO	WD05	255
HENRY, HENRY	1820	DUTC	REDH	115
HENRY, JAMES	1820	NYCO	WD04	215

NAME	YR	CO	TWP	PG
HENRY, JAMES	1830	DUTC	PLEA	308
HENRY, JAMES	1830	NYCO	WD14	432
HENRY, JAMES	1830	SARA	STIL	62
HENRY, JERRY	1820	NYCO	WD07	627
HENRY, JERRY	1820	NYCO	WD07	625
HENRY, JOHN	1820	NYCO	WD07	677
HENRY, JOHNATHAN	1830	NYCO	WD14	450
HENRY, JOSEPH	1820	QUEN	----	51
HENRY, JOSEPH	1820	QUEN	----	54
HENRY, PETER	1830	DUTC	REDH	370
HENRY, SAMUEL	1820	ABNY	ABNY	172
HENRY, THOMAS	1830	RICH	WEST	9
HENRY, WILLIAM	1800	NYCO	WD04	718
HENRY, WILLIAM	1800	NYCO	WD06	794
HENRY, WILLIAM	1800	NYCO	WD06	799
HENRY, WILLIAM	1800	NYCO	WD07	862
HENRY, WILLIAM	1810	NYCO	WD01	19
HENRY, WILLIAM	1810	NYCO	WD05	249
HENRY, WILLIAM	1820	NYCO	WD01	40
HENRY, WILLIAM	1830	NYCO	WD01	15
HENRY, WILLIAM	1830	ONID	UTIC	21
HENRY, WILLIAM	1830	RICH	CAST	39
HENSON, MOSES	1830	NYCO	WD10	6
HERCULES, THOMAS	1810	TIOG	ELMI	635
HERDER, PETER	1820	COLU	GHEN	5
HERDICH, P.	1820	COLU	HUDS	15
HERENY, ANTHONY	1820	NYCO	WD10	984
HERINGTON, LUCRETIA	1810	NYCO	WD01	23
HERMAME, JAMES	1800	COLU	HUDS	1138
HERRICK, PETER	1820	DUTC	PGKP	99
HERRID, FRANCIS	1820	NYCO	WD04	212
HESDRA, SOLOMON	1830	NYCO	WD08	130
HESTER	1790	QUEN	JAMA	150
HETFIELD, ROBERT	1810	NYCO	WD03	57
HEWIET, LEWIS	1830	NYCO	WD10	19
HEWLET, ISAAC	1830	NYCO	WD14	477
HEWLET, JAMES	1830	QUEN	NEWT	5
HEWLET, WILLIAM	1810	NYCO	WD04	162
HEWLET, WILLIAM	1830	NYCO	WD04	218
HEWLETT, ABRAHAM	1810	QUEN	NHEM	305
HEWLETT, ABRAHAM	1820	QUEN	----	10
HEWLETT, ABRAHAM	1820	QUEN	----	64
HEWLETT, GEORGE	1830	QUEN	JAMA	134
HEWLETT, HEAH	1810	QUEN	FLUS	203
HEWLETT, ISAAC	1820	QUEN	----	25
HEWLETT, JACOB	1830	QUEN	JAMA	134
HEWLETT, JACOB	1830	QUEN	FLUS	154
HEWLETT, JAMES	1810	QUEN	SHEM	305
HEWLETT, JAMES	1830	NYCO	WD08	258
HEWLETT, JAMES	1830	QUEN	SHEM	86

NAME	YR	CO	TWP	PG
HEWLETT, JOHN	1810	QUEN	OYST	255
HEWLETT, JOHN	1820	QUEN	----	68
HEWLETT, JOHN	1830	QUEN	NHEM	104
HEWLETT, KIES	1830	QUEN	JAMA	133
HEWLETT, NAT	1810	QUEN	NHEM	286
HEWLETT, ROBERT	1830	QUEN	FLUS	153
HEWLITT, PHILLIS	1810	QUEN	NHEM	307
HEWMAN, CHARLES	1830	DUTC	REDH	373
HEYER, ROBERT	1820	ABNY	ABNY	174
HEYTO, CALEB	1800	NYCO	WD07	859
HEZEKIAH	1790	QUEN	FLUS	150
HIBBARD, WILLIAM	1800	ULST	MARB	204
HIBBINS, COFFEE	1830	RENS	WD02	33
HICHCOCK, JOSEPH	1830	WEST	CORT	64
HICK, J.	1810	CLNT	PLAT	895
HICK, JACOB	1820	ORNG	WALL	794
HICK, JAMES	1810	CLNT	PLAT	895
HICK, JANE	1820	CLNT	BEEK	430
HICK, JANE	1830	CLNT	BEEK	299
HICK, JOSIAH	1820	CLNT	BEEK	430
HICK, LOUIS	1810	CLNT	PLAT	895
HICK, TAMAR	1830	CLNT	BEEK	299
HICKS, ADAM	1820	NYCO	WD07	698
HICKS, ANNA	1800	NYCO	WD06	808
HICKS, ANTHONY	1830	NYCO	WD08	269
HICKS, CANDUS	1820	NYCO	WD02	111
HICKS, CATO	1820	NYCO	WD04	242
HICKS, CHARLES	1820	QUEN	----	61
HICKS, CHARLES	1820	QUEN	----	71
HICKS, CHARLES	1830	NYCO	WD08	230
HICKS, CHARLES	1830	QUEN	OYST	41
HICKS, CHARLES	1830	QUEN	OYST	49
HICKS, COMENY	1830	KING	BRYN	366
HICKS, EDWARD	1830	NYCO	WD11	195
HICKS, GEORGE	1830	KING	BRYN	359
HICKS, GEORGE	1830	WEST	HARR	216
HICKS, HENRY	1820	QUEN	----	37
HICKS, ISAAC	1810	QUEN	OYST	232
HICKS, ISAAC	1820	NYCO	WD04	222
HICKS, ISAAC	1830	NYCO	WD14	433
HICKS, ISAAC	1830	QUEN	NHEM	112
HICKS, ISABELLA	1830	NYCO	WD06	368
HICKS, ISÁBELLA	1830	NYCO	WD06	421
HICKS, ISABELLA	1830	NYCO	WD07	116
HICKS, ISRAEL	1800	NYCO	WD06	833
HICKS, ISRAEL	1810	NYCO	WD07	552
HICKS, J.	1830	NYCO	WD11	133
HICKS, JACK	1800	NYCO	WD06	91
HICKS, JACOB	1830	NYCO	WD12	285

Hicks

NAME	YR	CO	TWP	PG
HICKS, JACOB	1830	WEST	SUMM	181
HICKS, JAMES	1820	NYCO	WD09	899
HICKS, JAMES	1820	QUEN	----	30
HICKS, JAMES R.	1830	NYCO	WD08	220
HICKS, JANE	1830	NYCO	WD07	43
HICKS, JOHN	1830	NYCO	WD14	526
HICKS, MORRIS	1820	QUEN	----	37
HICKS, MORRIS	1830	NYCO	WD10	26
HICKS, MRS.	1830	KING	WD04	310
HICKS, RICHARD	1830	QUEN	FLUS	147
HICKS, SARAH	1810	KING	BRYN	639
HICKS, SARAH	1820	QUEN	----	78
HICKS, SIMON	1810	KING	BRYN	631
HICKS, STEPHEN	1820	QUEN	----	55
HICKS, STEPHEN	1830	QUEN	FLUS	143
HICKS, TEHABUA	1820	QUEN	----	55
HICKS, THOMAS	1810	KING	BRYN	632
HICKS, THOMAS	1810	QUEN	SHEM	306
HICKS, THOMAS	1820	NYCO	WD07	702
HICKS, TOM	1790	QUEN	FLUS	149
HICKSON, MARCUS	1810	GENE	CALA	118
HICKY, EDWARD	1820	NYCO	WD10	984
HIDD, JAMES	1820	SARA	BALL	209
HIDDY, ROCHEL	1810	NYCO	WD06	445
HIDRO, JOSEPH	1830	NYCO	WD09	321
HIGGINS, PETER	1820	NYCO	WD05	352
HIGGINS, SAMUEL	1810	NYCO	WD06	436
HIGGS, STACY	1830	NYCO	WD06	414
HIGHT, HARRY	1820	GREN	NEWB	20
HILGROVE, JOHN	1830	NYCO	WD08	236
HILL	1830	NYCO	WD05	308
HILL, ADAM	1820	NYCO	WD03	165
HILL, ADAM	1830	NYCO	WD05	301
HILL, ANTHONY	1810	NYCO	WD03	84
HILL, CALEB	1810	NYCO	WD06	412
HILL, CAROLINE	1830	NYCO	WD11	133
HILL, DAVID	1830	NYCO	WD14	525
HILL, EBENEZER	1820	MADI	LENX	22
HILL, EBENEZER	1830	MADI	----	238
HILL, EPHRAM	1820	NYCO	WD10	981
HILL, GEORGE	1830	MADI	----	395
HILL, GEORGE	1830	ONTA	MANC	182
HILL, GRANTHAM	1820	NYCO	WD04	262
HILL, HARRY	1810	ORNG	MONT	962
HILL, HARRY	1820	DUTC	DOVE	49
HILL, HENRY	1820	SARA	STIL	191
HILL, JANE	1830	ORNG	WALL	139
HILL, JOB	1810	SCHR	BRON	160
HILL, JONATHAN	1820	PUTM	PHIL	101

NAME	YR	CO	TWP	PG
HILL, JONATHAN	1830	ORNG	MONR	235
HILL, JOSEPH	1800	DUTC	NORT	150
HILL, JOSEPH	1820	COLU	HUDS	15
HILL, JOSEPH	1820	NYCO	WD04	285
HILL, JOSEPH	1830	DUTC	DOVE	215
HILL, JOSEPH	1830	KING	WD03	291
HILL, LONDON	1790	DUTC	PAWL	88
HILL, LONDON JR.	1800	DUTC	PAWL	45
HILL, LONDON SR.	1800	DUTC	PAWL	44
HILL, MOSES	1820	ONTA	CANA	213
HILL, NICHOLAS	1830	GREN	ATHN	212
HILL, RACHEAL	1800	NYCO	WD07	86
HILL, RICHARD	1820	SCHR	BROM	412
HILL, RICHARD	1830	SCHR	BROM	88
HILL, SILAS	1830	TIOG	BART	165
HILL, THOMAS	1830	COLU	GHEN	152
HILL, WILLIAM	1820	NYCO	WD06	477
HILL, WILLIAM	1820	ORNG	MONT	821
HILL, WILLIAM	1830	ORNG	CRAW	187
HILL, WILLIAM	1830	ORNG	MONR	173
HILLIS, PHINE	1810	SUFF	SHAM	445
HILLS, ANDREW	1830	MADI	----	238
HILLS, E.	1810	MADI	BROK	774
HILLS, JOSEPH	1820	QUEN	----	63
HILLS, THOMAS	1830	COLU	HUDS	99
HILSON, ISAAC	1830	NYCO	WD13	336
HILSON, MRS.	1830	NYCO	WD06	443
HILTON, LEONARD	1810	NYCO	WD10	693
HIMY	1820	WEST	WEST	197
HINDERSON, JOE	1830	KING	WD04	308
HINE, HARRY	1830	PUTM	SOUT	50
HINNY, PETER	1820	DUTC	REDH	120
HINSON, SALLY	1830	NYCO	WD05	317
HITCH, ANDREW	1820	NYCO	WD06	494
HITCHCOCK	1810	NYCO	WD07	605
HITCHCOCK, AMOS	1820	ABNY	ABNY	174
HITCHCOCK, AMOS	1830	ABNY	BETH	536
HITCHCOCK, BARRENA	1810	NYCO	WD06	453
HITCHCOCK, HENRY	1820	DUTC	BEEK	11
HITCHCOCK, LEWIS	1800	WEST	CORT	812
HITCHCOCK, MOSES	1830	NYCO	WD10	73
HITCHCOCK, PETER	1810	NYCO	WD10	527
HITCHIOCH, MOSES	1820	NYCO	WD07	710
HITE, HENRY	1830	GREN	NEWB	174
HIX, MARTIN	1820	SCNE	WD02	129
HOASE, SUNN	1830	WASH	CAMB	121
HOBART, GEORGE	1810	ORNG	GOSP	1131
HOBART, JOHN H.	1810	NYCO	WD01	10
HOBART, NATHANIEL	1790	SUFF	SOUT	170

NAME	YR	CO	TWP	PG
HOBBY, KIFF	1810	WEST	RYE.	1164
HOBBY, PETER	1800	NYCO	WD07	859
HOBS, SALOMON	1810	QUEN	NHEM	205
HODGE, GEORGE	1820	NYCO	WD07	705
HODGE, SAMUEL	1820	NYCO	WD07	705
HODGE, WILLIAM	1830	LIVI	GROV	35
HODGES, DAVID	1810	NYCO	WD04	206
HODGES, JOSEPH	1800	ONTA	NOTH	310
HOES, SIMON	1830	COLU	KIND	137
HOFF, JOHN	1830	DUTC	WASH	450
HOFFMAN, ANN	1820	DUTC	REDH	120
HOFFMAN, F.	1830	NYCO	WD13	375
HOFFMAN, PETER	1830	ULST	KING	63
HOFFMAN, ROBERT	1820	COLU	HUDS	17
HOFFMAN, THOMAS	1830	NYCO	WD08	213
HOGABOOM, BARNEY	1830	RENS	BRUN	227
HOGABOOM, THOMAS	1830	RENS	BRUN	224
HOGAN, JOHN	1830	DUTC	PGKP	322
HOGAN, PETER	1820	NYCO	WD05	398
HOGANS, AARON	1830	NYCO	WD05	302
HOGART, GEORGE	1830	KING	WD04	320
HOGELAND, SAMUEL H.	1830	NYCO	WD14	488
HOGEMAN, SAMUEL	1810	QUEN	OYST	238
HOGHLAND, WILLIAM	1820	NYCO	WD09	946
HOGLAND, RICHARD	1810	QUEN	FLUS	201
HOGOBOOM, ANTHONY	1810	ULST	KING	757
HOIT, ABRAHAM	1830	COLU	HUDS	106
HOLAMBECK, PHILIP	1820	CHEN	SHER	337
HOLCOMB, ISAAC	1830	SCHR	MIDD	49
HOLD, JOHN	1810	NYCO	WD04	154
HOLDEN, JOB	1830	SCNE	GLEN	260
HOLEMBECK, PHILIP	1830	CHEN	SHER	137
HOLLAND, JEPTHA	1810	COLU	HUDS	147
HOLLAND, WILLIAM	1820	KING	BRYN	116
HOLLAND, WILLIAM	1820	ONTA	CANA	213
HOLLAND, WILLIAM	1830	ONTA	GORH	6
HOLLENBECK, BENJAMIN	1830	GREN	COXE	188
HOLLENBECK, GEORGE	1810	SARA	GALW	827
HOLLENBECK, HARRY	1820	SARA	SARA	189
HOLLENBECK, HERMAN	1830	GREN	ATHN	205
HOLLENBECK, JACK	1820	GREN	NEWB	25
HOLLENBECK, JACK	1830	GREN	ATHN	214
HOLLENBECK, JOSEPH	1830	GREN	ATHN	204
HOLLENBECK, PETER	1830	GREN	ATHN	202
HOLLENBECK, RICHARD	1820	SARA	EDIN	169
HOLLENBECK, RICHARD	1830	GREN	COXE	199
HOLLENBECK, RICHARD B.	1830	GREN	COXE	188
HOLLENBECK, THOMAS	1830	RENS	TROY	17
HOLLEY, WILLIAM	1820	WEST	NORS	387

NAME	YR	CO	TWP	PG
HOLLIDAY	1810	NYCO	WD07	557
HOLLIS, DANIEL	1820	NYCO	WD01	3
HOLLOCK, ISSAC	1810	ORNG	GOSH	1068
HOLMES, ANTHONY	1830	ABNY	WD02	245
HOLMES, CHARLOTTE	1810	NYCO	WD06	397
HOLMES, GEORGE	1820	WEST	BEDF	408
HOLMES, JACOB	1800	NYCO	WD05	786
HOLMES, JOHN	1830	RICH	SOUT	15
HOLMES, PETER	1800	NYCO	WD04	734
HOLMES, PETER	1830	KING	FLAN	412
HOLMES, THOMAS	1830	RICH	WEST	13
HOLMES, WILLIAM	1820	NYCO	WD06	498
HOLMS, MARY	1830	ONON	SALI	13
HOLSEY, PETER	1790	SUFF	SOUT	167
HOLSEY, YORK	1820	CHAT	HANO	104
HOLSTEAD, HARRY	1830	WEST	HARR	215
HOMER, ISRAEL	1790	QUEN	OYST	153
HON, MINK	1830	MONT	CANJ	35
HONEVILLE, EDWARD	1820	WEST	WTPL	461
HONEYWELL, ISAAC	1820	NYCO	WD06	475
HONNBECK, THOMAS	1820	ULST	ESOP	51
HOOFMAN, GEORGE	1800	SARA	CHAR	1072
HOOGEBOOM, ANTHONY	1800	ULST	KING	227
HOOKER, CHARLES	1810	ONTA	CANA	890
HOON, JOHN	1830	NYCO	WD06	410
HOONER, BENJAMIN	1830	NYCO	WD06	444
HOOSE, ABRAHAM	1820	COLU	HUDS	15
HOOSE, PETER	1830	ABNY	WD01	203
HOPKINS, ANTHONY	1800	NYCO	WD07	872
HOPKINS, CYRUS	1830	QUEN	OYST	43
HOPKINS, J.P.	1830	ERIE	BUFF	43
HOPKINS, JOSEPH	1820	NYCO	WD07	710
HOPKINS, PRINCE	1810	COLU	CANN	104
HOPPER, ANTHONY	1830	NYCO	WD09	430
HOPPIN, GELLIS	1820	NYCO	WD09	940
HORACE, PETER	1830	NYCO	WD08	269
HORBECK, PETER	1830	ULST	MARB	161
HORBROOK, SIMON	1810	NYCO	WD08	764
HORDEN, JAMES	1830	KING	BRYN	367
HORDON, WILLIAM	1830	NYCO	WD04	187
HORNBECK, HENRY	1820	ORNG	WALL	846
HORNBECK, HENRY	1830	SARA	SARA	146
HORNBECK, HENRY	1830	ULST	PLAT	260
HORNBECK, JACOBUS	1830	ULST	ROCH	170
HORNBECK, SAMUEL	1830	SULL	MAMA	79
HORNBECK, SIBYO	1830	ONON	SKAN	156
HORNBECK, THOMAS	1830	ULST	WAWA	191
HORTEN, ALEXANDER	1830	NYCO	WD04	187
HORTON, A.	1830	NYCO	WD11	162

NAME	YR	CO	TWP	PG
HORTON, CHARLES	1820	NYCO	WD04	285
HORTON, GEORGE	1830	QUEN	OYST	33
HORTON, JACK	1810	SUFF	SOUT	564
HORTON, OBEDIAH	1810	QUEN	FLUS	195
HORTON, OBET	1820	QUEN	----	60
HORTON, WILLIAM	1830	NYCO	WD05	334
HOSTADER, WILLIAM	1830	MONR	RWD1	196
HOSTER, RICHARD	1810	SUFF	SHAM	439
HOSTER, RICHARD	1810	SUFF	SHAM	445
HOTTENTAT, ESCOP	1810	QUEN	FLUS	203
HOTTENTAT, WILLIAM	1810	QUEN	FLUS	203
HOTTENTOT, EDWARD	1830	QUEN	FLUS	154
HOTTENTOT, ESOP	1830	QUEN	FLUS	154
HOTTENTOT, GEORGE	1830	QUEN	FLUS	144
HOTTENTOT, WILLIAM	1830	QUEN	FLUS	154
HOTTERTOT, GEORGE	1820	QUEN	----	54
HOTTONTOT, ESOP	1820	QUEN	----	57
HOTTONTOT, PHILLIS	1820	QUEN	----	57
HOTTONTOT, WILLIAM	1820	QUEN	----	57
HOUCH, JOE	1830	SCHR	SCHR	13
HOUCH, THOMAS	1830	SCHR	SCHR	14
HOUGH, EZEKL.	1830	ALLE	FDSP	94
HOUGH, STEPHEN	1830	ALLE	RUSH	175
HOUGHTAILING, JACK	1830	GREN	ATHN	203
HOUGHTAILING, JOHN	1830	GREN	NEWB	172
HOUGHTAILING, PETER	1830	GREN	NEWB	174
HOUGHTAILING, POMP	1830	ONID	NWHT	72
HOUGHTAILING, WILLIAM	1830	GREN	NEWB	176
HOUGHTALING, JACK	1820	GREN	NEWB	27
HOUGHTALING, POMP	1820	SCHR	BROM	412
HOUGHTALING, PRINCE	1820	ABNY	BETH	223
HOUGHTENBERGH, THOMAS	1830	SCHR	SCHR	16
HOUGHTENBURGH, ANDREW	1820	ORNG	WALL	778
HOUGHTENBURGH, JAMES	1830	SCHR	SCHR	20
HOUSMAN, J.	1830	NYCO	WD11	189
HOUSTEN, HARREY	1820	ORNG	NEWW	488
HOUSTON, HENRY	1830	ORNG	HBGH	124
HOUSTON, SILAS	1830	ORNG	MONR	168
HOUSTON, THOMAS	1830	NYCO	WD08	255
HOW, ABNEW	1810	WASH	CHES	401
HOW, JACOB	1830	ABNY	WD04	300
HOWARD, ARTHUR	1830	NYCO	WD06	427
HOWARD, CARNER	1810	QUEN	OYST	247
HOWARD, DANIEL	1830	QUEN	FLUS	152
HOWARD, HARRY	1830	SUFF	BROK	167
HOWARD, HENRY	1830	QUEN	FLUS	146
HOWARD, JAMES	1830	NYCO	WD10	24
HOWARD, PRINCE	1830	KING	WD04	305
HOWARD, ROBERT	1800	NYCO	WD06	800

NAME	YR	CO	TWP	PG
HOWARD, T.	1830	KING	WD04	319
HOWE, ABRAHAM	1830	NYCO	WD14	448
HOWE, JOHN	1800	NYCO	WD05	773
HOWE, JOSHUA	1820	ONID	WATE	303
HOWE, JOSHUA	1830	ONID	NWHT	70
HOWEL, CEASER	1810	SUFF	ISLP	498
HOWEL, CYRUS	1820	SUFF	SHAM	322
HOWEL, ELIZAH	1810	NYCO	WD07	545
HOWEL, GEORGE	1830	NYCO	WD10	19
HOWEL, PETER	1810	SUFF	BROK	490
HOWEL, PETER	1820	OTSG	UNAD	92
HOWEL, PETER	1820	SUFF	BROK	357
HOWELL, ABRAHAM	1820	SUFF	ISLP	309
HOWELL, CATHARINE	1790	SUFF	SOUT	169
HOWELL, EBO	1830	SUFF	BROK	162
HOWELL, GEORGE	1820	NYCO	WD06	531
HOWELL, HARRY	1830	ULST	NPAL	205
HOWELL, ISAAC	1830	SUFF	SHAM	215
HOWELL, OLIVER	1830	NYCO	WD05	261
HOWELL, PETER	1830	OTSG	UNAD	198
HOWELL, PETER	1830	SUFF	BROK	195
HOWELL, SIMAS	1820	SUFF	RIVH	355
HOWELL, THOMAS	1830	SUFF	SHAM	231
HOWLAND, DAVID	1830	NYCO	WD06	435
HOYT	1820	PUTM	PATE	101
HOYT, MARY	1830	NYCO	WD06	454
HOYT, RICHARD	1820	PUTM	PHIL	101
HUB, SOLOMON	1820	QUEN	----	60
HUBBARD, CHARLES	1830	NYCO	WD07	65
HUBBARD, GEORGE	1820	ORNG	GOSH	733
HUBBY, ROBERT	1820	DUTC	BEEK	20
HUBS, JACK	1820	WEST	NEWR	212
HUBS, JANE	1830	QUEN	FLUS	156
HUBS, JEFFERY	1820	QUEN	----	60
HUBS, SOLOMON	1830	QUEN	FLUS	155
HUDEY, LAZARIS	1820	WEST	NEWC	314
HUDSON, JACOB	1820	NYCO	WD06	482
HUDSON, JACOB	1820	NYCO	WD06	498
HUDSON, JACOB	1830	NYCO	WD06	375
HUDSON, LUCAS	1820	COLU	CHAT	7
HUDSON, WILLIAM	1800	NYCO	WD01	662
HUDSON, WILLIAM	1830	NYCO	WD06	435
HUDUD, BENJAMIN	1810	JEFF	CHAM	573
HUESTED, HENRY	1830	NYCO	WD06	447
HUFF, ANTHONY	1810	NYCO	WD06	442
HUFF, DAVID	1820	SENE	FAYE	382
HUFF, DAVID	1830	STEU	PRAT	440
HUFF, ISAIAH	1830	STEU	PRAT	454
HUFF, JACK	1820	DUTC	BEEK	12

NAME	YR	CO	TWP	PG
HUFF, JOHN	1800	ORNG	MINI	317
HUFF, JOHN	1830	ORNG	WARW	65
HUFF, JOSIAH	1820	SENE	ROMU	352
HUFFMAN, ROBERT	1830	NYCO	WD08	263
HUGABOOM, FRANCIS	1830	ABNY	WD02	274
HUGGET, EDWARD	1800	NYCO	WD05	764
HUGGET, EDWARD	1810	NYCO	WD04	194
HUGGET, EDWARD	1810	NYCO	WD06	396
HUGH	1810	NYCO	WD10	544
HUGHES, HARRY	1830	CAYU	AURE	186
HUGHES, HENRY	1820	SENE	FAYE	387
HUGHMAN, CATO	1800	NYCO	WD06	843
HUGHS, MARGARET	1830	NYCO	WD04	178
HUGHS, RICHARD	1830	GREN	CAIR	252
HUGSBEY, WILLIAM	1810	NYCO	WD10	693
HUIN, JOHN	1820	NYCO	WD07	631
HULET, HENRY	1810	SUFF	ISLP	499
HULET, PHILIP	1800	NYCO	WD05	764
HULETT, ROBERT	1820	NYCO	WD10	991
HULICK, WILLIAM	1800	NYCO	WD05	760
HULIS, JOHN	1820	NYCO	WD05	434
HULL, J.	1810	MADI	SMIT	880
HULL, JAMES	1810	NYCO	WD06	415
HULL, SUSAN	1810	KING	BRYN	630
HULL, THOMAS	1800	ONID	PARI	118
HULL, WILLIAM	1830	NYCO	WD05	272
HULMOT, NICOLAS	1830	SCNE	GLEN	261
HUMPHREY, ABEL	1820	ONON	MARC	238
HUMPHREY, ABEL	1830	ONON	CAMI	200
HUMPHREY, MOSES	1830	DUTC	PGKP	326
HUMPHRIES, JONAS	1830	JEFF	HOUN	187
HUNN, THOMAS	1820	KING	BRYN	126
HUNT, DAVID	1810	DUTC	BEEK	286
HUNT, FANNY	1810	NYCO	WD06	450
HUNT, FRANCES	1830	NYCO	WD05	338
HUNT, HARRY	1830	WEST	GREN	16
HUNT, JAMES	1810	COLU	HILL	123
HUNT, JAMES	1830	NYCO	WD06	386
HUNT, JESSE	1830	NYCO	WD09	330
HUNT, SAMUEL	1810	QUEN	FLUS	197
HUNT, THOMAS	1820	WEST	RYE	370
HUNT, TITUS	1810	QUEN	NHEM	306
HUNT, WILLET	1830	QUEN	FLUS	142
HUNTER	1790	NYCO	WEST	137
HUNTER, ABRAHAM	1810	SCHR	SCHR	28
HUNTER, ADAM	1830	SCHR	SCHR	6
HUNTER, BENJAMIN	1830	ONID	DEER	245
HUNTER, BENJAMIN	1830	ORNG	NEWB	42
HUNTER, ELIAS	1830	SUFF	HUNT	304

NAME	YR	CO	TWP	PG
HUNTER, EZAKIEL	1810	SUFF	SMIT	532
HUNTER, HENRY	1820	QUEN	----	80
HUNTER, JAMES	1820	QUEN	----	80
HUNTER, JAMES	1830	SUFF	SMIT	271
HUNTER, JAMES	1830	SUFF	SMIT	274
HUNTER, MOSES	1830	NYCO	WD13	336
HUNTER, MRS.	1830	NYCO	WD12	278
HUNTER, OLIVER	1820	SUFF	SHAM	319
HUNTER, OLIVER	1830	KING	BRYN	367
HUNTER, PETER	1830	WASH	KING	368
HUNTER, RICHARD	1830	ORNG	MONR	170
HUNTER, S.	1830	NYCO	WD11	155
HUNTER, SAMUEL	1800	ORNG	NEWC	305
HUNTER, SAMUEL	1820	ORNG	MONT	846
HUNTER, SAMUEL	1830	ORNG	NEWB	42
HUNTER, STEPHEN	1810	NYCO	WD10	648
HUNTER, STEPHEN	1820	NYCO	WD07	659
HUNTER, STEPHEN	1830	ORNG	MONR	161
HUNTER, THOMAS	1820	ABNY	ABNY	171
HUNTER, WILLIAM	1810	NYCO	WD02	116
HUNTER, WILLIAM	1830	NYCO	WD14	449
HUNTER, WILLIAM	1830	ORNG	BLOM	123
HUNTER, YORK	1830	ONID	VERN	99
HUNTING, NERO	1830	ORNG	GOSH	291
HUNTS, JAMES	1820	NYCO	WD08	827
HUNTTER, ELIAS	1820	SUFF	HUNT	274
HUNTTER, TAMOR	1820	SUFF	SMIT	316
HURSEY, HEZEKIAH	1820	ONTA	CANA	215
HURST, WILLIAM	1830	MONR	BRIG	32
HURWELL, NERO	1830	WEST	BEDF	150
HUSBAND, WILLIAMS	1810	NYCO	WD02	120
HUSBANDS, BETSEY	1820	NYCO	WD02	61
HUSBANDS, WILLIAM	1800	NYCO	WD03	704
HUSSEY, SYLVANUS	1820	GENE	LEIC	158
HUTCHINGS, DANIEL	1830	NYCO	WD05	345
HUTCHINGS, SAMUEL	1810	NYCO	WD02	127
HUTCHINS, CHARLES	1830	NYCO	WD05	271
HUTCHINS, SAMUEL	1820	NYCO	WD04	281
HUTCHINS, SAMUEL S.	1830	NYCO	WD14	427
HUTCHINSON, CHARLES	1830	PUTM	SOUT	46
HUTCHINSON, JAMES	1830	NYCO	WD08	214
HUTCHINSON, THOMAS	1830	NYCO	WD04	187
HUTET, HENRY	1820	SUFF	HUNT	304
HUTSON, WILLIAMS	1810	NYCO	WD05	252
HYALL, MINGO	1810	NYCO	WD06	457
HYAT, PETER	1810	NYCO	WD04	205
HYATT, HENRY	1820	NYCO	WD06	477
HYATT, JOSEPH	1830	SCHR	SCHR	13
HYERS, JOHN	1830	NYCO	WD05	315

NAME	YR	CO	TWP	PG
ICHABOD	1790	WEST	HARR	199
ICHOBED	1810	RENS	STEP	572
IMISS, SARAH	1830	NYCO	WD06	435
INDER, PETER	1820	ORNG	MINI	572
INGERSOLL, ALFRED	1830	NYCO	WD07	30
INGRAM, NATHANIEL	1810	GENE	RIGA	144
INURMISS, JOHN	1830	NYCO	WD06	454
IRVIN, FRANK	1810	WEST	HARR	1140
IRVING, JAMES	1820	NYCO	WD06	491
IRVING, JAMES	1830	NYCO	WD06	458
ISAAC	1790	QUEN	FLUS	149
ISAAC	1790	QUEN	JAMA	150
ISAAC	1790	QUEN	NHEM	152
ISAAC	1790	QUEN	OYST	154
ISAAC	1790	QUEN	SHEM	156
ISAAC	1800	QUEN	OYST	575
ISAAC	1800	QUEN	OYST	572
ISAAC	1800	QUEN	OYST	579
ISAAC	1800	QUEN	OYST	571
ISAAC	1800	SARA	PROV	1096
ISAAC	1810	DUTC	STAN	174
ISAAC	1810	ONTA	SENE	847
ISAAC	1820	QUEN	----	54
ISAAC, HANNAH	1810	SUFF	BROK	469
ISAAC, JOHN	1810	NYCO	WD05	334
ISAAC, JOHN	1830	NYCO	WD14	429
ISAAC, OSTIN	1830	KING	WD02	275
ISAACS, PEYTON	1830	NYCO	WD09	383
ISABELLA	1810	NYCO	WD06	442
ISAND	1800	SUFF	BROK	9
ISHMAEL	1790	QUEN	JAMA	150
ISHMAEL	1810	NYCO	WD10	773
ISRAEL	1790	NYCO	MONT	123
ISRAEL	1790	QUEN	JAMA	150
ISRAEL	1790	QUEN	OYST	154
ISRAEL	1790	QUEN	SHEM	156
ISRAEL	1800	QUEN	FLUS	540
IZZABEL	1790	QUEN	NHEM	152
JABEY	1800	SUFF	HUNT	44
JABUS (ETHOPHIAN)	1790	SUFF	SMIT	165
JACK	1790	NYCO	MONT	124
JACK	1790	NYCO	OUTW	128
JACK	1790	QUEN	FLUS	149
JACK	1790	QUEN	JAMA	150
JACK	1790	QUEN	NEWT	151
JACK	1790	QUEN	NHEM	152

NAME	YR	CO	TWP	PG
JACK	1790	QUEN	OYST	153
JACK	1790	QUEN	OYST	155
JACK	1790	QUEN	SHEM	156
JACK	1790	SUFF	SOUT	170
JACK	1800	ABNY	BETH	195
JACK	1800	QUEN	NEWT	656
JACK	1800	QUEN	NHEM	560
JACK	1800	QUEN	OYST	578
JACK	1800	QUEN	OYST	574
JACK	1800	QUEN	OYST	575
JACK	1800	QUEN	OYST	578
JACK	1800	QUEN	SHEM	559
JACK	1800	RENS	SCHO	837
JACK	1800	RENS	TROY	899
JACK	1800	SUFF	BROK	10
JACK	1800	SUFF	SMIT	27
JACK	1800	SUFF	ISLP	62
JACK	1810	QUEN	OYST	232
JACK	1810	RENS	SCHO	552
JACK	1810	RENS	TROY	387
JACK	1810	SUFF	BROK	493
JACK	1820	ABNY	COEY	130
JACK	1820	SUFF	BROK	353
JACK	1830	NYCO	WD11	151
JACK	1830	NYCO	WD13	362
JACK	1830	NYCO	WD13	374
JACK	1830	NYCO	WD13	406
JACK, BEN	1800	SUFF	EHAM	91
JACK, CLOE	1830	RENS	SHOD	253
JACK, DENCE	1820	SUFF	EAST	294
JACK, JACBOAM	1810	SUFF	SOUT	558
JACK, JAMES	1810	SUFF	HUNT	536
JACK, JAMES	1810	SUFF	SHAM	440
JACK, JOHN	1790	SUFF	BROK	162
JACK, LITTLE	1810	COLU	KIND	174
JACK, RICHARD	1820	DUTC	FISH	57
JACKLIN, COMFORD	1830	NYCO	WD06	387
JACKLIN, EDWARD	1820	OTSG	OTSG	100
JACKLIN, ISRAEL	1820	DUTC	FISH	74
JACKLIN, JAMES	1820	ONTA	CANA	210
JACKLIN, JOSEPH	1800	DELA	KORT	1317
JACKLIN, POMP	1830	ONID	AUGU	127
JACKLIN, ROBERT	1830	NYCO	WD14	487
JACKLIN, SU	1810	OTSG	MIDD	149
JACKLIN, TITUS	1810	DUTC	FISH	214
JACKLIN, TITUS	1820	DUTC	FISH	58
JACKNELL, EDWARD	1830	ABNY	WD04	318
JACKS, BENJAMIN	1810	SUFF	EAST	437
JACKS, JOHN	1830	LIVI	SPAR	136

Jackson

NAME	YR	CO	TWP	PG
JACKSON	1810	NYCO	WD06	449
JACKSON	1810	NYCO	WD07	549
JACKSON	1810	NYCO	WD10	699
JACKSON	1810	RENS	TROY	386
JACKSON	1820	NYCO	WD05	430
JACKSON	1820	PUTM	PATE	101
JACKSON, A.	1830	NYCO	WD11	144
JACKSON, ABIGAIL	1830	NYCO	WD05	278
JACKSON, ABRAHAM	1800	ABNY	WD01	263
JACKSON, ABRAHAM	1830	DUTC	HYPK	231
JACKSON, ABRAHAM	1830	ORNG	CRAW	195
JACKSON, ABRAM	1830	SENE	WL00	12
JACKSON, ANDREW	1820	WEST	WEST	184
JACKSON, ANDREW	1830	MONT	MIND	6
JACKSON, ANDREW	1830	WEST	YONK	10
JACKSON, ANN	1830	ABNY	WD01	221
JACKSON, ANTHONY	1820	NYCO	WD08	796
JACKSON, ANTHONY	1830	ONON	SALI	17
JACKSON, ANTHONY	1830	OTSG	BURL	278
JACKSON, BEN	1820	QUEN	----	6
JACKSON, BENJAMIN	1810	QUEN	SHEM	306
JACKSON, BENJAMIN	1830	NYCO	WD08	236
JACKSON, BENJAMIN	1830	NYCO	WD08	257
JACKSON, BENJIMEN	1820	NYCO	WD08	817
JACKSON, BETSEY	1820	NYCO	WD03	145
JACKSON, BETSEY	1830	GREN	CATS	237
JACKSON, BETSEY	1830	NYCO	WD08	245
JACKSON, BETTY	1820	COLU	HUDS	19
JACKSON, BRISTER	1800	NYCO	WD01	793
JACKSON, CAESAR	1800	NYCO	WD03	701
JACKSON, CAESAR	1800	NYCO	WD07	859
JACKSON, CAESAR	1830	NYCO	WD08	199
JACKSON, CAESAR	1830	NYCO	WD08	245
JACKSON, CATHERINE	1830	NYCO	WD06	388
JACKSON, CATO	1820	GREN	CATS	157
JACKSON, CATY	1820	GREN	COXE	35
JACKSON, CEASAR	1800	NYCO	WD07	859
JACKSON, CEASER	1820	GREN	CATS	170
JACKSON, CESAR	1830	RENS	SCHO	241
JACKSON, CEZAR	1830	HERK	DANU	185
JACKSON, CHARLES	1820	QUEN	----	7
JACKSON, CHARLES	1830	BROM	CHIN	15
JACKSON, CHARLES	1830	CHAT	RIPY	439
JACKSON, CHARLES	1830	QUEN	SHEM	78
JACKSON, CHARLES	1830	SUFF	BROK	162
JACKSON, CHRISTINA	1830	DUTC	FISH	462
JACKSON, CHRISTOPHER	1830	ABNY	WD01	197
JACKSON, COBUS	1830	SARA	MILT	28
JACKSON, CONGO	1810	NYCO	WD05	258
JACKSON, CORNELIUS	1830	RENS	TROY	17

NAME	YR	CO	TWP	PG
JACKSON, CORNELIUS	1830	WASH	FTED	305
JACKSON, CORNS	1830	NYCO	WD10	59
JACKSON, CYRUS	1830	WASH	KING	368
JACKSON, DANIEL	1830	RICH	SOUT	15
JACKSON, DAVID	1800	WEST	NEWR	623
JACKSON, DAVID	1810	NYCO	WD05	291
JACKSON, DAVID	1820	PUTM	SOUT	100
JACKSON, DAVID	1830	NYCO	WD07	46
JACKSON, DAVID	1830	QUEN	FLUS	147
JACKSON, DIANA	1830	NYCO	WD04	218
JACKSON, DIANNA	1830	SCNE	ROTT	250
JACKSON, DINAH	1830	ABNY	WD04	299
JACKSON, DINAH	1830	DUTC	FISH	501
JACKSON, EDWARD	1800	NYCO	WD04	741
JACKSON, EDWARD	1830	CHEN	NORW	175
JACKSON, ELIAS	1830	ORNG	NEWW	107
JACKSON, ELIJAH	1810	QUEN	OYST	256
JACKSON, ELIJAH	1830	QUEN	SHEM	78
JACKSON, ELIZABETH	1830	NYCO	WD06	368
JACKSON, ENOCH	1830	DUTC	REDH	375
JACKSON, ENOCH	1830	SUFF	HUNT	316
JACKSON, EVE	1830	KING	WD02	264
JACKSON, EVE	1830	KING	WD02	262
JACKSON, F.	1830	NYCO	WD11	201
JACKSON, FLORA	1830	COLU	HUDS	102
JACKSON, FRANCIS	1810	NYCO	WD08	714
JACKSON, FRANCIS	1820	NYCO	WD05	352
JACKSON, FRANCIS	1820	NYCO	WD10	984
JACKSON, FRANCIS	1820	ONID	UTIC	209
JACKSON, FRANCIS	1830	ORNG	MINI	255
JACKSON, GASHURN	1830	RENS	SCHO	251
JACKSON, GEORGE	1820	NYCO	WD03	182
JACKSON, H.	1830	NYCO	WD11	142
JACKSON, HANNAH	1810	NYCO	WD08	130
JACKSON, HANNIBAL	1790	ULST	WOOD	185
JACKSON, HANNIBAL	1800	ULST	WOOD	192
JACKSON, HARRIET	1830	NYCO	WD05	341
JACKSON, HARRY	1830	ONON	SALI	11
JACKSON, HENRY	1800	ABNY	SCNE	9
JACKSON, HENRY	1810	SCNE	WD02	946
JACKSON, HENRY	1820	NYCO	WD10	981
JACKSON, HENRY	1820	NYCO	WD10	983
JACKSON, HENRY	1820	SCNE	WD01	123
JACKSON, HENRY	1820	SCNE	WD02	129
JACKSON, HENRY	1830	ABNY	WD01	210
JACKSON, HENRY	1830	ABNY	WD04	312
JACKSON, HENRY	1830	COLU	CHAT	52
JACKSON, HENRY	1830	COLU	HUDS	102
JACKSON, HENRY	1830	FRAN	WEST	83

Jackson

NAME	YR	CO	TWP	PG
JACKSON, HENRY	1830	NYCO	WD05	337
JACKSON, HENRY	1830	NYCO	WD10	19
JACKSON, HENRY	1830	NYCO	WD12	310
JACKSON, HENRY JR.	1810	SCNE	WD02	953
JACKSON, ISAAC	1830	NYCO	WD09	347
JACKSON, ISABELLA	1830	NYCO	WD01	31
JACKSON, J.	1820	NYCO	WD08	789
JACKSON, JABIZ	1820	CHEN	NORW	378
JACKSON, JACK	1800	ABNY	WD01	263
JACKSON, JACK	1820	COLU	KIND	11
JACKSON, JACK	1820	ROCK	HAVE	102
JACKSON, JACK	1820	SCHR	SCHR	449
JACKSON, JACK	1830	ABNY	WD04	314
JACKSON, JACK	1830	ABNY	WD04	320
JACKSON, JACK	1830	ROCK	ORGT	114
JACKSON, JACOB	1810	NYCO	WD05	320
JACKSON, JACOB	1810	QUEN	NHEM	306
JACKSON, JACOB	1830	RENS	SHOD	253
JACKSON, JAMES	1810	DUTC	FISH	224
JACKSON, JAMES	1810	NYCO	WD05	298
JACKSON, JAMES	1820	ABNY	ABNY	177
JACKSON, JAMES	1820	KING	BRYN	149
JACKSON, JAMES	1820	NYCO	WD06	524
JACKSON, JAMES	1820	NYCO	WD08	807
JACKSON, JAMES	1820	QUEN	----	8
JACKSON, JAMES	1830	ABNY	WD01	221
JACKSON, JAMES	1830	CAYU	SEMP	317
JACKSON, JAMES	1830	COLU	AUST	180
JACKSON, JAMES	1830	DUTC	MILN	256
JACKSON, JAMES	1830	NYCO	WD10	95
JACKSON, JAMES	1830	NYCO	WD14	521
JACKSON, JAMES	1830	QUEN	FLUS	148
JACKSON, JAMES	1830	QUEN	SHEM	74
JACKSON, JANE	1810	NYCO	WD06	407
JACKSON, JANE	1810	NYCO	WD03	44
JACKSON, JANE	1810	NYCO	WD02	99
JACKSON, JANE	1810	NYCO	WD05	252
JACKSON, JANE	1810	NYCO	WD06	407
JACKSON, JANE	1820	NYCO	WD09	921
JACKSON, JANE	1830	NYCO	WD05	263
JACKSON, JANE	1830	NYCO	WD08	249
JACKSON, JEFFERY	1810	QUEN	SHEM	306
JACKSON, JENNET	1820	ABNY	GUID	247
JACKSON, JENNY	1830	ABNY	GUID	415
JACKSON, JOHN	1790	NYCO	WEST	134
JACKSON, JOHN	1800	ABNY	WD02	287
JACKSON, JOHN	1800	NYCO	WD01	667
JACKSON, JOHN	1810	DELA	DELH	531
JACKSON, JOHN	1810	KING	BRYN	640

NAME	YR	CO	TWP	PG
JACKSON, JOHN	1810	NYCO	WD05	331
JACKSON, JOHN	1810	NYCO	WD05	361
JACKSON, JOHN	1810	NYCO	WD06	397
JACKSON, JOHN	1810	ROCK	HEMP	668
JACKSON, JOHN	1820	ABNY	ABNY	177
JACKSON, JOHN	1820	COLU	HUDS	19
JACKSON, JOHN	1820	KING	BRYN	126
JACKSON, JOHN	1820	NYCO	WD02	120
JACKSON, JOHN	1820	NYCO	WD04	314
JACKSON, JOHN	1820	NYCO	WD05	422
JACKSON, JOHN	1820	NYCO	WD06	525
JACKSON, JOHN	1820	NYCO	WD09	872
JACKSON, JOHN	1820	ONTA	FREE	99
JACKSON, JOHN	1820	SARA	HALF	222
JACKSON, JOHN	1820	SARA	HALF	223
JACKSON, JOHN	1820	SCHR	SCHR	535
JACKSON, JOHN	1820	SCNE	WD01	123
JACKSON, JOHN	1820	SUFF	ISLP	307
JACKSON, JOHN	1820	WASH	FTED	159
JACKSON, JOHN	1830	ABNY	GUID	401
JACKSON, JOHN	1830	ABNY	BETH	548
JACKSON, JOHN	1830	ABNY	WD01	200
JACKSON, JOHN	1830	ABNY	WD01	212
JACKSON, JOHN	1830	ABNY	WD01	223
JACKSON, JOHN	1830	ABNY	WD02	258
JACKSON, JOHN	1830	ABNY	WD04	299
JACKSON, JOHN	1830	CHEN	GREN	48
JACKSON, JOHN	1830	COLU	STUY	57
JACKSON, JOHN	1830	COLU	STUY	65
JACKSON, JOHN	1830	COLU	HUDS	114
JACKSON, JOHN	1830	DUTC	LAGR	249
JACKSON, JOHN	1830	DUTC	FISH	478
JACKSON, JOHN	1830	GREN	CAIR	247
JACKSON, JOHN	1830	JEFF	WATE	67
JACKSON, JOHN	1830	KING	WD02	267
JACKSON, JOHN	1830	KING	WD04	313
JACKSON, JOHN	1830	KING	WD05	330
JACKSON, JOHN	1830	KING	WD05	332
JACKSON, JOHN	1830	LIVI	GENC	5
JACKSON, JOHN	1830	MONT	CANJ	26
JACKSON, JOHN	1830	MONT	AMST	119
JACKSON, JOHN	1830	MONT	JOHN	229
JACKSON, JOHN	1830	NYCO	WD01	31
JACKSON, JOHN	1830	NYCO	WD05	337
JACKSON, JOHN	1830	NYCO	WD06	379
JACKSON, JOHN	1830	NYCO	WD06	437
JACKSON, JOHN	1830	NYCO	WD08	194
JACKSON, JOHN	1830	NYCO	WD08	218
JACKSON, JOHN	1830	NYCO	WD08	220

Jackson

NAME	YR	CO	TWP	PG
JACKSON, JOHN	1830	NYCO	WD08	228
JACKSON, JOHN	1830	NYCO	WD08	245
JACKSON, JOHN	1830	NYCO	WD08	246
JACKSON, JOHN	1830	NYCO	WD09	310
JACKSON, JOHN	1830	NYCO	WD12	279
JACKSON, JOHN	1830	ORNG	BLOM	119
JACKSON, JOHN	1830	QUEN	NEWT	3
JACKSON, JOHN	1830	QUEN	NEWT	14
JACKSON, JOHN	1830	QUEN	FLUS	141
JACKSON, JOHN	1830	RENS	TROY	7
JACKSON, JOHN	1830	RICH	WEST	7
JACKSON, JOHN	1830	SARA	SASP	164
JACKSON, JOHN	1830	SCHR	COBL	143
JACKSON, JOHN	1830	SCNE	WD01	207
JACKSON, JOHN	1830	SUFF	ISLP	280
JACKSON, JOHN	1830	SULL	BETH	27
JACKSON, JOHN	1830	ULST	WOOD	124
JACKSON, JOHN	1830	WASH	FTED	314
JACKSON, JOHN C.	1820	KING	BRYN	134
JACKSON, JOHN J.	1830	DUTC	UNVA	422
JACKSON, JOHN JR.	1830	CHEN	GREN	38
JACKSON, JONATHAN	1810	ONTA	BLOM	612
JACKSON, JOSEPH	1790	ORNG	MINI	143
JACKSON, JOSEPH	1820	ABNY	ABNY	177
JACKSON, JOSEPH	1820	COLU	HUDS	19
JACKSON, JOSEPH	1830	ABNY	GUID	401
JACKSON, JOSEPH	1830	CHEN	NORW	165
JACKSON, JOSEPH	1830	DUTC	PLEA	312
JACKSON, JOSEPH	1830	NYCO	WD05	261
JACKSON, JOSEPH	1830	NYCO	WD06	438
JACKSON, JOSEPH	1830	RENS	TROY	14
JACKSON, JOSEPH	1830	ULST	HURL	142
JACKSON, JOSEPH W.	1830	QUEN	NEWT	17
JACKSON, JOSHUA	1820	CHEN	NORW	378
JACKSON, JOSHUA	1830	CHEN	OXFO	54
JACKSON, JOSIAH	1830	NYCO	WD09	301
JACKSON, JUDAH	1810	KING	BROK	632
JACKSON, JURDON	1830	NYCO	WD04	182
JACKSON, KESIAH	1810	NYCO	WD02	120
JACKSON, KEZIAH	1830	NYCO	WD05	335
JACKSON, KINGSAIL	1830	NYCO	WD10	59
JACKSON, LEWIS	1810	NYCO	WD07	535
JACKSON, LEWIS	1820	WEST	HARR	464
JACKSON, LEWIS	1830	NYCO	WD08	173
JACKSON, LEWIS	1830	NYCO	WD09	385
JACKSON, LEWIS	1830	NYCO	WD09	399
JACKSON, LEWIS	1830	QUEN	SHEM	78
JACKSON, MARDA	1820	NYCO	WD06	450
JACKSON, MARGARET	1820	SCNE	WD01	123

NAME	YR	CO	TWP	PG
JACKSON, MARGARET	1830	ABNY	WD02	239
JACKSON, MARGARET	1830	ABNY	WD02	255
JACKSON, MARIA	1830	NYCO	WD06	435
JACKSON, MARIA	1830	SCNE	WD02	223
JACKSON, MARY	1810	NYCO	WD05	318
JACKSON, MARY	1830	ABNY	WD01	212
JACKSON, MARY	1830	ABNY	WD02	261
JACKSON, MARY	1830	NYCO	WD08	244
JACKSON, MARY ANN	1830	NYCO	WD05	309
JACKSON, MICAH	1810	QUEN	SHEM	306
JACKSON, MICHAEL	1810	DUTC	DOVE	115
JACKSON, MICHAEL	1820	DUTC	DOVE	49
JACKSON, MINK	1830	RENS	BRUN	232
JACKSON, MORIS	1830	QUEN	SHEM	78
JACKSON, MORRIS	1830	ABNY	WD02	244
JACKSON, MOSES	1810	WEST	NORC	1172
JACKSON, MR.	1820	NYCO	WD05	395
JACKSON, MR.	1830	NYCO	WD06	458
JACKSON, MR.	1830	NYCO	WD13	378
JACKSON, MRS.	1820	KING	BRYN	127
JACKSON, MRS.	1820	NYCO	WD05	398
JACKSON, MRS.	1830	KING	WD05	332
JACKSON, MRS.	1830	NYCO	WD05	257
JACKSON, MRS.	1830	NYCO	WD11	177
JACKSON, NAIDER	1820	ABNY	ABNY	177
JACKSON, NANCY	1800	NYCO	WD01	663
JACKSON, NANCY	1820	ABNY	ABNY	176
JACKSON, NANCY	1830	ABNY	GUID	401
JACKSON, NANCY	1830	COLU	STUY	69
JACKSON, NANCY	1830	GREN	CATS	231
JACKSON, NANCY	1830	NYCO	WD09	341
JACKSON, NICHOLAS	1820	NYCO	WD04	266
JACKSON, OBEDIAH	1830	NYCO	WD05	344
JACKSON, OBY	1820	QUEN	----	7
JACKSON, PATIENCE	1820	NYCO	WD04	242
JACKSON, PAUL	1820	MONT	AMST	283
JACKSON, PAUL	1830	ONID	UTIC	45
JACKSON, PETER	1810	DELA	SIDN	558
JACKSON, PETER	1810	NYCO	WD02	127
JACKSON, PETER	1820	ORNG	NEWW	485
JACKSON, PETER	1820	QUEN	----	8
JACKSON, PETER	1830	DUTC	NORT	269
JACKSON, PETER	1830	KING	WD04	302
JACKSON, PETER	1830	KING	BRYN	353
JACKSON, PETER	1830	NYCO	WD13	336
JACKSON, PETER	1830	ONID	UTIC	30
JACKSON, PETER	1830	ORNG	NEWW	106
JACKSON, PETER	1830	QUEN	OYST	22
JACKSON, PHILIP	1830	LIVI	GENC	4

Jackson

NAME	YR	CO	TWP	PG
JACKSON, PHIP	1810	DUTC	RHIN	364
JACKSON, PIANA	1820	NYCO	WD04	322
JACKSON, POLLY	1830	ULST	SAUG	108
JACKSON, POMP	1820	CHEN	NORW	378
JACKSON, POMP	1830	ABNY	BETH	538
JACKSON, POMP	1830	CHEN	NORW	175
JACKSON, PRINCE	1830	ABNY	WATV	466
JACKSON, PRINCE	1830	NYCO	WD05	341
JACKSON, PRINCE	1830	NYCO	WD08	131
JACKSON, PRINCE	1830	OSWE	OSWE	135
JACKSON, PRINCE	1830	RENS	SCAS	111
JACKSON, RACHEL	1810	ULST	WOOD	821
JACKSON, RACHEL	1830	WASH	WTCK	187
JACKSON, REATUS	1830	QUEN	SHEM	77
JACKSON, RICHARD	1820	GREN	CATS	173
JACKSON, RICHARD	1820	NYCO	WD10	988
JACKSON, RICHARD	1820	SCNE	WD02	129
JACKSON, RICHARD	1820	WASH	SALE	186
JACKSON, RICHARD	1830	GREN	CATS	229
JACKSON, RICHARD	1830	GREN	CATS	230
JACKSON, RICHARD	1830	NYCO	WD05	304
JACKSON, RICHARD	1830	RENS	SCAS	108
JACKSON, RICHARD	1830	RENS	SCHO	243
JACKSON, RICHARD	1830	SUFF	ISLP	285
JACKSON, RICHARD	1830	WASH	FTED	315
JACKSON, ROBERT	1800	DUTC	PHIL	72
JACKSON, ROBERT	1800	DUTC	STAN	126
JACKSON, ROBERT	1810	COLU	HUDS	134
JACKSON, ROBERT	1810	NYCO	WD05	350
JACKSON, ROBERT	1820	ABNY	ABNY	177
JACKSON, ROBERT	1830	COLU	STUY	62
JACKSON, ROBERT	1830	NYCO	WD05	336
JACKSON, ROBERT	1830	NYCO	WD06	385
JACKSON, ROBERT	1830	NYCO	WD06	423
JACKSON, ROBERT	1830	NYCO	WD06	455
JACKSON, ROBERT	1830	ONID	UTIC	35
JACKSON, ROBERT	1830	WEST	CORT	63
JACKSON, ROBIN	1810	QUEN	SHEM	306
JACKSON, ROBINSON	1830	ONTA	SENE	74
JACKSON, RUBEN	1820	DUTC	FISH	62
JACKSON, S.	1830	KING	FLAT	400
JACKSON, SAM	1810	NYCO	WD04	159
JACKSON, SAMUEL	1810	NYCO	WD05	320
JACKSON, SAMUEL	1820	SCNE	ROTT	132
JACKSON, SAMUEL	1830	COLU	HUDS	114
JACKSON, SAMUEL	1830	KING	WD02	275
JACKSON, SAMUEL	1830	KING	WD04	298
JACKSON, SAMUEL	1830	MONT	AMST	122
JACKSON, SAMUEL	1830	NYCO	WD07	59

NAME	YR	CO	TWP	PG
JACKSON, SAMUEL	1830	SCNE	GLEN	272
JACKSON, SAMUEL	1830	SCNE	WD01	206
JACKSON, SAMUEL	1830	WASH	HART	304
JACKSON, SARAH	1830	HERK	HERK	52
JACKSON, SEASOR	1820	SCNE	WD02	129
JACKSON, SIMON	1830	ONON	SALI	17
JACKSON, SIPRAM	1810	MONT	CHAR	88
JACKSON, STEPHEN	1830	SCNE	WD02	219
JACKSON, SUCKEY	1820	NYCO	WD10	983
JACKSON, SYMON	1820	ONON	SALI	254
JACKSON, T.	1830	KING	WD04	310
JACKSON, THOMAS	1810	NYCO	WD01	19
JACKSON, THOMAS	1810	SCNE	WD02	952
JACKSON, THOMAS	1820	CHEN	NORW	378
JACKSON, THOMAS	1820	NYCO	WD01	30
JACKSON, THOMAS	1820	ONID	REMS	171
JACKSON, THOMAS	1820	SCNE	WD01	123
JACKSON, THOMAS	1820	SCNE	WD03	133
JACKSON, THOMAS	1830	ABNY	BETH	536
JACKSON, THOMAS	1830	ABNY	WATV	472
JACKSON, THOMAS	1830	ERIE	EVAN	112
JACKSON, THOMAS	1830	HERK	RUSS	20
JACKSON, THOMAS	1830	KING	WD05	325
JACKSON, THOMAS	1830	NYCO	WD01	16
JACKSON, THOMAS	1830	NYCO	WD05	330
JACKSON, THOMAS	1830	NYCO	WD08	186
JACKSON, THOMAS	1830	OSWE	OSWE	134
JACKSON, THOMAS	1830	RICH	CAST	42
JACKSON, THOMAS	1830	RICH	SOUT	16
JACKSON, THOMAS	1830	SARA	WATE	43
JACKSON, THOMAS	1830	SCNE	WD02	223
JACKSON, THOMAS	1830	ULST	KING	55
JACKSON, THOMAS M.	1830	NYCO	WD08	176
JACKSON, THOMAS S.	1820	SCNE	WD02	129
JACKSON, TITUS	1830	QUEN	SHEM	78
JACKSON, TITUS	1830	ROCK	CLAR	131
JACKSON, TUCKY	1820	NYCO	WD10	1016
JACKSON, WALTER	1860	ABNY	WD05	347
JACKSON, WILLIAM	1810	ROCK	ORNG	638
JACKSON, WILLIAM	1820	DUTC	BEEK	12
JACKSON, WILLIAM	1820	KING	BRYN	141
JACKSON, WILLIAM	1820	NYCO	WD06	497
JACKSON, WILLIAM	1820	NYCO	WD06	517
JACKSON, WILLIAM	1820	NYCO	WD08	789
JACKSON, WILLIAM	1820	ROCK	ORNG	88
JACKSON, WILLIAM	1830	COLU	KIND	137
JACKSON, WILLIAM	1830	DUTC	WASH	450
JACKSON, WILLIAM	1830	KING	BRYN	359
JACKSON, WILLIAM	1830	NYCO	WD06	384

Jackson

NAME	YR	CO	TWP	PG
JACKSON, WILLIAM	1830	NYCO	WD06	426
JACKSON, WILLIAM	1830	NYCO	WD08	220
JACKSON, WILLIAM	1830	OTSG	OTSG	41
JACKSON, WILLIAM	1830	ROCK	ORGT	109
JACKSON, WILLIAM	1830	ROCK	ORGT	114
JACKSON, WILLIAM	1830	ULST	MARB	166
JACKSON, WILLIAM	1830	WEST	EAST	131
JACKSTON, WILLIAM	1820	PUTM	CARM	101
JACKURY, JOHNNY	1820	ULST	WOOD	47
JACOB	1790	NYCO	HARL	137
JACOB	1790	NYCO	NORT	127
JACOB	1790	NYCO	OUTW	131
JACOB	1790	QUEN	FLUS	149
JACOB	1790	QUEN	NHEM	152
JACOB	1790	QUEN	NHEM	153
JACOB	1790	QUEN	OYST	153
JACOB	1790	QUEN	OYST	154
JACOB	1790	QUEN	SHEM	155
JACOB	1790	WEST	SALM	206
JACOB	1790	WEST	YORK	209
JACOB	1800	QUEN	FLUS	542
JACOB	1800	QUEN	NHEM	554
JACOB	1800	QUEN	OYST	571
JACOB	1800	QUEN	OYST	575
JACOB	1800	SUFF	SMIT	54
JACOB	1800	SUFF	ISLP	61
JACOB	1810	COLU	KIND	174
JACOB	1810	ONTA	CANA	886
JACOB	1810	QUEN	OYST	258
JACOB	1820	QUEN	----	57
JACOB	1820	QUEN	----	62
JACOB	1820	QUEN	----	72
JACOB	1820	QUEN	----	79
JACOB	1820	SUFF	SMIT	320
JACOB	1820	WEST	NEWR	217
JACOB, DUMB	1820	COLU	HUDS	19
JACOB, FRANCES	1800	NYCO	WD02	675
JACOB, JR.	1790	QUEN	OYST	153
JACOB, THOMAS	1800	NYCO	WD05	757
JACOB, TOBIAS	1820	DUTC	PAUL	92
JACOBS, AARON	1800	NYCO	WD04	720
JACOBS, AARON	1810	NYCO	WD05	318
JACOBS, FRANCIS	1830	ABNY	WATV	458
JACOBS, H.	1810	NYCO	WD06	410
JACOBS, HENRY	1830	NYCO	WD12	295
JACOBS, JANE	1830	NYCO	WD08	212
JACOBS, JOHN	1830	NYCO	WD12	271
JACOBS, PILLEMON	1830	WEST	EAST	131
JACOBS, STEPHEN	1830	ORNG	WARW	72

NAME	YR	CO	TWP	PG
JACOBS, TOBIAS	1830	DUTC	PAWL	285
JACOBS, TOBIAS	1830	WEST	SUMM	191
JACOBS, YAS	1810	KING	BRYN	633
JACOBUS, DION	1820	NYCO	WD05	398
JACOCKS, CORNELIUS	1830	DUTC	FISH	504
JACOCKS, JOSEPH	1830	DUTC	FISH	477
JACON, MRS.	1830	KING	WD05	338
JACQUELIN, DANIEL	1790	DUTC	NORT	86
JAFE, HENRY	1810	NYCO	WD05	250
JAGUA, GEORGE	1820	ALLE	NUND	43
JAM	1810	RENS	PITT	419
JAMAISON, JAMES	1820	NYCO	WD06	551
JAMAR	1790	NYCO	MONT	123
JAMER	1790	SUFF	SMIT	166
JAMER	1800	SUFF	ISLP	62
JAMES	1790	NYCO	MONT	120
JAMES	1790	NYCO	MONT	121
JAMES	1790	NYCO	NORT	125
JAMES	1790	NYCO	OUTW	130
JAMES .	1790	NYCO	WEST	134
JAMES	1790	NYCO	WEST	135
JAMES	1790	QUEN	OYST	154
JAMES	1790	QUEN	OYST	155
JAMES	1790	QUEN	SHEM	157
JAMES	1790	SUFF	ISLP	165
JAMES	1800	QUEN	FLUS	542
JAMES	1800	QUEN	OYST	568
JAMES	1800	QUEN	OYST	572
JAMES	1800	QUEN	OYST	571
JAMES	1800	QUEN	OYST	575
JAMES	1800	QUEN	OYST	573
JAMES	1800	QUEN	OYST	576
JAMES	1800	QUEN	OYST	578
JAMES	1800	QUEN	OYST	569
JAMES	1800	QUEN	OYST	580
JAMES	1800	SUFF	BROK	13
JAMES	1800	SUFF	ISLP	64
JAMES	1800	SUFF	SMIT	54
JAMES	1800	SUFF	SMIT	58
JAMES	1800	SUFF	SMIT	56
JAMES	1820	QUEN	----	65
JAMES	1820	QUEN	----	74
JAMES	1820	QUEN	----	77
JAMES	1820	RICH	SOUT	105
JAMES	1820	SUFF	SMIT	321
JAMES	1830	NYCO	WD13	391
JAMES, A.	1830	NYCO	WD11	155
JAMES, ABRAHAM	1800	NYCO	WD04	846
JAMES, ADELINE	1830	NYCO	WD05	317

James

NAME	YR	CO	TWP	PG
JAMES, ANDREW	1830	ABNY	WD02	257
JAMES, ANTHONY	1830	NYCO	WD07	59
JAMES, BENJAMIN	1810	NYCO	WD05	368
JAMES, CATO	1810	NYCO	WD05	271
JAMES, CHARLOTTE	1830	NYCO	WD01	31
JAMES, CYRUS	1800	NYCO	WD03	705
JAMES, DAVID	1810	ONTA	SENE	832
JAMES, DAVID	1820	ONTA	SENE	283
JAMES, DAVID	1830	ONTA	SENE	66
JAMES, F.	1810	RENS	TROY	376
JAMES, JOHN	1790	ABNY	WD02	13
JAMES, JOHN	1810	NYCO	WD06	453
JAMES, JOHN	1830	ESEX	JAY	293
JAMES, JOSHUA	1820	ORNG	WARW	639
JAMES, JOSHUA	1830	ORNG	WARW	72
JAMES, NANCY	1830	NYCO	WD14	448
JAMES, OLIVER	1810	SCNE	WD04	965
JAMES, OLIVER	1820	SCNE	GLEN	150
JAMES, PETER	1820	ESEX	JAY	16
JAMES, PETER	1820	ESEX	JAY	422
JAMES, PETER	1830	SUFF	BROK	193
JAMES, RICHARD	1820	NYCO	WD04	314
JAMES, RICHARD	1830	SARA	STIL	63
JAMES, ROBISON	1830	ONTA	PHEL	40
JAMES, ROSANAH	1820	SUFF	HUNT	276
JAMES, ROSANNAH	1830	QUEN	OYST	36
JAMES, SAMUEL	1830	RENS	SAND	324
JAMES, SARAH	1830	NYCO	WD05	331
JAMES, THOMAS	1810	NYCO	WD03	84
JAMES, THOMAS	1810	NYCO	WD06	494
JAMES, THOMAS	1820	NYCO	WD05	391
JAMES, THOMAS	1830	NYCO	WD01	36
JAMES, WILLIAM	1820	SCHR	SCHR	449
JAMISON, JESSE	1830	ORNG	NEWB	34
JAMISON, LEWIS	1820	WEST	MAMA	360
JAMISON, LEWIS	1830	NYCO	WD09	406
JAMMISON, HENRY	1830	NYCO	WD06	412
JANE	1790	NYCO	NORT	125
JANE	1790	NYCO	NORT	126
JANE	1790	QUEN	FLUS	149
JANE	1790	QUEN	JAMA	151
JANE	1790	QUEN	NEWT	151
JANE	1790	QUEN	NHEM	152
JANE	1790	QUEN	NHEM	153
JANE	1790	QUEN	OYST	153
JANE	1790	QUEN	SHEM	157
JANE	1800	ABNY	WD01	274
JANE	1800	NYCO	WD06	807
JANE	1800	RENS	SCAS	780

NAME	YR	CO	TWP	PG
JANE	1800	SUFF	EHAM	92
JANE	1810	SARA	HALF	722
JANE	1820	NYCO	WD07	620
JANE	1830	NYCO	WD05	241
JANES, THOMAS	1830	ABNY	BETH	536
JANNO	1810	NYCO	WD06	444
JANSEN, ABRAM	1820	MADI	HAMI	82
JANSEN, ABRAM	1820	MADI	HAML	82
JANSEN, ADAM	1830	ORNG	MINI	258
JANSEN, DIANA	1830	ULST	SHAW	246
JANSEN, ISAAC	1820	MADI	HAML	82
JANSEN, ISSAC	1820	MADI	HAMI	82
JANSEN, JACOBUS	1830	ULST	OLIV	137
JANSEN, JOHN C.	1830	ULST	HURL	145A
JANSEN, PETER	1820	ULST	MARB	53
JANSEN, TITUS	1830	ULST	OLIV	136
JANUARY, JOHN	1800	SUFF	ISLP	63
JANUARY, JOHN	1820	SUFF	ISLP	307
JAPETEY, MOSES	1820	CHEN	SHER	337
JAQUELIN, GEORGE	1800	NYCO	WD06	843
JAQUELIN, TITUS	1800	DUTC	FISH	32
JARRED	1800	SUFF	RIVH	18
JARRIS, WILLIAM	1830	KING	WD04	307
JARSON, PETER	1830	ABNY	WD01	221
JARTOLUS	1800	SUFF	ISLP	62
JARVIS	1800	QUEN	FLUS	540
JARVIS, ABBEY	1830	NYCO	WD10	106
JARVIS, DANIEL	1820	ORNG	MINI	587
JARVIS, FREDERICK	1800	TIOG	NEWN	324
JARVIS, FREDERICK	1810	TIOG	ELMI	631
JARVIS, FREDERICK	1820	TIOG	ELMI	304
JARVIS, FREDERICK	1830	TIOG	ELMI	221
JARVIS, HARRY	1830	STEU	BATH	268
JARVIS, JACOB	1810	NYCO	WD05	318
JARVIS, JAMES	1800	NYCO	WD01	666
JARVIS, JAS	1820	NYCO	WD08	836
JARVIS, JOHN	1800	ORNG	MINI	319
JARVIS, JOHN	1810	ORNG	MINI	1057
JARVIS, JOHN	1820	ORNG	MINI	603
JARVIS, JOHN	1830	ORNG	MINI	247
JARVIS, JOHN	1830	QUEN	SHEM	94
JARVIS, JOHN	1830	WANE	PALM	39
JARVIS, JOSEPH	1830	QUEN	OYST	20
JARVIS, JOSEPH	1830	QUEN	OYST	43
JARVIS, JOSIAH	1830	SUFF	SMIT	266
JARVIS, SEELY	1830	WANE	PALM	40
JARVIS, SURVILLIAN	1830	ONTA	CANA	120
JARVIS, TIMOTHY	1830	QUEN	JAMA	129
JAVER, ENOS	1810	SUFF	SHAM	440

Javis

NAME	YR	CO	TWP	PG
JAVIS, ANTHONY	1820	ULST	PLAT	58
JAY, ANTHONY	1810	NYCO	WD05	316
JAY, CEASAR	1820	WEST	RYE	368
JAY, NICHOLAS	1800	NYCO	WD05	380
JAY, PETER	1820	NYCO	WD06	455
JAY, PETER S.	1830	WEST	RYE	97
JAY, SEAZER	1830	WEST	WTPL	223
JAY, SILA	1830	MONR	RWD1	197
JAY, SOOLY	1830	MONR	RWD1	197
JAYNE, CATO	1830	SUFF	BROK	193
JEARST, JOHN	1800	NYCO	WD06	807
JEBECK, PHILLES	1830	ABNY	WD02	261
JEBEDIAH	1800	SUFF	SOUT	26
JEF	1830	ONTA	CANA	122
JEFERSON, JOHN	1820	QUEN	----	52
JEFF	1790	QUEN	NHEM	152
JEFF	1800	QUEN	OYST	577
JEFFERDS, JOSEPH	1830	MONR	BRIG	35
JEFFERSON, ANTHONY	1830	NYCO	WD09	437
JEFFERSON, BETSEY	1820	ABNY	ABNY	176
JEFFERSON, HENRY	1830	QUEN	JAMA	126
JEFFERSON, JOHN	1830	ROCK	RPOO	9J
JEFFERSON, SAMUEL	1830	KING	WD03	280
JEFFERY, PLAT	1820	ORNG	MINI	608
JEFFRY	1800	COLU	CLAV	164
JEHU	1790	QUEN	OYST	155
JEMISON, HENRY	1800	NYCO	WD04	722
JEMMY	1800	NYCO	WD07	550
JEN, FRANK	1800	ORNG	NEWB	923
JENKINS, ANDREW	1830	NYCO	WD05	339
JENKINS, ELIZA	1830	NYCO	WD10	26
JENKINS, FREDERICK	1830	WANE	MACE	93
JENKINS, HENRY	1830	NYCO	WD14	457
JENKINS, JOHN	1820	NYCO	WD07	635
JENKINS, JOHN	1830	NYCO	WD02	95
JENKINS, JOSEPH	1830	NYCO	WD01	54
JENKINS, JOSHUA	1830	NYCO	WD08	231
JENKINS, MAHOM	1830	DUTC	REDH	374
JENKINS, MAHOMET	1820	DUTC	REDH	115
JENKINS, MICHAEL	1830	QUEN	NHEM	104
JENKINS, PETER	1800	COLU	HUDS	141
JENKINS, PETER	1820	COLU	HUDS	19
JENKINS, PETER	1830	NYCO	WD06	409
JENKINS, PHILIP	1800	NYCO	WD07	553
JENKINS, PHILIP	1820	NYCO	WD07	635
JENKINS, RICHARD	1820	DUTC	CLNT	27
JENKINS, RICHARD	1830	DUTC	HYPK	234
JENKINS, SHADRICH	1820	ONTA	PALM	341
JENKINS, THOMAS	1800	NYCO	WD02	116

NAME	YR	CO	TWP	PG
JENKINS, THOMAS	1820	NYCO	WD02	111
JENKINS, THOMAS	1830	NYCO	WD02	97
JENKINS, THOMAS	1830	QUEN	FLUS	153
JENNINGS, EBENEZER	1830	ORNG	GOSH	278
JENNINGS, THOMAS L.	1830	NYCO	WD14	461
JENNY	1800	NYCO	WD06	490
JEOFFERY	1800	SUFF	ISLP	64
JEOFFRY	1790	QUEN	SHEM	155
JEOFRY	1790	NYCO	NORT	125
JEPTHA	1820	SUFF	SMIT	327
JEREMIAH	1820	SUFF	BROK	364
JERNON, CAESAR	1800	NYCO	WD03	710
JESSE	1790	QUEN	FLUS	149
JESSEE	1800	SUFF	EHAM	69
JESSU	1800	QUEN	OYST	573
JESSUP, RICE	1800	SUFF	BROK	486
JESSUP, THOMAS	1820	SARA	SARA	189
JESSUP, TOM	1830	SARA	SASP	164
JESUP, TOM	1830	SARA	MALT	50
JIM	1790	NYCO	MONT	121
JIMESAN, ISRAL	1820	KING	BRYN	117
JIMISON, CHARLES	1830	WEST	RYE	97
JIMMONS, ABRAHAM	1800	NYCO	WD01	659
JOCK, THOMAS	1800	SUFF	SHAM	67
JOCKLIN, JAMES	1790	COLU	HILL	63
JOCKSON, CHARLES	1820	NYCO	WD06	520
JOE	1790	QUEN	NEWT	151
JOE	1790	QUEN	NHEM	153
JOE	1790	WEST	SCAR	206
JOE	1800	DUTC	STEN	176
JOE	1800	RENS	TROY	388
JOE	1800	SARA	STIL	733
JOE, JOHN	1800	SUFF	EAST	437
JOE, RACHIAL	1830	SUFF	EAST	258
JOHN	1790	NYCO	MONT	120
JOHN	1790	NYCO	MONT	121
JOHN	1790	NYCO	MONT	122
JOHN	1790	NYCO	NORT	126
JOHN	1790	NYCO	OUTW	127
JOHN	1790	NYCO	OUTW	131
JOHN	1790	QUEN	FLUS	149
JOHN	1790	QUEN	JAMA	150
JOHN	1790	QUEN	JAMA	151
JOHN	1790	QUEN	NEWT	151
JOHN	1790	QUEN	OYST	153
JOHN	1790	QUEN	OYST	154
JOHN	1790	QUEN	SHEM	157
JOHN	1790	WEST	CORT	198
JOHN	1800	ABNY	WD01	265

NAME	YR	CO	TWP	PG
JOHN	1800	NYCO	WD05	308
JOHN	1800	NYCO	WD06	836
JOHN	1800	NYCO	WD06	399
JOHN	1800	NYCO	WD07	604
JOHN	1800	RENS	TROY	901
JOHN	1800	SUFF	SMIT	27
JOHN	1800	WEST	MAMA	633
JOHN	1820	QUEN	----	37
JOHN	1820	QUEN	----	63
JOHN	1820	QUEN	----	72
JOHN	1820	ROCK	HAVE	118
JOHN	1830	NYCO	WD13	379
JOHN	1830	QUEN	SHEM	87
JOHN, BETSY	1800	NYCO	WD01	667
JOHN, G.	1820	NYCO	WD10	977
JOHN, JACOB	1800	WEST	NEWR	1081
JOHN, JEANEWAY	1800	QUEN	NHEM	218
JOHN, JOSEPH	1800	DUTC	STAN	128
JOHN, JOSEPH	1820	DUTC	STAN	136
JOHN, JOSEPH	1830	DUTC	STAN	416
JOHN, MARY	1820	NYCO	WD05	337
JOHN, MRS.	1830	NYCO	WD06	431
JOHNATHAN, CHARLES	1820	NYCO	WD07	629
JOHNATHAN, JEFFERSON	1820	NYCO	WD07	618
JOHNES, CESAR	1820	NYCO	WD05	404
JOHNNIE	1800	QUEN	NHEM	550
JOHNNO	1790	QUEN	FLUS	149
JOHNS, ABRAHAM	1800	NYCO	WD01	662
JOHNS, JOHN	1800	NYCO	WD06	822
JOHNSON	1800	NYCO	WD01	666
JOHNSON	1800	NYCO	WD05	281
JOHNSON	1800	NYCO	WD06	461
JOHNSON, A.	1820	KING	BRYN	128
JOHNSON	1830	KING	WD04	310
JOHNSON, ABRAHAM	1800	NYCO	WD06	378
JOHNSON, ABRAHAM	1820	DUTC	FISH	66
JOHNSON, ABRAHAM	1820	DUTC	MILA	80
JOHNSON, ABRAHAM	1830	ABNY	WD01	221
JOHNSON, ABRAHAM	1830	DUTC	MILN	263
JOHNSON, ABRAHAM	1830	DUTC	STAN	405
JOHNSON, ABRAHAM	1830	NYCO	WD08	173
JOHNSON, ABRAHAM	1830	QUEN	NHEM	116
JOHNSON, ALEX	1830	NYCO	WD06	451
JOHNSON, AMOS	1830	SARA	BALL	13
JOHNSON, ANN	1830	NYCO	WD08	184
JOHNSON, ANTHONY	1830	KING	BUSH	387
JOHNSON, ANTHONY	1830	NYCO	WD06	451
JOHNSON, ANTHONY	1830	NYCO	WD08	213

NAME	YR	CO	TWP	PG
JOHNSON, ANTHONY	1830	WASH	KING	368
JOHNSON, BENJAMIN	1800	NYCO	WD10	717
JOHNSON, BENJAMIN	1800	ORNG	WARW	994
JOHNSON, BENJAMIN	1830	NYCO	WD03	110
JOHNSON, BENJAMIN	1830	NYCO	WD06	445
JOHNSON, BENJAMIN	1830	NYCO	WD08	246
JOHNSON, BENJAMIN	1830	NYCO	WD14	484
JOHNSON, BENJAMIN	1830	ORNG	GOSH	274
JOHNSON, BENJAMIN	1830	ORNG	MONR	163
JOHNSON, BETSEY	1820	NYCO	WD07	627
JOHNSON, BETSEY	1830	NYCO	WD08	173
JOHNSON, BETTY	1800	NYCO	WD06	820
JOHNSON, BRISTOL	1820	ABNY	ABNY	176
JOHNSON, CASAR	1830	NYCO	WD12	278
JOHNSON, CATHARINE	1830	ONID	KIRK	76
JOHNSON, CATHERINE	1820	NYCO	WD06	455
JOHNSON, CATHERINE	1820	SCNE	WD02	129
JOHNSON, CATHERINE	1830	NYCO	WD14	488
JOHNSON, CHARITY	1800	NYCO	WD05	309
JOHNSON, CHARLES	1800	NYCO	WD03	61
JOHNSON, CHARLES	1820	SCNE	WD01	123
JOHNSON, CHARLES	1830	NYCO	WD06	384
JOHNSON, CLARA	1830	NYCO	WD08	132
JOHNSON, CLOS	1800	COLU	CHAT	184
JOHNSON, CORNELIUS	1830	NYCO	WD05	340
JOHNSON, CORNELIUS	1830	QUEN	NEWT	11
JOHNSON, CURUS	1830	SARA	STIL	59
JOHNSON, DANIEL R.	1830	STEU	PRAT	453
JOHNSON, DARBY	1820	NYCO	WD03	145
JOHNSON, DAVID	1820	DUTC	BEEK	21
JOHNSON, DAVID	1820	OTSG	OTSG	100
JOHNSON, DAVID	1820	TOMP	HECT	7
JOHNSON, DAVID	1830	DUTC	LAGR	242
JOHNSON, DAVID	1830	NYCO	WD06	449
JOHNSON, DAVID	1830	NYCO	WD06	458
JOHNSON, DAVID	1830	ONID	UTIC	6
JOHNSON, DAVID	1830	TOMP	ITCA	332
JOHNSON, DIANA	1830	NYCO	WD08	200
JOHNSON, DOLLY	1800	NYCO	WD05	294
JOHNSON, EDWARD	1800	NYCO	WD05	752
JOHNSON, EDWARD	1820	NYCO	WD06	502
JOHNSON, ELIAS	1800	COLU	HUDS	140
JOHNSON, ELIAS	1820	COLU	HUDS	19
JOHNSON, ELIGTH	1820	NYCO	WD08	775
JOHNSON, ELIZABETH	1810	NYCO	WD05	309
JOHNSON, EPHRAIM	1830	NYCO	WD07	73
JOHNSON, F.	1810	ONID	----	346
JOHNSON, F.	1830	KING	FLAT	401
JOHNSON, FILLIS	1830	KING	WD01	253

Johnson

NAME		YR	CO	TWP	PG
JOHNSON,	FORTIN	1820	KING	BRYN	124
JOHNSON,	FRANCIS	1820	NYCO	WD06	495
JOHNSON,	FRANCES	1820	ONID	UTIC	208
JOHNSON,	FRANCIS	1830	KING	WD05	324
JOHNSON,	FRANCIS	1830	NYCO	WD10	66
JOHNSON,	FRANCIS	1830	NYCO	WD14	462
JOHNSON,	FRANCIS	1830	ORNG	NEWB	60
JOHNSON,	FREDERICK	1820	GREN	HUNT	105
JOHNSON,	FREDERICK	1820	NYCO	WD02	97
JOHNSON,	FREDERICK	1830	GREN	WIND	101
JOHNSON,	GEORGE	1810	NYCO	WD05	308
JOHNSON,	GEORGE	1810	NYCO	WD06	441
JOHNSON,	GEORGE	1830	NYCO	WD06	434
JOHNSON,	GEORGE	1830	NYCO	WD08	212
JOHNSON,	GES	1820	NYCO	WD08	784
JOHNSON,	GUY	1810	NYCO	WD03	60
JOHNSON,	HAGAR	1830	NYCO	WD05	309
JOHNSON,	HAGER	1820	NYCO	WD05	426
JOHNSON,	HANNAH	1830	NYCO	WD08	274
JOHNSON,	HARRY	1820	COLU	KIND	9
JOHNSON,	HARRY	1830	DUTC	PGKP	326
JOHNSON,	HARRY	1830	DUTC	FISH	489
JOHNSON,	HARRY	1830	NYCO	WD08	148
JOHNSON,	HAZARD	1810	WEST	MTPL	1111
JOHNSON,	HAZARD	1820	NYCO	WD06	494
JOHNSON,	HECTOR	1820	KING	BRYN	127
JOHNSON,	HENRY	1810	NYCO	WD02	127
JOHNSON,	HENRY	1810	SARA	SARA	848
JOHNSON,	HENRY	1820	ABNY	ABNY	176
JOHNSON,	HENRY	1820	NYCO	WD01	45
JOHNSON,	HENRY	1820	NYCO	WD06	572
JOHNSON,	HENRY	1820	NYCO	WD10	988
JOHNSON,	HENRY	1820	WEST	EAST	205
JOHNSON,	HENRY	1830	GREN	COXE	181
JOHNSON,	HENRY	1830	MONR	PENF	342
JOHNSON,	HENRY	1830	NYCO	WD05	338
JOHNSON,	HENRY	1830	NYCO	WD07	25
JOHNSON,	HENRY	1830	NYCO	WD08	230
JOHNSON,	HENRY	1830	NYCO	WD08	255
JOHNSON,	HENRY	1830	NYCO	WD09	387
JOHNSON,	HENRY	1830	NYCO	WD10	19
JOHNSON,	HENRY	1830	NYCO	WD10	28
JOHNSON,	HENRY	1830	ONID	UTIC	26
JOHNSON,	HENRY	1830	ONON	SKAN	152
JOHNSON,	HENRY	1830	ORNG	WALL	157
JOHNSON,	HENRY	1830	RENS	TROY	
JOHNSON,	HENRY	1830	WEST	EAST	134
JOHNSON,	HESTER	1830	NYCO	WD06	442
JOHNSON,	I.	1830	KING	WD04	310

NAME	YR	CO	TWP	PG
JOHNSON, ISAAC	1830	MADI	----	381
JOHNSON, ISAAC	1830	NYCO	WD14	472
JOHNSON, ISABEL	1830	RENS	LANS	100
JOHNSON, ISABELLA	1830	NYCO	WD08	262
JOHNSON, ISSAC	1820	OTSG	CHRV	19
JOHNSON, J.	1810	DUTC	PGKP	323
JOHNSON, J.	1820	NYCO	WD10	1028
JOHNSON, J.	1830	NYCO	WD05	271
JOHNSON, J.	1830	NYCO	WD11	162
JOHNSON, J.G.	1810	OTGS	MIDD	151
JOHNSON, J.J.	1830	NYCO	WD11	207
JOHNSON, JACK	1820	ABNY	ABNY	176
JOHNSON, JACK	1820	GENE	LEIC	160
JOHNSON, JACK	1830	KING	WD02	272
JOHNSON, JACK	1830	QUEN	NEWT	9
JOHNSON, JACOB	1800	NYCO	WD07	862
JOHNSON, JACOB	1810	NYCO	WD06	417
JOHNSON, JACOB	1820	ABNY	ABNY	176
JOHNSON, JACOB	1820	HERK	DANU	90
JOHNSON, JACOB	1820	NYCO	WD06	498
JOHNSON, JACOB	1820	OTSG	OTSG	107
JOHNSON, JACOB	1830	KING	WD05	325
JOHNSON, JACOB	1830	MADI	----	345
JOHNSON, JACOB	1830	NYCO	WD09	383
JOHNSON, JACOB	1830	QUEN	FLUS	
JOHNSON, JACOB	1830	QUEN	SHEM	94
JOHNSON, JAMES	1810	KING	BRYN	632
JOHNSON, JAMES	1810	NYCO	WD05	320
JOHNSON, JAMES	1820	DUTC	MILA	83
JOHNSON, JAMES	1820	NYCO	WD09	899
JOHNSON, JAMES	1820	BROM	UNON	27
JOHNSON, JAMES	1830	ABNY	WD01	224
JOHNSON, JAMES	1830	BROM	UNON	26
JOHNSON, JAMES	1830	KING	BRYN	359
JOHNSON, JAMES	1830	KING	WD04	313
JOHNSON, JAMES	1830	NYCO	WD12	273
JOHNSON, JAMES	1830	NYCO	WD13	364
JOHNSON, JANE	1800	NYCO	WD07	887
JOHNSON, JANE	1830	NYCO	WD11	174
JOHNSON, JEFFREY	1830	KING	FLAN	412
JOHNSON, JENKINS	1820	NYCO	WD06	571
JOHNSON, JEREMIAH	1830	MONR	RWD3	229
JOHNSON, JEREMIAH	1830	NYCO	WD08	198
JOHNSON, JESSE	1830	NYCO	WD13	336
JOHNSON, JOHN	1800	NYCO	WD03	705
JOHNSON, JOHN	1800	NYCO	WD03	706
JOHNSON, JOHN	1800	NYCO	WD07	859
JOHNSON, JOHN	1800	QUEN	NHEM	554
JOHNSON, JOHN	1810	NYCO	WD05	360

NAME	YR	CO	TWP	PG
JOHNSON, JOHN	1810	NYCO	WD06	491
JOHNSON, JOHN	1810	NYCO	WD06	418
JOHNSON, JOHN	1820	ABNY	ABNY	176
JOHNSON, JOHN	1820	DUTC	PAUL	95
JOHNSON, JOHN	1820	DUTC	FISH	57
JOHNSON, JOHN	1820	KING	BRYN	116
JOHNSON, JOHN	1820	NYCO	WD03	170
JOHNSON, JOHN	1820	NYCO	WD03	196
JOHNSON, JOHN	1820	NYCO	WD04	315
JOHNSON, JOHN	1820	NYCO	WD05	388
JOHNSON, JOHN	1820	NYCO	WD05	434
JOHNSON, JOHN	1820	NYCO	WD09	875
JOHNSON, JOHN	1820	NYCO	WD09	902
JOHNSON, JOHN	1820	NYCO	WD10	1016
JOHNSON, JOHN	1820	ONTA	CANA	212
JOHNSON, JOHN	1830	ABNY	WD01	220
JOHNSON, JOHN	1830	CAYU	OWAS	206
JOHNSON, JOHN	1830	KING	FLAN	411
JOHNSON, JOHN	1830	MONR	BRPT	382
JOHNSON, JOHN	1830	NYCO	WD05	308
JOHNSON, JOHN	1830	NYCO	WD05	345
JOHNSON, JOHN	1830	NYCO	WD07	46
JOHNSON, JOHN	1830	NYCO	WD07	107
JOHNSON, JOHN	1830	NYCO	WD08	129
JOHNSON, JOHN	1830	ONTA	CANA	119
JOHNSON, JOHN	1830	ORLE	ALBN	3
JOHNSON, JOHN R.	1830	NYCO	WD05	354
JOHNSON, JOHN T.	1820	NYCO	WD07	625
JOHNSON, JOHNATHAN	1830	NYCO	WD14	455
JOHNSON, JOHNATHAN	1830	NYCO	WD14	457
JOHNSON, JOHNATHAN	1830	NYCO	WD14	481
JOHNSON, JOSEPH	1810	NYCO	WD05	279
JOHNSON, JOSEPH	1820	KING	BRYN	132
JOHNSON, JOSEPH	1830	DUTC	WASH	442
JOHNSON, JOSEPH	1830	KING	FLAT	401
JOHNSON, JOSEPH	1830	KING	WD04	306
JOHNSON, JOSEPH	1830	NYCO	WD08	240
JOHNSON, JOSEPH	1830	ORNG	MONR	174
JOHNSON, JOSIAH	1830	NYCO	WD03	138
JOHNSON, JOSS	1820	NYCO	WD09	934
JOHNSON, L.	1830	NYCO	WD13	336
JOHNSON, LANAH	1810	NYCO	WD05	322
JOHNSON, LEONARD M.	1830	GENE	STAF	442
JOHNSON, LETTY	1800	NYCO	WD06	852
JOHNSON, LEWIS	1830	NYCO	WD14	500
JOHNSON, LEWIS	1830	QUEN	NHEM	103
JOHNSON, LOIS	1830	ONTA	SENE	85
JOHNSON, M.	1820	NYCO	WD10	1028
JOHNSON, MARGARET	1810	NYCO	WD06	401

NAME	YR	CO	TWP	PG
JOHNSON, MARGARETT	1820	NYCO	WD07	620
JOHNSON, MARINUS	1810	NYCO	WD05	355
JOHNSON, MARTIN	1830	ORNG	BLOM	119
JOHNSON, MARY	1810	NYCO	WD05	324
JOHNSON, MARY	1800	NYCO	WD06	820
JOHNSON, MARY	1810	NYCO	WD06	422
JOHNSON, MARY	1830	NYCO	WD08	227
JOHNSON, MARY	1830	NYCO	WD09	430
JOHNSON, MATILDA	1830	NYCO	WD10	28
JOHNSON, MICHAEL	1810	NYCO	WD03	82
JOHNSON, MICHAEL	1830	KING	WD04	307
JOHNSON, MOSES	1820	NYCO	WD05	348
JOHNSON, MOSES	1830	ONID	UTIC	20
JOHNSON, MR.	1830	NYCO	WD06	451
JOHNSON, MRS.	1820	KING	WILL	181
JOHNSON, MRS.	1830	NYCO	WD01	40
JOHNSON, MRS.	1820	NYCO	WD07	721
JOHNSON, NANCY	1830	NYCO	WD10	88
JOHNSON, NELLA	1820	DUTC	FISH	59
JOHNSON, NICHOLAS	1800	ABNY	SCNE	8
JOHNSON, NICHOLAS	1810	MONT	MIND	111
JOHNSON, NICHOLAS	1820	COLU	CHAT	11
JOHNSON, NICHOLAS	1830	KING	BRYN	367
JOHNSON, NICHOLAS	1830	NYCO	WD07	89
JOHNSON, PATIENCE	1830	RENS	STEP	293
JOHNSON, PERRY	1830	NYCO	WD08	246
JOHNSON, PETER	1800	ORNG	CHEE	384
JOHNSON, PETER	1810	NYCO	WD05	292
JOHNSON, PETER	1810	NYCO	WD05	713
JOHNSON, PETER	1820	DUTC	PGKP	104
JOHNSON, PETER	1820	DUTC	RHIN	122
JOHNSON, PETER	1820	GENE	RIGA	245
JOHNSON, PETER	1820	NYCO	WD05	338
JOHNSON, PETER	1820	NYCO	WD06	454
JOHNSON, PETER	1820	NYCO	WD07	721
JOHNSON, PETER	1820	NYCO	WD10	984
JOHNSON, PETER	1820	ORNG	NEWB	313
JOHNSON, PETER	1820	ORNG	NEWB	524
JOHNSON, PETER	1820	WEST	RYE	370
JOHNSON, PETER	1830	DUTC	RHIN	398
JOHNSON, PETER	1830	GENE	LROY	411
JOHNSON, PETER	1830	NYCO	WD06	437
JOHNSON, PETER	1830	NYCO	WD08	148
JOHNSON, PETER	1830	ONON	VANB	120
JOHNSON, PETER	1830	ORNG	NEWB	33
JOHNSON, PETER	1830	ORNG	MONR	163
JOHNSON, PETER	1830	QUEN	NEWT	5
JOHNSON, PETER	1830	SENE	WD01	206
JOHNSON, PETER	1830	SUFF	SHAM	217

Johnson

NAME	YR	CO	TWP	PG
JOHNSON, PETER	1830	ULST	MARL	285
JOHNSON, PHILIP	1820	ORNG	GOSH	750
JOHNSON, PHILIP	1830	ORNG	GOSH	291
JOHNSON, PHILIS	1810	KING	BRYN	632
JOHNSON, PHILIS	1810	NYCO	WD06	424
JOHNSON, PHILLIP	1820	NYCO	WD07	621
JOHNSON, PHILUP	1800	NYCO	WD05	748
JOHNSON, POLLY	1830	RENS	SAND	330
JOHNSON, POMPEY	1830	DUTC	FISH	477
JOHNSON, POMPEY	1830	ORNG	NEWW	97
JOHNSON, POMPY	1810	NYCO	WD06	460
JOHNSON, PRINCE	1810	NYCO	WD06	413
JOHNSON, PRINCE	1830	NYCO	WD05	338
JOHNSON, R.	1830	NYCO	WD11	189
JOHNSON, RACHEL	1810	NYCO	WD02	115
JOHNSON, RACHEL	1820	NYCO	WD04	281
JOHNSON, RICHARD	1800	ORNG	GOSH	360
JOHNSON, RICHARD	1820	DUTC	CLNT	27
JOHNSON, RICHARD	1820	NYCO	WD10	978
JOHNSON, RICHARD	1830	CHEN	SHER	137
JOHNSON, RICHARD	1830	KING	FLAT	399
JOHNSON, RICHARD	1830	NYCO	WD08	246
JOHNSON, RICHARD	1830	YATE	MILO	216
JOHNSON, ROBERT	1810	NYCO	WD03	68
JOHNSON, ROBERT	1800	NYCO	WD03	694
JOHNSON, ROBERT	1800	NYCO	WD03	702
JOHNSON, ROBERT	1800	NYCO	WD05	751
JOHNSON, ROBERT	1810	NYCO	WD05	249
JOHNSON, ROBERT	1830	NYCO	WD08	229
JOHNSON, ROBERT	1830	NYCO	WD08	231
JOHNSON, ROSANNA	1820	ABNY	ABNY	176
JOHNSON, ROSINDA	1830	NYCO	WD06	430
JOHNSON, S.	1830	KING	WD04	310
JOHNSON, SALLY	1820	NYCO	WD07	721
JOHNSON, SALLY	1820	NYCO	WD07	620
JOHNSON, SAMUEL	1800	DUTC	FISH	41
JOHNSON, SAMUEL	1810	WEST	NEWR	1079
JOHNSON, SAMUEL	1820	NYCO	WD02	106
JOHNSON, SAMUEL	1820	NYCO	WD08	789
JOHNSON, SAMUEL	1830	ABNY	WD02	239
JOHNSON, SAMUEL	1830	NYCO	WD09	370
JOHNSON, SAMUEL	1830	NYCO	WD10	46
JOHNSON, SAMUEL	1830	ORNG	NEWW	99
JOHNSON, SAMUEL	1830	OSWE	OSWE	134
JOHNSON, SAMUEL	1830	QUEN	FLUS	139
JOHNSON, SARAH	1820	NYCO	WD06	460
JOHNSON, SARAH	1830	NYCO	WD08	154
JOHNSON, SARAH	1830	NYCO	WD14	504
JOHNSON, SCIPIO	1820	STEU	READ	270

NAME		YR	CO	TWP	PG
JOHNSON,	SHADRACK	1830	NYCO	WD07	108
JOHNSON,	SIMON	1830	NYCO	WD05	339
JOHNSON,	STEPHEN	1810	KING	BRYN	632
JOHNSON,	STEPHEN	1830	CAYU	SCIP	263
JOHNSON,	STEPHEN	1830	KING	BUSH	384
JOHNSON,	STEPHEN	1830	NYCO	WD08	225
JOHNSON,	STEPHEN	1830	NYCO	WD09	430
JOHNSON,	SUSAN	1830	ORNG	NEWB	33
JOHNSON,	SUSSANNAH	1830	ABNY	WD04	314
JOHNSON,	THOMAS	1800	NYCO	WD03	696
JOHNSON,	THOMAS	1800	NYCO	WD04	724
JOHNSON,	THOMAS	1810	NYCO	WD05	303
JOHNSON,	THOMAS	1820	DUTC	FISH	67
JOHNSON,	THOMAS	1820	NYCO	WD08	788
JOHNSON,	THOMAS	1820	NYCO	WD10	1055
JOHNSON,	THOMAS	1830	DUTC	LAGR	246
JOHNSON,	THOMAS	1830	KING	WD05	327
JOHNSON,	THOMAS	1830	NYCO	WD05	262
JOHNSON,	THOMAS	1830	NYCO	WD05	354
JOHNSON,	THOMAS	1830	NYCO	WD07	56
JOHNSON,	THOMAS	1830	NYCO	WD10	13
JOHNSON,	THOMAS	1830	QUEN	JAMA	129
JOHNSON,	THOMAS	1830	QUEN	NEWT	13
JOHNSON,	THOMAS	1830	SARA	MALT	55
JOHNSON,	THOMAS	1830	WEST	EAST	131
JOHNSON,	TITUS	1800	ORNG	WARW	380
JOHNSON,	TOBIAS	1820	SARA	GALW	220
JOHNSON,	TROY	1820	NYCO	WD10	988
JOHNSON,	VIOLET	1830	NYCO	WD08	234A
JOHNSON,	WILLIAM	1800	DUTC	CARM	84
JOHNSON,	WILLIAM	1800	NYCO	WD05	775
JOHNSON,	WILLIAM	1800	NYCO	WD05	773
JOHNSON,	WILLIAM	1810	COLU	HUDS	147
JOHNSON,	WILLIAM	1810	SARA	MILT	798
JOHNSON,	WILLIAM	1810	WEST	NEWR	1085
JOHNSON,	WILLIAM	1820	NYCO	WD06	514
JOHNSON,	WILLIAM	1820	NYCO	WD10	987
JOHNSON,	WILLIAM	1820	SENE	FAYE	372
JOHNSON,	WILLIAM	1830	DUTC	LAGR	250
JOHNSON,	WILLIAM	1830	HERK	LTFA	90
JOHNSON,	WILLIAM	1830	KING	BRYN	367
JOHNSON,	WILLIAM	1820	NYCO	WD07	686
JOHNSON,	WILLIAM	1830	NYCO	WD04	195
JOHNSON,	WILLIAM	1830	NYCO	WD05	332
JOHNSON,	WILLIAM	1830	NYCO	WD06	370
JOHNSON,	WILLIAM	1830	NYCO	WD06	407
JOHNSON,	WILLIAM	1830	NYCO	WD14	488
JOHNSON,	WILLIAM	1830	PUTM	CARM	11
JOHNSON,	WILLIAM	1830	QUEN	OYST	52
JOHNSON,	WILLIAM P.	1830	NYCO	WD05	340

Johnson

NAME	YR	CO	TWP	PG
JOHNSON, ZEBULON	1830	ONID	VERN	111
JOHNSTON	1810	NYCO	WD07	556
JOHNSTON	1810	NYCO	WD07	592
JOHNSTON	1810	NYCO	WD10	644
JOHNSTON	1820	QUEN	----	46
JOHNSTON, ANTHONY	1830	NYCO	WD09	400
JOHNSTON, CLARRY	1830	PUTM	PHIL	63
JOHNSTON, CLASS	1790	ABNY	SCNE	44
JOHNSTON, DAVID	1800	NYCO	WD07	921
JOHNSTON, DANIEL	1800	NYCO	WD07	856
JOHNSTON, DANIEL	1810	NYCO	WD04	230
JOHNSTON, DAVID	1830	WASH	JACK	181
JOHNSTON, EDWARD	1830	NYCO	WD09	341
JOHNSTON, ELBERT	1830	NYCO	WD09	383
JOHNSTON, FRANCIS	1810	NYCO	WD07	617
JOHNSTON, GEORGE	1820	NYCO	WD04	303
JOHNSTON, GEORGE	1820	NYCO	WD06	487
JOHNSTON, GEORGE	1820	QUEN	----	30
JOHNSTON, HANNAH	1810	NYCO	WD10	525
JOHNSTON, HENRY	1820	QUEN	----	55
JOHNSTON, HENRY	1830	NYCO	WD09	302
JOHNSTON, JANE	1820	NYCO	WD07	655
JOHNSTON, JANE	1820	SUFF	SOUT	341
JOHNSTON, JASH	1820	NYCO	WD08	807
JOHNSTON, JEFFERY	1810	NYCO	WD10	531
JOHNSTON, JERMIAH	1820	NYCO	WD08	849
JOHNSTON, JOHN	1810	NYCO	WD04	186
JOHNSTON, JOHN	1810	NYCO	WD07	545
JOHNSTON, JOHN	1810	NYCO	WD07	579
JOHNSTON, JOHN	1830	NYCO	WD09	330
JOHNSTON, JOHN	1830	SARA	BALL	2
JOHNSTON, LEWIS	1810	NYCO	WD04	192
JOHNSTON, MARY	1820	NYCO	WD08	750
JOHNSTON, NATHANIEL	1800	NYCO	WD07	906
JOHNSTON, PETER	1810	NYCO	WD10	684
JOHNSTON, PETER	1810	NYCO	WD10	667
JOHNSTON, ROBERT	1820	NYCO	WD05	399
JOHNSTON, SAM	1810	NYCO	WD07	529
JOHNSTON, SAMUEL	1810	DUTC	FISH	220
JOHNSTON, SAMUEL	1810	NYCO	WD10	662
JOHNSTON, SAMUEL	1820	QUEN	----	51
JOHNSTON, SAMUEL	1830	NYCO	WD09	322
JOHNSTON, SIMON	1820	SUFF	SHAM	304
JOHNSTON, THOMAS	1800	NYCO	WD07	868
JOHNSTON, THOMAS	1810	NYCO	WD10	698
JOHNSTON, THOMAS	1820	QUEN	----	46
JOHNSTON, WILLIAM	1810	DUTC	CARM	138
JOHNSTON, WILLIAM	1820	PUTM	CARM	101
JOHNSTON, WILLIAM	1820	QUEN	----	46

NAME	YR	CO	TWP	PG
JOINER, CHARLES	1820	SARA	EDIN	169
JOINER, ISAAC	1810	SARA	EDIN	924
JOINER, ISAAC	1820	SARA	EDIN	169
JOINER, ISAAC	1830	SARA	EDIN	201
JOINER, THOMAS	1830	SARA	EDIN	201
JOINS, LUCY	1830	NYCO	WD07	83
JONAH	1800	SUFF	BROK	11
JONAS	1800	QUEN	FLUS	542
JONES, ABRAHAM	1830	NYCO	WD08	215
JONES, ALBERT	1820	QUEN	----	66
JONES, ALEXANDER	1830	WANE	LYON	110
JONES, ANN	1830	NYCO	WD06	443
JONES, ANTHONY	1830	NYCO	WD06	451
JONES, B.	1830	NYCO	WD11	163
JONES, BEN	1820	QUEN	----	30
JONES, BENJAMIN	1830	SUFF	BROK	194
JONES, BENJAMIN	1830	TOMP	ITCA	332
JONES, BETT	1820	SUFF	SHAM	309
JONES, CESAR	1830	NYCO	WD05	300
JONES, CHARLES	1820	ONTA	FREE	99
JONES, CLARISSA	1810	NYCO	WD02	112
JONES, CYRUS	1800	DUTC	AMEN	133
JONES, CYRUS	1810	RENS	BERL	501
JONES, CYRUS	1830	RENS	SAND	319
JONES, DARIA	1830	TOMP	NEWF	491
JONES, DAVID	1820	ONTA	CANA	210
JONES, DAVID	1830	NYCO	WD09	416
JONES, DENNIS	1810	NYCO	WD06	454
JONES, EDMOND	1820	QUEN	----	60
JONES, EDWARD	1830	ABNY	WD02	273
JONES, ELBERT	1830	QUEN	NHEM	111
JONES, ELSE	1830	NYCO	WD12	294
JONES, FRANCIS	1820	NYCO	WD10	976
JONES, FRANK	1810	QUEN	FLUS	202
JONES, FRANK	1830	QUEN	JAMA	135
JONES, FREDERICK	1820	DUTC	RHIN	123
JONES, FREDERICK	1820	NYCO	WD09	914
JONES, HARRIOT	1820	NYCO	WD10	967
JONES, HENRY	1800	NYCO	WD06	815
JONES, HENRY	1810	NYCO	WD05	298
JONES, HENRY	1830	NYCO	WD05	252
JONES, ISAAC	1820	DUTC	NORT	89
JONES, ISAAC	1830	DUTC	PINE	301
JONES, JACOB	1820	NYCO	WD06	503
JONES, JACOB	1830	SCNE	WD01	206
JONES, JAMES	1830	ABNY	WD02	255
JONES, JAMES	1830	MONR	RWD1	197
JONES, JAMES	1830	QUEN	OYST	50
JONES, JAMES	1830	SUFF	HUNT	318

Jones

NAME	YR	CO	TWP	PG
JONES, JAMES T.	1810	ULST	SHAW	692
JONES, JOHN	1810	COLU	CLAV	153
JONES, JOHN	1810	NYCO	WD06	435
JONES, JOHN	1810	NYCO	WD06	441
JONES, JOHN	1810	NYCO	WD07	549
JONES, JOHN	1820	NYCO	WD05	401
JONES, JOHN	1820	NYCO	WD07	686
JONES, JOHN	1820	NYCO	WD07	632
JONES, JOHN	1830	NYCO	WD08	215
JONES, JOHN	1830	NYCO	WD08	237
JONES, JOHN	1830	NYCO	WD10	121
JONES, JOHN	1830	SUFF	SHAM	217
JONES, JOSHUA	1820	NYCO	WD09	940
JONES, JOSIAH	1820	QUEN	----	54
JONES, JOY	1830	LIVI	YORK	50
JONES, L.	1820	NYCO	WD10	1056
JONES, LEVANY	1830	QUEN	FLUS	148
JONES, LEWIS	1810	NYCO	WD04	219
JONES, LEWIS	1810	QUEN	OYST	244
JONES, MARY	1830	NYCO	WD05	264
JONES, MENIS	1830	NYCO	WD08	180
JONES, MINGO	1810	ORNG	WALL	1109
JONES, NANCY	1820	QUEN	----	30
JONES, NANCY	1830	QUEN	OYST	20
JONES, NELLY	1830	MONR	RWD1	197
JONES, NELSON	1830	DUTC	FISH	480
JONES, PERRY	1830	ALLE	BIRD	54
JONES, PHILIP	1830	COLU	AUST	174
JONES, POMP	1810	SUFF	BROK	477
JONES, POMPY	1820	SUFF	BROK	346
JONES, PRINCE	1810	COLU	CHAT	190
JONES, PRINCE	1820	COLU	GHEN	7
JONES, PRINCE	1830	COLU	GHEN	159
JONES, R.	1830	NYCO	WD11	159
JONES, RICHARD	1810	NYCO	WD02	102
JONES, RICHARD	1810	QUEN	NHEM	220
JONES, RICHARD	1830	MONR	RWD3	230
JONES, RICHARD	1830	QUEN	JAMA	134
JONES, ROBERT	1830	KING	BRYN	346
JONES, ROGER	1800	ORNG	NEWB	278
JONES, SABUE	1820	SUFF	BROK	357
JONES, SAMUEL	1810	NYCO	WD05	336
JONES, SAMUEL	1810	SUFF	BROK	492
JONES, SAMUEL	1820	NIAG	CAMB	107
JONES, SAMUEL	1820	NIAG	CAMB	171
JONES, SAMUEL	1830	ABNY	WD01	210
JONES, SAMUEL	1830	NIAG	PEND	426
JONES, SAMUEL	1830	SUFF	BROK	194
JONES, SARAH	1830	QUEN	OYST	51

NAME	YR	CO	TWP	PG
JONES, SARAH	1830	SULL	THOM	39
JONES, SILAS	1820	ORNG	MONT	807
JONES, SILAS	1820	ORNG	MONT	841
JONES, SILAS	1830	DUTC	FISH	480
JONES, STEPHEN	1820	QUEN	----	57
JONES, STEPHEN	1830	NYCO	WD08	127
JONES, STRANDER	1830	NYCO	WD10	122
JONES, SUSAN	1830	NYCO	WD08	244
JONES, T.	1830	NYCO	WD13	387
JONES, THOMAS	1800	NYCO	WD05	755
JONES, THOMAS	1820	NYCO	WD06	455
JONES, WILLIAM	1810	NYCO	WD05	354
JONES, WILLIAM	1830	COLU	KIND	136
JONES, WILLIAM	1830	COLU	KIND	142
JONES, WILLIAM	1830	DELA	MIDD	154
JONES, WILLIAM	1830	QUEN	FLUS	141
JONES, WILLIAM	1830	QUEN	SHEM	94
JONES, WILLIS	1830	KING	WD03	292
JONHSON	1790	NYCO	MONT	124
JONHSON, BENJAMIN	1790	ORNG	WARW	147
JONHSON, BURTON	1790	COLU	HUDS	66
JONHSON, PETER	1790	ORNG	WARW	147
JONHSON, SAM	1790	QUEN	FLUS	149
JONHSON, SAMPSON	1790	DUTC	CLNT	77
JONHSON, TITUS	1790	ORNG	WARW	147
JONSON, STEPHEN	1830	MONR	PITS	96
JONSTON, NATHAN	1810	NYCO	WD04	160
JORDAN, ALFRED	1830	NYCO	WD09	385
JORDAN, EDWARD	1830	NYCO	WD08	259
JORDAN, JOHN	1830	COLU	GALA	249
JORDAN, MARY	1830	SUFF	EAST	253
JORDEN	1820	QUEN	----	72
JORDON, JOHN	1810	COLU	LIVN	225
JORDON, PATTY GRAY	1810	NYCO	WD08	772
JORNEE, THOMAS	1830	RICH	WEST	12
JOSEPH	1790	NYCO	MONT	122
JOSEPH	1790	NYCO	NORT	125
JOSEPH	1790	NYCO	NORT	127
JOSEPH	1790	NYCO	OUTW	128
JOSEPH	1790	QUEN	NHEM	152
JOSEPH	1790	QUEN	OYST	153
JOSEPH	1790	QUEN	OYST	155
JOSEPH	1790	QUEN	SHEM	158
JOSEPH	1790	SUFF	HUNT	165
JOSEPH	1800	NYCO	WD06	844
JOSEPH	1800	NYCO	WD07	866
JOSEPH	1800	QUEN	OYST	568
JOSEPH	1800	QUEN	OYST	572
JOSEPH	1810	NYCO	WD05	320

NAME	YR	CO	TWP	PG
JOSEPH	1810	NYCO	WD06	421
JOSEPH	1810	NYCO	WD07	611
JOSEPH	1810	RICH	COST	606
JOSEPH	1820	NYCO	WD05	394
JOSEPH	1820	QUEN	----	3
JOSEPH	1820	QUEN	----	64
JOSEPH	1830	RENS	SCHO	245
JOSEPH, AARON	1830	NYCO	WD08	233
JOSEPH, ABRAHAM	1800	NYCO	WD07	889
JOSEPH, CHARLES	1830	CLNT	PLAT	260
JOSEPH, ELLOE	1820	NYCO	WD06	490
JOSEPH, FRANCIS	1820	DUTC	PGKP	99
JOSEPH, GEORGE	1820	NYCO	WD02	122
JOSEPH, HENRY	1810	ORNG	NEWB	928
JOSEPH, JOHANNA	1830	DUTC	PGKP	326
JOSEPH, JOHN	1810	NYCO	WD05	289
JOSEPH, JOHN	1820	NYCO	WD04	314
JOSEPH, JOHN	1820	NYCO	WD10	1081
JOSEPH, JOHN	1830	KING	WD02	270
JOSEPH, JOHN	1830	NYCO	WD06	435
JOSEPH, JOHN	1830	NYCO	WD07	98
JOSEPH, PAUL	1820	NYCO	WD06	470
JOSEPH, SAMUEL	1810	NYCO	WD07	548
JOSHUA, JOHN	1800	NYCO	WD05	308
JOSIAH	1820	QUEN	----	59
JOT RAY & JOT-LEONARD	1820	NYCO	WD09	932
JOURDAN, JANE	1830	ONID	UTIC	41
JOURDAN, LEWIS	1830	NYCO	WD14	522
JOY, ANTHONEY	1820	NYCO	WD08	767
JOY, CANADAU	1820	CORT	VIRG	638
JOY, LINAS	1830	MONR	BRIG	35
JUBILER, ANTHONY	1820	ONON	POMP	149
JUDA	1820	SUFF	EHAM	300
JUDAS	1800	SUFF	EHAM	92
JUDE	1790	QUEN	SHEM	158
JUDE	1800	ABNY	SCNE	8
JUDE	1800	ABNY	WATV	95
JUDEY	1800	QUEN	NEWT	657
JUDEY	1800	QUEN	NHEM	561
JUINE, JOHN	1820	NYCO	WD06	472
JULETT, JOHN A.	1820	NYCO	WD06	476
JUNE, PHEBE	1800	NYCO	WD03	706
JUNE, POMP	1810	SUFF	BROK	481
JUPANE, PETER	1800	NYCO	WD07	927
JUPITER	1790	NYCO	MONT	120
JUPITER	1800	NYCO	WD06	847
JUPITER	1800	SUFF	HUNT	47
JUPITER	1830	NYCO	WD12	269
JUPITER, ANTHONY	1830	ONTA	SENE	76

NAME	YR	CO	TWP	PG
JURDEN	1800	QUEN	OYST	578
KANAH	1820	QUEN	----	69
KANDINE, KIMBY	1830	ABNY	WD01	196
KANE .	1810	COLU	CANN	105
KANE, JAMES	1830	QUEN	NEWT	6
KANE, LOTT	1820	SCHR	SCHR	449
KANE, MARY	1820	NYCO	WD07	721
KANN, CRESP	1790	ABNY	STIL	51
KATE	1790	QUEN	NHEM	152
KATE	1790	QUEN	NHEM	153
KATON, ISAAC	1830	DUTC	PLEA	316
KAWHISS, PETER	1820	MADI	SULL	10
KEAFFER, ANTHONY	1820	DUTC	RHIN	130
KEAMEY, ROBERT	1830	NYCO	WD12	309
KEE, THOMAS	1820	SENE	FAYE	373
KEELER	1790	NYCO	WEST	135
KEER, SARAH	1820	KING	BRAD	157
KEFF, JAMES	1830	COLU	STUY	64
KEGSLEY, RUFUS	1830	RENS	HOOS	155
KEIFER, NANCY	1830	DUTC	RHIN	400
KEIRL, WALKER	1830	QUEN	FLUS	144
KELDER, ROBERT	1830	ULST	MARB	167
KELLES, ALEXANDER	1830	ORNG	MONR	166
KELLEY, EDWARD	1820	ORNG	GOSH	762
KELLIS, JOSEPH	1810	SUFF	EAST	431
KELLY, ABRAHAM	1790	DUTC	WASH	96
KELLY, DOTTY	1830	QUEN	FLUS	142
KELLY, JAMES	1830	ORNG	NEWW	106
KELLY, PATIENCE	1830	NYCO	WD08	132
KELLY, STEPHEN	1830	NYCO	WD03	142
KELSO, JOSEPHUS	1830	GREN	CATS	237
KELSY, JOHN	1830	NYCO	WD06	427
KENNARD, SAMUEL	1810	SCHR	JEFF	122
KENNARD, SAMUEL	1830	CAYU	AUBN	165
KENNAW, JANE	1800	NYCO	WD06	833
KENSY, CHARLES	1830	ONTA	SENE	85
KENT, JOHN	1800	NYCO	WD04	722
KENT, JOHN	1810	NYCO	WD03	84
KERK, MICAH	1810	QUEN	OYST	260
KERK, THOMAS	1810	QUEN	OYST	238
KERLY, LICOM	1810	QUEN	OYST	242
KETTLE, GEORGE	1830	COLU	STUY	62
KETTLE, THOMAS	1830	COLU	GHEN	157
KETTLE, WILL	1830	COLU	GHEN	162
KEY, THOMAS	1800	NYCO	WD04	722
KEY, THOMAS	1830	STEU	PRAT	454
KEYERS, BETSEY	1820	NYCO	WD04	212

NAME	YR	CO	TWP	PG
KEYSER, MOSES	1830	ULST	MARB	163
KID, JAMES	1800	NYCO	WD07	862
KIDD, JAMES	1810	NYCO	WD07	613
KIDD, JAMES	1830	SARA	BALL	10
KIERSTEO, GARRET	1830	ULST	SAUG	108
KIF, DANIEL, JR.	1830	TOMP	ITCA	360
KIFF, DANIEL	1800	RENE	PITT	788
KIFF, DANIEL	1830	TOMP	ITCA	360
KILATED, HENRY	1820	ULST	SAUG	82
KILBORN, CYRUS	1820	COLU	HUDS	21
KILBORN, ELIZABETH	1810	NYCO	WD05	312
KILBORN, YORK	1820	BROM	UNON	29
KILBURN, YORK	1800	NYCO	WD04	725
KILBURN, YORK	1830	BROM	UNON	34
KILDAIR	1790	NYCO	MONT	121
KILGORE, ROBERT	1830	ONTA	MANC	174
KILLBURN, YORK	1790	ABNY	WD03	13
KILLIS	1820	SUFF	BROK	360
KILLIS, JANE	1820	SUFF	SHAM	314
KILLIS, JOHN	1820	SUFF	SHAM	313
KILLIS, JOSEPH	1820	SUFF	SHAM	300
KILLIS, ROBIN	1810	SUFF	BROK	488
KIN, CEASAR	1800	NYCO	WD01	656
KING, A.	1820	NYCO	WD10	987
KING, ABRAHAM	1830	KING	WD02	259
KING, ADAM	1830	ORNG	GOSH	291
KING, BETSEY	1810	NYCO	WD06	404
KING, CESAR	1830	NYCO	WD09	413
KING, CHARLES	1830	ORNG	GOSH	293
KING, CHARLOTTE	1830	KING	WD03	290
KING, GEORGE	1830	NYCO	WD10	19
KING, GEORGE	1830	ORNG	GOSH	289
KING, HENRY	1820	NYCO	WD10	988
KING, HENRY	1830	NYCO	WD10	26
KING, JANE	1820	ONID	WHTT	303
KING, JOHN	1800	NYCO	WD02	681
KING, JOHN	1810	WEST	NEWR	1086
KING, JOHN	1830	DUTC	RHIN	400
KING, NEWTON	1790	NYCO	MONT	120
KING, NEWTON	1800	NYCO	WD04	732
KING, NEWTON	1810	NYCO	WD03	56
KING, POMPEY	1820	NYCO	WD04	228
KING, RICHARD	1820	NYCO	WD08	850
KING, RICHARD	1830	DUTC	FISH	502
KING, SALLY	1820	NYCO	WD10	987
KING, SAMUEL	1830	NYCO	WD10	19
KING, THOMAS	1820	ORNG	MONT	805

NAME	YR	CO	TWP	PG
KING, THOMAS	1830	NYCO	WD14	478
KING, THOMAS	1830	ORNG	MONR	161
KING, WILLIAM	1830	ABNY	WATV	450
KINGSBURY, THOMAS	1800	ONID	CANT	257
KINGSLAND, RICHARD	1830	ORNG	BLOM	120
KINGSLEY, EZRA	1830	CHAT	POMF	421
KINGSLEY, WILLIAM	1820	ONTA	PHEL	296
KINGSLEY, WILLIAM	1830	ONTA	PHEL	26
KINGSTON	1790	NYCO	OUTW	129
KINNE, JOHN	1820	SENE	GALE	388
KINNEE, CHARLES	1820	ONTA	SENE	282
KINSEY, DAVID W.	1820	ONTA	SENE	265
KINZE, DADID W.	1820	ONTA	SODU	121
KINZEE, JAMES W.	1820	ONTA	SENE	269
KIP, JAMES	1810	NYCO	WD06	448
KIP, JOHN	1830	NYCO	WD05	332
KIP, JOHN	1830	NYCO	WD06	412
KIP, SARAH	1830	NYCO	WD08	237
KIPAM, WILLIAM	1820	QUEN	----	63
KIPMAN, PETER	1800	NYCO	WD06	797
KIPP, ABRAHAM	1830	ABNY	WATV	464
KIPP, HENRY	1820	NYCO	WD05	393
KIPP, JACOB	1820	ABNY	ABNY	178
KIPP, JANE	1830	NYCO	WD06	434
KIPP, MARY	1810	NYCO	WD05	249
KIPP, THOMAS	1800	DUTC	RHIN	162
KIPP, THOMAS	1810	DUTC	RHIN	366
KIPSAM, JACOB	1810	QUEN	NHEM	211
KIRKWAIN, ELIZA	1820	NYCO	WD08	738
KIRMS, SAMUEL	1830	NYCO	WD10	19
KIRTLAND, SILVIA	1820	GREN	COXE	39
KISSAM, CARNELIA	1810	NYCO	WD03	55
KISSAM, HENRY	1820	SARA	EDIN	169
KISSAM, JACOB	1800	NYCO	WD07	890
KISSAM, JAMES	1830	NYCO	WD12	254
KISSAM, JAMES	1830	QUEN	FLUS	
KISSAM, JEFFREY	1830	NYCO	WD10	116
KISSAM, JOHN	1830	NYCO	WD10	116
KISSAM, PETER	1830	NYCO	WD10	116
KISSAM, THOMAS	1810	QUEN	NHEM	212
KISSAM, WILLIAM	1810	QUEN	NHEM	213
KISSAN, JILL	1800	QUEN	FLUS	538
KISSEN, WILLIAM	1800	QUEN	NHEM	553
KISSMAN, MARRIS	1810	QUEN	JAMA	201
KITCHAIN, HARRY	1820	SUFF	BROK	338
KITCHAM, CHARLES	1820	NYCO	WD07	700
KITCHEN, CHARLES	1820	QUEN	----	54
KITCHUM, CHARLES	1810	QUEN	FLUS	201
KITTLE, JACK	1810	COLU	KIND	174
KITTLE, JACK	1820	COLU	GHEN	7

NAME	YR	CO	TWP	PG
KITTLE, JACOB	1820	COLU	KIND	11
KITTLE, PETER	1820	COLU	KIND	11
KITTLE, THOMAS	1820	COLU	GHEN	7
KLINE, BETSY	1800	NYCO	WD07	872
KNAPP, HENRY	1820	COLU	KIND	11
KNIGHT, ICHABOD	1830	QUEN	FLUS	149
KNIGHT, JAMES	1790	QUEN	FLUS	149
KNIGHT, WILLIAM	1810	NYCO	WD08	722
KNISKERN, JACOB	1830	SCHR	SCHR	13
KNOTT, JANE	1830	ABNY	WD02	258
KNOWER, HENRY	1830	GENE	ALAB	316
KNOWLES, BENJAMIN	1830	NYCO	WD05	347
KNOWLES, EBENEZER	1830	NYCO	WD05	262
KNOWLES, GEORGE S.	1830	NYCO	WD05	276
KNOX, HENRY	1830	NYCO	WD08	215
KNOX, JOHN	1820	ROCK	CLAK	90
KNOX, JOHN	1830	NYCO	WD08	140
KNOX, PETER	1830	OTSG	MIDD	103
KOEN, MOLLY	1830	DUTC	REDH	373
KOMBINE, KERMBY	1820	COLU	HUDS	19
KOON, LEONARD	1820	ORNG	NEWB	546
KOON, THOMAS	1820	ULST	NEWP	70
KORTRIGHT, DINAH	1830	NYCO	WD05	329
KORTRIGHT, HARRY	1830	ULST	MARB	150
KORTRIGHT, PETER	1830	ULST	MARB	161
KORTRIGHT, PHILIP	1830	ULST	ROCH	170
KORTRITE, HARRY	1800	ULST	MARB	203
KORTWRIGHT, JACOB	1810	NYCO	WD06	405
KRAW, GEOFFRY	1800	DUTC	WASH	106
KRITS, FREDERICK	1820	NYCO	WD07	627
KRUM, SAMUEL	1820	ULST	MARB	62
KUNTZ, JOHN	1800	DUTC	RHIN	153
KYPHER, AMANDA	1820	DUTC	PGKP	111
KYRNS, DERRY	1800	NYCO	WD04	725
KYSER, MOSES	1820	ULST	MARB	61
LABAN, ADAM	1830	DUTC	PGKP	345
LABORN, TIMOTHY	1830	QUEN	NHEM	104
LACEY, PHILIP	1830	NYCO	WD06	387
LA CROIX, JOHN	1830	NYCO	WD06	434
LACY, C.	1830	NYCO	WD13	374
LACY, JOHN	1830	NYCO	WD05	306
LACY, MRS.	1830	NYCO	WD11	162
LAFER, ROSANNA	1810	NYCO	WD08	768
LAFERT, JOHN	1810	NYCO	WD05	288
LAFFERS, MATSEY	1830	ABNY	WD02	239
LAFFUTS, P.	1800	ABNY	WATV	96
LAGRANGE, DIANA	1830	ABNY	GUID	403

NAME	YR	CO	TWP	PG
LA GRANT, ANN	1830	DUTC	PGKP	326
LAIN, PHINEAS	1790	ORNG	NEWC	144
LAIR, CESAR	1820	WEST	CORT	301
LAKE, JOSEPH	1800	NYCO	WD07	919
LAKE, JOSEPH	1810	ULST	MARB	793
LAKE, JOSEPH	1820	SARA	SARA	189
LAKE, SAMUEL	1820	DUTC	PGKP	97
LAKE, SHARP	1830	ULST	KING	70
LALLY, ANN	1820	NYCO	WD07	628
LAMB, S.	1820	BROM	BERK	35
LAMBERT, JAMES	1830	WEST	NORC	197
LAMBERT, MADAM	1810	NYCO	WD05	314
LAMBERT, WILLIAM	1810	NYCO	WD06	424
LAMBERT, WILLIAM	1810	NYCO	WD07	556
LAME, JACK	1830	SCHR	COBL	149
LAMOT, JOSEPH	1820	NYCO	WD01	54
LAMOT, JOSEPH	1830	NYCO	WD05	281
LAMPHERE, HANNAH	1830	ONTA	SENE	85
LANA	1790	NYCO	HARL	137
LANA	1790	QUEN	FLUS	149
LANAH	1820	SARA	WATE	240
LANARY, JOHN	1800	NYCO	WD06	836
LANCASTER, PERMELIA	1830	QUEN	FLUS	139
LANCE, WILLIAM	1810	NYCO	WD07	586
LANDER, JOHN	1800	NYCO	WD03	706
LANDERSON, DAVID	1800	NYCO	WD03	692
LANDO, AMES	1820	SARA	WATE	240
LANDRINE, BENJAMIN	1830	WEST	CORT	60
LANDRINE, JACOB	1830	WEST	NEWR	107
LANDRINE, JESS	1830	WEST	SCAR	77
LANDS, CATO	1810	QUEN	NHEM	212
LANDS, EDWARD	1820	QUEN	----	29
LANDS, HENRY	1830	MONT	CANJ	27
LANDS, THOMAS	1830	MONT	CANJ	32
LANDUEN, CESAR	1810	NYCO	WD05	255
LANE, DANIEL	1810	NYCO	WD06	407
LANE, E.	1820	NYCO	WD10	1028
LANE, HANNAH	1830	NYCO	WD04	225
LANE, HESTER	1830	NYCO	WD08	246
LANE, JOHN	1820	NYCO	WD05	383
LANE, JOHN	1830	NYCO	WD05	261
LANE, JOHN	1830	NYCO	WD08	175
LANE, JOHN	1830	NYCO	WD08	220
LANE, JOSEPH	1830	NYCO	WD10	121
LANE, NICHOLAS	1830	NYCO	WD05	310
LANE, PRIMUS	1800	ORNG	NEWC	395
LANE, RICHARD	1820	QUEN	----	46
LANE, S.	1830	NYCO	WD11	133
LANE, SAMUEL	1820	NYCO	WD05	399

Lane

NAME	YR	CO	TWP	PG
LANE, THOMAS	1830	NYCO	WD10	78
LANEN, GEORGE	1800	NYCO	WD06	831
LANG, CUFFY	1830	RICH	SOUT	16
LANG, JOHN	1830	QUEN	NEWT	2
LANG, NICHOLAS	1820	NYCO	WD05	429
LANGLEY, DINAH	1830	MADI	----	213
LANGLEY, THOMAS	1820	MADI	SULL	2
LANGO, JACK	1810	SCHR	BROM	160
LANKFORD, ARTHUR	1830	NYCO	WD06	387
LANLOCK, MOSES	1830	NYCO	WD06	438
LANNETT, SUSAN	1830	NYCO	WD06	443
LANSING, JAMES	1830	SCNE	WD02	223
LANSOM, E.	1830	NYCO	WD13	394
LANTMAN, PRINCE	1820	COLU	LAUG	9
LANTMAN, PRINCE	1830	COLU	COPA	207
LAPHAM, THOMAS	1830	DUTC	STAN	417
LAPLEAN, WIDOW	1810	NYCO	WD10	656
LAPPIN, SANDY	1830	NYCO	WD10	66
LAQUER, JACK	1830	KING	BUSH	383
LARDEN, JOSHUA	1830	QUEN	OYST	28
LAROD, JOHN	1820	SARA	EDIN	169
LAROE, JOHN	1830	MONT	BROA	148
LARR, ABRAHAM	1820	WEST	CORT	289
LARR, ROBERT	1830	OTSG	OTSG	59
LASHER, JOHN	1800	NYCO	WD06	826
LASHER, JOHN	1810	NYCO	WD05	289
LASHIN, LEWIS	1810	NYCO	WD05	291
LASHING, LEWIS	1830	NYCO	WD05	268
LASHLEY, HENRY	1820	WASH	JACK	190
LATHAM, JAMES	1810	NYCO	WD10	535
LATHAM, JAMES	1820	NYCO	WD04	228
LATHAM, JOSEPH	1830	NYCO	WD10	19
LATHROP, AUGUSTUS	1830	SCHR	SCHR	28
LATIMORE, CYNTHIA	1830	DUTC	PGKP	326
LATIN, E.	1830	NYCO	WD13	361
LATIN, JAMES	1830	NYCO	WD13	361
LATOUR, YORK	1830	ABNY	WATV	467
LATTEMORE, BENJAMIN	1830	ABNY	WD01	200
LATTEMORE, MARY	1830	NYCO	WD08	172
LATTEN, JAMES	1830	NYCO	WD08	181
LATTEN, THOMAS	1830	NYCO	WD07	116
LATTIMER, I.	1810	DUTC	PGKP	OIK
LATTIMER, WILLIAM	1830	SARA	HALF	82
LATTIMORE, BENJAMIN	1820	ABNY	ABNY	181
LATTIMORE, BENJAMIN	1830	ABNY	WD01	224
LATTIMORE, JOHN	1810	NYCO	WD06	442
LATTIMORE, TITUS	1810	NYCO	WD06	473
LATTIMORE, WILLIAM	1810	NYCO	WD10	672
LATTIN, EPHRAM	1820	NYCO	WD10	988

NAME	YR	CO	TWP	PG
LATTIN, JAMES	1790	QUEN	OYST	153
LATTIN, THOMAS	1820	NYCO	WD10	988
LATTING, ISAAC	1830	QUEN	NHEM	114
LATTING, JAMES	1810	QUEN	OYST	251
LATTING, LYDIA	1800	NYCO	WD07	900
LATTING, THOMAS	1830	QUEN	NEWT	5
LATTUS, JOHN	1810	NYCO	WD07	622
LATUI, SAM	1820	ABNY	ABNY	182
LATURE, WILLIAM	1830	ABNY	WD01	221
LAUGHLING, THOMAS M.	1820	ORNG	NEWB	514
LAURANCE, ANTHONY	1830	DUTC	PGKP	332
LAURENCE, ABRAHAM	1830	NYCO	WD06	426
LAURENCE, SARAH	1830	NYCO	WD06	388
LAUVIGNOR, ANTHONY	1810	NYCO	WD06	489
LAVENDER, FRANCIS	1830	RENS	SAND	323
LAVENDER, JOHN	1810	NYCO	WD10	522
LAVILS, A. FRENCH	1810	NYCO	WD06	420
LAVINAN, NICHOLAS	1830	RENS	BRUN	226
LAVINE, A.	1830	NYCO	WD11	171
LAW, MARTHA	1830	NYCO	WD05	300
LAWLEY, MRS.	1830	NYCO	WD06	394
LAWNSEND, CATO	1820	QUEN	----	55
LAWNSEND, JAMES	1820	QUEN	----	69
LAWRENCE, ABIGAL	1820	NYCO	WD05	401
LAWRENCE, ANDREW	1810	NYCO	WD03	44
LAWRENCE, ANDREW	1820	NYCO	WD05	423
LAWRENCE, ANDREW	1830	RICH	CAST	40
LAWRENCE, BRISTER	1830	NYCO	WD12	254
LAWRENCE, DAVID	1810	NYCO	WD04	323
LAWRENCE, EDWARD	1820	QUEN	----	51
LAWRENCE, FRANCIS	1820	DUTC	FISH	56
LAWRENCE, GEORGE	1830	NYCO	WD06	427
LAWRENCE, GILVANNS	1820	NYCO	WD10	1106
LAWRENCE, HARRY	1810	QUEN	FLUS	193
LAWRENCE, JACOB	1820	QUEN	----	56
LAWRENCE, JACOB	1820	ULST	MARB	54
LAWRENCE, JAMES	1810	NYCO	WD10	647
LAWRENCE, JAMES	1820	NYCO	WD07	648
LAWRENCE, JOANNA	1820	NYCO	WD07	627
LAWRENCE, JOHN	1800	COLU	LIVG	1128
LAWRENCE, JOHN	1820	COLU	ANCM	5
LAWRENCE, JOHN	1820	NYCO	WD07	600
LAWRENCE, JOHN	1830	NYCO	WD05	345
LAWRENCE, JOSEPH	1810	NYCO	WD05	309
LAWRENCE, JOSEPH	1830	QUEN	OYST	52
LAWRENCE, MARGARET	1830	QUEN	FLUS	143
LAWRENCE, MARIA	1830	NYCO	WD08	173
LAWRENCE, MARY	1820	NYCO	WD05	399
LAWRENCE, MARY	1830	NYCO	WD05	331

Lawrence

NAME	YR	CO	TWP	PG
LAWRENCE, MIAMI	1830	NYCO	WD06	400
LAWRENCE, PETER	1830	NYCO	WD06	367
LAWRENCE, PETER	1830	QUEN	FLUS	152
LAWRENCE, PEYER	1820	NYCO	WD05	336
LAWRENCE, POMPEY	1800	QUEN	NHEM	550
LAWRENCE, POMPEY	1820	QUEN	----	58
LAWRENCE, RICHARD	1830	NYCO	WD12	310
LAWRENCE, ROBERT	1830	ABNY	WD02	228
LAWRENCE, RODGER	1820	QUEN	----	63
LAWRENCE, SILVENIS	1810	QUEN	FLUS	194
LAWRENCE, SULAS	1800	ONID	CANT	257
LAWRENCE, THOMAS	1830	NYCO	WD10	89
LAWRENCE, VENUS	1820	QUEN	----	60
LAWRENCE, WILLIAM	1810	NYCO	WD04	220
LAWRENCE, WILLIAM	1820	QUEN	----	75
LAWRENCE, WILLIAM	1830	NYCO	WD12	262
LAWRENCE, YORK	1810	QUEN	NEWT	176
LAWS, THOMAS	1820	DUTC	PGKP	110
LAWS, THOMAS	1830	DUTC	PGKP	358
LAWSON, HENRY	1820	NYCO	WD06	474
LAWSON, HENRY	1830	NYCO	WD01	31
LAWSON, ISAAC	1830	OSWE	VOLN	193
LAWSON, JOHN	1830	NYCO	WD06	458
LAWYER, JACK	1830	SCHR	MIDD	36
LAWYER, PETER	1830	SCHR	MIDD	36
LAYMAN, JAMES	1820	QUEN	----	57
LAYMAN, JOHN	1830	NYCO	WD12	285
LAYTON, WILLIAM	1830	NYCO	WD08	264
LAZARUS	1790	WEST	NEWC	203
LAZARUS, SILVAN	1830	NYCO	WD05	302
LAZER, ABNER	1830	MONT	AMST	120
LEAH	1790	NYCO	OUTW	130
LEAMAN, JOSIAH	1820	QUEN	----	75
LEAMAN, MICHAEL	1820	QUEN	----	79
LEAMORE, SARAH	1810	NYCO	WD03	58
LEAN, MARY A.	1830	NYCO	WD06	387
LEANA, ROBERT	1810	NYCO	WD04	199
LEARING, THOMAS	1820	QUEN	----	61
LEATON, THANKFUL	1790	ABNY	SCNE	44
LEAVING, TIMOTHY	1810	QUEN	NHEM	221
LEAVOLLY, ARON	1810	NYCO	WD02	116
LECEL, THOMAS	1820	DELA	DELH	52
LECRUSE, JOHN	1830	NYCO	WD10	99
LEDGER, JOHN	1820	JEFF	HOUN	417
LEDISTINE, JOHN	1800	NYCO	WD06	831
LEDWELL, DANIEL	1820	QUEN	----	69
LEE, ALEXANDER	1820	ONTA	SODU	121
LEE, ANN	1830	ONTA	SENE	72
LEE, BENJAMIN	1820	GREN	COXE	32

NAME	YR	CO	TWP	PG
LEE, BENJAMIN	1830	GREN	COXE	199
LEE, C.	1830	ERIE	BUFF	26
LEE, CAESAR	1800	NYCO	WD06	800
LEE, CESAR	1790	NYCO	WEST	135
LEE, CHARLES	1820	DUTC	PGKP	106
LEE, CHARLOTTE	1830	ONTA	SENE	72
LEE, EDMOND	1820	ONTA	SENE	268
LEE, EDWARD W.	1830	NYCO	WD08	181
LEE, GABRIEL	1830	KING	BRYN	346
LEE, HANNAH	1820	WEST	YORK	341
LEE, HENRY	1810	ONTA	SENE	842
LEE, HENRY	1820	NYCO	WD06	456
LEE, HENRY	1820	ONTA	SENE	268
LEE, HENRY	1830	NYCO	WD05	337
LEE, ISAAC	1820	MONT	AMST	284
LEE, LOTT	1830	COLU	STUY	64
LEE, MOSES	1820	ONTA	SENE	268
LEE, PETER	1830	DUTC	PGKP	321
LEE, PHILEMON	1800	DUTC	PGKP	65
LEE, PHILO	1810	DUTC	PGKP	170
LEE, SANDY	1810	NYCO	WD05	320
LEE, WILLIAM T.	1830	NYCO	WD08	210
LEE, WILLIS	1810	ONTA	GENE	842
LEE, WILLIS	1820	ONTA	SENE	274
LEE, WILLIS	1830	ONTA	SENE	58
LEEDLY, ISAAC	1830	ORNG	NEWW	102
LEEGRANT, SIMON	1810	DUTC	STAN	179
LEFEVER, JAMES	1830	ULST	NPAL	215
LEFEVER, JANE	1830	DUTC	PGKP	322
LEFEVER, THOMAS	1830	ULST	NPAL	216
LEFEVRE, DAVID	1830	NYCO	WD08	263
LEFEVRE, DIANA	1830	NYCO	WD08	186
LEFOREST, M.	1830	NYCO	WD11	208
LEGETT, FREDERICK	1830	WEST	NEWR	111
LEGG, DIANA	1830	ULST	SAUG	111
LEGG, JOSEPH	1820	DUTC	RHIN	128
LEGG, JOSEPH	1830	DUTC	HYPK	227
LEGGEL, MARY	1810	NYCO	WD05	315
LEGGET, CHARLES	1800	ABNY	WD02	287
LEGGETT, AUGUSTUS	1830	COLU	STUY	61
LEGGETT, CEASAR	1830	COLU	KIND	136
LEGGETT, HENRY	1830	NYCO	WD10	6
LEGGETT, JAMES	1830	WEST	WEST	123
LEISA, ELIZABETH	1820	ROCK	ORNG	86
LEIST, JOHN	1820	NYCO	WD07	651
LEMM	1800	SUFF	RIVH	21
LEMORIS, DONATIONS	1830	NYCO	WD05	337
LEMORMAN, YORK	1820	DUTC	RHIN	114
LEMOUNT, JOSEPH	1820	NYCO	WD07	671

NAME	YR	CO	TWP	PG
LENARD, ELIAS	1810	SARA	GREN	837
LENER, SAMUEL	1830	NYCO	WD10	122
LENINGTON, JAMES	1820	NYCO	WD01	43
LENSEL, BENJAMIN	1820	NYCO	WD07	721
LENT, CHARLES	1800	DUTC	SOUT	177
LENT, CHARLES	1810	DUTC	SOUT	130
LENT, JOHN	1790	DUTC	FISH	81
LENT, JOHN	1800	DUTC	FISH	25
LENTS, CHARLES	1830	PUTM	SOUT	43
LEONARD, DANIEL	1830	ORLE	ALBN	3
LEONARD, ISAAC	1830	NYCO	WD06	437
LEONARD, JAMES	1830	NYCO	WD03	112
LEONARD, MRS.	1830	KING	WD04	298
LEONARD, NATHANIEL	1800	SARA	MILT	1070
LEONARD, WILLIAM	1830	SCHR	SCHR	8
LERRIN, PHILIP	1810	NYCO	WD03	45
LESHAW, ANDREW	1810	NYCO	WD05	254
LESTER, AMY	1830	NYCO	WD10	13
LESTER, ELANE	1820	QUEN	----	60
LESTER, LEW	1790	QUEN	SHEN	156
LEVERICH, TUI	1830	QUEN	NEWT	11
LEVI, ELEAKIM	1830	QUEN	NHEM	116
LEVI, LICUM	1830	QUEN	OYST	22
LEVI, LIDYA	1810	NYCO	WD03	83
LEVI, LICUM	1820	QUEN	----	79
LEVI, MOSES	1830	QUEN	OYST	22
LEVI, PETER	1810	NYCO	WD03	57
LEVIE, JOHN	1800	NYCO	WD06	830
LEVING, WILLIAM	1830	NYCO	WD01	46
LEVY	1800	QUEN	OYST	575
LEVY	1800	SUFF	SHAM	68
LEVY, BENJAMIN	1830	NYCO	WD07	99
LEVY, DAVID	1800	NYCO	WD03	711
LEVY, FRANCES	1800	NYCO	WD07	919
LEVY, LINKNEY	1810	QUEN	NHEM	219
LEVY, PETER	1830	NYCO	WD10	72
LEVY, RICHARD	1830	NYCO	WD06	389
LEW	1790	QUEN	NHEN	152
LEW	1790	QUEN	NHEN	153
LEW	1790	QUEN	OYST	155
LEW	1800	QUEN	NHEM	558
LEW	1800	QUEN	OYST	568
LEW	1800	SUFF	ISLP	62
LEW	1810	QUEN	NHEM	305
LEW, PETER	1800	NYCO	WD04	721
LEWIS	1790	WEST	CORT	198
LEWIS	1800	QUEN	NHEM	554
LEWIS	1800	SUFF	HUNT	37
LEWIS	1800	WEST	HARR	652

NAME	YR	CO	TWP	PG
LEWIS	1810	ORNG	CORN	1036
LEWIS, ALLEN	1830	NYCO	WD05	307
LEWIS, ANN	1820	NYCO	WD06	544
LEWIS, BUTTER	1820	ONTA	CANA	214
LEWIS, CHARLES	1820	SUFF	ISLP	306
LEWIS, CHARLES	1830	NYCO	WD04	215
LEWIS, CHARLES	1830	SUFF	ISLP	281
LEWIS, CHARLES	1830	WEST	YORK	180
LEWIS, DINAH	1830	HERK	LTFA	89
LEWIS, DIXON	1810	NYCO	WD04	223
LEWIS, ELIZA	1830	NYCO	WD08	173
LEWIS, EPHRAIM	1830	ONTA	SENE	74
LEWIS, FRIEDD	1820	DUTC	NORT	87
LEWIS, H.	1810	ONID	LISB	351
LEWIS, HANNAH	1800	NYCO	WD03	706
LEWIS, HANNAH	1810	NYCO	WD05	271
LEWIS, HENRY	1810	NYCO	WD05	321
LEWIS, HENRY	1820	QUEN	----	78
LEWIS, ISAAC	1830	COLU	HUDS	108
LEWIS, ISAAC	1830	QUEN	FLUS	143
LEWIS, ISABEL	1820	COLU	HUDS	21
LEWIS, JACK	1820	TOMP	ULYS	12
LEWIS, JACOB	1820	DUTC	PGKP	98
LEWIS, JACOB	1820	SUFF	SMIT	322
LEWIS, JEP	1830	WEST	SUMM	191
LEWIS, JOHN	1800	NYCO	WD06	806
LEWIS, JOHN	1810	NYCO	WD05	286
LEWIS, JOHN	1810	NYCO	WD05	313
LEWIS, JOHN	1820	BROM	UNON	25
LEWIS, JOHN	1820	NYCO	WD04	288
LEWIS, JOHN	1830	ABNY	COEY	513
LEWIS, JOHN	1830	BROM	VEST	73
LEWIS, JOHN	1830	JEFF	HOUN	173
LEWIS, JOHN	1830	NYCO	WD05	331
LEWIS, JOHN	1830	NYCO	WD06	384
LEWIS, JOHN	1830	NYCO	WD06	410
LEWIS, JOHN	1830	NYCO	WD07	58
LEWIS, JOHN	1830	ONID	UTIC	38
LEWIS, JOSEPH	1820	NYCO	WD06	482
LEWIS, LEW	1810	QUEN	NHEM	212
LEWIS, MARIA	1830	NYCO	WD10	125
LEWIS, MARY	1830	NYCO	WD05	334
LEWIS, MARY H.	1830	NYCO	WD06	385
LEWIS, MRS.	1810	NYCO	WD06	404
LEWIS, NANCY	1820	CLNT	PLAT	463
LEWIS, PETER	1810	NYCO	WD06	442
LEWIS, PETER	1820	NYCO	WD10	1030
LEWIS, PETER R.	1830	NYCO	WD08	178
LEWIS, PHOEBE	1830	NYCO	WD04	228

Lewis

NAME	YR	CO	TWP	PG
LEWIS, PHOEBE	1830	NYCO	WD10	98
LEWIS, PRIME	1830	DUTC	CLNT	206
LEWIS, PRINCE	1800	NYCO	WD03	694
LEWIS, RICHARD	1830	ABNY	WD01	210
LEWIS, ROSANAH	1830	NYCO	WD10	11
LEWIS, SAMUEL	1820	MADI	BROK	109
LEWIS, SAMUEL	1820	NYCO	WD05	409
LEWIS, SAMUEL	1830	NYCO	WD10	116
LEWIS, SARAH	1810	NYCO	WD02	116
LEWIS, SUSAN	1820	NYCO	WD07	621
LEWIS, SUSAN	1830	NYCO	WD06	446
LEWIS, THOMAS	1800	NYCO	WD05	770
LEWIS, THOMAS	1820	NYCO	WD05	386
LEWIS, TUSEY	1830	SUFF	HUNT	328
LEWIS, WILLIAM HENRY	1830	DUTC	REDH	374
LIBERTY J.	1810	ONID	LISB	362
LIBERTY, JEFFEEY	1790	DUTC	PAWL	87
LIBERTY, JORDAN	1830	ONID	WHTE	203
LIBERTY, THOMAS	1800	DUTC	PAWL	58
LIBRASES, THOMAS	1810	NYCO	WD10	690
LIDDES, JOHN P.	1820	DUTC	FISH	76
LIDDLE, L.	1810	NYCO	WD05	345
LIDELL, JAMES	1830	RICH	WEST	4
LIKE	1790	QUEN	OYST	155
LIKEUM	1790	QUEN	OYST	154
LIKUM	1820	QUEN	----	37
LILLEY, THAR	1810	WEST	CAST	1169
LILLY, THOMAS	1810	DUTC	FISH	258
LILVEY	1810	NYCO	WD10	546
LIMAN, ELIZABETH	1810	NYCO	WD05	345
LIME, J.	1830	NYCO	WD11	162
LIMUS	1810	ORNG	CORN	1036
LINCOLN, PETER	1830	ONTA	PHEL	47
LINCOM, PETER	1820	ONTA	PHEL	283
LINDSEY, JOHN	1830	NYCO	WD08	255
LINES, ISAAC	1810	QUEN	SHEM	306
LINES, ISAAC	1820	QUEN	----	10
LINES, SIMEOUS	1820	SUFF	ISLP	306
LINES, THOMAS	1810	NYCO	WD04	186
LINET, SAMUEL	1830	SARA	GREN	218
LINK, JACK	1830	COLU	CHAT	49
LINS, JOHN	1830	NYCO	WD10	13
LINSEY, JAMES	1820	NYCO	WD08	807
LINSKY, JACK	1830	ALLE	RUSH	174
LINYLETS, PETER	1820	ONID	BOON	177
LIPKINS, THOMAS	1800	NYCO	WD06	801
LIPKINS, THOMAS	1810	NYCO	WD08	723
LIRCE, FRANCIS	1810	NYCO	WD08	766
LISHER, SYBIL	1830	NYCO	WD07	46

NAME	YR	CO	TWP	PG
LITS, PETER	1830	RENS	NASS	303
LITTLE, ASA	1830	MONR	RWD3	231
LITTLE, JOHN	1800	ONID	LISB	255
LITTLE, JOHN	1830	ABNY	WD01	203
LITTLE, JOHN	1830	COLU	HUDS	111
LITTLE, JOHN	1830	NYCO	WD06	446
LITTLE, SABRINA	1830	GENE	CAST	151
LITTLE, THOMAS	1810	SCNE	WD02	953
LITTLE, TOWER	1830	ABNY	WD01	216
LITTLE, WILLIAM	1830	NYCO	WD08	218
LITTLETON, E.	1830	NYCO	WD13	337
LIVINGSTON, CIRUS	1800	NYCO	WD04	721
LIVINGSTON, DIAN	1830	MONT	CANJ	22
LIVINGSTON, HUTSON R.	1830	NYCO	WD05	252
LIVINGSTON, ISAAC	1830	QUEN	OYST	27
LIVINGSTON, JOHN	1810	NYCO	WD07	551
LIVINGSTON, JOHN D.	1800	DUTC	PGKP	63
LIVINGSTON, JOHN M.	1820	NYCO	WD06	462
LIVINGSTON, MARY	1830	NYCO	WD05	343
LIVINGSTON, PEGGY	1820	COLU	HUDS	21
LIVINGSTON, PUNCH	1810	COLU	HUDS	140
LIVINGSTON, RICHARD	1830	ONID	DEER	240
LIVINGSTON, SAMUEL	1830	COLU	HUDS	99
LIVINGSTON, SEARS	1800	COLU	HUDS	1149
LLODY, ABRAHAM	1830	NYCO	WD06	427
LLOYD, EDWARD	1810	NYCO	WD05	316
LLOYD, JAMES	1830	NYCO	WD06	445
LLOYD, ROSE	1830	WANE	SODU	130
LOAM	1810	NYCO	WD05	308
LOAN, CESAR V.	1830	GREN	WIND	113
LOANE, HENRY	1820	ABNY	ABNY	180
LOCAY, ROBERT	1820	ULST	SHAW	64
LOCKERSON, JOHN	1800	NYCO	WD05	766
LOCKLIN, ROBERT	1830	NYCO	WD04	164
LOCKWOOD, PHOEBE	1830	NYCO	WD04	159
LOCUS, JANE	1810	NYCO	WD02	130
LODAWICK, JACK	1830	COLU	STUY	60
LOFFERTY, TOBY	1810	NYCO	WD06	445
LOFFETS, RODNEY	1810	NYCO	WD06	59
LOGAN, J.	1830	NYCO	WD11	149
LOINS, GEORGE	1810	QUEN	FLUS	194
LOINS, JOSEPH	1830	QUEN	FLUS	139
LOINS, WILLIAM	1830	QUEN	NHEM	112
LONDON	1790	NYCO	MONT	121
LONDON	1790	QUEN	FLUS	149
LONDON	1790	QUEN	NHEM	152
LONDON, ABRAHAM	1830	ABNY	GUID	413
LONDON, HENRY	1830	ABNY	GUID	413
LONDON, JAMES W.	1830	NYCO	WD05	261

London

NAME	YR	CO	TWP	PG
LONDON, PETER	1830	RENS	PITT	144
LONDONDERRY, JOHN	1830	HERK	LTFA	85
LONG, BENJAMIN	1830	ORNG	NEWB	40
LONG, JAMES	1820	NYCO	WD05	331
LONG, JOB	1790	ORGN	ORGN	146
LONG, JOB	1800	ROCK	ORNG	1036
LONG, LEWIS	1820	NYCO	WD05	370
LONG, MARGARET	1830	NYCO	WD08	279
LONGMORE, THOMAS	1830	KING	WD04	316
LOOSELEY, TITUS	1790	COLU	HUDS	66
LOOSELY, TITUS	1800	COLU	HUDS	1143
LOOVSON, JAMES	1810	NYCO	WD08	772
LOPEZ, ARON	1810	NYCO	WD08	82
LOPEZ, LEWIS	1800	NYCO	WD05	752
LOPEZ, RACHEL	1820	NYCO	WD06	469
LOPP, WILLIAM	1830	MONT	JOHN	230
LORIE, MARTHA	1790	QUEN	SHEM	158
LORS, SARAH	1820	ULST	SAUG	81
LOSCE, PRIMUS	1800	DUTC	BEEK	18
LOSER, PRIMUS	1810	DUTC	FISH	206
LOSS, HEZEKIAH	1830	NYCO	WD05	285
LOTT	1820	ABNY	WEST	102
LOTT, LETTY	1830	NYCO	WD06	426
LOTT, SIMON	1810	NYCO	WD07	572
LOTT, SIMON	1820	NYCO	WD06	517
LOTTER, AMOS	1830	CHAT	HANO	382
LOUDON, HENRY	1810	COLU	CLAV	164
LOUIE	1830	NYCO	WD13	382
LOUIS	1820	QUEN	----	6
LOUIS	1820	QUEN	----	10
LOUIS	1820	QUEN	----	61
LOUIS	1820	QUEN	----	80
LOUIS, AARON	1800	NYCO	WD04	725
LOUIS, ISRAEL	1820	QUEN	----	79
LOUIS, TOBY	1800	NYCO	WD06	846
LOUISTON, DAVID	1810	QUEN	SHEM	306
LOUSTER, HAGER	1810	KING	BRYN	630
LOVE, DAUPHINE	1800	NYCO	WD06	800
LOVEAGE, P.	1810	MADI	BROK	759
LOVEGAW	1790	QUEN	OYST	154
LOVENDAL, JOHN	1800	NYCO	WD03	715
LOVERNA, JOHN	1820	NYCO	WD07	686
LOVET, PEGGY	1830	MADI	----	196
LOVET, ROBERT	1830	SCNE	GLEN	268
LOVETT, ROBERT	1820	SCNE	GLEN	150
LOW, ABRAHAM	1830	NYCO	WD08	237
LOW, HARRY	1830	ULST	KING	77
LOW, JAMES	1830	NYCO	WD06	445
LOW, MARGARET	1830	WEST	WEST	122

NAME	YR	CO	TWP	PG
LOW, SAMUEL	1830	DUTC	FISH	503
LOW, SARAH	1830	NYCO	WD08	214
LOW, WILLIAM	1830	NYCO	WD06	399
LOWDER, WILLIAM	1820	DUTC	PGKP	101
LOWE, ROBERT	1820	OTSG	OTSG	100
LOWERRE, ELIZABETH	1830	NYCO	WD05	294
LOWERRY, JANE	1830	NYCO	WD05	333
LOWERY, PETER	1810	NYCO	WD05	257
LOWIS, PETER	1820	NYCO	WD08	735
LOWNSBURG, WILLIAM	1830	LEWI	DENM	407
LOWNSOND, BENJAMIN	1820	QUEN	----	61
LOWRENCE, JOSEPH	1820	NYCO	WD06	476
LOWREY, PETER	1790	NYCO	WEST	133
LOWREY, PETER	1820	NYCO	WD06	449
LOWRY, GEORGE	1830	YATE	MILO	215
LOYD, BERNJAMIN	1810	SUFF	HUNT	528
LOYD, THOMAS	1800	DUTC	PGKP	59
LOYD, THOMAS	1820	ONTA	SODU	121
LOYNE, ISRAEL	1800	QUEN	NHEM	554
LOYNS, ISREAL	1810	QUEN	NHEM	220
LOYNS, JOHN	1810	QUEN	NHEM	220
LUALUM, AMOS	1820	ORNG	MONT	843
LUCAN, JOHN	1830	SCNE	PRIN	254
LUCAR, JOHN	1820	NYCO	WD04	227
LUCAS, AARON	1830	ONTA	SENE	85
LUCAS, BELINDA	1790	NYCO	SOUT	131
LUCAS, H.	1830	KING	FLAT	401
LUCAS, HARRY	1830	STEU	BATH	273
LUCAS, LUKE	1810	NYCO	WD06	443
LUCAS, RELANDA	1820	NYCO	WD10	969
LUCEY	1790	QUEN	FLUS	150
LUCHEY, JOHN	1810	NYCO	WD06	448
LUCUS	1800	CHEN	CARN	982
LUDDINGTON, CAESAR	1830	COLU	CHAT	40
LUDLEY, NANCY	1830	ORNG	NEWB	28
LUDLOW, AARON	1810	NYCO	WD06	425
LUDLOW, ANTHONY	1810	DUTC	BEEK	274
LUDLOW, ISAAC	1830	ORNG	MONR	163
LUDLUM, THOMAS	1830	NYCO	WD10	114
LUE	1800	SUFF	HUNT	40
LUELLY, H.L.	1820	NYCO	WD07	620
LUGRANT, ANNY	1820	DUTC	STAN	135
LUGREE, JOSEPH	1830	NYCO	WD14	499
LUIO	1800	QUEN	OYST	568
LUISTER, ELFY	1830	QUEN	FLUS	154
LUKE	1790	NYCO	NORT	127
LUKES, WILLIAM	1820	NYCO	WD05	429
LUN, NERO	1820	KING	BRYN	171
LUNN, NERO	1830	KING	FLAN	413

NAME	YR	CO	TWP	PG
LUNSON, SAMUEL	1830	NYCO	WD06	426
LUNYEA, ADAM	1820	NYCO	WD04	228
LUSH, JACK	1830	COLU	CANN	30
LUSH, JACK	1820	COLU	CANN	9
LUSH, PETER	1830	TOMP	ITCA	332
LUSTER, JOHN	1830	NYCO	WD12	252
LUSTRE, LEWIS	1830	NYCO	WD07	31
LUTLIFF, ALEXANDER	1810	NYCO	WD03	81
LYLE, JACOB	1820	DUTC	MILA	82
LYLE, JACOB	1830	DUTC	MILN	257
LYLESWORTH, ARTER	1810	SUFF	BROK	471
LYMAN, J.	1830	NYCO	WD11	133
LYMAN, MINEAS	1830	SUFF	BROK	178
LYNCH, JOHN	1830	MONR	RWD3	231
LYNCH, RICHARD	1820	NYCO	WD06	518
LYON, JACOB	1830	WEST	RYE	102
LYON, JACOB	1830	WEST	RYE	103
LYON, JAMES	1820	NYCO	WD05	430
LYON, JOSEPH	1800	NYCO	WD07	927
LYON, JUDY	1830	WEST	EAST	134
LYON, PETER	1820	ULST	SHAW	67
LYON, PETER	1830	ULST	SHAW	242
LYON, SILVEY	1820	WEST	RYE	372
LYONS, ABRAHAM	1820	NYCO	WD07	702
LYONS, CESAR	1830	NYCO	WD07	51
LYONS, ELBERT	1800	NYCO	WD02	677
LYONS, GEORGE	1810	DUTC	BEEK	282
LYONS, GEORGE	1830	NYCO	WD09	390
LYONS, JOSEPH	1810	NYCO	WD06	443
LYONS, JOSEPH	1830	NYCO	WD08	148
LYONS, JOSEPH	1830	NYCO	WD09	391
LYONS, PERO	1830	SCNE	WD02	219
LYONS, RICHARD	1830	QUEN	FLUS	139
LYONS, RICHARD 2nd.	1830	QUEN	FLUS	139
LYONS, WILLIAM	1830	NYCO	WD06	381
LYTER, ROBERT	1830	RICH	SOUT	19
MAAIMORE, PETER	1800	NYCO	WD04	717
MCCARTY, HELLEN	1830	ABNY	WD02	263
MCCLAUREY, EDSALL	1830	ORNG	WALL	140
MCCLAUREY, ISAAC	1830	ORNG	WALL	144
MCCLAUREY, JOHNIAM	1830	ORNG	WALL	140
MCCLAUREY, PETER	1830	ORNG	WALL	140
MCCLAUREY, THOMAS	1830	ORNG	WALL	140
MCCLAUREY, WILLIAM	1830	ORNG	WALL	140
MCCLELLAN, ROBERT	1830	WANE	LYON	109
MCCLOUD, LAWRENCE	1830	NYCO	WD08	231
MCCLURE, WILLIAM	1830	ONTA	SENE	81

NAME	YR	CO	TWP	PG
MCCOLLIN, OBADIAH	1830	NYCO	WD05	261
MCCOMBS, THOMAS	1830	NYCO	WD12	294
MCCOON, JOSEPH	1830	QUEN	FLUS	142
MCCOUN, POMP	1800	RENS	GREN	899
MC COY, C.	1830	NYCO	WD11	201
MC COY, FLORA	1800	NYCO	WD05	782
MCCOY, HENRY	1830	RENS	TROY	14
MC CRADY, HANNAH	1810	NYCO	WD03	84
MCDONALD, CHARLES	1830	NYCO	WD04	159
MAC DONALD, JOHN	1810	WASH	THUR	406
MCDONALD, LUCY	1830	MONR	RWD1	201
MC DOUGAL, JAMES	1820	NYCO	WD05	390
MCDOUGAL, JAMES	1830	NYCO	WD08	258
MC DOUGULL, JOHN	1820	WASH	WHIT	195
MC DUGALD, ROBERT	1830	GREN	CATS	237
MACE, JOHN	1820	NYCO	WD03	185
MCELROY, ROBERT	1830	NIAG	NEWF	341
MC ERBACK, DYCK	1830	ABNY	RENV	420
MC EVEN, JAMES	1810	NYCO	WD03	89
MC EVERS, JAMES	1810	NYCO	WD03	53
MC EWEN, SARAH	1820	NYCO	WD06	485
MACEY, HARRY	1830	COLU	STUY	69
MCFARLAND, ROBERT	1820	ABNY	ABNY	184
MC FARLANG, DANIEL	1830	NYCO	WD10	125
MC FARLIN, THOMAS	1820	SCHR	BLEN	476
MC GAVENY, EDMUND	1830	NYCO	WD12	287
MC GEE, THOMAS	1810	MONT	PALA	117
MC GEE, WILLIAM	1820	ESEX	KENE	19
MC GEE, WILLIAM	1820	ESEX	KENE	428
MCGERT, ANN	1830	ABNY	WD04	311
MC GILL, JOHN	1810	NYCO	WD05	249
MC GILL, MARY	1810	NYCO	WD02	116
MCGINNIS, BRYAN	1800	ORNG	WARW	380
MC GINNIS, FRANCIS	1810	NYCO	WD08	716
MCGLAUGHRY, JOHN	1800	ORNG	WALL	341
MCGLAUGHRY, JOHN	1800	ORNG	WARW	341
MCGLAUGHRY, THOMAS	1800	ORNG	WALL	341
MCGLAUGHRY, WILLIAM	1800	ORNG	WALL	341
MCGOMERY, THOMAS	1830	WEST	WEST	123
MCGREGOR, NANCY	1830	NYCO	WD08	224
MACGRUDY, THOMAS	1830	QUEN	NHEM	112
MC GULLY, CHARLES	1820	QUEN	----	28
MCHINNEE, LEWIS	1820	MONT	JOHN	367
MACHY, BETSY	1810	NYCO	WD05	281
MC INTYRE, ARCHIBALD	1830	ORNG	GOSH	289
MACK, ABRAHAM	1820	NYCO	WD10	981
MCKAY, DARBY	1820	ABNY	ABNY	185
MCKAY, SARAH	1830	NYCO	WD08	183
MCKEE, ABRAHAM	1830	NYCO	WD14	444

NAME	YR	CO	TWP	PG
MCKEE, DANIAL	1830	MONT	PALA	170
MCKEE, THOMAS	1830	MONT	CANJ	21
MCKENNA, JOHN	1830	NYCO	WD07	72
MCKENZIE, MARIA	1830	NYCO	WD05	278
MCKERZIE, CATHARINE	1830	ONTA	SENE	72
MACKEY, DAVID	1830	NYCO	WD08	240
MACKILL	1810	NYCO	WD07	585
MCKINNE, G.	1830	NYCO	WD13	375
MCKINNEY, JACOB	1800	NYCO	WD07	861
MCKINNEY, WILLIAM	1830	NYCO	WD06	458
MCKINNY, PETER	1820	NYCO	WD07	685
MCKINNY, WID. DINA	1830	MONT	JOHN	227
MCKINS, JOHN	1830	WEST	WEST	127
MC KINSEY, VOLL	1820	STEU	BATH	227
MC KINZEY, MARGARET	1820	NYCO	WD05	393
MCKINZY, MARY	1830	ALLE	ANGE	5
MCKOY, THOMAS	1830	SARA	WATE	37
MC LAUGHLIN, CHARLES	1810	ORNG	GOSH	1071
MCLAUGHLIN, THOMAS	1830	ORNG	NEWB	40
MC LAUGHRY, JOHN	1810	ORNG	WALL	1112
MC LAUGHRY, THOMAS	1810	ORNG	WALL	1112
MC LAUGHTY, THOMAS	1810	ORNG	WALL	1110
MC LAUGHTY, WILLIAM	1810	ORNG	WALL	1110
MCLAURY, JOSEPH	1830	ORNG	WALL	139
MCLAURY, WILLIAM JR.	1830	ORNG	WALL	140
MC MORE, PETER	1820	NYCO	WD08	850
MC NEAL, CARSON	1820	NYCO	WD09	918
MC NEIL, PETER	1820	NYCO	WD05	404
MCPHERSON, JOHN	1800	NYCO	WD07	794
MCPHERSON, JOHN	1830	NYCO	WD05	274
MCQUOIN, GEORGE	1830	SENE	FAYE	59
MC PHERSON, MORE	1810	NYCO	WD05	249
MC PHERSON, WILLIAM	1820	NYCO	WD05	369
MACRABACK, DIKE	1820	GREN	GREN	68
MADDE, LEWIS	1810	NYCO	WD05	368
MADDEN, SAMUEL	1830	NYCO	WD05	302
MADER, HENRY	1830	QUEN	SHEM	78
MAEINTIER, ELIZABETH	1830	STEU	PRAT	454
MAGARD, A.	1830	NYCO	WD03	113
MAHEW, CHARLES	1820	QUEN	----	7
MAHEW, LURANNA	1820	NYCO	WD07	659
MAHUE, JAMES	1790	QUEN	NEWT	151
MAHUE, NANCY	1810	QUEN	OYST	244
MAHUE, RYER	1820	WEST	NEWR	190
MAINES, ROBERT	1830	TOMP	ITCA	332
MAKER, LOUIS	1800	DUTC	BEEK	17
MALISS, QUACO	1800	COLU	HUDS	1140
MAN, ARON	1810	WEST	HARR	1131
MAN, CHARLES B.	1810	WEST	HARR	1131

NAME	YR	CO	TWP	PG
MAN, ELI	1830	OTSG	CHRV	163
MAN, JEREMIAH B.	1810	WEST	RYE	1163
MAN, JOHN	1830	ROCK	RPOT	100
MAN, PETER	1810	NYCO	WD05	767
MAN, ROBIN B.	1810	WEST	MTPL	1115
MAN, SPONUTS B.	1810	WEST	WEST	1152
MANCHESTER, ANN	1810	RENS	PETE	342
MANDEVILLE	1790	NYCO	OUTW	129
MANDLYNE, NANCY	1800	NYCO	WD06	802
MANDO, JOEL	1790	DUTC	AMEN	73
MANDO, THOMAS	1830	RENS	SCAS	115
MANFIELD, NIK	1810	QUEN	NHEM	215
MANHISON, GABRIEL	1820	WEST	EAST	202
MANLY, CEASAR	1800	NYCO	WD04	722
MANN, JAMES	1820	ORNG	GOSH	738
MANN, JAMES	1830	ORNG	GOSH	281
MANN, PETER	1810	NYCO	WD04	214
MANN, PHILIP	1810	ROCK	HEMP	661
MANN, THOMAS	1830	OTSG	OTSG	42
MANNASER, PRINCE	1820	DUTC	STAN	139
MANNERS, THOMAS	1830	NYCO	WD06	448
MANNING, CHARLES	1820	NYCO	WD08	784
MANNING, CHARLES	1830	NYCO	WD09	417
MANNING, HENRY	1830	NYCO	WD10	13
MANNING, JEFFERY	1830	KING	WD04	301
MANNING, WILLIAM	1830	WEST	GREN	25
MANNWELL, MARY	1800	NYCO	WD03	701
MANO, UMPKINS	1810	NYCO	WD04	205
MANSFIELD, CYRUS	1820	COLU	HUDS	23
MANSFIELD, EDWARD	1800	NYCO	WD06	791
MANSFIELD, HANNAH	1830	NYCO	WD04	218
MANSFIELD, PETER	1790	DUTC	CLNT	76
MANSFIELD, SARAH	1810	NYCO	WD06	397
MANSON, AMOS	1830	OSWE	VOLN	193
MANSON, RICHARD	1820	NYCO	WD07	721
MANUEL, JOSEPH	1830	QUEN	NEWT	15
MANUS, JAMES M.	1830	NYCO	WD09	437
MAPELYN, FRANCIS	1820	QUEN	----	63
MARANDA, ISAAC	1820	NYCO	WD08	790
MARANDER, ANTHONY	1800	NYCO	WD03	693
MARANDUM, JOHN	1810	NYCO	WD05	362
MARCADE, ROSE	1800	NYCO	WD06	820
MARCH, FRANCIS	1800	ABNY	WATV	93
MARCH, FRANCIS	1830	ABNY	WD01	224
MARCH, PETER	1820	NYCO	WD06	472
MARCY	1820	WEST	NORC	442
MARCY, HARRY	1820	COLU	KIND	15
MARGARET	1790	QUEN	FLUS	149
MARGARET	1790	QUEN	NHEM	152

NAME	YR	CO	TWP	PG
MARGARET	1800	NYCO	WD06	818
MARGARET	1810	NYCO	WD01	33
MARGARET	1810	NYCO	WD05	322
MARGARET	1820	QUEN	----	50
MARGARETTE	1820	SUFF	BROK	340
MARGON, JAMES	1820	NYCO	WD06	502
MARIA	1790	QUEN	OYST	154
MARIAN	1810	NYCO	WD06	404
MARIAN	1820	COLU	KIND	15
MARIATH	1820	WASH	WHIT	195
MARINER, WILLIAM	1820	NYCO	WD05	337
MARK	1800	NYCO	WD07	885
MARK, ABRAM	1820	SUFF	BROK	360
MARK, SHARP	1790	SUFF	BROK	162
MARKE, LORITTE	1810	SUFF	EAST	434
MARKHAM, JOHN	1800	ONTA	HART	376
MARKIL, POMP	1810	SUFF	SHAM	456
MARKISSON, GABRAEL	1830	WEST	EAST	137
MARKS, ABRAHAM	1830	NYCO	WD14	448
MARLETT, AUGUSTUS	1830	NYCO	WD06	389
MARLOW, JOE D.	1810	NYCO	WD08	772
MARRS, JOHN	1830	COLU	GHEN	152
MARSELL, GILBERT	1820	QUEN	----	55
MARSH	1800	QUEN	SHEM	559
MARSH	1810	NYCO	WD06	402
MARSH, PETER	1810	NYCO	WD07	600
MARSH, WILLIAM	1820	NYCO	WD05	353
MARSH, WILLIAM	1830	NYCO	WD08	264
MARSHAL, JAMES	1820	NYCO	WD10	983
MARSHALL, ADAM	1810	NYCO	WD05	298
MARSHALL, ADAM	1820	KING	BRYN	116
MARSHALL, ELIZABETH	1830	NYCO	WD06	442
MARSHALL, JACOB	1820	NYCO	WD06	520
MARSHALL, JAMES	1830	NYCO	WD11	207
MARSHALL, PETER	1830	NYCO	WD05	301
MARTHA	1810	NYCO	WD06	430
MARTIN, ABRAHAM	1820	NYCO	WD10	975
MARTIN, ANDREW	1800	NYCO	WD06	822
MARTIN, BENJAMIN	1830	DUTC	HYPK	234
MARTIN, BURWICK	1800	NYCO	WD07	927
MARTIN, CATY	1830	COLU	CANN	23
MARTIN, CHARLES	1830	ABNY	WD01	198
MARTIN, CHARLES	1830	NYCO	WD08	249
MARTIN, DAVID	1820	ONTA	PALM	336
MARTIN, DAVID	1830	KING	WD04	301
MARTIN, ELIZABETH	1830	DUTC	HYPK	234
MARTIN, GRIFFEN	1830	DUTC	HYPK	231
MARTIN, GRIFFIN	1820	DUTC	CLNT	27
MARTIN, H.	1810	RENS	TROY	387

NAME	YR	CO	TWP	PG
MARTIN, HARRIOT	1830	NYCO	WD06	448
MARTIN, HARRY	1820	WEST	HARR	466
MARTIN, HENRY	1820	WEST	HARR	466
MARTIN, HENRY	1830	RENS	TROY	8
MARTIN, HENRY	1830	WEST	HARR	214
MARTIN, J.	1830	NYCO	WD03	113
MARTIN, JACK	1820	HERK	MANH	15
MARTIN, JACK	1830	HERK	MANH	119
MARTIN, JOHN	1800	NYCO	WD01	657
MARTIN, JOHN	1800	NYCO	WD07	888
MARTIN, JOHN	1830	NYCO	WD05	261
MARTIN, JOHN B.	1810	NYCO	WD06	448
MARTIN, LEWIS	1820	WEST	HARR	467
MARTIN, LIAR	1820	COLU	HUDS	23
MARTIN, PHILIP	1830	NYCO	WD05	275
MARTIN, PRIMUS	1790	DUTC	CLNT	76
MARTIN, PRIMUS	1800	DUTC	CLNT	107
MARTIN, PRIMUS	1820	DUTC	CLNT	26
MARTIN, PRIMUS	1820	DUTC	PGKP	103
MARTIN, PRIMUS	1830	NYCO	WD04	153
MARTIN, PRINCESS	1810	DUTC	CLNT	395
MARTIN, SAMUEL	1800	NYCO	WD04	735
MARTINA, JERMAIN	1830	NYCO	WD06	428
MARTINE, HARRY	1830	WEST	HARR	220
MARTINE, PETER	1800	NYCO	WD07	890
MARTINO, JACK	1830	RICH	SOUT	15
MARVEL, SQUIRE	1830	QUEN	OYST	49
MARVIN, ANDREW	1830	ORNG	NEWW	100
MARVIN, HARRY	1820	NYCO	WD09	916
MARVIN, HENRY C.	1830	NYCO	WD08	224
MARVIN, JAMES	1830	ORNG	GOSH	282
MARVIN, JEFFERY	1810	NYCO	WD10	635
MARVIN, LUCY	1830	ORNG	NEWW	108
MARVIN, WILLIAM	1830	NYCO	WD08	258
MARY	1790	NYCO	MONT	121
MARY	1790	NYCO	NORT	127
MARY	1790	QUEN	FLUS	149
MARY	1790	QUEN	FLUS	150
MARY	1790	QUEN	NHEM	152
MARY	1790	QUEN	OYST	153
MARY	1790	QUEN	SHEM	157
MARY	1800	ABNY	WD02	282
MARY	1810	NYCO	WD02	124
MARY	1810	NYCO	WD06	416
MARY	1810	RENS	TROY	387
MASDORE, PEGGY	1810	NYCO	WD01	33
MASIER, ANTHONY	1820	KING	BRYN	126
MASON, ALFRED	1830	NYCO	WD08	227
MASON, EDWARD	1810	DUTC	BEEK	268

NAME	YR	CO	TWP	PG
MASON, EDWARD	1820	NYCO	WD05	422
MASON, JAMES	1830	NYCO	WD06	387
MASON, JOHNATHAN	1830	NYCO	WD09	431
MASON, OLIVER	1820	ONID	WHIT	303
MASON, OLIVER	1820	ONID	WATE	303
MASON, OLIVER	1830	ONID	NWHT	62
MASON, STEPHEN	1830	NYCO	WD05	340
MASON, THOMAS	1820	HERK	FRAN	61
MASON, THOMAS	1830	NYCO	WD06	435
MASON, WILLIAM	1820	TOMP	HECT	7
MASON, WILLIAM	1830	NYCO	WD04	201
MASON, WILLIAM	1830	SENE	LODI	118
MASON, WILLIAM	1830	STEU	HOWA	417
MASONER, WILLIAM	1820	SENE	COVE	300
MASS	1810	ROCK	CLAK	678
MASSIER, MISS	1830	KING	NEUT	395
MATER, JOHN	1820	NYCO	WD05	337
MATHEW, GEORGE	1830	NYCO	WD06	459
MATHEWS, ABRAHAM	1800	NYCO	WD04	723
MATHEWS, ABRAHAM	1810	NYCO	WD05	315
MATHEWS, ABRAHAM	1820	NYCO	WD08	742
MATHEWS, EDWARD	1820	SUFF	BROK	352
MATHEWS, MR.	1830	NYCO	WD10	101
MATHEWS, MRS. CORNELIA	1820	NYCO	WD01	62
MATHEWS, WIDOW	1830	NYCO	WD13	369
MATHIAS, F.	1830	NYCO	WD10	87
MATHIS, JOHN	1810	NYCO	WD07	551
MATICE, HORACE	1830	ORNG	WARW	83
MATILDA	1810	SUFF	SHEL	466
MATOON, ELI	1800	SARA	MILT	1062
MATT, NATHANIEL	1830	RENS	SAND	323
MATTACK, JOSEPH	1800	QUEN	NHEM	555
MATTHERS, ABRAM	1790	NYCO	WEST	133
MATTHEW	1790	QUEN	NEWT	151
MATTHEW, ABRAHAM	1830	NYCO	WD14	487
MATTHEWS, ABRAHAM	1810	NYCO	WD08	717
MATTHEWS, DANIEL	1810	DELA	HARP	588
MATTHEWS, JACOB	1810	NYCO	WD05	317
MATTHEWS, JACOB	1830	NYCO	WD08	213
MATTHEWS, JANE	1830	ABNY	WD02	239
MATTHEWS, PETER	1830	CAYU	SPRG	314
MATTHEWS, SALLY	1820	NYCO	WD10	990
MATTHEWS, WILLIAM	1810	NYCO	WD05	322
MATTHEWS, WILLIAM	1830	NYCO	WD05	261
MATTICE, JESSE	1830	ORNG	GOSH	289
MATTIN, PETER	1830	SCHR	MIDD	36
MATTISS, JONATHON	1830	NYCO	WD03	143
MATTY, ABRAHAM	1790	NYCO	WEST	134
MAUDY, CHARLES	1820	STEU	READ	270

NAME	YR	CO	TWP	PG
MAURICE, MR.	1830	NYCO	WD06	435
MAWKINS, THOMAS	1790	DUTC	PWKP	90
MAXFIELD, JOHN	1810	NYCO	WD05	280
MAXWELL, SARAH	1830	NYCO	WD05	348
MAY, JAMES	1790	DUTC	PWKP	87
MAY, JOSEPH	1830	DUTC	PINE	295
MAY, RICHARD	1830	NYCO	WD09	428
MAY, SAMPSON	1820	DUTC	BEEK	105
MAY, THOMAS	1790	DUTC	WASH	94
MAY, THOMAS	1800	DUTC	WASH	104
MAY, THOMAS	1830	DUTC	AMEN	173
MAY, WILLIAM	1820	NYCO	WD09	924
MAYHEW, CHARLES	1790	QUEN	OYST	155
MAYHEW, CHARLES	1830	QUEN	SHEM	78
MAYHEW, JOHN	1790	QUEN	FLUS	149
MAYNARD, JOSEPH JR.	1800	ONTA	SENE	498
MAYNE, PHILIP	1830	ROCK	RPOO	100
MAYO, J'AMES	1830	NYCO	WD14	499
MAYO, PHILIP	1830	NYCO	WD08	247
MAYREE	1800	ABNY	WATV	95
MEAD, WILL	1820	KING	BRYN	114
MEAD, WILLIAM	1830	NYCO	WD06	413
MEADOW, ANDREW	1830	KING	WD04	316
MEAZEL, JACOB	1830	COLU	STUY	59
MEDDOCK, HENRY	1820	KING	BRYN	117
MEDFORD, JAMES	1830	NYCO	WD06	465
MEDGE, JOHN	1820	QUEN	----	77
MEED, ABSALEM	1830	WEST	NORS	81
MELAWS, A.	1830	NYCO	WD11	163
MELILDA	1800	SUFF	SHEL	85
MENARD, MIDDLETON	1830	ULST	SHAW	249
MENDON, JEANTHAN	1830	DELA	MIDD	147
MENISER, PRINCE	1830	COLU	GALA	230
MENTIS, THOMAS	1830	MONT	MAYF	283
MEREN, JOSEPH	1820	ORNG	NEWB	510
MERMIA, BENJAMIN	1830	NYCO	WD06	399
MERN, THOMAS	1820	QUEN	----	57
MERRIT, HANNAH	1830	WEST	EAST	131
MERRYMAN, JUDITH	1830	NYCO	WD05	275
MERTINE, HENRY	1810	WEST	HARR	1132
MERVIN, H.	1820	NYCO	WD10	1068
MERVIN, JEFFREY	1820	NYCO	WD06	489
MESECK, HENRY	1830	COLU	HUDS	93
MESEROLE, SAMUEL	1830	NYCO	WD07	28
MEYER, CAPES	1830	NYCO	WD06	423
MEYERS, JACOB	1820	NYCO	WD10	1028
MICAH	1790	QUEN	OYST	154
MICAH	1790	QUEN	SHEM	157
MICHAEL	1790	WEST	YORK	209

NAME	YR	CO	TWP	PG
MICHAEL	1800	NYCO	WD07	887
MICHAEL	1800	QUEN	OYST	571
MICHAEL	1800	QUEN	OYST	573
MICHAEL	1800	WEST	HARR	657
MICHAEL	1820	QUEN	----	10
MICHAEL	1820	QUEN	----	54
MICHAEL	1820	QUEN	----	60
MICHAEL	1820	QUEN	----	65
MICHAEL, HENRY	1830	NYCO	WD05	333
MICHAELS, HENRY	1830	NYCO	WD06	389
MICHEL, JACOB	1820	SUFF	EAST	290
MICHEL, JERIMIAH	1810	QUEN	NHEM	207
MICHELL, JEREMIAH	1820	QUEN	----	63
MICHERSON, GEORGE	1820	QUEN	----	56
MICKERSON, JOHN	1820	QUEN	----	56
MIDDLETON, ISAAC	1800	CAYU	MINT	614
MIERS, ACHEW	1830	STEU	HOWA	416
MIFFIN, RID.	1830	NYCO	WD06	442
MIGGINS, JOHN	1820	WEST	WEST	188
MIHANDER, JOHN	1800	NYCO	WD06	794
MIKE	1790	QUEN	OYST	155
MIKE	1820	SUFF	BROK	330
MIKE, JOHN	1820	SUFF	SHAM	318
MILBOUR, REUBEN	1800	DUTC	WASH	105
MILBOURN, DEVEREUX	1790	DUTC	PGKP	90
MILBOURN, DEVEREUX	1800	DUTC	PGKP	68
MILBUR, D.	1810	DUTC	PGKP	329
MILBURNE, RICHARD	1830	NYCO	WD08	213
MILDEN, PETER	1830	ULST	MARL	279
MILES, DAVID	1810	NYCO	WD04	158
MILES, JOHN	1830	KING	BRYN	346
MILES, JOHN	1830	SUFF	BROK	163
MILES, MARY	1830	NYCO	WD08	243
MILIGAN, SAMUEL	1830	ORNG	WARW	75
MILL, LOTT	1830	COLU	CHAT	52
MILLER, AARON T.	1830	NYCO	WD14	473
MILLER, ABRAHAM	1820	NYCO	WD05	348
MILLER, ABRAHAM	1830	NYCO	WD07	33
MILLER, ADELIA	1830	NYCO	WD06	430
MILLER, B.	1830	SUFF	SHAM	204
MILLER, BETT	1790	SUFF	BROK	161
MILLER, BRISTER	1810	SUFF	SHAM	449
MILLER, BRISTER	1820	SUFF	NHAM	300
MILLER, CHARLES	1830	DUTC	STAN	409
MILLER, CHARLES	1830	NYCO	WD07	65
MILLER, CHARLES	1830	ROCK	ORGT	114
MILLER, CHARLES	1830	SUFF	SHAM	209
MILLER, CHARLOTTE	1820	NYCO	WD07	620
MILLER, CHATHAM	1830	ORNG	GOSH	274

NAME	YR	CO	TWP	PG
MILLER, CLAUS	1830	GREN	NEWB	179
MILLER, COLLY	1830	ORNG	MONR	161
MILLER, F.	1830	NYCO	WD11	201
MILLER, FRANK	1830	SUFF	SHAM	206
MILLER, FRANK	1830	SUFF	SHAM	215
MILLER, HANNUEL	1820	NYCO	WD09	918
MILLER, HOP	1830	GREN	NEWB	169
MILLER, ISHMAN	1830	NYCO	WD13	336
MILLER, JACK	1820	GREN	COXE	35
MILLER, JACK	1830	COLU	HUDS	98
MILLER, JACK	1830	GREN	COXE	195
MILLER, JAMES	1820	DUTC	CLNT	28
MILLER, JAMES	1830	NYCO	WD06	451
MILLER, JAMES	1830	NYCO	WD10	46
MILLER, JANE	1830	NYCO	WD06	380
MILLER, JARED	1830	SUFF	BROK	175
MILLER, JEFFERSON	1830	ABNY	WD02	263
MILLER, JEREMIAH	1820	ORNG	CORN	698
MILLER, JEREMIAH	1830	NYCO	WD07	105
MILLER, JEREMIAH	1830	ORNG	MONR	173
MILLER, JEREMIAH	1830	ORNG	NEWB	54
MILLER, JEREMIAH B.	1820	ORNG	MONT	804
MILLER, JOE	1830	NYCO	WD09	390
MILLER, JOHN	1800	NYCO	WD03	703
MILLER, JOHN	1820	COLU	HUDS	9
MILLER, JOHN	1820	NYCO	WD07	626
MILLER, JOHN	1820	NYCO	WD07	612
MILLER, JOHN	1820	SUFF	HUNT	274
MILLER, JOHN	1830	NYCO	WD06	426
MILLER, JOHN	1830	SUFF	HUNT	310
MILLER, JOHN	1830	WASH	WTCK	195
MILLER, JONAH	1790	SUFF	BROK	161
MILLER, JONAH	1810	SUFF	BROK	486
MILLER, JONAH	1820	SUFF	BROK	363
MILLER, JONAH	1830	SUFF	BROK	177
MILLER, JONAH	1830	SUFF	HUNT	310
MILLER, JOSEPH	1800	ULST	NAVI	184
MILLER, JOSEPH	1810	NYCO	WD03	83
MILLER, JOSEPH	1820	NYCO	WD04	294
MILLER, MAGTO	1820	SUFF	HUNT	290
MILLER, MARK	1830	SUFF	EAST	258
MILLER, MARY	1830	ONTA	SENE	83
MILLER, NANCY	1830	GREN	COXE	190
MILLER, PETER	1830	NYCO	WD05	334
MILLER, PETER	1830	NYCO	WD06	377
MILLER, PETRE	1830	CAYU	AUBN	168
MILLER, PHILIP	1830	ABNY	WD01	210
MILLER, POLLY	1800	NYCO	WD05	748
MILLER, POMP	1820	GREN	COXE	41

NAME	YR	CO	TWP	PG
MILLER, PRESS	1790	SUFF	BROK	161
MILLER, RICHARD	1830	ROCK	ORGT	105
MILLER, ROBERT	1820	STEU	READ	270
MILLER, SAMPSON	1820	SUFF	HUNT	292
MILLER, SAMPSON	1830	SUFF	HUNT	303
MILLER, SARAH	1830	NYCO	WD08	263
MILLER, STEPHEN	1830	WEST	RYE	102
MILLER, STEVE	1810	SUFF	EAST	438
MILLER, THOMAS	1800	NYCO	WD06	846
MILLER, THOMAS	1800	NYCO	WD03	699
MILLER, THOMAS	1810	NYCO	WD06	424
MILLER, THOMAS	1820	NYCO	WD06	494
MILLER, THOMAS	1820	ORNG	CORN	708
MILLER, THOMAS	1830	DUTC	REDH	374
MILLER, THOMAS	1830	ORNG	NEWW	100
MILLER, THOMAS	1830	ROCK	CLAR	122
MILLER, THOMAS JR.	1810	NYCO	WD06	460
MILLER, TOM	1820	GREN	COXE	43
MILLER, TONATO	1820	SUFF	HUNT	274
MILLER, WILLIAM	1800	NYCO	WD06	846
MILLER, WILLIAM	1810	NYCO	WD06	460
MILLER, WILLIAM	1820	NYCO	WD06	503
MILLER, WILLIAM	1830	NYCO	WD06	451
MILLER, YAT	1830	JEFF	WATE	62
MILLER, YATT	1820	ONON	SALI	255
MILLES, RICHARD	1820	ROCK	ORNG	85
MILLEY	1790	NYCO	MONT	121
MILLIGAN, FREDERICK	1830	RENS	TROY	10
MILLIGAN, ROBERT	1800	NYCO	WD03	722
MILLIGAN, AUSTIN	1830	ORNG	MONR	176
MILLS, CLARRISSA	1830	SUFF	HUNT	321
MILLS, EDWARD	1830	DUTC	PGKP	322
MILLS, ELIJAH	1830	NYCO	WD06	410
MILLS, F.	1830	ERIE	BUFF	33
MILLS, FRANKLIN	1830	SUFF	SMIT	275
MILLS, JAMES	1800	NYCO	WD03	701
MILLS, JENNY	1830	DUTC	PLEA	312
MILLS, JOHN	1820	NYCO	WD07	636
MILLS, JONAH	1820	SUFF	HUNT	285
MILLS, JOSEPH	1820	NYCO	WD06	498
MILLS, MRS.	1830	KING	WD03	290
MILLS, MRS.	1830	NYCO	WD05	245
MILLS, ROBIN	1830	SUFF	SMIT	276
MILLS, THOMAS	1800	NYCO	WD03	693
MILLS, THOMAS	1830	NYCO	WD08	174
MILLSPAUGH, GEORGE	1830	ORNG	WALL	147
MILLY	1790	QUEN	NHEM	152
MILTCO, ANN	1820	ABNY	ABNY	187
MIMA	1820	SUFF	RIVH	360

NAME	YR	CO	TWP	PG
MIME, BILL	1790	QUEN	NEWT	151
MIMI	1790	QUEN	NHEM	153
MIMY, WILLIAM	1820	DUTC	FISH	56
MINAH, SUSAN	1830	NYCO	WD05	354
MINDAS	1810	NYCO	WD06	575
MINDERSE, MOSES	1830	DUTC	RHIN	397
MINDOW, THOMAS	1830	RENS	PITT	126
MINER, JOHN	1830	ABNY	WD05	338
MINER, JOHN	1830	NYCO	WD14	520
MINFIELD, ANNAMIS	1800	QUEN	NHEM	552
MINGO	1790	QUEN	NEWT	151
MINGO	1790	QUEN	SHEM	157
MINGO	1820	ONTA	BENT	261
MINGO	1820	SUFF	SMIT	320
MINGO, GEORGE	1830	YATE	BENT	302
MINGO, HOSA	1820	ORNG	GOSH	763
MINGO, HOSEA	1830	ORNG	HBGH	128
MINGO, JAMES	1820	SUFF	SMIT	319
MINGO, JAMES	1830	SUFF	SMIT	271
MINGO, JOHN	1800	ORNG	NEWB	284
MINGO, JOHN	1800	SUFF	HUNT	39
MINGO, JONATHAN	1830	SUFF	HUNT	314
MINGO, PETER	1800	NYCO	WD05	768
MINGO, PETER	1820	ABNY	ABNY	185
MINISEE, QUACKO	1830	NYCO	WD08	255
MINISING, QUANS	1810	NYCO	WD05	371
MINISING, QUANS JR.	1810	NYCO	WD05	371
MINISSEE, ADAM	1830	NYCO	WD05	337
MINK	1810	RENS	SCHO	555
MINK	1820	ABNY	COEY	133
MINKS, NYTIE	1800	NYCO	WD05	749
MINNE	1800	QUEM	OYST	575
MINNESEE, QUAQUO	1800	NYCO	WD06	828
MINNIMAN, WILLIAM	1830	TOMP	ULYS	394
MINS, SARAH	1800	NYCO	WD06	832
MINSE, LUCUS	1790	COLU	CLAV	62
MINSER, REBECCA	1830	COLU	CHAT	35
MINTFIELA, ANASSIOR	1820	QUEN	----	77
MINTFIELD, RACHAEL	1800	NYCO	WD07	886
MINTFULA, EDWARD	1820	QUEN	----	74
MINTON, JAMES	1810	NYCO	WD06	405
MINUS, MIDDLETON	1820	ORNG	MONT	846
MIRES, JAMES	1830	MONR	GREC	190
MIRRITT, GEORGE	1820	WEST	YORK	341
MISSESUR, JOSEPH	1820	COLU	CHAT	13
MITCHEL, ISAAC	1830	QUEN	FLUS	141
MITCHEL, LEWIS	1830	QUEN	FLUS	
MITCHEL, MRS.	1820	KING	BRYN	116
MITCHELL, CASAR	1830	ORNG	NEWW	99

NAME	YR	CO	TWP	PG
MITCHELL, HENRY	1820	NYCO	WD05	419
MITCHELL, JEREMIAH	1830	QUEN	NHEM	110
MITCHELL, JERRY	1810	WEST	HARR	1133
MITCHELL, JOHN	1810	NYCO	WD01	21
MITCHELL, JOHN	1830	NYCO	WD06	421
MITCHELL, JOHN	1830	QUEN	NHEM	108
MITCHELL, JOHNATHAN	1830	NYCO	WD09	395
MITCHELL, LEWIS J.	1830	NYCO	WD07	34
MITCHELL, MICHAEL	1830	SUFF	SMIT	272
MITCHELL, PETER	1800	NYCO	WD01	661
MITCHELL, THOMAS	1810	NYCO	WD03	67
MITCHELL, TONE	1820	DUTC	PGKP	96
MITCHELL, WILLIAM	1830	NYCO	WD06	442
MITCHELL, WILLIAM	1830	NYCO	WD09	390
MITCHILL, OLIVER	1830	QUEN	OYST	28
MITTACK, JOSEPH	1800	QUEN	NHEM	555
MIXER, JOHN	1800	NYCO	WD04	725
MOCKERSON, GEORGE	1830	QUEN	FLUS	153
MOCKERSON, LAURA	1830	QUEN	FLUS	153
MODDO, MAR	1810	KING	BRYN	631
MODE, WILLIAM	1830	KING	BRYN	359
MOFFAT, ROBERT	1810	ORNG	GOSH	1128
MOFFATT, ZEDICK	1830	ORNG	BLOM	123
MOFFETT, ASHAEL	1820	NYCO	WD05	393
MOGER, CUFF	1800	DUTC	BEEK	17
MOGGY	1790	QUEN	NHEM	153
MOLAT, SUSANNAH	1790	ABNY	WD01	12
MOLESTON, SOLOMON	1830	NYCO	WD01	32
MOLINEAUX, WILLIAM	1820	NYCO	WD06	484
MOLLY	1790	NYCO	NORT	124
MOLLY	1790	SUFF	ISPL	165
MONCLIEF	1810	NYCO	WD06	444
MONDAY	1790	NYCO	NORT	125
MONDAY, ABRAM	1830	GREN	CATS	242
MONDORE, JUDTHUN	1810	DUTC	AMEN	441
MONEY, ANN	1820	WEST	NORS	391
MONFORT, JACOB	1820	QUEN	----	76
MONFORT, WILLIAM	1820	QUEN	----	73
MONK, FLOUR	1830	SCHR	SCHR	26
MONROE, ANTHONY	1820	DUTC	FISH	72
MONROE, ANTHONY	1830	DUTC	LAGR	245
MONROE, FRANCIS	1830	KING	WD05	327
MONSON, HARVEY	1830	ABNY	WD02	255
MONTAGNIE, THEODORE	1830	NYCO	WD05	267
MONTAGUE, FLORA	1810	NYCO	WD03	80
MONTAGUE, GEORGE	1800	NYCO	WD04	724
MONTAY, M.	1830	NYCO	WD06	403
MONTAYNE, THEODORE	1830	NYCO	WD05	336

NAME	YR	CO	TWP	PG
MONTER, DAVID	1810	NYCO	WD05	272
MONTGOMERY, MICHAEL	1830	KING	WD04	299
MONTGOMERY, ROSANNA	1800	NYCO	WD04	836
MONTGOMERY, WILLIAM	1810	NYCO	WD05	313
MONTGOMERY, WILLIAM	1820	NYCO	WD05	385
MONTIER, MR.	1830	NYCO	WD10	18
MONTROP, JACK	1810	WEST	MTPL	1103
MONTROSS, PETER	1830	WEST	YORK	167
MOODE, THOMAS	1830	KING	WD04	305
MOODY, CATHERINE	1800	NYCO	WD05	786
MOODY, ELIZABETH	1830	NYCO	WD10	13
MOODY, ISAAC	1820	TIOG	SPEN	276
MOOKISON, PETER	1820	NYCO	WD05	364
MOONDONE, JEDUTHAM	1820	DUTC	AMEN	7
MOONEY, PHILIP	1790	WEST	NORS	203
MOONY, ABSALOM	1800	WEST	NORS	756
MOOR, GILBUT	1820	NYCO	WD07	627
MOOR, SUSANNAH	1820	DUTC	REDH	119
MOORE, ALEXANDER	1820	NYCO	WD10	982
MOORE, ALEXANDER	1830	NYCO	WD05	263
MOORE, ALEXANDER	1830	NYCO	WD06	443
MOORE, ANN	1820	NYCO	WD01	19
MOORE, ANTHONY	1820	ABNY	ABNY	185
MOORE, ANTHONY	1820	NYCO	WD07	636
MOORE, ANTHONY	1830	KING	FLAN	411
MOORE, C.	1820	NYCO	WD10	998
MOORE, CADE	1800	SUFF	SHEL	85
MOORE, CEASAR	1810	COLU	HUDS	150
MOORE, COOK	1790	SUFF	SHEL	165
MOORE, CUMMINGS	1830	NYCO	WD09	430
MOORE, DORSEY	1820	BROM	OWEG	33
MOORE, EDWARD H.	1830	NYCO	WD06	436
MOORE, GEORGE	1830	NYCO	WD06	458
MOORE, GEORGE E.	1800	NYCO	WD04	724
MOORE, HARRY	1810	NYCO	WD05	370
MOORE, HENRY	1810	NYCO	WD02	126
MOORE, HENRY	1830	COLU	STUY	64
MOORE, HENRY	1830	KING	WD04	303
MOORE, HESTER	1830	ABNY	WD02	274
MOORE, JACOB	1820	ABNY	ABNY	187
MOORE, JAMES	1810	NYCO	WD05	255
MOORE, JAMES	1820	NYCO	WD04	212
MOORE, JAMES	1820	NYCO	WD08	758
MOORE, JAMES	1820	QUEN	----	52
MOORE, JAMES	1830	NYCO	WD04	159
MOORE, JAMES	1830	NYCO	WD08	241
MOORE, JAYNE	1830	SUFF	SOUT	342
MOORE, JOHN	1810	ROCK	ORNG	637
MOORE, JOHN	1820	KING	BRYN	126

NAME	YR	CO	TWP	PG
MOORE, JOHN	1830	NYCO	WD06	387
MOORE, JOHN	1830	NYCO	WD08	248
MOORE, JOHN S.	1810	NYCO	WD05	255
MOORE, JOSEPH	1810	ROCK	ORNG	638
MOORE, LEWIS	1830	NYCO	WD05	343
MOORE, LUCINDA	1830	NYCO	WD05	313
MOORE, LUCKY	1830	NYCO	WD10	11
MOORE, MARGARET	1820	NYCO	WD04	281
MOORE, MARTHA	1810	NYCO	WD06	449
MOORE, MARY	1820	NYCO	WD07	721
MOORE, MERKANDER	1800	ORNG	NEWC	395
MOORE, MOSES	1800	NYCO	WD07	887
MOORE, MRS.	1820	KING	NEUT	161
MOORE, PETER	1810	NYCO	WD03	83
MOORE, PETER	1820	GREN	COXE	36
MOORE, PETER	1820	NYCO	WD07	636
MOORE, REUBEN	1830	NYCO	WD06	383
MOORE, RICHARD	1820	ABNY	ABNY	187
MOORE, RICHARD	1820	NYCO	WD08	859
MOORE, RICHARD	1830	DUTC	REDH	368
MOORE, SAMUEL	1820	ROCK	CLAK	99
MOORE, SIMON	1810	ORNG	WALL	1110
MOORE, SOLOMON	1810	DUTC	BEEK	294
MOORE, SOLOMON	1820	DUTC	BEEK	20
MOORE, SOLOMON	1830	DUTC	UNVA	427
MOORE, SUSAARAH	1800	NYCO	WD03	696
MOORE, T.	1830	KING	WD04	310
MOORE, THOMAS	1800	NYCO	WD01	657
MOORE, THOMAS	1800	NYCO	WD07	904
MOORE, THOMAS	1810	NYCO	WD05	255
MOORE, THOMAS	1830	NYCO	WD07	46
MOORE, THOMAS	1830	SUFF	SHAM	215
MOORHOUSE, EZRA	1820	BROM	WIND	15
MOORIS, JACK	1830	ULST	MARB	159
MOORIS, SUSAN	1830	COLU	HUDS	101
MOORSE, WILLIAM	1830	NYCO	WD13	336
MOOVUS, ISAAC	1830	ERIE	BUFF	6
MORE	1810	NYCO	WD07	606
MORE, ALEXANDER	1810	NYCO	WD07	535
MORE, CADE	1810	SUFF	SOUT	565
MORE, CUFFEE	1830	KING	BRYN	358
MORE, J.	1830	NYCO	WD11	162
MORE, JACOB	1830	GREN	CATS	244
MORE, JOHN	1830	KING	WD03	290
MORE, JOHN	1830	ONID	UTIC	7
MORE, JOHN	1830	WEST	CORT	71
MORE, MARTIN	1810	SUFF	SHAM	448
MORE, NICHOLAS	1820	ROCK	ORNG	88
MORE, NICHOLAS	1830	ONID	UTIC	6

NAME	YR	CO	TWP	PG
MORE, PETER	1830	GREN	COXE	198
MORE, SIMON	1820	ORNG	WALL	786
MOREAU, MARY	1830	NYCO	WD08	237
MOREHOUSE, EZRA	1810	DELA	FRAN	548
MOREHOUSE, GEORGE	1830	TIOG	VETR	175
MOREHOUSE, JOSEPH	1810	DUTC	NORT	339
MOREKINS, RICHARD	1810	NYCO	WD04	192
MORES, THOMAS	1820	ULST	SAUG	•83
MORFORD, ELIZABETH	1800	COLU	HUDS	1144
MORGAN, ANN	1830	NYCO	WD10	124
MORGAN, ELI	1830	MADI	----	416
MORGAN, GEORGE	1830	KING	WD05	327
MORGAN, J.	1810	MADI	BROK	765
MORGAN, JOHN	1830	MADI	----	416
MORGAN, JOHN	1830	NYCO	WD06	442
MORGAN, JOSEPH	1830	GREN	CATS	232
MORGAN, MARY	1830	NYCO	WD06	385
MORGAN, NOAN	1830	RICH	WEST	9
MORIA, PELON	1820	NYCO	WD06	458
MORILLO, CATO	1830	NYCO	WD06	431
MORREL, ELIZABETH	1810	KING	BRYN	641
MORREL, JAMES	1830	NYCO	WD10	59
MORRELL, ISAAC	1830	KING	WD04	313
MORRICE, GEORGE	1820	SUFF	BROK	364
MORRIL, PETER	1830	WEST	RYE	106
MORRIS	1790	QUEN	FLUS	149
MORRIS	1790	QUEN	OYST	153
MORRIS	1790	QUEN	OYST	154
MORRIS	1800	QUEN	FLUS	540
MORRIS	1800	QUEN	OYST	573
MORRIS	1800	QUEN	NHEM	550
MORRIS	1800	QUEN	OYST	578
MORRIS	1800	QUEN	OYST	570
MORRIS	1800	QUEN	SHEM	558
MORRIS	1810	NYCO	WD07	591
MORRIS	1820	QUEN	----	65
MORRIS	1820	QUEN	----	70
MORRIS	1820	QUEN	----	72
MORRIS, AARON	1800	NYCO	WD06	840
MORRIS, AARON	1820	NYCO	WD05	336
MORRIS, ANSON	1820	NYCO	WD02	128
MORRIS, BENJAMIN	1830	ABNY	WEST	483
MORRIS, BETSEY	1810	NYCO	WD06	430
MORRIS, BETSEY	1830	NYCO	WD10	11
MORRIS, C.	1810	OTSG	MIDD	151
MORRIS, C.	1830	NYCO	WD10	24
MORRIS, CAPER	1810	NYCO	WD06	407
MORRIS, CARON	1820	NYCO	WD06	467
MORRIS, CHRISTIANA	1820	NYCO	WD06	481

NAME	YR	CO	TWP	PG
MORRIS, COOPER	1810	NYCO	WD06	414
MORRIS, EDWARD	1830	NYCO	WD08	133
MORRIS, ELIZABETH	1800	NYCO	WD07	887
MORRIS, EZRA	1830	NYCO	WD05	315
MORRIS, GABRIEL	1830	NYCO	WD06	427
MORRIS, GEORGE	1830	NYCO	WD09	301
MORRIS, ISAAC	1820	NYCO	WD04	242
MORRIS, JAMES	1810	NYCO	WD06	441
MORRIS, JAMES	1820	COLU	AUST	9
MORRIS, JAMES	1820	DELA	WALT	93
MORRIS, JAMES	1820	NYCO	WD08	841
MORRIS, JAMES	1820	SARA	WATE	240
MORRIS, JAMES	1830	DELA	WALT	215
MORRIS, JAMES	1830	NYCO	WD07	116
MORRIS, JAMES	1830	RENS	WD02	28
MORRIS, JOHN	1810	NYCO	WD05	291
MORRIS, JOHN	1820	NYCO	WD06	567
MORRIS, JOHN	1830	NYCO	WD08	244
MORRIS, JOSEPH	1810	NYCO	WD03	89
MORRIS, JOSEPH	1820	ABNY	ABNY	184
MORRIS, JOSIAH	1830	STLR	OSWE	229
MORRIS, NANCY	1830	NYCO	WD08	216
MORRIS, NERO	1800	DUTC	PGKP	68
MORRIS, NERO	1810	DUTC	PGKP	323
MORRIS, NERO	1820	NYCO	WD05	404
MORRIS, NERO	1830	NYCO	WD08	172
MORRIS, PETER	1800	NYCO	WD06	805
MORRIS, PETER	1810	DUTC	FISH	228
MORRIS, PETER	1820	DUTC	PGKP	113
MORRIS, PHEBE	1830	NYCO	WD14	440
MORRIS, RICHARD	1830	YATE	MILO	223
MORRIS, SAMUEL	1800	NYCO	WD07	929
MORRIS, SUSAN	1820	NYCO	WD10	988
MORRIS, WIDOW	1810	NYCO	WD10	635
MORRIS, WILLIAM	1830	ROCK	ORGT	114
MORRISON, JACOB	1830	NYCO	WD05	347
MORRISON, LARRY	1830	ONON	CICE	110
MORRISON, POMPEY	1830	ORNG	BLOM	122
MORRISON, RICHARD	1800	NYCO	WD03	704
MORRISON, SAMUEL	1820	COLU	HUDS	7
MORRISON, SAMUEL	1830	COLU	HILL	186
MORRISON, SAMY	1820	ONON	CICE	189
MORRISON, SIRAS	1810	QUEN	NHEM	220
MORRISON, THOMAS	1830	ORNG	MONR	182
MORROW, ROBERT	1830	RENS	TROY	16
MORSE, MATILDA	1830	NYCO	WD14	504
MORSRE, CARSEL	1810	NYCO	WD04	205
MORTIMER, CHARLES	1830	NYCO	WD05	345
MORTIN, LIAS	1820	COLU	HUDS	25

NAME	YR	CO	TWP	PG
MORTON, ANSTED	1830	NYCO	WD10	91
MORTON, CORNELIA	1810	NYCO	WD05	255
MORTON, MATHIAS	1800	NYCO	WD05	778
MORTON, THOMAS	1810	NYCO	WD05	312
MOSBY, MIKEL	1810	NYCO	WD07	530
MOSEERANS, PHILLIP	1800	DUTC	FISH	22
MOSELY, CESAR	1810	NYCO	WD05	309
MOSES	1790	QUEN	OYST	154
MOSES	1790	QUEN	SHEM	157
MOSES	1800	QUEN	OYST	576
MOSES	1800	QUEN	SHEM	557
MOSES, MR.	1830	NYCO	WD11	165
MOSHER, FRANK	1800	WEST	CORT	813
MOSIER, HARRY	1830	ROCK	HVER	156
MOSIER, THOMAS	1810	WASH	BOTT	399
MOSS, PRIME	1820	ABNY	ABNY	188
MOTT, BENJAMIN	1820	KING	BRYN	134
MOTT, CHARLES	1830	QUEN	OYST	39
MOTT, FRANCIS	1820	DUTC	BEEK	12
MOTT, FRANCIS	1820	KING	BRYN	141
MOTT, GEORGE	1830	WASH	WHIT	352
MOTT, ..HABB	1810	QUEN	OYST	247
MOTT, JEREMIAH	1830	NYCO	WD07	46
MOTT, MARY	1820	NYCO	WD06	494
MOTT, PETER	1830	WEST	EAST	137
MOTT, RICHARD	1800	NYCO	WD07	864
MOTT, STEPHEN	1800	QUEN	NHEM	552
MOTT, STEPHEN	1810	QUEN	NHEM	205
MOTT, STEPHEN	1830	KING	BRYN	363
MOTT, THOMAS	1830	KING	WD04	299
MOTT, WILLIAM	1820	KING	REDH	105
MOTT, WILLIAM	1830	SARA	CONC	187
MOUND, ANTHONY	1830	NYCO	WD14	467
MOUNTS, DAVID	1820	NYCO	WD08	780
MOUSAC, CRIZZLE	1820	NYCO	WD04	307
MOWER, THOMAS	1830	ULST	SAUG	106
MOXTERSON, TONEY	1810	QUEN	FLUS	193
MUBEN, DARCAS	1810	SUFF	SOUT	565
MUCRAY, WILLIAM	1830	ORNG	NEWB	60
MUDGE, LEONARD	1830	QUEN	NHEM	104
MULFORD, JOSEPH	1810	SUFF	SMIT	540
MULFORD, LYMAS	1830	SUFF	BROK	178
MULLEN, PATTY	1820	NYCO	WD06	470
MULLEN, THOMAS	1790	DUTC	PAWL	87
MULLEN, THOMAS	1810	SCHR	BROM	154
MUMFORD, ELIZABETH	1820	COLU	HUDS	23
MUMFORD, JOHN	1830	NYCO	WD05	337
MUMFORD, JOHN	1830	NYCO	WD06	441
MUMFORD, MARY	1830	ONTA	SENE	69
MUMFORD, TIMOTHY	1820	NYCO	WD07	705

NAME	YR	CO	TWP	PG
MUNDIN, JOHN	1830	GREN	ATHN	203
MUNDIN, THOMAS	1830	GREN	ATHN	203
MUNDOOR, JEDUTHAN	1800	DUTC	AMEN	138
MUNDY (?)	1830	NYCO	WD02	63
MUNFORT, JACOB	1830	QUEN	OYST	32
MUNGS, RICHARD	1830	MONT	CANJ	35
MUNN	1810	NYCO	WD07	585
MUNN, JOHN	1830	DUTC	FISH	489
MURPHY, DINE	1820	GREN	COXE	33
MURPHY, HENRY	1830	RENS	SCHO	240
MURPHY, JAMES	1830	NYCO	WD12	251
MURPHY, JOHN	1830	SCHR	BROM	78
MURPHY, PETER	1810	GREN	COXE	288
MURPHY, PETER	1820	NYCO	WD09	944
MURRA, JEWLE	1810	KING	BRYN	634
MURRAY, ANDREW	1830	ORNG	NEWB	40
MURRAY, BECCA	1830	SUFF	ISLP	284
MURRAY, BENJAMIN	1790	DUTC	PGKP	90
MURRAY, BENJAMIN	1800	DUTC	PGKP	67
MURRAY, BETSEY	1820	NYCO	WD04	242
MURRAY, CHARLES	1830	NYCO	WD06	457
MURRAY, DEBORAH	1830	ORNG	BLOM	117
MURRAY, GEORGE	1820	NYCO	WD03	190
MURRAY, GEORGE	1820	NYCO	WD04	226
MURRAY, GEORGE	1830	NYCO	WD07	30
MURRAY, HANNAH	1800	NYCO	WD06	799
MURRAY, HANNAH	1830	ORNG	BLOM	123
MURRAY, ISAAC	1830	OTSG	BURL	278
MURRAY, JANE	1820	NYCO	WD04	303
MURRAY, JOHN	1800	SUFF	ISLP	63
MURRAY, JOHN	1830	NYCO	WD06	435
MURRAY, JOHN	1830	SUFF	ISLP	280
MURRAY, JOSEPH	1820	ABNY	ABNY	184
MURRAY, MARGARET	1810	NYCO	WD02	116
MURRAY, NANCY	1800	NYCO	WD07	857
MURRAY, PETER	1810	NYCO	WD05	313
MURRAY, PETER	1810	NYCO	WD05	315
MURRAY, PETER	1820	NYCO	WD06	570
MURRAY, PHILIP	1810	NYCO	WD06	434
MURRAY, PHILLIP	1820	NYCO	WD04	227
MURRAY, RICHARD	1800	SUFF	ISLP	61
MURRAY, S.	1830	KING	WD05	330
MURRAY, STEPHEN	1800	SUFF	ISLP	61
MURRAY, STEPHEN	1820	KING	BRYN	142
MURRAY, STEPHEN	1820	NYCO	WD09	909
MURRAY, STEPHEN	1830	NYCO	WD05	300
MURRAY, WILLIAM	1820	ORNG	CORN	699
MURRAY, WILLIAM	1820	ORNG	MONT	841
MURRAY, WILLIAM	1820	WEST	HARR	463

NAME	YR	CO	TWP	PG
MURRY, APPOLLES	1810	SUFF	ISLP	499
MURRY, CEASER	1810	ORNG	NEWB	926
MURRY, DAVID	1830	NYCO	WD10	125
MURRY, ELIZABETH	1830	NYCO	WD10	89
MURRY, JAMES	1820	SCNE	WD01	125
MURRY, JAMES	1820	SCNE	WD02	129
MURRY, JOHN	1820	SUFF	ISLP	306
MURRY, LEWIS	1820	NYCO	WD07	636
MURRY, POLLUS	1820	SUFF	ISLP	308
MUST, WILLIAM	1830	SCHR	MIDD	36
MUTHONEY, ELIZA	1830	NYCO	WD14	444
MYER, HARRY	1830	ULST	HURL	146
MYER, HARRY	1830	ULST	KING	74
MYER, HARRY	1830	ULST	SAUG	97
MYER, JACK	1830	ULST	SAUG	97
MYER, ROBERT	1820	ULST	SAUG	81
MYER, SAMUEL	1830	ULST	HURL	146
MYERS	1810	NYCO	WD07	549
MYERS, ABRAHAM	1810	NYCO	WD04	203
MYERS, ANTHONY	1800	NYCO	WD02	675
MYERS, ANTHONY	1830	MONR	GREC	190
MYERS, ELIZA	1830	DUTC	PGKP	322
MYERS, HARRY	1810	DUTC	FISH	242
MYERS, JANNIS	1820	WEST	MAMA	362
MYERS, JOHN	1800	NYCO	WD05	779
MYERS, JOHN	1810	NYCO	WD05	316
MYERS, JOHN	1830	NYCO	WD05	305
MYERS, JOHN N.	1820	ULST	SAUG	82
MYERS, NANCY	1800	NYCO	WD06	814
MYERS, NANCY	1830	GREN	CATS	226
MYERS, PHILLIS	1830	ROCK	HVER	148
MYERS, SANDY	1820	ROCK	HVER	103
MYRICK, RICHARD	1810	NYCO	WD08	765
MYRIS, JAMES	1830	WEST	MAMA	228
MYSCO, CLOSS	1820	NYCO	WD05	393
NABON, CHARLES	1820	DUTC	PGKP	99
NALES, WALLIS	1800	NYCO	WD07	857
NAMES, ERNA	1820	GREN	CAIR	116
NAN	1790	QUEN	NHEM	152
NAN	1800	ABNY	WD01	263
NANCY, W.	1810	MADI	SULL	794
NANN	1810	ROCK	CLAK	674
NANNEY	1790	QUEN	FLUS	149
NANNY, TONY	1800	QUEN	NEWT	537
NANSY	1810	KING	BRYN	632
NAPHY, MRS. JUDITH	1820	NYCO	WD01	17
NARMON, JOSEPH	1810	NYCO	WD10	671

NAME	YR	CO	TWP	PG
NARNES, EZRA	1830	CHEN	MCDN	95
NARSISE, FRANCIS	1800	NYCO	WD07	879
NASEY, JUDAH	1830	NYCO	WD01	31
NASH, JAMES	1830	STLR	OSWE	228
NASHEROU, FLOE	1800	NYCO	WD06	844
NAT	1790	QUEN	OYST	153
NAT	1790	QUEN	SHEM	157
NATHAN, CHRISTOPHER	1830	NYCO	WD04	203
NATHANIEL	1790	SUFF	ISLP	165
NATHANIEL	1800	NYCO	WD05	760
NATHANIEL	1800	QUEN	SHEM	557
NATION, ISAAC	1790	QUEN	OYST	155
NATION, LEWIS	1810	QUEN	OYST	256
NATT, THOMAS	1830	GREN	ATHN	205
NATUS, FORTIND	1810	NYCO	WD04	199
NAVIENS, RICHARD	1810	NYCO	WD01	28
NAVY, AGNES	1820	NYCO	WD02	129
NAWSI, ANN	1820	WEST	YORK	330
NE--/--TER (?)	1810	SUFF	SMIT	539
NEAL	1820	SUFF	SMIT	320
NEAL, CHARLES	1820	NYCO	WD10	1028
NEAL, RICHARD	1810	NYCO	WD07	549
NED	1790	QUEN	NHEM	153
NED	1790	QUEN	SHEM	156
NED	1810	WEST	NORC	1170
NEDDY, LAZARUS	1810	WEST	NEWR	1092
NEDWELL, JACOB	1830	GREN	ATHN	211
NEGRO	1800	QUEN	FLUS	541
NEGRO, BINAH	1820	SUFF	SHAM	322
NEGRO, CAMBRIDGE	1820	SUFF	SHAM	319
NEGRO, DANIEL	1810	SUFF	ISLP	518
NEGRO, EDWARD	1810	SUFF	BROK	494
NEGRO, JOHN	1810	SUFF	SHAM	461
NEGRO, PERO	1810	SUFF	RIVH	551
NEGRO, PRINCE	1810	ORNG	MINI	1137
NEGRO, VIOLET	1810	SUFF	SHEL	466
NEHR, HANNAH	1800	DUTC	RHIN	153
NEILSON, CESAR	1810	NYCO	WD05	271
NEILSON, JOHN	1810	NYCO	WD05	272
NEILSON, JOHN	1810	NYCO	WD03	80
NELSON, BENJAMIN	1830	QUEN	NEWT	17
NELSON, CESAR	1830	NYCO	WD05	335
NELSON, CHARLES	1830	WEST	CORT	59
NELSON, JAMES	1810	NYCO	WD05	285
NELSON, JAMES	1830	KING	WD03	279
NELSON, JOSEPH	1820	NYCO	WD05	362
NELSON, JUDITH	1820	NYCO	WD03	144
NELSON, PETER	1830	WASH	CAMB	113
NELSON, SAMUEL	1830	WEST	EAST	137

NAME	YR	CO	TWP	PG
NELSON, THOMAS	1830	ONTA	SENE	86
NEPTUNE	1800	QUEN	OYST	577
NERO	1810	COLU	CLAV	157
NERO, ABRAHAM	1810	NYCO	WD07	589
NERVEMAN, THOMAS	1830	MONR	RWD3	229
NESS, JAMES	1800	NYCO	WD05	770
NETER, CALEB	1810	NYCO	WD07	622
NETTUS, HENRY	1800	NYCO	WD06	831
NEWARK, CHARLES	1830	TIOG	OWGO	274
NEWENS, JACOB	1810	KING	BRYN	639
NEWKERK, SAMUEL	1830	ULST	KING	63
NEWKIRK, JAMES	1830	ULST	MARB	163
NEWMAN, ISAAC	1830	MONR	MEND	107
NEWMAN, JOHN	1820	ULST	MARB	63
NEWMAN, JOHN	1830	RENS	TROY	14
NEWMAN, JOHN	1830	ULST	OLIV	141
NEWPORT	1800	SUFF	BROK	8
NEWPORT, ELEPHALET	1800	NYCO	WD01	668
NEWPORT, JANE	1830	NYCO	WD05	304
NEWPORT, WILLIAM	1820	ONTA	SODU	121
NEWPORTE	1810	NYCO	WD10	672
NEWRY, N.	1830	NYCO	WD02	81
NEWTON, JOHN	1800	NYCO	WD07	903
NICALL, SEASOR	1820	ORNG	NEWW	493
NICHOL, CADE	1800	SUFF	SHEL	85
NICHOL, RICHARD	1800	NYCO	WD06	826
NICHOL, SILVA	1800	NYCO	WD06	845
NICHOLAS	1800	QUEN	OYST	576
NICHOLAS	1800	WEST	HARR	652
NICHOLAS, ANTHONY	1820	NYCO	WD07	602
NICHOLAS, BETTY	1820	KING	BRYN	141
NICHOLAS, DINU	1810	NYCO	WD04	160
NICHOLAS, JOSEPH	1820	NYCO	WD09	936
NICHOLAS, MRS.	1830	NYCO	WD12	311
NICHOLAS, PETER	1810	NYCO	WD06	442
NICHOLAS, PETER	1820	NYCO	WD09	933
NICHOLAS, PHAEBIE	1820	NYCO	WD10	1000
NICHOLAS, WILLIAM	1820	NYCO	WD09	935
NICHOLAS, WILLIAM L.	1830	NYCO	WD08	226
NICHOLASS, JOSEPH	1830	NYCO	WD12	255
NICHOLLS, ANTHONY	1830	NYCO	WD12	276
NICHOLLS, ELIZA	1830	SUFF	SHEL	291
NICHOLS	1810	NYCO	WD07	557
NICHOLS, BILLY	1820	SENE	FAYE	370
NICHOLS, BRISTOL	1830	WASH	HAMP	275
NICHOLS, HAGAR	1810	NYCO	WD05	329
NICHOLS, HENRY	1810	NYCO	WD04	182
NICHOLS, HENRY	1830	NYCO	WD07	82
NICHOLS, ISREAL	1830	CHAT	ELCT	335

Nichols

NAME	YR	CO	TWP	PG
NICHOLS, JACOB	1810	NYCO	WD10	647
NICHOLS, JOHN	1830	DUTC	FISH	477
NICHOLS, PETER	1830	DUTC	FISH	462
NICHOLS, SUSAN	1830	DUTC	FISH	502
NICHOLS, THOMAS	1820	NYCO	WD05	411
NICHOLS, YORK	1830	DUTC	FISH	477
NICHOLSON, FRANCIS	1830	ORNG	HBGH	124
NICHOLSON, PAMELLA	1830	ORNG	NEWB	28
NICHOLSON, ROBERT	1820	ORNG	NEWB	513
NICHOLUS	1820	SUFF	SMIT	323
NICK	1790	NYCO	OUTW	130
NICKELS, BETTY	1810	KING	BRYN	639
NICKINS, JAMES	1810	NYCO	WD05	298
NICKOLS, DANIEL	1830	QUEN	NHEM	117
NICKOLS, JACK	1820	DUTC	FISH	61
NICKOLS, PETER	1820	DUTC	FISH	66
NICKOLS, YORK	1820	DUTC	FISH	61
NICOB, ELIZABETH	1820	SUFF	SHEL	331
NICOLAS, CAESAR	1820	NYCO	WD10	976
NICOLE, HAGAR	1800	NYCO	WD03	705
NICOLES, SAMUEL	1830	NYCO	WD06	404
NICOLL, JACOB	1800	NYCO	WD03	870
NICOLL, SEASOR	1820	ORNG	CORN	711
NICOLLS, CADE	1810	SUFF	SHEL	466
NICOLLS, CHARLES	1830	NYCO	WD12	255
NICOLLS, J.B.	1830	NYCO	WD12	255
NICOLSON, JAMES	1830	NYCO	WD10	125
NIGHT, JAMES	1800	NYCO	WD03	706
NIGHT, JAMES	1810	QUEN	NHEM	304
NILBEE, ROBERT	1810	NYCO	WD05	345
NILE, JOSAPHUS	1820	SARA	STIL	195
NILES, JOSEPH	1830	SARA	SARA	153
NIMROD	1820	SUFF	BROK	361
NIX, JACK	1810	WEST	BEDF	1077
NIXEN, GEORGE	1820	NYCO	WD05	398
NIXON, GEORGE	1810	NYCO	WD05	317
NIXON, JOHN	1820	NYCO	WD07	654
NIXON, JOHN	1830	NYCO	WD10	79
NOAH	1800	QUEN	OYST	570
NOAILLES, CHARLES	1830	NYCO	WD05	260
NOBLE, JACOB	1830	SCHR	SCHR	16
NOBLE, THOMAS	1830	ONTA	SENE	85
NOBLE, WILLIAM	1830	NYCO	WD06	446
NOEL, CHARLES	1800	NYCO	WD06	840
NOELL, FRANCIS	1800	NYCO	WD06	830
NOLES, JAMES	1820	NYCO	WD05	392
NOLT, JANE	1820	GREN	ATHE	8
NOLT, THOMAS	1820	GREN	ATHE	3
NORE, JOHN	1810	NYCO	WD07	530

NAME	YR	CO	TWP	PG
NORRIS, MARIA	1830	NYCO	WD06	432
NORTHROP, FREDERICK	1820	DUTC	STAN	135
NORTHUP, MINTRUS	1810	WASH	GRAN	432
NORTHUP, MINTUS	1820	WASH	FTED	159
NORTHUP, SOLOMAN	1830	WASH	KING	362
NOTT, GARRETT	1830	ABNY	BETH	536
NOTT, JACK	1820	ABNY	ABNY	189
NOTT, PETER	1830	NYCO	WD03	142
NOTT, PRIME	1830	ABNY	BETH	536
NOTTINGHAM, CATHERINE	1820	ULST	MARB	62
NOTTINGHAM, FORTUNE	1830	ULST	MARL	282
NOTTINGHAM, FORTUNE	1830	ULST	PLAT	267
NOTTINGHAM, SAMUEL	1830	ULST	MARB	157
NOVENESS, NATHANIEL	1830	ABNY	WD04	299
NOXON, ZACKO	1830	RENS	BRUN	230
NUDHAM, JOHN	1800	NYCO	WD07	888
NYMHAM, HENRY	1800	WEST	WESF	593
OAK, JOSEPH	1810	NYCO	WD07	538
OAKHOUSE, JEREMIAH	1800	SUFF	SHAM	67
OAKLEV, THOMAS	1830	OTSG	OTSG	57
OAKLEY	1820	PUTM	PATE	101
OAKLEY, CATO	1810	NYCO	WD06	424
OAKLEY, FANNY	1830	WEST	WTPL	224
OAKLEY, JACOBUS	1830	WEST	NORC	199
OAKLEY, ROBERT	1820	WEST	WTPL	461
OATFIELD, ANDREW	1830	NYCO	WD08	237
OATFIELD, CHRISTOPHER	1820	ABNY	ABNY	190
OATFIELD, CHRISTOPHER	1830	ABNY	WD04	299
OATFIELD, SARAH	1830	ABNY	WD04	299
OATHANDT, NEHEMIAH	1830	HERK	LTFA	85
OATOUT, R.	1810	RENS	TROY	378
OBARE, SALLY	1820	NYCO	WD06	482
OBDIAH	1820	QUEN	----	74
OBE	1790	QUEN	NHEM	152
OBE	1800	QUEN	OYST	575
OBE, JACK	1810	WEST	WEST	1148
OBE, JAMES	1810	SUFF	SMIT	538
OBED	1790	QUEN	OYST	154
OBEEDIAH	1800	QUEN	OYST	576
OBER, ADELE	1830	NYCO	WD05	334
OBRIEN, DANIEL	1830	SARA	SASP	163
OBRIEN, DANIEL	1810	SARA	MILT	797
OBRIEN, DANIEL	1820	SARA	SARA	189
OBRIEN, DENNIS	1820	QUEN	----	78
O BRIEN, WESLEY	1830	NYCO	WD10	33
OCAS, HUAH	1810	SUFF	SHAM	445
OCHO	1790	WEST	YORK	209

NAME	YR	CO	TWP	PG
OCUS, HEZIAH	1830	SUFF	SHAM	215
ODELL, C.	1830	NYCO	WD11	213
ODELL, HARRY	1830	WEST	HARR	214
ODELL, PETER	1830	NYCO	WD11	224
ODELL, SILAS	1810	SUFF	BROK	492
ODETT, P.	1820	NYCO	WD10	1115
ODLE, JOHN	1820	ORNG	GOSH	754
OGDEN, JOHN	1790	ULST	NPAL	179
OGDEN, JONATHAN	1800	SARA	CHAR	1075
OGDEN, PETER	1830	NYCO	WD05	245
OGDEN, SAMUEL	1830	CATT	RAND	234
OGDON, ROBERT	1830	QUEN	FLUS	138
OHAM, FLORA	1800	NYCO	WD03	704
OHEA, THOMAS	1820	NYCO	WD07	707
OKEEFE, ANDREW	1810	ONON	CICE	584
OLAND, LEWIS	1810	NYCO	WD05	301
OLBONES, MARY	1830	ABNY	ABNY	191
OLCOTT, CHARLES	1830	ABNY	WD02	268
OLCOTT, THOMAS	1820	ABNY	ABNY	190
OLDBOY, SIKY	1800	NYCO	WD03	701
OLDBY, LABAN	1820	MADI	BROK	109
OLDREDAS, DANIEL	1820	NYCO	WD08	785
OLIVER	1800	QUEN	FLUS	542
OLIVER, ALBERT	1830	KING	FLAT	402
OLIVER, BLACK	1810	GREN	CAIR	248
OLIVER, CATHERINE	1830	NYCO	WD01	31
OLIVER, FRANK	1830	NYCO	WD09	288
OLIVER, ISAAC	1790	MONT	OTSE	113
OLIVER, J.	1830	NYCO	WD01	35
OLIVER, JACOB	1820	NYCO	WD10	1002
OLIVER, JAMES	1820	NYCO	WD03	164
OLIVER, JOHN	1820	NYCO	WD05	399
OLIVER, JOHN	1830	NYCO	WD05	336
OLIVER, LEWIS	1830	ULST	MARB	155
OLIVER, MARGARET	1830	DUTC	FISH	462
OLIVER, POMP	1830	ULST	HURL	145
OLIVER, ROBERT	1820	NYCO	WD09	924
OLLIVER, FRANCIS	1810	NYCO	WD08	733
OLLY, JOSEPH	1800	NYCO	WD03	696
OMPEDORE	1810	DUTC	PGKP	325
ONDERDONK, JOHN	1830	QUEN	NHEM	107
ONDERDONK, OSBURN	1810	QUEN	OYST	238
ONDERDUNK, WILL	1820	ROCK	ORNG	86
ONEIL, HENRY	1800	NYCO	WD07	890
OOTHOUT, RACHEL	1830	RENS	WD02	28
OPHUS	1810	WASH	CAMB	491
ORANGE, JUNY	1810	KING	FLAT	655
ORANGE, ROBERT	1830	QUEN	NHEM	100
ORANGE, TERRY	1820	KING	NLOT	176

NAME	YR	CO	TWP	PG
ORCHARD, SAMUEL	1830	NYCO	WD13	336
ORCOTT, THOMAS	1830	ABNY	WD03	278
ORFEY, PETER	1830	NYCO	WD05	300
ORIAN, GEORGE	1800	ABNY	WD02	287
ORIST, PHILIP	1830	ULST	MARB	150
ORM, REUBEN	1830	ONTA	MANC	181
ORM, RICHARD	1790	NYCO	WEST	133
ORR, SAMUEL	1800	NYCO	WD07	887
OSBORNE, JOHN	1830	NYCO	WD01	32
OSGOOD, THOMAS	1810	QUEN	NEWT	165
OSTERHONDT, PHILIP	1830	ULST	SAUG	110
OSTERHONDT, THOMAS	1830	ULST	ROCH	184
OSTERHONDT, TOM	1830	ULST	SAUG	92
OSTRANDER, HENRY	1830	ABNY	WD05	329
OSTRANDER, JACK	1830	GREN	CATS	226
OSTRANDER, MINK	1830	MONT	CANJ	39
OSTRAUT, STEPHEN	1820	ULST	NEWP	72
OSTROM, JACK	1830	DUTC	PLEA	317
OVERBAGH, RICHARD	1830	ULST	SAUG	109
OVERTON, SUSANNA	1810	SUFF	SOUT	563
OWENS, HENRY	1830	SUFF	SHAM	233
PADDOCK, JAMES	1810	ONON	CAMI	566
PAGE, BRISTER JR.	1830	NYCO	WD08	215
PAGE, HENRY	1830	NYCO	WD10	99
PAIN, JOSEPH G.	1820	NYCO	WD09	939
PAINE, BENJAMIN	1830	RENS	LANS	93
PAINE, THOMAS	1810	NYCO	WD03	76
PAKE, HARRY	1830	ROCK	ORGT	114
PALL, ANTHONY	1800	WASH	BOTT	396
PALL, THOMAS	1800	WEST	EAST	621
PALM, NATHAN	1820	ONTA	PHEL	304
PALMER, ABEATHER	1800	WASH	GRAN	522
PALMER, ABEATHER	1820	WASH	GRAN	136
PALMER, JAMES	1830	NYCO	WD06	385
PALMER, JOHN	1830	GREN	COXE	188
PALMER, JOHN	1830	ROCK	ORGT	106
PALMER, JOSEPH	1820	SCNE	GLEN	149
PALMER, JOSEPH	1830	ORNG	WARW	92
PALMER, NANCY	1800	NYCO	WD05	754
PALMER, SAMUEL	1820	WASH	GRAN	136
PALMER, SAMUEL	1830	OSWE	SCRI	159
PALMER, THOMAS	1830	ROCK	ORGT	106
PAMELAS	1820	SUFF	BROK	361
PAMPY	1820	RICH	NORT	112
PANCO, JOSEPH	1830	ONID	UTIC	6
PANKAKE, PETER	1790	QUEN	FLUS	149
PANTON, RICHARD	1800	ABNY	COEY	244

NAME	YR	CO	TWP	PG
PAPER, JANE	1820	NYCO	WD07	721
PAPPAW, JOHN	1830	KING	FLAN	411
PARDELLS, CHARLES	1830	NYCO	WD05	269
PARISH, JAMES	1830	OTSG	PITT	313
PARK	1820	SUFF	RIVH	366
PARKER, EDMUND	1830	KING	WD05	342
PARKER, ELISABETH	1820	NYCO	WD05	424
PARKER, GABRIEL	1800	NYCO	WD07	884
PARKER, ISAAC	1810	ORNG	NEWB	925
PARKER, JAMES	1800	NYCO	WD07	904
PARKER, JAMES	1810	NYCO	WD07	624
PARKER, JOHN	1830	CAYU	VENI	352
PARKER, JOSEPH	1810	DUTC	FISH	258
PARKER, JOSEPH	1810	KING	BRYN	630
PARKER, JOSEPH	1820	DUTC	FISH	56
PARKER, JOSEPH	1820	KING	BRYN	149
PARKER, JOSEPH	1830	DUTC	FISH	491
PARKER, JOSEPH	1830	DUTC	FISH	495
PARKER, LUDWILL	1830	NYCO	WD04	170
PARKER, MARVIN	1810	SUFF	EHAM	431
PARKER, MARY	1830	NYCO	WD05	344
PARKER, PEGGY	1830	RENS	TROY	7
PARKER, SAMUEL	1830	NYCO	WD05	328
PARKER, THOMAS	1810	NYCO	WD05	331
PARKER, THOMAS	1820	NYCO	WD10	966
PARKER, THOMAS	1830	NYCO	WD05	312
PARKER, THOMAS	1830	NYCO	WD10	13
PARKINSON, PETER	1830	NYCO	WD06	448
PARKS, RICHARD	1820	NYCO	WD06	466
PARKS, WILLIAM	1810	NYCO	WD06	438
PARON, PETER	1810	NYCO	WD06	414
PARRETSON, JOHN	1830	KING	WD02	262
PARRETSON, JOHN	1830	KING	WD02	264
PARRISH, PLATO	1830	QUEN	OYST	47
PARRYN, HANNAH	1820	ABNY	ABNY	190
PARSER, THOMAS	1830	SCNE	WD02	219
PARSOL, JOHN	1830	DUTC	WASH	451
PARSON, CHRISTINA	1830	ABNY	WD02	239
PARSON, PETER	1820	SCHR	SUMM	549
PARSONS, GEORGE	1830	ABNY	WD04	319
PARSONS, HENRY	1810	NYCO	WD04	204
PARSONS, JACOB	1820	ABNY	ABNY	190
PARSONS, PETER	1810	COLU	LIVG	228
PASCAL, MARION	1820	NYCO	WD06	482
PASTLEY, ISAAC	1830	DELA	TOMP	205
PATEON, SAMUEL	1810	NYCO	WD10	641
PATERSON	1820	PUTM	PATE	101
PATERSON, ANN	1820	NYCO	WD07	636
PATERSON, SUSAN	1830	ABNY	WD01	226

NAME	YR	CO	TWP	PG
PATERSON, YORK	1830	MONT	AMST	119
PATIENCE	1810	ULST	SHAW	639
PATIENCE, ANN	1820	NYCO	WD02	97
PATROT, BENJAMIN	1830	DELA	HARP	88
PATT	1790	QUEN	SHEM	156
PATT, POMP	1810	SUFF	BROK	468
PATTEN, JAMES	1810	NYCO	WD06	415
PATTERSON, AARON	1820	NYCO	WD06	509
PATTERSON, JACK JR.	1830	COLU	CHAT	34
PATTERSON, JOHN	1800	NYCO	WD06	829
PATTERSON, JOHN	1800	NYCO	WD06	805
PATTERSON, JOHN	1820	NYCO	WD09	910
PATTERSON, JOHN	1830	COLU	HUDS	103
PATTERSON, JOHN	1830	NYCO	WD06	431
PATTERSON, JOHN	1830	NYCO	WD06	458
PATTERSON, M.	1810	NYCO	WD05	371
PATTERSON, MARCUS	1830	CAYU	GENO	290
PATTERSON, SAMUEL	1790	ORNG	WARW	147
PATTERSON, THOMAS	1830	NYCO	WD09	370
PATTERSON, WILLIAM	1830	NYCO	WD10	59
PATTERSON, WILLIAM	1830	ONTA	FARM	203
PATTERSON, WILLIAM	1830	QUEN	FLUS	142
PATTILLO, WILLIAM J.	1820	TIOG	CARO	316
PAUL	1810	RENS	TROY	388
PAUL, BENJAMIN	1830	ABNY	WD04	303
PAUL, BENJAMIN	1830	NYCO	WD08	175
PAUL, BRYSTER	1800	NYCO	WD03	696
PAUL, JOHN	1800	NYCO	WD06	846
PAUL, JOHN	1820	NYCO	WD07	620
PAUL, NATHANIEL	1830	ABNY	WD01	196
PAUL, PETER	1800	NYCO	WD03	706
PAUL, PETER A.	1820	DUTC	REDH	115
PAUL, PETER S.	1810	DUTC	RHIN	434
PAUL, SARAH	1810	NYCO	WD02	99
PAUL, SIMON	1800	NYCO	WD03	699
PAUL, SIMON	1800	ORNG	GOSH	357
PAUL, SIMON	1820	ORNG	MINI	586
PAUL, SIMON	1830	ORNG	MINI	258
PAULDING, CUFF	1830	WEST	NORC	201
PAULIN, FRANCIS	1800	NYCO	WD08	802
PAULON, FRANCIS	1810	NYCO	WD05	277
PAYNE, ABSALEN	1830	QUEN	NHEM	106
PAYNE, BRESTOW	1820	NYCO	WD06	520
PAYNE, CEASAR	1830	SUFF	HUNT	304
PAYNE, CEASER	1810	SUFF	HUNT	305
PAYNE, CEAZER	1820	SUFF	HUNT	274
PAYNE, CHARLES	1820	SUFF	BROK	327
PAYNE, ENOS	1830	ORNG	NEWB	40
PAYNE, HANNAH	1820	SUFF	HUNT	274

Payne

NAME	YR	CO	TWP	PG
PAYNE, LILLE	1810	SUFF	RIVH	346
PAYNE, MAHALY L.	1830	QUEN	NHEM	112
PEAN, CATHERINE	1800	NYCO	WD06	835
PEAR, M.	1810	NYCO	WD05	288
PEARCE, BEM	1820	NYCO	WD09	900
PEARCE, POMP	1800	OTSG	UNAD	616
PEARCE, POMPEY	1790	DUTC	BEEK	74
PEARSALE, MARY	1820	QUEN	----	77
PEARSALL, ISAAC	1830	QUEN	NHEM	108
PEARSON, BENJAMIN	1830	NYCO	WD08	240
PEARSON, CATHERINE	1800	NYCO	WD03	705
PEARSON, GEORGE	1830	QUEN	FLUS	139
PEARSON, HENRY	1830	RENS	BRUN	235
PEARSON, SARAH	1830	NYCO	WD08	226
PEAS, PHILLIP	1820	SUFF	EAST	291
PEASE, KINGSTON	1800	NYCO	WD05	886
PEASE, PHILIP	1830	SUFF	EAST	255
PEASE, WILLIAM	1830	ONID	UTIC	23
PECK, JOHN	1810	SCNE	WD01	935
PECK, NOAH	1810	ULST	WOOD	824
PECK, SARAH	1830	NYCO	WD05	262
PEER, HANNAH	1810	NYCO	WD05	323
PEER, HENRY	1810	NYCO	WD03	80
PEES, JAMES	1830	STEU	WHEL	389
PEG	1790	QUEN	JAMA	150
PEG	1790	QUEN	NHEM	152
PEG	1790	QUEN	OYST	155
PEG	1790	QUEN	SHEM	156
PEG	1800	RENS	SCHO	825
PEGE	1790	NYCO	OUTW	131
PEGGY	1820	SUFF	SHAM	313
PEGGY, MRS.	1820	KING	BRYN	110
PEIS, ANTHONY	1830	WEST	NEWR	113
PELHAM, FRANCIS	1810	NYCO	WD05	258
PELITUS, PETER	1830	NYCO	WD08	201
PELL, A.	1810	ONID	----	414
PELL, BENJAMIN	1820	WEST	NEWR	209
PELL, HANNAH	1830	WEST	PELH	115
PELL, HARRY	1820	SCHR	BROM	167
PELL, HERCULUS	1830	WEST	EAST	134
PELL, JACK	1820	WEST	EAST	198
PELL, JOHN	1830	NYCO	WD10	39
PELL, JOSEPH	1830	COLU	HUDS	112
PELL, OLIVER	1830	SCHR	SHAR	110
PELLET, THOMAS	1820	ORNG	GOSH	741
PEMBLETON, N.	1810	MADI	SMIT	877
PENCE, JAMES	1810	NYCO	WD02	138
PENDLETON, JOHN	1830	ABNY	WD01	203
PENTZ, CHARLES	1830	NYCO	WD10	9

NAME	YR	CO	TWP	PG
PEOOMAN, THOMAS	1830	SCHR	SHAR	110
PEPPER, BILL	1800	ABNY	WD02	280
PEPPER, WILLIAM	1790	ABNY	WATV	52
PERCIER, SALLY	1830	NYCO	WD10	8
PERDUN, CATO	1800	SARA	NORT	1132
PERDUN, CATO	1810	ROCK	MALT	783
PERDY, JAMES	1830	PUTM	PATE	25
PERKENS, CHARLOTTE	1830	MONR	RWD1	197
PERO	1790	NYCO	NORT	127
PERO, EDWARD	1820	NYCO	WD02	130
PERO, JACK	1820	DUTC	CLNT	42
PERO, JOHN	1810	ULST	NPAL	706
PERO, LABAN	1830	CHAT	BUST	267
PERRIE, WILLIAM	1830	NYCO	WD10	26
PERRIO, JOSEPH	1810	NYCO	WD06	396
PERRY, MILTON	1830	NYCO	WD08	220
PERRY, PELES	1820	CHEN	SMYA	334
PERRY, RICHARD	1830	ROCK	ORGT	109
PERRY, SAMUEL	1810	NYCO	WD05	312
PERRY, SAMUEL	1820	NYCO	WD02	110
PERRY, SOLOMON	1820	SENE	FAYE	373
PERRY, SOLOMON	1830	STEU	PRAT	453
PERRY, WILLIAM	1820	NYCO	WD09	940
PERSONS, HENRY	1830	COLU	GALA	263
PERVORS, LEWIS	1810	WEST	HARR	1130
PESER	1820	QUEN	----	79
PETER	1790	NYCO	MONT	122
PETER	1790	NYCO	MONT	123
PETER	1790	NYCO	MONT	124
PETER	1790	NYCO	NORT	125
PETER	1790	NYCO	NORT	126
PETER	1790	NYCO	OUTW	131
PETER	1790	QUEN	FLUS	149
PETER	1790	QUEN	JAMA	150
PETER	1790	QUEN	OYST	153
PETER	1790	QUEN	OYST	154
PETER	1800	ABNY	SCNE	3
PETER	1800	NYCO	WD06	831
PETER	1800	NYCO	WD07	883
PETER	1800	QUEN	FLUS	539
PETER	1800	QUEN	NEWT	538
PETER	1800	QUEN	OYST	577
PETER	1800	QUEN	OYST	579
PETER	1800	QUEN	OYST	575
PETER	1800	QUEN	SHEM	559
PETER	1800	SUFF	BROK	9
PETER	1800	SUFF	HUNT	48
PETER	1800	SUFF	RIVH	19
PETER	1800	SUFF	SHAM	68

Peter

NAME	YR	CO	TWP	PG
PETER	1810	DUTC	STAN	179
PETER	1810	NYCO	WD06	400
PETER	1810	NYCO	WD07	540
PETER	1810	NYCO	WD06	462
PETER	1810	RENS	STEP	570
PETER	1810	RENS	TROY	387
PETER	1820	QUEN	----	25
PETER	1820	QUEN	----	56
PETER	1820	QUEN	----	58
PETER	1820	QUEN	----	77
PETER	1820	SUFF	SHAM	309
PETER	1830	NYCO	WD05	257
PETER, CESAR	1830	ROCK	CLAR	122
PETER, JAMES	1820	SUFF	SMIT	324
PETER, LAWRENCE	1820	NYCO	WD05	337
PETER, SAMPSON	1830	SUFF	SMIT	269
PETER, SAMUEL	1810	NYCO	WD06	425
PETER, SAMUEL	1810	SUFF	SHAM	439
PETER, SAMUEL	1820	NYCO	WD07	620
PETER, TOM	1820	COLU	KIND	15
PETERMAN	1790	QUEN	JAMA	151
PETERMAN, HENRY	1830	RENS	PETE	169
PETERS, ABRAHAM	1810	CHEN	SHER	1076
PETERS, BOSTON	1820	SCNE	WD01	122
PETERS, CHARLES	1820	SUFF	SMIT	315
PETERS, CHARLES	1830	SUFF	ISLP	287
PETERS, CIPIO	1800	NYCO	WD04	728
PETERS, DORUS	1830	NIAG	PEND	426
PETERS, F.	1830	NYCO	WD13	364
PETERS, FRANCES	1810	DUTC	CLNT	392
PETERS, FRANCIS	1820	DUTC	CLNT	27
PETERS, FRANCIS	1830	DUTC	HYPK	239
PETERS, FRANK	1810	DUTC	CLNT	406
PETERS, HENRY	1800	ORNG	MINI	326
PETERS, HENRY	1830	QUEN	NHEM	115
PETERS, JAMES	1800	CHEN	CARN	932
PETERS, JAMES	1800	NYCO	WD07	916
PETERS, JOHN	1810	NYCO	WD06	420
PETERS, JOHN	1810	WEST	WEST	1147
PETERS, JOHN	1820	NYCO	WD06	528
PETERS, JOHN	1830	NYCO	WD06	466
PETERS, JOHN	1830	TOMP	ITCA	332
PETERS, JOHN	1830	YATE	ITAL	347
PETERS, JUDAS	1830	NYCO	WD14	475
PETERS, LAMAN	1820	QUEN	----	79
PETERS, MARGARET	1810	DUTC	FISH	244
PETERS, MRS.	1820	KING	BRYN	136
PETERS, NICHOLAS	1800	NYCO	WD03	715
PETERS, PETER	1800	WASH	WHIT	593

NAME	YR	CO	TWP	PG
PETERS, SALLE	1800	SUFF	EHAM	95
PETERS, SAMUEL	1830	ULST	NPAL	225
PETERS, SIMON	1830	GREN	CAIR	255
PETERS, SIMON	1830	QUEN	OYST	33
PETERS, SYRUS	1830	SUFF	SHAM	221
PETERS, THOMAS	1810	NYCO	WD05	299
PETERS, WILLIAMS	1820	CLNT	PLAT	466
PETERS, WILLIAMS	1830	RENS	HOOS	166
PETERSON	1790	NYCO	NORT	126
PETERSON	1820	QUEN	----	46
PETERSON, ALEXANDER	1820	NYCO	WD07	721
PETERSON, AMEY	1830	STEU	PRAT	453
PETERSON, ANCHERO	1810	WEST	YORK	1024
PETERSON, ANDREW	1830	ORNG	GOSH	289
PETERSON, ANTHONY	1820	ORNG	GOSH	734
PETERSON, BENJAMIN	1800	ORNG	WALL	341
PETERSON, BENJAMIN	1830	ORNG	WARW	90
PETERSON, BETSEY	1830	NYCO	WD08	131
PETERSON, BILL	1820	COLU	CHAT	15
PETERSON, CATHERINE	1830	NYCO	WD07	29
PETERSON, CATO	1820	NYCO	WD07	721
PETERSON, CHARLES	1790	ULST	NEWB	182
PETERSON, CHARLES	1820	WEST	YORK	332
PETERSON, CHARLES	1830	ORNG	WARW	71
PETERSON, CHARLES	1830	WEST	YORK	169
PETERSON, CLAE	1820	ORNG	NEWB	510
PETERSON, CORA	1820	COLU	HUDS	29
PETERSON, DENNIS	1810	NYCO	WD02	116
PETERSON, DORCAS	1830	ORNG	NEWB	40
PETERSON, ELLEN	1830	NYCO	WD05	339
PETERSON, EUSAW	1820	WEST	YORK	332
PETERSON, F.	1830	NYCO	WD12	288
PETERSON, HANNAH	1830	KING	WD02	268
PETERSON, HENRY	1830	ONID	WEST	327
PETERSON, HENRY	1830	RENS	TROY	19
PETERSON, ISAAC	1820	NYCO	WD06	486
PETERSON, ISREAL	1830	KING	WD05	340
PETERSON, JACK	1800	WEST	CORT	811
PETERSON, JACK	1830	COLU	CHAT	35
PETERSON, JACK	1830	WEST	CORT	74
PETERSON, JACOB	1820	WEST	CORT	285
PETERSON, JACOB	1820	WEST	YORK	333
PETERSON, JACOB	1830	NYCO	WD06	434
PETERSON, JACOB	1830	NYCO	WD07	24
PETERSON, JACOB	1830	QUEN	NEWT	17
PETERSON, JACOB	1830	WEST	CORT	73
PETERSON, JACOB	1830	WEST	YORK	168
PETERSON, JEFFREE	1810	KING	BRYN	641
PETERSON, JOHN	1800	NYCO	WD07	877

Peterson

NAME	YR	CO	TWP	PG
PETERSON, JOHN	1810	NYCO	WD06	447
PETERSON, JOHN	1810	NYCO	WD06	457
PETERSON, JOHN	1810	NYCO	WD03	84
PETERSON, JOHN	1810	WEST	CORT	1016
PETERSON, JOHN	1820	NYCO	WD06	485
PETERSON, JOHN	1820	SENE	GALE	428
PETERSON, JOHN	1820	WEST	CORT	310
PETERSON, JOHN	1830	NYCO	WD05	334
PETERSON, JOHN	1830	NYCO	WD08	214
PETERSON, JOHN	1830	ONID	UTIC	18
PETERSON, JOHN	1830	QUEN	NEWT	4
PETERSON, JOHN	1830	QUEN	NEWT	15
PETERSON, JOHN	1830	STEU	PRAT	453
PETERSON, JOHNATHAN	1830	NYCO	WD14	461
PETERSON, JOHNATHAN	1830	NYCO	WD14	487
PETERSON, JOSEPH	1820	DUTC	WASH	143
PETERSON, JOSEPH	1830	DUTC	WASH	438
PETERSON, MARY	1810	NYCO	WD05	316
PETERSON, MORRIS	1830	DUTC	FISH	494
PETERSON, MRS.	1830	KING	BRYN	367
PETERSON, OCHOO	1830	WEST	YORK	174
PETERSON, PAUL	1800	NYCO	WD04	743
PETERSON, PETER	1800	NYCO	WD07	859
PETERSON, PETER	1810	NYCO	WD06	444
PETERSON, PETER	1810	NYCO	WD06	494
PETERSON, PETER	1820	NYCO	WD10	991
PETERSON, PETER	1830	COLU	STUY	60
PETERSON, PETER	1830	NYCO	WD01	16
PETERSON, PETER	1830	NYCO	WD08	175
PETERSON, PETER	1830	QUEN	NEWT	17
PETERSON, PETER	1830	QUEN	FLUS	151
PETERSON, RACHEL	1830	NYCO	WD10	125
PETERSON, RICHARD	1810	NYCO	WD05	312
PETERSON, RICHARD	1830	ABNY	BETH	536
PETERSON, SALAMON	1830	QUEN	NEWT	17
PETERSON, SAMUEL	1800	ORNG	WARW	380
PETERSON, SAMUEL	1830	NYCO	WD08	219
PETERSON, SILAS	1830	KING	WD05	332
PETERSON, SOLOMAN	1800	NYCO	WD04	798
PETERSON, SUSAN	1830	NYCO	WD04	159
PETERSON, THOMAS	1800	NYCO	WD06	817
PETERSON, THOMAS	1810	NYCO	WD05	340
PETERSON, THOMAS	1830	WEST	MAMA	228
PETERSON, WILLIAM	1810	COLU	CHAT	191
PETERSON, WILLIAM	1820	NYCO	WD07	624
PETERSON, WILLIAM	1820	SENE	ROMU	363
PETERSON, WILLIAM	1830	COLU	CHAT	43
PETERSON, WILLIAM	1830	NYCO	WD08	230
PETERSON, WILLIAM	1830	STEU	PRAT	453

NAME	YR	CO	TWP	PG
PETERSON, WILLIAM	1830	SUFF	ISLP	287
PETISS, JOHN	1820	ONTA	RICH	38
PETTER, PATIENCE	1800	NYCO	WD06	846
PETTERSON, ROBERT	1830	DUTC	PGKP	322
PETTERSON, THOMAS	1830	COLU	GHEN	165
PETTIBONE, PRINCE	1820	WASH	HAMP	127
PETTIBONE, PRINCE	1830	WASH	WHIT	349
PETTIS, HANNAH	1830	ABNY	WATV	455
PETTYFOOT, JOHN	1830	DUTC	PGKP	321
PEYTON, SAMUEL	1820	NYCO	WD04	314
PHARO, DANIEL	1800	NYCO	WD07	893
PHAROAH	1810	NYCO	WD07	591
PHEANON, MARTINUS	1810	SCHR	SCHR	10
PHEBE	1810	CLNT	PLAT	897
PHEBE	1820	QUEN	----	10
PHELIX, MATHEW	1830	NYCO	WD06	408
PHELPS, CHARLES	1830	ABNY	WD04	311
PHELPS, OLIVER	1820	ONID	WHTT	303
PHELPS, TERROR	1810	COLU	HUDS	143
PHELPS, WILLIAM	1830	NYCO	WD10	28
PHENIX, MARTINUS	1820	SCHR	SCHR	455
PHEONIX, GEORGE	1830	WEST	SUMM	187
PHILIP	1800	SUFF	EHAM	91
PHILIP	1810	RENS	SCHO	553
PHILIP	1810	SUFF	EHAM	431
PHILIP, ENOS	1830	ORNG	GOSH	290
PHILIP, MR.	1830	NYCO	WD11	140
PHILIPS, BENJAMIN	1830	OTSG	OTSG	63
PHILIPS, CEZAR	1810	NYCO	WD04	194
PHILIPS, DANIEL	1830	WEST	BEDF	151
PHILIPS, DAVID	1830	NYCO	WD13	344
PHILIPS, DICK	1830	COLU	GHEN	167
PHILIPS, FLORA	1830	COLU	HUDS	114
PHILIPS, HENRY	1830	MONT	JOHN	205
PHILIPS, J.	1830	NYCO	WD13	394
PHILIPS, JAMES	1820	MONT	MIND	387
PHILIPS, JAMES	1830	MONT	MIND	13
PHILIPS, JOHN	1810	NYCO	WD04	177
PHILIPS, JOHN	1810	NYCO	WD06	443
PHILIPS, JUDE	1810	NYCO	WD06	450
PHILIPS, LYDIA	1830	SUFF	BROK	178
PHILIPS, NERO	1820	ORNG	GOSH	744
PHILIPS, SCIPIO	1810	NYCO	WD06	486
PHILIS	1790	NYCO	MONT	120
PHILLIP	1800	NYCO	WD01	667
PHILLIP	1800	QUEN	NEWT	537
PHILLIP	1800	SUFF	ISLP	61
PHILLIP, CHARLES	1830	RENS	WD02	36

Phillips

NAME	YR	CO	TWP	PG
PHILLIPS, ALDEN	1830	NYCO	WD05	282
PHILLIPS, ANGELIS	1820	NYCO	WD06	449
PHILLIPS, CHANCY	1830	JEFF	ELIS	36
PHILLIPS, CHARLES	1820	WEST	YONK	228
PHILLIPS, CHARLES	1830	NYCO	WD08	244
PHILLIPS, CHARLES	1830	WEST	YONK	8
PHILLIPS, FRADERICH	1820	PUTM	PHIL	101
PHILLIPS, GEORGE	1820	ORNG	NEWW	494
PHILLIPS, GEORGE	1830	NYCO	WD06	451
PHILLIPS, GEORGE	1830	ORNG	CORN	204
PHILLIPS, HENRY	1790	ORNG	GOSH	138
PHILLIPS, HENRY	1800	ORNG	GOSH	358
PHILLIPS, HENRY	1830	KING	WD04	316
PHILLIPS, IRA F.	1830	NYCO	WD08	179
PHILLIPS, J.	1820	NYCO	WD10	976
PHILLIPS, JACK	1810	DUTC	BEEK	268
PHILLIPS, JACK	1820	DUTC	BEEK	21
PHILLIPS, JACK	1830	DUTC	UNVA	428
PHILLIPS, JAMES	1830	NYCO	WD05	338
PHILLIPS, JOHN	1820	KING	BRYN	123
PHILLIPS, JOHN	1830	NYCO	WD06	384
PHILLIPS, JOHN	1830	NYCO	WD08	258
PHILLIPS, JOHN	1830	NYCO	WD09	334
PHILLIPS, JOSEPH	1830	DUTC	PGKP	327
PHILLIPS, JOSEPH	1830	NYCO	WD06	384
PHILLIPS, PETER	1820	SUFF	RIVH	354
PHILLIPS, RICHARD	1820	COLU	HUDS	13
PHILLIPS, RICHARD	1830	SUFF	ISLP	286
PHILLIPS, SAMPSON	1820	SUFF	SMIT	319
PHILLIPS, SAMUEL	1830	NYCO	WD09	399
PHILLIPS, SARAH	1800	NYCO	WD03	711
PHILLIPS, SQUIRE	1810	QUEN	FLUS	192
PHILLIPS, STEPHEN	1830	NYCO	WD06	455
PHILLIPS, YORK	1830	NYCO	WD08	249
PHILLIS	1790	KING	BRYN	96
PHILLIS	1790	QUEN	FLUS	150
PHILLIS	1790	QUEN	NHEM	152
PHILLIS	1790	QUEN	NHEM	155
PHILLIS	1800	NYCO	WD06	832
PHILLIS	1810	WEST	CORT	1018
PHILLIS, JAMES	1820	NYCO	WD09	934
PHILP, WARD	1820	NYCO	WD05	430
PHINNY	1810	NYCO	WD07	601
PICK, NOAH	1800	ULST	MARB	199
PICK, NOAH	1830	ULST	MARB	160
PICKNEY, MR.	1810	NYCO	WD07	605
PIER	1800	SUFF	RIVH	19
PIERCE, ISAAC	1830	NYCO	WD14	530

NAME	YR	CO	TWP	PG
PIERCE, JACK	1830	GREN	CATS	222
PIERCE, JACK	1830	GREN	CATS	228
PIERCE, JOHN	1830	NYCO	WD08	190
PIERCE, SAMUEL	1830	GREN	CATS	229
PIERE, HENRY	1800	NYCO	WD04	724
PIERE, THOMAS	1830	NYCO	WD10	96
PIEREE, DAVID	1830	DUTC	RHIN	391
PIERPOINT, THOMAS	1800	NYCO	WD03	692
PIERPOINT, THOMAS	1810	NYCO	WD06	489
PIERRE, ANN	1810	NYCO	WD06	419
PIERRE, JOHN	1810	NYCO	WD06	403
PIERSALL, WILLIAM	1830	WEST	HARR	216
PIERSON, ANN	1830	NYCO	WD05	300
PIERSON, HESTER	1830	WEST	YONK	10
PIERSON, LEVI	1830	NYCO	WD12	289
PIERSON, RICHARD	1830	NYCO	WD14	450
PIFER, JOHN	1830	DUTC	PLEA	312
PIGRA, MARIAH	1830	ROCK	RPOO	100
PIGRIT, HENRY	1830	TOMP	ITCA	332
PIGRUT, HENRY	1820	TOMP	LANS	37
PILE, FRANCIS	1820	ABNY	ABNY	191
PILES, JINNY	1800	NYCO	WD03	705
PILL	1810	NYCO	WD06	461
PINE, CEZAR	1810	WEST	NEWR	1088
PINE, DAVID	1830	NYCO	WD09	409
PINE, DAVID	1830	NYCO	WD12	308
PINE, HANNAH	1820	WEST	NORC	433
PINE, HENRY	1820	NYCO	WD10	984
PINE, HENRY	1830	KING	BUSH	382
PINE, ISAAC	1810	QUEN	OYST	242
PINE, JOHN	1830	NYCO	WD11	139
PINE, M.	1820	NYCO	WD10	975
PINE, P.	1830	NYCO	WD12	308
PINE, ROBERT	1830	WEST	NEWC	94
PINER, BENJAMIN	1830	NYCO	WD08	175
PINER, JOHN	1830	NYCO	WD07	65
PINT, THOMAS	1830	ABNY	BETH	536
PINT, THOMAS	1830	ULST	SHAW	251
PINTIER, SIMON	1800	NYCO	WD03	704
PIPER, ABNER	1820	DUTC	AMEN	9
PIPER, ISAAC	1830	NYCO	WD07	110
PIPER, JOHN	1830	DUTC	AMEN	181
PIPEROD, PETER	1820	LEWI	LOWV	251
PLACE, LEWIS	1820	NYCO	WD06	462
PLANK, LANK	1820	ORNG	MONT	820
PLASS, PETER	1820	COLU	HUDS	29
PLATE, CHARLES A.	1830	WEST	WTPL	222
PLATE, JOHN	1820	NYCO	WD05	353
PLATER, GEORGE	1830	NYCO	WD10	37

NAME	YR	CO	TWP	PG
PLATO	1790	QUEN	SHEM	157
PLATO	1800	QUEN	FLUS	543
PLATO	1800	QUEN	SHEM	558
PLATO	1800	SUFF	EHAM	92
PLATO, ANASTASIA	1830	NYCO	WD06	378
PLATO, GEAR	1820	NYCO	WD10	1010
PLATO, ISAAC	1800	SUFF	EHAM	91
PLATO, ISAAC	1810	SUFF	EHAM	434
PLATO, ISAAC	1820	SUFF	HUNT	290
PLATO, ISAAC	1830	SUFF	EAST	264
PLATO, MARTIN	1810	SUFF	EHAM	434
PLATO, MARTIN	1830	SUFF	EAST	259
PLATT, CIPIO	1800	NYCO	WD03	696
PLATT, DAVID	1830	QUEN	FLUS	151
PLATT, PHILIP	1800	QUEN	FLUS	541
PLATT, SCIPIO	1790	NYCO	WEST	133
PLET, CHERRY	1830	NYCO	WD05	335
PLET, JOHN	1830	NYCO	WD05	276
PLIT, LOUIS	1810	NYCO	WD04	207
PLUTT, ROSE	1810	NYCO	WD06	445
PLYMOTH	1800	CHEN	CARN	940
POAS, SYLVIA	1820	NYCO	WD02	120
POINTER	1820	WEST	WEST	86
POKE, HARRY	1810	GREN	CAIR	254
POKE, HENRY	1820	GREN	CAIR	116
POKE, HENRY	1830	GREN	DURH	273
POLET, BURNS	1820	ORNG	NEWW	506
POLHAMUS, JUDAH	1830	QUEN	JAMA	134
POLHEMUS, CAESAR	1830	OSWE	HANN	236
POLHEMUS, JAMES	1830	NYCO	WD09	315
POLINET, MARGARET	1810	NYCO	WD06	399
POLL	1790	QUEN	FLUS	149
POLSTON, ALEXANDER	1830	NYCO	WD08	230
POMEROY, MARY	1820	OTSG	OTSG	98
POMP	1790	QUEN	SHEM	157
POMP	1810	RENS	TROY	369
POMP	1820	ROCK	CLAK	93
POMPEY	1790	NYCO	MONT	121
POMPEY	1790	NYCO	OUTW	130
POMPEY	1790	QUEN	NHEM	152
POMPEY	1800	QUEN	NHEM	554
POMPEY	1800	SUFF	RIVH	19
POMPEY	1800	SUFF	EHAM	70
POMPY	1800	ABNY	WD01	263
POMS, ANDREW	1810	SUFF	BROK	490
PONTIER, SAMUEL	1830	NYCO	WD10	21
PONTUS	1800	WEST	PCHE	604
PONTUS, ABRAHAM	1830	WEST	WEST	128
POORNEY, JOHN	1820	NYCO	WD06	470
POPPAW, COMONEY	1830	KING	GRAV	405

NAME	YR	CO	TWP	PG
PORTAGER, JOHN	1800	QUEN	SHEM	557
PORTEGUE, HENRY	1820	ONTA	SENE	267
PORTER	1830	NYCO	WD08	199
PORTER, DAVID	1810	COLU	CANN	106
PORTER, FREDERIC	1830	KING	BRYN	370
PORTER, GEORGE	1830	NYCO	WD04	206
PORTER, ISAAC	1830	ERIE	BUFF	12
PORTER, ISAAC	1830	NYCO	WD09	361
PORTER, JACOB	1790	QUEN	NHEM	152
PORTER, TITE	1810	ULST	SHAW	687
PORTER, WILLIAM	1830	NYCO	WD06	415
PORTLAND	1790	QUEN	NEWT	151
PORTLAND	1800	QUEN	NEWT	660
PORTLAND, JACK	1820	KING	WILL	182
PORTLAND, JOHN	1820	NYCO	WD06	517
PORTLAND, JOHN	1830	KING	BRYN	367
PORTLAND, JOHN	1830	KING	BUSH	382
PORTLAND, TITUS	1830	KING	BRYN	367
PORTLEY, NATHANIEL	1820	NYCO	WD06	572
POSEY, HUMPHREY	1810	NYCO	WD06	449
POST, ABRAHAM	1830	SUFF	ISLP	286
POST, ADAM	1830	WEST	YONK	6
POST, CONSTANT	1820	DUTC	CLNT	27
POST, MR.	1820	NYCO	WD05	391
POST, REBASTIAN	1820	GREN	CATS	171
POST, THEODORE	1830	WASH	JACK	177
POST, THOMAS	1830	GREN	ATHN	212
POST, WILLIAM	1810	ULST	KING	766
POST, WILLIAM	1830	ULST	SAUG	101
POTTER, BAKER	1830	YATE	BENT	302
POTTER, BOSTON	1810	QUEN	OYST	234
POTTER, BOSTON	1830	QUEN	OYST	35
POTTER, CATHARINE	1830	NYCO	WD08	243
POTTER, CHARLES	1790	SUFF	HUNT	165
POTTER, CHARLES	1810	SUFF	HUNT	516
POTTER, DANIEL	1820	QUEN	----	63
POTTER, ELLIS	1830	NYCO	WD14	520
POTTER, FRANCIS	1820	SARA	WATE	240
POTTER, HENRY	1830	BROM	CHIN	15
POTTER, ISRAEL	1830	QUEN	FLUS	140
POTTER, ISRAEL	1830	QUEN	FLUS	143
POTTER, JACOB	1790	QUEN	OYST	154
POTTER, JACOB	1810	QUEN	NHEM	216
POTTER, JAMES	1820	ONTA	JERU	203
POTTER, JAMES	1830	COLU	HILL	197
POTTER, JOHN	1830	DUTC	FISH	463
POTTER, JOHN	1830	QUEN	NEWT	4
POTTER, JOSEPH	1820	QUEN	----	62
POTTER, JOSEPH	1830	QUEN	NHEM	114

Potter

NAME	YR	CO	TWP	PG
POTTER, LLOYD	1820	NYCO	WD05	377
POTTER, MORRIS	1820	QUEN	----	63
POTTER, MORRIS	1830	NYCO	WD04	190
POTTER, MORRIS	1830	QUEN	FLUS	143
POTTER, MOSES	1820	QUEN	----	34
POTTER, MRS.	1830	KING	WD05	325
POTTER, PETER	1820	BROM	WIND	13
POTTER, PETER	1820	CHEN	BAIN	150
POTTER, PETER	1830	BROM	CHIN	15
POTTER, PHEBE	1810	QUEN	OYST	256
POTTER, POMP	1820	ONID	DEER	241
POTTER, RICHARD	1820	QUEN	----	25
POTTER, RICHARD	1830	DUTC	PAWL	285
POTTER, RICHARD	1830	QUEN	OYST	50
POTTER, STEPHEN	1830	QUEN	JAMA	134
POTTER, STEPHEN	1830	QUEN	OYST	51
POTTER, WILLIAM	1830	NYCO	WD14	525
POTTS, JOHN G.	1820	ONID	BOON	177
POTTS, MARY	1810	COLU	HUDS	133
POTTS, SALLY	1800	NYCO	WD06	844
POULSON, ARTHUR	1830	NYCO	WD07	55
POULSTON, ABRAHAM	1820	NYCO	WD05	382
POWELL	1810	NYCO	WD07	546
POWELL, JAMES	1820	NYCO	WD07	672
POWELL, JAMES	1830	NYCO	WD13	336
POWELL, JOHN	1800	NYCO	WD07	910
POWELL, JOHN	1810	NYCO	WD06	450
POWELL, JOHN	1820	NYCO	WD06	519
POWELL, JOHN	1830	KING	WD05	339
POWELL, JOHN	1830	NYCO	WD14	522
POWELL, THOMAS	1830	ABNY	WATV	464
POWELLS, SAMUEL	1830	KING	GRAV	406
POWEN, JANE	1810	NYCO	WD06	449
POWERS, THEODORE	1820	LEWI	DENM	277
POWERS, TOM	1820	ABNY	WATV	267
POWERS, YOT	1830	COLU	GHEN	167
POWTUS, W.	1830	KING	FLAT	400
POYER, AARON	1830	NYCO	WD03	114
POYER, AARON L.	1820	NYCO	WD03	248
POYER, WILLIAM J.	1830	NYCO	WD05	308
POYRER, BONE	1810	NYCO	WD05	273
PRAETON, JOHN	1810	NYCO	WD07	540
PRALL, JOHN	1830	NYCO	WD05	343
PRANKS, MERCY	1820	ABNY	ABNY	190
PRATT, HENRY	1820	NYCO	WD03	192
PRATT, HENRY	1830	NYCO	WD07	59
PRAY	1830	NYCO	WD05	341
PRESTON, ALEXANDER	1830	NYCO	WD04	187
PRICE, JACOB	1820	GENE	LROY	145

NAME	YR	CO	TWP	PG
PRICE, JOHN	1830	WEST	BEDF	146
PRICE, PETER	1830	WEST	BEDF	146
PRICE, RICHARD R.	1830	ABNY	WD01	197
PRICE, SAMUEL	1830	RICH	CAST	39
PRICE, THOMAS	1810	NYCO	WD01	33
PRICE, THOMAS	1830	NYCO	WD08	236
PRICE, THOMAS	1830	NYCO	WD10	88
PRICE, ZADOCK	1820	SARA	BALL	208
PRICE, ZADOCK	1830	SARA	BALL	14
PRIDE, JOSEPH	1800	NYCO	WD03	709
PRIDER, TOM	1800	QUEN	SHEM	557
PRIM, EDWARD	1800	NYCO	WD06	794
PRIME	1800	SUFF	BROK	14
PRIME	1800	SUFF	EHAM	74
PRIME	1800	SUFF	EHAM	92
PRIME	1810	ORNG	BLOM	1022
PRIME, JOE	1830	SCHR	MIDD	36
PRIME, JOSEPH	1810	SCHO	SCHO	20
PRIME, JULIUS C.	1830	LEWI	LOWV	390
PRIME, RICHARD	1820	GREN	ATHE	11
PRIME, RICHARD	1830	COLU	STUY	66
PRIME, SEASOR	1830	ABNY	BETH	536
PRIME, SIMEON	1830	TOMP	HECT	426
PRIME, THOMAS	1830	MONT	ROOT	42
PRIME, TITUS	1830	SUFF	SHAM	215
PRIME, WILLIAM	1830	SUFF	SHAM	222
PRIMES, CEASAR	1810	ULST	NPAL	711
PRIMM	1810	RENS	TROY	376
PRIMUS	1790	NYCO	HARL	137
PRIMUS	1790	NYCO	SOUT	131
PRIMUS	1800	TIOG	LISL	246
PRIMUS, PETER	1810	SUFF	SHAM	447
PRIMUS, PETER	1820	SUFF	ISLP	312
PRIMUS, PRIME	1800	RENS	PITT	798
PRINCE	1790	QUEN	OYST	154
PRINCE	1790	WEST	HARR	199
PRINCE	1800	QUEN	JAMA	545
PRINCE	1800	SUFF	BROK	3
PRINCE	1800	SUFF	BROK	11
PRINCE	1800	WEST	PHEL	643
PRINCE	1810	RENS	LANS	430
PRINCE	1810	SUFF	SHAM	443
PRINCE	1820	QUEN	----	79
PRINCE	1820	QUEN	----	80
PRINCE	1820	SUFF	BROK	356
PRINCE	1830	GREN	COXE	185
PRINCE, ACHILLES	1830	SUFF	SHAM	209
PRINCE, BETSEY	1830	SUFF	BROK	177
PRINCE, BETSY	1820	SUFF	BROK	363

Prince

NAME	YR	CO	TWP	PG
PRINCE, BRAY	1830	WEST	MTPL	45
PRINCE, H.	1830	NYCO	WD13	388
PRINCE, HARRY L.	1810	SARA	MALT	765
PRINCE, HECTOR	1810	NYCO	WD05	367
PRINCE, HENRY	1820	NYCO	WD07	619
PRINCE, HENRY	1830	RICH	NORT	28
PRINCE, HUNTER	1820	NYCO	WD08	814
PRINCE, JACK	1830	COLU	KIND	147
PRINCE, JAMES	1830	QUEN	NEWT	10
PRINCE, NATHAN	1820	NYCO	WD07	670
PRINCE, NICHOLAS	1830	HERK	FAIR	14
PRINCE, NOAH	1820	CHEN	SHER	337
PRINCE, NOAH	1830	CHEN	SHER	136
PRINCE, PEGGY	1810	NYCO	WD03	83
PRINCE, PETER	1820	SUFF	HUNT	288
PRINCE, PETER	1830	ORNG	NBGH	124
PRINCE, RICHARD	1810	MONT	MANH	210
PRINCE, RICHARD	1830	CAYU	GENO	290
PRINCE, RICHARD	1830	GREN	ATHN	212
PRINCE, RICHARD	1830	HERK	MANH	128
PRINCE, RICHARD JR.	1830	HERK	GERM	142
PRINCE, SAMUEL	1820	NYCO	WD07	633
PRINCE, SAMUEL	1820	SUFF	BROK	355
PRINCE, SANDERS	1830	ABNY	WD01	216
PRINCE, SIMEON	1830	SUFF	EAST	253
PRINCE, SUSAN	1830	QUEN	OYST	28
PRINCE, SUSSANAH	1830	NYCO	WD08	148
PRINCE, SYLVESTER	1820	NYCO	WD07	709
PRINCE, TEMPERENCE	1820	SUFF	SHAM	305
PRINCE, THOMAS	1820	NYCO	WD01	30
PRINCE, THOMAS	1820	NYCO	WD05	393
PRINCE, THOMAS	1830	NYCO	WD01	15
PRINCE, TIMOTHY	1800	ESEX	PINT	996
PRINCE, TIMOTHY	1800	ESEX	PINT	1003
PRINCE, W.	1830	NYCO	WD13	401
PRINCE, WILLIAM	1790	DUTC	PAWL	89
PRINCE, WILLIAM	1820	OTSG	PITT	108
PRINDEWELL, ROBERT	1830	NIAG	LOCK	396
PRINE, A.	1830	NYCO	WD11	153
PRINE, JOSEPH	1830	STEU	BATH	266
PRIX	1790	QUEN	NHEM	152
PROCTER, SALLY	1820	NYCO	WD07	656
PROCTOR, THOMAS	1800	NYCO	WD04	722
PROPHET, MOSES	1830	CORT	SCOT	138
PROPTER, SALLY	1830	NYCO	WD10	46
PROUT, ELIZA	1830	NYCO	WD06	435
PROVOST, PETER	1810	NYCO	WD06	397
PROVVE, LEVI	1830	MONT	JOHN	192
PRUYNE, JOHN	1830	HERK	LTFA	91

NAME	YR	CO	TWP	PG
PRYEN, WILLIAM	1810	NYCO	WD05	282
PUDDING, HARRY	1800	NYCO	WD07	926
PUGESLY, SAMUEL	1830	NYCO	WD14	455
PUGGSLEY, CHARLES	1830	WEST	NEWR	107
PUGOLEY, SAMUEL	1820	NYCO	WD06	568
PUGSHY, HANNAH	1820	WEST	NEWR	215
PUGSLEY, JACK	1830	COLU	CLAV	78
PUGSLEY, PLATO	1800	WEST	EAST	619
PUGSLEY, THOMAS	1830	HERK	DANU	185
PUNCH, DANIEL	1830	COLU	HUDS	111
PUNCH, THOMAS	1830	COLU	HUDS	115
PURBY, CLAUS	1830	ROCK	CLAR	122
PURDU, ABRAM	1830	SUFF	BROK	159
PURDU, HENRY	1830	SUFF	BROK	159
PURDY, AANON	1830	WEST	HARR	214
PURDY, AARON	1820	WEST	HARR	468
PURDY, DANIEL	1820	WEST	NORS	381
PURDY, FRANK	1810	WEST	RYE	1167
PURDY, GEORGE	1830	WEST	HARR	214
PURDY, HARRY	1820	WEST	CORT	293
PURDY, HARRY	1830	WEST	NORC	203
PURDY, JACK	1830	WEST	WTPL	223
PURDY, JAMES	1830	WEST	YORK	170
PURDY, JOHN	1810	WEST	GREN	1122
PURDY, LEWIS	1830	WEST	WTPL	223
PURDY, PRINCE	1810	WEST	GREN	1122
PUROLIN, SAMUEL	1810	DUTC	FISH	244
PURSON, GILBERT	1820	WEST	SUMM	353
PUSH, CHRISTOPHER	1820	NYCO	WD06	455
PUTMAN, HARRY	1830	SARA	SASP	164
PUTMAN, JOHN P.	1820	WASH	WHIT	191
PUTNAM, JACOB	1820	WASH	YOUC	205
PUTTER, JOHN	1820	DUTC	FISH	68
PUTTER, POMP	1820	ONID	DARF	241
QUAAK, SAMUEL	1800	ORNG	WARW	379
QUACK, DAVID	1830	QUEN	SHEM	87
QUACKENBUSH, QUACK	1830	DUTC	HYPK	234
QUACKENBUSH, ROBERT	1820	DUTC	CLNT	25
QUACKINGBUSH	1810	DUTC	CLNT	403
QUACKINGBUSH, ROBERT	1810	DUTC	CLNT	403
QUAK, JOHN	1800	ORNG	WARW	365
QUAMBO, DAVID	1830	QUEN	NHEM	99
QUAMENO	1790	WEST	BEDF	196
QUAND, MARK	1830	NYCO	WD05	343
QUARTAS, M.	1810	DUTC	PGKP	315
QUARTER, JOISAH	1810	ORNG	GOSH	1132
QUARTERS, ANNA	1820	ORNG	MINI	588

NAME	YR	CO	TWP	PG
QUARTERS, JOSIAH	1800	ORNG	GOSH	362
QUARTERS, NEWBURRY	1830	RENS	WD03	47
QUARTERS, SILVANUS	1810	ORNG	MINI	1057
QUARTERS, SILVANUS	1820	ORNG	MINI	576
QUARTERS, SYLVANUS	1800	ORNG	MINI	320
QUARTERS, SYLVERNUS	1790	ORAN	GOSH	139
QUARTERS, WILLIAM	1820	ORNG	DEER	661
QUARTERS, WILLIAM	1830	ORNG	DEER	3
QUASH	1800	ABNY	BERN	150
QUAW, PETER	1830	SUFF	EAST	257
QUEEN, WILLIAM	1830	NYCO	WD08	162
QUERO, ROBERT	1830	MONT	FLOR	88
QUIDZ, JOHN	1810	NYCO	WD07	574
QUIN, EDWARD	1830	RENS	WD03	47
QUIN, GEORGE	1830	NYCO	WD10	91
QUIN, WILLIAM P.	1830	NYCO	WD14	451
QUINN, WILLIAM	1820	NYCO	WD05	419
QUOCK, JOHN	1790	QUEN	NEWT	151
QUOK, ELIAS	1810	ORNG	WARW	994
QUOM	1790	SUFF	ISLP	165
QUOUGH	1800	SUFF	EHAM	92
RACE, PETER	1830	COLU	CLAV	73
RACHEL	1810	NYCO	WD06	406
RACHEL	1810	NYCO	WD06	447
RACHEL, ANN	1820	ABNY	ABNY	195
RACKET, SAM	1800	ABNY	WATV	88
RADLEY, JACOB	1820	ABNY	ABNY	195
RAILMORE, CATO	1800	NYCO	WD04	725
RAINHART, FRANK	1790	QUEN	FLUS	149
RAINMIRE, PHOEBE	1810	NYCO	WD06	443
RAINWARD, JAMES	1810	NYCO	WD06	445
RAINWOOD, CATO	1800	NYCO	WD05	770
RAJMAN, FIZU	1820	ULST	ROCH	75
RAKINS, SAMUEL	1820	SARA	SARA	189
RALTNY, JOHN	1830	JEFF	BRON	280
RAMPTON, EPHRAIM	1820	NYCO	WD06	469
RAND, JACOB	1800	NYCO	WD05	774
RAND, MARY	1830	NYCO	WD12	289
RANDAL	1810	ONTA	GENE	847
RANDAL, JAMES	1820	NYCO	WD09	922
RANDALL, AMOS	1820	CHEN	NORW	378
RANDALL, JACK	1820	CHEN	NORW	378
RANDALL, JACK	1830	CHEN	OXFO	54
RANDALL, MRS.	1830	NYCO	WD12	278
RANDLE, AMOS	1830	CHEN	NORW	165
RANDLE, HENRY	1830	ABNY	WD01	212
RANDOLF, WILLIAM B.	1820	NYCO	WD08	810

NAME	YR	CO	TWP	PG
RANDOLPH, JOHN	1810	NYCO	WD06	449
RANDOLPH, PETER	1830	CAYU	CATO	429
RANDOLPH, WILLIAM B.	1830	NYCO	WD04	187
RANGER	1790	NYCO	OUTW	130
RANGER, EBENEZER	1800	NYCO	WD07	910
RANKIN, ANDREW	1820	NYCO	WD06	485
RANKIN, CHARLES	1830	NYCO	WD10	72
RANKIN, HENRY	1800	NYCO	WD07	886
RANKIN, HENRY	1830	NYCO	WD05	336
RANKISS, HENRY	1820	NYCO	WD05	355
RANN, JACOB	1800	NYCO	WD03	696
RANNELLS, ABRAHAM	1820	NYCO	WD06	498
RANNY, GEORGE	1830	MONR	RWD3	226
RANSOM, CEASAR	1810	ULST	ROCH	779
RANSON, HENRY	1830	MONR	BRIG	16
RANTO, TRAY	1810	QUEN	FLUS	202
RANTUS, JAMES	1830	QUEN	FLUS	143
RANTUS, VENUS	1810	QUEN	FLUS	201
RAPELYE, PATTY	1800	NYCO	WD05	771
RAPELYE, SARAH	1810	NYCO	WD06	422
RAPLEYEA, C.	1830	NYCO	WD11	159
RAPPALYE, SIMON	1830	QUEN	NHEM	108
RATLER, ISAAC	1830	QUEN	OYST	43
RATOON, ALFRED	1830	NYCO	WD04	187
RATTERRY, JOHN	1820	JEFF	BRON	364
RAY, ISSAC	1820	SENE	FAYE	372
RAY, J.R.	1830	ALLE	RUSH	175
RAY, JAMES A.	1830	ONON	ONON	189
RAY, NICHOLAS A.	1830	NYCO	WD08	271
RAY, PETER	1820	GENE	BERG	41
RAY, PETER	1830	NYCO	WD08	225
RAY, WILLIAM	1830	BROM	CONK	67
RAY, WILLIAM, JR.	1830	BROM	CONK	67
RAYMOND, CHARLES	1820	NYCO	WD10	1074
RAYMOND, JAMES	1820	NYCO	WD06	494
RAYMOND, JOHN	1820	NYCO	WD06	473
RAYNEY, DAVID	1820	ORNG	MONT	819
RAYNEY, PETIN	1820	DUTC	DOVE	51
READ, A.	1810	MADI	SMIT	880
READ, ANTHONY	1800	NYCO	WD04	722
READ, ELIZABETH	1820	NYCO	WD06	533
READ, J.	1810	MADI	SMIT	877
READ, PETER	1810	NYCO	WD05	255
READ, SAMUEL	1810	NYCO	WD03	68
READER, DAVID	1830	STEU	WHEL	393
READER, JACOB	1830	STEU	WHEL	389
READHEADS, CORNELIUS	1820	QUEN	----	4
REASONER, ANTHONY	1830	KING	BRYN	359
REASOR, MITCHEL	1820	NYCO	WD07	671

NAME	YR	CO	TWP	PG
REAVY, RICHARD	1810	NYCO	WD05	318
RECHARD	1820	QUEN	----	57
REDDEN, EDWARD	1830	DUTC	LAGR	249
REDDEN, GEORGE	1820	NYCO	WD04	285
REDDIN, EDWARD	1810	DUTC	FISH	196
REDDING, CHARLES	1830	RENS	BRUN	222
REDDING, NEDE	1820	DUTC	FISH	59
REDIN, DANIEL	1830	DUTC	FISH	458
REED, ABRAHAM	1820	DUTC	DOVE	51
REED, ABRAHAM	1830	DUTC	DOVE	220
REED, ANTHONY	1810	NYCO	WD04	192
REED, BURRILE	1820	GENE	GATE	124
REED, CHARLES	1810	NYCO	WD04	220
REED, CHESTER	1830	NYCO	WD08	229
REED, JAMES	1830	NYCO	WD05	333
REED, JOHN	1800	OTSG	PITT	630
REED, JOHN	1820	OTSG	PITT	115
REED, MARY	1820	GREN	COXE	35
REED, MORIAH	1830	MONR	RWD3	226
REED, PETER	1820	KING	WATA	159
REED, POWELL P.	1830	ONON	SALI	32
REED, QUASH	1830	GREN	COXE	195
REED, SAMUEL	1830	NYCO	WD14	484
REED, SERVILLA	1830	NYCO	WD08	219
REED, T.	1810	RENS	TROY	387
REED, WILLIAM	1820	SARA	CHAR	213
REED, ZEPHANIAH	1830	DUTC	UNVA	422
REEVE, ELIMUS	1830	SUFF	SOUT	347
REEVES, JAYNE	1830	SUFF	SOUT	349
REEVEY, JOSEPH	1830	NYCO	WD06	450
REID, SAMUEL	1820	COLU	AUST	13
REID, WILLIAM	1820	SARA	CHAR	213
REIFER, HARRY	1830	PUTM	SOUT	53
RELPH, BENJAMIN	1830	SUFF	BROK	193
RELSON, JOSEPH	1830	KING	BUSH	378
REMSEN, BENJAMIN	1830	QUEN	NEWT	9
REMSEN, BETTY	1810	KING	BRYN	632
REMSEN, MOLLY	1820	QUEN	----	69
REMSEN, SOPHIA	1800	ULST	MARB	21
REN, JOSEPH	1800	NYCO	WD06	847
RENAULT, MARY	1830	NYCO	WD05	260
RENNE	1800	NYCO	WD06	830
RENTIS, JAMES	1820	QUEN	----	54
RERVEY, RICHARD P.	1830	NYCO	WD10	28
RESNORE, JOHN	1830	NYCO	WD08	213
RESTSON, RICHARD	1820	NYCO	WD08	784
RETUS	1810	RENS	SCHO	549
REUBEN, DARCUS	1830	SUFF	SOUT	339
REUBEN, HARRIET	1830	SUFF	SHAM	230

NAME	YR	CO	TWP	PG
REUBUS	1820	SUFF	SOUT	349
REUBY, GEORGE	1820	DUTC	WASH	143
REVY, RICHARD P.	1820	NYCO	WD05	429
REYNOLDS, ABRAHAM	1830	ORNG	WALL	145
REYNOLDS, JAMES	1820	ONTA	SENE	268
REYNOLDS, STEPHEN	1820	TIOG	ELMI	307
REYNOLDS, STEPHEN	1830	TIOG	SOPO	212
REYNOLDS, THOMAS	1810	TIOG	ELMI	633
REYNOLDS, THOMAS	1830	TIOG	VETR	181
REYNOLDS, WILLIAM	1830	DUTC	FISH	462
REYNOLDS, WILLIAM	1830	ONON	SALI	3
RHIDY, HANNAH	1820	QUEN	----	41
RHINEY, GEORGE	1820	ONTA	SODU	121
RHOADES, CUFF	1830	QUEN	NEWT	2
RHOADS, SAMUEL	1830	NYCO	WD06	437
RHODES, ABEGAIL	1820	QUEN	----	40
RHODES, DAVID	1830	NYCO	WD06	444
RHODES, RECHARD	1820	QUEN	----	41
RIALL, FON	1800	NYCO	WD07	860
RICE, JOHN	1820	NYCO	WD06	567
RICE, TOBIAS	1830	TIOG	CATH	196
RICE, WILLIAM	1830	KING	WD02	262
RICE, WILLIAM	1830	KING	WD02	264
RICH, HENRY	1820	NYCO	WD10	988
RICH, INS.	1820	NYCO	WD10	1002
RICH, JAMES	1810	NYCO	WD05	319
RICH, JOHN	1830	NYCO	WD05	340
RICH, MARY	1820	NYCO	WD05	394
RICHARDSON, ANN M. MRS.	1830	NYCO	WD01	9
RICHARD	1790	NYCO	NORT	125
RICHARD	1790	NYCO	NORT	126
RICHARD	1800	NYCO	WD07	912
RICHARD	1800	NYCO	WD05	755
RICHARD	1800	SUFF	ISLP	62
RICHARD	1800	SUFF	ISLP	61
RICHARD	1810	NYCO	WD06	447
RICHARD	1810	SARA	STIL	733
RICHARD	1820	QUEN	----	63
RICHARD	1820	QUEN	----	67
RICHARD	1830	KING	BUSH	386
RICHARD, DEWITT	1820	TIOG	OSWE	118
RICHARD, FREEMAN	1830	MADI	----	189
RICHARD, THOMAS	1820	NYCO	WD06	533
RICHARD, WILLIAM	1800	RENS	GREN	721
RICHARD, WILLIAM	1830	SUFF	SHAM	215
RICHARDS, ELIPHALIT	1830	CHEN	SHER	136
RICHARDS, JAMES	1820	DUTC	REDH	114
RICHARDS, JANE	1830	NYCO	WD08	244
RICHARDS, JOSEPH	1800	NYCO	WD06	806

NAME	YR	CO	TWP	PG
RICHARDS, LEWIS	1830	NIAG	NIAG	419
RICHARDS, MOSES	1800	NYCO	WD06	847
RICHARDS, RICHARD	1810	NYCO	WD05	331
RICHARDS, ROBERT	1820	NYCO	WD06	517
RICHARDS, THOMAS	1800	NYCO	WD07	921
RICHARDS, WILLIAM	1810	NYCO	WD03	84
RICHARDSON, BENJAMIN	1830	NYCO	WD05	330
RICHARDSON, EDWARD	1800	NYCO	WD07	863
RICHARDSON, EDWARD	1830	NYCO	WD07	8
RICHARDSON, HENRY	1830	NIAG	NIAG	420
RICHARDSON, HETTY	1830	NYCO	WD05	342
RICHARDSON, ISAAC	1810	NYCO	WD06	492
RICHARDSON, ISAIAH	1820	NYCO	WD06	494
RICHARDSON, JAMES	1830	NYCO	WD13	380
RICHARDSON, JAMES	1830	NYCO	WD14	472
RICHARDSON, JOHN	1830	NYCO	WD05	337
RICHARDSON, JOHNATHAN	1830	NYCO	WD14	435
RICHARDSON, JOS	1820	NYCO	WD08	742
RICHARDSON, MARY	1810	NYCO	WD01	2
RICHARDSON, NANNY	1810	ROCK	CLAR	674
RICHARDSON, PAUL	1810	NYCO	WD06	492
RICHARDSON, PETER	1830	NYCO	WD01	15
RICHARDSON, RICHARD	1810	NYCO	WD06	496
RICHARDSON, S.	1830	NYCO	WD11	163
RICHARDSON, STEPHEN	1810	NYCO	WD06	484
RICHERDSON, BETSEY	1820	NYCO	WD07	686
RICHERSON, CHARLES	1810	ORNG	NEWW	912
RICHERSON, HENRY	1820	ROCK	CLAK	93
RICHMOND, CALEB	1830	NYCO	WD07	55
RICHMOND, FRANCES	1830	NYCO	WD08	246
RICHMOND, JACK	1820	COLU	CHAT	17
RICHMOND, JACK	1830	COLU	CHAT	44
RICHMOND, PAUL	1820	NYCO	WD07	686
RICKETS, DINAH	1800	NYCO	WD06	813
RICKETS, ROBERT	1830	NYCO	WD13	336
RICKS, GEORGE	1820	KING	BRYN	186
RICKS, SAMUEL	1830	KING	BUSH	384
RICKS, STEPHEN	1830	KING	WD04	299
RIDDLE, BETSEY	1830	DUTC	HYPK	233
RIDDLES, FREDERICK	1820	DUTC	CLNT	27
RIDER	1800	SUFF	RIVH	21
RIDER, LEWIS	1820	SUFF	ISLP	308
RIDER, PRINCE	1800	DUTC	AMEN	138
RIDGELY, RICHARD	1800	NYCO	WD07	898
RIDLIE, PETER	1790	QUEN	FLUS	149
RIES, JOSEPH	1830	RICH	CAST	41
RIGHT, ISAAC	1820	SUFF	EAST	295
RIGHT, PHOEBE	1830	NYCO	WD10	88
RIGHT, RUFUS	1810	SUFF	EAST	437

NAME	YR	CO	TWP	PG
RIGHT, SILVENUS	1820	SUFF	EAST	294
RIGHT, STEPHEN	1810	SUFF	SHAM	440
RIGHT, SUTHER	1820	SUFF	EAST	295
RIGS, DIANA	1830	NYCO	WD11	144
RIKER, ANTHONY	1830	WEST	GREN	26
RIKER, FRANCIS	1820	NYCO	WD07	698
RIKER, JOHN	1820	NYCO	WD06	467
RIKER, PETER	1830	WEST	YONK	6
RIKER, PETER	1830	WEST	YONK	9
RIKES, NANCY	1830	NYCO	WD05	270
RILEY, JACOB	1830	KING	WD04	304
RILEY, M.	1830	NYCO	WD10	97
RILEY, SILAS	1820	NYCO	WD06	454
RILEY, W.	1830	NYCO	WD13	392
RILEY, WILLIAM	1820	NYCO	WD07	686
RILEY, WILLIAM	1830	ABNY	WD02	249
RINEY, HAM	1830	ONTA	PHEL	23
RINGAM, J.	1830	NYCO	WD11	162
RIPLEY, DAVID	1820	COLU	HUDS	29
RIPLEY, JOBS	1820	COLU	HUDS	31
RIPLEY, JOSEPH	1790	COLU	KIND	68
RIPLEY, JOSEPH	1800	COLU	HUDS	1143
RIPLEY, JOSEPH	1830	COLU	HUDS	104
RIPLY, JO	1810	COLU	HUDS	147
RISOS, DAN---(?)	1820	COLU	HUDS	29
RITCHINSON, WILLIAM	1830	NYCO	WD08	162
RITKER, RICHARD	1830	NYCO	WD06	384
RITT, HENRY	1820	NYCO	WD04	279
RITT, SUSAN	1830	NYCO	WD06	368
RITTER, ANNA	1810	NYCO	WD03	89
RITTER, BENJAMIN	1830	ROCK	HVER	151
RITTER, CAMBRIDGE	1830	NYCO	WD12	278
RITTER, H.	1830	NYCO	WD12	313
RITTER, HANABLE	1830	WEST	YONK	6
RIVERS, HUDSON	1820	NYCO	WD06	572
RIVERS, WILLIAM	1810	NYCO	WD06	397
RIX, BENJAMIN	1830	NYCO	WD08	231
RIX, GEORG	1810	NYCO	WD07	540
ROACH, ANDREW	1810	NYCO	WD04	203
ROACH, ANDREW	1820	NYCO	WD06	502
ROACH, ANDREW	1830	NYCO	WD04	188
ROACH, JOHN	1830	NYCO	WD01	48
ROACH, RICHARD	1810	NYCO	WD03	80
ROAH, SAMUEL	1830	NYCO	WD09	294
ROBART, HARRY	1800	NYCO	WD06	820
ROBBERTON, PETER	1830	RICH	WEST	4
ROBBIN	1790	QUEN	OYST	153
ROBBIN	1790	WEST	NORC	203
ROBBIN	1800	QUEN	NEWT	655

NAME	YR	CO	TWP	PG
ROBBIN	1800	QUEN	SHEM	561
ROBBIN	1800	SUFF	BROK	11
ROBBIN	1810	SUFF	BROK	489
ROBBIN	1820	QUEN	----	62
ROBBINS, HAGER	1820	NYCO	WD07	723
ROBBINS, HOSEA	1820	CHEN	SHER	337
ROBBINS, JACOB	1820	NYCO	WD04	288
ROBBINS, JAMES	1830	NYCO	WD10	102
ROBBINS, JOBIN	1820	CHEN	SHER	337
ROBBINS, JOEL	1820	CHEN	SHER	337
ROBBINS, JONATHAN	1820	ONID	BRID	232
ROBBINS, JONATHAN	1830	HERK	WINF	170
ROBBINS, JONATHAN C.	1820	ONID	BRID	232
ROBBINS, JOSEPH	1830	SCHR	FULT	53
ROBBINS, JOY	1820	CHEN	NORW	338
ROBBINS, JUDE	1820	CHEN	SHER	337
ROBBINS, PELES	1820	CHEN	SHER	337
ROBBINS, RIMAS	1810	NYCO	WD07	549
ROBBINS, THOMAS	1830	RENS	SCAS	108
ROBENSON, CATO	1820	NYCO	WD10	987
ROBENSON, CORNELIUS	1820	ULST	MARB	62
ROBENSON, JACK	1820	DUTC	CLNT	28
ROBERIS, GEORGE	1830	NYCO	WD10	18
ROBERSON, CATOW	1810	KING	BRYN	628
ROBERSON, JOHN	1830	TOMP	DANB	440
ROBERSON, MARGARET	1800	NYCO	WD01	661
ROBERT	1790	NYCO	MONT	121
ROBERT	1790	NYCO	OUTW	128
ROBERT	1790	WEST	YONK	208
ROBERT	1800	ABNY	BETH	198
ROBERT	1800	QUEN	OYST	572
ROBERT	1800	SUFF	HUNT	46
ROBERT	1810	DUTC	PGKP	325
ROBERT	1830	NYCO	WD12	262
ROBERT, LETT	1810	SUFF	BROK	469
ROBERT, ONDERDONK	1810	NYCO	WD05	308
ROBERTS	1830	NYCO	WD09	342
ROBERTS, DAVID	1830	NYCO	WD10	18
ROBERTS, DENNIS	1830	NYCO	WD08	226
ROBERTS, EDWARD	1830	NYCO	WD08	216
ROBERTS, ISABELLA	1830	NYCO	WD01	31
ROBERTS, JAMES	1820	NYCO	WD06	449
ROBERTS, JAMES	1820	NYCO	WD07	686
ROBERTS, JAMES	1820	QUEN	----	39
ROBERTS, JOHN	1810	NYCO	WD01	31
ROBERTS, JOHN	1810	NYCO	WD02	108
ROBERTS, JOHN	1820	NYCO	WD01	53
ROBERTS, JOHN	1820	NYCO	WD06	488
ROBERTS, JOHN	1830	NYCO	WD04	225

NAME	YR	CO	TWP	PG
ROBERTS, JOHN	1830	NYCO	WD08	213
ROBERTS, MARY	1810	NYCO	WD03	84
ROBERTS, PHILLIS	1830	NYCO	WD01	31
ROBERTS, ROBERT	1800	NYCO	WD05	770
ROBERTS, THOMAS	1790	DUTC	WASH	95
ROBERTS, THOMAS	1800	DUTC	STAN	128
ROBERTS, THOMAS	1810	COLU	CHAT	190
ROBERTS, THOMAS	1810	DUTC	STAN	174
ROBERTS, WILLIAM	1810	NYCO	WD03	64
ROBERTSON, BENJAMIN	1830	NYCO	WD05	300
ROBERTSON, CHARLES	1820	NYCO	WD08	819
ROBERTSON, CHARLES	1820	ORNG	CORN	713
ROBERTSON, CLUE	1810	NYCO	WD06	442
ROBERTSON, EDWARD	1810	NYCO	WD07	574
ROBERTSON, GRACE	1810	NYCO	WD06	448
ROBERTSON, ISSAC	1800	NYCO	WD06	819
ROBERTSON, JACOB	1820	QUEN	----	38
ROBERTSON, JAMES	1830	ABNY	BETH	538
ROBERTSON, JAMES	1830	NYCO	WD14	469
ROBERTSON, JASPER	1810	NYCO	WD06	442
ROBERTSON, JESSE	1820	ORNG	NEWB	516
ROBERTSON, JOHN	1810	NYCO	WD06	439
ROBERTSON, JOHN	1810	NYCO	WD08	713
ROBERTSON, JOHN	1820	NYCO	WD09	918
ROBERTSON, JOHN	1830	NYCO	WD05	328
ROBERTSON, JOHN	1830	NYCO	WD14	484
ROBERTSON, MARSEY	1820	NYCO	WD03	189
ROBERTSON, MIKEL	1810	NYCO	WD07	536
ROBERTSON, PEGGY	1810	NYCO	WD06	422
ROBERTSON, RICHARD	1810	NYCO	WD05	370
ROBERTSON, ROBERT	1820	ABNY	ABNY	195
ROBERTSON, ROBERT	1830	NYCO	WD09	302
ROBERTSON, ROBERT	1830	NYCO	WD10	9
ROBERTSON, SAMUEL	1810	NYCO	WD07	574
ROBESON, JOHN	1820	NYCO	WD10	1077
ROBISN, FRANCIS	1830	ABNY	WD02	254
ROBIN	1790	QUEN	SHEM	158
ROBIN	1800	SUFF	BROK	12
ROBIN, SAMUEL	1830	ULST	WAWA	197
ROBINS, G.	1820	NYCO	WD10	985
ROBINS, HOSEA	1810	CHEN	SHER	1076
ROBINS, JACOB	1810	NYCO	WD02	127
ROBINS, JAY	1810	CHEN	SHER	1076
ROBINS, JOEL	1810	CHEN	SHEN	1076
ROBINS, JOEL	1830	CHEN	SHER	137
ROBINS, JOY	1830	CHEN	SHER	137
ROBINS, JUDE	1830	CHEN	NBER	238
ROBINS, MARGARET	1830	CHEN	SHER	137
ROBINS, PETER	1810	CHEN	SHER	1076

Robins

NAME	YR	CO	TWP	PG
ROBINS, THOMAS	1810	SARA	SARA	856
ROBINS, TITUS	1830	WASH	CAMB	116
ROBINSON	1830	NYCO	WD08	178
ROBINSON, AMANDA	1820	NYCO	WD07	628
ROBINSON, ANTHONY	1830	ULST	MARB	157
ROBINSON, AUGUSTUS	1800	ORNG	NEWB	282
ROBINSON, BEN	1810	ORNG	MONT	959
ROBINSON, CATO	1800	NYCO	WD03	704
ROBINSON, CHARLES	1830	ULST	SAUG	106
ROBINSON, CORNELIUS	1800	ULST	MARB	199
ROBINSON, DAN S.	1830	ONID	DEER	244
ROBINSON, DORAS	1820	ONID	WHTT	303
ROBINSON, ESQUIRE	1820	NYCO	WD09	932
ROBINSON, ESTHER	1820	NYCO	WD10	954
ROBINSON, FRANCIS	1820	ABNY	ABNY	194
ROBINSON, FRANCIS	1830	SARA	BALL	2
ROBINSON, GEORGE	1830	NYCO	WD12	262
ROBINSON, HARRIET	1830	NYCO	WD05	241
ROBINSON, JACK	1830	DUTC	HYPK	231
ROBINSON, JACK	1830	GREN	DURH	269
ROBINSON, JANE	1810	NYCO	WD02	120
ROBINSON, JESS	1810	ORNG	NEWW	906
ROBINSON, JESSE	1830	ORNG	BLOM	123
ROBINSON, JOHN	1800	DUTC	PGKP	66
ROBINSON, JOHN	1810	NYCO	WD06	424
ROBINSON, JOHN	1820	ABNY	ABNY	193
ROBINSON, JOHN	1820	ONTA	BRIS	53
ROBINSON, JOHN	1830	NYCO	WD01	49
ROBINSON, JOHN	1830	NYCO	WD10	21
ROBINSON, JOSEPH	1830	COLU	GALA	264
ROBINSON, LEWIS	1810	NYCO	WD03	44
ROBINSON, LEWIS	1810	NYCO	WD05	307
ROBINSON, LEWIS	1830	ORNG	NEWB	32
ROBINSON, MINGO	1830	ULST	ESOP	89
ROBINSON, NANCY	1830	ORNG	WALL	137
ROBINSON, ORLANDO	1820	NYCO	WD05	427
ROBINSON, PETER	1830	ORNG	MONR	176
ROBINSON, PRINCE	1830	SCHR	MIDD	36
ROBINSON, RICHARD	1830	NYCO	WD08	212
ROBINSON, ROBERT	1810	SCNE	WD01	934
ROBINSON, ROBERT	1830	DUTC	REDH	378
ROBINSON, SAMUEL	1830	NYCO	WD09	323
ROBINSON, SARAH	1830	NYCO	WD05	300
ROBINSON, SUSAN	1830	NYCO	WD06	372
ROBINSON, THOMAS	1820	SARA	MITL	233
ROBINSON, TOBIAS	1830	KING	WD02	268
ROBINSON, WIDOW	1830	ULST	MARB	157
ROBINSON, WILLIAM	1830	FRAN	CONS	31

NAME	YR	CO	TWP	PG
ROBINSON, WILLIAM	1830	NYCO	WD05	339
ROBINSON, WILLIAM	1830	ULST	SHAW	255
ROBISON, CORNELIUS	1810	ULST	MARB	808
ROBISON, FLORA	1810	ULST	KING	757
ROBSON, BENJAMIN	1830	MONT	ROOT	43
ROCK, GEORGE	1830	DUTC	WASH	437
ROCK, JAMES	1810	DUTC	WASH	160
ROCK, JAMES	1820	DUTC	WASH	146
ROCK, POMPY	1810	QUEN	NHEM	203
ROCK, RUTH	1830	NYCO	WD06	458
ROCKET, JOHN	1800	ABNY	WD02	276
ROCKETTS, HANNAH	1830	NYCO	WD05	334
ROCKINS, SAMUEL	1830	SARA	SASP	169
RODCLIFF, THOMAS	1820	ULST	SHAW	64
RODGERS, PRIMUS	1830	RENS	BRUN	230
RODMAN, EDMUND	1830	RENS	WD03	42
RODMAN, ISAAC	1830	ONTA	HOPE	90
RODMAN, ISAAC	1830	RENS	LANS	87
ROE, ARCANA	1800	SARA	CHAR	1071
ROE, CHARITY	1830	QUEN	FLUS	143
ROE, HENRY	1830	SUFF	HUNT	326
ROE, ISRAEL G.	1830	KING	WD05	340
ROE, JACOB	1810	QUEN	FLUS	195
ROE, MARTIN	1810	COLU	CLER	219
ROE, MATTHEW	1830	DUTC	REDH	371
ROE, MINGO	1810	SUFF	BROK	494
ROE, MINGO	1820	SUFF	SMIT	320
ROE, PETER	1830	QUEN	NHEM	102
ROE, STEPHEN	1830	SUFF	ISLP	285
ROE, THOMAS	1830	DUTC	REDH	371
ROGERS, ADAM	1830	WASH	FTED	313
ROGERS, ADAM W.	1820	WASH	FTED	159
ROGERS, ALEXANDER	1830	ONON	SALI	9
ROGERS, CATO	1800	WASH	EATN	442
ROGERS, CATO	1800	WASH	ARGY	485
ROGERS, FRANK	1830	MONT	MAYF	285
ROGERS, HARRY	1810	COLU	HILL	129
ROGERS, HARRY	1830	WEST	RYE	106
ROGERS, HENRY	1830	COLU	AUST	174
ROGERS, ISAAC	1830	NYCO	WD08	214
ROGERS, JOHN	1830	OTSG	SPFD	72
ROGERS, LEVI	1830	SUFF	SOUT	351
ROGERS, POMP	1830	COLU	CHAT	36
ROGERS, ROBERT	1830	RENS	PITT	123
ROGERS, STEPHEN	1830	NYCO	WD14	488
ROGERS, URIAH	1820	PUTM	PHIL	101
ROGERS, WILLIAM	1830	NIAG	LOCK	403
ROLINSON, ABIGAIL	1830	NYCO	WD04	158
ROLLIN, BETSY	1810	NYCO	WD06	415

Rollin

NAME	YR	CO	TWP	PG
ROLLIN, NELSON	1830	NYCO	WD05	344
ROLLINGS, ELIJAH	1830	NYCO	WD04	230
ROLLOSON, JOHN	1830	NYCO	WD06	436
ROMAN, PETER	1810	COLU	CLAV	155
ROMANS, MINGO	1810	ORNG	NEWB	927
ROME, SABINA	1830	NYCO	WD10	35
ROMEO	1810	NYCO	WD06	443
ROMEYN, DOMINGO	1800	ORNG	HAVE	280
RONSOM, SAMUEL	1830	NYCO	WD10	42
RONTTE, JAMES	1810	QUEN	FLUS	202
ROONEY, GEORGE	1820	NYCO	WD06	446
ROOS, THOMAS	1830	ULST	SHAW	255
ROOSA, ABRAHAM	1830	ULST	SHAW	237
ROOSA, ADAM	1810	ULST	WARW	798
ROOSA, ANDRIES	1830	ULST	WAWA	187
ROOSA, CHARLES	1830	ULST	SHAW	235
ROOSA, ISSAC	1820	ULST	MARB	61
ROOSA, WILLIAM	1810	ULST	MARB	793
ROOSA, WILLIAM	1830	ULST	HURL	145
ROOSA, WILLIAM	1830	ULST	MARB	167
ROOSA, WILLIAM, JR.	1830	ULST	MARB	167
ROOSEVELT, ADAM	1800	NYCO	WD05	761
ROOSEVELT, MINGS	1800	NYCO	WD06	848
ROOT, DANIEL	1830	ULST	SAUG	106
ROPER, BETSEY	1810	NYCO	WD06	452
RORHOVE, JOHN	1830	NYCO	WD06	457
ROSANA	1810	RENS	TROY	387
ROSANNAH	1790	NYCO	OUTW	130
ROSE	1790	QUEN	FLUS	149
ROSE	1800	NYCO	WD06	832
ROSE, BILL	1820	SUFF	BROK	330
ROSE, CATHI	1810	NYCO	WD01	11
ROSE, CEASAR JR.	1810	ULST	NPAL	714
ROSE, DOCTOR	1800	NYCO	WD03	696
ROSE, ELIJAH	1830	CAYU	AUBN	165
ROSE, ELYMUS	1830	SUFF	SHAM	221
ROSE, GARRET	1830	ORNG	NEWB	55
ROSE, ISSAC	1820	ULST	MARB	60
ROSE, JACOB	1830	NYCO	WD04	159
ROSE, LEMIA	1820	SUFF	SOUT	347
ROSE, LEWIS	1800	NYCO	WD05	775
ROSE, LEWIS	1810	SUFF	ISLP	496
ROSE, LUCAS	1810	NYCO	WD05	312
ROSE, MARY	1810	NYCO	WD06	437
ROSE, SAMUEL	1830	ORNG	CRAW	194
ROSE, SARAH	1830	NYCO	WD07	22
ROSE, WILLIAM	1820	ULST	MARB	60
ROSE, WILLIAM	1810	SUFF	BROK	469
ROSEBOOM, SUSAN	1820	ABNY	ABNY	195

NAME	YR	CO	TWP	PG
ROSEKRANTZ, JACK	1830	ULST	SHAW	238
ROSEKRANTZ, JOHN	1830	ULST	ROCH	184
ROSEKRAUSE, JACK	1820	ULST	MARB	61
ROSEWELL, BETTY	1830	KING	WD04	319
ROSEWELL, HARRY	1830	KING	WD04	319
ROSHART, E.	1830	NYCO	WD02	81
ROSS, AARON	1830	NYCO	WD06	410
ROSS, CHARLES	1830	NYCO	WD05	331
ROSS, GREENBURG	1820	ONID	UTIC	208
ROSS, GREENBURY	1820	ONID	UTIC	208
ROSS, JACOB	1830	NYCO	WD07	5
ROSS, JAMES	1820	NYCO	WD06	455
ROSS, JAMES	1830	ONTA	SENE	69
ROSS, JOHN	1830	NYCO	WD08	231
ROSS, MARY	1830	NYCO	WD06	372
ROSS, P.	1830	NYCO	WD11	133
ROSS, PETER	1820	ORNG	NEWB	516
ROSS, RICHARD	1830	NYCO	WD12	262
ROSS, ROBERT	1800	NYCO	WD06	851
ROSS, SUSAN	1830	NYCO	WD06	372
ROSWITT, TITUS	1820	KING	BRYN	139
ROTH, HERY	1810	NYCO	WD08	772
ROUIFELLER, JACOB	1820	WASH	SALE	186
ROUSE, ANN	1830	WEST	YORK	180
ROUSE, BENJAMIN	1830	GREN	ATHN	205
ROUSE, CUFF	1830	COLU	KIND	138
ROW, FRANCIS	1830	NYCO	WD05	345
ROW, MATT	1820	DUTC	REDH	114
ROW, THOMAS	1830	DUTC	STAN	405
ROWLAND, FREDERICK	1830	QUEN	OYST	21
ROWLAND, JAMES	1830	QUEN	JAMA	135
ROWLAND, JOHN	1830	RENS	WD02	37
ROWMAN, PETER	1810	COLU	CLAV	155
ROYAL, PRINCE	1830	WANE	LYON	125
RUBA, GEORGE	1830	GREN	CAIR	261
RUBEN	1810	SUFF	SOUT	556
RUBEN, DAREAS	1810	SUFF	SOUT	555
RUBIN	1800	SUFF	SMIT	27
RUBIN	1820	SUFF	BROK	364
RUD, T.	1810	RENS	TROY	387
RUFUS	1800	SUFF	EHAM	92
RUGGLES, PAUL	1820	SUFF	SHAM	316
RUGLIS, DAVID	1830	RICH	CAST	44
RUMJUICE, BEN	1790	QUEN	OYST	155
RUMPERS, MARGARET	1830	QUEN	OYST	28
RUMPES, BENJAMIN	1810	QUEN	OYST	258
RUMPES, JOHN	1830	SUFF	HUNT	324
RUMPUS, SAMUEL	1830	SARA	HALF	85
RUNNELS, WILLIAM	1820	DUTC	FISH	66

NAME	YR	CO	TWP	PG
RUNTUS, TROY	1830	QUEN	FLUS	139
RUSH, CHRISTOPHER	1830	NYCO	WD14	462
RUSHMAN, THOMAS	1830	GREN	COXE	195
RUSHMORE, HENRY	1800	NYCO	WD07	889
RUSHMORE, JAMES	1830	QUEN	NHEM	106
RUSHMORE, SAMUEL	1820	QUEN	----	75
RUSHMURE, LEWIS	1810	QUEN	SHEM	306
RUSS---, TOM	1820	COLU	HUDS	31
RUSSEL, ISAAC	1820	NYCO	WD04	236
RUSSEL, JAMES	1830	DUTC	RHIN	400
RUSSEL, JOHNATHAN	1830	NYCO	WD10	89
RUSSELL, BENJAMIN	1830	NYCO	WD06	436
RUSSELL, DIANA	1830	NYCO	WD06	435
RUSTIN, PHILIP	1830	RICH	NORT	23
RUSTON, PHILLIP	1820	NYCO	WD06	458
RUTGER, R.	1810	DUTC	PGKP	325
RUTGERS, BENJAMIN	1820	NYCO	WD06	502
RUTGERS, ROBERT	1820	DUTC	PGKP	99
RUTTENFIELD, JAMES	1800	NYCO	WD07	884
RUVE, WILLIAM	1810	COLU	HUDS	147
RYA, ISAAC	1830	NYCO	WD08	246
RYAL, SAMUEL	1810	NYCO	WD08	716
RYDER, HENRY	1830	QUEN	JAMA	134
RYDER, SUE	1800	ABNY	COEY	232
RYDER, THOMAS	1810	QUEN	SHEM	305
RYEM, JAMES	1810	NYCO	WD05	368
RYERSON, SUSAN	1830	NYCO	WD14	448
RYERSS, JOSEPH	1820	RICH	CAST	115
RYKER, HARVY	1830	ROCK	CLAR	124
RYNA, B.	1820	WEST	GREN	248
RYNE, PERO	1820	SCNE	WD02	129
RYNOLDS, NELSON	1820	ORNG	NEWB	512
RYOR, HANNAH	1810	SUFF	ISLP	499
RYOS, THOMAS	1830	RICH	CAST	45
S---, THOMAS	1820	NIAG	BUFF	156
SACK, SOLOMON	1810	WEST	NORS	1045
SACKETT, JENNY	1810	NYCO	WD01	21
SACKETT, JOSEPH	1830	NYCO	WD14	525
SACKETT, PRIMUS	1800	NYCO	WD06	836
SADLER, WILLIAM	1830	NYCO	WD08	230
SAGAR, GEORGE	1830	ALLE	GROV	105
SAGE, JOHN	1830	NYCO	WD04	164
SAHLER, CEZAR	1830	ULST	MARB	168
SAHLER, JOHN	1830	ULST	MARB	154
SAIDELER, SAMUEL	1820	NYCO	WD03	152
SAIDLER, MARGARET	1830	NYCO	WD09	302
SAILS, FRANCES	1820	DUTC	FISH	56

NAME	YR	CO	TWP	PG
ST. JOHN, EMANUEL	1820	ULST	MARB	54
ST. JOHN, JOHN	1800	SARA	MILT	1064
ST. JOHN, MANUEL	1830	ULST	PLAT	264
ST. PAUL, DIANA	1830	DUTC	REDH	378
SALES, CHARLES	1830	NYCO	WD06	458
SALES, FRANCIS	1810	DUTC	FISH	210
SALES, HARRY	1810	DUTC	FISH	230
SALES, HARRY	1820	DUTC	FISH	67
SALES, HARRY JR.	1810	DUTC	FISH	250
SALES, HAXOR	1830	NYCO	WD06	458
SALES, HENRY	1830	DUTC	PLEA	312
SALES, J.	1830	NYCO	WD11	155
SALISBURY, SAMUEL	1830	GREN	CATS	245
SALL	1790	NYCO	NORT	126
SALL	1790	SUFF	HUNT	164
SALLES, EDWARD	1830	DUTC	PLEA	303
SALLY	1810	NYCO	WD06	410
SALLY	1830	NYCO	WD13	392
SALSBERRY, ASA	1830	CHEN	NBER	247
SALSBURY, PLATO	1820	ULST	KING	78
SALTER, ---	1820	ONID	AUGU	320
SALTER, HENRY	1830	ABNY	WD01	219
SALTER, JOHN	1800	NYCO	WD06	844
SALTER, V.	1810	ONID	MADR	385
SALTERS, CAROLINE	1830	NYCO	WD05	334
SALTERS, EDWARD	1830	NYCO	WD07	55
SALTERS, ELIZABETH	1830	NYCO	WD07	42
SALTERS, JOHN	1820	NYCO	WD07	701
SALTPAW, ROBERT	1830	GREN	CATS	241
SALTUS, FRANCIS	1820	NYCO	WD06	469
SALTUS, JOHN	1800	NYCO	WD04	722
SALTUS, SAMUEL	1810	NYCO	WD05	258
SAM	1790	NYCO	MONT	120
SAM	1790	NYCO	MONT	121
SAM	1790	NYCO	OUTW	127
SAM	1790	NYCO	OUTW	131
SAM	1790	QUEN	JAMA	150
SAM	1790	QUEN	OYST	154
SAM	1790	QUEN	OYST	155
SAM	1790	QUEN	SHEM	157
SAM	1800	QUEN	OYST	577
SAM	1800	QUEN	OYST	579
SAM	1800	QUEN	OYST	571
SAM	1800	QUEN	OYST	573
SAM	1800	RENS	TROY	892
SAM	1800	SUFF	BROK	9
SAM	1800	SUFF	BROK	10
SAMBERT, JOHN	1820	NYCO	WD02	104
SAMBO	1790	QUEN	OYST	154

NAME	YR	CO	TWP	PG
SAMBO, JAMES	1810	SUFF	ISLP	498
SAMMERS, EPHRAIM	1830	ULST	SHAW	247
SAMMON, WILLIAM	1820	NYCO	WD04	295
SAMMONS, EPHRAIM	1820	ORNG	MONT	844
SAMMONS, EPHRAIM	1830	ORNG	NEWB	41
SAMO, JOHN	1810	NYCO	WD05	286
SAMONS, CHARLES	1810	QUEN	FLUS	198
SAMOS, M.	1810	NYCO	WD05	292
SAMPSON	1790	SUFF	ISLP	165
SAMPSON	1800	SUFF	ISLP	64
SAMPSON	1810	SARA	MALT	769
SAMPSON, CATHARINE	1830	HERK	LTFA	90
SAMPSON, ENOCH	1800	NYCO	WD07	903
SAMPSON, ENOCH	1820	SUFF	HUNT	288
SAMPSON, HARRY	1830	DUTC	FISH	484
SAMPSON, HARRY	1830	MONT	GLEN	75
SAMPSON, JOHN	1830	ULST	MARB	15
SAMPSON, JOHN	1830	ULST	MARB	157
SAMPSON, JOSEPH	1830	DUTC	LAGR	242
SAMPSON, KILLIS	1820	SUFF	BROK	355
SAMPSON, MARGARET	1810	NYCO	WD04	224
SAMPSON, NICHOLAS	1820	DUTC	FISH	76
SAMPSON, RICHARD	1830	DUTC	FISH	500
SAMPSON, SAM	1830	SUFF	SMIT	275
SAMPSON, SAMBO	1800	NYCO	WD07	919
SAMPSON, SAMUEL	1820	ONTA	PALM	378
SAMPSON, SAMUEL	1830	DUTC	LAGR	243
SAMPSON, SILAS	1790	DUTC	PAWL	88
SAMSON, CORNELIUS	1820	QUEN	----	79
SAMSON, GEORGE	1830	MONR	RWD3	230
SAMSON, JOHN	1820	SULL	THOM	151
SAMSON, JOHN	1820	ULST	MARB	62
SAMSON, RICHARD	1820	SCNE	WD01	124
SAMSON, RICHARD	1830	SCNE	WD02	223
SAMSSON, JOHN	1810	NYCO	WD04	424
SAMSSON, RICHARD	1810	SCNE	WD02	953
SAMUEL	1790	NYCO	WEST	136
SAMUEL	1800	QUEN	JAMA	545
SAMUEL	1800	QUEN	OYST	571
SAMUEL	1800	QUEN	OYST	572
SAMUEL	1800	SUFF	ISLP	62
SAMUEL	1820	QUEN	----	64
SAMUEL	1820	QUEN	----	65
SAMUEL	1820	QUEN	----	75
SAMUEL	1820	SUFF	BROK	355
SAMUEL, ERNEST	1820	NYCO	WD04	277
SAMUEL, WILLIAM	1820	NYCO	WD10	1008
SAMUELS, GATTY	1800	NYCO	WD05	752
SANCHO, SAMUEL	1790	DUTC	CLNT	78

NAME	YR	CO	TWP	PG
SANCO, SAMUEL	1810	DUTC	FISH	236
SAND, DAVID	1830	NYCO	WD13	336
SANDER, ELIZABETH	1820	NYCO	WD06	474
SANDERS, DICK	1810	SCNE	WD01	933
SANDERS, DICK	1830	SCNE	WD01	206
SANDERS, E.	1810	MADI	LENX	776
SANDERS, JOHN	1820	FRAN	FORC	75
SANDERS, JOHN	1830	DUTC	WASH	451
SANDERS, THOMAS	1810	NYCO	WD04	196
SANDERS, THOMAS	1810	NYCO	WD08	728
SANDERS, THOMAS	1830	NYCO	WD05	300
SANDERS, WILLIAM	1820	JEFF	HOUN	417
SANDERS, WILLIAM	1830	ABNY	WD01	212
SANDERSON, ABRAHAM	1830	ULST	KING	72
SANDERSON, DICK	1810	SCNE	WD01	933
SANDFORD, THOMAS	1810	NYCO	WD08	760
SANDS	1810	NYCO	WD06	438
SANDS, ANDREW	1800	ORNG	WARW	381
SANDS, ANTHONY	1810	QUEN	NHEM	212
SANDS, ANTHONY	1820	QUEN	----	65
SANDS, ANTHONY	1830	KING	WD05	330
SANDS, ANTHONY	1830	NYCO	WD07	46
SANDS, CATHERINE	1830	QUEN	FLUS	139
SANDS, CATO	1820	QUEN	----	64
SANDS, CATO	1830	QUEN	NHEM	110
SANDS, CESAR	1830	ORNG	NEWW	103
SANDS, CHARLES	1800	NYCO	WD06	774
SANDS, CHARLES	1810	NYCO	WD04	194
SANDS, DANIEL	1820	QUEN	----	54
SANDS, ELIAS	1830	QUEN	NHEM	116
SANDS, GEORGE	1830	WEST	SUMM	191
SANDS, HARRY	1830	WEST	YORK	174
SANDS, HARVY	1830	WEST	NORC	198
SANDS, JACOB	1810	QUEN	OYST	284
SANDS, JACOB	1820	DUTC	RHIN	128
SANDS, JACOB	1830	NYCO	WD10	10
SANDS, JACOB	1830	NYCO	WD13	345
SANDS, NATHAN	1830	NYCO	WD09	409
SANDS, NICHOLAS	1820	DUTC	CLNT	43
SANDS, RICHARD	1820	WEST	NEWC	325
SANDS, RICHARD	1830	WEST	CORT	71
SANDS, SAMUEL	1830	NYCO	WD12	256
SANDS, SEASON	1820	ORNG	NEWB	509
SANDS, THOMAS	1830	NYCO	WD12	254
SANDS, W.L.	1820	NYCO	WD09	909
SANDS, WALTER	1830	SUFF	BROK	173
SANERS, DAVID	1820	NYCO	WD07	621
SANFORD, EDWARD	1830	HERK	LTFA	91
SANFORD, SARAH	1830	ABNY	WD01	220

NAME	YR	CO	TWP	PG
SANFORD, THOMAS	1830	NYCO	WD09	385
SANFORD, THOMAS	1830	ONTA	SENE	72
SANGLEY, RICHARD	1820	CHEN	PLYM	324
SANGO, DYKE	1810	SCHR	BROM	160
SANNETE, M.	1810	NYCO	WD05	314
SANNICK, J.W.	1830	CHEN	OXFO	66
SANNICK, SAMUEL B.	1830	CHEN	OXFO	66
SANSER, ROBERT	1830	ULST	SAUG	110
SANSINIT, JOHN	1830	ONTA	PHEL	23
SANTEE	1790	WEST	YORK	209
SANTHAN, JERIMIAH	1820	WEST	EAST	200
SANTICA, JOSHUA	1820	ORNG	DEER	660
SANTON, CHARLES	1830	QUEN	FLUS	152
SANTON, JOHN	1790	ORAN	WARW	148
SANTON, ORRY	1830	QUEN	FLUS	141
SANTON, TOWNSEND	1790	QUEN	JAMA	150
SAOCE, JAMES	1820	ONID	FLOR	194
SARAH	1790	NYCO	SOUT	131
SARAH	1790	QUEN	FLUS	150
SARAH	1790	QUEN	OYST	155
SARAH	1790	WEST	HARR	199
SARAH	1820	QUEN	----	45
SARAH	1820	SUFF	SMIT	324
SARJEANT, ESSEY	1790	NYCO	WEST	133
SARLES, QUAMBO	1820	CHEN	NORW	378
SARSNET, JOHN	1820	ONTA	PHEL	296
SARVEN, WILLIAM	1830	ROCK	CLAR	123
SATCHEL, WILLIAM	1830	KING	WD03	288
SATEPIER, F.C.	1830	NYCO	WD13	349
SATIMORE, TITUS	1820	NYCO	WD08	784
SATTER, NICHOLAS	1800	NYCO	WD04	740
SATTIN, SANDY	1810	NYCO	WD05	345
SAUDERS, PEGGY	1800	NYCO	WD03	701
SAUGHTER, JAMES	1820	NYCO	WD07	702
SAUNDERS, CHARLES	1830	DUTC	CLNT	203
SAUNDERS, SHARP	1800	NYCO	WD05	751
SAUNDERS, THOMAS	1830	NYCO	WD06	403
SAUNDERS, THOMAS	1830	NYCO	WD06	405
SAUNDERS, WILLIAM	1830	MONR	RWD1	196
SAUTECKE, HENRY	1830	ORNG	DEER	8
SAUTTER, PEGGEY	1820	ONTA	SODU	121
SAVILLA, PETER	1800	NYCO	WD07	891
SAXE, JAMES	1820	ONID	FLOR	194
SAYES, LEWIS	1800	NYCO	WD04	737
SAYING, SIBA	1820	DUTC	RHIN	124
SAYRE, ANTHONY	1830	ORNG	WARW	64
SAYRE, WILLIAM	1830	GREN	COXE	181
SCANK, SAMUEL	1830	WEST	NEWR	114
SCARBOROUGH, DANIEL	1830	NYCO	WD07	14

NAME	YR	CO	TWP	PG
SCEREK, JOSEPH	1820	QUEN	----	64
SCHAMERHORN, PETER	1830	HERK	RUSS	20
SCHANK, JACK	1800	QUEN	NHEM	553
SCHANK, JOSEPH	1810	QUEN	NHEM	207
SCHAPMOUSE, SAMUEL	1830	COLU	GALA	262
SCHELLINGER, SCIPIO	1830	SUFF	EAST	259
SCHELLUYNE, ANTHONY	1820	ABNY	ABNY	200
SCHEMERHORN, JACK	1830	MONT	EPHR	183
SCHENCK, HENRY	1830	QUEN	NHEM	111
SCHENCK, JAMES	1830	QUEN	OYST	42
SCHENCK, SAMUEL	1830	NYCO	WD13	344
SCHENCK, SAMUEL	1830	QUEN	NHEM	104
SCHENK, HENRY	1830	QUEN	JAMA	128
SCHERMENHORN, JACOB	1820	NYCO	WD09	933
SCHERMERHONE, HENRY	1830	RENS	SCHO	243
SCHERMERHONE, JOHN	1830	RENS	SCHO	247
SCHERMERHONE, POMPEY	1830	RENS	SCHO	249
SCHERMERHORN, AUGUSTUS	1830	COLU	STUY	66
SCHERMERHORN, JACOB	1830	NYCO	WD08	212
SCHERMERHORN, JOHN	1830	NYCO	WD05	245
SCHERMERHORN, PETER	1820	MONT	CHAR	337
SCHERMERHORN, PETER	1830	SARA	HALF	74
SCHERMERHORN, PRINCE	1820	MONT	CHAR	337
SCHERMERHORN, THOMAS	1820	SCNE	GLEN	617
SCHERMERHORN, THOMAS	1830	ABNY	WD01	221
SCHERMUHORN, PRINCE	1810	MONT	CHAR	68
SCHMIDT, ALEXANDER R.	1830	NYCO	WD08	243
SCHONOVER, PRINCE	1830	OTSG	CHRV	163
SCHOONER, FEDRICK	1820	ONID	UTIC	207
SCHOONER, FREDERICK	1820	ONID	UTIC	208
SCHOONER, FREDERICK	1830	ONID	UTIC	6
SCHOONER, JOHN	1800	WASH	EAST	463
SCHOONER, JOHN	1820	ONID	UTIC	207
SCHOONER, JOHN	1820	ONID	UTIC	208
SCHOONHOVEN, SARAH	1810	SCHR	SCHR	5
SCHOONMAKER, CAESAR	1830	ULST	SAUG	111
SCHOONMAKER, EPHRAIM	1830	ORNG	MONR	173
SCHOONMAKER, M.	1820	KING	BRYN	173
SCHOONMAKER, PETER	1830	ORNG	MONR	161
SCHOONMAKER, PETER	1830	ORNG	NEWB	32
SCHOONMAKER, POMP	1830	ULST	SAUG	108
SCHOONMAKER, PRINCE	1830	ULST	ROCH	182
SCHOONMAKER, RICHARD	1830	ORNG	MONR	160
SCHOONMAKER, THOMAS	1830	ULST	WAWA	202
SCHOONMAKER, TOM	1810	ULST	ROCH	776
SCHOORMAKER, RICHARD	1820	ULST	MARB	63
SCHOORMAKER, THOMAS	1820	ULST	ROCH	75
SCHULTZ, ANDREW	1820	NYCO	WD09	916
SCHULTZ, SAMUEL	1830	ORNG	WARW	65

NAME	YR	CO	TWP	PG
SCHULYER, JAMES	1830	WASH	CAST	137
SCHUREMAN, HERCULES	1800	DUTC	PHIL	78
SCHUREMAN, HERCULUS	1820	NYCO	WD05	421
SCHUREMAN, MR.	1830	NYCO	WD06	414
SCHUREMUR, HARRY	1820	GREN	CATS	157
SCHUYLER, HARRY	1830	NYCO	WD08	279
SCHUYLER, JAMES	1810	WASH	EAST	505
SCHUYLER, JAMES	1820	WASH	EAST	174
SCHUYLER, JIM	1800	WASH	EAST	460
SCHUYLER, MILFORD	1830	NYCO	WD06	430
SCHUYLER, PETER	1830	COLU	AUST	179
SCHUYLER, PETER	1830	LEWI	LEYD	438
SCHUYLER, PETER J.	1820	HERK	MANH	12
SCHUYLER, PHILIP	1820	DUTC	FISH	58
SCHUYLER, PHILIP	1830	DUTC	PGKP	327
SCHUYLER, PHILIP	1830	SARA	STIL	68
SCHUYLER, POLLY	1830	ABNY	WD02	260
SCHUYLER, SAMUEL	1820	ABNY	ABNY	201
SCHUYLER, SAMUEL	1830	ABNY	WD01	220
SCHUYLER, THOMAS	1820	ABNY	ABNY	197
SCHUYLER, THOMAS	1830	ABNY	WD01	213
SCHUYLER, TOBIAS	1830	QUEN	FLUS	155
SCHUYLER, YACHT	1830	ABNY	WATV	448
SCHUYLOR, ...	1820	NYCO	WD08	840
SCINIFSON, MATHEW	1820	NYCO	WD06	484
SCINO, PETER	1820	NYCO	WD08	750
SCIPEO	1820	SUFF	EAST	295
SCIPEO, CATO	1820	SUFF	EAST	295
SCIPIO	1790	NYCO	MONT	120
SCIPIO	1790	NYCO	NORT	126
SCIPIO	1800	SUFF	SHAM	65
SCIPIO, CATO	1830	SUFF	EAST	259
SCIPIO, SOLOMON	1800	ONTA	CHAR	368
SCIPIO, SOLOMON	1800	ONTA	HART	376
SCIPIO, SOLOMON	1810	ONTA	AVON	595
SCIPIO, SOLOMON JR.	1810	ONTA	AVON	595
SCISCO, BETSEY	1830	NYCO	WD07	14
SCOFIELD, DAVID	1820	NYCO	WD05	352
SCOFIELD, MILLER	1830	WEST	NEWR	108
SCOFIELD, PETER	1830	NYCO	WD05	275
SCOGGINS, JACOB	1820	KING	BRYN	127
SCOLFIELD, JOHN	1830	ABNY	BETH	536
SCOOT, MATTHEW	1830	LEWI	WATS	378
SCOOT, PETER	1830	SCNE	GLEN	273
SCOT, JOSEPH	1820	NYCO	WD09	934
SCOTLAND, BUTHERFIELD	1800	NYCO	WD06	830
SCOTT	1810	NYCO	WD10	695
SCOTT, --	1820	KING	BRYN	141
SCOTT, AMOS	1800	ONON	LYSO	224

NAME	YR	CO	TWP	PG
SCOTT, ELIJAH	1830	QUEN	FLUS	146
SCOTT, ELIZA	1820	NYCO	WD06	476
SCOTT, HENRY	1810	NYCO	WD05	360
SCOTT, HENRY	1810	NYCO	WD06	430
SCOTT, HENRY	1820	NYCO	WD05	396
SCOTT, HENRY	1830	NYCO	WD05	332
SCOTT, HENRY	1830	NYCO	WD05	341
SCOTT, ISAAH	1830	MONR	SWED	368
SCOTT, ISAIAH	1820	GENE	SWEN	280
SCOTT, J.	1830	NYCO	WD11	162
SCOTT, JAMES	1820	NYCO	WD06	515
SCOTT, JAMES	1830	NYCO	WD13	374
SCOTT, JOHN	1810	NYCO	WD05	360
SCOTT, JOHN	1810	NYCO	WD05	275
SCOTT, JOHN	1820	ABNY	GUID	253
SCOTT, JOHN	1820	NYCO	WD05	393
SCOTT, JOHN	1820	NYCO	WD06	509
SCOTT, JOHN	1820	NYCO	WD07	715
SCOTT, JOHN	1830	ABNY	WD04	312
SCOTT, JOHN	1830	NYCO	WD08	237
SCOTT, JOHN	1830	NYCO	WD08	240
SCOTT, JOHN	1830	NYCO	WD12	271
SCOTT, JOHN	1830	NYCO	WD12	278
SCOTT, JONAS	1800	NYCO	WD06	848
SCOTT, JONAS	1810	NYCO	WD06	482
SCOTT, JOS	1820	NIAG	BUFF	148
SCOTT, JOSEPH	1810	NYCO	WD04	159
SCOTT, JOSEPH	1820	NIAG	BUFF	63
SCOTT, JOSEPH	1820	NYCO	WD03	187
SCOTT, JOSEPH	1830	NYCO	WD08	236
SCOTT, MARY	1830	NYCO	WD06	435
SCOTT, RICHARD	1810	NYCO	WD06	446
SCOTT, ROBERT	1820	ONTA	SENE	273
SCOTT, ROBERT	1830	MONR	RWD1	196
SCOTT, ROBERT	1830	NIAG	CAMB	314
SCOTT, STEPHEN	1800	NYCO	WD07	912
SCOTT, WILLIAM	1830	NYCO	WD03	117
SCOTT, WILLIAM	1830	NYCO	WD09	310
SCOTT, WILLIAM	1830	NYCO	WD14	487
SCOTTRIN, SAMUEL	1820	NYCO	WD07	686
SCOTTS, JOHN	1820	SUFF	SHAM	313
SCOVENHOVEN, PRINCE	1820	OTSG	CHRV	4
SCROGGEN, GEORGE	1830	TIOG	ELMI	229
SCROGGINS, GEORGE	1830	JEFF	HOUN	173
SCROMEL, PATIENCE	1800	NYCO	WD05	768
SCUDAER, SIMON	1830	SUFF	BROK	178
SCUDDER, ABRAHAM	1820	SUFF	ISLP	309
SCUDDER, POMPEY	1810	NYCO	WD03	59
SCUDDER, SAMUEL	1820	SUFF	HUNT	294

Scudder

NAME	YR	CO	TWP	PG
SCUDDER, SAMUEL	1830	SUFF	SMIT	273
SCUREMAN, SUSAN	1830	NYCO	WD04	159
SCUYLER, ANTHONY	1830	RENS	TROY	15
SEABURY, CORNELIUS	1810	QUEN	NHEM	306
SEABURY, HANNAH	1810	SUFF	HUNT	505
SEABURY, JAMES	1810	SUFF	HUNT	507
SEABURY, JAMES	1810	SUFF	SOUT	557
SEABURY, JOHN	1820	NYCO	WD06	482
SEACOR, JACK	1810	WEST	RYE	1168
SEALS, WILLIAM	1830	NYCO	WD07	58
SEAMAN, ANTHONY	1810	QUEN	SHEM	306
SEAMAN, ANTHONY	1830	QUEN	SHEM	78
SEAMAN, B.	1830	NYCO	WD11	166
SEAMAN, CUFFE	1820	DUTC	FISH	56
SEAMAN, DAVID	1820	NYCO	WD04	228
SEAMAN, DAVID	1830	NYCO	WD05	346
SEAMAN, EDMUN	1810	QUEN	SHEM	306
SEAMAN, HANNAH	1830	QUEN	OYST	38
SEAMAN, HEWLETT	1830	QUEN	OYST	34
SEAMAN, ISAAC	1810	QUEN	OYST	234
SEAMAN, JACOB	1820	NYCO	WD05	385
SEAMAN, JACOB	1830	NYCO	WD08	236
SEAMAN, JAMES	1830	QUEN	OYST	30
SEAMAN, JAMES	1830	QUEN	SHEM	75
SEAMAN, JOSEPH	1810	QUEN	OYST	244
SEAMAN, JOSIAH	1810	QUEN	OYST	247
SEAMAN, MOSES	1800	ORNG	NEWB	280
SEAMAN, MRS.	1830	KING	WD04	310
SEAMAN, PETER	1800	ORNG	GOSH	358
SEAMAN, SAMPSON	1830	QUEN	NHEM	112
SEAMAN, STEAPHEN	1830	QUEN	SHEM	77
SEAMAN, STEPHEN	1810	QUEN	SHEM	306
SEAMAN, STEPHEN	1820	WEST	YONK	222
SEAMAN, TIMOTHY	1810	NYCO	WD04	162
SEAMAN, TIMOTHY	1820	NYCO	WD04	228
SEAMAN, WRIGHT	1820	NYCO	WD05	394
SEAMAN, WRIGHT	1830	NYCO	WD05	276
SEAMANS, GEORGE	1810	ROCK	HEMP	663
SEAMEN, HENRY	1830	NYCO	WD04	218
SEAMEN, JAMES	1820	QUEN	----	8
SEAMEN, SMITH	1830	NYCO	WD10	75
SEAMEN, TIMOTHY	1830	NYCO	WD04	218
SEAMOR, SIMON	1830	WEST	HARR	217
SEAMORE, HARRY	1830	RICH	WEST	12
SEAMOUR, THOMAS	1800	NYCO	WD07	878
SEANDLIN, THOMAS	1830	NYCO	WD09	409
SEARING, JACK	1810	QUEN	NHEM	299
SEARING, TIMOTHY	1830	QUEN	NHEM	113
SEARLER, IRA	1820	NYCO	WD10	966

NAME	YR	CO	TWP	PG
SEARS	1800	SUFF	SOUT	26
SEARS, HENRY	1830	GREN	CATS	238
SEATH, ELIZA	1820	NYCO	WD08	788
SEBB, SAMUEL	1810	SUFF	BROK	491
SEBITT, ARABELLA	1830	NYCO	WD14	477
SEBRING, REBECCA	1830	NYCO	WD06	436
SEBY	1800	QUEN	SHEM	560
SECOND, MILES	1830	WEST	MAMA	227
SEDGWICK	1820	KING	BRYN	153
SEDLIN, DINAH	1800	NYCO	WD03	706
SEE, EDWARD W.	1820	NYCO	WD08	781
SEE, JOHN	1830	RENS	PITT	123
SEELEY, ISAAC	1820	WEST	RYE	370
SEELY, ISAAC	1830	WEST	WTPL	223
SEERS, GEORGE	1830	MONT	JOHN	203
SEGAR, JOSEPH	1830	COLU	AUST	173
SEGUINE, ABRAHAM	1830	NYCO	WD06	442
SEHERER, YORKER	1800	DUTC	PGKP	66
SELA, JOHN	1810	ROCK	ORNG	639
SELARIE, FRANCIS	1820	NYCO	WD04	307
SELBY, THOMAS	1810	DUTC	CLNT	378
SELISTIAN, BERNARD	1820	NYCO	WD03	190
SELIX, CIPEO	1820	ORNG	BLOM	727
SELLICK, GEORGE	1830	RENS	WD04	75
SELLINGTON, WILLIAM	1830	NYCO	WD09	391
SELLS, JOSEPH	1830	QUEN	NHEM	111
SEMORE, PRINCE	1830	WEST	YORK	167
SEMOUR, ABRAHAM	1830	QUEN	NHEM	109
SENECA	1800	RENS	SCAS	777
SENIOR, ROBERT	1830	NYCO	WD12	288
SENSOR, NICHOLAS	1820	SCNE	WD02	573
SENT, AARON	1830	NYCO	WD08	257
SENTEW, ANTHONY	1800	WASH	ARGY	482
SERINGTON, GILBERT	1830	NYCO	WD08	268
SERINGTON, SAMUEL	1830	WEST	NEWR	109
SERRING, WILLIAM	1800	QUEN	NHEM	553
SERVIS, DANIEL	1830	ORNG	MINI	250
SETH	1800	QUEN	OYST	573
SEURFER, JOHN	1830	ROCK	CLAR	133
SEVAN, NERO	1830	RENS	PITT	123
SEVAN, TRUMAN	1830	RENS	WD02	39
SEWAL, B.·	1830	NYCO	WD13	395
SEWAL, S.	1830	NYCO	WD13	417
SEWARD, S.	1810	ONID	LISB	442
SEWEL, JUBITER	1830	CHEN	SHER	136
SEWEL, JOHN	1830	RICH	NORT	31
SEWEL, PHILLIP	1810	CHEN	SHER	1083
SEWELL, JOHN	1830	NYCO	WD08	229
SEWEN, JOHN	1810	ROCK	CLAR	675

Seymour

NAME	YR	CO	TWP	PG
SEYMOUR, ALLEN	1830	NYCO	WD08	219
SEYMOUR, CATHARINE	1830	QUEN	NEWT	4
SEYMOUR, CHARLES	1830	ONID	UTIC	6
SEYMOUR, JACOB	1830	NYCO	WD08	236
SEYMOUR, JOHN	1830	NYCO	WD06	386
SEYMOUR, JOSEPH	1810	NYCO	WD06	442
SEYMOUR, JOSEPH	1820	NYCO	WD06	449
SEYMOUR, MOSES	1810	NYCO	WD07	551
SEYMOUR, PETER	1810	ORNG	GOSH	1134
SEYMOUR, PETER	1830	NYCO	WD08	192
SEYMOUR, ROBERT	1810	NYCO	WD04	236
SEYMOUR, S.	1830	NYCO	WD11	143
SEYMOUR, SEAMAN	1820	WEST	RYE	370
SHADLEY, JONAH	1830	SUFF	BROK	173
SHAFER, CEACER	1830	SCHR	SCHR	26
SHAFER, CEASAR	1820	SCHR	SCHR	468
SHAFFLER, HENRY	1810	NYCO	WD08	760
SHANEWAY, AKIN	1810	NYCO	WD05	280
SHANKLIN, CATO	1830	NYCO	WD05	302
SHANKS, BENJAMIN	1810	QUEN	OYST	256
SHAPE, PETER	1820	JEFF	CHAM	386
SHARK, JAMES	1830	JEFF	CHAM	132
SHARP	1800	SUFF	BROK	10
SHARP, AMOS	1820	BROM	OWEG	33
SHARP, CALVIN	1830	JEFF	CHAM	140
SHARP, CHARLES	1820	NYCO	WD06	468
SHARP, HARRY	1830	COLU	GHEN	155
SHARP, ISAAC	1810	TIOG	OWGO	667
SHARP, ISAAC	1820	TIOG	TIOG	292
SHARP, ISSAC	1800	DUTC	SOUT	177
SHARP, JOSEPH	1830	STLR	OSWE	231
SHARP, LEVI	1820	SCHR	BROM	423
SHARP, LOT	1830	GREN	COXE	196
SHARP, PETER	1810	JEFF	CHAM	572
SHARP, PETER	1820	KING	BRYN	136
SHARP, PETER	1830	KING	WD02	262
SHARP, PRIMEY	1820	NYCO	WD10	1003
SHARP, RICHARD	1830	GREN	CATS	242
SHARP, RICHARD	1830	NYCO	WD14	459
SHARPE, ISAAC	1800	WEST	NORT	756
SHARPE, PETER	1830	JEFF	CHAM	132
SHARPER	1810	SUFF	BROK	491
SHAVER, JOHN	1830	STLR	OSWE	231
SHAVERS, A.	1830	NYCO	WD13	402
SHAW, ABRAHAM	1820	NYCO	WD05	393
SHAW, JOHN	1810	NYCO	WD05	252
SHAW, JOHN	1830	TOMP	ITCA	332
SHAW, PETER	1830	ORNG	WALL	141
SHAW, TIM	1820	SUFF	ISLP	306

NAME	YR	CO	TWP	PG
SHAWBUM, SAMUEL	1820	DELA	ROXB	84
SHEALD, ELIJAH	1830	GENE	ALAB	318
SHEAR, YORK	1820	DUTC	PGKP	101
SHEARER, JOHN	1820	CORT	PREB	570
SHEDAR, DAVID	1800	DUTC	PAWL	50
SHEEP, CEZAR	1830	ULST	SAUG	91
SHEFFIELD, THOMAS	1820	SULL	THOM	164
SHEFFIELD, THOMAS	1830	SULL	THOM	72
SHELBY, H.	1830	ERIE	BUFF	6
SHELDEN, DAVID	1820	GENE	GATE	125
SHELDON, DAVID	1830	WANE	PALM	40
SHELLEY, SIMON	1830	OSWE	HAST	222
SHELLY, ABRAHAM	1800	DUTC	PAWL	43
SHELLY, LEWIS	1810	NYCO	WD06	484
SHELP, DANIEL	1820	ORNG	MONT	831
SHEM, DUINCEE	1830	RENS	LANS	100
SHEPARD, MICHAEL	1830	STEU	READ	333
SHEPHERD, DAVID	1820	NYCO	WD06	477
SHEPHERD, M.A.	1820	NYCO	WD10	988
SHEPHERD, SAMUEL	1830	NYCO	WD08	131
SHEPHERD, SAMUEL	1830	NYCO	WD12	310
SHEPHERD, THOMAS	1810	NYCO	WD03	81
SHEREN, JESEY	1830	NYCO	WD10	97
SHERMAN, CHARLES	1830	ONON	OTIS	330
SHERMAN, CHRISTOPHER	1810	SCNE	WD02	954
SHERMAN, JESSE	1820	SARA	SARA	189
SHERMAN, JOHN	1830	DUTC	WASH	439
SHERWOOD, LEYMAN	1820	PUTM	SOUT	100
SHEWETT, JOSEPH	1830	ORNG	WARW	77
SHIELDS, CATO	1820	ONTA	CANA	215
SHIELDS, ELIJAH	1830	GENE	BATA	329
SHIELDS, JANE	1810	NYCO	WD06	396
SHIELDS, TRUSTOM	1820	ONTA	PHEL	287
SHILBURN, JAMES	1810	NYCO	WD07	527
SHILTON, PHILON	1820	PUTM	PHIL	101
SHINN, RICHARD	1820	SARA	STIL	191
SHIPLEY, HENRY	1830	DUTC	WASH	448
SHOALS, C.	1830	NYCO	WD12	288
SHOEMAKER, FRANK	1820	TIOG	ELMI	309
SHOOD, HENRY	1830	NYCO	WD08	219
SHOOTS, JACK	1830	COLU	KIND	140
SHORT, BASIL	1820	NYCO	WD08	731
SHORTER	1820	NYCO	WD05	434
SHORTER, CHARLES	1830	CAYU	AURE	186
SHORTER, CLEMENT	1830	ALLE	RUSH	174
SHORTER, GERARD	1830	NYCO	WD05	310
SHORTER, JANE	1830	NYCO	WD06	450
SHORTER, NASE	1810	NYCO	WD03	79
SHOTTER, JANE	1810	NYCO	WD05	318

NAME	YR	CO	TWP	PG
SHOUPER, ALLEN	1820	CLNT	PLAT	452
SHOVE, S.	1830	NYCO	WD03	116
SHOWERS, JAMES	1830	ORNG	HBGH	129
SHOWN, C.	1810	ONID	LISB	431
SI--S, WILLIAM	1810	ONON	ONON	497
SIAH	1790	QUEN	OYST	154
SIAH	1790	QUEN	SHEM	157
SIAH	1800	QUEN	OYST	573
SIB	1790	QUEN	SHEM	156
SIBB, SAMUEL	1810	SUFF	BROK	491
SICKELS, GIN	1810	ROCK	CLAR	687
SICKINS, WILLIAM	1820	DUTC	PGKP	107
SICKLER, GEORGE	1800	SARA	HALF	1044
SICKLES, HARRY	1830	WEST	YONK	11
SICKLES, MARY	1820	NYCO	WD07	671
SICKLES, SIBBY	1830	WEST	NORS	84
SIDNEY, FAME	1810	NYCO	WD05	255
SIDNEY, JACK	1830	DELA	STAM	183
SIDNEY, JOSEPH	1810	NYCO	WD05	254
SIDNEY, MARY	1820	NYCO	WD07	626
SIDNEY, ROBERT	1820	NYCO	WD08	769
SIDNEY, STEPHEN	1810	NYCO	WD04	213
SIEBONEY, STEPHEN	1820	NYCO	WD07	603
SILAMAN, HARRY	1830	WEST	MTPL	46
SILAS	1790	QUEN	NEWT	151
SILAS	1800	SUFF	BROK	9
SILAS	1810	RICH	SMIT	628
SILAS	1820	RICH	SOUT	106
SILAS, PHEBE	1820	DUTC	PGKP	101
SILAS, R.	1810	DUTC	PGKP	325
SILAS, ROBERT	1810	NYCO	WD04	158
SILES, JAMES	1830	NYCO	WD06	385
SILKINS, HENRY	1820	NYCO	WD08	769
SILKINS, THOMAS	1820	NYCO	WD08	769
SILL	1820	SUFF	BROK	353
SILLS, JAMES	1810	NYCO	WD06	458
SILLS, PETER	1830	SUFF	BROK	178
SILLS, PETTER	1810	SUFF	BROK	492
SILLS, TITUS	1830	SUFF	BROK	176
SILLS, TUTUS	1810	SUFF	BROK	486
SILVA	1800	WEST	RYE	661
SILVAN, WILLIAM	1820	NYCO	WD06	473
SILVENUS	1790	SUFF	ISLP	165
SILVESTER	1810	DUTC	PGKP	22
SILVESTER, JACK	1830	COLU	STUY	62
SILVIA	1830	NYCO	WD13	398
SILVY, PETER	1830	SENE	OVID	108
SIMAS	1820	SUFF	BROK	362
SIMEON	1790	SUFF	ISLP	165

NAME	YR	CO	TWP	PG
SIMEON	1800	SUFF	EHAM	95
SIMES, REBECCA	1830	NYCO	WD09	399
SIMESON, EDWARD	1830	KING	NEUT	391
SIMMERMAN, YORK	1830	DUTC	REDH	375
SIMMOND, JOHN	1830	MADI	----	196
SIMMONDS, JANE	1830	NYCO	WD14	489
SIMMONS, ABRAHAM	1810	NYCO	WD06	484
SIMMONS, AMELLA	1830	NYCO	WD10	18
SIMMONS, AMOS	1830	DUTC	DOVE	218
SIMMONS, ANN	1810	NYCO	WD05	330
SIMMONS, BETSY	1830	NYCO	WD05	341
SIMMONS, CHARLES	1810	RENS	GREN	458
SIMMONS, ENOCH	1790	COLU	CANN	61
SIMMONS, FRANCIS	1830	ONON	SALI	5
SIMMONS, GEORGE	1820	ORNG	CORN	711
SIMMONS, HANNAH	1800	NYCO	WD03	701
SIMMONS, HENRY	1820	MADI	BROK	101
SIMMONS, ISAAC	1820	QUEN	----	29
SIMMONS, JAMES	1810	NYCO	WD04	200
SIMMONS, JAMES	1820	NYCO	WD07	710
SIMMONS, JAMES	1830	NYCO	WD08	246
SIMMONS, JAMES	1830	ORNG	GOSH	289
SIMMONS, JANE	1800	NYCO	WD07	874
SIMMONS, JANE	1830	COLU	AUST	172
SIMMONS, MARGARET	1830	NYCO	WD07	44
SIMMONS, MARY	1820	COLU	HUDS	33
SIMMONS, MOSES	1820	NYCO	WD04	295
SIMMONS, MOSES	1830	NYCO	WD06	435
SIMMONS, NICHOLAS	1830	NYCO	WD09	391
SIMMONS, PRINCE	1830	KING	WD04	319
SIMMONS, RACHEL	1830	RENS	WD02	35
SIMMONS, RICHARD	1820	KING	BRYN	144
SIMMONS, RICHARD	1830	ORNG	GOSH	285
SIMMONS, TIMOTHY	1820	SCNE	WD02	574
SIMMONS, WILLIAM	1810	WEST	HARR	1131
SIMMONS, WILLIAM	1830	KING	WD05	327
SIMMS, GEORGE	1830	NYCO	WD04	228
SIMMS, JACOB	1830	NYCO	WD05	339
SIMON	1790	NYCO	OUTW	129
SIMON	1790	QUEN	NEWT	151
SIMON	1790	QUEN	OYST	157
SIMON	1800	QUEN	NHEM	553
SIMON	1800	QUEN	FLUS	538
SIMON	1800	QUEN	SMIT	57
SIMON	1820	ABNY	RENV	75
SIMON, J.	1810	MADI	BROK	774
SIMON, JOHN	1810	SUFF	BROK	474
SIMON, MOTHER	1820	SUFF	BROK	363
SIMON, PHEBE	1810	NYCO	WD03	89

Simon

NAME	YR	CO	TWP	PG
SIMON, SAMUEL	1830	ROCK	ORGT	117
SIMONS, ABBEY	1830	SUFF	BROK	179
SIMONS, ABRAHAM F.	1830	WEST	PELH	116
SIMONS, JAMES	1820	MADI	BROK	102
SIMONS, JAMES	1830	CORT	CORT	70
SIMONS, JAMES	1830	WARR	QUEN	80
SIMONS, JOHN	1820	MADI	BROK	101
SIMONS, JOHN	1830	SUFF	SHAM	228
SIMONS, MIMA	1830	SUFF	ISLP	282
SIMONS, MINGO	1820	NYCO	WD05	337
SIMONS, MOSES	1830	ORNG	MONR	166
SIMONS, PHEBE	1830	NYCO	WD08	243
SIMONS, PRINCE	1810	QUEN	NHEM	221
SIMONSON, ABRAHAM	1790	RICH	SOUT	159
SIMONSON, ABRAHAM	1800	RICH	SOUT	953
SIMONSON, ABRAHAM	1830	QUEN	OYST	29
SIMONSON, ELIZA	1830	SUFF	EAST	259
SIMONSON, WIDOW	1830	NYCO	WD09	408
SIMPLINS, HENRY	1830	NYCO	WD06	385
SIMPOO, BENJAMIN	1800	NYCO	WD06	847
SIMPSON, CATO	1810	NYCO	WD04	162
SIMPSON, CATO	1820	NYCO	WD06	503
SIMPSON, CATO	1820	ORNG	NEWB	546
SIMPSON, CATO	1830	ORNG	NEWB	39
SIMPSON, EPHRAIM	1810	RENS	GREN	458
SIMPSON, FORTUNE	1830	ABNY	WD02	241
SIMPSON, GEORGE	1830	NYCO	WD08	173
SIMPSON, HAGAR	1800	NYCO	WD03	696
SIMPSON, HENRY	1830	ULST	OLIV	141
SIMPSON, ISAAC	1830	NYCO	WD12	252
SIMPSON, JACOB	1830	NYCO	WD06	424
SIMPSON, JOHN	1830	NYCO	WD06	443
SIMPSON, JOHN	1830	NYCO	WD13	341
SIMPSON, JOHN H.	1830	NYCO	WD06	380
SIMPSON, MARY	1830	NYCO	WD02	69
SIMPSON, MATTHEW	1830	NYCO	WD05	341
SIMPSON, MISS	1830	KING	WD03	288
SIMPSON, PETER	1830	COLU	HUDS	99
SIMPSON, PETER	1830	NYCO	WD10	66
SIMPSON, T.	1810	NIAG	BUFF	235
SIMPSON, THOMAS	1820	NYCO	WD08	811
SIMPSON, WILLIAM	1830	NYCO	WD07	64
SIMS, JOHN	1830	NYCO	WD06	465
SIMS, MICHAEL	1810	NYCO	WD06	473
SIMS, PETER	1830	NYCO	WD12	262
SIMS, ROBERT	1830	LIVI	LEIC	172
SIMSBERRY, JACK	1800	NYCO	WD03	706
SIMSON, DOLLY	1800	NYCO	WD04	721
SIMSON, FORTUNE	1820	SCNE	WD02	572

NAME	YR	CO	TWP	PG
SIMSON, FOTIN	1810	SCNE	PRIN	998
SIMSON, JENNY	1810	NYCO	WD05	789
SIMSON, JOHN	1800	WEST	CORT	800
SIMSON, THOMAS	1830	MONR	BRIG	16
SINCLAR	1820	SUFF	HUNT	290
SINCLAIR, DANIEL	1810	NYCO	WD06	407
SINES, GEORGE	1820	NYCO	WD02	104
SINES, NEMUS	1820	SUFF	ISLP	310
SINES, SIMEON	1810	SUFF	ISLP	496
SINNEN, ISAAC	1830	NYCO	WD14	426
SIPKINES, WILLIAM	1830	NYCO	WD13	336
SIPKINS, THOMAS	1830	NYCO	WD14	518
SIPP, WILLIAM	1830	ORNG	NEWB	46
SIRLEY, JOHN	1800	NYCO	WD07	922
SIRUS	1800	SUFF	EHAM	92
SIRUS	1800	SUFF	SHAM	77
SISCO, ISAAC	1830	SUFF	HUNT	325
SISCO, JACOB	1810	SUFF	SOUT	536
SISCO, JOHN	1830	QUEN	FLUS	151
SISCO, NICHOLAS	1830	NYCO	WD09	372
SISCO, SAMUEL	1820	ONON	ONON	207
SISCO, SAMUEL	1820	OTSG	OTSG	5
SISCO, SAMUEL	1830	ONON	ONON	188
SISCO, WILLIAM	1830	ONON	CAMI	201
SISIO, AURAN	1820	NYCO	WD09	886
SISIO, PETER & NICK	1820	NYCO	WD09	893
SISSON, DIANA	1830	NYCO	WD06	367
SKERRIT, MATTHEW	1830	NYCO	WD05	337
SKIDMON, STEPHEN	1830	QUEN	OYST	29
SKIDMORE, CAIN	1810	SUFF	RIVH	545
SKIDMORE, SAMUEL	1830	ORNG	CORN	201
SKIDMORE, STEPHEN	1820	QUEN	----	27
SKINNER, EBEN	1810	NYCO	WD06	424
SKINNER, EBENEZER	1830	NYCO	WD08	213
SKINNER, EDWARD	1830	NYCO	WD08	256
SKINNER, THOMAS	1830	OTSG	OTSG	37
SLATER	1820	ONID	AUGU	73
SLATER, ANDREW B.	1830	OSWE	VOLN	194
SLATER, HANNAH	1830	NYCO	WD10	66
SLATER, THOMAS	1830	NYCO	WD06	382
SLATER, THOMAS	1830	NYCO	WD14	475
SLATER, VENUS	1830	OSWE	VOLN	193
SLATER, WIDOW	1820	ONID	WHIT	303
SLATER, WIDOW	1820	ONID	WATE	303
SLAUGHTER, DEMSEY	1800	ABNY	SCNE	18
SLAUTER, ABRAHAM	1810	KING	BRYN	632
SLAUTER, JAMES	1790	ORNG	GOSH	138
SLAUTER, JAMES	1810	KING	BRYN	632
SLAYTER, ABRAHAM	1800	ULST	NPAL	243

NAME	YR	CO	TWP	PG
SLAYTER, JOHN	1830	ONID	UTIC	26
SLINGLELANDT, JACK	1830	COLU	KIND	141
SLOCUM, CHARLES	1830	JEFF	HOUN	173
SLOUGHTER, MARGARET	1830	SCHR	SCHR	13
SLOUNTENBERGH, JAMES	1820	SCHR	SCHR	189
SLOWTER, JAMES	1820	NYCO	WD07	602
SLUMBUST, CHRISTOPHER	1800	NYCO	WD04	725
SLUYTER, ABRAHAM	1810	ULST	MARB	799
SLUYTER, JAMES	1800	ORNG	GOSH	357
SLYTOR, BENJAMIN	1810	NYCO	WD05	319
SMALLWOOD, CHARLES	1830	WANE	PALM	37
SMART, JOSEPH	1830	SARA	STIL	64
SMART, WILLIAM	1800	NYCO	WD06	797
SMART, WILLIAM	1810	NYCO	WD03	44
SMEDES, DICK	1810	ULST	WOOD	824
SMEDES, MARGARET	1830	ULST	KING	67
SMEDES, MARY	1830	NYCO	WD08	243
SMEDES, PHILIP	1810	ULST	KING	757
SMEDO, MARGARET	1820	ULST	KING	78
SMILA, JOHN	1830	HERK	STAR	235
SMILEY, NICHOLAS	1830	ONON	ONON	188
SMILEY, PATIENCE	1830	ABNY	WD02	255
SMITH	1800	NYCO	WD07	889
SMITH	1810	NYCO	WD07	572
SMITH	1810	NYCO	WD07	574
SMITH	1820	ESEX	ELIZ	416
SMITH, ABNER	1830	SUFF	SMIT	274
SMITH, ABRAHAM	1810	NYCO	WD04	198
SMITH, ABRAHAM	1820	SUFF	SMIT	320
SMITH, ABRAHAM	1830	NYCO	WD06	435
SMITH, ADAM	1820	KING	BRYN	123
SMITH, ALEXANDER	1830	NYCO	WD01	31
SMITH, ALEXANDER	1830	OSWE	OSWE	139
SMITH, AMILIA	1820	NYCO	WD08	788
SMITH, ANDREW	1820	NYCO	WD06	485
SMITH, ANDREW	1830	NYCO	WD07	55
SMITH, ANN MRS.	1830	NYCO	WD01	28
SMITH, ANTHONY	1820	SENE	FAYE	372
SMITH, ANTHONY	1820	WEST	EAST	204
SMITH, ANTHONY	1830	SENE	VARI	83
SMITH, ARCH	1810	SUFF	SMIT	353
SMITH, ARCHABOLD	1820	SUFF	SMIT	322
SMITH, BENJAMIN	1800	DUTC	FISH	31
SMITH, BENJAMIN	1810	NYCO	WD02	101
SMITH, BENJAMIN	1820	ABNY	ABNY	200
SMITH, BENJAMIN	1820	NYCO	WD01	60
SMITH, BENJAMIN	1820	NYCO	WD03	140
SMITH, BENJAMIN	1820	NYCO	WD10	1028
SMITH, BENJAMIN	1830	ABNY	WD03	284

NAME	YR	CO	TWP	PG
SMITH, BENJAMIN	1830	NYCO	WD05	315
SMITH, BENJAMIN	1830	QUEN	FLUS	142
SMITH, BETSEY	1830	NYCO	WD10	28
SMITH, BETSY	1820	NYCO	WD10	988
SMITH, CEASAR	1810	ULST	MARB	731
SMITH, CEASAR	1820	SARA	STIL	195
SMITH, CEAZAR	1810	WASH	EAST	497
SMITH, CESAR	1810	NYCO	WD08	766
SMITH, CHARLES	1820	ABNY	ABNY	198
SMITH, CHARLES	1820	ULST	ROCH	75
SMITH, CHARLES	1830	ABNY	WD01	220
SMITH, CHARLES	1830	KING	WD04	311
SMITH, CHARLES	1830	NYCO	WD03	116
SMITH, CHARLES	1830	NYCO	WD06	447
SMITH, CHARLES	1830	NYCO	WD09	360
SMITH, CHARLES	1830	TIOG	ELMI	228
SMITH, CHARLES	1830	ULST	WAWA	187
SMITH, CHARLOTTE	1830	ALLE	ANGE	3
SMITH, CHRISTEEN	1800	COLU	CLAV	1216
SMITH, COBB	1810	ORNG	DEER	1079
SMITH, CROZER	1830	KING	BUSH	379
SMITH, CUFF	1820	GREN	CATS	157
SMITH, CUFF	1820	ONID	NWHT	64
SMITH, D.	1830	NYCO	WD13	369
SMITH, DANIAL	1830	MONT	JOHN	186
SMITH, DANIEL	1830	ONON	SALI	24
SMITH, DANIEL T.	1830	NYCO	WD08	229
SMITH, DAVID	1810	QUEN	FLUS	201
SMITH, DAVID	1830	QUEN	OYST	22
SMITH, E.	1830	NYCO	WD06	464
SMITH, E.	1830	NYCO	WD13	367
SMITH, EBOW	1830	NYCO	WD08	215
SMITH, EDWARD	1790	ORNG	GOSH	139
SMITH, EDWARD	1800	ORNG	WALL	333
SMITH, EDWARD	1810	NYCO	WD04	193
SMITH, ELIJAH	1810	SUFF	SMIT	534
SMITH, ELIZABETH	1830	NYCO	WD06	428
SMITH, ELIZABETH	1830	SUFF	SHAM	215
SMITH, ENOCH	1820	WEST	SUMM	355
SMITH, ENOCH	1830	NYCO	WD14	443
SMITH, EPHRAIM	1820	ORNG	MONT	835
SMITH, EPHRAIM	1830	NYCO	WD07	61
SMITH, FANNY	1830	ABNY	WD04	293
SMITH, FORTUNE	1800	NYCO	WD07	891
SMITH, FORTUNE	1810	NYCO	WD10	696
SMITH, FRANCIS	1830	NYCO	WD08	136
SMITH, FRANK	1830	SUFF	SMIT	274
SMITH, G.	1830	NYCO	WD13	344
SMITH, G.N.	1830	NYCO	WD13	345

NAME	YR	CO	TWP	PG
SMITH, GEORGE	1830	NYCO	WD04	178
SMITH, GEORGE	1830	QUEN	FLUS	141
SMITH, GILBERT	1810	NYCO	WD02	124
SMITH, GO	1810	ROCK	ORNG	636
SMITH, H.	1830	SUFF	SMIT	271
SMITH, HANNAH	1830	NYCO	WD14	460
SMITH, HARRY	1810	NYCO	WD01	23
SMITH, HARRY	1810	ORNG	GOSH	1128
SMITH, HARRY	1830	WEST	NEWC	94
SMITH, HENRY	1820	NYCO	WD04	212
SMITH, HENRY	1820	NYCO	WD06	450
SMITH, HENRY	1820	NYCO	WD09	882
SMITH, HENRY	1830	KING	BRYN	360
SMITH, HENRY	1830	ORNG	GOSH	289
SMITH, HETTY	1830	NYCO	WD10	91
SMITH, INDA	1820	NYCO	WD10	978
SMITH, ISAAC	1810	DUTC	PGKP	172
SMITH, ISAAC	1820	DUTC	PGKP	104
SMITH, ISAAC	1830	DUTC	PGKP	343
SMITH, ISRAEL	1830	NYCO	WD11	133
SMITH, J.	1820	NYCO	WD10	1104
SMITH, J.	1830	KING	WD04	319
SMITH, JACOB	1810	NYCO	WD06	449
SMITH, JACOB	1810	QUEN	NHEM	215
SMITH, JACOB	1820	NYCO	WD05	331
SMITH, JACOB	1830	NYCO	WD08	240
SMITH, JACOB	1830	QUEN	NHEM	104
SMITH, JAMES	1800	NYCO	WD03	710
SMITH, JAMES	1800	NYCO	WD06	799
SMITH, JAMES	1810	NYCO	WD10	676
SMITH, JAMES	1820	DUTC	DOVE	47
SMITH, JAMES	1820	JEFF	HOUN	417
SMITH, JAMES	1820	NYCO	WD07	606
SMITH, JAMES	1820	QUEN	----	23
SMITH, JAMES	1820	SCHR	BROM	426
SMITH, JAMES	1830	DUTC	DOVE	212
SMITH, JAMES	1830	GREN	GREN	156
SMITH, JAMES	1830	KING	WD02	259
SMITH, JAMES	1830	KING	WD05	342
SMITH, JAMES	1830	NYCO	WD04	199
SMITH, JAMES	1830	NYCO	WD06	403
SMITH, JAMES	1830	NYCO	WD07	31
SMITH, JAMES	1830	ONON	SKAN	136
SMITH, JAMES	1830	QUEN	NHEM	117
SMITH, JAMES	1830	ULST	ROCH	172
SMITH, JANE	1800	ABNY	WD02	278
SMITH, JANE	1810	NYCO	WD03	80
SMITH, JANE	1810	NYCO	WD05	371
SMITH, JANE	1830	NYCO	WD14	517

NAME	YR	CO	TWP	PG
SMITH, JANE MRS.	1830	NYCO	WD01	31
SMITH, JEREMIAH	1820	NYCO	WD06	501
SMITH, JEREMIAH	1830	SUFF	SMIT	276
SMITH, JOHN	1810	DUTC	STAN	174
SMITH, JOHN	1810	DUTC	STAN	180
SMITH, JOHN	1810	SUFF	SOUT	445
SMITH, JOHN	1810	WEST	EAST	1158
SMITH, JOHN	1820	NYCO	WD05	393
SMITH, JOHN	1820	NYCO	WD06	531
SMITH, JOHN	1830	CLNT	PERU	350
SMITH, JOHN	1830	KING	BUSH	383
SMITH, JOHN	1830	NYCO	WD04	204
SMITH, JOHN	1830	NYCO	WD05	300
SMITH, JOHN	1838	NYCO	WD05	338
SMITH, JOHN	1830	NYCO	WD05	350
SMITH, JOHN	1830	NYCO	WD06	433
SMITH, JOHN	1830	NYCO	WD12	304
SMITH, JOHN	1830	ONTA	SENE	54
SMITH, JOHN	1830	QUEN	NHEM	109
SMITH, JOHN	1830	SUFF	SMIT	271
SMITH, JOHN	1830	WEST	NEWR	113
SMITH, JOS	1820	NYCO	WD08	738
SMITH, JOSEPH	1800	NYCO	WD03	709
SMITH, JOSEPH	1810	KING	BRYN	633
SMITH, JOSEPH	1810	NYCO	WD10	635
SMITH, JOSEPH	1820	KING	BRYN	126
SMITH, JOSEPH	1830	ROCK	ORGT	116
SMITH, JUDAH	1830	SARA	STIL	59
SMITH, JUDITH	1830	NYCO	WD06	429
SMITH, LAURENCE	1830	NYCO	WD06	388
SMITH, LAWRENCE	1820	NYCO	WD04	212
SMITH, LAWRENCE	1830	NYCO	WD04	159
SMITH, LEAVEN	1830	NYCO	WD12	288
SMITH, LETTICE	1830	NYCO	WD14	510
SMITH, LEVI	1820	NYCO	WD10	957
SMITH, LEWIS	1830	NYCO	WD04	228
SMITH, LONDON	1830	SUFF	BROK	162
SMITH, LUCY	1800	QUEN	NHEM	553
SMITH, LYDIA	1800	NYCO	WD06	844
SMITH, M.	1830	NYCO	WD11	209
SMITH, MARY	1810	ROCK	ORNG	636
SMITH, MARY	1820	NYCO	WD06	517
SMITH, MARY	1830	NYCO	WD06	444
SMITH, MASHE	1830	SUFF	BROK	162
SMITH, MICHAEL	1830	NYCO	WD05	345
SMITH, MINGO	1830	SUFF	SMIT	274
SMITH, MINK	1830	COLU	STUY	62
SMITH, MORRIS	1810	NYCO	WD06	424
SMITH, MORRIS	1820	ORNG	GOSH	761
SMITH, MORRIS	1820	QUEN	----	67

Smith

NAME	YR	CO	TWP	PG
SMITH, MOSES	1820	GREN	ATHN	10
SMITH, MOSES	1830	GREN	ATHN	210
SMITH, MRS.	1810	NYCO	WD01	28
SMITH, MRS.	1820	NYCO	WD06	461
SMITH, NATHAN	1810	NYCO	WD06	427
SMITH, NOAH	1820	ULST	WAWA	73
SMITH, NOAH	1830	ULST	ROCH	173
SMITH, PETER	1810	NYCO	WD05	258
SMITH, PETER	1810	NYCO	WD06	411
SMITH, PETER	1810	QUEN	NHEM	204
SMITH, PETER	1820	ORNG	NEWB	512
SMITH, PETER	1820	ULST	MARB	54
SMITH, PETER	1830	ORNG	NEWB	40
SMITH, PETER	1830	QUEN	OYST	22
SMITH, PETER	1830	RENS	NASS	298
SMITH, PHILIP	1820	TOMP	ULYS	12
SMITH, PHILLIP	1830	TOMP	ITCA	332
SMITH, PLATO	1810	NYCO	WD06	484
SMITH, PLATT	1820	PUTM	CARM	101
SMITH, R.	1820	WEST	SALM	392
SMITH, REBECCA	1820	ONTA	SENE	264
SMITH, REUBEN	1830	SUFF	BROK	159
SMITH, RICHARD	1800	NYCO	WD07	891
SMITH, RICHARD	1810	NYCO	WD07	552
SMITH, RICHARD	1810	QUEN	OYST	250
SMITH, RICHARD	1820	WEST	NEWR	211
SMITH, RICHARD	1830	GREN	CATS	237
SMITH, RICHARD	1830	MONT	JOHN	188
SMITH, RICHARD	1830	NYCO	WD07	30
SMITH, RICHARD	1830	SUFF	SMIT	267
SMITH, RICHARD	1830	WEST	NEWR	114
SMITH, ROBBIN	1820	QUEN	----	7
SMITH, ROBERT	1810	QUEN	FLUS	199
SMITH, ROBERT	1820	NYCO	WD06	445
SMITH, ROBERT	1820	QUEN	----	55
SMITH, ROMEO	1800	NYCO	WD01	660
SMITH, ROMEO	1810	NYCO	WD04	192
SMITH, SALLY	1810	NYCO	WD06	417
SMITH, SALLY	1810	NYCO	WD06	457
SMITH, SAMEUL	1830	NYCO	WD05	344
SMITH, SAMUAL	1800	NYCO	WD05	763
SMITH, SAMUEL	1810	NYCO	WD05	362
SMITH, SAMUEL	1820	WEST	NORC	433
SMITH, SAMUEL	1830	NYCO	WD04	187
SMITH, SAMUEL	1830	NYCO	WD07	39
SMITH, SAMUEL	1830	NYCO	WD12	290
SMITH, SAMUEL	1830	ORNG	DEER	8
SMITH, SAMUEL	1830	WEST	NEWC	94
SMITH, SARAH	1830	NYCO	WD06	428

NAME	YR	CO	TWP	PG
SMITH, SARAH	1830	QUEN	NHEM	105
SMITH, SILVANNIS	1830	KING	WD04	319
SMITH, SIMEON	1830	SUFF	SMIT	275
SMITH, SIMON	1810	NYCO	WD05	259
SMITH, SIMON	1830	NYCO	WD08	229
SMITH, STEPHEN	1820	NYCO	WD08	750
SMITH, STEPHEN	1830	QUEN	FLUS	143
SMITH, STEPHEN	1830	SUFF	BROK	162
SMITH, SUBMIT	1820	NYCO	WD07	686
SMITH, SUSAN	1830	NYCO	WD08	218
SMITH, T.	1820	NYCO	WD09	881
SMITH, T.A.	1830	NYCO	WD10	26
SMITH, THEO. A.	1830	NYCO	WD11	239
SMITH, THOMAS	1800	NYCO	WD03	698
SMITH, THOMAS	1810	ONTA	MIDD	770
SMITH, THOMAS	1820	NYCO	WD05	404
SMITH, THOMAS	1820	NYCO	WD06	557
SMITH, THOMAS	1820	ONTA	MIDD	74
SMITH, THOMAS	1820	QUEN	----	54
SMITH, THOMAS	1830	KING	WD04	297
SMITH, THOMAS	1830	KING	WD04	309
SMITH, THOMAS	1830	NYCO	WD05	310
SMITH, THOMAS	1830	NYCO	WD10	36
SMITH, THOMAS	1830	QUEN	NHEM	110
SMITH, THOMAS	1830	QUEN	FLUS	142
SMITH, THOMAS	1830	ROCK	ORGT	109
SMITH, TIM	1810	NYCO	WD06	473
SMITH, TIMOTH	1830	QUEN	OYST	45
SMITH, TIMOTHY	1820	QUEN	----	70
SMITH, TIMOTHY	1830	ONID	ROME	406
SMITH, TOPHEN	1820	SUFF	SMIT	315
SMITH, TOWER	1800	COLU	HUDS	1138
SMITH, TOWER	1810	COLU	HUDS	140
SMITH, TOWN	1790	COLU	HUDS	66
SMITH, TYS	1810	DUTC	FISH	259
SMITH, WARNER	1830	NYCO	WD08	229
SMITH, WILLIAM	1810	DELA	WALT	567
SMITH, WILLIAM	1810	NYCO	WD05	279
SMITH, WILLIAM	1820	NYCO	WD06	454
SMITH, WILLIAM	1820	NYCO	WD07	721
SMITH, WILLIAM	1820	NYCO	WD07	701
SMITH, WILLIAM	1820	NYCO	WD07	654
SMITH, WILLIAM	1820	QUEN	----	29
SMITH, WILLIAM	1830	KING	FLAT	402
SMITH, WILLIAM	1830	NYCO	WD06	395
SMITH, WILLIAM	1830	NYCO	WD07	98
SMITH, WILLIAM	1830	ONID	DEER	226
SMITH, WILLIAM	1830	QUEN	NHEM	109
SMITH, WILLIAM	1830	WEST	MAMA	228

NAME	YR	CO	TWP	PG
SMITH, WILLIAM A.	1830	NYCO	WD14	525
SMITHE, LUCY	1830	NYCO	WD04	154
SMOCK, HAGAR	1810	NYCO	WD03	87
SNEDEKER, JOHN	1830	QUEN	JAMA	127
SNEDEMER, SYLVESTER	1800	DUTC	PGKP	63
SNELL, BONELBY	1830	MONT	EPHR	174
SNIDER, JACK	1810	ORNG	MONT	954
SNIFFEN, KUFF	1810	WEST	RYE	1161
SNIP, SIAH	1810	QUEN	NHEM	206
SNUTHKINS, LEWIS	1810	NYCO	WD05	318
SNYDAM, LEWIS	1830	QUEN	OYST	46
SNYDER, ADAM	1820	ULST	MARB	62
SNYDER, CEASER	1830	SCHR	SCHR	27
SNYDER, CEASAR	1820	SCHR	SCHR	459
SNYDER, EDWARD	1830	ULST	MARB	156
SNYDER, JACK	1830	SCHR	COBL	149
SNYDER, JEREMIAH	1830	COLU	STUY	64
SNYDER, JOHN	1830	NYCO	WD08	231
SNYDER, LUKE	1830	ULST	NPAL	224
SNYDER, NELLY	1830	ORNG	MONR	173
SO, CURRYAND	1810	QUEN	SHEM	306
SOBRISKY, THOMAS	1800	NYCO	WD07	870
SOCANY, WIDOW	1810	NYCO	WD37	519
SOLES, CHARITY	1830	DUTC	FISH	471
SOLES, ROBERT	1830	DUTC	FISH	489
SOLES, ROBERT	1830	DUTC	FISH	502
SOLOMAN	1800	SUFF	BROK	8
SOLOMAN	1810	RENS	PITT	405
SOLOMAN	1810	RENS	TROY	49
SOLOMAN, JACK	1810	QUEN	NEWT	171
SOLOMAN, JOHN	1810	SUFF	SHAM	460
SOLOMAN, SAMUEL	1810	SUFF	EAST	431
SOLOMON	1790	QUEN	JAMA	150
SOLOMON	1790	QUEN	NEWT	151
SOLOMON, ABRAHAM	1800	SUFF	SHAM	74
SOLOMON, JACOB	1790	QUEN	NEWT	151
SOLOMON, JOHN	1800	SUFF	SHAM	74
SOLOMON, JOHN	1820	SUFF	SHAM	309
SOLOMON, SAMUEL	1820	SUFF	EAST	288
SOLOMON, SAMUEL	1830	SUFF	SHAM	210
SOLVENUS	1800	SUFF	ISLP	62
SOMENCE, PETER	1820	DUTC	FISH	70
SOMERSETT, LEVI	1830	NYCO	WD09	414
SOMMERVILLE, ABRAHAM	1820	NYCO	WD04	282
SOPER, SAMPSAN	1820	CLNT	PLAT	468
SOPER, SAMPSON	1830	CLNT	PLAT	263
SOPHIA	1810	NYCO	WD06	399
SORRELS, AMOS	1810	DELA	WALT	572
SOURING, PHILIP	1820	NYCO	WD03	149

NAME	YR	CO	TWP	PG
SOUTH, J.S.	1820	NIAG	LEWS	230
SOUTH, P.G.	1820	NIAG	LEWS	221
SOUTHERLAND, PRINCE	1830	COLU	CHAT	50
SOUTHERLAND, ROBERT	1820	ORNG	WARW	654
SOUTHERLAND, WILLIAM	1820	ORNG	CORN	707
SOUTHERLAND, WILLIAM	1830	COLU	CHAT	39
SOUW	1810	ULST	ROCH	785
SPACK, NICHOLAS	1820	SCNE	WD02	568
SPACK, SUSAN	1820	SCNE	WD01	559
SPADER, ANTHONY	1830	KING	WD04	298
SPADES, JAMES	1830	QUEN	SHEM	67
SPAIN, ASIA	1830	NYCO	WD05	288
SPAK, NICHOLAS	1810	SCNE	WD01	933
SPARKS, ROBERT	1820	NYCO	WD06	454
SPARKS, SOPHIA	1820	NYCO	WD06	525
SPAUCK, JOHN	1830	SCNE	WD02	219
SPAUK, OLAS	1810	SCNE	WD01	938
SPEARMAN, NICHOLAS	1830	MONT	JOHN	205
SPECK, ABRAHAM	1800	ABNY	WATV	96
SPECK, ABRAHAM	1820	SARA	MILT	236
SPECK, CATHARINE	1790	ABNY	SCNE	44
SPECK, MARGEY	1790	ABNY	SCNE	44
SPECK, PETER	1800	ABNY	WATV	89
SPECKERMAN, PETER	1800	COLU	CLAV	1217
SPEDER, MRS.	1830	KING	WD04	313
SPEEDER, FRANCIS	1830	KING	WD04	316
SPEEDER, HENRY	1830	NYCO	WD08	140
SPENCER, BEN	1810	NYCO	WD06	425
SPENCER, CATO	1800	NYCO	WD03	708
SPENCER, JAMES	1830	NYCO	WD10	110
SPENCER, MICHAEL	1830	ABNY	COEY	503
SPENCER, ROBERT	1830	ABNY	GUID	407
SPENCER, ----	1810	ONTA	SENE	842
SPENSER, DANIEL	1830	NYCO	WD11	147
SPIDER, AND.	1820	KING	BRYN	141
SPIKERMAN, AUGUSTUS	1830	COLU	STUY	69
SPINIER, CATO	1810	NYCO	WD07	535
SPINSER, PHILLIS	1800	NYCO	WD07	878
SPOOR, SIMON	1830	GREN	COXE	188
SPOOX, HARRY	1830	ABNY	WD05	342
SPRAGER, ELEAZER	1820	PUTM	SOUT	100
SPRINGFIELD, COZER	1830	KING	WD04	309
SPRINGFIELD, ZERAH	1820	KING	BRYN	118
SPRINGSTEAD, RICHARD	1830	ABNY	COEY	513
SPRINGSTED, JOHN	1830	ABNY	WD02	239
SPRINGSTEEL, GEORGE	1810	NYCO	WD02	113
SPRINGSTEEN, THOMAS	1830	QUEN	NEWT	2
SPRINGSTREET, JOHN	1830	ABNY	WD02	245
SPUR, PETER	1830	DUTC	PGKP	322

NAME	YR	CO	TWP	PG
SPURR, PETER	1820	DUTC	PGKP	97
SQUIRE	1790	QUEN	OYST	155
SQUIRE	1800	QUEN	FLUS	540
SQUIRE, ISMAL	1830	QUEN	SHEM	78
SQUIRES, CHARLES	1820	QUEN	----	3
SQUIRES, CHARLES	1830	QUEN	OYST	27
SQUIRES, JOSEPH	1800	NYCO	WD05	782
SQUIRES, LOUIS	1820	QUEN	----	7
SQUIRES, PETER	1820	QUEN	----	7
SQUIRES, PETER	1830	QUEN	SHEM	78
SQUIRES, WILLIAM	1830	ONON	SALI	32
SREIK, ABRAHAM	1800	ABNY	SCNE	8
STAATS, RICHARD	1830	ABNY	WD04	299
STANFORD, JAMES	1830	NYCO	WD13	343
STANFORD, NICHOLAS	1830	NYCO	WD13	339
STANGHTON, PHEBE	1830	NYCO	WD14	435
STANLEY, PETER	1830	ONTA	CANA	115
STANSLEY, PETO	1820	ONTA	PALM	341
STANSON, EVERETT	1790	ABNY	WATV	52
STANTON, AARON	1820	KING	WATA	159
STANTON, J.	1830	NYCO	WD13	369
STANTON, THOMAS	1830	MADI	----	327
STANTON, THOMAS	1830	NYCO	WD04	228
STAPLE, PHOEBE	1830	NYCO	WD01	36
STAPLES, PHEBE	1800	NYCO	WD04	734
STAR, OLIVER	1820	WEST	NORS	382
STARE, STEPHEN	1810	WEST	SUMM	1038
STARES, ARCHOBALL	1820	WEST	NORS	383
STARES, OLIVER	1830	SULL	THOM	72
STARES, RACHEL	1830	SULL	THOM	71
STARLING	1820	ROCK	CLAK	92
STATE, POMPY	1810	NYCO	WD08	716
STATES, JOHN	1830	WEST	YORK	167
STATIA, MARY	1810	NYCO	WD05	353
STATTS, PETER	1810	COLU	CLAV	158
STATTS, PETER	1830	COLU	STUY	63
STAUNCH, BENJAMIN	1830	QUEN	OYST	47
STEARNS, M.	1830	NYCO	WD11	237
STEBBINS, ANTHONY	1830	DUTC	PAWL	288
STEBBINS, HARRY	1830	WEST	SUMM	183
STEBBINS, PETER	1830	NYCO	WD06	407
STEDLE, JOHN	1820	PUTM	SOUT	100
STEDWELL, JOHN	1830	PUTM	SOUT	50
STEEL, DAVID	1820	SUFF	HUNT	274
STEEL, DAVID	1830	SUFF	HUNT	310
STEEL, GEORGE	1810	SUFF	HUNT	505
STEEL, GEORGE	1820	SUFF	HUNT	274
STEEL, GEORGE	1830	SUFF	HUNT	304
STEEL, PRINCE	1830	WEST	NORS	84

NAME	YR	CO	TWP	PG
STEEL, TOM	1790	QUEN	FLUS	149
STEELE, SARAH	1830	NYCO	WD08	214
STEINBURGH, ROBERT	1830	COLU	GALA	232
STEN	1800	SUFF	RIVH	18
STEP, AMOS	1830	SUFF	RIVH	245
STEPENNY, TOM	1790	QUEN	FLUS	149
STEPHEN	1790	QUEN	NHEM	152
STEPHEN	1790	QUEN	NHEM	153
STEPHEN	1790	QUEN	NHEM	155
STEPHEN	1790	QUEN	OYST	155
STEPHEN	1800	QUEN	JAMA	545
STEPHEN	1800	QUEN	OYST	575
STEPHEN	1800	QUEN	SHEM	559
STEPHEN	1800	QUEN	SHEM	67
STEPHEN	1800	SUFF	SMIT	55
STEPHEN	1820	QUEN	----	61
STEPHEN, SAMPSON	1810	SUFF	ISLP	498
STEPHEN, TOM	1790	QUEN	NHEM	153
STEPHENS	1810	NYCO	WD07	550
STEPHENS	1820	PUTM	PATE	101
STEPHENS, EDWARD	1820	ROCK	CLAK	98
STEPHENS, FANNY	1830	NYCO	WD09	301
STEPHENS, HANNAH	1810	QUEN	OYST	256
STEPHENS, JAMES	1810	NYCO	WD05	255
STEPHENS, JOE	1830	NYCO	WD09	391
STEPHENS, JOHN	1830	ORNG	BLOM	119
STEPHENS, JOHN	1830	ORNG	GOSH	275
STEPHENS, MOSES	1830	WEST	NEWR	113
STEPHENS, NICHOLAS	1820	NYCO	WD07	705
STEPHENS, NICHOLAS	1830	NYCO	WD14	473
STEPHENS, PLATO	1830	ABNY	WATV	464
STEPHENS, R.	1810	MADI	SMIT	879
STEPHENS, RICHARD	1830	MADI	----	416
STEPHENS, WILLIAM	1830	WEST	NEWR	109
STERIP, W.	1830	NYCO	WD10	26
STERLING, NICHOLAS	1830	ROCK	HVER	150
STERNBERGH, CEASAR	1820	SCHR	SCHR	468
STERNBERGS, SAMUEL	1830	SCHR	SCHR	20
STEVE	1790	QUEN	NHEM	152
STEVEN, WILLIAM	1800	NYCO	WD06	811
STEVENS, DANIEL	1790	QUEN	OYST	154
STEVENS, EDWARD	1830	NYCO	WD09	312
STEVENS, HENRY	1800	NYCO	WD06	814
STEVENS, HENRY	1830	NYCO	WD07	56
STEVENS, HENRY	1830	NYCO	WD08	173
STEVENS, HORACE	1800	NYCO	WD05	765
STEVENS, JACK	1830	WEST	EAST	132
STEVENS, JAMES	1830	NYCO	WD07	58
STEVENS, JAMES	1830	NYCO	WD09	416

NAME	YR	CO	TWP	PG
STEVENS, JOHN	1800	NYCO	WD05	722
STEVENS, JOHN	1820	NYCO	WD04	261
STEVENS, MALIA	1800	ORNG	NEWW	293
STEVENS, MARTIN	1810	MONT	FLOR	35
STEVENS, MARTIN	1820	SCNE	WD01	561
STEVENS, PETER	1820	NYCO	WD09	912
STEVENS, PLATO	1810	QUEN	NHEM	304
STEVENS, REUBIN	1800	NYCO	WD06	840
STEVENS, REUBIN	1810	NYCO	WD06	435
STEVENS, RICHARD	1820	MADI	SMIT	46
STEVENSON, ANTHONY	1810	NYCO	WD05	330
STEVENSON, J.	1830	NYCO	WD11	179
STEVENSON, JARED	1820	DUTC	CLNT	40
STEVENSON, JOHN H.	1830	NYCO	WD06	451
STEVENSON, PETER	1800	NYCO	WD06	925
STEVENSON, PHEBE	1800	NYCO	WD06	842
STEVES, LOTT	1830	RENS	SCHO	250
STEVINS, JOHN	1830	NYCO	WD06	437
STEVINSON, HARRY	1810	NYCO	WD03	93
STEVINSON, PETER	1830	RICH	CAST	47
STEWARD, GEORGE	1820	ONID	UTIC	208
STEWARD, PETER	1830	KING	BUSH	386
STEWART, ANN	1820	NYCO	WD06	528
STEWART, ANTHONY	1820	OTSG	BUTT	52
STEWART, ANTHONY	1830	OTSG	BUTT	336
STEWART, AUSTIN	1820	ONTA	BTON	165
STEWART, AUSTIN	1830	MONR	BRIG	14
STEWART, BENJAMIN	1820	NYCO	WD06	456
STEWART, CATHERINE	1820	DUTC	MILA	80
STEWART, CHARLES	1830	NYCO	WD05	262
STEWART, DAVID	1830	ONID	UTIC	15
STEWART, GARISON	1830	NYCO	WD12	298
STEWART, GEORGE	1800	NYCO	WD01	663
STEWART, GEORGE	1800	NYCO	WD06	827
STEWART, GEORGE	1820	ONID	UTIC	208
STEWART, GEORGE	1830	ONID	UTIC	6
STEWART, HENRY	1810	NYCO	WD06	424
STEWART, JACOB	1830	NYCO	WD01	35
STEWART, JAMES	1830	NYCO	WD06	424
STEWART, JAMES	1830	NYCO	WD12	271
STEWART, JOHN G.	1830	ABNY	WD01	212
STEWART, N.	1830	NYCO	WD11	159
STEWART, WILLIAM	1830	KING	WD02	258
STEWART, ZACHARIAH	1810	NYCO	WD06	425
STICO, WILLIAM	1820	OSWE	VOLN	62
STILE, AMOS	1820	DUTC	PAUL	95
STILES, CAROLINE	1830	ULST	SHAW	250
STILES, STACY	1830	NYCO	WD01	40
STILL, ELIZABETH	1820	ORNG	MONT	808

NAME	YR	CO	TWP	PG
STILL, GRACE	1810	DUTC	DOVE	74
STILL, SOPHIA	1810	ORNG	MONT	965
STILWELL, THOMAS	1830	NYCO	WD10	6
STOCKBRIDGE, SILAS	1830	NYCO	WD09	430
STOKELY, DAVID	1830	NYCO	WD07	29
STOKES, FRANCIS	1830	NYCO	WD14	448
STOKES, JOHN	1830	NYCO	WD08	257
STONE, HECTOR	1800	NYCO	WD06	835
STONE, MR.	1830	NYCO	WD06	451
STONES, ABRAHAM	1820	DUTC	MILA	78
STOOP, THOMAS	1830	ORNG	CORN	201
STORMS, POMP	1830	WEST	BEDF	151
STORMS, POMPI	1820	WEST	BEDF	410
STORTS, ABRAHAM	1830	DUTC	DOVE	214
STORUM, JOHN	1830	CHAT	BUST	267
STORUM, WILLIAM	1830	CHAT	BUST	267
STORUMS, CHARLES	1820	JEFF	HOUN	417
STORY, SAMUEL	1810	HERK	WARR	463
STORY, SAMUEL	1820	ONTA	RICH	38
STORY, SAMUEL	1830	LIVI	GROV	35
STOUGHTON, MARY	1830	NYCO	WD05	339
STOUGHTON, W.	1820	NYCO	WD05	418
STOUT, ACUON	1830	TOMP	HECT	426
STOUT, LEVINA	1820	WEST	HARR	470
STOUT, NATHANIEL	1830	NYCO	WD10	78
STOUT, PHILIP	1830	TOMP	HECT	426
STOUT, TINGO	1830	RENS	PITT	136
STOUT, ZING	1810	WEST	HARR	1131
STOUTENBURGH, JOHN	1790	DUTC	WASH	94
STOW, LEVI	1830	SUFF	EAST	259
STRANG, ROBERT	1830	WEST	MTPL	45
STRAS, STEPHEN	1800	DUTC	PAWL	53
STREET, JAMES D.	1830	NYCO	WD14	466
STREVER, JOSEPH	1830	DUTC	STAN	405
STRINGER, MINGS	1830	NYCO	WD06	437
STRINGHAM	1820	ESEX	ELIZ	416
STRINGHAM, THOMAS	1830	KING	WD04	303
STRONG, ABEL	1830	SUFF	BROK	173
STRONG, CHARLES	1830	SUFF	ISLP	282
STRONG, DENNIS	1830	ORNG	BLOM	116
STRONG, EPHRAIGHM	1830	SUFF	ISLP	285
STRONG, FABIAS	1820	ORNG	MONR	673
STRONG, JAMES	1830	ORNG	BLOM	117
STRONG, JOHN	1820	ONID	WEST	218
STRONG, JOHN	1820	ONID	UTIC	218
STRUBERS, JANE	1810	NYCO	WD06	424
STRUTINE, JACOB	1800	NYCO	WD06	799
STUARD, CHARLES	1830	NYCO	WD10	98
STUARD, WILEY	1830	NYCO	WD10	117

NAME	YR	CO	TWP	PG
STUARD, WILLIAM	1830	NYCO	WD10	116
STUART, CESAR	1830	BROM	UNON	38
STUART, CHARLES	1830	NYCO	WD06	375
STUART, CHARLES	1830	NYCO	WD06	458
STUART, GEORGE	1810	NYCO	WD05	298
STUART, HARVEY	1820	HERK	DANU	90
STUART, JOSEPH	1820	OTSG	OTSG	97
STUDDER, JAMES	1830	WEST	PELH	115
STUKELY, JACK	1830	NYCO	WD08	246
STUKES, JAICK	1820	WEST	YERK	340
STURGES, JOHNATHAN	1830	NYCO	WD14	495
SUCUS, HARRY	1820	STEU	BATH	227
SUDAM, HARRY	1830	ULST	KING	67
SUE	1810	ROCK	CLAR	685
SUITS, JOHN	1820	MONT	JOHN	376
SUITS, PETER	1830	HERK	HERK	52
SULLIVAN, DAVID	1830	ORNG	WARW	72
SULLIVAN, JAMES	1830	QUEN	NHEM	110
SULLIVAN, JOB	1820	NYCO	WD06	467
SULLIVAN, JOB	1830	NYCO	WD05	299
SULLIVAN, JOSEPH	1810	NYCO	WD04	177
SUMMERVILLE, HENRY	1810	NYCO	WD05	323
SUMMOVER, BETSY	1810	NYCO	WD05	356
SUNLEY, JOHN	1830	ERIE	HAMB	155
SUORE, ROBERT	1810	NYCO	WD07	531
SURREY, ANDREW	1830	NYCO	WD14	434
SUSAN	1800	NYCO	WD06	805
SUSAN	1800	NYCO	WD06	822
SUSAN	1830	GREN	CATS	237
SUSAN, BLACK	1830	MONT	JOHN	191
SUSAN, PETER	1810	ONON	MANL	553
SUSAN, PETER	1820	ONON	SALI	253
SUSANNA	1790	QUEN	OYST	154
SUSANNA	1800	ABNY	SCNE	8
SUSANNA	1800	ABNY	SCNE	9
SUSANNA	1800	ABNY	WD03	293
SUSANNAH	1790	QUEN	NEWT	151
SUSANNAH	1800	NYCO	WD01	660
SUSSEX, STEPHEN	1830	NYCO	WD08	244
SUTBAN, TITUS	1830	ONID	ROME	394
SUTLIFF, ALEXANDER	1830	NYCO	WD08	131
SUTTEN, JOHN	1830	NYCO	WD14	438
SUTTER, ISAAC	1820	SUFF	RIVH	366
SUTTON, GILBERT	1830	WEST	SCAR	78
SUTTON, JOHN	1830	ORNG	MONR	176
SUTTON, LEW	1810	QUEN	NHEM	210
SUTTON, LOUIS	1820	QUEN	----	65
SUTZ, YORK	1830	MONT	JOHN	191
SUZAN	1800	NYCO	WD05	753

NAME	YR	CO	TWP	PG
SWAIN, CALEB	1810	NYCO	WD05	320
SWAN, ELISHA	1810	RENS	PITT	396
SWAN, HENRY	1830	DUTC	FISH	494
SWAN, JOHN	1830	MONR	RWD3	223
SWAN, NERO	1810	SARA	GALW	826
SWAN, ROBERT	1810	DUTC	BEEK	270
SWAN, ROBERT	1820	DUTC	BEEK	17
SWAN, ROBERT	1820	DUTC	BEEK	15
SWANN, NERO	1790	ABNY	HOSS	31
SWARROW, JOSEPH	1810	DUTC	BEEK	280
SWART, JOHN	1810	DUTC	FISH	250
SWART, JOHN	1830	DELA	KORT	112
SWART, JOSEPH	1820	SARA	STIL	191
SWARTOUT, JOHN	1830	ORNG	DEER	4
SWARTOUT, POMPEY	1830	ORNG	DEER	4
SWARTWONT, THOMAS	1800	DUTC	AMEN	44
SWARTWORET, JACK	1820	ORNG	DEER	658
SWATTS, JOHN	1830	CAYU	AUBN	171
SWATWOOD, DISMALL	1830	MONR	PERT	74
SWEEZY, RICHARD	1830	CHAT	BUST	283
SWIFT, POMPEY	1800	DUTC	WASH	100
SWIFT, WILLIAM TITUS	1830	COLU	HUDS	106
SYDNEY, JOSEPH	1800	NYCO	WD01	667
SYKES, JAMES	1830	NYCO	WD09	307
SYKES, JAMES	1830	ONID	FLOR	360
SYLVA, DRAPER	1830	NYCO	WD04	197
SYLVAN, CHARLES	1830	NYCO	WD08	224
SYLVANUS	1790	QUEN	OYST	154
SYLVESTER	1790	QUEN	FLUS	149
SYLVESTER	1790	QUEN	JAMA	150
SYLVESTER, ROSANNA	1820	WASH	SALE	186
SYLVIA	1790	NYCO	EAST	118
SYLVIA	1790	NYCO	WEST	135
SYLVIA, JOHN	1830	NYCO	WD13	345
SYMOR, WILLIAM	1810	NYCO	WD06	419
SYRUS	1800	QUEN	OYST	574
TAB	1790	QUEN	NHEM	152
TAB	1790	QUEN	SHEM	156
TABOR, JETHRO	1790	DUTC	PAWL	87
TACK, THOMAS	1830	ULST	MARB	165
TAIT, JOHN	1820	NYCO	WD06	452
TALBERT, LEVY	1830	NYCO	WD10	102
TALBOT, ABSALEM	1830	ONON	ONON	192
TALEBUSY, ASU	1820	CHEN	PLYM	324
TALK, D'AVIN	1790	ULST	MARB	174
TALLMAN, ELIZA	1820	DUTC	STAN	135
TALLMAN, HARVEY	1830	DUTC	BEEK	188

NAME	YR	CO	TWP	PG
TALLMAN, JAMES	1810	NYCO	WD05	277
TALLMAN, JANE	1830	DUTC	DOVE	218
TALLMAN, LEWIS	1820	DUTC	PAUL	92
TALLMAN, LEWIS	1830	DUTC	PAWL	282
TALLMAN, SANFORD	1810	DUTC	DOVE	110
TALLOW, JONNET	1820	NYCO	WD02	97
TALMAN, LEWIS	1790	DUTC	PAWL	88
TALMAN, LOUIS	1800	DUTC	PAWL	57
TALON, SAMUEL	1810	NYCO	WD07	550
TALUUS, ELLENOR	1800	NYCO	WD06	839
TAM, TOM	1810	QUEN	FLUS	202
TAMBELSON, HENRY	1810	NYCO	WD07	553
TANKARD, GEORGE	1830	CLNT	PLAT	263
TANKARD, MARY	1800	ORNG	NEWW	290
TANKARD, RICHARD	1810	NYCO	WD06	460
TANNER, AARON	1830	RENS	NASS	311
TANNER, QUAM	1810	RENS	PETE	348
TANNER, QUAUN	1800	RENS	HOOS	758
TANNER, THOMAS	1830	RENS	LANS	89
TANSTY, LUCY	1820	NYCO	WD10	988
TAP, JOHN	1800	ABNY	WD01	266
TAP, MICHAEL	1830	KING	WD02	277
TAPPAN, JOHN	1830	TOMP	ITCA	332
TAPPIN, MOSES	1830	ONTA	CANA	112
TAPPIN, R.	1830	NYCO	WD11	134
TAR & TAITT	1820	ULST	SHAW	67
TARSON, CHARLES	1830	NYCO	WD14	463
TATE, JOHN	1830	TOMP	ITCA	332
TATE, JOHNATHAN T.	1830	NYCO	WD09	370
TATE, PHEBE	1830	NYCO	WD05	354
TATE, THOMAS	1830	WEST	CORT	60
TAUPSUM, JANE	1820	NYCO	WD09	909
TAYLOR, ANTONIO	1810	NYCO	WD06	419
TAYLOR, BENJAMIN	1830	NYCO	WD07	108
TAYLOR, BILL	1810	COLU	CANN	101
TAYLOR, CHARLES	1830	CAYU	GENO	289
TAYLOR, JACOB	1820	ORNG	GOSH	756
TAYLOR, JOHN	1820	MADI	LEBN	70
TAYLOR, JOHN	1820	ONTA	ONTA	139
TAYLOR, JOHN	1830	NYCO	WD06	377
TAYLOR, JOHN	1830	NYCO	WD08	204
TAYLOR, JOHN	1830	NYCO	WD13	336
TAYLOR, JOHN	1830	RICH	SOUT	19
TAYLOR, JOHN	1830	SENE	WLOO	3
TAYLOR, JOSEPH	1830	NYCO	WD06	380
TAYLOR, JOSEPH	1830	NYCO	WD06	430
TAYLOR, M.L.	1830	ERIE	BUFF	30
TAYLOR, PETER	1820	PUTM	SOUT	100
TAYLOR, PRINCE	1820	ESEX	TICO	30

NAME	YR	CO	TWP	PG
TAYLOR, PRINN	1820	ESEX	SCON	451
TAYLOR, RICHARD	1830	MADI	----	354
TAYLOR, ROBERT	1810	NYCO	WD03	88
TAYLOR, SAMUEL	1820	NYCO	WD02	97
TAYLOR, SAMUEL	1830	NYCO	WD06	380
TAYLOR, THOMAS	1800	NYCO	WD06	850
TAYLOR, THOMAS	1810	NYCO	WD03	82
TAYLOR, THOMAS	1820	NYCO	WD09	916
TAYLOR, WILLIAM	1820	COLU	CHAT	21
TAYLOR, WILLIAM	1820	NYCO	WD04	216
TAYLOR, WILLIAM	1830	COLU	CHAT	49
TAYLOR, WILLIAM	1830	COLU	HUDS	112
TAYLOR, WILLIAM	1830	NYCO	WD06	462
TEABOUT, DANIAL	1830	MONT	JOHN	185
TEABOUT, MOSES	1830	SCHR	SCHR	15
TEABOUT, PETER	1830	MONT	JOHN	186
TEABOUT, TOM	1830	SCHR	SCHR	31
TEASMAN, JOHN	1800	NYCO	WD06	837
TEASMAN, JOHN	1810	NYCO	WD05	279
TEBERA, SYLVERA	1830	ABNY	WD02	246
TED	1790	SUFF	SOUT	169
TELMAN, JACOB	1820	NYCO	WD03	144
TEMPERANCE	1790	QUEN	OYST	153
TEMPERANCE	1800	SUFF	SHAM	72
TEN BROECK, ANTHONY	1830	ULST	KING	64
TEN BROECK, JACK	1830	COLU	GALA	264
TEN BROECK, JACOB JR.	1830	COLU	CLAV	73
TEN BROECK, POMP	1830	COLU	HUDS	99
TEN BROECK, SAMUEL	1830	ULST	KING	64
TEN BROEK, THOMAS	1830	GREN	CATS	228
TEN EYCK, ANTHONY	1830	ABNY	BETH	528
TEN EYCK, BETSEY	1830	SCNE	WD02	223
TEN EYCK, CHARLES	1830	ABNY	COEY	513
TEN EYCK, HARRY	1830	GREN	COXE	183
TEN EYCK, HENRY	1830	ULST	SAUG	96
TEN EYCK, RICHARD	1830	ULST	HURL	146
TEN EYCK, THOMAS	1820	SCNE	WD02	572
TEN EYCK, WILLIAM	1830	GREN	COXE	183
TEN EYK, THOMAS	1830	GREN	CAIR	255
TENBROOK, FRANCES	1820	NYCO	WD05	396
TENBROUCH, NINO	1820	COLU	HUDS	34
TENSY	1800	QUEN	FLUS	542
TENT, CHARLES	1820	PUTM	SOUT	100
TENYCK, CEASER	1820	ONON	ONON	218
TERREL, JOHN	1830	ABNY	GUID	403
TERREY, BITHIAH	1790	SUFF	SOUT	169
TERREY, JULIUS	1830	JEFF	HOUN	178
TERRY	1800	QUEN	OYST	568
TERRY, BARNABAS	1820	SUFF	SOUT	346

NAME	YR	CO	TWP	PG
TERRY, JOHN	1830	RENS	SCAS	109
TERRY, JULIUS	1820	JEFF	HOUN	417
TERRY, MARGARET	1830	ULST	KING	72
TERRY, PRINCE	1810	ULST	KING	745
TEWAN, BENJAMIN	1800	QUEN	NHEM	554
TEWAN, PRINCE	1800	QUEN	NHEM	554
THELE, PRINCE	1810	WEST	RYE	1164
THEODORE, ADONIS	1830	NYCO	WD06	389
THEW, MORRIS	1830	ORNG	HBGH	130
THOM, PRIMUS	1810	QUEN	NHEM	211
THOMAS	1790	NYCO	MONT	120
THOMAS	1790	NYCO	MONT	121
THOMAS	1790	NYCO	NORT	125
THOMAS	1790	NYCO	WEST	133
THOMAS	1790	QUEN	OYST	153
THOMAS	1800	NYCO	WD07	878
THOMAS	1800	QUEN	OYST	576
THOMAS	1800	SUFF	ISLP	61
THOMAS	1810	DUTC	STAN	180
THOMAS	1820	DUTC	CLNT	32
THOMAS	1820	NIAG	BUFF	78
THOMAS	1820	QUEN	----	20
THOMAS	1820	QUEN	----	54
THOMAS	1820	QUEN	----	72
THOMAS	1820	RICH	WEST	702
THOMAS, A.	1830	KING	WD01	246
THOMAS, ABRAHAM	1820	DELA	MASO	78
THOMAS, ABRAHAM	1830	COLU	STUY	60
THOMAS, ABRAM	1830	LEWI	BRAN	435
THOMAS, ANDREW	1820	COLU	AUST	15
THOMAS, ANDREW	1830	SARA	HALF	81
THOMAS, BELLA	1800	NYCO	WD05	778
THOMAS, BENJAMIN	1830	NYCO	WD04	197
THOMAS, BETSEY	1820	NYCO	WD07	628
THOMAS, CATHERINE	1800	NYCO	WD08	237
THOMAS, CHARLOTTE	1830	NYCO	WD06	435
THOMAS, DANIEL	1830	NYCO	WD04	228
THOMAS, DAVID	1830	LEWI	BRAN	435
THOMAS, EUNICE	1830	NYCO	WD05	300
THOMAS, HARRY	1830	MONT	CANJ	32
THOMAS, HARRY	1830	OTSG	OTSG	63
THOMAS, HARRY	1830	SUFF	SOUT	350
THOMAS, HENRY	1820	NYCO	WD10	990
THOMAS, HENRY	1820	SUFF	SHEL	329
THOMAS, HENRY	1830	NYCO	WD06	427
THOMAS, HENRY	1830	NYCO	WD11	197
THOMAS, HENRY	1830	RENS	TROY	7
THOMAS, ISAAC	1820	NYCO	WD04	307
THOMAS, ISAAC	1820	NYCO	WD08	758

NAME	YR	CO	TWP	PG
THOMAS, J.	1830	NYCO	WD02	77
THOMAS, JACK	1790	QUEN	FLUS	150
THOMAS, JACOB	1800	NYCO	WD04	721
THOMAS, JACOB	1810	NYCO	WD03	82
THOMAS, JACOB	1810	NYCO	WD03	85
THOMAS, JACOB	1820	NYCO	WD02	118
THOMAS, JACOB	1830	NYCO	WD10	21
THOMAS, JACOB	1830	NYCO	WD14	457
THOMAS, JAMES	1800	NYCO	WD07	865
THOMAS, JAMES	1810	NYCO	WD08	713
THOMAS, JAMES	1810	NYCO	WD08	213
THOMAS, JAMES	1810	NYCO	WD08	717
THOMAS, JAMES	1820	NYCO	WD06	529
THOMAS, JAMES	1830	KING	WD01	247
THOMAS, JAMES	1830	NYCO	WD06	379
THOMAS, JEREMIAH	1830	ULST	WAWA	200
THOMAS, JOB	1820	NYCO	WD07	636
THOMAS, JOHN	1800	NYCO	WD05	757
THOMAS, JOHN	1800	NYCO	WD06	831
THOMAS, JOHN	1800	NYCO	WD07	910
THOMAS, JOHN	1810	NYCO	WD05	310
THOMAS, JOHN	1810	NYCO	WD06	414
THOMAS, JOHN	1810	NYCO	WD07	535
THOMAS, JOHN	1810	NYCO	WD07	549
THOMAS, JOHN	1820	NYCO	WD06	515
THOMAS, JOHN	1820	NYCO	WD06	544
THOMAS, JOHN	1820	NYCO	WD10	1068
THOMAS, JOHN	1820	ONTA	VICT	327
THOMAS, JOHN	1830	ABNY	WD02	261
THOMAS, JOHN	1830	KING	WD01	252
THOMAS, JOHN	1830	NYCO	WD01	17
THOMAS, JOHN	1830	NYCO	WD04	159
THOMAS, JOHN	1830	NYCO	WD04	185
THOMAS, JOHN	1830	NYCO	WD10	116
THOMAS, JOHN	1830	NYCO	WD11	133
THOMAS, JOHN	1830	STEU	BATH	269
THOMAS, JOHNATHAN	1830	NYCO	WD09	417
THOMAS, JOSEPH	1830	DUTC	FISH	477
THOMAS, JOSEPH S.	1830	CLNT	BEEK	283
THOMAS, JOSOPH S.	1820	CLNT	PLAT	472
THOMAS, MANUEL	1810	NYCO	WD05	271
THOMAS, MARY	1810	NYCO	WD06	420
THOMAS, MICHAEL	1800	NYCO	WD04	742
THOMAS, MOSES	1800	SARA	MILT	1062
THOMAS, NANCY	1830	ABNY	WD01	197
THOMAS, PETER	1800	DUTC	RHIN	158
THOMAS, PETER	1810	DUTC	RHIN	372
THOMAS, PETER	1830	DUTC	REDH	381
THOMAS, PHILIP	1830	ORNG	MINI	265

Thomas

NAME	YR	CO	TWP	PG
THOMAS, PLATO	1830	NYCO	WD08	248
THOMAS, PRINCE	1810	SUFF	SHAM	447
THOMAS, RICHARD	1800	NYCO	WD07	861
THOMAS, RICHARD	1810	NYCO	WD02	124
THOMAS, RICHARD	1820	NYCO	WD02	108
THOMAS, RICHARD	1830	LEWI	BRAN	435
THOMAS, RICHARD	1830	NYCO	WD10	83
THOMAS, RICHARD	1830	NYCO	WD14	437
THOMAS, S.	1830	NYCO	WD11	156
THOMAS, SAM	1800	RENS	TROY	899
THOMAS, SILVEY	1820	NYCO	WD04	236
THOMAS, SIMON	1810	NYCO	WD03	68
THOMAS, SIMON	1820	NYCO	WD05	332
THOMAS, SUSAN	1830	NYCO	WD10	46
THOMAS, THOMAS	1810	KING	BYKN	628
THOMAS, THOMAS	1810	NYCO	WD04	204
THOMAS, THOMAS	1810	SCNE	WD01	940
THOMAS, THOMAS	1810	SCNE	WD02	953
THOMAS, THOMAS	1820	SCNE	WD02	572
THOMAS, TOM	1810	NYCO	WD05	277
THOMAS, W. CO.	1830	NYCO	WD13	396
THOMAS, WILLIAM	1800	NYCO	WD05	771
THOMAS, WILLIAM	1800	NYCO	WD06	849
THOMAS, WILLIAM	1810	NYCO	WD03	81
THOMAS, WILLIAM	1810	NYCO	WD05	285
THOMAS, WILLIAM	1820	NYCO	WD01	17
THOMAS, WILLIAM	1820	NYCO	WD02	108
THOMAS, WILLIAM	1820	NYCO	WD06	520
THOMAS, WILLIAM	1820	NYCO	WD10	1054
THOMAS, WILLIAM	1820	NYCO	WD08	807
THOMAS, WILLIAM	1830	NYCO	WD05	342
THOMAS, WILLIAM	1830	NYCO	WD08	174
THOMAS, WILLIAM	1830	NYCO	WD10	21
THOMPKINS, ISAAC	1820	WEST	NORC	429
THOMPKINS, JOHN	1820	PUTM	PHIL	101
THOMPKINS, LEONARD	1820	WEST	NORC	442
THOMPSON	1810	NYCO	WD07	550
THOMPSON	1830	KING	GRAV	405
THOMPSON	1830	NYCO	WD09	358
THOMPSON, ABRAHAM	1800	NYCO	WD07	848
THOMPSON, ABRAHAM	1820	NIAG	NIAG	215
THOMPSON, ABRAHAM	1820	NIAG	NIAG	227
THOMPSON, ABRAHAM	1820	NYCO	WD06	498
THOMPSON, ABRAHAM	1830	DUTC	MILN	258
THOMPSON, ABRAHAM	1830	KING	WD03	287
THOMPSON, ABRAM	1830	HERK	LTFA	91
THOMPSON, ACHILLES	1830	SUFF	BROK	172
THOMPSON, AMOS	1830	KING	WD05	331
THOMPSON, ANTHONY	1830	KING	BUSH	379

NAME	YR	CO	TWP	PG
THOMPSON, ANTHONY	1830	NYCO	WD08	190
THOMPSON, BELINDA	1830	ABNY	WD01	212
THOMPSON, CAROLINE	1830	SUFF	EAST	259
THOMPSON, CATHERINE	1820	NIAG	MTPL	250
THOMPSON, CESAR	1830	NYCO	WD14	462
THOMPSON, CHARITY	1820	ABNY	ABNY	204
THOMPSON, CHARLES	1800	NYCO	WD05	754
THOMPSON, CHARLES	1800	NYCO	WD07	916
THOMPSON, CHARLES	1830	MONT	AMST	114
THOMPSON, CHRISTOPHER	1830	NYCO	WD06	444
THOMPSON, CHRISTOPHER	1830	RENS	BRUN	223
THOMPSON, CORNELIUS	1810	KING	BKYN	632
THOMPSON, DANIEL	1830	NYCO	WD08	213
THOMPSON, DANIEL	1830	OSWE	OSWE	135
THOMPSON, DANIEL W.	1830	ONID	AMIS	343
THOMPSON, DAVID	1810	NYCO	WD05	256
THOMPSON, DAVID	1830	NYCO	WD05	334
THOMPSON, DIANA	1830	NYCO	WD01	35
THOMPSON, EDMUND	1830	NYCO	WD10	42
THOMPSON, EDWARD	1830	KING	FLAT	398
THOMPSON, EDWARD	1830	NYCO	WD08	240
THOMPSON, EDWARD	1830	NYCO	WD08	248
THOMPSON, ELIZA	1830	ALLE	ANGE	8
THOMPSON, ELIZABETH	1790	KING	NEUT	98
THOMPSON, ELIZABETH	1810	KING	NEUT	667
THOMPSON, ELIZABETH	1820	DUTC	PGKP	98
THOMPSON, ELIZABETH	1830	DUTC	PGKP	327
THOMPSON, ELLEN	1830	NYCO	WD08	175
THOMPSON, EZEKEL	1830	NYCO	WD10	78
THOMPSON, FRANCES	1800	NYCO	WD07	896
THOMPSON, FRANCIS	1830	KING	WD04	313
THOMPSON, FRANCIS	1830	NYCO	WD14	462
THOMPSON, FRANK	1830	COLU	AUST	181
THOMPSON, G.	1830	NYCO	WD13	375
THOMPSON, GEORGE	1810	NYCO	WD07	574
THOMPSON, GRAEL	1810	NYCO	WD05	271
THOMPSON, H.C.	1820	KING	BRYN	112
THOMPSON, H.C.	1830	KING	BUSH	387
THOMPSON, H.H.	1820	NYCO	WD07	621
THOMPSON, H.L.	1820	NYCO	WD07	712
THOMPSON, HANNAH	1830	NYCO	WD08	220
THOMPSON, HENRIETTA	1830	RENS	TROY	14
THOMPSON, HENRY	1810	KING	BKYN	632
THOMPSON, HENRY	1820	KING	BRYN	126
THOMPSON, HENRY	1820	KING	BRYN	186
THOMPSON, HENRY	1830	ABNY	WD01	224
THOMPSON, HENRY	1830	DUTC	REDH	380
THOMPSON, HENRY	1830	KING	FLAN	412
THOMPSON, HENRY	1830	RENS	BRUN	208

Thompson

NAME	YR	CO	TWP	PG
THOMPSON, HENRY	1830	RENS	SCHO	256
THOMPSON, HENRY	1830	RICH	CAST	45
THOMPSON, HENRY C.	1830	KING	WD03	280
THOMPSON, ISAAC	1830	RENS	BRUN	223
THOMPSON, ISACC	1830	NYCO	WD14	450
THOMPSON, JACK	1800	NYCO	WD07	862
THOMPSON, JACOB	1820	SARA	MITL	227
THOMPSON, JACOB	1830	COLU	KIND	137
THOMPSON, JACOB	1830	NYCO	WD09	385
THOMPSON, JACOB	1830	SARA	CTPK	136
THOMPSON, JAMES	1810	KING	BKYN	632
THOMPSON, JAMES	1820	ABNY	ABNY	204
THOMPSON, JAMES	1820	KING	BRYN	116
THOMPSON, JAMES	1820	NYCO	WD05	429
THOMPSON, JAMES	1820	NYCO	WD07	634
THOMPSON, JAMES	1820	NYCO	WD08	845
THOMPSON, JAMES	1830	ABNY	WD04	294
THOMPSON, JAMES	1830	ABNY	WD04	319
THOMPSON, JAMES	1830	DUTC	PGKP	327
THOMPSON, JAMES	1830	KING	WD03	280
THOMPSON, JAMES	1830	NYCO	WD05	354
THOMPSON, JAMES	1830	NYCO	WD06	443
THOMPSON, JAMES	1830	NYCO	WD08	231
THOMPSON, JAMES	1830	SCNE	WD02	211
THOMPSON, JANE	1820	NYCO	WD06	472
THOMPSON, JANE	1830	NYCO	WD05	278
THOMPSON, JEREMIAH	1830	RENS	SCHO	256
THOMPSON, JO	1820	SARA	STIL	190
THOMPSON, JOHN	1800	ABNY	SCNE	2
THOMPSON, JOHN	1810	NYCO	WD05	473
THOMPSON, JOHN	1820	COLU	HUDS	35
THOMPSON, JOHN	1820	KING	BRYN	123
THOMPSON, JOHN	1820	NYCO	WD02	124
THOMPSON, JOHN	1820	NYCO	WD06	572
THOMPSON, JOHN	1820	NYCO	WD07	636
THOMPSON, JOHN	1820	PUTM	PATE	101
THOMPSON, JOHN	1820	SARA	STIL	190
THOMPSON, JOHN	1820	SCNE	WD02	572
THOMPSON, JOHN	1830	COLU	CANN	29
THOMPSON, JOHN	1830	LIVI	GENC	5
THOMPSON, JOHN	1830	MONR	RUSH	71
THOMPSON, JOHN	1830	MONT	FLOR	100
THOMPSON, JOHN	1830	NYCO	WD05	252
THOMPSON, JOHN	1830	NYCO	WD10	52
THOMPSON, JOHN	1830	ONTA	SENE	85
THOMPSON, JOHN	1830	ORNG	WARW	92
THOMPSON, JOHN	1830	PUTM	PHIL	63
THOMPSON, JOHN	1830	RENS	BRUN	223
THOMPSON, JOHN	1830	SCHR	SHAR	109

NAME	YR	CO	TWP	PG
THOMPSON, JOHN	1830	SCNE	WD02	219
THOMPSON, JOHN	1830	SCNE	WD02	223
THOMPSON, JOHN	1830	STLR	OSWE	230
THOMPSON, JOHNATHAN C.	1830	NYCO	WD10	5
THOMPSON, JOSEPH	1810	NYCO	WD05	275
THOMPSON, JOSEPH	1810	SUFF	SHAM	445
THOMPSON, JOSEPH	1820	ABNY	ABNY	203
THOMPSON, JOSEPH	1820	NYCO	WD05	430
THOMPSON, JOSEPH	1830	GREN	ATHN	212
THOMPSON, JOSEPH	1830	HERK	COLU	210
THOMPSON, JOSEPH	1830	MONR	RWD3	228
THOMPSON, JOSEPH	1830	NYCO	WD08	201
THOMPSON, JOSEPH	1830	NYCO	WD09	349
THOMPSON, JOSEPH	1830	SUFF	SHAM	228
THOMPSON, LEWIS	1830	NYCO	WD04	228
THOMPSON, LONDON	1830	ABNY	WD01	220
THOMPSON, MAGDALEN	1830	ABNY	WATV	447
THOMPSON, MARGARET	1810	NYCO	WD05	367
THOMPSON, MARY	1830	NYCO	WD08	234A
THOMPSON, MICHAEL	1820	KING	BRYN	140
THOMPSON, MICHAEL	1830	ABNY	WATV	462
THOMPSON, MICHAEL	1830	KING	WD04	307
THOMPSON, MICHAEL	1830	SARA	MALT	54
THOMPSON, MRS.	1820	KING	BRYN	116
THOMPSON, MRS.	1820	KING	BRYN	139
THOMPSON, MRS.	1820	KING	NEUT	161
THOMPSON, NANCY	1820	ABNY	ABNY	204
THOMPSON, PAUL	1830	ABNY	WATV	457
THOMPSON, PERO	1820	NYCO	WD01	40
THOMPSON, PERO	1830	NYCO	WD07	97
THOMPSON, PHEBE	1830	SUFF	HUNT	312
THOMPSON, PHEBY	1830	SCNE	WD02	223
THOMPSON, PRINCE	1830	KING	WD02	262
THOMPSON, PRINCE	1830	MONT	BROA	142
THOMPSON, PRINCE	1830	NYCO	WD14	521
THOMPSON, RACHEL	1810	NYCO	WD05	298
THOMPSON, REBECCA	1830	NYCO	WD05	336
THOMPSON, RICHARD	1820	SCNE	WD01	559
THOMPSON, RICHARD	1830	ABNY	WD02	237
THOMPSON, RICHARD	1830	ABNY	WD05	329
THOMPSON, RICHARD	1830	CHEN	OXFO	63
THOMPSON, RICHARD	1830	NYCO	WD08	242
THOMPSON, RICHARD	1830	SCNE	WD01	206
THOMPSON, RICHARD	1830	TOMP	CARO	498
THOMPSON, ROBERT	1810	NYCO	WD04	177
THOMPSON, ROBERT	1830	ORNG	CRAW	189
THOMPSON, RULIN	1830	KING	BUSH	383
THOMPSON, S.	1830	NYCO	WD11	184
THOMPSON, SAMUEL	1820	ABNY	GUID	253

Thompson

NAME	YR	CO	TWP	PG
THOMPSON, SAMUEL	1820	NYCO	WD05	425
THOMPSON, SAMUEL	1820	NYCO	WD05	429
THOMPSON, SAMUEL	1820	NYCO	WD06	470
THOMPSON, SAMUEL	1820	NYCO	WD08	814
THOMPSON, SAMUEL	1820	SCNE	WD01	563
THOMPSON, SAMUEL	1830	DUTC	FISH	490
THOMPSON, SAMUEL	1830	GREN	ATHN	211
THOMPSON, SAMUEL	1830	NYCO	WD06	388
THOMPSON, SAMUEL	1830	NYCO	WD08	154
THOMPSON, SAMUEL	1830	NYCO	WD08	247
THOMPSON, SAMUEL	1830	NYCO	WD08	255
THOMPSON, SAMUEL	1830	RENS	BRUN	208
THOMPSON, SAMUEL	1830	SCNE	WD01	202
THOMPSON, SAMUEL	1830	SCNE	WD02	219
THOMPSON, SHARPER	1830	SUFF	BROK	193
THOMPSON, SIMON	1830	SUFF	BROK	194
THOMPSON, T.C.	1830	KING	WD04	319
THOMPSON, THO--	1820	KING	BRYN	186
THOMPSON, THOMAS	1800	NYCO	WD07	858
THOMPSON, THOMAS	1820	ABNY	ABNY	202
THOMPSON, THOMAS	1820	NYCO	WD05	436
THOMPSON, THOMAS	1820	NYCO	WD09	885
THOMPSON, THOMAS	1820	SCNE	WD02	572
THOMPSON, THOMAS	1830	ABNY	WD01	222
THOMPSON, THOMAS	1830	ABNY	WD01	223
THOMPSON, THOMAS	1830	DUTC	PGKP	326
THOMPSON, THOMAS	1830	GREN	ATHN	212
THOMPSON, THOMAS	1830	NYCO	WD05	331
THOMPSON, THOMAS	1830	NYCO	WD07	42
THOMPSON, THOMAS	1830	NYCO	WD08	259
THOMPSON, THOMAS	1830	NYCO	WD09	324
THOMPSON, THOMAS	1830	NYCO	WD14	525
THOMPSON, THOMAS	1830	ROCK	ORGT	113
THOMPSON, THOMAS	1830	SCNE	WD01	202
THOMPSON, THOMAS	1830	WASH	FTED	311
THOMPSON, THOMAS	1860	ABNY	WATV	465
THOMPSON, THOMAS I.	1810	NYCO	WD05	346
THOMPSON, TOM	1830	SARA	SASP	163
THOMPSON, W.	1830	KING	WD04	310
THOMPSON, WILLIAM	1820	ESEX	ESEX	411
THOMPSON, WILLIAM	1820	GENE	LEIC	161
THOMPSON, WILLIAM	1820	GREN	CATS	157
THOMPSON, WILLIAM	1820	KING	BRYN	133
THOMPSON, WILLIAM	1820	NYCO	WD05	434
THOMPSON, WILLIAM	1820	NYCO	WD06	571
THOMPSON, WILLIAM	1820	ROCK	ORNG	89
THOMPSON, WILLIAM	1830	ESEX	ESEX	323
THOMPSON, WILLIAM	1830	GREN	CATS	237
THOMPSON, WILLIAM	1830	JEFF	HOUN	174

NAME	YR	CO	TWP	PG
THOMPSON, WILLIAM	1830	LIVI	LEIC	166
THOMPSON, WILLIAM	1830	NYCO	WD05	276
THOMPSON, WILLIAM	1830	NYCO	WD08	215
THOMPSON, WILLIAM	1830	NYCO	WD08	247
THOMPSON, WILLIAM	1830	QUEN	OYST	44
THOMPSON, WILLIAM	1830	ROCK	ORGT	109
THOMPSON, YAH	1810	NYCO	WD05	342
THOMPSON, YORK	1820	ONID	VERN	261
THOMPSON, YORK	1830	ONON	ONON	171
THOMSON, CHRISTOPHER	1810	SCNE	WD02	954
THOMSON, JACOB	1830	ABNY	WD03	288
THOMSON, JAMES	1810	NYCO	WD05	371
THOMSON, JAMES	1810	SCNE	WD03	958
THOMSON, JAMES	1830	MONT	AMST	125
THOMSON, JOHN	1790	DUTC	RHIN	93
THOMSON, JOHN	1810	QUEN	OYST	239
THOMSON, JOHN	1810	SCNE	WD02	952
THOMSON, MATHIAS	1830	MONT	EPHR	183
THOMSON, MRS.	1810	NYCO	WD06	460
THOMSON, NICHOLAS	1810	SCNE	WD02	953
THOMSON, NICHOLAS	1830	NYCO	WD08	274
THOMSON, SAM	1810	SCNE	WD01	933
THOMSON, THOMAS	1810	NYCO	WD05	346
THOMSON, THOMAS	1810	NYCO	WD05	370
THOMSON, WILLIAM	1820	JEFF	HOUN	417
THOMSON, WILLIAM	1830	NYCO	WD05	325
THORN, HANNAH	1820	NYCO	WD10	996
THORN, HANNAH	1830	NYCO	WD08	275
THORN, HEREKIAH	1830	RENS	WD02	28
THORN, ISAAC	1810	QUEN	OYST	260
THORN, ISAAC	1820	SUFF	HUNT	288
THORN, JEFFERY	1830	COLU	CHAT	55
THORN, JEFFRY	1800	COLU	CLAV	1217
THORN, MICHAEL	1830	ABNY	WD02	239
THORN, MICHEAL	1810	COLU	KIND	173
THORN, SLAB	1810	DUTC	NORT	338
THORN, TIMOTHY	1800	QUEN	NHEM	25
THORNE, F.	1830	NYCO	WD13	382
THORNE, ISAAC	1830	QUEN	OYST	46
THORNTON, DAVID	1830	NYCO	WD06	426
THURSTON, CHARLES	1800	COLU	HUDS	1144
THURSTON, CHARLES	1810	COLU	HUDS	147
THURSTON, JOHN	1810	NYCO	WD06	444
TIBUS	1820	QUEN	----	45
TICE, JOHN	1820	ONTA	PENF	149
TIEBOUT, ANTHONY	1820	GREN	DURH	132
TIEBOUT, CORNELIUS	1820	SCHR	SCHR	463
TIEBOUT, CORNELIUS	1830	SCHR	SCHR	13

NAME	YR	CO	TWP	PG
TIEBOUT, JOHNATHAN	1830	NYCO	WD09	416
TIEBOUT, THOMAS	1820	NYCO	WD09	940
TIEPOUT, HARY	1830	SCHR	MIDD	36
TIGHMAN, WILLIAM	1830	NYCO	WD05	344
TILDER, WILLIAM	1830	NYCO	WD11	156
TILLER	1800	NYCO	WD06	811
TILLESON, LEUIS	1790	SUFF	HUNT	165
TILLMAN, ELIJAH	1830	NYCO	WD04	203
TILLMAN, WILLIAM	1830	NYCO	WD06	403
TILMAN, JACOB	1830	DUTC	FISH	478
TILMAN, JAMES	1830	NYCO	WD13	336
TILMAN, JOHN	1830	ERIE	BUFF	28
TILMAN, MATILDA	1830	NYCO	WD08	227
TILMAN, WILLIAM	1830	NYCO	WD08	217
TILUS, THOMAS	1820	MONT	CHAR	339
TIM	1790	QUEN	NHEM	152
TIM, POMPEY	1830	SUFF	BROK	161
TIMES, JANET	1830	NYCO	WD10	21
TIMOTHY	1790	SUFF	ISLP	165
TIMOTHY	1800	QUEN	NHEM	553
TIMOTHY	1800	QUEN	OYST	571
TIMOTHY	1800	SUFF	ISLP	61
TINA	1790	ABNY	STIL	50
TINBROOK, JENNY	1820	ABNY	ABNY	204
TINES, WILLIAM	1830	NYCO	WD07	66
TINKHORA, WALLY	1800	NYCO	WD05	753
TINMAN, DINA	1820	DUTC	CLNT	29
TISON, WILLIAM	1820	COLU	HUDS	35
TITE, SAMUEL	1820	SUFF	SHAM	317
TITUS	1790	QUEN	FLUS	149
TITUS	1790	QUEN	NHEM	153
TITUS	1790	QUEN	OYST	155
TITUS	1800	ABNY	BETH	195
TITUS	1800	COLU	HUDS	1143
TITUS	1800	TIOG	LISL	246
TITUS	1810	COLU	CANN	101
TITUS	1810	NYCO	WD06	424
TITUS	1810	SUFF	SMIT	538
TITUS	1820	QUEN	----	60
TITUS	1820	SUFF	BROK	362
TITUS, ABRAHAM	1820	NYCO	WD07	651
TITUS, ABRAHAM	1830	NYCO	WD06	367
TITUS, ABSOLOM	1790	DUTC	PAWL	87
TITUS, ANTHONY T.	1830	NYCO	WD05	305
TITUS, BOS	1830	BROM	CHIN	8
TITUS, DIANA	1820	DUTC	RHIN	129
TITUS, JACOB	1820	ABNY	ABNY	204
TITUS, JACOB	1820	KING	BRYN	126
TITUS, JAMES	1800	ORNG	WALL	346

NAME	YR	CO	TWP	PG
TITUS, JAMES	1820	ORNG	WALL	788
TITUS, JAMES	1830	ABNY	WD01	221
TITUS, JOSEPH	1800	QUEN	NHEM	553
TITUS, JOSEPH	1810	QUEN	NHEM	219
TITUS, JOSEPH	1820	ABNY	ABNY	203
TITUS, JOSEPH	1830	KING	WD04	319
TITUS, JOSEPH	1830	NYCO	WD11	133
TITUS, LEWIS	1830	NYCO	WD11	133
TITUS, MARGARET	1820	COLU	HUDS	35
TITUS, RICHARD	1830	ABNY	COEY	513
TITUS, RICHARD	1830	COLU	STUY	60
TITUS, RICHARD	1830	NYCO	WD07	59
TITUS, ROBERT	1820	NYCO	WD05	427
TITUS, ROBERT	1830	NYCO	WD08	148
TITUS, SAMUEL	1830	ESEX	ESEX	326
TITUS, SAMUEL	1830	SUFF	SHAM	229
TITUS, SARAH	1830	DUTC	REDH	371
TITUS, SYLVANUS	1830	QUEN	FLUS	
TITUS, THOMAS	1830	NYCO	WD14	520
TITUS, TONS	1820	DUTC	REDH	114
TOBBY, HARRY	1810	QUEN	NHEM	206
TOBEY	1790	COLU	HUDS	66
TOBIAS, ANGELICA	1830	RENS	LANS	100
TOBIAS, BENJAMIN	1830	GREN	ATHN	204
TOBIAS, ISAAC	1830	SUFF	SMIT	268
TOBIAS, JOHN	1810	NYCO	WD05	281
TOBIAS, SUSAN	1830	COLU	HUDS	124
TOBIAS, TOBE	1830	COLU	CHAT	50
TOBINS, CHARLES	1810	SUFF	BROK	491
TOBY, ISAAC	1820	SUFF	SMIT	319
TOBY, MARTHA	1830	MADI	----	416
TODD, JOSEPH	1830	NYCO	WD14	526
TODD, JOSHUA	1810	NYCO	WD04	193
TODD, SAMUEL	1810	NYCO	WD06	492
TOLBERT, WILLIAM	1830	NYCO	WD05	257
TOLIVER, WILLIAM	1830	STEU	BATH	264
TOLL, PETER	1830	MONT	MIND	13
TOLL, SAMUEL	1830	SCNE	GLEN	261
TOLLIVE, BILLY	1820	STEU	BATH	227
TOM	1790	NYCO	NORT	126
TOM	1790	NYCO	WEST	133
TOM	1790	WEST	SALM	206
TOM	1800	ABNY	WD02	284
TOM	1800	ABNY	WD01	4
TOM	1800	ONON	MANL	176
TOM	1810	DUTC	PGKP	168
TOM	1810	SARA	STIL	731
TOM	1820	ABNY	COEY	141
TOM	1820	RICH	NORT	108

NAME	YR	CO	TWP	PG
TOM, JAJER	1810	QUEN	NHEM	217
TOMAS, EZRA	1820	SUFF	SHAM	319
TOMIS, JOSEPH	1830	WEST	PELH	115
TOMISON, DAVID	1830	RENS	PITT	123
TOMKINS, NERO	1820	ONID	VERN	261
TOMM, SAMUEL	1800	DUTC	FISH	25
TOMMAS, PETER	1820	DUTC	REDH	118
TOMMIS, MOSES	1830	WEST	SCAR	78
TOMPHINS, HENRY	1820	NYCO	WD07	659
TOMPKINS, ABRAHAM	1810	NYCO	WD06	424
TOMPKINS, ABRAHAM	1820	DUTC	MILA	83
TOMPKINS, ALBERT	1830	NYCO	WD10	99
TOMPKINS, AMELIN	1820	NYCO	WD10	992
TOMPKINS, ANDREW	1830	WEST	GREN	16
TOMPKINS, ANDREW	1830	WEST	GREN	19
TOMPKINS, CESAR	1830	COLU	CLAV	79
TOMPKINS, EDWARD	1830	STEU	BATH	271
TOMPKINS, ELIZA	1830	ORNG	NEWB	41
TOMPKINS, JOHN	1820	NYCO	WD05	382
TOMPKINS, JOHN	1830	NYCO	WD05	260
TOMPKINS, L.	1830	NYCO	WD10	98
TOMPKINS, NOAH	1820	ULST	PLAT	58
TOMPKINS, RICHARD	1800	WEST	GREN	681
TOMPKINS, SAMUEL	1830	RENS	SAND	320
TOMPKINS, SEZAR	1830	WEST	CORT	60
TOMPSON, EZEKIEL	1830	STEU	BATH	272
TOMPSON, JOHN	1830	NYCO	WD06	401
TOMPSON, JOHN	1830	WEST	MTPL	47
TOMPSON, JOSEPH	1820	SUFF	SHAM	314
TOMPSON, THOMAS	1810	NYCO	WD10	698
TOMPSON, THOMAS	1830	SCNE	WD02	223
TOMS, BOWMAN	1810	WEST	GREN	1121
TOMSON, WILL	1810	ROCK	ORNG	640
TONE	1800	WEST	PELM	642
TONE	1810	DUTC	PGKP	170
TONE	1810	SUFF	SOUT	555
TONE	1810	ULST	SHAW	693
TONEY	1790	QUEN	NEWT	151
TONEY	1790	QUEN	NHEM	152
TONEY	1790	QUEN	SHEM	157
TONEY	1790	WEST	HARR	199
TONEY	1790	WEST	WTPL	207
TONEY	1800	QUEN	FLUS	542
TONEY	1800	QUEN	FLUS	543
TONEY	1800	QUEN	NHEM	551
TONEY	1800	QUEN	OYST	578
TONEY	1800	QUEN	SHEM	558
TONEY	1800	SUFF	ISLP	62
TONEY, JETHRO	1800	COLU	HUDS	1141

NAME	YR	CO	TWP	PG
TONEY, LUDOCK	1830	SUFF	SHAM	220
TONEY, TONY	1800	QUEN	NEWT	537
TONSON, WILLIAM	1820	SUFF	SHAM	315
TONY	1820	QUEN	----	51
TONY, TADOR	1820	SUFF	SHAM	309
TOOLE, ZACHARIAH	1820	NYCO	WD06	462
TOOLER, BEN	1820	SUFF	ISLP	306
TOOLER, BENJAMIN	1810	SUFF	ISLP	497
TOOLER, HENRY	1830	SUFF	ISLP	284
TOOLER, JEREMIAH	1820	SUFF	ISLP	309
TOOLER, STEPHEN	1830	NYCO	WD14	451
TOOLERS, PAUL	1810	SUFF	HUNT	514
TOOLY, MARY	1830	NYCO	WD14	451
TOP, JOHN	1830	ABNY	WD01	224
TOPP, LEWIS	1820	ABNY	ABNY	203
TOPP, LEWIS	1830	ABNY	WD04	318
TOPPINS, MOSES	1820	ONTA	CANA	225
TORIN, SAMUEL	1830	DUTC	BEEK	185
TOUKARD, GEORGE	1820	CLNT	PLAT	472
TOUSANT, PETER	1830	NYCO	WD03	103
TOWNSAND, CORNELIUS	1820	SUFF	ISLP	306
TOWNSAND, EDMOND	1820	QUEN	----	64
TOWNSAND, NATHANIEL	1800	SARA	HALF	1033
TOWNSAND, PHILLIS	1820	NYCO	WD10	970
TOWNSAND, STEPHEN	1820	QUEN	----	78
TOWNSEN	1810	NYCO	WD07	557
TOWNSEN, SYLVANUS	1810	NYCO	WD07	535
TOWNSEND, ABRAHAM	1830	QUEN	OYST	32
TOWNSEND, BENJAMIN	1830	QUEN	OYST	23
TOWNSEND, BENJAMIN	1830	QUEN	NHEM	113
TOWNSEND, CANAH	1810	QUEN	NHEM	218
TOWNSEND, CAROLINE	1830	QUEN	FLUS	146
TOWNSEND, CATO	1830	QUEN	FLUS	139
TOWNSEND, CATO	1830	SUFF	BROK	162
TOWNSEND, CHARLES	1830	NYCO	WD07	46
TOWNSEND, CHARLES	1830	QUEN	FLUS	152
TOWNSEND, CORNELIUS	1830	NYCO	WD08	204
TOWNSEND, COROLINE	1830	QUEN	NHEM	106
TOWNSEND, CRANDUS	1830	QUEN	OYST	31
TOWNSEND, DAVID	1830	QUEN	FLUS	143
TOWNSEND, EDMUND	1830	QUEN	NHEM	109
TOWNSEND, EDMUND	1830	QUEN	OYST	28
TOWNSEND, EDWARD	1810	QUEN	OYST	237
TOWNSEND, EDWARD	1830	QUEN	FLUS	143
TOWNSEND, ENOCH	1800	QUEN	NHEM	553
TOWNSEND, ENOCH	1810	QUEN	NHEM	218
TOWNSEND, ENOCH	1810	QUEN	OYST	234
TOWNSEND, ENOCH	1830	QUEN	NHEM	106
TOWNSEND, EVE	1830	QUEN	OYST	39

NAME	YR	CO	TWP	PG
TOWNSEND, GERANDUS	1810	QUEN	OYST	241
TOWNSEND, GERANDUS	1810	QUEN	OYST	239
TOWNSEND, HARRY	1830	NYCO	WD07	16
TOWNSEND, HENRY	1830	QUEN	OYST	28
TOWNSEND, HENRY	1830	QUEN	OYST	33
TOWNSEND, ISAAC	1830	QUEN	JAMA	135
TOWNSEND, JACOB	1800	QUEN	NHEM	553
TOWNSEND, JACOB	1810	QUEN	FLUS	302
TOWNSEND, JACOB	1810	QUEN	OYST	234
TOWNSEND, JACOB	1830	PUTM	PHIL	56
TOWNSEND, JACOB	1830	QUEN	OYST	20
TOWNSEND, JACOB JR.	1830	QUEN	FLUS	146
TOWNSEND, JAMES	1810	NYCO	WD01	31
TOWNSEND, JAMES	1830	QUEN	OYST	29
TOWNSEND, JAMES	1830	QUEN	OYST	39
TOWNSEND, JAMES	1830	QUEN	NHEM	106
TOWNSEND, JAMES JR.	1830	QUEN	OYST	39
TOWNSEND, JEFFEE	1830	WEST	WTPL	223
TOWNSEND, JEFFERY	1810	QUEN	OYST	234
TOWNSEND, JEFFERY	1810	QUEN	OYST	241
TOWNSEND, JEFFERY	1820	WEST	HARR	466
TOWNSEND, JOSEPH	1800	DUTC	FRAN	170
TOWNSEND, JOSEPH	1810	DUTC	PATT	120
TOWNSEND, JOSEPH	1820	DUTC	PAUL	90
TOWNSEND, JOSEPH	1830	PUTM	PATE	27
TOWNSEND, JOSIAH	1830	QUEN	FLUS	138
TOWNSEND, LETTY	1830	NYCO	WD10	11
TOWNSEND, MITCHEL	1820	NYCO	WD07	705
TOWNSEND, MRS.	1830	KING	WD03	288
TOWNSEND, NATHANIEL	1820	DUTC	PGKP	101
TOWNSEND, NATHANIEL	1830	DUTC	PGKP	327
TOWNSEND, NECKOLAS	1830	QUEN	OYST	38
TOWNSEND, OBEDIAH	1830	QUEN	OYST	41
TOWNSEND, PETER	1810	QUEN	OYST	244
TOWNSEND, PETER	1830	NYCO	WD10	84
TOWNSEND, PETER	1830	SUFF	HUNT	324
TOWNSEND, RICHARD	1810	QUEN	NHEM	217
TOWNSEND, STEPHEN	1830	QUEN	OYST	38
TOWNSEND, SYLVANUS	1830	QUEN	FLUS	143
TOWNSEND, THOMAS	1810	NYCO	WD07	620
TOWNSEND, THOMAS	1810	NYCO	WD07	525
TOWNSEND, TITUS	1810	QUEN	OYST	247
TOWNSEND, WILLIAM	1830	NYCO	WD10	24
TOWSAND, THOMAS	1820	WASH	FTED	159
TOY	1820	QUEN	----	50
TRADWELL, CHARLES	1820	NYCO	WD06	571
TRANG, JAMES GOLD	1810	NYCO	WD05	350
TRAVIS, LEAH	1830	NYCO	WD07	46
TRAY	1800	QUEN	FLUS	538

NAME	YR	CO	TWP	PG
TREADWELL, ANTHONY	1830	QUEN	FLUS	147
TREADWELL, CYRUS	1810	NYCO	WD02	99
TREADWELL, JAMES	1830	QUEN	OYST	38
TREADWELL, MORRIS	1830	NYCO	WD10	66
TREADWELL, PETER	1830	NYCO	WD09	430
TREADWELL, SENECA	1830	SUFF	HUNT	306
TREADWELL; SQUIRE	1800	DUTC	FISH	32
TREAWELL, MORRIS	1820	SUFF	ISLP	309
TREDDLE, DAVID	1810	KING	BYKN	638
TREDWELL, CAISAR	1830	NYCO	WD08	139
TREDWELL, CHARETY	1830	QUEN	SHEM	78
TREDWELL, CHARLES	1820	QUEN	----	60
TREDWELL, CHARLES	1830	NYCO	WD06	407
TREDWELL, CHARLES	1810	NYCO	WD06	441
TREDWELL, DAVID	1830	QUEN	OYST	24
TREDWELL, DAVID	1830	QUEN	OYST	31
TREDWELL, DAVID	1830	QUEN	JAMA	126
TREDWELL, ESQUIRE	1810	DUTC	FISH	196
TREDWELL, GEORGE	1830	NYCO	WD04	174
TREDWELL, GEORGE	1830	NYCO	WD09	431
TREDWELL, GEORGE	1830	QUEN	NHEM	112
TREDWELL, GILBERT	1800	NYCO	WD05	786
TREDWELL, ISRAEL	1830	QUEN	NHEM	114
TREDWELL, JAMES	1800	NYCO	WD05	774
TREDWELL, JAMES	1810	QUEN	NHEM	221
TREDWELL, JAMES	1830	DUTC	LAGR	249
TREDWELL, JAMES	1830	QUEN	NEWT	2
TREDWELL, JAMES	1830	SUFF	ISLP	284
TREDWELL, JANE	1830	NYCO	WD08	244
TREDWELL, JOHN	1830	QUEN	OYST	20
TREDWELL, JOSEPH	1830	NYCO	WD08	198
TREDWELL, JOSEPH	1830	QUEN	NHEM	108
TREDWELL, LEWIS	1830	QUEN	FLUS	141
TREDWELL, LEWIS	1830	SUFF	HUNT	324
TREDWELL, MILLE	1810	SUFF	HUNT	520
TREDWELL, MORIS	1810	SUFF	ISLP	498
TREDWELL, MORRIS	1810	QUEN	NHEM	218
TREDWELL, MORRIS	1810	QUEN	SHEM	303
TREDWELL, MORRIS	1830	SUFF	ISLP	284
TREDWELL, MOSES	1810	QUEN	NHEM	305
TREDWELL, PHILIP	1830	NYCO	WD14	477
TREDWELL, RICHARD	1830	NYCO	WD08	243
TREDWELL, ROBERT	1830	QUEN	FLUS	142
TREDWELL, SEEZAR	1830	QUEN	OYST	45
TREDWELL, SIRAS	1820	NYCO	WD05	409
TREDWELL, THOMAS	1830	QUEN	NEWT	5
TREDWELL, WILLIAM	1820	NYCO	WD09	945
TREDWELL, WILLIAM	1830	DUTC	LAGR	249
TREDWIL, MRS.	1830	KING	WD04	303

NAME	YR	CO	TWP	PG
TREDWILL, CHARLES	1820	NYCO	WD08	738
TREE, DEEN	1800	ULST	SHAW	250
TREE, HANNAH	1800	DUTC	NORT	152
TRENDWEL, WILLIAM	1820	DUTC	FISH	72
TRENDWELL, VININE	1820	DUTC	FISH	72
TREWEY, ALEXANDER	1830	RENS	WD02	26
TRI---FE(?)	1820	PUTM	PATE	101
TRIMBLE, SOLOMON	1830	NYCO	WD13	339
TRIPHENA	1820	ONTA	SENE	268
TRISCONE, JOHN	1830	NYCO	WD11	154
TRITHENE	1800	SUFF	SHAM	70
TROINS, THOMAS	1820	ULST	ESOP	52
TROWBRIDGE, CYREN	1820	ONID	BOON	177
TROWBRIDGE, SUSAN	1830	ABNY	WD04	326
TRUSTY, WILLIAM	1830	NYCO	WD13	378
TILLISSON, CHESTER	1830	WEST	SUMM	191
TUBA	1790	QUEN	NHEM	152
TUCK, PETER T.	1820	ULST	KING	79
TUCKER, AARON	1830	SUFF	BROK	167
TUCKER, BENJAMIN H.	1830	NYCO	WD07	17
TUCKER, CHRISTOPHER	1830	NYCO	WD06	385
TUCKER, ISSAC	1810	NYCO	WD06	492
TUCKER, JOHN	1830	NYCO	WD05	300
TUCKER, NANCY	1800	NYCO	WD06	848
TUCKER, POMPEY	1830	ONTA	CANA	126
TUCKER, THOMAS	1830	SUFF	EAST	253
TUCKER, TUMOR	1820	SUFF	EAST	288
TUCKER, WILLIAM	1830	QUEN	FLUS	139
TUDER, HENRY	1810	WEST	NEWR	1081
TUDER, JAMES	1810	WEST	NEWR	1081
TUHTEM	1790	NYCO	OUTW	127
TULAH, SAM	1790	SUFF	ISLP	165
TULLEY, ABRAHAM	1830	SCHR	MIDD	36
TULOR, BENJAMIN	1800	SUFF	ISLP	61
TUNISON, SYLVESTER	1820	DUTC	PGKP	97
TUNISON, SYLVESTER	1830	DUTC	PGKP	321
TUNN, BENJERMAN	1810	QUEN	NHEM	220
TURK, PETER	1810	ULST	KING	756
TURK, PETER	1830	ULST	KING	70
TURNER, BENJAMIN	1800	WASH	THUR	386
TURNER, BENJAMIN	1810	NYCO	WD06	460
TURNER, BENJAMIN	1820	WEST	EAST	199
TURNER, BENLAMIN	1830	WEST	EAST	137
TURNER, CHARLES	1820	NYCO	WD07	721
TURNER, CHARLES	1830	ABNY	WD01	223
TURNER, D.	1830	NYCO	WD11	191
TURNER, FREDERICK	1830	NYCO	WD08	248
TURNER, HARRIOT	1830	NYCO	WD09	302
TURNER, JAMES	1820	NYCO	WD10	998

NAME	YR	CO	TWP	PG
TURNER, JOSEPH	1830	ALLE	HAIG	122
TURNER, MARGARET	1820	NYCO	WD10	987
TURNER, PHEBE	1820	NYCO	WD07	620
TURNER, RICHARD	1820	NYCO	WD04	242
TURNER, THOMAS	1830	NYCO	WD10	13
TURNER, THOMAS	1830	NYCO	WD14	434
TURNER, THOMAS	1830	NYCO	WD14	491
TURNER, WIDOW	1830	NYCO	WD13	400
TURNER, WILLIAM	1810	NYCO	WD03	85
TURNER, WILLIAM	1820	NYCO	WD04	242
TURNPIKE, JOHN	1830	QUEN	OYST	38
TURVEY, MR.	1830	NYCO	WD06	403
TUTER, WILLIAM	1830	WEST	SCAR	77
TUTHILL, ISAAC	1830	SUFF	RIVH	240
TUTHILL, JEREMIAH	1830	ORNG	BLOM	122
TUTOR, HENRY	1810	NYCO	WD07	569
TUTTLE, PETER	1830	HERK	NORW	79
TWINE, SAMUEL	1830	ABNY	WD02	261
TYCE, JOHN	1830	MONR	PENF	339
TYLER, JOHN	1810	NYCO	WD05	262
TYLER, JOHN	1820	MADI	SULL	10
TYLER, JOHN	1820	MADI	SULL	10
TYLY, SARAH	1830	RENS	TROY	7
UDLE, SAMUEL	1830	QUEN	OYST	35
UMBER	1790	NYCO	NORT	125
UNDER, JOHN	1830	KING	WD04	307
UNDER, MIME	1810	NYCO	WD03	262
UNDERDUNK, SAMUEL	1830	WEST	MAMA	228
UNDERHILL	1810	NYCO	WD07	575
UNDERHILL, BENJAMIN	1810	QUEN	OYST	236
UNDERHILL, BENJAMIN	1820	QUEN	----	75
UNDERHILL, BENJAMIN	1830	QUEN	NHEM	106
UNDERHILL, CALEB	1790	QUEN	OYST	153
UNDERHILL, CUFFEY	1800	QUEN	NHEM	554
UNDERHILL, EDWARD	1830	WEST	SCAR	78
UNDERHILL, GEORGE	1830	QUEN	FLUS	138
UNDERHILL, JACOB	1820	WEST	MTPL	255
UNDERHILL, JAMES	1820	WEST	MTPL	261
UNDERHILL, JAMES	1830	NYCO	WD07	14
UNDERHILL, JEFRE	1810	WEST	NEWR	1087
UNDERHILL, JESSE	1820	WEST	SCAR	280
UNDERHILL, JOHN	1820	QUEN	----	56
UNDERHILL, JOSEPH	1820	QUEN	----	67
UNDERHILL, ROBERT	1820	QUEN	----	50
UNDERHILL, ROBERT	1830	QUEN	FLUS	138
UNDERHILL, SAMUEL	1820	WEST	GREN	242
UPHAM, MINGO	1790	QUEN	NEWT	151

Upton

NAME	YR	CO	TWP	PG
UPTON, ANNA	1800	NYCO	WD06	847
URIAH	1790	QUEN	SHEM	156
URIAH	1800	QUEN	NHEM	559
UTTER, MORRES	1810	QUEN	NHEM	216
VADER, THOMAS	1820	HERK	RUSS	170
VAGOT, MARY	1820	GREN	ATHE	8
VAIL, CUFF	1820	DUTC	FISH	58
VAIL, FRANCIS	1820	DUTC	FISH	72
VAIL, RICHARD	1820	WEST	HARR	470
VALANTINE, S.	1830	MONR	RWD3	221
VALED, SAMUEL	1820	SCNE	WD01	557
VALENTINE	1800	NYCO	WD06	813
VALENTINE, ABSOLAM	1830	NYCO	WD14	461
VALENTINE, BALB	1810	QUEN	NHEM	217
VALENTINE, D.	1830	NYCO	WD11	212
VALENTINE, ELY	1810	NYCO	WD05	310
VALENTINE, HENRY	1820	KING	BRYN	173
VALENTINE, HENRY	1830	KING	FLAT	397
VALENTINE, HEZEKIAH	1830	NYCO	WD14	487
VALENTINE, HEZEKIAH	1830	QUEN	NHEM	112
VALENTINE, JOHN	1830	NYCO	WD06	368
VALENTINE, JOSEPH	1800	WEST	YONK	610
VALENTINE, LEWIS	1830	NYCO	WD09	385
VALENTINE, LITUS	1800	QUEN	NHEM	552
VALENTINE, MORRIS	1830	WEST	RYE	100
VALENTINE, POMPEY	1800	NYCO	WD06	802
VALENTINE, RICHARD	1830	ONTA	CANA	115
VALENTINE, RICHARD	1830	QUEN	NHEM	106
VALENTINE, ROBERT	1820	QUEN	----	67
VALENTINE, ROBERT	1830	QUEN	NHEM	100
VALENTINE, THOMAS	1820	QUEN	----	67
VALENTINE, TITUS	1810	QUEN	NHEM	217
VALENTINE, TOM	1810	QUEN	NHEM	217
VALES, HAGAR	1820	DUTC	FISH	57
VALINTINE, THOMAS	1820	NYCO	WD08	789
VAN ALEA, JACK	1830	COLU	STUY	69
VAN ALEN, DICK	1810	COLU	KIND	172
VAN ALEN, HENRY	1830	COLU	KIND	147
VAN ALEN, JOHN	1810	COLU	KIND	168
VAN ALEN, JOHN	1830	COLU	GALA	254
VAN ALEN, PETER	1830	COLU	KIND	142
VAN ALLEN, ANTHONY	1820	COLU	HILL	7
VAN ALLEN, BRACE	1830	COLU	KIND	133
VAN ALLEN, JACK	1830	COLU	KIND	147
VAN ALLEN, PHILIP	1830	RENS	NASS	298
VAN ALSTIN, JACK	1820	COLU	HUDS	37
VAN ALSTIN, PETER	1820	COLU	HUDS	37

NAME	YR	CO	TWP	PG
VAN ALSTINE, BRIDGE	1820	COLU	KIND	25
VAN ALSTINE, DICK	1820	COLU	KIND	29
VAN ALSTINE, HARRY	1820	COLU	KIND	25
VAN ALSTINE, JACK	1820	COLU	KIND	27
VAN ALSTINE, POMP	1820	COLU	KIND	29
VAN ALSTINE, TOM	1820	COLU	CHAT	21
VAN ALSTINE, WILLIAM	1820	COLU	HUDS	37
VAN ALSTYN, MINK	1830	COLU	KIND	136
VAN ALSTYN, YORES	1830	COLU	STUY	62
VAN ALSTYNE, AUGUSTUS	1830	COLU	HUDS	102
VAN ALSTYNE, JACK	1830	COLU	HUDS	105
VAN ALSTYNE, JEREMIAH	1830	COLU	HUDS	120
VAN ALSTYNE, JOHN	1830	COLU	KIND	135
VAN ALSTYNE, JOHN	1830	ULST	SHAN	126
VAN ALSTYNE, POMP	1830	COLU	STUY	67
VAN ALSTYNE, RICHARD	1830	COLU	STUY	67
VAN ALSTYNE, RICHARD	1830	COLU	HUDS	94
VAN ALSTYNE, SUSAN	1830	COLU	HUDS	101
VAN ALSTYNE, WILLIAM	1810	COLU	HUDS	139
VAN ALSTYNE, WILLIAM	1830	COLU	HUDS	108
VAN ATTEN, HENRY	1830	GREN	CATS	238
VAN AULER, JACK	1820	DELA	KORT	67
VAN BASER, KETTLE	1830	MONT	JOHN	191
VAN BENTHUYSEN, MINK	1830	DUTC	RHIN	388
VAN BERGEN, ANTHONY	1830	GREN	COXE	190
VAN BERGEN, SAMUEL	1830	GREN	NEWB	175
VAN BERGEN, THOMAS	1830	GREN	NEWB	174
VAN BERGEN, TONE	1820	GREN	COXE	43
VAN BEUREN, CATO	1830	COLU	GHEN	160
VAN BEUREN, GEORGE	1830	COLU	KIND	146
VAN BLACK, DENNIS	1830	ABNY	WD01	212
VAN BLANK, SIMON	1830	NYCO	WD10	52
VAN BLERCON, DINAH	1790	DUTC	PGKP	91
VAN BONK, JOHN	1830	WASH	ARGY	104
VAN BROCK, ANDREW	1830	ABNY	WD02	274
VAN BRUNT, FRANCIS	1820	DUTC	FISH	69
VAN BRUNT, HARRY	1820	DUTC	CLNT	42
VAN BRUNT, HARRY	1830	DUTC	PLEA	313
VANBRUNT, JACK	1830	WEST	YONK	6
VAN BRUNT, S.	1830	SUFF	BROK	196
VAN BUREN, AUGUSTUS	1830	TIOG	BERK	322
VAN BUREN, CAP	1830	MONT	MAYF	283
VAN BUREN, CROWN	1820	ONON	ONON	212
VAN BUREN, CROWN	1830	ONON	CAMI	200
VAN BUREN, FRANCIS	1830	RENS	PITT	126
VAN BUREN, HARRY	1800	RENE	TROY	900
VAN BUREN, HENRY	1800	WASH	EAST	451
VAN BUREN, JAMES	1830	ABNY	WD01	201
VAN BUREN, JOHN	1830	WASH	CAST	138

Van Buren

NAME	YR	CO	TWP	PG
VAN BUREN, LUCRETIA	1830	ONON	SALI	11
VANBUREN, RICHARD	1820	SARA	SARA	197
VAN BUREN, RICHARD	1830	ABNY	WD01	225
VAN BUREN, RICHARD	1830	SARA	SARA	157
VAN BUREN, THOMAS	1830	COLU	GHEN	158
VAN BUREUN, HENDRICK	1810	WASH	EAST	501
VAN BURIN, AUGUSTUS	1820	BROM	BERK	37
VAN BURIN, THOMAS	1820	COLU	GHIN	15
VAN BURREN, HENRY	1800	RENE	TROY	897
VANBURY, RICHARD	1810	SARA	SARA	873
VANBURY, TOM	1800	SARA	STIL	1116
VANCAMP, PRINCE	1830	OTSG	BUTT	319
VANCE, HANNAH	1820	NYCO	WD04	222
VANCE, MR.	1830	NYCO	WD06	410
VANCLEEF, GAFF	1820	NYCO	WD06	477
VAN CLEEFF, YAFF	1830	NYCO	WD06	399
VAN CORTLANDT, ISAAC	1820	ORNG	GOSH	742
VAN DAM, GEORGE	1830	ORNG	HBGH	128
VAN DEBERG, JUDE	1810	NYCO	WD03	79
VAN DEBILK, HENRY	1820	DUTC	PGKP	101
VAN DEBILK, WILLIAM	1820	DUTC	PGKP	101
VAN DEN BURGH, JACK	1820	ABNY	ABNY	205
VANDER, ABRAHAM	1820	SCNE	WD02	572
VANDERBELT, PHILIP	1830	ULST	KING	55
VANDERBELT, WILLIAM	1830	GREN	COXE	185
VANDERBERG, CHLOE	1830	ONTA	CANA	119
VAN DERBERGH, CATHARINE	1790	ULST	MARB	174
VAN DERBILT, H.	1810	DUTC	PGKP	324
VANDERBILT, HARRY	1800	DUTC	PGKP	68
VANDERBILT, HENRY	1830	DUTC	PGKP	328
VANDERBILT, WILLIAM	1830	DUTC	PGKP	326
VANDERBOUGH, POMP	1830	WASH	SALM	214
VAN DER BURGH, PETER	1830	DUTC	NORT	269
VANDERBURGH, THOMAS	1820	SARA	STIL	189
VANDERENTER, MARY	1800	NYCO	WD07	912
VANDERHEYDEN, HARRY	1830	SARA	MORE	242
VAN DER LYN, PETER	1830	ULST	KING	62
VANDERMARK, JAMES	1830	ULST	MARB	154
VANDERPOOL, ANTHONY	1830	RENS	SCHO	245
VANDERPOOL, POMPY	1830	RENS	SCHO	243
VAN DER POOL, SHARK	1830	COLU	STUY	67
VAN DER POOL, SHARK JR.	1830	COLU	STUY	69
VAN DERSEN, LUNN	1810	COLU	KIND	177
VANDERVEER, HECK	1830	QUEN	NEWT	9
VANDERVOORT, DINAH	1830	ABNY	WD04	314
VAN DERZCE, JACK	1830	ABNY	COEY	513
VAN DERZEE, PRINCE	1820	ABNY	BETH	237
VAN DERZER, JACK	1820	GREN	NEWB	29
VAN DEUSEN, JOSEPH	1830	COLU	HUDS	115

NAME	YR	CO	TWP	PG
VAN DEUSEN, WIDOW	1810	COLU	HUDS	147
VANDEVER, HARRY	1830	ONTA	CANA	115
VAN DEVERE, PETER	1820	DUTC	CLNT	40
VAN DEVIER, JOHN	1830	KING	BRYN	370
VANDEVINDOR, THOMAS	1830	RICH	SOUT	16
VAN DEVORT, HENRY	1830	WANE	LYON	111
VAN DICK, JOHN	1820	ORNG	MINI	586
VAN DIERM, JOSEPH	1820	COLU	HUDS	37
VANDIKE, PETER	1830	NYCO	WD05	275
VAN DINE, D.	1830	NYCO	WD10	121
VANDOOSEN, THOMAS	1830	CHEN	SHER	136
VAN DORNE, PRINE	1830	KING	WD02	272
VAN DORUS, DOMINGO	1790	DUTC	AMEN	72
VANDORUS, JUNE	1820	DUTC	AMEN	10
VANDORUS, TIM	1820	DUTC	AMEN	10
VAN DOURS, MACK	1800	DUTC	AMEN	138
VAN DUNK, JOHN	1800	ORNG	WARW	380
VAN DUNK, JOHN	1810	ORNG	WARW	994
VANDUZAR, PETER	1830	RICH	CAST	41
VAN DUZEN, FRANCIS	1830	ULST	WOOD	118
VAN DYCK, NANCY	1830	COLU	GALA	252
VAN DYCK, PETER	1830	COLU	STUY	69
VAN DYCK, TOBE	1830	COLU	KIND	133
VAN DYCKE, MINK	1830	COLU	STUY	67
VAN DYKE, AUGUSTUS	1830	TIOG	BERK	321
VAN DYKE, PETER	1820	NYCO	WD06	472
VAN EPPS, JEREMIAH	1830	RENS	SHOD	244
VAN ETTEN, HARRY	1830	ULST	SAUG	94
VAN EVERA, JACK	1830	MONT	CANJ	39
VAN EVERENM, JACK	1820	SCHR	SHAR	532
VAN GAASBECK, HENRY	1830	ULST	KING	57
VAN GAPEPUH, DANIEL	1820	ULST	KING	78
VAN GASSBECK, JOHN	1830	ULST	SHAW	246
VAN GEESEN, SAMUEL	1810	NYCO	WD03	76
VAN GOSBECK, THOMAS	1830	NYCO	WD08	266
VAN HAR, P.	1810	ORNG	MONR	997
VAN HARRIS, JOHN	1830	NYCO	WD06	404
VAN HAUTEN, TOM	1830	SENE	VARI	80
VAN HENSEN, SIMON	1830	ULST	ROCH	170
VAN HEUSEN, FRANK	1810	ORNG	MONT	963
VAN HEUSEN, DINAH	1820	GREN	ATHE	7
VAN HEYCK, HARRY	1820	DUTC	PGKP	107
VANHOESEN, ISAAC	1820	ABNY	ABNY	206
VAN HOESEN, JOHN	1830	COLU	CHAT	43
VAN HOESEN, NICK	1810	COLU	HUDS	149
VAN HOESEN, PETER	1830	COLU	KIND	146
VANHONTEN, HENRY	1830	ROCK	CLAR	124
VANHONTEN, JOHN	1820	ROCK	HAVE	120
VAN HOOSEN, BENJAMIN	1830	GREN	ATHN	210

NAME	YR	CO	TWP	PG
VAN HOOSEN, DANIEL	1830	GREN	COXE	187
VAN HORN, CHARLES	1830	RENS	LANS	88
VAN HORN, DAVID	1830	ABNY	WD01	225
VAN HORN, HARRY	1830	WANE	PALM	40
VAN HORN, HENRY	1820	ONTA	SENE	268
VAN HORN, JOHN	1810	NYCO	WD05	262
VAN HORN, JUDY	1830	NYCO	WD08	249
VANHORN, PETER	1830	NYCO	WD12	290
VANHORNE, ALEXANDER	1820	NYCO	WD06	480
VAN HORNE, HECTOR	1830	ORNG	NEWW	97
VAN HORNE, JACK	1800	NYCO	WD06	791
VAN HORNE, THOMAS	1810	NYCO	WD06	438
VAN HOSEN, NANCY	1800	COLU	HUDS	1142
VAN HOSEN, PETER	1800	COLU	HUDS	1143
VANHOUTEN, ANTHONY	1820	ROCK	CLAK	93
VAN HOUTEN, JAMES	1810	NYCO	WD06	408
VANHOUTEN, JOHN	1830	ROCK	RPOO	85
VANHUSEN, ISAAC	1830	ABNY	WD02	261
VAN HYKE, JACK	1820	SCHR	BROM	429
VAN KEURIN, SAMUEL	1830	ORNG	CALH	18
VAN KUCEN, FRANCIS	1820	ORNG	MONT	837
VAN KUREN, FRANCES	1830	ORNG	MONR	163
VAN LOAN, ABRAHAM	1820	GREN	ATHE	3
VAN LOAN, ABRAM	1830	GREN	COXE	190
VAN LOAN, ANTHONY	1830	GREN	COXE	190
VAN LOAN, PETER	1820	GREN	ATHE	4
VAN LOAN, PETER	1830	GREN	COXE	187
VAN LOAN, TOBIAS	1830	GREN	ATHN	211
VAN MARTER, FRANCES	1820	KING	NEUT	159
VAN MATER, FRANCES	1830	KING	NEUT	389
VAN MEHTER, JACOB	1820	GREN	ATHE	1
VAN METER, FRANK	1810	KING	NEUT	668
VAN MUNN, JOHN	1820	DUTC	FISH	64
VANNE, JACK	1810	COLU	CLAV	157
VAN NESS, ABRAHAM	1820	COLU	HUDS	37
VAN NESS, ANTHONY	1830	COLU	STUY	69
VAN NESS, FRANCIS	1830	NYCO	WD03	109
VAN NESS, FRANK	1830	COLU	KIND	146
VAN NESS, JACK	1820	COLU	HUDS	37
VAN NESS, JACK	1830	COLU	HUDS	128
VAN NESS, PETER	1820	COLU	KIND	25
VAN NETS, TOM	1810	COLU	CHAT	186
VAN NICKTON, NICHOLAS	1820	COLU	HUDS	37
VAN NOLER, JOHN	1830	NYCO	WD10	64
VAN NOSTRAND, TOM	1830	QUEN	JAMA	134
VAN ORDEN, ANDREW	1820	GREN	DURH	133
VAN ORDEN, ANDREW	1830	GREN	COXE	185
VAN ORDEN, ANDREW	1830	ULST	SAUG	104
VANPELT, ELEANOR	1830	NYCO	WD05	336

NAME	YR	CO	TWP	PG
VANPELT, JOHN	1820	ABNY	ABNY	206
VAN RANSALAER, MARY	1830	ONTA	SENE	81
VAN RANSILVER, THOMAS	1830	NYCO	WD03	135
VAN RENSELAER, CAESAR	1830	COLU	CLAV	78
VAN RENSELLAER, JACOB	1830	COLU	HUDS	102
VAN RENSSLAER, MOLLY	1820	ONTA	SENE	268
VAN SCHAICK, JOHN	1820	ABNY	WATV	270
VAN SCHAICK, JOHN	1830	SARA	WILT	260
VAN SCHAICK, PETER	1810	COLU	CANN	102
VAN SCHAICK, RICHARD	1830	CAYU	BRUT	194
VAN SCHAICK, RUP	1810	WASH	EAST	502
VAN SCHUYCH, PHILES	1800	WASH	EAST	460
VAN SCOICK, THOMAS	1830	GREN	CATS	243
VAN SCOLK, CAESAR	1830	GREN	CATS	228
VAN SITZ, HENRY	1800	NYCO	WD01	667
VANSLIKE, FRANCIS	1830	ABNY	WD01	197
VAN SLUYCH, JACK	1830	COLU	KIND	142
VAN SLYCK, FRANK	1820	GREN	COXE	41
VAN SLYCK, HENRY	1830	ONON	MANI	362
VAN SLYCK, JACK	1830	SCHR	BROM	89
VAN SLYCK, PRINCE	1820	GREN	NEWB	28
VAN SLYK, JACK	1830	GREN	NEWB	178
VAN SLYK, PRINCE	1830	GREN	NEWB	177
VAN SLYK, THOMAS	1830	GREN	NEWB	179
VAN SOON, WILLIAM	1830	RENS	TROY	19
VANSURLY, MARGARET	1830	NYCO	WD05	269
VAN TASSEL, HENRY	1830	NYCO	WD10	99
VANTHORN, THOMAS	1820	MONT	CHAR	339
VANTINE, JOHN	1820	NYCO	WD02	98
VAN TINE, PETER	1830	NYCO	WD08	176
VAN VALKENBURGH, JOHN	1830	GREN	CATS	238
VAN VALKENBURGH, THOMAS	1830	RENS	NASS	298
VAN VALKUBURG, THOMAS	1810	SARA	STIL	739
VAN VECHTEN, HARRY	1830	GREN	CATS	242
VAN VECHTEN, NICHOLAS	1830	GREN	ATHN	203
VAN VEIGHTON, THOMAS	1830	RENS	PITT	127
VAN VENCHTEN, ABRAM	1830	GREN	CATS	229
VAN VIECK, THOMAS	1830	DELA	KORT	112
VAN VLACK, THOMAS	1820	DELA	KORT	68
VAN VLECK, PETER	1820	ABNY	ABNY	206
VAN VORST, PETER	1820	SCNE	GLEN	609
VAN VRANK, THOMAS	1830	RENS	PITT	136
VAN VRANKEN, DAVID	1820	SARA	HALF	221
VAN VRONK, MARGARETT	1830	RENS	TROY	17
VAN WAGENEN, SAMUEL	1830	ULST	ROCH	179
VAN WART, SAMUEL	1830	WEST	MTPL	27
VANWECK, ELIAS	1810	QUEN	NHEM	205
VAN WERKER, ROBERT	1830	RENS	LANS	87
VAN WEYAN, SAMUEL	1830	ULST	SHAW	250

NAME	YR	CO	TWP	PG
VAN WICK, WAN	1810	COLU	HUDS	134
VAN WIE, DINAH	1830	SARA	STIL	65
VAN WIE, PETER	1830	RENS	TROY	4
VAN WIE, THOMAS	1830	ABNY	BETH	536
VAN WINKLE, JOHN	1810	NYCO	WD05	258
VAN WINKLE, WILLIAM	1830	NYCO	WD05	269
VAN WOAK, FRANCES	1820	WASH	JACK	190
VAN WYAN, SAMUEL	1820	ULST	SHAW	65
VAN WYCK, CHARLES	1810	DUTC	FISH	246
VAN WYCK, ELIAS	1830	QUEN	NHEM	100
VAN WYCK, ISAAC	1830	QUEN	OYST	34
VAN WYCK, ISRAEL	1830	QUEN	FLUS	148
VAN WYCK, NEOB	1820	QUEN	----	55
VAN WYCK, PETER	1830	QUEN	NHEM	112
VAN WYCK, THOMAS	1830	QUEN	SHEM	85
VAN WYCK, W---	1820	COLU	HUDS	37
VAN WYCKE, JACOB	1830	QUEN	FLUS	143
VARIAN, ISAAC	1830	WEST	HARR	219
VARICK, AURELIA	1830	NYCO	WD10	59
VARICK, DANIEL	1830	NYCO	WD11	183
VARICK, JAMES	1810	NYCO	WD06	445
VARICK, JAMES	1820	NYCO	WD06	493
VARROT, DINAH	1800	NYCO	WD01	667
VAUHN, NERO	1830	MONR	PENF	349
VAUXHALL, WILLIAM	1830	NYCO	WD06	427
VEAL, SIB	1810	WEST	NORS	1043
VEDDER, THOMAS	1830	HERK	RUSS	20
VEILE, PHOEBE	1830	RENS	TROY	17
VEMUNG, PETER	1830	DUTC	PGKP	330
VENOE, THOMAS	1830	CAYU	AUBN	165
VENUS	1800	NYCO	WD01	661
VENUS	1800	QUEN	NHEM	554
VER BURAN, HARY	1820	WASH	EAST	174
VERPLANCK, RICHARD	1810	NYCO	WD06	455
VER PLANK, HARRY	1830	DUTC	HYPK	231
VER VALEN, ANTHONY	1820	DUTC	FISH	74
VERVALEN, JANE	1810	DUTC	FISH	218
VER VALEN, SAMUEL	1820	DUTC	FISH	74
VER VALERN, SAMUEL	1830	DUTC	FISH	477
VER VLEET, JAMES	1820	ULST	ESOP	53
VER ZELMAC, JOHN	1800	NYCO	WD07	877
VEWALEN, JOHN	1810	ROCK	ORNG	635
VILLIER, JOHN	1800	.NYCO	WD07	855
VINCEN, JACOB	1830	WASH	GRAN	258
VINCENT	1820	SUFF	SHAM	313
VINCENT, DAVID	1830	OTSG	MIDD	101
VINCENT, DOROTHY	1820	COLU	AUST	15
VINCENT, ISAAC	1830	RENS	TROY	13
VINCENT, J.	1830	NYCO	WD11	173

NAME	YR	CO	TWP	PG
VINCENT, SHARP	1800	NYCO	WD06	846
VINCENT, SOLOMON	1800	RENS	PITT	796
VINCENT, SOLOMON	1830	RENS	GRAF	191
VIOR	1790	QUEN	SHEM	156
VIRGIL	1790	NYCO	MONT	120
VIRGIL	1800	SUFF	EHAM	92
VIRGINIA, GEORGE	1830	ESEX	JAY	293
VIRGINIA, STEPHEN	1830	FRAN	MALO	72
VOLGAR, SAMUEL	1830	SCNE	WD01	206
VOLGER, JAMES	1830	SCNE	WD01	206
VOMORS, DANIEL	1810	DUTC	CLNT	414
VOSBURGH, JAMES	1830	DELA	STAM	183
VOSBURGH, POWS	1820	COLU	CLAV	7
VRAMETT, CASPER	1810	COLU	CLAV	155
VROMAN, JACK	1830	SCHR	SCHR	19
VROMAN, PETER	1830	COLU	HUDS	98
VROMAN, PETER	1830	SCHR	MIDD	36
VROMAN, SAMUEL	1830	SCHR	MIDD	36
VROMAN, SAMUEL S.	1830	SCHR	MIDD	36
VROMAN, WILLIAM	1830	SCHR	SCHR	19
WADDEN, STEPHEN	1800	QUEN	NHEM	553
WADDIN, ENOCH	1820	QUEN	----	79
WADDIN, STEPHEN	1820	QUEN	----	78
WADDING, ENOCH	1830	QUEN	NHEM	112
WADDING, STEPHEN	1830	QUEN	NHEM	115
WAGENAN, SUSAN	1810	NYCO	WD01	27
WAGGONER, JAMES	1830	ONON	SALI	11
WAGGONER, THOMAS	1830	ONTA	SENE	52
WAGLIN, GEORGE	1810	ORNG	WARW	973
WAIT, REUBEN	1810	WASH	BOTT	399
WAKE, RANSOM F.	1830	NYCO	WD05	341
WAKE, SARAH	1830	NYCO	WD04	158
WAKER, JOHN	1800	CLNT	PERU	1059
WALCH, ELIZABETH	1810	NYCO	WD05	280
WALDEN, PHEBE	1830	NYCO	WD08	237
WALDON, WILLIAM	1830	NYCO	WD01	49
WALDRON, JACOB	1810	COLU	HUDS	137
WALDRON, JACOB	1830	ABNY	WD01	197
WALDRON, RICHARD	1830	ABNY	COEY	513
WALES, ELIZABETH	1830	DUTC	FISH	481
WALES, FRANCES	1830	DUTC	LAGR	245
WALES, ISAAC	1830	ONON	SALI	11
WALES, PRINCE OF	1790	DUTC	FISH	79
WALES, SAMUEL	1820	DUTC	FISH	56
WALES, THOMAS	1830	ABNY	GUID	413
WALES, THOMAS	1830	NYCO	WD05	339
WALKER, BENJAMIN	1830	NYCO	WD08	237

NAME	YR	CO	TWP	PG
WALKER, DINAH	1810	NYCO	WD01	27
WALKER, J.	1830	NYCO	WD13	375
WALKER, JONAS	1830	NYCO	WD05	310
WALKER, POPLAR	1830	NYCO	WD10	11
WALKER, SAMUEL	1830	SUFF	SHAM	224
WALL, PETER	1810	NYCO	WD05	276
WALL, POMPEY	1800	NYCO	WD07	925
WALL, TOBY	1800	COLU	HUDS	1140
WALL, TOBY	1810	COLU	HUDS	147
WALLACE	1830	NYCO	WD02	79
WALLACE, ABRAHAM	1830	NYCO	WD01	32
WALLACE, ANTHONY	1830	NYCO	WD13	358
WALLACE, JOHN	1820	ORNG	GOSH	750
WALLACE, JOHN	1830	ORNG	GOSH	289
WALLACE, ROBERT	1830	NYCO	WD10	14
WALLACE, ROSANNAH	1800	NYCO	WD01	667
WALLACE, ROSANNAH	1810	NYCO	WD06	404
WALLACE, ZACHERSAK	1810	RENS	BRUN	500
WALLER, WILL	1790	NYCO	DOCK	116
WALLIN, ELIAS	1820	NYCO	WD02	115
WALLINBECK, DIRK	1810	GREN	COXE	290
WALLIS, THOMAS	1830	NYCO	WD09	301
WALMSLEY, JAMES	1820	MADI	MADI	92
WALRADT, MARIA	1830	HERK	HERK	50
WALTERS, HENRY	1820	NYCO	WD04	316
WALTERS, JAMES	1830	NYCO	WD10	88
WALTERS, REUBEN	1830	SUFF	SHAM	225
WALTERS, RICHARD	1800	QUEN	FLUS	542
WALVAATH, THOMAS	1820	HERK	FRAN	61
WAMPUM, CATO	1810	SCHR	BROM	160
WAMSLEY, ANDREW	1820	CHEN	NORW	378
WAMSLEY, JAMES	1800	CHEN	BROK	818
WAMSLEY, SMITH	1830	CHEN	NORW	176
WANDELL, FRANCIS	1820	SARA	BALL	212
WANDELL, FRANCIS	1830	ONON	SALI	31
WANDELL, RICHARD	1830	ONON	SALI	23
WANTON, CAESAR	1790	NYCO	SOUT	132
WAR, ELIJAH	1830	MONR	RWD3	228
WARD, FRANK	1810	SUFF	SHEL	466
WARD, J.	1830	ERIE	BUFF	37
WARD, JACK	1820	SUFF	BROK	330
WARD, JACOB	1830	SUFF	BROK	161
WARD, JANE	1830	NYCO	WD09	395
WARD, JOHN	1830	KING	WD03	279
WARD, JOSEPH	1830	NYCO	WD14	512
WARD, LONDON	1810	SUFF	SHEL	466
WARD, LONDON	1820	SUFF	SHEL	331
WARD, LONDON	1830	SUFF	SHEL	291
WARD, PHILIP	1830	NYCO	WD08	257

NAME	YR	CO	TWP	PG
WARD, PHILLIP	1810	NYCO	WD06	449
WARD, THOMAS	1830	NYCO	WD08	179
WARD, THOMAS	1830	SUFF	BROK	179
WARD, WILLIAM	1820	ORNG	GOSH	763
WARD, WILLIAM	1830	NYCO	WD06	447
WARD, WILLIAM	1830	NYCO	WD14	472
WARD, WILLIAM	1830	WANE	GALE	154
WARDENBURG, SHARP	1820	ORNG	MONT	841
WARE, WILLIAM	1830	NYCO	WD11	151
WAREING, PETER	1830	QUEN	OYST	35
WARING, JACOB	1830	QUEN	NEWT	10
WARM, JOSEPH	1800	NYCO	WD05	774
WARNER, JACK	1810	ORNG	MONT	957
WARNER, JACK	1820	ORNG	WALL	778
WARNER, JOHN	1830	ORNG	WALL	147
WARNER, JOSEPH	1800	NYCO	WD07	863
WARNER, STEPHEN	1830	ORNG	MONR	181
WARNER, WILLIAM	1810	NYCO	WD06	444
WARREN, MORDECAI	1790	DUTC	PAWL	87
WARREN, RICHARD	1800	NYCO	WD06	823
WARREN, THOMAS	1810	DUTC	FISH	254
WARREN, WILLIAM	1800	NYCO	WD06	844
WASHINGHAM, ABRAHAM	1810	NYCO	WD06	492
WASHINGHAM, MARY	1810	NYCO	WD06	410
WASHINGTON, GEORGE	1830	NYCO	WD08	175
WASHINGTON, GEORGE	1830	NYCO	WD08	246
WASHINGTON, JOHN	1820	NYCO	WD02	112
WASHINGTON, JOHN	1830	NYCO	WD06	458
WASHINGTON, ROBERT	1820	NYCO	WD06	515
WATERMAN, AMA	1820	SENE	JUNU	417
WATERMAN, JACOB	1830	NYCO	WD14	439
WATERMAN, LEVI	1820	NYCO	WD07	709
WATEROUS, THAYMER	1830	DUTC	AMEN	175
WATERS, ABEL	1830	NYCO	WD06	437
WATERS, ANTHONY	1830	NYCO	WD06	421
WATERS, ANTHONY & MORSE W.	1830	NYCO	WD13	338
WATERS, CAESAR	1800	NYCO	WD01	667
WATERS, CATHERINE	1820	NYCO	WD06	449
WATERS, CHARLES	1820	SUFF	BROK	360
WATERS, CHARTIS	1810	SUFF	BROK	488
WATERS, DICK	1800	QUEN	FLUS	538
WATERS, FRANCIS	1830	MONT	JOHN	209
WATERS, HAGAEN	1820	OTSG	CHRV	27
WATERS, HENRY	1810	SUFF	SOUT	536
WATERS, HENRY	1830	NYCO	WD06	429
WATERS, JAMES	1800	NYCO	WD07	923
WATERS, JAMES	1830	DUTC	AMEN	177
WATERS, JOE	1820	SUFF	BROK	362
WATERS, JOSEPH	1810	NYCO	WD05	380

NAME	YR	CO	TWP	PG
WATERS, MOSES	1830	DUTC	RHIN	400
WATERS, MULBERRY	1820	DUTC	CLNT	28
WATERS, POMP	1830	WARR	QUEN	80
WATERS, ROBERT	1790	DUTC	AMEN	73
WATERS, ROBERT	1800	DUTC	AMEN	138
WATERS, ROBERT	1820	DUTC	AMEN	7
WATERS, SAMUEL	1820	DUTC	AMEN	7
WATERS, SAMUEL	1830	DUTC	AMEN	175
WATERS, SARAH	1810	NYCO	WD04	159
WATERS, THOMAS	1800	NYCO	WD07	857
WATKINS, JACOB	1830	SULL	BETH	31
WATKINS, KING	1820	STEU	BATH	227
WATKINS, KING	1830	STEU	BATH	264
WATKINS, OMY	1820	QUEN	----	28
WATKINS, POMP	1810	ORNG	WALL	1113
WATKINS, SIMON	1820	STEU	BATH	227
WATKINS, SIMON	1830	STEU	BATH	263
WATKINS, THOMAS	1820	ONTA	FARM	317
WATKINS, THOMAS	1830	STEU	BATH	271
WATRONS, ROBERT	1810	DUTC	AMEN	441
WATROUP, POMP	1810	WASH	GREN	505
WATSON, ELIZABETH	1830	NYCO	WD05	252
WATSON, GEORGE	1820	NYCO	WD09	935
WATSON, GEORGE	1830	NYCO	WD12	252
WATSON, HARRIS	1820	WEST	NORC	432
WATSON, HENRY	1830	NYCO	WD07	56
WATSON, HORACE	1830	WEST	NORC	198
WATSON, JOHN	1820	NYCO	WD05	384
WATSON, JOHN	1830	KING	WD04	307
WATSON, JOHN	1830	NYCO	WD12	251
WATSON, MRS.	1830	NYCO	WD10	28
WATSON, PHILIP	1810	NYCO	WD07	552
WATSON, WILLIAM	1820	NYCO	WD06	570
WATSON, WILLIAM	1830	NYCO	WD06	380
WATSON, WILLIAM	1830	NYCO	WD07	56
WATTERS, HAYDEN	1830	OTSG	MIDD	108
WATTERS, RICHARD	1800	QUEN	FLUS	542
WATTS, GEORGE	1830	ABNY	WD05	333
WATTS, JAMES	1830	YATE	MSEX	336
WATTS, SAMUEL	1830	NYCO	WD07	83
WAUTSEX, LUTUS	1810	SUFF	SHAM	445
WAY, ISAAC	1830	COLU	HILL	191
WAY, TUSBEY	1830	RENS	LANS	89
WAYS, ELIZABETH	1820	ABNY	WATV	271
WAYWOOD, CATO	1810	NYCO	WD07	543
WEAKS, CESAR	1830	NYCO	WD05	314
WEALCH, H.	1810	MADI	SMIT	877
WEALCH, W.	1810	MADI	SMIT	877
WEAVER, J.	1820	NYCO	WDII	191
WEAVER, JOHN	1820	ABNY	ABNY	212

NAME	YR	CO	TWP	PG
WEAVER, JOSEPH	1800	NYCO	WD06	847
WEBB, PETER	1830	TOMP	CARO	506
WEBSTER, SAMUEL	1830	NYCO	WD11	168
WEDDEN, ROBERT	1830	NYCO	WD09	431
WEDDER, CHARLES	1830	NYCO	WD06	379
WEEDS, SOLOMON	1830	NYCO	WD06	444
WEEKS, BENJAMIN	1830	QUEN	OYST	32
WEEKS, CAROLINE	1830	QUEN	FLUS	155
WEEKS, CUFFEE	1830	QUEN	JAMA	128
WEEKS, DOROTHY	1820	SARA	CHAR	213
WEEKS, HENRY	1810	NYCO	WD07	590
WEEKS, JOHN	1830	WASH	JACK	181
WEEKS, MICHAEL	1810	QUEN	FLUS	194
WEEKS, MICHAEL	1830	QUEN	NHEM	113
WEEKS, MRS.	1820	NYCO	WD07	627
WEEKS, NATHANIEL	1800	NYCO	WD06	846
WEEKS, SHUBACH	1800	DUTC	AMEN	133
WEEKS, THOMAS	1830	NYCO	WD11	212
WEESE, JOHN	1810	NYCO	WD05	295
WEISER, HINSEY	1810	NYCO	WD05	154
WELCH, D.	1810	MADI	SMIT	880
WELCH, DAVID	1830	ONON	ONON	188
WELCH, DAVID	1830	OSWE	HAST	222
WELCH, H.	1810	MADI	SMIT	880
WELCH, HENRY	1830	OSWE	HAST	222
WELCH, LAWRENCE	1830	NYCO	WD06	412
WELCH, WILLIAM	1830	OSWE	HAST	222
WELDING, ELIJAH	1830	DUTC	DOVE	218
WELDING, ELIJAH	1830	DUTC	STAN	405
WELDING, STEPHEN	1790	DUTC	FRDK	84
WELDON, JACOB	1830	NYCO	WD14	435
WELL, JOHN	1800	NYCO	WD04	722
WELLER, JACOB	1830	NYCO	WD05	347
WELLER, JANE	1830	ULST	SHAW	242
WELLER, JOSIAH	1830	ULST	SHAW	251
WELLES, A.	1810	DUTC	WASH	164
WELLS, AMELIA	1810	NYCO	WD06	448
WELLS, AMELIA	1820	NYCO	WD06	502
WELLS, AMELIA	1830	NYCO	WD06	380
WELLS, DAVID	1820	JEFF	HOUN	427
WELLS, JACOB	1830	NYCO	WD12	283
WELLS, JAMES	1830	NYCO	WD06	368
WELLS, JANE	1810	NYCO	WD05	359
WELLS, JANE	1820	NYCO	WD07	636
WELLS, JUDAH	1830	NIAG	LOCK	385
WELLS, MR.	1830	NYCO	WD06	410
WELLS, NOAH	1820	SUFF	SHAM	317
WELLS, NOAH	1830	SUFF	SHAM	229
WELLS, S.	1810	ONID	DEER	450

Wells

NAME	YR	CO	TWP	PG
WELLS, SIMON	1810	SENS	ROMU	228
WELLS, SIMON	1820	NIAG	HART	164
WELLS, WILLIAM	1810	DUTC	CLNT	417
WELSH, JOHN	1830	ORNG	NEWB	40
WELSH, SOLOMAN	1830	NYCO	WD14	475
WENDLE, JOHN	1830	SCNE	WD01	206
WERTMAN, HANNAH	1830	NYCO	WD10	122
WESCOT, ANTHONY	1820	PUTM	SOUT	100
WEST, ANTHONY	1830	NYCO	WD01	31
WEST, EDWARD	1800	NYCO	WD04	721
WEST, EDWARD	1810	NYCO	WD05	301
WEST, EDWARD	1820	NYCO	WD05	337
WEST, GEORGE	1810	NYCO	WD05	293
WEST, GEORGE	1830	NYCO	WD08	173
WEST, HECTOR	1830	ULST	KING	77
WEST, JAMES	1830	NYCO	WD13	350
WEST, LINDLY	1820	NYCO	WD05	333
WEST, P.	1830	ERIE	BUFF	26
WEST, SAM	1810	SENE	ROMU	222
WEST, STEPHEN	1820	DUTC	RHIN	123
WESTBROOK, CALVIN	1830	ULST	ROCH	184
WESTBROOK, DAVID	1830	OSWE	OSWE	135
WESTBROOK, HENRY	1830	NYCO	WD08	217
WESTBROOK, JOHN	1830	DUTC	FISH	467
WESTBROOK, PETER	1830	ULST	ROCH	176
WESTBROOK, PHILIP	1830	ULST	ROCH	177
WESTBROOK, POMP	1820	ORNG	MONT	807
WESTBROOK, POMPEY	1830	ORNG	GOSH	292
WESTCOT, ANTHONY	1800	DUTC	SOUT	176
WESTCOTT, ANTHONY	1790	DUTC	FRDK	82
WESTCOTT, ENOS	1820	ORNG	GOSH	750
WESTERN, GEORGE	1830	NYCO	WD08	184
WESTERVELT, HENRY	1820	ORNG	WARW	616
WETBECK, JOSEPH	1820	GREN	NEWB	27
WETSEL, PETER	1830	ABNY	WD02	262
WEUB, ZENUS	1830	WEST	GREN	21
WHEATLEAY, JOHN	1830	CAYU	LEDY	276
WHEELER, PETER	1830	COLU	AUST	179
WHEELER, RICHARD	1820	MADI	HAML	82
WHEELER, SARY	1810	SUFF	SMIT	538
WHEELER, YORK	1800	DUTC	AMEN	133
WHESNER, PRIME	1820	ORNG	GOSH	756
WHIBAIN, JACK	1820	ULST	PLAT	58
WHILLETS, CALEB	1830	NYCO	WD10	118
WHILTINE, JACK	1820	COLU	KIND	31
WHIPLE, JONATHAN	1810	DELA	MIDD	494
WHIPPIE, ANTHONY	1830	QUEN	SHEM	85
WHIPPLE, JONATHAN	1800	DELA	MIDD	1288
WHISTLOW, ALEXANDER	1810	NYCO	WD03	62

NAME	YR	CO	TWP	PG
WHISTTO, ABNES	1820	NYCO	WD08	780
WHITBECK, JACK	1830	DUTC	REDH	369
WHITBECK, JACOB	1830	COLU	CLAV	79
WHITBECK, JACOB	1830	SCHR	SHAR	120
WHITBECK, JOSEPH	1830	GREN	NEWB	174
WHITBECK, ROBERT	1810	COLU	KIND	166
WHITE, ABRAM	1830	KING	WD05	325
WHITE, CATHERINE	1830	NYCO	WD06	382
WHITE, GEOGE	1800	NYCO	WD05	752
WHITE, GEORGE	1810	NYCO	WD04	177
WHITE, GEORGE	1820	NYCO	WD04	212
WHITE, GEORGE	1830	NYCO	WD05	241
WHITE, GEORGE	1830	WEST	YORK	171
WHITE, HARY	1810	KING	BRYN	632
WHITE, HENRY	1820	DUTC	CLNT	44
WHITE, HENRY	1820	KING	BRYN	149
WHITE, HENRY	1820	WEST	YORK	340
WHITE, HENRY	1830	DUTC	HYPK	234
WHITE, HENRY	1830	NYCO	WD11	139
WHITE, JACKSON	1830	KING	WD04	305
WHITE, JAMES	1800	SARA	HALF	1045
WHITE, JARVIS	1830	MONR	PITS	98
WHITE, JOEL	1820	STEU	READ	270
WHITE, JOHN	1820	NYCO	WD10	1066
WHITE, JOHNATHAN	1830	NYCO	WD14	429
WHITE, JOSEPH	1810	STEU	BATH	376
WHITE, JOSEPH	1830	STEU	URBA	285
WHITE, MORRIS	1830	NYCO	WD03	121
WHITE, PETER B.	1830	DELA	TOMP	208
WHITE, PHOEBE	1790	QUEN	OYST	154
WHITE, RACHEL	1810	NYCO	WD06	398
WHITE, ROMEMO	1830	KING	WD03	280
WHITE, SCIPIO	1810	NYCO	WD06	494
WHITE, THOMAS	1810	NYCO	WD04	214
WHITE, THOMAS	1810	NYCO	WD06	484
WHITE, TULLY	1800	NYCO	WD05	760
WHITEHEAD, J.	1810	MADI	MADI	837
WHITEHEAD, JOHN	1820	ONID	AUGU	320
WHITEHEAD, JOHN	1830	ONID	AUGU	114
WHITEING, ANTHONY	1810	NYCO	WD04	212
WHITFIELD, JOSEPH	1810	NYCO	WD03	78
WHITLOCK, JACOB	1820	COLU	HUDS	39
WHITNEY	1820	PUTM	PATE	101
WHITNEY, JOHN	1830	NYCO	WD08	148
WHITS, LEMUEL	1830	NYCO	WD06	402
WHITSON, MR.	1820	NYCO	WD05	418
WICKHAM, STEPHEN	1830	ABNY	WD02	268
WICKOFF, THOMAS	1830	SENE	COVE	134
WICKOFF, TOM	1810	SENE	HECT	318

NAME	YR	CO	TWP	PG
WICKS & QUINBY, NATHANIEL	1790	ABNY	BALL	18
WICKS, ANTHONY	1830	NYCO	WD12	304
WICKS, DAGIE	1810	SUFF	HUNT	527
WICKS, JACK	1820	SARA	STIL	194
WICKS, JAMES	1830	NYCO	WD11	144
WICKS, JOHN	1830	SARA	WILT	263
WIDIFIELD, AMANIAS	1830	QUEN	NHEM	106
WIGGIN, MARY	1830	ALLE	FDSP	94
WIGGINS, JAMES	1830	NYCO	WD07	49
WIGGINS, MOSES	1820	SUFF	SOUT	345
WIGGINS, W.	1830	NYCO	WD06	403
WIGTON, BEN	1820	SENE	RAMU	351
WILBER, JOSEPH	1820	ONTA	SODU	121
WILBER, JOSEPH	1830	CAYU	AUBN	165
WILCOX, CHARLES L.	1830	NYCO	WD06	368
WILCOX, MOSES	1830	ONID	UTIC	15
WILDEN, JACOB	1820	KING	BRYN	113
WILDER, JACOB	1830	NYCO	WD14	457
WILDER, TOBE	1830	COLU	CHAT	41
WILDING, ELIJAH	1820	DUTC	NORT	84
WILDS, RACHEL	1820	NYCO	WD06	502
WILES, FRANCIS	1830	NYCO	WD05	266
WILES, WASHINGTON	1810	NYCO	WD06	473
WILISON, HENRY	1790	ORNG	WARW	147
WILISON, SARAH	1830	NYCO	WD06	447
WILKES, ANN	1830	NYCO	WD05	269
WILKES, JOHN	1810	NYCO	WD06	443
WILKHAM, JACK	1810	SUFF	SHAM	449
WILKINS, ALEXANDER	1830	NYCO	WD06	386
WILKINS, JOHN	1800	NYCO	WD07	899
WILKINS, ROBERT	1830	MONR	RWD3	222
WILKINS, WILLIAM	1830	NYCO	WD03	112
WILKINSON, PATRICK	1830	NYCO	WD04	206
WILL	1790	WEST	MAMA	200
WILL	1810	RICH	CAST	613
WILL, LUSA	1810	SUFF	SHAM	444
WILL, PETER	1820	NYCO	WD06	469
WILL, SHADRACH	1830	SUFF	SHAM	232
WILL, STEINBURGH	1820	ABNY	BARN	31
WILLARD, HENRY	1830	QUEN	FLUS	148
WILLARD, JAMES	1820	NYCO	WD10	1028
WILLET, GEORGE	1820	KING	BRYN	137
WILLET, NATHANIEL	1830	DUTC	WASH	446
WILLET, SIMON	1830	QUEN	FLUS	139
WILLETS, TIMOTHY	1810	SUFF	ISLP	497
WILLETT, CALEB	1820	NYCO	WD06	498
WILLETT, MOSES	1830	WEST	WEST	117
WILLETT, WILLIAM	1820	QUEN	----	51

Williams

NAME	YR	CO	TWP	PG
WILLETTS, HECKEAH	1820	QUEN	----	30
WILLETTS, SILVANUS	1810	QUEN	OYST	256
WILLETTS, WILLIAM	1810	QUEN	SHEM	291
WILLGROWS, JOHN	1830	QUEN	NHEM	115
WILLIAM	1790	NYCO	MONT	120
WILLIAM	1790	NYCO	MONT	123
WILLIAM	1790	NYCO	NORT	124
WILLIAM	1790	NYCO	OUTW	128
WILLIAM	1790	NYCO	WEST	136
WILLIAM	1790	QUEN	FLUS	149
WILLIAM	1790	QUEN	NHEM	153
WILLIAM	1800	QUEN	OYST	573
WILLIAM	1800	QUEN	NHEM	554
WILLIAM	1800	QUEN	NHEM	551
WILLIAM	1800	SUFF	BROK	12
WILLIAM	1800	SUFF	BROK	6
WILLIAM	1800	SUFF	BROK	13
WILLIAM	1800	SUFF	SHAM	75
WILLIAM	1800	WEST	HARR	652
WILLIAM	1810	NYCO	WD07	545
WILLIAM	1810	RENS	STEP	578
WILLIAM	1820	QUEN	----	74
WILLIAM	1820	QUEN	----	80
WILLIAM	1820	WEST	RYE	370
WILLIAM	1830	NYCO	WD11	234
WILLIAM	1830	NYCO	WD12	262
WILLIAM	1830	NYCO	WD13	388
WILLIAM, ADDY	1810	QUEN	FLUS	192
WILLIAM, BENJAMIN	1830	NYCO	WD08	201
WILLIAM, JACOB	1820	COLU	HUDS	39
WILLIAM, JOHN	1830	NYCO	WD06	458
WILLIAM, LEONARD	1810	DUTC	FISH	192
WILLIAM, PAUL	1790	NYCO	EAST	118
WILLIAM, PRINCE	1820	SARA	MALT	230
WILLIAM, RICHARD	1820	COLU	KIND	27
WILLIAM, RICHARD	1820	NYCO	WD07	634
WILLIAMS	1810	NYCO	WD05	323
WILLIAMS	1810	NYCO	WD07	593
WILLIAMS, ABBY	1820	STEU	BATH	227
WILLIAMS, ABRAHAM	1830	KING	FLAT	398
WILLIAMS, ADDY	1830	NYCO	WD05	345
WILLIAMS, ALEXANDER	1820	GREN	HUNT	110
WILLIAMS, ALLEN	1830	NYCO	WD05	300
WILLIAMS, ALMIRA	1830	ONTA	CANA	113
WILLIAMS, AMANDA	1810	NYCO	WD05	316
WILLIAMS, ANDREW	1820	ABNY	ABNY	209
WILLIAMS, ANDREW	1830	ABNY	WD01	215
WILLIAMS, ANDREW	1830	NYCO	WD12	288
WILLIAMS, ANTHONY	1830	DUTC	WASH	442

NAME	YR	CO	TWP	PG
WILLIAMS, ARMISTED	1820	NYCO	WD06	501
WILLIAMS, BELLA	1800	NYCO	WD04	722
WILLIAMS, BENJAMIN	1820	NYCO	WD04	281
WILLIAMS, BENJAMIN	1830	NYCO	WD10	20
WILLIAMS, BENJEMEN	1820	NYCO	WD10	983
WILLIAMS, BETSEY	1830	NYCO	WD07	59
WILLIAMS, CATHERINE	1820	DUTC	REDH	114
WILLIAMS, CEASAR	1820	NYCO	WD09	936
WILLIAMS, CHARLES	1820	NYCO	WD09	933
WILLIAMS, CHARLES	1830	GREN	COXE	185
WILLIAMS, CHARLES	1830	NYCO	WD08	214
WILLIAMS, CHARLES	1830	NYCO	WD10	68
WILLIAMS, CHARLOTT	1810	NYCO	WD04	214
WILLIAMS, CHESTER	1830	NYCO	WD08	224
WILLIAMS, CORINGTON	1830	WEST	WEST	117
WILLIAMS, CORNELIUS	1800	NYCO	WD06	801
WILLIAMS, DANIEL	1830	ABNY	WD02	268
WILLIAMS, DIANA	1830	SCHR	BROM	79
WILLIAMS, DIANN	1820	NYCO	WD04	215
WILLIAMS, DIANNA	1820	SUFF	SHEL	329
WILLIAMS, DIANNA	1830	SUFF	SHEL	290
WILLIAMS, EDWARD	1830	NYCO	WD14	432
WILLIAMS, EDWIN	1830	SUFF	SHAM	225
WILLIAMS, ELIZA	1830	NYCO	WD06	377
WILLIAMS, ELIZABETH	1810	WEST	CORT	1000
WILLIAMS, ELIZABETH	1830	ABNY	WD01	212
WILLIAMS, ELIZABETH	1830	ABNY	WD04	300
WILLIAMS, ELIZABETH	1830	NYCO	WD08	197
WILLIAMS, ESTER	1830	SUFF	SHAM	225
WILLIAMS, FANNY	1830	ORLE	MURR	43
WILLIAMS, FRANCES	1830	SUFF	SHAM	225
WILLIAMS, FRANCIS	1790	DUTC	FISH	81
WILLIAMS, FRANCIS	1810	NYCO	WD04	160
WILLIAMS, FRANCIS	1820	NYCO	WD05	372
WILLIAMS, FRANCIS	1820	WEST	YONK	227
WILLIAMS, FRANCIS	1830	NYCO	WD05	300
WILLIAMS, FRANCIS	1830	NYCO	WD08	199
WILLIAMS, FRANK	1830	QUEN	FLUS	143
WILLIAMS, FREDRICK	1820	NYCO	WD07	632
WILLIAMS, GEORGE	1800	NYCO	WD03	705
WILLIAMS, GEORGE	1830	MONR	GATE	235
WILLIAMS, H.	1820	NYCO	WD10	1072
WILLIAMS, H.	1830	NYCO	WD03	116
WILLIAMS, H.	1830	NYCO	WD11	162
WILLIAMS, HANNAH	1830	NYCO	WD01	35
WILLIAMS, HANNAH	1830	NYCO	WD05	331
WILLIAMS, HARKNESS	1820	ONTA	FREE	99
WILLIAMS, HARRIET	1820	NYCO	WD06	447
WILLIAMS, HARRY	1820	COLU	KIND	31
WILLIAMS, HARRY	1820	DUTC	RHIN	128

NAME	YR	CO	TWP	PG
WILLIAMS, HARRY	1830	DUTC	RHIN	400
WILLIAMS, HARRY	1830	KING	GRAV	405
WILLIAMS, HARRY	1830	SUFF	BROK	180
WILLIAMS, HAXULUS	1830	LIVI	CONE	100
WILLIAMS, HEBER	1830	GREN	CATS	230
WILLIAMS, HEBERT	1810	ULST	WARW	798
WILLIAMS, HENRY	1810	WEST	RYE	1162
WILLIAMS, HENRY	1820	KING	BRYN	126
WILLIAMS, HENRY	1830	COLU	LABN	15
WILLIAMS, HENRY	1830	COLU	KIND	146
WILLIAMS, HENRY	1830	DUTC	PGKP	321
WILLIAMS, HENRY	1830	NYCO	WD05	300
WILLIAMS, HENRY	1830	NYCO	WD06	449
WILLIAMS, HENRY	1830	NYCO	WD12	288
WILLIAMS, HERBERT	1820	ULST	MARB	61
WILLIAMS, HESTER	1820	NYCO	WD02	129
WILLIAMS, INS.	1820	NYCO	WD10	998
WILLIAMS, ISAAC	1830	ABNY	WD04	314
WILLIAMS, ISAAC	1830	KING	WD04	313
WILLIAMS, ISHAM	1830	LEWI	DENM	410
WILLIAMS, ISSABELLA	1810	NYCO	WD03	69
WILLIAMS, J.	1830	NYCO	WD13	364
WILLIAMS, JACOB	1800	NYCO	WD06	799
WILLIAMS, JACOB	1810	NYCO	WD02	113
WILLIAMS, JACOB	1830	ABNY	WD04	319
WILLIAMS, JACOB	1830	COLU	CLAV	79
WILLIAMS, JACOB	1830	DUTC	REDH	377
WILLIAMS, JACOB	1830	NYCO	WD10	6
WILLIAMS, JAMES	1800	NYCO	WD04	718
WILLIAMS, JAMES	1810	NYCO	WD02	98
WILLIAMS, JAMES	1810	NYCO	WD03	83
WILLIAMS, JAMES	1810	NYCO	WD02	127
WILLIAMS, JAMES	1820	NYCO	WD05	429
WILLIAMS, JAMES	1820	NYCO	WD06	503
WILLIAMS, JAMES	1820	NYCO	WD07	670
WILLIAMS, JAMES	1820	NYCO	WD07	621
WILLIAMS, JAMES	1820	SCNE	DUNN	590
WILLIAMS, JAMES	1830	NYCO	WD05	252
WILLIAMS, JAMES	1830	NYCO	WD07	37
WILLIAMS, JAMES	1830	NYCO	WD10	84
WILLIAMS, JAMES	1830	NYCO	WD11	162
WILLIAMS, JAMES	1830	NYCO	WD13	344
WILLIAMS, JAMES R.	1830	NYCO	WD10	17
WILLIAMS, JANE	1820	ABNY	ABNY	209
WILLIAMS, JANE	1820	NYCO	WD02	120
WILLIAMS, JANE	1830	NYCO	WD04	216
WILLIAMS, JASPER	1830	NYCO	WD08	227
WILLIAMS, JEPTHA	1810	ORNG	MONT	960
WILLIAMS, JEPTHA	1820	ORNG	MONT	845

Williams

NAME	YR	CO	TWP	PG
WILLIAMS, JEPTHA	1830	ORNG	MONR	177
WILLIAMS, JOHN	1790	NYCO	SOUT	131
WILLIAMS, JOHN	1800	NYCO	WD06	792
WILLIAMS, JOHN	1800	NYCO	WD06	838
WILLIAMS, JOHN	1800	NYCO	WD03	696
WILLIAMS, JOHN	1810	NYCO	WD02	116
WILLIAMS, JOHN	1810	NYCO	WD02	124
WILLIAMS, JOHN	1810	NYCO	WD05	258
WILLIAMS, JOHN	1810	NYCO	WD05	287
WILLIAMS, JOHN	1810	NYCO	WD04	225
WILLIAMS, JOHN	1810	NYCO	WD07	522
WILLIAMS, JOHN	1810	NYCO	WD10	699
WILLIAMS, JOHN	1820	COLU	ANCM	10
WILLIAMS, JOHN	1820	NYCO	WD03	140
WILLIAMS, JOHN	1820	NYCO	WD03	184
WILLIAMS, JOHN	1820	NYCO	WD07	705
WILLIAMS, JOHN	1820	NYCO	WD10	1028
WILLIAMS, JOHN	1820	ULST	MARB	61
WILLIAMS, JOHN	1830	KING	WD03	282
WILLIAMS, JOHN	1830	KING	BRYN	365
WILLIAMS, JOHN	1830	NYCO	WD06	389
WILLIAMS, JOHN	1830	NYCO	WD06	427
WILLIAMS, JOHN	1830	NYCO	WD08	219
WILLIAMS, JOHN	1830	NYCO	WD09	301
WILLIAMS, JOHN	1830	NYCO	WD10	26
WILLIAMS, JOHN	1830	NYCO	WD10	65
WILLIAMS, JOHN	1830	NYCO	WD10	107
WILLIAMS, JOHN	1830	NYCO	WD13	336
WILLIAMS, JOHN	1830	NYCO	WD13	364
WILLIAMS, JOHN	1830	ORNG	CORN	201
WILLIAMS, JOHN	1830	ROCK	ORGT	115
WILLIAMS, JOHN	1830	ULST	KING	67
WILLIAMS, JOHNATHAN	1830	NYCO	WD10	91
WILLIAMS, JOSEPH	1810	NYCO	WD05	290
WILLIAMS, JOSEPH	1820	NYCO	WD07	706
WILLIAMS, L.	1830	NYCO	WD13	396
WILLIAMS, LEAH	1820	NYCO	WD03	189
WILLIAMS, LEONARD	1820	DUTC	PGKP	111
WILLIAMS, LEONARD	1830	DUTC	PGKP	321
WILLIAMS, LEWIS	1820	KING	BRYN	126
WILLIAMS, LIVINGSTON	1830	CAYU	AUBN	168
WILLIAMS, LOU	1820	NYCO	WD08	789
WILLIAMS, LUCY	1820	NYCO	WD04	314
WILLIAMS, LYDIA	1820	NYCO	WD10	1006
WILLIAMS, MANDO	1800	NYCO	WD06	810
WILLIAMS, MARGARET	1830	NYCO	WD08	201
WILLIAMS, MARGRET	1830	WEST	CORT	63
WILLIAMS, MARY	1810	NYCO	WD16	460
WILLIAMS, MARY	1820	NYCO	WD05	404

NAME	YR	CO	TWP	PG
WILLIAMS, MARY	1830	ABNY	WD01	219
WILLIAMS, MARY	1830	NYCO	WD08	220
WILLIAMS, MINARD	1830	DUTC	PLEA	308
WILLIAMS, MINGO	1800	NYCO	WD03	696
WILLIAMS, MOSES	1830	WEST	YONK	9
WILLIAMS, MOSSES	1830	NYCO	WD09	430
WILLIAMS, MR.	1830	NYCO	WD10	116
WILLIAMS, MR.	1830	NYCO	WD11	162
WILLIAMS, MRS.	1830	KING	WD02	272
WILLIAMS, MRS.	1830	NYCO	WD03	143
WILLIAMS, MRS.	1830	NYCO	WD13	394
WILLIAMS, NATHAN	1830	CAYU	AUBN	169
WILLIAMS, NED	1830	DUTC	FISH	480
WILLIAMS, NICHOLAS	1810	NYCO	WD04	153
WILLIAMS, NOAH	1830	SUFF	SHAM	212
WILLIAMS, NOBLE	1810	NYCO	WD04	193
WILLIAMS, P.	1830	KING	WD04	310
WILLIAMS, PATIENCE	1820	NYCO	WD03	189
WILLIAMS, PAUL	1800	NYCO	WD06	846
WILLIAMS, PAUL	1810	NYCO	WD06	396
WILLIAMS, PAUL	1810	NYCO	WD08	761
WILLIAMS, PEGGY	1830	RENS	TROY	8
WILLIAMS, PEGGY	1830	ULST	SAUG	108
WILLIAMS, PETER	1810	KING	BKYN	635
WILLIAMS, PETER	1810	NYCO	WD03	90
WILLIAMS, PETER	1820	ABNY	ABNY	210
WILLIAMS, PETER	1820	DUTC	RHIN	123
WILLIAMS, PETER	1820	NYCO	WD02	86
WILLIAMS, PETER	1820	NYCO	WD08	735
WILLIAMS, PETER	1830	KING	WD03	288
WILLIAMS, PETER	1830	NYCO	WD01	48
WILLIAMS, PETER	1830	NYCO	WD06	448
WILLIAMS, PETER	1830	NYCO	WD09	391
WILLIAMS, PETER	1830	ONID	DEER	230
WILLIAMS, PETER	1830	RENS	SCAS	114
WILLIAMS, PETER	1830	WASH	CAMB	121
WILLIAMS, PETER JR.	1830	NYCO	WD14	481
WILLIAMS, PHILIP	1820	GREN	CATS	173
WILLIAMS, PHILLIP	1820	COLU	KIND	33
WILLIAMS, POMP	1830	GREN	COXE	186
WILLIAMS, POMP	1830	RENS	TROY	14
WILLIAMS, POMP	1830	SARA	MILT	32
WILLIAMS, PRIMROSE	1830	NYCO	WD06	455
WILLIAMS, PRINCE	1820	DUTC	FISH	71
WILLIAMS, PRINCE	1820	SARA	MITL	230
WILLIAMS, PRINCE	1830	CHEN	NBER	238
WILLIAMS, PRINCE	1830	DUTC	FISH	498
WILLIAMS, PRINCE	1830	SARA	MILT	32
WILLIAMS, RACHEL	1830	NYCO	WD08	134

NAME	YR	CO	TWP	PG
WILLIAMS, RACHEL	1830	NYCO	WD08	224
WILLIAMS, RICHARD	1820	ONTA	CANA	210
WILLIAMS, RICHARD	1830	KING	WD04	303
WILLIAMS, RICHARD	1830	NYCO	WD06	389
WILLIAMS, RICHARD	1830	NYCO	WD06	448
WILLIAMS, ROB	1790	QUEN	NEWT	151
WILLIAMS, ROBERT	1810	NYCO	WD05	255
WILLIAMS, ROBERT	1810	NYCO	WD07	552
WILLIAMS, ROBERT	1820	DUTC	FISH	67
WILLIAMS, ROBERT	1820	NYCO	WD05	372
WILLIAMS, ROBERT	1820	NYCO	WD06	506
WILLIAMS, ROBERT	1830	COLU	CLAV	75
WILLIAMS, ROBERT	1830	DUTC	FISH	480
WILLIAMS, ROBERT	1830	NYCO	WD10	125
WILLIAMS, ROBERT	1830	QUEN	NEWT	4
WILLIAMS, ROBERT	1830	QUEN	SHEM	73
WILLIAMS, ROBERT	1830	QUEN	SHEM	89
WILLIAMS, SALLY	1820	NYCO	WD04	322
WILLIAMS, SAMUEL	1810	NYCO	WD04	174
WILLIAMS, SAMUEL	1810	NYCO	WD06	427
WILLIAMS, SAMUEL	1820	QUEN	----	54
WILLIAMS, SAMUEL	1830	NYCO	WD12	254
WILLIAMS, SAMUEL	1830	ORNG	CRAW	194
WILLIAMS, SAMUEL	1830	TIOG	NICH	296
WILLIAMS, SAMUEL	1830	WEST	NEWR	107
WILLIAMS, SARAH	1830	NYCO	WD05	339
WILLIAMS, SARAH	1830	NYCO	WD06	404
WILLIAMS, SAWL	1810	QUEN	NHEM	206
WILLIAMS, SEME	1830	COLU	HUDS	110
WILLIAMS, SETH	1830	DELA	DELH	36
WILLIAMS, SOPHIA	1830	NYCO	WD06	403
WILLIAMS, SQUIRE	1800	NYCO	WD05	752
WILLIAMS, SQUIRE	1810	NYCO	WD05	321
WILLIAMS, SQUIRE	1810	NYCO	WD06	460
WILLIAMS, STEPHEN	1800	NYCO	WD07	876
WILLIAMS, SUSAN	1820	NYCO	WD07	627
WILLIAMS, SUSAN	1820	ROCK	ORNG	86
WILLIAMS, THOMAS	1800	NYCO	WD04	725
WILLIAMS, THOMAS	1800	NYCO	WD07	875
WILLIAMS, THOMAS	1810	NYCO	WD03	84
WILLIAMS, THOMAS	1810	NYCO	WD05	338
WILLIAMS, THOMAS	1810	SUFF	SHEL	466
WILLIAMS, THOMAS	1820	DUTC	DOVE	51
WILLIAMS, THOMAS	1820	NYCO	WD06	503
WILLIAMS, THOMAS	1820	ONID	UTIC	208
WILLIAMS, THOMAS	1830	ABNY	WD04	311
WILLIAMS, THOMAS	1830	DUTC	UNVA	427
WILLIAMS, THOMAS	1830	HERK	LTFA	89
WILLIAMS, THOMAS	1830	KING	FLAT	398

NAME	YR	CO	TWP	PG
WILLIAMS, THOMAS	1830	QUEN	NHEM	111
WILLIAMS, W.	1830	NYCO	WD12	283
WILLIAMS, WILLIAM	1800	NYCO	WD02	672
WILLIAMS, WILLIAM	1800	NYCO	WD06	809
WILLIAMS, WILLIAM	1800	NYCO	WD06	836
WILLIAMS, WILLIAM	1810	DUTC	FISH	204
WILLIAMS, WILLIAM	1810	NYCO	WD04	181
WILLIAMS, WILLIAM	1810	NYCO	WD04	179
WILLIAMS, WILLIAM	1810	NYCO	WD05	309
WILLIAMS, WILLIAM	1810	NYCO	WD01	15
WILLIAMS, WILLIAM	1810	QUEN	FLUS	198
WILLIAMS, WILLIAM	1820	DUTC	FISH	75
WILLIAMS, WILLIAM	1820	KING	BRYN	115
WILLIAMS, WILLIAM	1820	NYCO	WD09	930
WILLIAMS, WILLIAM	1820	NYCO	WD10	1014
WILLIAMS, WILLIAM	1820	QUEN	----	54
WILLIAMS, WILLIAM	1830	NYCO	WD05	326
WILLIAMS, WILLIAM	1830	NYCO	WD06	385
WILLIAMS, WILLIAM	1830	NYCO	WD07	14
WILLIAMS, WILLIAM	1830	NYCO	WD08	160
WILLIAMS, WILLIAM	1830	NYCO	WD08	173
WILLIAMS, WILLIAM	1830	NYCO	WD10	18
WILLIAMS, WILLIAM	1830	ONID	AUGU	124
WILLIAMS, WILLIAM	1830	ORNG	WALL	138
WILLIAMS, WILLIAM	1830	QUEN	FLUS	142
WILLIAMS, WILLIAM P.	1830	QUEN	FLUS	143
WILLIAMSON, CAPTAIN J.	1830	NYCO	WD10	6
WILLIAMSON, JOHN	1830	NYCO	WD07	73
WILLIAMSON, JOSEPH	1830	NYCO	WD07	46
WILLIAMSON, PETER	1830	KING	WD02	262
WILLIAMSON, PETER	1830	KING	WD02	264
WILLIAMSON, SAMUEL	1820	ROCK	CLAK	97
WILLIAMSON, SAMUEL	1830	ROCK	ORGT	119
WILLIAMSON, THOMAS	1810	NYCO	WD06	410
WILLIARD, GEORGE	1830	QUEN	SHEM	63
WILLIS	1790	QUEN	NHEM	152
WILLIS	1810	NYCO	WD07	556
WILLIS, ANTHONY	1820	DUTC	WASH	140
WILLIS, CHARLES	1830	NYCO	WD11	201
WILLIS, FRANCIS	1830	RENS	HOOS	166
WILLIS, GEORGE	1800	NYCO	WD07	863
WILLIS, HEZEKIAH	1830	QUEN	OYST	21
WILLIS, ISREAL	1830	DUTC	PGKP	322
WILLIS, JOHN	1830	OTSG	BUTT	313
WILLIS, MRS.	1820	NYCO	WD07	628
WILLIS, NATHANIEL	1820	DUTC	WASH	141
WILLIS, RACHEL	1820	NYCO	WD04	228
WILLIS, REUBEN	1830	QUEN	NHEM	116
WILLIS, RICHARD	1830	ONID	NWHT	64

NAME	YR	CO	TWP	PG
WILLIS, SAMUEL	1830	ABNY	BETH	548
WILLIS, SILVANUS	1830	QUEN	OYST	53
WILLIS, SIMON	1820	NIAG	HART	93
WILLIS, THOMAS	1800	NYCO	WD03	696
WILLIS, TIMOTHY	1820	WEST	HARR	470
WILLIS, TIMOTHY	1820	WEST	WHPL	459
WILLIS, WILLIAM	1830	QUEN	OYST	32
WILLIT, JOSEPH	1810	NYCO	WD10	644
WILLIT, SAMUEL	1830	WEST	CORT	72
WILLITS, WILLIAM	1830	QUEN	FLUS	150
WILLITT, BILL	1810	QUEN	FLUS	201
WILLITT, JAMES	1810	QUEN	OYST	242
WILLITT, SIMON	1810	QUEN	FLUS	202
WILLOTE, SIMON	1820	QUEN	----	51
WILLS, HANNAH	1800	NYCO	WD05	771
WILLS, JAMES	1820	QUEN	----	78
WILLS, JOHN	1820	NYCO	WD05	338
WILLS, MRS.	1820	ONID	UTIC	208
WILLS, PETER	1810	NYCO	WD05	307
WILLS, RICHARD	1820	ONID	WHIT	303
WILLS, RICHARD	1820	ONID	WATE	303
WILLS, TIM	1830	SUFF	ISLP	280
WILLSON	1830	NYCO	WD02	96
WILLSON, HENRY	1830	NYCO	WD06	431
WILLSON, JAMES	1820	NYCO	WD05	350
WILLSON, JOHN	1830	DELA	TOMP	205
WILLSON, JOHN	1830	NYCO	WD06	410
WILLSON, JOSEPH	1830	NYCO	WD04	203
WILLSON, MARY	1830	NYCO	WD06	393
WILLSON, RICHARD	1830	TOMP	ULYS	394
WILLSON, ROBERT	1830	NYCO	WD06	443
WILLSON, STEPHEN	1830	QUEN	FLUS	147
WILLSON, THOMAS	1820	HERK	MANH	14
WILLSON, TOBIAS	1830	ABNY	WD02	273
WILLSON, WILLIAM	1810	NYCO	WD08	763
WILLSON, YENIX	1830	MONR	RWD3	231
WILMORE, CHARLES	1830	NYCO	WD10	68
WILMORE, HENRY	1830	NYCO	WD08	231
WILMOT, PHILIP	1830	DUTC	PGKP	363
WILMUR, HENRY	1830	QUEN	JAMA	130
WILSON	1830	NYCO	WD10	27
WILSON, ADIAN	1820	DUTC	DOVE	46
WILSON, ADIN	1830	OSWE	AMBO	267
WILSON, ALEXANDER	1830	NYCO	WD09	430
WILSON, ANDREW	1830	HERK	DANU	185
WILSON, BENJAMIN	1830	DELA	STAM	186
WILSON, CATO	1820	NYCO	WD10	1055
WILSON, CESAR	1820	NYCO	WD10	1110
WILSON, DINAH	1810	NYCO	WD01	18

NAME	YR	CO	TWP	PG
WILSON, GEORGE	1810	NYCO	WD05	322
WILSON, GEORGE	1830	KING	WD04	295
WILSON, GEORGE	1830	NYCO	WD08	261
WILSON, HANNAH	1820	NYCO	WD10	998
WILSON, ISAAC	1830	NYCO	WD01	9
WILSON, J.	1830	NYCO	WD13	382
WILSON, JAMES	1810	NYCO	WD05	249
WILSON, JAMES	1820	NYCO	WD04	211
WILSON, JAMES	1820	NYCO	WD04	266
WILSON, JAMES	1830	NYCO	WD08	200
WILSON, JAMES	1830	NYCO	WD13	380
WILSON, JOHN	1800	NYCO	WD03	705
WILSON, JOHN	1800	NYCO	WD07	916
WILSON, JOHN	1810	NYCO	WD05	276
WILSON, JOHN	1830	GREN	NEWB	174
WILSON, JOHN	1830	KING	BUSH	378
WILSON, JOSEPH	1830	NYCO	WD13	378
WILSON, LIBA	1820	DELA	STAN	86
WILSON, LUCY	1800	NYCO	WD06	808
WILSON, MANN	1830	RICH	WEST	13
WILSON, MARY	1810	NYCO	WD03	84
WILSON, PETER	1830	NYCO	WD08	250
WILSON, PETER	1830	NYCO	WD09	430
WILSON, PHILLIP	1820	KING	BRYN	133
WILSON, R.	1830	NYCO	WD13	358
WILSON, RICHARD R.	1800	NYCO	WD07	910
WILSON, ROBERT	1830	GREN	ATHN	206
WILSON, ROBERT	1830	KING	BUSH	378
WILSON, ROBERT	1830	SCHR	MIDD	36
WILSON, SAMUEL	1800	NYCO	WD06	830
WILSON, SAMUEL	1820	JEFF	WATE	491
WILSON, SAMUEL	1830	KING	BUSH	382
WILSON, SAMUEL	1830	ONON	SALI	11
WILSON, SARAH	1830	NYCO	WD08	246
WILSON, SARAH	1830	NYCO	WD10	26
WILSON, THOMAS	1800	NYCO	WD03	701
WILSON, THOMAS	1820	NYCO	WD06	498
WILSON, THOMAS	1820	NYCO	WD08	731
WILSON, THOMAS	1830	HERK	LTFA	87
WILSON, THOMAS	1830	KING	BUSH	379
WILSON, THOMAS	1830	MONT	CANJ	31
WILSON, THOMAS	1830	MONT	MIND	6
WILSON, THOMAS	1830	NYCO	WD09	370
WILSON, WILLIAM	1830	NYCO	WD12	271
WILSON, WILLIAM	1830	NYCO	WD13	378
WILSON, WILLIAM	1830	NYCO	WD14	525
WILSON, WILLIAM	1830	SCNE	GLEN	272
WILSON, YEAT	1830	WANE	PALM	41
WILSON, ZIAB	1810	DELA	STAN	582

NAME	YR	CO	TWP	PG
WILTER, HENRY	1820	NYCO	WD10	1006
WINANS, ABIGAIL	1830	NYCO	WD10	27
WINECUP, THOMAS	1820	ORNG	MONT	807
WINEKOOP, JAMES	1830	GREN	CATS	234
WINEROD, JAMES	1800	NYCO	WD03	706
WINES, HEDER	1810	SUFF	BROK	488
WINFIELD, J.	1830	NYCO	WD13	402
WING, PETER	1820	NYCO	WD09	943
WINNAN, DAVID	1830	OSWE	OSWE	134
WINNE, LUM	1830	ABNY	RENV	439
WINNE, PETER	1830	WASH	JACK	177
WINNE, THOMAS	1830	WASH	WTCK	193
WINNER, DAVID	1820	JEFF	HOUN	417
WINNER, DAVID	1830	JEFF	HOUN	187
WINSLOW, CAROLINE	1830	NYCO	WD05	267
WINSLOW, DINNAH	1800	NYCO	WD04	734
WINSLOW, W.	1830	KING	WD04	310
WINSLOW, WILLIAM	1820	KING	BRYN	132
WINTERS, RICHARD	1830	YATE	MILO	214
WINTFERRY, P.	1830	ERIE	BUFF	5
WIPPLE, ANTHONY	1820	QUEN	----	20
WISEMAN, CHRISTOPHER	1800	NYCO	WD05	764
WISHINGHAM, ABRAHAM	1800	NYCO	WD03	843
WISNER, THOMAS	1830	NYCO	WD05	331
WIST, STEPHEN	1830	DUTC	HYPK	239
WISTAR, JOHN	1800	NYCO	WD07	888
WITHERINGTON, HOSEA	1830	NYCO	WD11	233
WITMORE, JAMES	1820	WEST	RYE	370
WITSON, GEORGE	1830	KING	WD02	275
WITT, ALEXANDER LEE	1820	ONON	MANL	167
WOEKS, PRINCE	1820	GREN	COXE	41
WOGLAM, HARRY	1830	RICH	WEST	12
WOLLEY, GEORGE	1830	KING	BRYN	366
WOLSEY, HENRY	1830	MONR	RWD3	223
WOMBSLY, J.	1810	MADI	BROK	753
WOOBY, JOHN	1830	ONTA	CANA	111
WOOD, AAREN	1830	NYCO	WD04	184
WOOD, AARON	1820	NYCO	WD04	228
WOOD, AARON	1830	SUFF	HUNT	323
WOOD, BENJAMIN	1830	WEST	RYE	102
WOOD, CEZAR	1800	ABNY	BETH	193
WOOD, H.	1830	NYCO	WD11	133
WOOD, H.L.	1820	NYCO	WD07	633
WOOD, HARRY	1820	NIAG	NIAG	215
WOOD, HARRY	1820	NIAG	NIAG	227
WOOD, HARRY	1830	MADI	----	398
WOOD, HARRY	1830	NIAG	NIAG	418
WOOD, ISHAMEL	1810	DUTC	FISH	242
WOOD, ISHMAEL	1800	DUTC	FISH	26

NAME	YR	CO	TWP	PG
WOOD, JACOB	1830	QUEN	JAMA	129
WOOD, JAMES	1820	ORNG	GOSH	742
WOOD, JAMES	1830	LIVI	SPAR	133
WOOD, JAMES	1830	ORNG	GOSH	290
WOOD, JEAN	1810	DELA	KORT	622
WOOD, JEMIMA	1830	NYCO	WD05	340
WOOD, JUDA	1830	MONR	RWD3	230
WOOD, LETTA	1810	NYCO	WD05	299
WOOD, LYDIA	1830	ORNG	NEWB	59
WOOD, METTY	1830	ONTA	MANC	181
WOOD, MORRIS	1830	MONR	RWD3	230
WOOD, MOSES	1810	QUEN	OYST	244
WOOD, MOSES	1830	NYCO	WD13	358
WOOD, MOSES	1830	SUFF	HUNT	318
WOOD, POMP	1830	RENS	TROY	14
WOOD, RICHARD	1830	HERK	STAR	228
WOOD, ROBERT	1830	NYCO	WD05	337
WOOD, SAMSON	1800	RENE	PITT	826
WOOD, SAMSON	1820	GENE	GATE	122
WOOD, SAMUEL	1820	SUFF	HUNT	299
WOOD, SIMPSON	1810	RENS	SCHO	548
WOOD, STEPHEN	1820	DUTC	REDH	120
WOOD, STEPHEN	1820	ORNG	NEWW	487
WOOD, WILLAIM	1830	NYCO	WD05	263
WOOD, WILLIAM	1800	NYCO	WD07	862
WOOD, WILLIAM	1810	NYCO	WD05	322
WOOD, WILLIAM	1820	NYCO	WD03	190
WOOD, WILLIAM	1820	NYCO	WD06	465
WOOD, WILLIAM	1820	NYCO	WD06	498
WOODENDYKE, CHARLES	1830	NYCO	WD08	187
WOODHUL, TITUS	1790	SUFF	BROK	162
WOODHULL, ABRAHAM	1830	SUFF	BROK	193
WOODHULL, BENJAMIN	1810	SUFF	BROK	469
WOODHULL, HARKNESS	1830	SUFF	HUNT	301
WOODHULL, HENRY	1830	SUFF	BROK	193
WOODHULL, JANE	1820	DUTC	WALL	791
WOODHULL, JOHN	1820	SUFF	BROK	355
WOODHULL, JOHN	1830	SUFF	BROK	195
WOODHULL, LUNN	1830	ORNG	HBGH	124
WOODHULL, PHILIP	1830	ORNG	BLOM	123
WOODHULL, ROBIN	1830	SUFF	BROK	179
WOODHULL, TOBIAS	1830	ORNG	BLOM	114
WOODMAN, JAMES	1830	NYCO	WD12	262
WOODNORTH, CEZAR	1830	SCNE	WD02	223
WOODRIFF, CYRUS	1810	SUFF	SHAM	461
WOODRUFF, ISAAC	1830	ERIE	BUFF	11
WOODRUFF, JERRY	1830	SUFF	ISLP	280
WOODRUFF, SAMUEL	1830	NIAG	LOCK	405
WOODRUFF, WILLIAM S.	1830	NYCO	WD14	456

Woods

NAME	YR	CO	TWP	PG
WOODS, MARY	1830	NYCO	WD08	161
WOODS, MOSES	1820	SUFF	HUNT	279
WOODWARD, ANN	1830	NYCO	WD05	276
WOODWARD, EXODUS	1820	OTSG	BUTT	55
WOODWARD, JAMES	1830	ORNG	CALH	17
WOODWORTH, EXODUS	1830	OTSG	PITT	313
WOOL, DANIEL	1810	DUTC	RHIN	376
WOOL, DAVID	1790	DUTC	RHIN	92
WOOL, DAVID	1800	DUTC	RHIN	153
WOOLFOOT, LEVI	1830	QUEN	FLUS	142
WOOLS, STEPHEN	1830	DUTC	REDH	375
WOOLSEY, CHARLES	1830	NYCO	WD10	99
WOOLSEY, ELLEN	1830	NYCO	WD14	526
WOOLSEY, ISAAC	1810	QUEN	OYST	237
WOOLSEY, ISABELLA	1830	NYCO	WD06	446
WOOLSEY, LUTUS	1810	SUFF	SMIT	445
WORLDS, JOSEPH	1810	NYCO	WD04	154
WORMSKY, JAMES	1830	MADI	----	363
WORRALE, LAETITIA	1830	NYCO	WD06	366
WORSAL, ELIZA	1830	NYCO	WD06	368
WORTH, JAMES	1810	NYCO	WD10	642
WORTHINGTON, JOHN	1820	NYCO	WD04	241
WORTMAN, JACK	1830	NYCO	WD12	313
WORTMAN, TOM	1790	QUEN	FLUS	149
WRAY, ISAAC	1830	NYCO	WD06	436
WRENT, SIMEON	1830	SUFF	SMIT	275
WRIGHT, ABRAHAM	1800	ONTA	HART	376
WRIGHT, ABRAHAM	1810	ONTA	AVON	595
WRIGHT, ABRAHAM	1830	CHAT	ELCT	331
WRIGHT, AMANDA	1800	NYCO	WD04	722
WRIGHT, AMANTHA	1810	NYCO	WD05	362
WRIGHT, BENJAMIN	1820	DUTC	GOSH	748
WRIGHT, BENJAMIN	1830	ORNG	MINI	244
WRIGHT, DANIEL	1800	ONTA	HART	376
WRIGHT, DANIEL	1810	ONTA	AVON	595
WRIGHT, DAVID	1800	ONTA	LYSO	193
WRIGHT, ELIZA	1830	NYCO	WD06	387
WRIGHT, ENOS	1820	PUTM	PHIL	101
WRIGHT, GEORGE	1800	NYCO	WD06	811
WRIGHT, GEORGE	1830	NYCO	WD05	261
WRIGHT, HAMILTON	1800	SARA	CHAR	1076
WRIGHT, HENRY	1830	NYCO	WD07	66
WRIGHT, HENRY	1830	QUEN	NHEM	109
WRIGHT, ISIAH	1830	CHAT	ELCT	335
WRIGHT, JAC.	1810	ONTA	CANA	900
WRIGHT, JACOB	1800	ONTA	HART	376
WRIGHT, JACOB	1810	ONTA	AVON	595
WRIGHT, JACOB	1820	ONTA	RICH	38
WRIGHT, JACOB	1830	LIVI	SPWT	116

NAME	YR	CO	TWP	PG
WRIGHT, JAMES	1820	PUTM	PHIL	101
WRIGHT, JOHN	1800	ONTA	HART	376
WRIGHT, JOHN	1810	ONTA	AVON	595
WRIGHT, JOHN	1830	WEST	GREN	18
WRIGHT, JOSEPH	1800	ONTA	HART	376
WRIGHT, JOSEPH	1810	ONTA	AVON	597
WRIGHT, JOSEPH	1830	NYCO	WD06	403
WRIGHT, JUDITH	1820	ABNY	ABNY	209
WRIGHT, JULIA	1830	ABNY	WD04	300
WRIGHT, LEBUSS	1800	ONTA	CHAR	366
WRIGHT, LIBBRUS	1820	ONTA	RUSH	183
WRIGHT, LIBEUS	1820	NIAG	BUFF	72
WRIGHT, LIBUIS	1810	ONTA	AVON	595
WRIGHT, MRS.	1830	NYCO	WD13	331
WRIGHT, NANCY	1830	CHAT	ELCT	311
WRIGHT, NANCY	1830	SUFF	EAST	259
WRIGHT, OLIVER	1810	NYCO	WD10	676
WRIGHT, OLIVER	1830	MONR	RWD3	22
WRIGHT, OLIVER	1830	NYCO	WD12	287
WRIGHT, P.G.	1820	SCNE	WD02	569
WRIGHT, RICHARD P.G.	1810	SCNE	WD02	954
WRIGHT, RICHARD P.G.	1830	SCNE	WD02	217
WRIGHT, ROBERT	1830	CATT	PERY	219
WRIGHT, SARAH	1820	NYCO	WD10	1016
WRIGHT, SGGIBERT	1810	QUEN	FLUS	198
WRIGHT, SYLVESTER	1830	SUFF	SHAM	223
WRIGHT, WILLIAM	1820	NYCO	WD06	505
WRIGHT, WILLIAM	1830	NYCO	WD14	526
WRIGHT, YORK	1800	NYCO	WD01	667
WRIGHT, YORK	1810	NYCO	WD05	289
WRIGHT, YORK	1810	NYCO	WD06	430
WRIGHT, YORK	1810	NYCO	WD07	928
WRIGHT, ZIBEUS	1820	NIAG	BUFF	153
WRIGTH, JAMES	1830	DUTC	FISH	484
WRIT, HENRY	1810	NYCO	WD03	59
WURNER, WILLIAM	1820	NYCO	WD10	1084
WYCHOFF, JACK	1820	MONT	CHAR	341
WYCHOFF, JOHN	1830	NYCO	WD10	46
WYCHOFF, R.	1830	KING	WD04	310
WYCKOFF, JOSEPH	1820	NYCO	WD06	515
WYCOFF, DAVID	1830	ONID	UTIC	18
WYCOFF, TOM	1820	TOMP	HECT	4
WYLLIS, ISAAC	1800	QUEN	NHEM	553
WYLLS, ANTHONY	1800	DUTC	WASH	97
WYLLYS, ANTHONY	1790	DUTC	WASH	96
WYNKODD, JOHN	1800	ULST	HURL	20L
WYNKOOP, CHARLES	1820	NYCO	WD01	59
WYNKOOP, CHARLES	1830	ULST	HURL	146
WYNKOOP, DAGO	1830	ULST	SAUG	105

NAME	YR	CO	TWP	PG
WYNKOOP, HARRY	1830	ULST	NPAL	214
WYNKOOP, JOHN	1810	ULST	WOOD	824
WYNKOOP, JOHN	1830	ULST	KING	78
WYNKOOP, RICHARD	1830	ULST	MARB	163
WYNKOOP, SINDRED	1830	ULST	SHAW	253
WYNKOOP, THOMAS	1810	ULST	KING	764
WYNKOOP, THOMAS	1820	ULST	SAUG	83
WYNKOOP, TOM	1830	ULST	NPAL	212
WYNKOP, THOMAS	1830	ULST	SAUG	107
XEINE, EDWARD S.	1830	NYCO	WD01	32
YAFF	1820	QUEN	----	38
YALES, SARAH	1800	NYCO	WD07	896
YANSEN, HENDRICK	1810	MONT	AMST	179
YATÈS, ANTHONY	1830	COLU	AUST	175
YATES, CEASAR	1830	ABNY	ABNY	213
YATES, CEZAR	1830	ABNY	WD02	257
YATES, JACK	1830	MONT	CANJ	32
YATES, JANE	1820	GREN	GREN	67
YATES, JOHN	1830	WEST	RYE	98
YATES, JOHN T.	1830	MONT	JOHN	224
YEEKLEY, SAMUEL S.	1820	ORNG	NEWB	514
YONGS, ABSOLOM	1810	QUEN	FLUS	203
YONGS, TIMOTHY	1810	QUEN	NHEM	219
YORICK, PHILLIS	1830	NYCO	WD08	253
YORK	1790	QUEN	FLUS	149
YORK	1800	OTSG	BURL	652
YORK	1810	CLNT	PLAT	895
YORK	1820	QUEN	----	45
YORK	1820	ROCK	CLAK	99
YORK, CEZAR	1830	SCNE	WD01	206
YORK, CHARLES	1830	CLNT	BEEK	299
YORK, COLONEL DEXTER	1830	ONID	UTIC	6
YORK, DAVID	1830	ORNG	WARW	73
YORK, JACOB	1800	ORNG	WALL	341
YORK, JAMES	1810	ULST	MARB	733
YORK, JAMES	1830	ULST	MARL	283
YORK, JOHN	1830	NYCO	WD08	253
YORK, JOHN	1830	QUEN	NEWT	15
YORK, JOSEPH	1830	MONT	FLOR	98
YORK, JOSEPH	1830	NYCO	WD12	294
YORK, SAMUEL	1810	NYCO	WD04	179
YORK, SAMUEL	1810	NYCO	WD04	181
YORKSHIRE	1810	DUTC	PGKP	325
YORKSON, PETER	1820	SCNE	WD02	572

NAME	YR	CO	TWP	PG
YORKSON, SEASOR	1820	SCNE	WD01	563
YOUNG, A.	1830	ERIE	BUFF	30
YOUNG, BRISTER	1830	SUFF	RIVH	246
YOUNG, CAMMANG	1830	KING	WD05	327
YOUNG, EZEBEL	1810	KING	BRYN	639
YOUNG, FRANCES	1820	NYCO	WD08	781
YOUNG, FRANCIS	1830	NYCO	WD06	368
YOUNG, JERIMIAH	1810	ONTA	BLOM	612
YOUNG, JESSE	1810	NYCO	WD04	186
YOUNG, JOHN	1800	NYCO	WD06	844
YOUNG, JOHN	1830	NYCO	WD08	219
YOUNG, JOHN	1830	WANE	ONTA	58
YOUNG, JOSHUA	1820	NYCO	WD06	517
YOUNG, JOSHUA	1830	NYCO	WD14	442
YOUNG, PETER	1820	NYCO	WD10	981
YOUNG, THOMAS	1830	DUTC	STAN	418
YOUNGELL, THOMAS	1820	ABNY	ABNY	213
YOUNGER, JACOB	1830	QUEN	FLUS	154
YOUNGS, --	1820	KING	BRYN	136
YOUNGS, BROWSTER	1810	SUFF	RIVH	548
YOUNGS, ELIMUS	1830	SUFF	RIVH	237
YOUNGS, FRANCES	1820	KING	BRYN	141
YOUNGS, HARVEY	1830	ALLE	ANGE	4
YOUNGS, ISAAC	1830	GREN	ATHN	203
YOUNGS, ISAAC	1830	GREN	CATS	244
YOUNGS, JEREMIAH	1820	ONTA	FARM	315
YOUNGS, JOHN	1820	KING	BRYN	141
YOUNGS, LIMAS	1810	SUFF	SHAM	464
YOUNGS, PERO	1830	SUFF	BROK	173
YOUNGS, RANDEL	1830	GREN	ATHN	205
YOUNGS, SAUL	1830	CAYU	LEDY	281
YOURK, ELIZA	1800	NYCO	WD03	706
YUFFER, JOHN	1820	NYCO	WD05	337
ZABRISKIES, JOSEPH	1820	NYCO	WD05	404
ZAMOT, JOSEPH	1820	NYCO	WD01	54
ZANDT, ANDREW	1830	SCHR	SCHR	25
ZEBEY, SYLVA	1820	ABNY	ABNY	213
ZEBRA, BRISTOR	1800	ABNY	RENV	175
ZEBULON	1800	QUEN	OYST	571
ZEBULON	1800	SUFF	HUNT	37
ZELMAC, JOHNSON	1800	NYCO	WD07	877
ZEOCAH	1820	SUFF	SOUT	352
ZINGO	1790	WEST	HARR	199
ZOBRISHEE	1810	NYCO	WD06	492
ZOGART, FRANK	1820	MONT	MAYF	391
ZOPHER	1800	SUFF	SMIT	55
ZOULMIN, JOHN B.	1820	QUEN	----	55

www.ingramcontent.com/pod-product-compliance
Lightning Source LLC
Chambersburg PA
CBHW060144280326
41932CB00012B/1627